Teaching Dance as Art in Education

Brenda Pugh McCutchen

MFA Dance • Dance Education Consultant

Human Kinetics

Library of Congress Cataloging-in-Publication Data

McCutchen, Brenda Pugh, 1943-
  Teaching dance as art in education / Brenda Pugh McCutchen.
    p. cm.
  Includes bibliographical references and index.
  ISBN-13: 978-0-7360-5188-0 (hard cover)
  ISBN-10: 0-7360-5188-0 (hard cover)
  1. Dance--Study and teaching (Elementary)--United States. 2. Dance--Study and teaching (Secondary)--United States. 3. Dance--Curricula--United States. 4. Public schools--Curricula--United States. I. Title.
  GV1589.M33 2006
  792.8071--dc22

                        2006002873

ISBN-10: 0-7360-5188-0
ISBN-13: 978-0-7360-5188-0

The Web addresses cited in this text were current as of December 2005, unless otherwise noted.

Acquisitions Editor: Judy Patterson Wright, PhD
Developmental Editor: Ray Vallese
Assistant Editor: Derek Campbell
Copyeditor: Julie Anderson
Proofreader: Erin Cler
Indexer: Bobbi Swanson
Permission Manager: Carly Breeding
Graphic Designer: Bob Reuther
Graphic Artist: Tara Welsch
Photo Manager: Sarah Ritz
Cover Designer: Keith Blomberg
Photographer (cover): © William Frederking; dancers: Brian Jeffery and Julia Rhoads, XSIGHT! Performance Group
Photographer (interior): Steve Clarke, except where otherwise noted
Art Manager: Kelly Hendren
Illustrator: Mic Greenberg; dancer icon on cover and title page (and throughout this book) © Cecily Bradford Morris
Printer: Sheridan Books

Printed in the United States of America   10 9 8 7 6 5 4 3 2 1

Human Kinetics
Web site: www.HumanKinetics.com

United States: Human Kinetics
P.O. Box 5076
Champaign, IL 61825-5076
800-747-4457
e-mail: humank@hkusa.com

Canada: Human Kinetics
475 Devonshire Road Unit 100
Windsor, ON N8Y 2L5
800-465-7301 (in Canada only)
e-mail: orders@hkcanada.com

Europe: Human Kinetics
107 Bradford Road
Stanningley
Leeds LS28 6AT, United Kingdom
+44 (0) 113 255 5665
e-mail: hk@hkeurope.com

Australia: Human Kinetics
57A Price Avenue
Lower Mitcham, South Australia 5062
08 8277 1555
e-mail: liaw@hkaustralia.com

New Zealand: Human Kinetics
Division of Sports Distributors NZ Ltd.
P.O. Box 300 226 Albany
North Shore City
Auckland
0064 9 448 1207
e-mail: info@humankinetics.co.nz

I dedicate this book to the memory of my mother, **Mary Agnes Caldwell Pugh** (1910-1997). She was a long-time educator who epitomized how a caring teacher affects the lives of students. She saw the magic in their creativity and the delight in their questions and thus showed me how necessary creative expression and inquiry are to education.

Contents

PART I | Why —Understanding Dance as Arts Education | 1

PART III How —Presenting Dance as Art in Education 293

Preface

If you are a dancer considering a career as a certified dance teaching specialist, this book is for you! It is a comprehensive book for dancers going into K-12 dance education. It connects the dots of teacher certification in dance and adds some new dots. It is particularly useful if you are majoring in dance education with teacher certification (a preservice dance specialist), are a dancer hired to teach in K-12, or are a dance educator already in the schools.

This book enables you to envision what school-based dance education really is, then it shows you how to make it happen. It marries dance with education in a way that makes K-12 dance education clear and distinct. Meanwhile, it distinguishes a standards-oriented, aesthetically driven program in the schools from other settings in dance teaching. With this book you harness your wealth of dance knowledge and skills for the educational benefit of children. You find out what you need to know to design and deliver a comprehensive dance education for students as they progress from kindergarten through 12th grade.

Reason for Writing the Book

I wrote this text to give dance specialists a "leg up" on how to make dance the dynamic, vital subject it can be in school-based programs. I so want dance to achieve its educational and artistic potential there. Therefore, the text presents a standards-oriented curriculum that ensures dance students meet, and even surpass, baseline expectations. I want to be sure the text's content is steeped in national standards without being driven by them, because dance has to be far more than merely what can be measured.

Serendipity

Some may think it coincidental, but I think it serendipitous: The very week this completed manuscript went into production (in October 2005) was the week the *National Standards for Learning and Teaching in Dance Ages 5-18* (LTS) came into my hands, freshly released to states by the National Dance Education Organization. Even though both the LTS and this textbook developed totally independently of each other without benefit of any connection or conversation, they speak the same language. (The LTSs identify integrated K-12 dance standards, which would ideally be facilitated by a "master teacher" who has been working successfully in the field and who has proven excellence. While the LTSs do not directly impact preservice licensure in dance education, they inform your ideal of becoming that master teacher.) I am gratified that this text so acutely aligns with those standards as well as the *National Standards for Dance Education* (NSDEs). The decade between 1995 and 2005 has seen dance education come of age from the momentum generated through the 1994 national arts education consensus project's first national standards in dance education.

How to Use This Book

Much thought was given to the organization of the book. Chapters are ordered to systematically deliver you into the world of dance education with increasing confidence and skill. One by one each chapter constructs the foundations. It is best used in the order presented since the chapters organically take the basics from one chapter and expand them with greater depth later on.

Whether you are a practicing or a preservice dance specialist, use this book's content to

- identify the way students grow in dance year by year and how to get them to where they need to be at each grade level,
- achieve the national achievement standards in dance without being driven by them, and
- create a model program based on the six defining characteristics of educational dance.

Organization

The first five chapters (part I) are the bridge you must cross from being a dancer to becoming a dance education specialist. Until you cross that bridge, what is on the other side—the land of educational dance—can be bewildering and foreign. However, after you cross the bridge, you find yourself on solid ground, ready to encounter the cornerstones of the dance discipline (part II), *what* you teach in dance as art. You learn how to use the full dance discipline so that your students advance in dance while also achieving standards. Standards are interwoven into the text. Thus you need to keep a copy of the *National Standards for Dance Education* handy as a map to cross-reference the content and achievement standards that keep you grounded in this new land. (See appendix C to find out how to order *National Standards for Dance Education* from National Dance Association.)

Part III focuses on *how* you teach dance as art. Here you acquire the infrastructure to turn dance curriculum into coherent, lasting learning experiences for students. By the end, the two culminating chapters bring you to the high ground of your profession so that you can look back to see where you have traveled and where you are.

Part I

Specifically, part I (chapters 1 to 5) creates the context that enables you to assimilate the rest of the book:

- **Chapter 1** invites you into dance from a perspective of arts education.
- **Chapter 2** depicts the external factors that govern your workplace: how you are accountable to externally driven student standards and assessments.
- **Chapter 3** describes life as a dance specialist in a school-based program (skills and attributes, roles and responsibilities). This chapter also introduces teacher preparation standards.
- **Chapter 4** emphasizes a student-centered curriculum driven internally by the readiness and the developmental needs of your particular students. Together chapters 2 and 4 explain the external and internal factors you must continually mitigate in K-12.
- **Chapter 5** helps you balance those two factors. It also introduces the four dance cornerstones as unchangeable pillars of teaching dance from an arts education perspective. It explains each cornerstone's unique method of inquiry into dance as one of the essential artistic processes. This chapter prepares you to cross the bridge into part II.

Part II

Part II (chapters 6 to 9) delineates content: what to teach and how to sequence the major skills and concepts in each cornerstone:

- **Chapter 6** focuses on dance techniques and skills—dancing and performing.
- **Chapter 7** focuses on choreographing—creating and composing.
- **Chapter 8** focuses on dance heritage—knowing and applying history, culture, and context.
- **Chapter 9** focuses on dance criticism—analyzing and critiquing.

Part III

Part III (chapters 10 to 16) provides practical "how tos" for teaching dance and also asks you to reflect on the big issues of teaching:

- **Chapter 10** interfaces dance with other subjects to maximize learning in dance.

- **Chapter 11** shows how to set up and maintain an effective learning environment.

- **Chapter 12** interfaces curriculum, instruction, and assessment so that you learn the mechanics of organizing units.

- **Chapter 13** shows how to merge the four cornerstones into integrated units of study. It features the Eight-Step Plan—an integrated delivery system—and ways to adapt it to vary instruction.

- **Chapter 14** enables you to synthesize chapters 1 through 13 to create contextual units of study with individual lesson plans.

- **Chapter 15** asks you to be a reflective practitioner who considers the ethical implications of teaching dance.

- **Chapter 16** helps you organize two professional documents that show what you know.

Appendixes

Three appendixes give you accessible materials.

- Appendix A gives you easy access to the most-often-used lists in the text that are integral to understanding the content as well as to teaching dance as art in education.

- Appendix B contains the forms, long checklists, sample items, and articles referred to in the text.

- Appendix C lists some of the professional organizations that are useful for dance specialists. Along with key players in arts education, it also includes initiatives and legislation pertaining directly to dance.

Special Features

Five features make this text unique and innovative.

- **The K-12 Dance Cornerstone Curriculum Framework** outlines the content of a dance curriculum, from the big picture to the details. It shows you how to sequence learning in dance with increasing levels of complexity as students advance from grade to grade. The Dance Cornerstone Curriculum Framework (DCC Framework) appears in chapters 6, 7, 8, and 9. The Framework consists of three parts in each chapter:

  1. Goals and objectives (big picture)
  2. Content outline (overview)
  3. Content details (chart of sequential outcomes)

  All three parts of the framework in these four chapters combine to make up the entire DCC Framework.

- The book clarifies the **developmental areas dance must advance in K-12**: kinesthetic–motor, cognitive–intellectual, aesthetic–artistic, and psychological–social. It explains how to move students through stages of development in each one so that you make educationally appropriate choices for different ages.

- **Notebook/Portfolio** features direct you to prepare materials as you go along so that by the end of the book you have the materials with which to create two professional documents: a Perspectives Notebook and your Professional Teaching Portfolio. You will find out all about these in chapter 16, but you might look ahead at them anytime you get curious along the way.

- The innovative **Eight-Step Plan** is unique to this book. It is a delivery model for integrating the artistic processes of dance.

- The practical orientation to the field of educational dance is unlike any other because it instills a comprehensive inquiry-based model throughout the book—and especially as part of the first five chapters.

Recurring features in each chapter stretch your perspective:

- Questions to Ponder ask you to reflect on what you have just learned and to act on it.

- Rich Resources enable you to go further than the text.

- Quotes let you hear what others have to say on the topic.

- Queries in the text (marked with ▩) ask you to reflect on the idea you just encountered.

- Reflect and Respond highlights issues to investigate further.

The real journey toward being a fine dance educator is the marriage of what you teach with how you teach it. Your students deserve the best you can give them. They also deserve to be challenged to be their best. To this end I invite you to learn as much as you can about dance education and about dance so that you may teach with great satisfaction and joy.

Brenda Pugh McCutchen, MFA

Acknowledgments

I am indebted to several icons whose concepts are integrally woven into the fabric of this text: Elliot Eisner, John Goodlad, Benjamin Bloom, and Howard Gardner.

I acknowledge educators Arrie Boyd and Robin Nicholson, who kept a professional eye on the process and product, and who ensured I didn't give up before finishing the manuscript. I am also grateful to colleagues who contributed to this book, among them Ellen Harrison, Wrenn Cook, Jan Scott, Karen Buchheim, Pat Cohen, Karen Hubbard, Anuradha Murali, April Barber, Kesha Nichols, Nicole Almeida, Kellie Romanstine, and Deborah Martin.

I also pay tribute to the Dance Cornerstone Curriculum (DCC) Framework's roots. Its long evolution started in 1986 when Jody Lunt and I wrote our state's K-12 discipline-based dance framework for the SC Department of Education. Jody's good work is still embedded in it; however, in the last 20 years, I have greatly expanded the substance of that original framework as I put it into practice in K-12 and in higher education. By now, the framework has matured into a fuller, integrated curriculum base that I am pleased to share with you.

I acknowledge the first group of extraordinary certified professional dance educators in South Carolina whom I mentored as professor, supervisor, and adviser while they were students at Columbia College. They lit my fire to write this book. A very special acknowledgment goes to former students Heather Riley Shealy and Nicole Manuel Almeida, who assisted me as I developed the manuscript. They transcribed notes and dictation, typed for hours, offered insight, and gave their energy to make this book happen.

How grateful I am to the strong professional team at Human Kinetics, whose expertise and attention enabled this text to be the best possible. Each person's contribution was an incalculable asset. It was the magic touch of developmental editor Ray Vallese that made everything fall into place and the close supervision of assistant editor Derek Campbell that kept the important details of the book miraculously on track. I have the utmost respect for all listed in the credits for this text.

I thank the child models that worked with Jan Scott and me at the photo shoot for this book: Essence Evans, Abigail and Elijah Hassett, Brian Koh, Dylan McCrorey, and Katie Payne. I thank dance photographer Steve Clarke for all the exquisite images he provided.

To Martha McLure and Arrie Boyd go my unending gratitude. They trudged with me through each chapter to get the manuscript into its finished product. Without their competent, wise, and steadfast assistance as well as their inspiration, this book may never have been realized.

Introduction

Thinking About Dance Education

"It
is easier to
complete someone
else's thinking and act
out their plan than it is to be
original in your own thinking
and responsible for what you
do. Yet doubt, ambiguity, and
struggle have a contribution to
make to learning. Easy routes
to learning, however, seldom
(if ever) result in lasting
growth."

—Ralph Peterson (1992,
pp. 121-122)

The introduction provides the underlying principles that support this book. It asks you to reflect on what you believe and to expand your ability to express the main premises that support dance as art in education.

What Do You Believe About Dance Education?

Ask yourself these questions:

- "Do I think dance should be a part of the basic education of all children in K-12?"
- "What else do I believe about dance education in a school-based program?"
- "What do I want to accomplish by being a teacher?"

This inquiry launches you into the kind of reflective thinking that I hope will become part of your teaching practice.

Before you read further, stop and list your most strongly held beliefs about K-12 dance education. They will allow to you focus on where you are going, what you want to accomplish, and why you want to teach dance. Title the list, "Statements of Belief as of __(today's date)__." Include statements about

- what you believe about students,
- what you believe about teaching dance in K-12, and
- what you believe to be the characteristics of a well-rounded school-based dance program.

Consider your Statements of Belief an ongoing work in progress. Glean from each chapter that which helps you refine your own philosophical position. Incorporate all you can to broaden your teaching perspective and strengthen your professional commitment. Refer to your Statements of Belief often, update them regularly, and increase your ability to articulate what you believe. It is the personal philosophy that pilots you through your entire career and determines most of what you do as a teacher.

When you get to chapter 16, "Developing an Arts-Oriented Teaching Portfolio," you will use your Statements of Belief to compose a well-developed philosophical statement to anchor the first part of your Professional Teaching Portfolio. Therefore, absorb the ideas in this book, make them your own, and be ready to use them.

The beliefs that drive this book will undergird you while you develop your own skills, knowledge, and philosophy of teaching. The first five chapters lay the important foundation for understanding your profession. Reflect on them and incorporate what you learn. The remaining content in this book depends on the information in these chapters.

Operational Definitions for Terms Used in This Book

To start, these are terms you need to know:

classroom—Large teaching space for dance (studio, multipurpose room, or large classroom).

dance education—Every model of teaching dance, private and public, group or individual, in all settings. Out of a dance education context, the K-12 model called "educational dance" emerges.

dance inquiry—A problem-solving, questioning, and investigative approach to dance by students.

dance specialist—A dancer who is a dance educator and is certified to teach dance as an art form in K-12 education.

educational dance (ED)—This term broadly encompasses all aspects of dance used to educate and inspire the young. It assumes that dance is taught as an art form by using knowledge and skills in all the varied dance processes—dancing, creating, performing, responding, and critical thinking about dance—to affect the total education of a child.

inquiry approach—A method used by a teacher or dance specialist to facilitate students' dance inquiry.

school-based program—A dance education program in a public or private K-12 school district that serves students in primary, elementary, middle, and high school during the school day as part of the basic school curriculum. Although after-school programs take place in the schools, they are not referred to as school-based programs.

Understanding Dance as Arts Education

Viewing Educational Dance From an Arts Education Perspective

"'In dreams begins responsibility' observed the Irish poet William Butler Yeats, for he understood that no lasting achievement is possible without a vision, and no dream can become real without action and responsibility."

—Rosabeth Moss Kanter (1989, p. 1)

This chapter explains what an arts education perspective is and how dance is part of it. It lays the foundation for understanding all aspects of a school-based dance program. The chapter describes the purpose of school-based dance, its defining characteristics, and the scope of educational dance for all students as part of the basic curriculum. This chapter enables you, the **dance specialist,** to distinguish how educational dance differs from other teaching models and to determine what is desired in education. In this chapter, you will examine what drives dance in the context of arts education in K-12.

What Is an Arts Education Perspective?

All of the arts are vital, complex subjects worth serious attention in education. Dance should be taught in the context of arts education in **school-based programs.** Teaching dance from an **arts education perspective** is different from teaching other dance education models. Let's examine this perspective and the purpose of K-12 educational dance.

As stated by the National Coalition for Education in the Arts, a consortium of 28 national arts organizations, arts education is the process of teaching and learning how to create and produce the visual and performing arts and how to understand and evaluate art forms created by others. With language, mathematics, the natural sciences, and the social sciences, the arts constitute a fundamental curriculum.

At a minimum, such a curriculum encompasses four basic aspects with the expectation that students will

- create and perform the arts;
- understand the role and importance of the arts in culture and history;
- perceive and respond to the qualities of the arts; and
- make sound judgments about the arts and understand the bases on which those judgments rest. (Arts Education Partnership Working Group 1993, p. 5)

Beliefs Underlying This Perspective

An arts education perspective aims to further aesthetic education. It uses expressive arts languages to communicate meaning, creates learning environments to support creative **expression** and the **refinement** of such expression, values the major art works and artists of the discipline, and moves students to achieve all national arts education standards.

An arts education perspective emphasizes the art forms themselves. It values cross-curricular learning only as long as qualitative objectives of each discipline are met. An arts education perspective expects critical thinking in all the artistic processes: **creating, performing, and responding (c/p/r).** This perspective also promotes knowing dance as art and human expression from across time and place. Thus, doing the art is not enough.

More specifically, an arts education perspective in dance is student centered. It investigates how children learn from preschool to high school so as to advance their artistic, **cognitive,** social, and **kinesthetic** development. This perspective uses complex thinking and challenging subject matter, as do all core subjects.

Aesthetic perception increases as students learn to make informed artistic judgments about what they and others do in dance. Aesthetic education permeates all teaching and learning in dance.

The following 14 premises are basic to an arts education perspective on dance in K-12. They are recurring themes throughout this text. They underpin teaching dance as art in education.

1. Dance is one of the four major art forms (dance, music, theatre, and visual arts), and children should study all its styles, facets, and processes.
2. Dance is for all children—no matter what their age or abilities.
3. Dance is core curriculum. Dance is on par with the other arts and is studied, like they are, continuously from K through grade 12.
4. Dance should be taught during the school day; it should not be relegated to an after-school activity or reserved for a few.
5. Reflective and critical thinking are essential skills to build through dance, as essential as the ability to dance.
6. A complete program necessitates learning to create, perform, and respond to dance as well as to apply dance knowledge, aesthetics, and critical judgment.
7. Dance learning comes first. To learn concepts from other subjects through dance enhances, but is not a substitute for, a complete standards-oriented dance program.
8. National dance standards are baseline measures for dance education, and all children should be given the opportunity to achieve them.
9. Children should personally integrate learning by simultaneously engaging body, mind, and spirit.
10. Educational dance is more than activity-based lessons. It contributes vitally to a child's overall education about dance, the world, the arts, and the self.
11. Every child in a democracy should have access to comprehensive educational dance, which begins in elementary school and continues uninterrupted through high school.
12. Dance should integrate aesthetic and kinesthetic learning so a child learns dance as an expressive language with which to communicate.
13. Fully certified dance specialists from accredited institutions should teach dance in school-based programs.

Every child should have the opportunity to study dance from elementary through high school.

14. To teach dance as art, dance specialists must have skills in the expressive art of dance, in educational dance, in world dance, and in aesthetic education.

Thus, the goal of dance education is to see that all students have access to a comprehensive education in dance, which is taught in such a way that aesthetic education develops through students' total engagement with the **kinetic** art of dance.

Defining K-12 Educational Dance

Many seem to have trouble defining school-based dance education. But the real issue here is to define its purpose. After its purpose is clear—and distinguished from other models—the defining characteristics become clear.

Its Purpose

Educational dance's purpose in K-12 is *to broadly educate all students in dance as an art form in all its facets*—that is, to teach students from the time they enter kindergarten until they graduate to know about dance and to use the **artistic processes** inherent in dance. This purpose distinguishes educa-

tional dance from all other types of dance instruction. Teachers of K-12 dance are to inspire students to inquire into dance as art and acquire artistic skills in creating, performing, and responding. The mantra of educational dance is inspire, inquire, and acquire.

Dance is also used for a multitude of purposes other than education. Some purposes are to perform (performance dance), to heal (therapeutic dance), to worship and communicate (ritual dance and liturgical dance), to become fit (aerobic dance), to entertain (theatrical dance and spectacle), and to socialize (social dance). In K-12, dance should educate rather than produce professional performers (thus the term *educational dance*).

But in school-based programs, dance's educational purpose comes first. Its educational purpose governs what you teach. It is based on the desired educational results for students. Until you know what is expected from educational dance, how can you know what to teach or where to start? As you will discover, there are multiple purposes, goals, and objectives for teaching dance in K-12. You need to know them all to communicate about teaching dance and to design effective instruction.

This text uses the term **educational dance** rather than **dance education** to refer to school-based K-12 dance. The reason is that *dance education* is a general term to describe all situations in which one person teaches dance to another. *Dance education* is too generic a term to convey the complex nature of how dance functions in K-12.

The term *educational dance* describes dance taught as an art form in school-based programs to effect learning in and about dance. This term identifies dance as a rich discipline of study in all its facets as well as a means to fully educate the young. Educational dance describes dance from an arts education perspective. Educational dance is for all children: It broadly educates, it embraces all aspects of dance that have educational value, it increases **aesthetic education,** and it affects the total education of a child. Educational dance is dance that educates and inspires the young. It stretches the body and the mind. Note: Our term is not to be confused with the British term based on Laban's work where *educational dance* means creative dance for children.

How Educational Dance's Purpose Distinguishes It From Other Teaching Models

Dance is taught in many different venues for distinct purposes. How do you determine what is appropriate for a school-based program? How do you distinguish it from what is appropriate in other familiar models?

Look in the telephone directory. You'll find all sorts of dance instruction available: private studios, physical education classes, college dance classes, community classes such as contra dance and square dance, and professional dance company classes. Curriculum and methods vary widely in different settings depending on the purposes and desired outcomes of the instruction.

You won't find K-12 dance in the telephone directory. But if you did, how would it be described? What would you see if you walked into a dance class in a public school? How would it differ from dance instruction somewhere else? What is expected in a school-based program? In becoming a dance specialist, what are you getting yourself into?

The emerging field of school-based educational dance (ED) is often confused with models that serve school-aged children in other settings. It is vital at this point to differentiate ED from other such dance education models.

How ED Differs From a Gifted Education Model Educational dance is for all, not just for those labeled gifted and talented. Dance is for the same groups of students who during the school day go to academic subjects, related arts, and physical education. In these homogeneous classes you find the most un-homogeneous individuals! They'll have an array of abilities, talents, skills, and interests. They'll come from an array of cultures, languages, experiences, and socioeconomic backgrounds. They will bring varied levels of arts experiences. No doubt, some will be gifted in dance. But the basic dance curriculum is not meant to make dance performers out of all these students. You are there to broaden their educational horizons through a broad-based curriculum in dance. You will teach them to dance, create dances, and know about dance as human expression. You will also teach them to analyze, value, and critique dance with their new dance vocabularies.

Artistically gifted and talented (AG/T) programs, on the other hand, serve selected students identified in a particular art form according to state-approved criteria for artistic giftedness. AG/T programs operate during the school day, in the summer, after school, or a mix. Approximately 5 percent of all U.S. dance students are artistically **gifted,** which means they have exceptional ability to conceptualize and outstanding compositional and choreographic skills. A larger percent will be artistically **talented,** which means they will exhibit outstanding performance skills. Advanced instruction in such programs is aimed at increasing artistic excellence in **choreography** and performance. Many of these students will seek dance careers. A small percentage of U.S. middle and high

School-based dance is sometimes confused with other models that teach school-age children dance, such as private studios or specialized after-school classes.

6

schools are designated as schools for the artistically gifted or performing arts academies.

In the course of teaching all students, you will no doubt identify some as gifted or talented in dance who need further specialized training. Recommend that they audition for gifted programs in the school district. Also channel them to reputable local studios for advanced training. Impress on both of these programs that your basic curriculum program provides broad dance training to complement theirs—not to compete with it.

How ED Differs From and Is Similar to an After-School Model Educational dance's mandate is to serve all students during the school day, not after school. As basic curriculum for all students, ED connects to other academic instruction as part of the core curriculum. National standards govern school day programs to promote consistent, ongoing curricular goals.

However, after-school models give some students, but not all, a chance for dance instruction. Typically, activity-based instruction predominates. Some after-school programs are performance oriented. It is one way for students to extend their dance experiences and polish their skills. After-school programs are generally not regulated by quantity or quality, so what is taught varies widely. Some are funded by parent–teacher organizations (PTOs), some are private pay, some are state or federally funded, and some are offered through arts education umbrella organizations like the Kennedy Center, which funds after-school programs in designated communities throughout the country. Most are taught by instructors with a background in dance who are not certified dance specialists.

How ED Differs From a Private Dance Studio Model Many students discover that they want more dance experience than they can get during the school day and enroll in studios for further instruction. Private studios provide an excellent way to master technique and refine performing abilities. Indeed, serious dance students should and must consistently study in high-quality studios.

School-based and private studios complement each other with different purposes. Each offers students different skills:

- Private studios stress technique and performance. Most studio classes are activity based.
- ED is comprehensive. It emphasizes creating and composing, studying dancing technique and performing, and knowing about and

responding to dance from a broad variety of dance styles and cultures.

- Private studios train dancers (and others who want to study dance) to dance.
- ED introduces all students to dance to strengthen body and mind.
- Private studios refine specialized skills.
- ED provides more generalized instruction.
- Private studios specialize in particular styles (e.g., tap, ballet, character, musical theatre) and options (e.g., Pilates mat classes, yoga, pointe classes).
- ED emphasizes many styles of dance, including a broad spectrum of dance across cultures, and also connects with the other arts and academics as well as performing.
- Private studios have specific performance criteria by which to measure and promote student success.
- ED follows state and national accountability standards that delineate learning outcomes.

In addition, some studios offer conservatory-level instruction for highly skilled performers. Some studios that are affiliated with a dance company offer junior company classes to those who qualify.

Therefore, the private studio, conservatory, and dance company models are not the models for K-12. Both private study and ED aim to create the best dancers possible, but rarely does a basic curriculum during the school day offer enough time to create highly proficient performers who would not also need outside instruction. Motivated students get the best of both when they get schools that teach dance broadly and studios that further refine dance technique and give them additional performance venues.

 How does this school model differ from your studio experience? How does it complement studio classes? How might you work with a local studio to enhance both programs?

How ED Differs From a Physical Education Model Aspects of dance are easily adapted to physical education. Indeed, physical educators historically brought dance into the curriculum and made a place for it long before there were dance specialists in K-12. Dance training for certified physical educators is usually activity based. Rarely do physical educators study dance performance, choreography, criticism, and dance history. Their dance goals relate to fitness, skill development, recreation, rhythmic acuity, locomotor skills and sequences, movement exploration, and lifelong learning. Many physical educators have strong backgrounds in folk, social, and recreational dance, and many offer quality programs in movement exploration and creative dance. Their professional preparation makes them strong collaborators and collegial resources in **kinesiology,** movement analysis, class management, assessment, and adaptive activities for physically challenged students. Most physical education standards include physical skills in dance as an activity. Collaborations between the dance specialist and physical educator are important to nurture.

On the other hand, a dance specialist's rigorous study of technique, performance, dance history, criticism, and composition prepares him or her to bring dance to the level of aesthetic presentation required to teach dance as an art form. The expectations of aesthetic education by a dance specialist are that dance will be taught as an expressive art form in all its facets rather than strictly as activity-based learning.

Dance can be taught in both ED and physical education with the highest integrity. A supportive partnership between physical education and ED gives students the best of both approaches to dance. Both the physical educator and dance specialist bring specific skills and backgrounds to dance, and both ably teach dance to achieve their goals and standards.

Some states emphasize dance and movement exploration in the physical education curriculum more than others. What about your state? How do its physical education dance standards interface with the dance and arts standards?

How ED Differs From a Traditional Classroom Model The dance specialist sets out to achieve educational goals similar to those of every other classroom teacher in the building, although the way of achieving these goals and the teaching spaces differ. Both ED and the traditional classroom model educate broadly. Where overlapping goals exist between other subjects and dance, both classroom teachers and dance specialists should address these goals (see chapter 10). Growing numbers of elementary classroom teachers value movement-

"Do not forget—never forget it!—that dance-educational work is an artistically conditioned task."

—Mary Wigman
(1966, p. 107)

based education to increase conceptual learning in subject areas. They openly incorporate dance. You can become a resource for such generalists seeking age-appropriate dance and movement material to support academic learning.

What Are the Defining Characteristics of Educational Dance?

Educational dance has six defining characteristics:

1. Comprehensive (broad in scope)
2. Substantive (challenging and significant)
3. Sequential (ordered and incremental)
4. Aesthetically driven (seeking fine quality)
5. Contextually coherent (relevant and related)
6. Inquiry based (participatory and investigative)

To educate broadly in, about, and through dance in school-based programs, we must maximize each of these six defining characteristics. The first three characteristics are the basis for the rest. Without the first three, the last three would be ineffective and impotent. As we examine all six characteristics, keep in mind that all fit together to complete an arts education perspective on dance. We refer to these six throughout the text as the **6DC Cornerstone Model of Inquiry-Based Educational Dance,** or the 6DC Cornerstone Model.

Comprehensive

Characteristic 1: **Comprehensive** means that dance education is broad in scope, covering the many facets of dance including diverse styles and experiences. To be comprehensive, educational dance must encompass the full spectrum of the dance discipline: the dance processes (dancing, dance making, and dance critiquing), dance science (anatomy, somatics, kinesiology, injury prevention), dance knowledge (**dance elements, dance history** and anthropology, and cultural dance forms), and everything that affects dance (e.g., theatrical terms, stage lighting, and performance techniques). ED addresses psychomotor, cognitive, and **affective domains,** and it parallels the

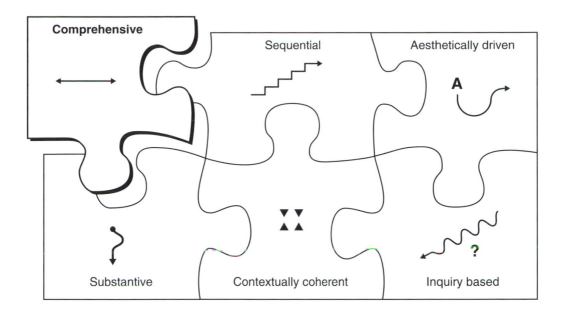

breadth of national and state standards. It emphasizes dance as an art form and makes connections to other art forms but also draws from other aspects of dance such as social, recreational, and ritual dance. ED is diverse: It calls on dances from our time and dances of the past, and it explores world cultures through dance to create knowledgeable world citizens.

Comprehensive dance study in ED is inclusive in every sense of the term—including all students, using all dance styles, engaging the full self in all aspects of dance. The interactions between each of the artistic processes (c/p/r) strengthen learning in dance. What Stephen Mark Dobbs said about teaching art applies to dance: "A single . . . experience in [dance] is unlikely to provide students with the effective array of experiences and benefits that a comprehensive approach envisions" (Dobbs 1998, p. 56).

To deliver a comprehensive program, teachers use numerous ways to invite learners to move, dance, create, critique, edit, refine, study, perform, label, and reflect. Through such a wide range of experiences, we build dance literate students.

 How does this affect the knowledge and skills you must acquire to teach K-12?

Substantive

Characteristic 2: A **substantive** dance program must contain stimulating, content-rich subject matter worthy of study, thought, and investigation. It brings

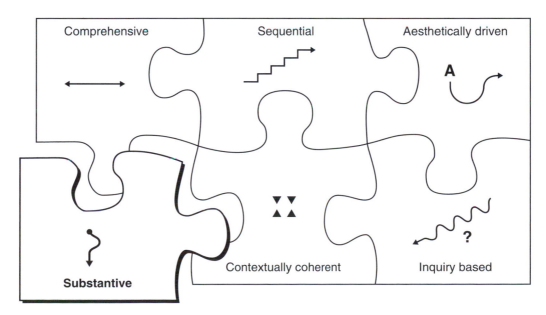

students into the complexity of the subject matter. Teachers engage students deeply—physically, mentally, and aesthetically—to explore movement and concepts to advance their education. Students develop a context for dance by delving into all its facets and relating them to each other. Students do both creative and re-creative work. Inquiry leads students further and deeper, beyond superficiality.

Students need to acquire depth in all aspects of dance and the dance processes to be educated in dance (i.e., to be dance literate). Dancing is vital to learning the art. However, dancing activities alone are neither comprehensive nor substantive enough for a standards-oriented curriculum. Elliot Eisner agrees: "We must ask students to think critically as well as to articulate about these experiences in order to ensure the experiences take on significance and are processed into the total learning experience" (1985, p. 2). Children must see dance performed to develop visual sensitivity to dance. Harry Broudy called these "skills of 'impression' as well as 'expression'" (Brandt 1987/1988, p. 7).

Substantive educational dance rigorously challenges students to reach for academic, aesthetic, and kinetic achievements. We are asked to teach technique classes with purpose because demanding technique classes develop world-class dancing and performing skills. We are asked to teach with somatic integrity to emphasize the inner workings of the neuromusculoskeletal system. We are asked to refine our own skills so we can refine those of our students. We are asked to involve students at different levels of thinking and reflection.

Substantive study requires substantial interaction with the material and with classmates as well as between student and teacher. Successful teachers constantly challenge students to deal with complex material in and outside class. ED is intense and stimulating; it educates with quality, for quality.

 What implications does a substantive K-12 dance program have for universities who certify dance specialists?

Sequential

Characteristic 3: **Sequential** content and instruction systematically build one skill on another. Because instruction develops from one concept to the next, from simple to complex, this characteristic determines how you select, plan, and order content at each grade level. Because you teach multiple grade levels, you must learn to sequence content to layer skills year by year. **Sequencing** keeps content from being haphazard, redundant, and repetitive. Introduce concepts at one stage and develop them later. Grow today's concepts on previous foundations to challenge students to achieve the next level. Plan 13 independent, yet interdependent, years. Once begun, dance education should continue uninterrupted for all remaining school years to make a K-12 program sequentially effective. One of the best ways to grow educational dance programs is to start the new program in elementary school and add one year at a time as students move up, until all grade levels are in place.

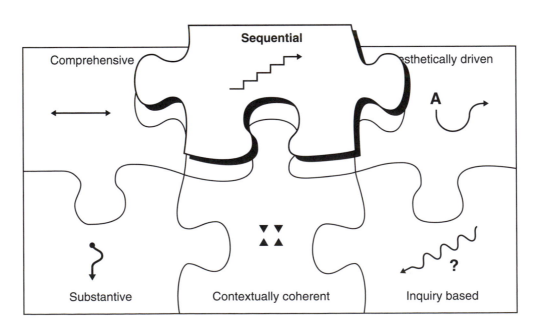

Stephen Mark Dobbs' belief about visual art education applied to dance: "A written sequential curriculum facilitates competent instruction and cumulative learning. As youngsters move through their school years they require [a dance] program that reinforces and builds rather than merely repeats the previous lessons" (Dobbs 1989, p. 10).

Unless there is a sequential framework to follow, the teacher will not know what experiences have preceded. Dobbs also reminds us that "well designed curricula are not formulas or blueprints; they provide a resource to be mediated by sensitive, informed teaching . . . endless possibilities exist for the expansion of imagination and the development of divergent problem-solving skills, both in the teacher's instructional technique and in student learning" (Dobbs 1989, p. 10).

There are three ways to keep content and instruction sequentially progressing.

- Ensure that learning is nonrepetitive.
- Use a spiral approach.
- See the big picture before you start to plan the details.

To ensure that learning is nonrepetitive, progress from simple to complex. Sequence learning during each school year as well as from one year to the next to consistently build new skills on the old. Review and extend old skills rather than repeat the same material year after year. Move students forward, toward specific growth-oriented goals and objectives. Sequence each year, each unit, and each lesson according to sequenced objectives, while keeping in mind student need and readiness.

Spiral through dance content so that it grows richer and deeper year by year. Spiral back to material introduced earlier to extend it to the next level. Revisit the main concepts and topics to expand them year by year so tasks become more challenging and complex. Construct curriculum goals today on those reached previously to get an ever-increasing tapestry of student accomplishment. Go from what students know to what they need to know in a continuing spiral to keep content student focused. Remember that spiraling weaves the student's artistic tapestry by attaching new threads to those previously woven.

To keep students moving forward, look at the multiyear continuum they experience as they go from kindergarten through high school (the big picture). Teaching is more than determining where

Consistently spiral through space concepts of shape, level, and focus to bring students to a keen awareness of how they interact.

students are right now and what they need to learn next. Step back to take a broader look at what each grade level should add to students' knowledge and skills in dance, even as you take a child-centered approach. Consider Johna, a kindergartener, who has 12 more years of school dance. How can you keep her from experiencing the same thing year after year or, just as bad, experiencing isolated activities that have no bearing on what she already learned in dance or what she will acquire next year? How can you avoid starting her over at the beginning of each year and giving her only experiences instead of a systematic progression of knowledge and skills in dance?

Keep a perspective on how learning at one age level affects learning at the next age level. Sequence instruction year by year to prepare students to succeed at the next level. Identify the main educational goals first, and from that vantage point plan instruction for any age based on (a) what students already know, (b) what they should already know but may not have grasped to determine whether you need to repeat material, (c) what specific skills they must acquire during this grade level, and (d) how those skills prepare them for their next level of educational dance.

Chapter 4's developmental descriptions enable you to make conscious decisions about the nature and needs of students at different ages. Notice in the discussion of *National Standards for Dance Education* (NSDEs) in chapter 2 that achievement standards are grouped in grade clusters (such as grades K-4), which tells you what students should know and do by the time they get to the last grade level in the cluster (in that case, grade 4). That perspective enables you to see the big picture and then use the developmental descriptions in chapter 4 to decide how to sequence instruction. From that vantage point you can plan the sequential progression for the age range you teach so as to achieve all the standards during those years.

Aesthetically Driven

Characteristic 4: **Aesthetics** are the branch of philosophy that deal with the nature of beauty and our response to it. Aesthetics seek that which is beautiful, well designed, and artistic. Dance in aesthetic education shows students diverse ways to create and appreciate quality and beauty. Aesthetic education deals with the nature of dance as art and especially values quality dance performance. Aesthetics drive teaching and learning in K-12 dance.

Aesthetics seek the exquisite, the balanced, the correct artistic form, and that which has artistic value. We apply aesthetics when we refine our own performing and creating as well as when we ana-

"The arts need to be incorporated into every child's learning—not to improve test scores, but to provide individuals with the necessary tools to make and find meaning. . . . The arts need to be incorporated into every child's learning for the more important purpose of enabling a future generation to participate across circumstance, culture, and time in the ongoing human conversation that is perpetuated through the arts."

—Jessica Davis (1996, p. 33)

lyze and **evaluate** the arts. Aesthetics include our response to things of beauty around us. Something aesthetic satisfies. Developing an aesthetic perspective is a driving factor for teaching dance as art in education.

Aesthetics call up feelings from the participant:

- Being personally moved by something
- Being satisfied with an accomplishment
- Being driven to do one's best work

Although aesthetics is an individual feeling response (of the heart), aesthetic quality is also evaluated (by the mind) by what is collectively believed to be of good quality and form. Arts education advances both.

Although definitions of *aesthetics* are illusive, art educator Stephen Mark Dobbs (1998) explains:

[T]he field of *aesthetics* is that branch of philosophy in which questions are raised and examined about the nature, meaning, and value of art, and other things, from an aesthetic point of view. The study of aesthetics in this sense helps students to understand what distinguishes art from other kinds of phenomena. . . . (p. 46)

The goal of aesthetic education is to help students establish an aesthetic perspective or an aesthetic viewpoint. Aesthetic education helps students uphold artistic standards and take an artistic viewpoint while creating, performing, or responding to dance. In turn aesthetic education is developed through each of these experiences. As a teacher well versed in the art of dance, you must consistently hold an aesthetic perspective so you can lead students to a refined level of discernment about what is quality work and what is not.

An **aesthetically driven** curriculum relates all dance experiences to matters of artistry and the degree to which artistry can be achieved for the satisfaction of the doer and the beholder. Such a curriculum aims to help students attain proficiency and the best in terms of art making and performing. NSDEs are aesthetically driven, and so is your K-12 curriculum. Herein is the defining line between

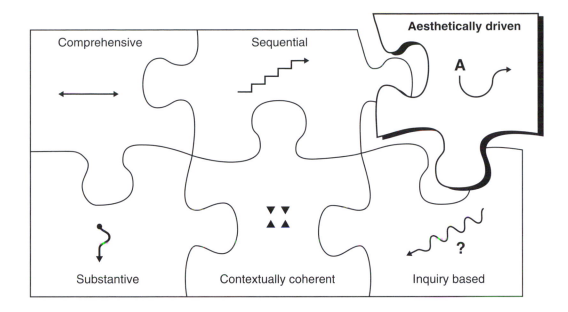

teaching *dance* and teaching *dance as art in education.*

Aesthetic education seeks the highest point of refinement, the ultimate in beauty, the magnificent. It does not seek what is merely pleasing or useful; rather it describes or seeks to attain what is extraordinary in its achievement of excellence and refinement. As we increase our artistic awareness, we perceive exquisite beauty through the senses and process it cognitively. We have to see the great works and masterpieces of choreography to begin to understand dance in an aesthetically driven curriculum.

Aesthetic education fosters artistic thought and expression. In dance, it teaches how to transform ideas into movement symbols, how to create and compose with artistic skill, and how to dance and increase technical skills of performing. Aesthetic education teaches a vocabulary with which to analyze and critique dance for its compositional quality and performance quality. Artistic quality informs all aesthetic decisions and choices when creating, leads learners toward qualitative judgments from multiple viewpoints (i.e., performer, creator, critic), and asks for discriminating choices. In total, aesthetic education not only increases artistic expression—it builds a perspective for looking at the world.

Aesthetic education in dance should increase the quality of student output in

- dancing and performing (refined technique, fluidity of motion, artistic presentation),
- choreographing (use of artistic principles), and

- observation of dance (analysis of quality, critiquing).

We develop a sense of aesthetics from two perspectives:

1. **Collective aesthetics**—a perspective of what is of artistic quality based on the artistic **principles of design** while also factoring in aspects of **aesthetic pluralism.** One's collective aesthetic is acquired through education and experience. Thus it evolves from the artistic values of the arts and design community and stretches to include or embrace the aesthetic norms of varied cultures.

2. **Personal aesthetics**—an individual response from our unique inner aesthetic perception. It is enhanced by educational experiences in the arts.

Collective Aesthetics

Collective aesthetics are shaped by the **design principles** of the art form. In dance the principles apply to a dance work's overall choreographic design and form. The principles of design underpin the choreographic structure of all major dance works of art. The principles give us benchmarks for describing artistry. They are necessary to an educational dance curriculum.

In addition, the collective aesthetic needs to stretch to include aesthetic perspectives from different world cultures. Cultural aesthetic norms vary according to what is satisfying, what uniquely pleases, or what suits the taste of a particular culture. You must be prepared to shift aesthetic perspectives as you teach dance of different cultures.

Also include the perspective of the cultures represented in your **classroom.** To study dance from our own familiar collective cultural norms grounds us in those norms. No matter where you are in the world, your students will call on their own cultural values to make sense of other cultures' aesthetic differences and similarities. Recognizing norms does not inhibit students from making their own satisfying choices to express their unique perspectives.

Personal Aesthetics

By middle school, dance students begin to develop personal aesthetic discrimination within the context of the broad collective (i.e., communal and cultural) aesthetics. High school students find their own artistic voices—to branch out and create what is freer and less predictable. Norms, however, prevent them from running nude down the street and expecting to hear that this is a beautiful, aesthetically pleasing "dance."

It is your responsibility to uphold artistic standards to increase aesthetic discrimination at all ages. As you anchor students of any age in the ability to recognize artistic quality according to the collective aesthetic norms, you help them develop standards for excellence. By bringing in varied cultural norms, you help students expand their aesthetic viewpoint. By bringing in a variety of cultures, you help students cultivate their own personal taste. Thus, aesthetic education in dance helps individuals make refined

personal artistic choices within the context of what is considered good by collective artistic standards without feeling rigidly bound to those norms.

Contextually Coherent

Characteristic 5: **Contextual coherence** relates dance to other aspects of learning. It gives dance instruction relevance and relatedness. What is learned is related to what is known in other aspects of dance and in other subjects. A dance experience is not a stand-alone event.

A single dance class risks becoming a random event, not connected to anything else and not even connected to other aspects of dance. In the past we have tended to teach dance so our students learn piecemeal, in fragments. We isolated aspects of the dance discipline: one class to learn the techniques of a certain style, another class to learn repertory, another to focus on great dances of the past, another to choreograph, another to critique dance works. But school-based programs for all children need to make dance understandable and coherent as an art form. You can easily infuse relevant aspects of dance history while dancing, or compare two dance styles' similarities and differences, or integrate all the artistic processes around a theme. You certainly will continue to teach technique-based classes in the studio. But you must also add related content from the full dance discipline to support what you are teaching there.

You may have been taught in a piecemeal way and will now need to evaluate how contextual

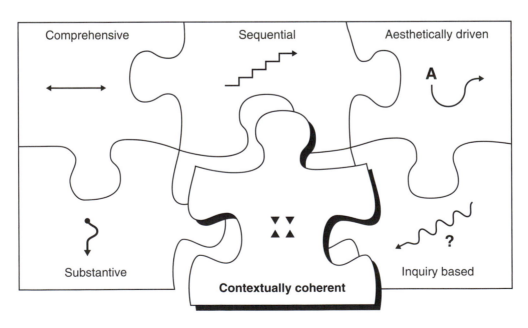

learning might have increased your knowledge of dance alongside your dancing abilities. School-based dance education requires a paradigm shift toward integrated, sustained learning experiences that build a context, an enlarged grid for learning. Dance instruction can no longer be fragmented. It must include all aspects of dance learning within a broad perspective about the art form of dance and dancing.

Educational coherence is critical to learning. When parts are related to the whole in a sustained learning environment, students achieve and understand what they learn. An isolated event in dance is of little value. It is just one part of the total picture. "Content without context is pretext," said Warren Bennis (lecture at Wilson Learning Client Conference, 1982, Minneapolis, MN).

You must guarantee that learning is not random. Help students connect their learning to the larger world of dance and when possible apply it in relevant ways to the rest of the world. If not, how will they know what dance can be? How will they understand dance? For example, the context of a choreographic work might be its relationship to its creator, to the place it was created, or to the way it fulfills artistic or societal purposes. Although some dance works are obscure, many have accessible histories. Contextual information enables us to classify dance works by style, function, and genre. A dance's context is its environment. This environment sheds light on the work itself. Relate dance to music and art. Look for notable visual artworks to compare that have a similar theme, share the same time period, have a similar **rhythm,** or connect through shapes and **textures.**

Build context by relating concepts (parts) to the whole:

- Interrelate aspects of the dance discipline that reinforce each other to increase aesthetic education.
- Relate dance across disciplines to increase overall arts education.

Interrelate the artistic processes of creating, performing, and responding to dance (c/p/r) for optimum coherence. For example, if one unit connects to a dance work such as Pilobolus' *Bonsai,* the choreographic work itself stimulates students in multiple ways. Not only do students learn about Pilobolus and its evolution, they work on techniques and movements inspired by *Bonsai*'s partner shapes and balances. Students analyze the work aesthetically and critique the choreography and the performance they are viewing. They compare symmetrical and asymmetrical shapes in dance to shapes in math. They contrast original shapes seen in the work to **geometric** and mathematical shapes. They take ideas from the work to stimulate their own dance making with a partner. They then evaluate and critique their dance work by discussing time, body shape, **dynamics,** and **relationships** in their own composition. The context has been built by a dance work that gives students a greater understanding of what dance is and how what they are doing relates to what a major dance company does in one particular style (modern dance). Without the context of the work, isolated learning experiences would not have achieved greater dance understanding.

Inquiry Based

Characteristic 6: **Dance inquiry** is about investigating. **Inquiry-based dance** is both a teaching style and a learning process that invites students to participate and to problem solve. Inquiry produces an active learning environment where students uncover diverse topics essential to their growth. Meaningful inquiry stimulates learning. Aesthetic inquiry leads learners to make discriminating choices about what they do and what they see in dance.

Dance inquiry relies on creative and **critical thinking.** Individuals delve into complexities with a questioning attitude. They use their senses and at times their whole self—body, mind, and spirit—to question and to explore. This process deepens their experiences and advances their education. Inquiry engages learners on many levels (see chapter 5).

Student inquiry is facilitated when you invite movement exploration and pose meaningful dance questions. Target questions that stimulate your students to analyze (left brain function) and to imagine (right brain function). Use inquiry to put students at the center of learning so they acquire a personal understanding of dance. For example, when you pose a movement problem to solve in dance improvisation, each person solves it in her or his own way. Or when you invite older students to research a topic of interest and make a dance study about it, the lesson goes from an abstract inquiry-based project to a unique form of individual expression. To a great extent, inquiry personalizes and individualizes learning. It leads each student to take ownership of learning to personally seek out

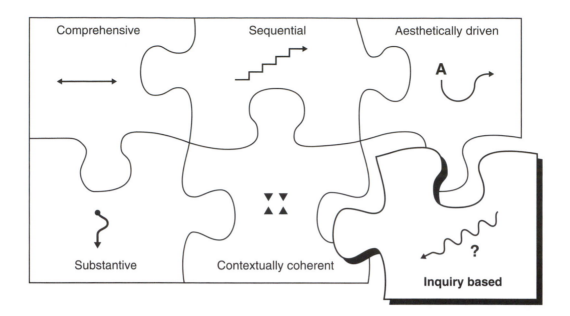

relevant information and experiences. Inquiry can be investigative, creative, evaluative, or reflective, as shown in later chapters.

Dance inquiry refers to a student's process of investigating dance that generates higher-order and critical thinking about significant content in a comprehensive, substantive dance curriculum. An **inquiry approach** refers to the teacher's process of incorporating comprehensive content in dance with student inquiry to increase active learning, **higher-order and critical thinking,** and artistic production. An inquiry approach expects a lot from students *and*

teachers. It expects teachers to engage students, promote artistic standards, and facilitate aesthetic inquiry. It also expects learners to be responsible for learning—to actively participate, investigate, question, and problem solve.

6DC Cornerstone Model

Educational dance programs must exhibit all six characteristics in order to be complete, as shown in figure 1.1. Each puzzle piece fits together to make the whole picture. Students in such programs are

Six Characteristics of Educational Dance

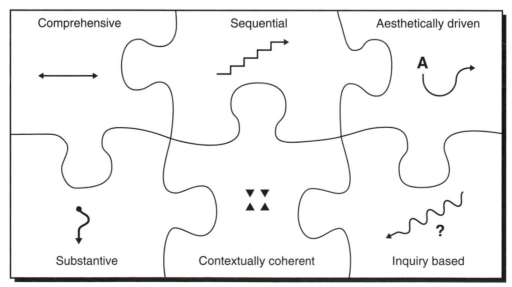

FIGURE 1.1 When all six characteristics work together, learners get a complete model of educational dance.

expected to achieve national dance standards. These characteristics comprise what this text calls the 6DC Cornerstone Model of Inquiry-Based Educational Dance.

Reflect and Respond

1. Stop reading now and pull together what you have learned.

   > How do you explain what should be found in a school-based program?

   > What is your concise definition for *educational dance* based on its six defining characteristics and its purpose? (Don't read ahead until you answer this!)

2. After you finish writing your definition for *educational dance*, read this one. How does yours compare with this?

   > Educational dance: A comprehensive, substantive, and sequential contextually based dance program that integrates the arts processes of performing, creating, and responding into all children's education. Such a dance program is investigative. It furnishes the necessary knowledge, skills, and artistic perspectives to support aesthetic growth in all aspects of dance. Its aim is to educate broadly in and through dance to develop learners who understand dance as an art form and are skilled in the artistic processes.

3. What exactly did you describe? What will it look like in the classroom? What are outcomes of a complete program?

What Drives an Arts Education Perspective?

An arts education perspective emerges out of all the beliefs presented so far in the **six defining characteristics (6DC) of educational dance.** In addition, three other factors are always at play in arts education:

1. Student-centered learning
2. National standards, part of the arts education reform agenda
3. Cornerstones of the discipline

Putting students at the center of learning is an internal matter. But following the national standards arts education agenda is an external matter. Why and how do these standards help drive dance as art in education?

Student-Centered Learning

Student needs help drive the dance curriculum. It is up to you to determine student needs. You must assess where your students are and where they need to go. Then you become the catalyst to bring standards-oriented curriculum content and experiences to real individuals.

You are responsible for student growth in all these aspects when you teach dance: the physical, the psychosocial, the aesthetic, and the cognitive. To reach the whole child, you combine the kinesthetic with the cognitive, social, and aesthetic. You also increase critical thinking and motor development. This is a pretty tall order, but this book helps you achieve each goal (see chapter 4).

Such all-encompassing student-centered learning gives up nothing. Students are to accept responsibility for their aesthetic growth—but you design the tasks and set the standards. You are the one who draws them into discussion and dialogue about significant dance topics. You ask the kind of questions that turn their wheels and send them off to inquire further into this dynamic activity or that world-class dance form. In this process, they find what is personally relevant to them in dance. This process results in students who understand dance, appreciate it, and are able to express themselves through it.

Students need to grow whether they are gifted and talented or have disabilities. Inquiry personalizes the experience so all students can grow in a way that is appropriate for them.

Arts Education Reform Agenda

The enabling legislation for arts education was enacted by Congress in 1989. It was the Goals 2000—Educate America Act. It named the arts, including dance, as basic subjects for every child. Goal 3 of Goals 2000 states the following:

> All students will leave grades 4, 8, and 12 having demonstrated competency over challenging subject matter including English, mathematics, science, foreign languages, civics and government, economics, arts, history and geography. (National Endowment for the Arts 1994, p. 3)

Thus, the arts were legitimized as core academic disciplines alongside math, science, and language arts, creating the need to have national standards in **all the arts.**

National Arts Standards (K-12)

In 1989, the United States became a nation of standards-based education, which includes arts education. National arts standards followed in 1994. Under the aegis of the **Consortium of National Arts Education Associations (DAMT for Dance, Art, Music, and Theatre)** (consisting of the American Alliance for Theatre & Education, MENC: The National Association for Music Education, the National Art Education Association, and the National Dance Association), the *National Standards for Arts Education* (NSAEs) were published. Their purpose was to stop the marginalization of the arts in American education and to ensure a place for the arts in the K-12 curriculum. The standards were developed as world-class standards of what American young people should know and be able to do in all the arts. The standards are to help students keep pace with other countries that emphasize arts education. Although voluntary as of 2005, these standards help drive arts education's reform agenda.

In writing the national arts standards, recognized arts educators in each discipline laid out realistic content and achievement standards in the arts. Working long and hard, they debated issues, stood their ground, and reached consensus to design a document with far-reaching implications for both education and all the arts. After considering commonalities across the arts, as well as unique needs of each individual art form, these arts educators prepared comprehensive standards that guide school arts programs. This process was jointly funded by the U.S. Department of Education, the National Endowment for the Arts, and the National Endowment of the Humanities.

There are two separate documents that are connected. The NSAEs call for measurable student achievement in all **four arts disciplines** K-12 (dance, music, theatre, and visual arts). The document is targeted to educational administrators, government leaders, and general lay audiences. The NSAEs contain standards for all four arts. The NSDEs, one section of the NSAEs, are also printed as a separate document and are written for dance

> **"Most curriculums pay no attention at all to aesthetics, a branch of philosophy that deals with questions, What is art?, Must all art be beautiful?, Does art provide knowledge? . . . [S]omewhere between kindergarten and twelfth grade students ought to be introduced to such questions in order to participate in an intellectual dialogue that has been going on for two thousand years."**
>
> —Elliot Eisner (in Brandt 1987/ 1988, p. 7)

specialists. NSAEs and NSDEs inform our tasks and externally drive our programs toward quality. The dance standards are the subject of chapter 2.

It is helpful to first study the NSAEs to identify the commonalities among art disciplines before you focus on dance standards alone. Grasp parallel processes across the arts. See how all the arts expand the ways learners think, reason, intuit, imagine, and express themselves. Again, see the big picture. Learn to think like an arts educator—not just a dance educator! From this perspective you will understand how what you do in dance needs to contribute to the desired outcomes stated for and expected of every twelfth grader in America:

- *to communicate at a basic level in all four of the arts,* by using the basic vocabularies, materials, tools, techniques, and intellectual methods of each of the arts disciplines;
- *to communicate proficiently in one art form;*
- *to analyze works of art* (including dance) from various structural, historical, and cultural perspectives;
- *to be familiar with exemplary works of art from various cultures across history;* and
- *to relate arts knowledge and skills in each discipline as well as across the arts.*

Adapted with permission of the National Dance Association (NDA).

Uniform standards promote consistency among national programs. Students and school districts across state lines may now be compared. Standards stabilize the field as well as serve students who move to another state. The benchmarks are reasonable and attainable. Teach students to master arts competencies and dance expectations for their benefit first and for your program accountability second. Learn how all standards affect your work, but closely focus on the NSDEs to inform your accountability in dance.

Accountability

Accountability to world-class standards also drives arts education: for teachers, for schools, and for higher education.

- Teachers are accountable for student achievement.
- Schools are accountable for quality programs.
- Higher education is accountable for preparing qualified arts specialists (including dance specialists).

Teacher Accountability   You are expected to prepare students to achieve national arts standards. As a certified dance specialist, you are to produce individuals from kindergarten through grade 12 who at least meet defined standards in dance as arts education.

School Accountability Programs   Dance as part of the basic curriculum adheres to different guidelines than those of specialized programs in dance.

• **Basic Curriculum Programs.** Schools are morally accountable to offer uninterrupted programs from kindergarten through high school. Schools are accountable to state and national guidelines as well as to district policies that affect logistics and delivery of school arts. Schools professionally evaluate all arts and academic programs. Schools formally assess teachers' efforts in the classroom based on state and national guidelines. Specialists are expected to meet specific educational and artistic standards according to quality teacher standards.

• **Specialized Programs.** Some states in the United States are required to have a specialized artistically gifted and talented (AG/T) curriculum available for all who qualify. Their legislation mandates that a percentage of educational funds serve identified G/T or AG/T students in grades 2 through 12. If you are in such a state, this should not affect your budget for comprehensive dance education because the AG/T curriculum is usually funded from a different source. Neither should it affect your program that is part of the basic curriculum. AG/T students are usually also in basic curriculum at the elementary level. Because you will teach all students, you are a valu-

"If imagination and creativity alone made art, we could all be artists."

—New York Council on the Arts postcard

As you teach dance in the basic curriculum, help identify students who seem gifted or talented to recommend for special study.

able resource to identify all who seem *gifted* (i.e., conceptually, compositionally, and choreographically outstanding) and those who are *talented* (outstanding performers) in dance.

Higher Education Accountability   Higher education is accountable to state teacher licensure standards in dance, which are regulated by national accrediting bodies such as the National Association of Schools of Dance and the National Council for the Assessment of Teacher Education. State and national accrediting agencies determine the standards for university dance programs. Standards say what criteria are to be accomplished. Assessments measure the extent to which teachers reach or accomplish the standards. Standards and assessments drive everything from student learning to school programs to teacher preparation, as you will see in chapters 2 and 3.

Quality teaching hinges on quality teacher preparation. Your ability to shape a standards-oriented, outcome-based K-12 program depends on the quality of your education. Excellence in one fosters excellence in the other. Dance education is a continuous K-16 cycle. Just as kindergarten through grade 5 lay the foundation for all that follows through twelfth grade, your undergraduate college education determines how fully prepared you, the dance specialist, are to teach K-12. (See figure 1.2.) The implications of an aesthetically driven K-12 curriculum thus dictate to a great extent how your 13-16 experiences must be shaped.

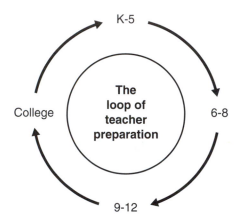

FIGURE 1.2 Quality K-12 dance programs depend on quality teacher preparation at the college or university level.

Cornerstones of the Curriculum

Although standards affect dance and arts education from the outside, professionals in the field have no trouble embracing standards as baseline to student success. Not only do dance specialists ensure that their students reach standards, but specialists also reach beyond standard achievement, to excellence. Excellence in the arts is always an appropriate benchmark.

So what is the core dance content? What practices ensure that students achieve the standards or surpass them? It is the dance **cornerstones** that contain the core body of knowledge and skills that all students should possess: dancing and performing; creating and composing; knowing dance history, culture, and context; and analyzing and critiquing. Cornerstone content is comprehensive (broad) and substantive (deep), is infused in aesthetics, and is able to be sequenced from kindergarten to grade 12. Cornerstone content encourages dance inquiry. The cornerstones provide a contextual grid for dance, so one aspect relates to another within the dance discipline rather than being taught as isolated skills. Cornerstone content brings the full dance discipline to students. This is the subject of chapters 5 through 9.

What Is Best Practice?

Dance's best practices—rather than being the latest trends—are in fact the practices that are tried and true, those that work best, and those rooted in the dance discipline itself. Best practices are those that educate students broadly in and through dance. Best practices grow out of and build on the 14 premises stated earlier (page 4) and the **dance cornerstones.** Best practices take forward the most enduring understanding about dance and artistic expression and go far beyond what can be measured by tests or listed as a standard. Best practices factor in the richness of dance and recognize the intrinsic value (and corresponding personal satisfaction) of performing your best, refining your choreography, analyzing a professional choreographer's well-crafted composition, and learning about dance's social, political, or artistic impact on the world.

Teaching from the 6DC Cornerstone Model sets the stage for best practice, because it aims to incorporate—yet go beyond—what is measured in the national standards. This model combines knowing about dance as art and applying the artistic processes (c/p/r) to increase dance skills and deepen aesthetic education.

There is no **codified** list of best practices. Best practices evolve based on what gets the best results in the context of the 6DC. Because "best" is not quantifiable and is highly **subjective,** teachers share their own best practices through journal articles, ongoing research, dance conferences, and dialogue with state and national leaders in dance education. With these activities teachers take the field forward. Plan to share your best teaching practices that result in artistic growth so you continue to add to the development of best practice in dance.

How Does This Mesh With National Standards?

No matter what the current version of the standards, the 6DC Cornerstone Model, rooted in the four dance cornerstones, gives a consistently stable base from which to teach the discipline. A program anchored in the cornerstones incorporates the complete dance discipline. Best practices in arts education centered on artistic application of the cornerstones keep the field growing in new ways and sharing what seems to work well. Chapter 2 goes into greater detail about national standards.

What Should Dance Specialists Know and Be Able to Do?

What are *you* supposed to know and do? What kind of background prepares you to teach dance as art in education? That is the subject of the rest of this book. Chapter 2 describes the externally driven accountability of your program. It emphasizes the standards you are to teach by. Chapter 3 explains your roles and responsibilities as well as the standards that determine how you are prepared to teach. Chapter 4 explains the four ways you keep dance education student centered (internally driven). Chapters 5 through 9 explain the comprehensive content, which is substantive and sequential. These chapters show you how to create an aesthetically driven, contextually coherent, and inquiry-based curriculum for your students. Chapters 10 through 16 further develop your skills. Meanwhile, study dance in all its aspects to be the most knowledgeable and creative dancer you can be. And we will go from there.

> **"It is widely acknowledged that arts education is integral to educational excellence. While recognized as essential fields of learning in and of themselves, the arts can deepen and enliven learning in all subject areas. Experience in the arts provides significant opportunities for critical thinking, creative problem solving, collaborative learning, autonomous judgment, and constructive community involvement. The arts provide knowledge of our own cultural heritage and enlighten us about other cultures, past and present. Moreover, the arts invite students of all ages to address fundamental human issues such as values, feelings, ethics, standards, and social or environmental concerns."**
>
> —Alliance of SC Arts Education Organizations in Visual Art, Dance, Music, and Theatre (1991, p. 22)

experiences grow with a student from the time she or he enters school until graduation?

4. What educational advantage is achieved by including choreography in the schools? By discussing dance as a nonverbal art form? By studying varied dance styles?

5. What is the purpose of educational dance, and how does it serve students? What should dance's educational impact be on an average learner who isn't preparing to be a professional performer?

6. What is an arts education perspective?

7. What are the six distinguishing characteristics of educational dance from an arts education perspective?

8. How does a K-12 educational dance curriculum differ from that of a private studio? Why is a studio model inappropriate for a school-based program?

Rich Resources

State frameworks are available from the following:

- South Carolina Department of Education: www.myscschools.com
- Utah State Office of Education: www.usoe.k12.ut.us
- New Jersey Department of Education: www.state.nj.us/education
- Arizona Department of Education: www.ade.state.az.us
- California Department of Education: www.cde.ca.gov
- Texas Education Agency: www.tea.state.tx.us
- Wyoming Department of Education: www.k12.wy.us/index.asp

Questions to Ponder

1. What do you believe about curriculum in dance in K-12? How does this affect what you need to know?

2. How does your college work prepare you to design and teach a comprehensive dance program? A substantive program? A sequential program?

3. Why is a sequential curriculum important? How is context built? How might dance

Examining How National Arts Initiatives Affect Dance

"A comprehensive, articulated arts education program also engages students in a process that helps them develop the self-esteem, self-discipline, cooperation, and self-motivation necessary for success in life."

—Consortium of National Arts Education Associations (1994, p. 7)

This chapter describes the national arts education landscape and tells how it affects initiatives in dance education today. It is necessary information for starting a school-based dance program. The way you design your dance education curriculum and measure its success depends on national and state standards. National arts assessment plans are explained so you understand your accountability to state and national evaluation. The information shows how dance affects the overall education of students. Find the external factors that shape and affect dance education in this chapter. In addition, read the complete formal documents introduced in this chapter to grasp the vitally important details contained in them.

Dance education is to a large extent defined by the landscape that surrounds it. As the century turned 21, dance education also came of age in America—manifesting a growing presence in public education. Future generations will see the last decade of the 20th century as the time when goals for the art of movement, dance, aligned with the goals of education: a time when arts education, arts focus schools, arts magnet schools, and dance education increased in quantity and quality in U.S. schools.

Take a look at the simultaneous developments in the 1990s that positioned dance to be part of this educational renaissance:

- The education pendulum swung away from basic skills toward higher-order and reflective thinking.

- The arts were included as a core subject in the bipartisan Goals 2000—Educate America Act passed by Congress.

- National dance standards—the first ever—identified what students should know and be able to do in dance along with standards in other subjects (arts and other academics).

- The arts were added to the **"nation's report card."** The National Assessment of Educational Progress (NAEP assesses all core academic subjects) designed ways to measure skills, achievement, and knowledge in the arts, including dance, as a way to measure national standards and validate student learning in the arts.

- State departments of education across the United States began to add dance as an area of teacher certification. With the help of national agencies, states developed standards to measure what teachers should know and be able to do in the arts, including dance. Interdisciplinary and integrated arts were viewed as ways to promote learning in the arts and across other academic areas.

- Universities in those states started new teacher certification degrees in dance education.

- Howard Gardner's multiple intelligences theory gained acceptance from educators. Three of the intelligences or "ways of knowing"—kinesthetic, spatial, and musical—are significant to dance and acknowledge movement as an important mode of learning.

- Educational research on diverse learning styles also acknowledged arts modalities as effective avenues to learning.

- The arts were added to college educational methods courses for classroom teacher candidates, giving the arts broad entree into the classroom.

- Inquiry became a popular way to get students personally invested in learning in all disciplines.

Of the arts education landmark initiatives addressed in this chapter, three are of primary importance. The three with direct impact on dance are these:

1. National Standards for Dance Education (NSDEs): dance's content and achievement standards as part of the NSAEs

2. National Assessment of Education Progress (NAEP): dance's arts assessment

3. Opportunity-to-Learn Standards (OTLS): school program delivery standards

Each of these initiatives helped define the new path for dance in education in the United States. Collectively they sparked a proliferation of arts programs that included dance. Let's examine the landmarks in this educational landscape that continue to have direct impact on dance.

You need several primary reference documents close at hand as you prepare to be certified in dance. Because they affect how, when, where, and what you teach, you need to refer to them often. Become thoroughly familiar with the contents and application

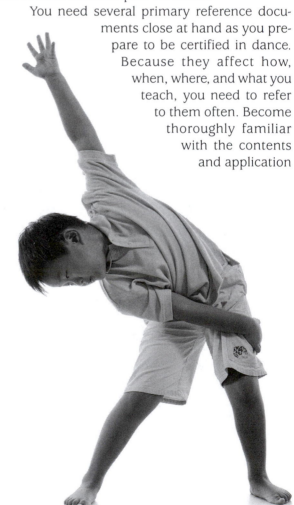

Research into diverse learning styles shows dance to be an effective learning modality for many children.

24

of these resources (for order information, see the Rich Resources section at the end of the chapter):

- *National Standards for Dance Education* (for dance specialists)
- *National Standards for Arts Education* (NSAEs)
- Your state dance education framework; achievement standards
- Local district scope and sequence guidelines

National Dance Content and Achievement Standards

The Consortium of National Arts Education Associations (which uses the acronym DAMT for dance, art, music, and theatre) oversaw the writing of national arts standards. Not only did this group set out to establish world-class standards, but it aimed to reflect the field of dance's aspirations—not the status quo. The consortium listed seven **content standards** that describe in general what students should know and do in dance. The consortium then wrote **achievement standards** that describe specific levels of competence expected at different grades for each content standard. Together, content and achievement standards identify what every young American should know and be able to competently do in dance in K-12.

> *Competence* is defined in the arts standards as
>
> the ability to combine the content, perspectives, and techniques associated with the various elements to achieve specific artistic and analytical goals. Students work toward comprehensive competence from the very beginning, preparing in the lower grades for deeper and more rigorous work each succeeding year. As a result, the joy of experiencing the arts is enriched and matured by the discipline of learning and the pride of accomplishment. (Consortium of National Arts Education Associations 1994, p. 18)

Reprinted with permission of the National Dance Association (NDA).

The dance standards from the National Standards for Arts Education K-12 are printed in a stand-alone publication titled *National Standards for Dance Education: What Every Young American Should Know and Be Able to Do* (National Dance Association 1996), so order your personal copy as soon as possible. Learn the seven dance content standards. Knowing them enables you to know what students are expected to learn (and thus what you are expected to teach

by grades 4, 8, and 12, no matter which state you teach in). Use the national standards document for reference as you read this book.

NSDE Content Standards

The seven content standards in dance are the same for all students in all grade levels. They are broad and comprehensive. They identify the seven main areas of expected growth. Notice that they drive the achievement standards. Memorize them.

> Content Standard 1: Identifying and demonstrating movement elements and skills in performing dance
>
> Content Standard 2: Understanding choreographic principles, processes, and structures
>
> Content Standard 3: Understanding dance as a way to create and communicate meaning
>
> Content Standard 4: Applying and demonstrating critical and creative thinking skills in dance
>
> Content Standard 5: Demonstrating and understanding dance in various cultures and historical periods
>
> Content Standard 6: Making connections between dance and healthful living
>
> Content Standard 7: Making connections between dance and other disciplines

This material is reprinted from the *National Standards for Dance Education and the Opportunity-to-Learn Standards in Dance Education* with permission of the National Dance Association (NDA). The original source may be purchased from: National Dance Association, 1900 Association Drive, Reston, VA 20191-1599.

The Dance Standards were completed as part of the Arts Standards, a project developed by the Consortium of National Arts Education Associations (American Alliance for Theatre & Education, Music Educators National Conference, National Arts Education Association & National Dance Association). This project was under the guidance of the National Committee for Standards in the Arts, & prepared under a grant from the U.S. Dept. of Education, the National Endowment for the Arts and the National Endowment for the Humanities.

NDA is an association of the American Alliance for Health, Physical Education, Recreation & Dance (AAHPERD).

Look closer at the seven content standards. Notice the difference between the first five and the last two. The first five standards reflect the substance of dance content and skills. The last two extend that dance substance into broader arenas of healthful living and across disciplines. You may consider the last two as important enhancement standards. This text emphasizes the first five content standards because they contain the substance of the dance curriculum. The last two are well integrated into the text.

NSDE Achievement Standards

The achievement standards are grouped into three grade level divisions: grades K-4, grades 5-8, and grades 9-12. After you have learned the seven content standards, spend time with the three levels of achievement standards that apply specifically to grades K-4, grades 5-8, and grades 9-12. Notice how learners are expected to gradually and consistently progress through these three divisions from early elementary through high school. Notice that grades 9-12 have two levels of achievement standards to differentiate between what is expected of an experienced dancer (advanced achievement) and what is expected of a beginner or novice (proficient achievement). Specific language explains:

> It is recognized that not all students study dance in grades 9-12. "Proficient" and "Advanced" levels of achievement have been identified at this level in the hope that students may learn about dance in settings other than the dance classroom. No link is necessarily implied between achievement and the election of formal course work in dance in grades 9-12. In general however, the proficient level is designed to apply to the student who has elected a dance course involving relevant skills or knowledge for one to two years beyond grade eight, and the advanced level is designed to apply to the student who has elected a dance course involving relevant skills or knowledge for three to four years beyond grade eight. (National Dance Association 1995, p. 27)

For example, compare the different expectations for one twelfth grader's critical and creative thinking at the proficient level with another twelfth grader's at the advanced level. Think of Steve as the novice and Luke as advanced. (NSDE Content Standard 4—*Applying and demonstrating critical and creative thinking skills in dance.*) One student is to meet the proficient level and the other the advanced, specified as follows:

SAMPLE 1: GRADE 12 ACHIEVEMENT STANDARD (PROFICIENT)

Students:

a. create a dance and revise it over time, articulating the reasons for their artistic decisions and what was lost and gained by those decisions

b. establish a set of aesthetic criteria and apply it in evaluating their own work and that of others

c. formulate and answer their own aesthetic questions (such as, What is it that makes a particular dance that dance? How much can one change that dance before it becomes a different dance?) (Consortium of National Arts Education Associations 1994, pp. 56-57)

SAMPLE 2: GRADE 12 ACHIEVEMENT STANDARD (ADVANCED)

Students:

d. discuss how skills developed in dance are applicable to a variety of careers

e. analyze the style of a choreographer or cultural form; then create a dance in that style

f. analyze issues of ethnicity, gender, social/economic class, age and/or physical condition in relation to dance (Consortium of National Arts Education Associations 1994, p. 57)

Reprinted with permission of the National Dance Association (NDA).

 How do Luke's expectations differ from Steve's according to this achievement standard?

The NSDEs are actually student content and achievement standards. But they go beyond that in implication:

- The authority for a standards-oriented curriculum comes from the standards.

- The standards influence the significant aspects of a well-rounded K-12 dance program in order for students to achieve competence.

- The standards affect how teachers are trained to facilitate such a K-12 program.

By their very existence, these standards raise the level of minimum expectation in dance. By their authority, they require educational dance curricula to be comprehensive, substantive, and sequential. They expect instruction to be aesthetically driven. Make such a program educationally viable by also making it contextually coherent and inquiry based.

Even though U.S. national standards inform both K-12 curriculum and undergraduate teacher preparation, they are not the source of either. What they do is point to the need for a broad-based dance curriculum founded on the cornerstones of the dance discipline: dancing and performing; creating and composing (dance making); knowing history, culture, and context (dance knowing); and analyzing and criticizing dance—all taught from an aesthetic perspective (which is explained further in chapter 5).

National standards, rather than mandated by law, are suggested or voluntary. Achievement standards convey clear and attainable age-level benchmarks for each art form. Ensure the viability of the dance education program you build by keeping the NSDEs at the forefront of your planning and instruction. Keep students focused on their achievement goals by posting the standards so they consistently see them. See figure 2.1 for suggestions.

Minimum Program

The NSDEs are world-class standards, and their benchmarks are attainable for most students in a quality program. Obviously your students must meet minimum standards, but it is hoped that you challenge them to exceed standards by excelling in all of dance's artistic processes: creating, performing, and responding (c/p/r). Aim instruction higher than the standards to ensure that all students grasp sufficient content and skills to place well on the nation's arts report card. In the next section you will learn how the standards are to be measured. There are three levels of achievement. Will your students rank as at least "basic"? Or will they rank higher—either proficient or advanced?

Do not use standards to drive the curriculum. Drive your curriculum based on the 6DCs and on your state's curriculum frameworks, which are mandatory, not voluntary like the national standards. All three documents define more closely how students are to be broadly educated in and about dance. Some states' standards also parallel the national standards but describe in more detail what is expected. They are there to help you. Use them.

The "Nation's Report Card" in Dance

Enter the National Assessment of Educational Progress (NAEP), a governmental entity that oversees national student assessments. "The National Assessment of Educational Progress is a Congressionally mandated project of the National Center for Education Statistics, U.S. Department of Education.

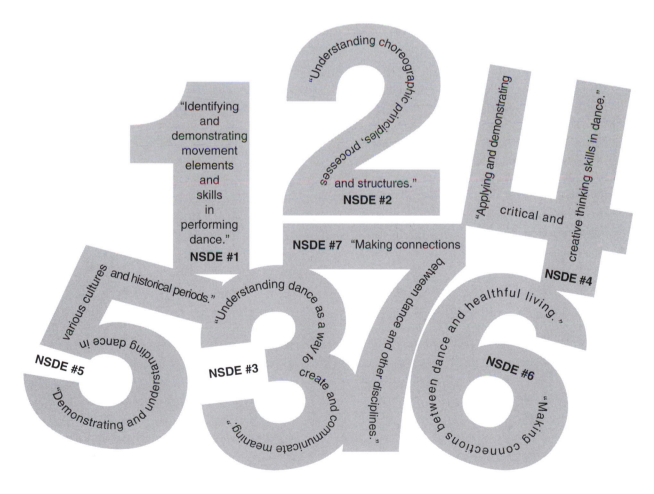

FIGURE 2.1   Make banners or posters for each national dance content standard for your classroom to emphasize them.

In 1988, Congress created the National Assessment Governing Board (NAGB) to set policy for NAEP" (NAGB 1994, p. 1).

Between 1992 and 1994, a common vision was acutely needed for arts education between the group developing national arts education standards and the different group planning their assessment. Through the Arts Education Consensus Project, a coalition of arts partners articulated this common vision in the *NAEP Arts Education Assessment Framework* (1994). The framework states: "The development of the *NAEP Arts Education Assessment Framework* has coincided with the development of the *National Standards for Education in the Arts*. This confluence of a standards-setting process and its immediate application in creating a national assessment provide an unprecedented opportunity to align standards and assessment in a model for arts education" (NAGB 1994, p. 2).

NAGB approved the consensus framework in 1994 as the basis for a planned arts assessment. The consensus framework was then translated into a national standardized assessment instrument (by a different group) to measure all that the NSDEs propose. Although NAEP assesses all core subject areas, their 1997 assessment was actually to have been the first national assessment of all the arts: dance, music, theatre, and the visual arts (NAGB 1994, pp. 1-2).

Due to budgetary constraints, the 1997 national arts assessment was only administered for grade 8. However, dance was dropped from the actual 1997 assessment because "In its survey, NAEP identified only nine schools in the nationally representative sample with significant dance programs at the eighth-grade level. At least 50 were needed for a statistically valid survey" (U.S. Department of Education Office of Educational Research and Improvement 1998b, p. 5).

Nonetheless, future assessments measure student ability to create, perform, and respond to dance at the same three junctures in schooling—at the end of grades 4, 8, and 12. Although NAEP assessment is voluntary, as are the NSDEs, there is incentive to have NAEP assess all the core subjects in a school. Invite NAEP to field test these assessments at your school to see how effective the test instruments

Future NAEP assessments will measure your students' ability to create, perform, and respond to dance.

are and how to better prepare your students to succeed. The NAEP documents explain the nature of the tests, samples of test items, the achievement level expected at each grade level tested, and the criteria that will be assessed.

Authentic testing on a national level is complicated when you consider how complex the creating, performing, and responding processes in dance are. The tests take time and expertise to administer and to evaluate. Only one dance class at a time can be tested, so time alone translates into money and makes national testing cumbersome and costly. The national dance community urges NAEP to use qualified dance specialists to administer the performance-based assessments. Even if fewer students are assessed, it is better that assessment be done correctly rather than administered and scored by non-dance specialists.

Measuring the National Standards for the National Report Card

The consensus framework and the national standards depict the kind of integrated arts experiences for America's youth that are educationally meaningful and rigorous, yet doable. The tests involve students in a way that shows what they know connected with what they can do. The consensus framework admits

> The *NAEP Framework* process and the National Standards have framed a vision of arts education that integrates the aesthetic, social, cultural, and historical contexts of the arts with the knowledge and skills necessary to participate in the arts. Skills will not be considered as separable, and it has been decided to report the achievement of students as a whole according to the various artistic processes, not on separate scales for isolated knowledge or technical skills. The image of arts education portrayed by the NAEP Arts Education will be as close to a vision of the arts as basic, unified, and pervasive as practically possible. (NAGB 1994, p. 11)

Thus in dance you will notice they measure in three areas: creating, performing, and responding to dance. See figure 2.2 for a page from the NAEP 1997 Arts Report Card explaining how the assessments are structured in five blocks.

NAEP is a formidable force in education. You have to know about NAEP to teach in the schools because national accountability is a frequent topic from school administrators and because they are accountable to high-stakes testing. NAEP tells administrators if their students measure up to national standards. You must learn to speak the NAEP language to communicate with your principal about the actual assessments and who administers them.

Placing NAEP Into Context

Here is a profile of NAEP.

- NAEP conducts the next arts assessments in 2008 and 2016. The assessments are paid for by funds allocated by Congress.
- The 1995 field test in all four arts at grades 4 and 8 showed that comprehensive educational dance and theatre programs were scarce. This random sample found that only 3 percent of

America's students receive dance instruction in school three to four times a week.

- NAEP assessments aim to reflect the **cultural pluralism** of America.
- NAEP only assesses comprehensive or complete dance education programs.
- NAEP assessments are nicknamed "the nation's report card." The logo, "The Nation's Report Card: NAEP," appears on all documents that pertain to the NAEP assessments (e.g., *The 1996 NAEP Arts Education Assessment Framework* [1994], *The NAEP 1997 Arts Report Card* [1998], and the NCES publications called *Focus on NAEP,* several of which are devoted entirely to the arts assessment). After NAEP added arts assessments, they are sometimes called "the nation's *arts* report card."

The National Center for Education Statistics tells us that

> NAEP is an important resource for understanding what students know and can do. NAEP assessments have explored students' abilities in a range of subject areas including reading, science, US history, and mathematics. Based on assessment results, NAEP reports levels of student achievement and the instructional, institutional, and demographic variables associated with those levels of achievement. In 1997, NAEP conducted a national assessment in the arts at Grade 8. The assessment included music, theater, and visual arts. (Though an assessment was developed for dance, it was not implemented because a statistically suitable sample could not be located.) (U.S. Department of Education, Office of Educational Research and Improvement, National Center for Education Statistics 1998a, p. i)

NAEP assessments take 60 minutes for grade 4 and 90 minutes for grades 8 and 12. The assessment evaluates students actually doing the arts **(authentic assessment)** and also includes a paper test. The assessment rates students as basic, proficient, or advanced. Dance assessment exercises include the following:

- Authentic tasks that measure students' knowledge and skills in creating and performing (such as performing dances, creating one's own dance and evaluating it)
- Multiple choice and constructed-response questions, which have students describe, analyze, and evaluate works of art in written form

Chapter Five

Dance

Creating, Performing, and Responding in Dance: A Close Look at the Exercises for the NAEP 1997 Dance Assessment

The Content of the Dance Assessment

As previously explained, the grade 8 assessment developed for dance was not administered. Results from the 1995 grades 4 and 8 NAEP field test in dance indicated that comprehensive dance programs are rare in the nation's schools. This is also the case according to the National Center for Education Statistics publication, *Arts Education in Public Elementary and Secondary Schools.*[1]

Those schools that do offer dance do not always teach a wide range of dance forms, or studies of dance aesthetics and the social, cultural, and historical contexts of dance. Many students of dance pursue their activities in classes outside a school context.

To ensure that students taking the dance assessment would have some solid exposure to dance, a range of arts policymakers, members of the National Center for Education Statistics, the National Assessment Governing Board, and dance teachers decided that students taking the dance assessment should be chosen from schools offering a reasonably comprehensive dance program. In this way, assessment results would supply rich information about what students exposed to dance in schools know and can do.

A lengthy process was undertaken to identify what number and kinds of dance course work ought to characterize students in the dance sample. NAEP staff responsible for identifying and locating NAEP samples and administering NAEP assessments worked extensively with dance policymakers and teachers to make these decisions, and then to locate a sample of schools and students with the national distribution necessary for NAEP assessments. After much effort, it was found that, given the nature of dance education, a statistically suitable sample could not be located.

So that readers will have a picture of the performance assessment in dance that was developed based on the arts framework, the dance exercises that were intended for administration to students are included in this *Report Card.* (The lessons learned from the development, administration, and scoring of the 1995 and 1997 dance field tests will be featured in the *NAEP Arts Process Report.*)

These exercises were created to reflect the view of a complete dance education presented in the (voluntary) *Standards for Education in the Arts* and the NAEP *Arts Education Assessment Framework.* According to these documents, significant dance learning in schools should include Creating, Performing, and Responding.

---

1 National Center for Education Statistics. (1995). *Arts education in public elementary and secondary schools.* Publication No. NCES 95-082. Washington, DC: U.S. Department of Education. (See also http://nces.ed.gov/surveys/frss.html)

(continued)

FIGURE 2.2   Chapter Five in the NAEP 1997 Arts Report Card details the plan to measure how well students achieve national dance standards. To discern what the assessment intends to incorporate, read the last two paragraphs of the material reprinted above and all of page 31.

U.S. Department of Education, Institute of Education Sciences, National Center for Education Statistics.

In a comprehensive dance program, students would learn how to convey ideas and feelings using movement and elements of choreography. They would be taught dance knowledge, skills, and techniques that would enable them to use their bodies with confidence and insight when Creating and Performing. Through being taught how to Create and Perform, students would gain spatial and bodily awareness, musicality, and an ability to observe and refine movement.[2]

In learning how to Respond to their own dance work or that of others, students would be taught how to identify compositional elements; notice details; identify stylistic, cultural, social, and historical contexts of dance; and make informed critical observations about technical and artistic components of dance.[3]

Creating the NAEP dance assessment posed interesting challenges. In educational settings, students and teachers of dance can discuss and experiment with different ways of solving movement problems to communicate ideas and feelings. This is not the case in a timed assessment. To give students as much of an opportunity as possible to demonstrate their dance knowledge and skills, it was necessary to create context for the assessment exercises. This was done in three important ways.

First, instructions for Creating and Performing tasks were carefully crafted to lead students through complex exercises step by step. This included extensive warm-up exercises to prepare students to dance, and as much information as possible about what students were being asked to demonstrate. At the same time, instructions were designed not to "overteach" students, and hence damage assessment results.

Second, since a substantial part of dance instruction involves understanding and learning movement from live demonstration, trained dancers and dance educators were to administer and lead students through the dance Creating and Performing tasks. This would help to increase students' comfort level with dancing in an unfamiliar context. Third, Responding exercises were built around videotape selections from two, three, or at most four dances, so that students could focus their attention on a small selection of works. This would give students the opportunity to think more deeply about the assessment tasks, and ensure that students would not be asked isolated questions about unrelated dances.

An overview of the grade 8 dance assessment "blocks" (a group of exercises administered as separate units to be completed in a set time frame) is presented in Figure 5.1. As shown in the figure, the assessment consists of five blocks. Three of those blocks feature Responding exercises. These are multiple-choice and constructed-response questions asking students to analyze, describe, and identify different aspects of dance. The dances students are asked to observe represent a wide range of cultures, genres, and historical periods. The remaining two blocks consist of a Performing block asking students to learn a dance phrase and a Creating/Performing block asking students to create and perform a brief composition.

2 National Assessment Governing Board. (1994) *Arts Education Assessment Framework* (pre-publication ed.) Washington, D.C.: Author, 22–23.

3 Ibid.

FIGURE 2.2   *(continued)*

Therefore, authentic tasks are performance based as well as written, whereas the constructed-response or multiple-choice items are written.

Creating Proportional Dance Programs

NAEP uses kinetic assessments to measure what students know by what they can do in dance. NAEP assessments allot a good portion of time to moving. Be sure your dance program also features dancing at all grade levels, and include movement assessments.

NAEP emphasizes different artistic processes (creating, performing, and responding) more at one age than another. Notice by the percentages in table 2.1 which artistic processes the national assessment emphasizes at each grade level. For example, at grade 4, creating gets more emphasis than performing or responding because creative dance is a best practice in the K-4 curriculum. Likewise, the proportion of student time spent creating in the grade 8 assessment is less than at grades 4 and 12 because middle school students prefer to be "alike" more than "original." Thus, NAEP mirrors the best practice in educational dance without driving it.

Bring these facts to your study of human development in chapter 4. To increase student growth, design proportional dance programs at different ages to capitalize on their strengths and receptivity throughout K-12. Accentuate their strong points at all grade levels while also developing their weaker ones. For example, Bill's receptivity to creating in K-4 will be great, but it will give way to a better ability to refine his motor skills when he gets to middle school technique class and to analyze and critique dance works in high school. Therefore, emphasize content that builds on his innate receptivity at each age to ensure that Bill graduates with the highest achievement possible in all artistic processes (NAGB 1994, p. 48).

Reflect and Respond

One part of the NAEP field tests at grades 4, 8, and 12 includes a paper-and-pencil test. Look at the following sample from the twelfth-grade written test. Do you believe that the questions are (a) reflective of a quality program and of what students should understand in dance, (b) too rigorous, or (c) too simplistic? This test is given as part of a dance performance viewing exercise on videotape:

Sample Questions for Twelfth Grade Field Test Scoring

Multiple Choice
- The movements performed by the dancers in Dance 1 can best be described as (a) flowing, (b) sharp, (c) heavy, (d) slow.
- Which of the following technical skills are most often demonstrated by the dancers in Dance 2? (a) abdominal control, (b) fluidity of the spine, (c) use of muscular tension, (d) high kicks

Short Constructed Response
- Describe two specific ways in which costumes are an important part of Dance 1.

Extended Constructed Response
- Compare the way the feet of the dancers are used in Dance 1 and Dance 2.

U.S. Department of Education (1998b, p. 4)

Seeking Program Accountability

This is how national dance standards (NDSEs) correspond to the national assessments (NAEP):

- National standards say what is to be learned; NAEP measures if and how well it was learned.

Table 2.1   National Assessment Percentages for Dance (NAEP)

	Grade 4	Grade 8	Grade 12
Creating	40%	20%	30%
Performing	30%	40%	30%
Responding	30%	40%	40%

- NAEP artistic processes (c/p/r) measure NSDE content areas (chapter 5, table 5.3). Order a *NAEP Arts Education Assessment Framework* to read and study. It tells what ought to be learned, but it does not specify how to get there. That's what you add. See figure 2.3 for a sample assessment.

Not only must teachers and administrators uphold the NSDEs, which promote a complete curriculum taught during the school day at all grade levels, but it is also equally important for students to know they have achieved according to a national standard measure. National assessment helps keep students focused on achievement, knowing their scores will be part of the national statistics of educational progress in dance. It also keeps you focused on student outcomes and challenges you to teach at a high level so that your students achieve at that level.

School administrators notice success even though they may not yet fully understand what you do in dance education. One thing is for sure: Getting a good grade on the nation's report card is a mark of excellence and prestige. It helps earn administrative support for what you do from decision makers (e.g., principals, superintendents, states, and government) who allocate the funds to dance programs. *What gets tested gets taught.* When student learning is evident, programs with successful test scores get funded and they usually stay in the curriculum.

Will your program be eligible for a NAEP assessment? Here are some eligibility criteria:

- Students must attend schools that offered at least 17 contact hours of dance per semester.
- Students must have been enrolled in dance classes in the previous year.
- Course work must include more than dance in an athletic context.
- Course work must include more than knowledge-based courses in aesthetics and criticism.

Find all specifications in the primary resource, *NAEP Arts Education Assessment Framework* (1994), for the 1996 National Assessment of Educational Progress. It can be ordered online. You can find more information in Rich Resources.

Chapters 6 through 10 help you build a complete program for NAEP to assess. Notify the U.S. Department of Education and NAEP that your program is ready to be assessed at the next scheduled arts assessment. Volunteer for either a full-scale assessment (grades 4, 8, and 12) or offer to be part of a targeted sample such as NAEP selected for the 1997 theatre assessment. Dance must be represented in future NAEP arts assessments so as to have a statistical place in education. Only after it is apparent that standards-oriented programs flourish will educational dance increase in recognition and respect. Be counted for the good work you do. It paves the way for others.

As important as the NAEP assessment framework and the NSDEs are, they are not documents made for designing dance curriculum. NSDE standards are organized in three 4-year blocks (i.e., K-4, 5-8, and 9-12) not because that is the best pedagogical division but more because it is the most practical division to accommodate the NAEP assessment. For example, kindergarten through grade 4 is too broad an age range to be helpful in curriculum design because children between those ages have such a wide range of physical, artistic, and mental maturity and ability. As you design your curriculum, incorporate all the standards and criteria from the nation's report card, but don't see them as your curriculum guides. Use them to inform your curriculum.

Other Initiatives That Affect Dance Education

Just as the arts education reform agenda affects your dance education program, so do other educational agendas such as school delivery standards, No Child Left Behind, the SCANS Report, and the 21st Century Skills.

Opportunity-to-Learn Standards

Whereas you are accountable to prepare students according to NSDEs, schools are accountable to what the field refers to as "school delivery standards" to make quality dance programs accessible to every child. Officially called **Opportunity-to-Learn Standards for Dance Education (OTLS),** they are published inside the second printing of the NSDE document (1995). They maintain that it is unfair to expect students to meet dance achievement standards unless given reasonable opportunities to acquire the skills and knowledge to do so (see chapter 11 for more details). They convey the national guidelines for scheduling, facilities, and resources for dance education.

Sample Questions from the "Philippine" Block

In this block, students observe three dances: a Philippine Singkal dance, an Irish Step dance, and a West African dance. These dances may be viewed on the CD that accompanies this report. They can be found by clicking on the Philippine menu in the dance section or on the video icon below.

 Video Link to Dances

Question 1 measures students' abilities to identify compositional elements in dance, relating the use of props to time and space in a performance.

1. Describe two specific ways the poles are an important part of the Philippine dance (Dance 1).

Question 2 measures students' abilities to analyze compositional elements in dance, such as time, space, and energy.

2. Describe the Philippine dance (Dance 1). In your answer, discuss in detail: use of timing (rhythm and tempo), use of space (how the dancers moved in and through the performance space and around one another); and the use of force/energy (the qualities and mood of the movements the dancers made).

    1. Use of timing:

    2. Use of space:

    3. Use of force/energy:

Question 3 measures students' abilities to make informed critical observations about technical and artistic components of dance in relation to shape.

3. Describe two specific ways the group of dancers in the Irish dance (Dance 2) physically connect to one another, and describe the shape the group forms each time the dancers connect.

    1. Way the dancers physically connect:
       Shape they form when they physically connect:

    2. Way the dancers physically connect:
       Shape they form when they physically connect:

Question 4 measures students' abilities to identify compositional elements in dance by comparing two dance compositions in terms of shape.

4. What group formation did the dancers make in both the Irish dance (Dance 2) and the West African dance (Dance 3)?

    (A) Lines

    (B) Semicircles

    (C) Square

    (D) Star

(continued)

FIGURE 2.3 The material above and on page 35, reprinted from the NAEP 1997 Arts Report Card, addresses the eighth grade assessment. The original document includes a video link to a CD (not part of this book) showing dance samples related to the written questions.

U.S. Department of Education, Institute of Education Sciences, National Center for Education Statistics.

Question 5 measures students' abilities to distinguish movement styles (changes in the use of body parts, levels, and timing) in dances of different cultures.

5. Describe two specific differences between the ways the dancers use their upper bodies (torsos and arms) in the Irish and West African dances (Dances 2 and 3).

Question 6 measures students' abilities to identify compositional elements in dance by comparing two compositions in terms of the style of footwork.

6. Describe one difference and one similarity between the ways the dancers use their feet in the Irish dance (Dance 2) and in the West African dance (Dance 3).

    Difference:

    Similarity:

Question 7 measures students' abilities to identify compositional elements in dance by comparing two compositions.

7. Compare the dancers' facial expressions and the mood in the Philippine dance (Dance 1) with the dancers' facial expressions and the mood in the West African dance (Dance 3). Be specific.

Question 8 measures students' abilities to identify technical components of dance composition.

8. The performers' arms change levels in which dance?

   Ⓐ The West African only

   Ⓑ The Philippine and the Irish only

   Ⓒ The Philippine and the West African only

   Ⓓ The West African, the Philippine, and the Irish

Question 9 measures students' abilities to make informed critical observations about dance by comparing the movement qualities of several compositions.

9. Which dance or dances demonstrated the largest range of body movement?

   Ⓐ The West African

   Ⓑ The Irish

   Ⓒ The Philippine

   Ⓓ The Philippine and the Irish

Question 10 measures students' abilities to identify the compositional elements of dance by recognizing specific methods of choreography used in a performance.

10. Which kind of choreographic form was used in only ONE of the three dances?

   Ⓐ Solo movement

   Ⓑ Unison movement

   Ⓒ Canon movement

   Ⓓ Call-and-response movement

NAEP 1997 Arts Report Card

FIGURE 2.3   *(continued)*

No Child Left Behind

In 2002, seven years after Goals 2000, the No Child Left Behind Act (NCLB) was passed by Congress. NCLB recognizes the arts as core subjects, but it fails to fund them or to identify standards or assessments in arts education. NCLB's emphasis on reading and math scores tips the scales away from arts and back toward the old "basics." Few incentives encourage schools to develop arts curricula. So the local arts education community—including dance—must see that authentic performance-based assessments based on national standards are administered at the local level to measure growth as well as to keep student progress consistent with other academics. Lacking direct funding support for the arts, arts educators have to find other funded aspects in NCLB where the arts contribute to learning so as not to have the arts left behind.

There are limited sources to call on. Explore using Title I, Part A funds to improve the arts for disadvantaged kids. Use Title II Teacher Quality Enhancement Grants to address professional development needs of arts specialists and Title II funds to support partnerships with local nonprofit organizations.

NCLB expects arts specialists to be as highly qualified as teachers of other academics. This is admirable in theory, but in practice it breaks down. As yet, there is no official definition of what a highly qualified dance specialist is. NCLB recognizes National Board for Professional Teaching Standards (NBPTS) certification for most subjects, but there is no NBPTS for dance. We need to advocate for official dance teacher quality standards. It behooves the field to articulate what "highly qualified" means for teaching dance as art in education. In the interim, the National Dance Education Organization developed a document akin to the NBPTS called the Professional Teaching Standards that might suffice if you need to be assessed under the NCLB law in your state.

(Access the PTS at www.ndeo.org.) Often laws have unintended consequences, and in this case, NCLB could be the leverage dance needs to get official national teacher quality standards! (Chapter 3 further addresses teacher preparation standards in dance.)

SCANS Report

To take the broadest view yet of dance's place in education, attune yourself to how dance contributes to the education of the whole child. All subject areas, including dance, are also expected to educate broadly so learners are prepared to live good lives and contribute to society. All of education contributes. And to some extent, our existence in K-12 partly depends on how we contribute to overall education—as in all disciplines.

What Work Requires of Schools: A SCANS Report for America 2000 was presented in 1991 to the U.S. Congress by the Labor Department's Secretary's Commission on Achieving Necessary Skills (SCANS). It identifies what is expected of all *literate persons* of the future. It states,

> We understand that schools do more than simply prepare people to make a living. They prepare people to lead full lives—to participate in their communities, to raise families, and to enjoy the leisure that is the fruit of their labor. A solid education is its own reward. (U.S. Department of Labor 1991, p. v)

To that end, U.S. schools have an educational role beyond each isolated discipline. They must build life skills that contribute substantially to the American democracy and to a strong workforce.

The SCANS Report compels us to integrate social and cognitive goals into our unit plans in dance. For the privilege of having the arts in education, we also need to broadly educate students for high levels of adult productivity and higher-order thinking (i.e., creative and critical thinking). For example, it is natural for dance's creative process to develop social skills

> **"Creating refers to expressing ideas and feelings in the form of an original work of art, for example, a dance, a piece of music, a dramatic improvisation, or a sculpture.**
>
> **"Performing refers to performing an existing work, a process that calls upon the interpretive or recreating skills of the student.**
>
> **"Responding refers to observing, describing, analyzing, and evaluating works of art."**
>
> —U.S. Department of Education, Office of Educational Research and Improvement, National Center for Education Statistics (1998a, p. i)

and group collaboration as you compose group dances. Address SCANS competencies and skills as simultaneous goals alongside the NSDEs. SCANS competencies and skills enhance the kinds of artistic processes and experiences described in this book. Intentionally add SCANS goals to your long-range and short-range dance plans to ensure that dance improves students' ability

- to make decisions that improve overall quality,
- to understand the cultural and historic context of their decisions,
- to collaborate and problem solve,
- to communicate well in different media, and
- to work for the good of all in our democracy.

Celebrate different cultures through dance and bring them to life as an ongoing part of your curriculum.

Partnership for 21st Century Skills

The Partnership for 21st Century Skills stands on the shoulders of the SCANS Report and continues to develop the concept of the need for creative functioning in the 21st century. While it does not replace SCANS, it moves SCANS to the next level. Its seven areas of emphasis are global awareness; civic literacy; financial, economic, and business literacy; information and communication skills; thinking and problem-solving skills; interpersonal and self-directional skills; and information and communication technology literacy.

Educational dance has a role to play in all seven of their goals. 21st Century Skills focuses attention on the "creative economy" that No Child Left Behind seems to have left behind in its emphasis on basic skills. The partnership stresses the need to educate students for their future rather than our past by noting that the majority of the job market in the 21st century will be in areas around the creative economy rather than the mass-production emphasis of the 20th century. 21st Century Skills supports

visionary leaders to teach our children now so that they are able not only to solve problems but also to look beyond the problem they're solving to solutions for the next problem, to discern what lies ahead. The 21st Century Skills report values relevant, real-world experiences that connect to the real world that students will live in, as well as the kinds of authentic assessments that measure those 21st century skills. Both the National Governors Association (NGA) and the Education Commission of the States (ECS) focus on the vital role the arts in education play in supporting the creative economy. "The Arts are not extraneous, not extravagant, and not extra-curricular. They are essential in education" (Huckabee 2005).

For companies and organizations to remain competitive and cutting-edge, they must attract and retain individuals who can think creatively, adapt to rapidly changing environments and demands, and solve problems from new perspectives. These skills are part of the creative capital that will drive the US economy in the foreseeable future. (Education Commission of the States [ECS] brochure 2005, The Arts, Education and the Creative Economy)

Reflect and Respond

When our students enter the workforce they need specific competencies and skills. Can you develop them while you are developing dance skills?

1. Competencies
   - Resources: identifies, organizes, plans
     - > Schedules time and arranges space effectively
     - > Uses resources effectively
   - Interpersonal: works with others
     - > Contributes to group efforts as a team member
     - > Teaches others new skills, negotiates, and works toward agreements
     - > Exercises leadership, justifies own position, persuades and convinces others
     - > Works well with both genders and diverse backgrounds
   - Information: acquires and uses information
     - > Evaluates information
     - > Organizes information
     - > **Interprets** and communicates information
   - Systems: understands complex interrelationships
     - > Knows how social, organizational, and technological systems work
     - > Operates effectively with these systems
     - > Monitors and corrects performance problems
     - > Improves on or designs new systems; suggests modifications to existing systems and designs alternative systems to improve performance

Creative and critical thinking in dance deepen analytical skills. How can you make long- and short-range plans to increase these SCANS foundation skills and qualities?

2. Foundation skills
   - Basic skills: reading, writing, analytical reasoning and problem solving, listening, and speaking
   - Thinking skills: creative thinking, decision making, problem solving, seeing things in the mind's eye, knowing how to learn, and reasoning
   - Personal qualities: individual responsibility, sociability, self-esteem, self-management, and integrity

U.S. Department of Labor, *A SCANS Report for America 2000* (1991).

Educational dance plays a critical role in developing many of these 21st century skills, such as working with diverse cultures; creativity and intellectual curiosity; self-direction; the ability to frame, analyze, and solve problems; social responsibility; and interpersonal skills.

See Rich Resources for further information.

Interplay of State and National Initiatives

National standards stand behind and give credence to state standards. Each state has its own mandated laws, curricula, standards, and guidelines. Although state and national headings may differ, the substance is normally equivalent or parallel. State standards are mandated by state law, whereas national standards are voluntary. So state standards can be more specific than national standards because they are part of the state's educational system and as such are regulated by the state. When all standards converge, they affect the quality of every child's education (figure 2.4). The standards assessments hold students accountable to achieve and dance specialists accountable to deliver the best practices in dance that are available.

State Curriculum Frameworks (K-12)

Your state may have a dance curriculum framework to show what is to be achieved by K-12 students in your state. The goals and objectives in this framework give consistency, quality, and uniformity among the schools in your state (similar to how national standards give consistent benchmarks across the country). Therefore, students who change in-state schools are more assured of curricular continuity. Few states have comprehensive frameworks like the one provided in chapters 6 through 9 of this text.

Local and District Initiatives

You will ultimately design your local school curriculum according to your state curriculum framework and factor in all the content and achievement standards from the NSDEs. Ask if your school district also has a curriculum **scope and sequence,** which is like a framework that shows what to teach (content) and how to develop it for consecutive years. It usually gives additional strategies, methods, and resources to help you achieve state and national standards.

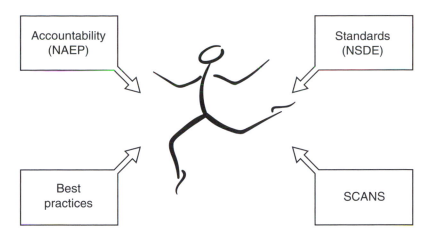

FIGURE 2.4 External factors affect the dancing child in school-based programs.

Amalgamate local, state, and national curriculum and standards documents. Base unit plans on the outcomes described in these documents. Curriculum and standards documents will be compatible and in some cases almost the same.

Always plan and teach to the curriculum with the higher standard to ensure that students achieve all requirements. Base the goal's objectives for each unit on the particular standards you intend to meet. Over time, you should achieve all the goals named in your district guide, state framework, and the national standards in dance because you will have included all of these goals in the curriculum, used them in the classroom, and assessed them to see whether students mastered required knowledge and skills.

> **"The education of feeling may not be measurable, yet it is very important that it is not lost or put aside in favor of what can be assessed."**
>
> —Jacqueline Smith-Autard (2002, p. 36)

Need for Arts Alliances

Arts alliances produced our pivotal national arts initiatives in the last decade: Goals 2000 Act, INTASC teacher licensure standards in the arts, and the National Standards for Arts Education and Dance Education. Arts alliances continue to forge a path for quality arts in education. The Consortium of National Arts Organizations (DAMT) is the coalition that brings together dance, art, music, and theatre.

So what does dance gain and lose by being part of the national arts coalition with uniform broad-based standards? Politically, dance gains more than it loses as part of a national arts coalition (i.e., DAMT, NAEP, NSAEs, and others), but arts alliances dictate the overall shape of their initiatives. Keeping all the arts categories uniform and the formats parallel dictates how national dance standards are written. Headings in the arts documents are made to be parallel as well as their terms. One prime example is the NAEP arts assessment. As noted, because NAEP assesses at certain grade levels, the national dance standards are written to correspond to those grade clusters. The tail sometimes wags the dog. However, we need each other.

POTENTIAL GAINS

- A broad base of support
- An advocacy network with a common voice
- Parallel design elements expressed across disciplines
- Documents such as arts standards
- A louder voice and ability to lobby as one group

POTENTIAL LOSSES

- Specialized needs of each discipline
- Exclusion of areas that are not parallel
- Force fitting language to serve all four arts

Two professional organizations serve the national reform agenda in dance education and represent us in various arts education coalitions: the National Dance Education Organization **(NDEO)** and the National Dance Association **(NDA).** Both lead advocacy efforts on behalf of dance. Your personal alliance with one or both brings you into the national dialogue to keep abreast of what is happening not only in dance education but also in arts education. In addition, both organizations' annual conferences provide professional development in varied aspects of dance. Both organizations give member discounts on a large selection of high-quality dance books. Join and actively participate in one or both to meet the leaders in your field, share ideas, network, and have your voice heard in a broader arena than your school. As you align nationally, you not only gain a broad arts education perspective but also add momentum to the profession as you continue your professional growth.

Advocacy

Advocacy translates to program survival. Advocate for your school dance program consistently and continuously. Constantly defend and express the educational value of the arts. Advocacy determines where money gets allocated at all levels of decision making: school building, district office, state department of education, state legislature, and U.S. Congress. Large numbers of voices speaking a consistent message get heard. Part of your job is to increase your community's understanding of the worthwhile outcomes of educational dance. There is no better advocacy than an outstanding program.

Advocate for a quantity of quality art education programs:

- The *quality* of programs is determined by the content taught, the effectiveness of instructional delivery, and the thoroughness of assessment.
- The *quantity* of programs is determined by equity, access for all, and availability of resources.

Join forces with dance specialists in your district. Join your state arts advocacy network to put your voice out to a broader community. You will get e-mail alerts to political action—national and

Look at arts coalitions from both sides to gain a perspective on why we must build them.

statewide. For information, contact your state arts commission or council. Join the Arts Education Partnership at www.aep-arts.org.

Reflect and Respond

How will you keep your program alive and well?

List eight aspects of your program that make an educational impact on the school, students, and educational system. Pare them down to concise, clear statements. Post the list where you and others see it. Periodically change its location in the school. Use these items as "talk points" in presentations to the parent–teacher organization or school council, teacher in-services, civic leaders, and the legislature. Regularly articulate these items to your principal and to your students.

Notebook/Portfolio:

Perspectives Notebook

1. Prepare a two-page paper titled "How National Dance Standards Affect My Teaching."

2. Download the full national dance standards from www.menc.org for your notebook.

Questions to Ponder

1. The *National Standards for Dance Education* identify what students should know and be able to do in dance. How does this affect what teachers should know and be able to do in dance education?

2. How would you explain the difference between the national content and achievement standards? How are they related to each other?

3. How would you restate the seven national dance content standards in your own words?

4. How do dance's national content standards mesh with your state standards?

5. How will the NAEP assessment affect your program? How can you design and teach a comprehensive dance education curriculum so that students will pass the nation's report card? What implications does NAEP assessment have for your curriculum and your instruction?

6. How can you teach dance education and also contribute important life skills to broaden the education of your students?

Rich Resources

RESOURCES

- *The NAEP 1997 Arts Report Card: Eighth Grade Findings from the National Assessment of Educational Progress* is a book. It may be found electronically at http://nces.ed.gov/naep. It is available in CD-ROM from Educational Testing Service. In general refer to NAEP 1997 Arts

Report Card to learn more about dance assessment (pp. 130-133). Order it from the National Center for Education Statistics (NCES). Access the free publication, *Arts Education in Public Elementary and Secondary Schools,* for statistics on existing dance education programs. Order them online at www.ed.gov/pubs/edpubs.html.

- Write to the U.S. Department of Education to subscribe to the free NCES newsletter, *Focus on NAEP.*

- Read the six-page National Center for Education Statistics document called "NAEP and Dance: Framework and Field Tests," *Focus on NAEP,* August 1998, Volume 3, No. 1. It presents an overview of the Dance Assessment Framework's content and processes, the field test samples in dance, the student tasks, and much pertinent information about the dance assessment. Access it through the U.S. Department of Education, Office of Educational Research and Improvement at http://nces.ed.gov/NAEP.

WEB SITES

- www.menc.org: Order *National Standards for Arts Education* (NSAEs).

- www.aahperd.org: Order *National Standards for Dance Education* (NSDEs).

- http://nces.ed.gov/NAEP: Web site for the National Center for Education Statistics (NCES) at the U.S. Department of Education, Office of Educational Research and Improvement. This is the source from which to order *The NAEP 1997 Arts Report Card* (1998) and the *NAEP Arts Education Assessment Framework* (1994).

- http://artsedge.kennedy-center.org: The ArtsEdge Web site contains an excellent collection of lesson plans in dance.

- http://kennedy-center.org/education/kcaaen: The Kennedy Center Alliance for Arts Education Network is a programmatic affiliate of the Education Department, JFK Center for Performing Arts, Washington, DC. It partners with state affiliates to promote the arts and support of policies, practices, and partnerships that ensure the arts are woven into the fabric of American education. It builds community partnerships for effective school arts programs, serves as an information exchange, and actively participates in the development of arts education policy in partnership with other national arts and arts in education organizations.

- www.aep-arts.org: The Arts Education Partnership Web site contains the ArtsEd listserve. The Web site and listserve are the most dependable sources for arts education information and important events affecting arts education. Visit regularly.

- http://arts.endow.gov: The National Endowment for the Arts is a federal agency with grants to support arts education, professional performances, and professional choreographers in the United States.

- www.ed.gov: The U.S. Department of Education Web site for general information regarding No Child Left Behind, Goals 2000—Educate America Act, and other federal initiatives and laws that affect education, including arts education.

- http://wdr.doleta.gov/SCANS: Get information about the U.S. Department of Labor's SCANS Report.

- www.21stcenturyskills.org/assess21/assess_definitions.php: Access the Partnership for 21st Century Skills to read the specific goals and objectives for each of the 21st-century skills. See how dance can contribute to the "creative economy."

- www.ecs.org/CreativeEconomy: Learn more about the creative economy on the ECS Web site.

- www.ndeo.org: Access NDEO Professional Teaching Standards to describe highly qualified teachers in dance in the absence of NBPTS in dance.

Adopting Your Roles and Responsibilities for Teaching

This chapter helps you decide whether the educational dance profession is a good choice for you. It enables you to zero in on the varied roles and responsibilities asked of a school-based dance specialist, and it helps you take stock of your personal and professional traits for teaching. This chapter will show you how to view teaching as an "art" with its own technique and skills. It shows you where to look for the professional competencies you should acquire in the art of dance, in the art of teaching (education), and in dance education. From this overview of the profession and the competency checklists, you can see how well suited you are for a career in teaching.

Why Become a Dance Specialist?

Take stock of why you want to become a dance specialist. Although it's not for everyone, it is an excellent way to advance dance. Teaching is one of the most demanding, challenging, and rewarding of the dance careers. Although most dancers end up teaching in some capacity, not all choose to become certified K-12 dance specialists.

This profession needs educators who understand the significance and the magnitude of their work. It needs those prepared and able to deliver substantive learning experiences for students. It needs teachers excited by dance who believe there is no better way to learn than through movement and dance. The profession furthers aesthetic education for children. It is missionary work.

List reasons to—and not to—go into the profession. This list will help you decide whether entering the profession is a wise personal choice not only for you but also for the impressionable students in your future.

CHOOSE THIS PROFESSION IF

- you want to share the joy of dance with others,
- you like to see kids achieve,
- you want to take the dance field forward,
- you are eager to demonstrate what educational dance is and what it can do for students,
- you want to encourage others to set high expectations and achieve them, and
- you want to be a role model in dance.

DON'T CHOOSE THE PROFESSION IF

- you want job security,
- you want to showcase your specialty area of dance,
- you want to showcase your talent,
- you enjoy dancing so much you want to dance all day,
- another person thinks this would be a good career for you, or
- you feel you have no other career options.

 If you really love to dance, is that reason enough to become a dance specialist? Explain.

Let's get the tough stuff out first. This profession isn't easy. It takes energy, time, and thought to attain personal teaching excellence. You need to be as highly skilled in teaching as you are in dancing, choreographing, and performing. In addition to teaching, you also prepare, assess, research, and plan for upcoming goals. You keep fit, take dance classes yourself, and keep abreast of a growing profes-

> **"Some people go into teaching because it is a job. Some people go into teaching to make a difference."**
>
> —Harry K. and Rosemary T. Wong (1998, p. i)

sion. You must embrace multicultural diversity, nurture students' minds and bodies, advocate for quality educational dance programs, and ensure that dance is accessible to all students. So take stock of your personal traits and abilities. How well do they match up with what is required? Here are seven top traits to cultivate.

Trait 1: Desire to Let Others Shine

Take joy in your students' achievements and creativity. Understand the difference between seeking your own praise and giving praise away. Teach to make dance happen for others. Choose to generously give dance to others and light candles for them to glow by. For example, some dance teachers walk into the room like performers. Coveting the spotlight, they want to be the main attraction in their classrooms as well as on stage. Instead of taking the spotlight, *be the spotlight* to shine on others. Shine outside of school, but keep students the focus in your classroom.

Give students your full attention in the classroom so they grow in body and mind and flourish in spirit.

Trait 2: Determination and Perseverance

Never give up. Once you choose this career, become a standard bearer for the profession. Keep your eye on its goals. If just one teacher devalues dance education, it jeopardizes the entire profession. You are a pioneer blazing a trail. Blaze a clear path for those who follow.

Trait 3: Dual Perspective

"See" through your students' eyes. Up to now, you have been learning only for yourself. To teach you have to be both teacher and student at the same time. Extend yourself as though you were a student in your class. "Be" where they are, see from their perspective. Think from their viewpoint—from the outside in. What do they already know? What do they not yet have? Take yourself to that place. Be intuitive so you can better target instruction. This is part of teaching from a child-centered perspective (see chapter 4).

Trait 4: Broad View of Dance

Call on a wide range of styles, aesthetic viewpoints, cultures, and periods. Only comprehensive programs meet national standards. Acquire a range of techniques to prepare yourself: modern, ballet, and culturally diverse styles. For example, what kind of dancer are you? Are you a ballerina, a jazz dancer, a Bharata Natyam dancer? Of course you'll bring what you love and do best to your students. But you must also branch out and learn and enjoy the wide spectrum of modern dance, ballet, and culturally balanced styles so your students grasp a world of variety in dance.

Trait 5: Energy

Your energy fuels each class. It also activates you to recue music between classes, get the room ready for the next group, call class to order, and get your students going. Your energy motivates you to do all the things you do in class: be animated, demonstrate, encourage, monitor learning, move around the room, and make corrections on bodies. You must be fit to keep up with the sheer physical demands of the work. The day doesn't end with the last bell. You need the stamina to take classes that maintain your own technique, to organize lecture–demonstrations and showings of student work, and to attend dance concerts and other arts events.

Trait 6: Positive Professional Attitude

Adjust your attitude before class starts so you are emotionally ready to motivate students to do their best and stay focused on their tasks. Be upbeat. Keep a "can-do" spirit. Your class needs your positive energy. Students thrive only in positive environments. Good teachers keep personal problems, fatigue, and disappointments out of the classroom. Complaining teachers demoralize students. Some days you just have to remember the rules of teaching:

- It's not about you.
- Don't take it personally.
- Murphy's law: Whatever can go wrong will go wrong. Expect the unexpected.
- "Mama said there'd be days like this."

Trait 7: Willingness to Learn New Forms of Dance

Be acquisitive in dance. There's much to know. Take time to increase your dance skills and knowledge over the course of your career. Seek out what you lack. Add new dance styles to your repertory to expand your aesthetic perspective. Treat yourself and your students to guest artists who will share their expertise with you. Be continually captivated by the diverse dance forms available to study today.

 Are you jazzed by what you have read? Then get busy making your list of personal reasons to be a dance specialist. Is it a good career match for your personal traits? Read further to decide. Interview several professional dance specialists about their programs.

Examining K-12 Teaching Roles and Responsibilities

The art of teaching dance requires you (1) to dance, (2) to know about dance as art and human expression, and (3) to possess the skills to facilitate learning for others in dance. In the process of challenging students to "own" their own learning, you will engage them in dance inquiry that will be personally significant to them—cognitively and kinesthetically as well as artistically. Your role will be more of a facilitator and source of inspiration than a fount of knowledge. "Carl Rogers has written movingly on the point that no one can teach another; we can only learn together" (Drews 1975, p. 39).

From "The Gifted Student: A Researcher's View," by Elizabeth Monroe Drews, in *The Gifted and Talented: Developing Elementary and Secondary School Programs,* edited by Bruce O. Boston, 1975. Copyright 1975 by Council for Exceptional Children. Reprinted with permission.

> **"...responsibility means the ability to respond."**
>
> —Richard L. Loveless (1992, p. 136)

To take on your roles, you must have a content-rich curriculum. The more knowledgeable and skilled you are in dance, the better you can facilitate dance and enable students to incorporate these aspects of dance into their own learning. You'll need your own broad knowledge that spans the four main disciplines of dance (performance, choreography, dance history, and dance criticism). You must be a dancer to know the art of dancing and impart such applied skills to students: performing, anatomy and kinesiology, sound technique principles, body therapies, classical dance, health and nutrition, and dancing techniques from varied cultures and times. Be patient. You have a lifetime to acquire new knowledge and skills for these responsibilities. Congratulate yourself on "packing your bag" full of useful facts and skills for teaching right now.

Dance Specialist Roles

You have two main roles as a dance specialist: one primary and the other secondary. As a dance specialist your primary role is to teach dance. You are to ensure that your students get a quality dance education to at least achieve the minimum state and national dance standards. In addition to these primary dance roles, you are expected to generate opportunities for dance across the curriculum.

Roles in Dance

Just as the art of performance requires managing multiple roles on stage, the art of teaching means managing multiple roles in the school and in your own classroom. (The details you need to perform these roles are examined in other chapters.) Here are the main dance roles to take on and learn to manage with ease.

Design and Evaluate the Dance Curriculum You will design a year-long plan that consists of short-term, contextually coherent units of study made up of individual lessons. You will design the dance curriculum to ensure that its content, instruction, and student assessment are seamlessly integrated. Your curriculum will be informed by the national standards but driven by aesthetic goals and objectives consistent with the dance standards. The curriculum should be comprehensive and substantive. You must find ways to continually evaluate the curriculum based on student achievement and program effectiveness (educational relevance).

Facilitate Substantive Aesthetic Experiences in Dance You will focus on developing individuals' artistic skills and expressivity by steeping them in the artistic processes (c/p/r). You need to teach students about important dance works and people who contributed vitally to the art to increase students' knowledge of and appreciation for dance as an art form. You should facilitate creative and critical thinking as you construct curriculum experiences around the 6DCs.

Create a Laddered Aesthetic Environment You should ensure that students emerge each year more artistically aware and more able to create, perform, and respond to dance as a powerful art form than the year before.

Focus on Individual Growth You will see that dance is personally satisfying and increases skills in four growth areas: cognitive, kinesthetic, psychological, and aesthetic. Your driving goal is for your students to achieve at minimum the national dance standards (chapter 2).

Collaborative Roles Across Disciplines

In elementary buildings—where all academic subjects are taught by classroom teachers—there should be at least one dance specialist. Partner with teachers and other specialists so they extend movement concepts into other lessons. Take both an initiatory and a supportive role.

Be a Center Point for Collaboration Your main goal is to teach dance as art, but always look outside of dance for concepts to stimulate creative ideas and to extend learning in and about dance and the body. For example, what are your students studying in body science, music, visual art, physical education and fitness, injury prevention, and social studies? What guest artist can teach a new dance skill to you and your students? How can you enrich dance study with information from other disciplines and draw parallels to other subject areas? Can you find colleagues ready to share what they know or what they are teaching? Where are opportunities to mix disciplines that extend learning in dance?

Deliver concepts from other subjects in your dance class (such as science levers and hinges). Make dance a component in someone else's classroom (such as bringing history to life through period dances). A cardinal rule of collaboration: Don't try to force-fit an arts idea into someone else's academic idea unless both disciplines are well served.

Share your ideas and dance skills with colleagues and encourage them to use dance to teach appropriate aspects of their subject areas. Notice opportunities they might miss and call attention to their options. Learning through dance in other classrooms not only increases learning time in dance in the school day but also reinforces how dance is a vibrant way to learn and a vital form of artistic expression.

To illustrate, let's use the analogy of a wagon wheel. A wheel needs a strong hub to keep it stable and to provide a place for the spokes to attach. At the other end of the spokes, the outside of the wheel carries the load of the wagon and moves it along. Without a stable hub, the wheel wobbles and does not turn smoothly. Likewise, with insuf-ficient connecting spokes to evenly distribute the weight of the wagon, it doesn't function well or get very far.

Dance education is like that wheel. As your school's authority in dance, you are the hub of the dance wheel that gives stability to the entire wheel. In figure 3.1, see how the spokes reach out to others in the school to share dance with them. Also notice that they are two-way spokes, through which cross-curricular information flows back and forth linking you (dance) to others in the school. The spokes are avenues for you to help others teach through dance and opportunities for you to bring in links that enhance learning in dance in your classroom. Interdisciplinary and intradisciplinary ideas open up all kinds of new places for the wheel to go. Just as energy exchanged back and forth from hub to spoke gives a stable wheel the mobility to move toward its destination, these spokes move us toward our ultimate destination: an educated child.

Consider each professional mentioned on the wheel chart. How might you build educational relationships with each one? Because dance education

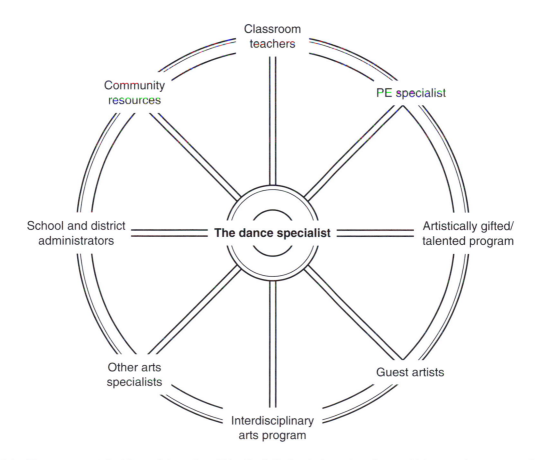

FIGURE 3.1 Become a catalyst for collaboration. Take the initiative to import and export ideas and processes that build momentum for dance learning.

Find obvious, and not so obvious, links between arts disciplines. For example, visual art teaches how to use changes in value to add interest and variety; dance choreography teaches how to use changes of dynamics and accents to add interest and variety.

- Collaborate on multimedia and multidisciplinary arts projects.
- Discuss and share content across the arts.
- Draw on similar themes (e.g., *texture* in visual arts is similar to *qualities* in dance).
- Take creative projects across disciplines (e.g., musical theatre, opera).
- Be a dance resource to other arts teachers.

Share effective instructional methods with each other. Collaboration between arts specialists not only helps you to better understand the other arts but also helps other specialists to learn about yours. Creative partnerships reinforce your artistic vocabulary and increase your artistic options. Forge partnerships to maximize artistic skills that benefit both you and your students.

Which partnerships will you build first? How will you initiate this conversation?

Take creative projects across disciplines. Collaborate especially with other arts specialists.

is for all students—not just for gifted and talented students or for those who audition—your mandate is to educate broadly in dance. This also means building coalitions in the school to all who are committed to achieving quality education for children.

Especially important is your relationship to physical educators. You and they contribute learning experiences not duplicated anywhere else in the school curriculum. You both share the goals of increasing student dexterity, fitness, and physical skills. Team up with physical educators in folk dance, social dance, world dance, and other areas of mutual interest.

Build Bridges to Other Arts Your closest "job-alikes" at school are other arts specialists (music, theatre, literary, and visual arts). Each contributes educational experiences not duplicated anywhere else in the curriculum. Because you share the same students, communicate regularly with each other.

Collaborate With Classroom Teachers Bring in other academics to feed outside ideas into dance class and to meaningfully connect to other concepts your students are studying. Connect links for students so that they see them. Then from your examples help them learn to make their own connections.

Be a dance resource to primary and elementary teachers whose students naturally learn through the arts. Help these teachers bridge their fears of turning a group of students loose in an empty space. Invite them to a demonstration of creative dance.

Collaborate at all age levels. Ensure that upper-level students experience the power of dance

- as a form of composition and expression (English teachers),
- as cultural expression (foreign language teachers), and
- as science (science teachers).

Work cooperatively on a theme-based project to cross-pollinate ideas across disciplines. Although it takes time to customize such experiences, this

48

process can generate some of the best work you do. Such projects frequently take you into areas you would have missed on your own and lead you into fresh, uncharted waters. Incorporate standards from other disciplines alongside your dance standards when this is productive.

Collaborate with students as well as adults (see chapter 10). For example, renowned hoofer Savion Glover was to perform nearby, and Mark, who had been taking tap dance classes, heard about it. He brought a lot of information about Glover's upcoming performance, photos, and a press release to class. The dance specialist saw the level of student interest it raised, and although she had limited tap experience, she designed a unit on tap dance that featured some of the great tappers, got Mark to demonstrate, lined up a guest teacher in tap, asked the students to gather more materials about Glover's performance and tap dancing greats, and made an exhibit for the school hallway. It generated so much interest that a bus was needed to transport all the students to Glover's performance.

Dance Specialist Responsibilities

Whereas roles are distinct, responsibilities are diverse. Prepare to assume multiple, overlapping responsibilities. There are too many to list, and invariably some crop up unexpectedly and present themselves unannounced. Responsibilities are as different as students.

Responsibility comes from the same root word as *responsible* and *responsive*. The current educational term is *accountability*. Not only must you know your subject, your goals, and your plan of action, but you must be able to articulate them to whoever asks. You are directly accountable to your students, to their parents, to administrators, and, indirectly, to your chosen profession of school-based dance education. It sounds like a heavy load, and it is. Be ready.

Teaching is a serving profession. You are responsible to manage students on one hand and nurture them on the other. You hold educational dance goals paramount yet occasionally abandon the day's goals when unplanned opportunities arise to share vital insights (i.e., "the teachable moment"). A level head helps you learn to exert your authority so you can handle the unexpected, smooth ruffled feathers, and calm troubled waters. Show that any situation in dance can be handled when approached as a win–win with everyone's best interest at heart. Separate what is professional from what is personal so your feelings do not get in the way of professional situations. Step back from difficult situations, breathe, and then handle them as you need to.

What areas of responsibility should you expect? The next section looks at five areas of responsibilities. They all revolve around your students, your dance program, and yourself and how they interact.

As we examine your responsibilities, list the skills you possess and those you want to cultivate. As you come to understand how demanding educational dance is and how rewarding, you will also see why it draws the best and brightest with the most to give to dance and to others.

Consider what modern dance choreographer Murray Louis has to say on the subject of dance teachers:

> Who are these people that teach? These people who so desperately care for their profession, their students, their art? Where do they come from? Where are they found? Why do they teach? . . . There must be a designed order that spots great teachers throughout the world in strategic places and another order that leads the potential artist to those places. In the triumvirate of dancer, teacher, and choreographer, I've always felt the teacher an equally important member, because everything that takes place on stage begins in the classroom. . . . What makes a good teacher as opposed to a bad one? . . . A good teacher feeds the class, and a bad one feeds from it. What they feed, and how they feed the class constitute their uniqueness. If the students absorb, then the teacher has taught. The absorption can range from an intellectual flickering to an artistic mastery of the body. (Louis 1980, p. 84)

Responsibilities to Students

Teach children, not subjects. In dance, give individuals information on which to build ideas and opinions and experiences on which to build artistic skills.

Inspire Students   Good teachers do more than teach; they *inspire*. Inspire children to use their acquired skill and knowledge, to do something unique with it, and to want to dance. Inspire them to transcend what they think they can do in dance and empower them to surpass their wildest dreams. Measure success less with test grades and more by artistic growth and pride in accomplishment.

Nurture Students Through Dance   Provide a nurturing, safe, stimulating learning environment. Nurture the basic dance roots that support students, and nourish their developing skills year to year. Roots do not prevent a tree from growing but provide the means for deep nourishment to grow strong and reach for the sky. Likewise, good technique development is the solid base (taproot) that builds strong dancers. At the same time, make opportunities for students to create and perform. Support students so they can learn to grow. With the strength of the basics (roots), they grow to creatively reach for the sky, to attempt creative solutions and find unique ways of expressing themselves (see "Scaffolding" in chapter 4, page 96).

Teach Individuals Within the Group   Although the bell rings and students enter your room in a group, they are not a block of students. Recognize and relate to each person for her or his individual differences and unique cluster of needs. Each one is at a different stage of development. Although you put them into motion as a group and keep the group on task, you must simultaneously see individual needs and address varied levels while they move. This requires vigilance, yet dance's impact on individuals has the power to change their lives. How can you do less?

Value Students   Be a champion for children. Take their side and when necessary be their advocate. You can still value dance standards while you care deeply about the impact your experiences will have on learners. Praise success. Validate successful attempts as well as signs of artistic growth and then use them as inspirational models. This legitimately increases dance confidence. Remember, too, that children learn from you, but they should also learn from each other.

Keep the Group on Task   Be consistent with expectations, fair with all, and yet generous with deserved praise. (Counterfeit praise is damaging.) Be a ringmaster who watches over all rings at once, keeping the pace of learning steady and assessing dance activities to keep all members on task and performing to standard. At the same time, be aware of the traits and interests of each one in the ring so you can adjust the pace to maximize each individual's experience (within the group). Maximize every moment of a dance class. Immediately redirect unproductive into productive energy. For example, when a class drags in as though they just expended their last drop of energy and are about to collapse before the class begins, go straight to the CD player, put on some high-energy music, and announce that they have to be dressed and in their places by the time the next cut (of music) comes on—about 3 minutes. Hurrying the dressing process gives students a focus and energy. Another example is to keep a hand jive (rhythmic clap—stamp call and response) ready to pull out. You clap and they respond. Diagnose the unproductive symptom (a lack of energy) and find a prescription to get students focused and on task before they realize what you've done!

Empower Learners to Grow   Set performance expectations and then motivate students to reach them. Empower students to achieve by expecting achievement. Give them the power to create and the skills to refine their creations. Be the catalyst that incrementally moves your students from where they are artistically to where they need to go. Encourage individual inquiry and the kind of curiosity that motivates them to formulate good questions and to make decisions for themselves, with or without a teacher present.

Engage the Whole Child   Reach the whole child in dance—body, mind, and spirit. Keep learners mentally alert, challenged, and focused as they

> *"To lead out is the literal meaning of the Latin verb educere, from which the word education is derived."*
>
> —Elizabeth Monroe Drews (1975, p. 35)
>
> From "The Gifted Student: A Researcher's View," by Elizabeth Monroe Drews, in *The Gifted and Talented: Developing Elementary and Secondary School Programs,* edited by Bruce O. Boston, 1975. Copyright 1975 by Council for Exceptional Children. Reprinted with permission.

move. Invite movement investigation and invention. Use creative thinking to stimulate the imagination, feed the creative spirit, and activate the body. Ask students questions to think about while they move, such as these:

- "What is initiating this particular movement?"
- "Can you find a way to hold your balance longer by reaching out in opposite directions . . . by bending your knees?"
- "Show or demonstrate your answers to my exploratory questions while we move rather than speak answers. Show me you are thinking about my questions and comments by the movement responses you make."
- "What can your body do? Show different ways you can reshape your spine as the drum sounds."

Program Responsibilities

In addition to moving students forward, keep your overall program's health and well-being in mind. Challenge yourself to develop well-rounded skills as a professional.

Be Accountable   It's not enough to be a dancer who wants to teach. Teaching requires results. You are accountable to deliver quality standards-oriented dance education to every grade level from kindergarten through high school. You must produce students who achieve. They must demonstrate

- a broad knowledge of dance and the dance elements,
- creative and expressive abilities,
- movement vocabulary,
- the ability to make discriminating judgments about dance,
- dancing skill and good technique, and
- safe use of the body.

Be Visible   Share dance education beyond the walls of your classroom. Show the valuable educational contribution that dance makes as an academic subject during the school day. Because you help define the profession by what you do, do it well. For example, invite the principal to visit your classroom, or invite parents on special days (e.g., once a quarter) to observe. Visit local dance studios to show and tell how educational dance (ED) relates to and differs from studio models. Build bridges between schools and private studios to emphasize how each enhances the other, not competes with it. Ongoing advocacy is vital.

Facilitate Higher-Order and Critical Thinking   Educational dance includes more than dancing skills. You must put creative and critical thinking to work so students grow creatively and aesthetically. Involve students in problem solving, analyzing, and evaluating dance. These are required skills for arts educators. (You will learn how to do this in chapters 4 and 9 with Bloom's taxonomy.)

Know the Expressive Vocabularies of Dance   Be an expert in describing movement. Learn and teach the languages of dance. Whether you use Laban terms, general dance elements terms, **Language of Dance (LOD),** or a combination is less important than that you use standard, universally understood vocabulary to describe movement so students learn to *speak* dance, *hear* dance, *see* dance, and *dance* dance (chapter 6). This calls on you to develop two kinds of language: one for moving (kinetic) and the other for conceptualizing (using words). We call the first the **kinetic dance vocabulary** and the latter **conceptual dance vocabulary.**

Analyze Movement   Become a movement analyst. You have to break down dance into its elements of body, space, time, energy and dynamics, and relationship **(BSTER)** to communicate about it. You have to be able to say exactly how the body moves in space (chapter 6). The dance elements enable you to "read" movement, explain it, evaluate it, ask for adjustments in technique, and talk about choreography. For example, in middle and high school, movement analysis is more than analyzing placement or proper lines. It calls attention to such aspects as a movement's timing, quality, shape, and flow and its relationship to the rest of the body or to the accompaniment. Breaking movement down through the elements this way helps students learn how to execute movement technique and discern movement options with attention to nuance.

Match Instruction With Clear Goals and Objectives   Teach purposefully. National standards keep you focused on some of what to accomplish at different ages. Dance frameworks delineate in more detail what students should know and be able to do at each grade level. Create lessons and units that achieve those specific goals. Assess whether the goals are met and to what level (chapter 12). For

51

example, without a thorough understanding of the desired outcomes for learning, teachers might be tempted to recycle other people's movement combinations. Unless you teach with clear artistic and educational goals, how will you know where you're taking your students educationally or artistically? Avoid stringing together familiar steps from someone else's choreography without clear justification for why you are teaching those steps.

Take Dance Seriously You have to take dance seriously for others to value it. To call class activities "having fun" creates the perception that dance is neither serious nor educational—that it's just play. Or worse, to make dance all fun

Your personal experience dancing, performing, and choreographing makes you a primary arts resource and role model.

and games misses the point. Dance *is* fun when it challenges the mind and body. Students should be so pleased with their dance work that their accomplishments legitimately boost their self-confidence and self-esteem. Expect students to thrive and grow, and praise their growth. But to call students' work "cute" trivializes their effort. Take care not to undermine your students or your program's educational value this way.

Ask for Quality Consistently teach students how to refine all aspects of their dance work. Foster aesthetic judgment so students of all ages increasingly refine their own work and perceive aesthetic quality in the work of others. Activities that are directed, purposeful, and complete have educational value. But only activities that are artful, discriminating, and refined have lasting aesthetic value. For example, it is not enough just to do a movement; you must stress how it is done and how well it is done. Putting movements together is just the start. Teach qualitative skills so students address how the movements flow, how they fit, and how well the dance is crafted. Teach students of all ages to make discriminating choices. Teach them how to design well-crafted dances. For example, most students above grade 2 can edit compositions and polish them to perform and critique in class. Urge older students to improve

movement quality, placement, and alignment in technique class.

Responsibility to Be a Role Model

Be a role model as a dancer and teacher. Be broadly educated, enjoy learning, and become an expert in the art of dance. Show that you are a thoughtful, **reflective practitioner** who evaluates the effectiveness of your teaching and who models excellence. Be the kind of authority in dance who earns the respect of others.

Be a Dancer To be effective at all grade levels, especially middle and high school, you must dance to know the dancing. A classroom rides not only on your dancer energy but also on your deep understanding of what it is to dance. With technique inside your neuromusculature, you can better call forth correct technique in others. One who brings personal **somatic** awareness into the classroom offers more than one who does not. Your personal experience dancing, performing, and composing makes you a primary arts resource with valuable firsthand dance experience. In some instances, nondancers build strong programs in the schools, but as national standards are raised for K-12, teacher expectations must keep pace. Gain as much dancing proficiency as possible.

Murray Louis reminds us about this:

A good teacher, out of simple reason, has to have in some way participated in his art and, through this participation, come to teaching. It is true that many performers consider teaching or coaching after their performing career has ended. Their contribution is invaluable and essential. Professional experience can only enhance professional teaching. (1980, p. 85)

Be a Dance Scholar Your teaching success hinges on how well you know your subject. Acquire new skills. Attend national and state dance education conferences for ongoing professional development. Engage in professional research not only to get information but also to contribute to the developing scholarly database in dance education. The U.S. Department of Education funded the National Dance Education Organization (NDEO) to develop the Research in Dance Education Database (RDE db), which lists more than 2,700 studies and articles from 1926 to the present. It has continuous updates from dance education and grows as new research is produced (see Rich Resources at the end of the chapter). There are other ways to research dance. For example, there are extensive dance archives at the New York City Public Library, the American Dance Festival, and others given in more detail in chapter 8.

Be an Arts Educator Develop the artistic, expressive side of students. Show them how to decode the language of dance. Show them how you might express ideas and feelings as well as abstract images and pure movement **patterns.** Relate dance to the other arts.

Be a Choreographer Show students how to transform a thought into movement and translate reality into abstract gesture. Show them how to find the best movements to convey intent. Show how to select, edit, polish, and rework to model a refined sense of compositional craft. Instead of praising everything your students create, show them how to reshape a work to increase its clarity and quality. Be a model choreographer who can talk about, use, and demonstrate the choreographic process.

Be Politically Savvy Stay tuned to the national scene to incorporate evolving national educational

perspectives into local programs. Keep current with arts education initiatives and how they affect you and your students. Run a tight ship and achieve all expectations. Learn when the National Assessment of Educational Progress assessments are being planned in dance at your grade level (see chapter 2).

Responsibility to Take Responsibility (Authority)

Learn how to orchestrate and balance teacher authority with a nurturing pedagogy. Set boundaries for student participation at the same time you empower students to take responsibility for their own learning. Assert authority by structuring the day for everyone's maximum output and **time on task.** Use your authority to insist on discipline and rules adherence for the well-being of all. At the same time, facilitate a nurturing pedagogy that compels students to learn. The protocols you set determine how effectively your class operates, which determines the quality of the educational experience. And the quality of the educational experience determines the quality of the aesthetic experiences.

Observe arts specialists who model effective management to see *authority* and *nurture* simultaneously in action. Because arts environments are interactive and creative, arts models help you figure out how to maintain an active learning environment as the "coach on the side" more than the "sage on the stage." That said, new teachers need to build in more structure rather than less to ensure that students stay on task and achieve goals and objectives.

Responsibility to Unite the Arts

The arts are in education together. We have talked about collaborating with other arts specialists, advocating for the arts, and what the arts gain and lose by sticking together, but the bottom line is—now you are an arts educator. Dance gained widespread acceptance because of the strides of arts education as a whole since 1985. Collaboration among arts leaders moved all the arts forward. Collaboration is a far more successful strategy than separating dance from the pack. Many states passed dance as an area

> **"... it is not sheer revolt against things as they are which stirs human endeavor to its depths, but vision of what might be and is not. . . ."**
>
> John Dewey in 1938 (Boydston 1985, p. 114)

of teacher certification because it was presented as one of the four arts disciplines instead of an isolated subject area with a lone voice. The arts—as multiple disciplines—can speak about parity with each other and advocate for equity with other academic subjects.

Dance benefited when the arts were seen to be at the forefront of education reform in the 1990s. For example, when *assessment* was education's hot new buzzword, the arts led out with portfolios and performance assessments, which had been used in arts education for some time. When the theory of multiple intelligences was the rage, the creative and artistic intelligences were part of it. When divergent learning was big, the arts had them down pat (i.e., kinesthetic, visual, auditory, and tactile modalities for learning). When higher-order thinking skills (HOTS) was touted, the arts showed how their educational processes relied on HOTS (i.e., questioning techniques, critiquing, journaling, creating, problem solving, editing, and refining activities). Arts specialists in countless schools increased the arts' visibility by demonstrating the merits of each educational discovery when the topic was hot—and still do it today because educational substance is so vital to learning.

Stick together to show what the arts do for education. Take every opportunity to justify the significance of what you do, to show the merit of the artistic processes, and to demonstrate the valuable knowledge and skills contained in all arts disciplines.

Arts specialists and dance specialists must speak with a common voice to promote all the arts in education. Although each art discipline accentuates different expressive modalities, together these disciplines cultivate the full range of verbal and nonverbal human expression. To lose sight of the connection between the arts—or worse, to put one art form above another—is neither wise nor practical. One way to lose collective political gains is for the arts to splinter into factions or to fight inter-arts turf wars. To divide the arts weakens each one, leaving it more vulnerable than if unified. Each one contributes uniquely to the well-rounded education we seek and promote.

Arts education, always on the fringe of being considered a frill and therefore on the edge of extinction in public education, requires vigilance and constant advocacy from all arts practitioners. Think like a wolf. Run as a pack. It's harder to marginalize a group of four than one alone.

That said, don't forget to continually justify the necessity of dance's place in the curriculum by showcasing exemplary work and adhering to quality standards. Use "education language" to talk with all who need to know—colleagues, administrators, school board members, parents, and students—about how arts education and dance affect the total education of children. Your role as an arts and dance advocate cannot be overstated. Don't be a lone voice in the wilderness. Join forces with other arts specialists to extol the virtues of arts education. Find strength in numbers.

Preparing to Teach Dance as Art in K-12

Of the three largest dance teaching professions—private studios, K-12, and higher education—K-12 is the most highly regulated. It requires the most diverse training, education, skills, and experience. It is the one that is accountable to state and national teaching standards (i.e., through certification and accreditation). Of course, the quality of the K-12 program you create depends on the completeness and quality of your preparation for teacher certification.

So you ask, what am I supposed to know and be able to do? Where do I get the main skills I need to teach dance as art? Let's examine where you get the content, experiences, materials, and expertise with which to teach dance as art in education.

Three-Pronged Teaching Skills You Need

There are three specialized areas of preparation:

1. The content and skills in the art of dance
2. The theories and practices specific to dance education
3. The theories and practices of education

Dance education has specific content, distinct methods and theories, and unique facilitation skills. It is erroneous to assume that one acquires integrated dance education skills by isolated study of dance and of education. Neither dance courses nor education courses address comprehensive educational dance (ED). You get essential skills in both, but they are not dance education skills. You need specialized knowledge and skills in three dis-

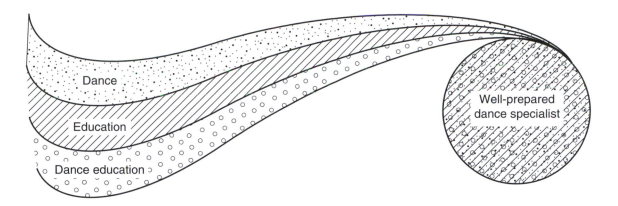

FIGURE 3.2   Dance expertise + education methods + dance education methods, experiences, and skills prepare you to teach educational dance in K-12.

tinct areas: dance, education, and dance education (figure 3.2).

In Dance

K-12 demands a teacher highly qualified in dance to teach dance as art. (The No Child Left Behind Act also requires highly qualified teachers, as you learned in chapter 2.) Dance specialists whose dance background is strong in the four dance cornerstones are the ones who can design and deliver complete, comprehensive K-12 programs (see chapter 5). If preparation is mostly performance based—without emphasis also on dance history, choreography, and criticism—the specialist is at a great teaching disadvantage.

Immerse yourself in a content-rich curriculum in the dance discipline—one that emphasizes both dance technique and dance academics. You need them for yourself; you need them to teach. Find universities with dance programs that emphasize diverse dance techniques, including dance styles across cultures. You need strong skills in ballet and modern. You need also to have danced some classical dances of the East, African dance forms, and world folk dance to possess the well-rounded credentials to teach a comprehensive dance curriculum. Try to be well balanced in dancing, dance making, dance appreciation, and dance-related knowledge. You need these dance competencies:

DANCE COMPETENCIES

1. Certified K-12 dance specialists use

   - anatomy, kinesiology, and somatics for safe practice and for technique development;

   - prevention and treatment for common dance injuries;

   - dance aesthetics and criticism;

   - dance history as well as the cultural underpinnings of each dance style;

   - non-Western dance forms (and perform at least one non-Western classical dance style);

   - major choreographic works from different dance styles; and

   - movement analysis, some dance notation, and the dance elements.

2. Certified K-12 dance specialists demonstrate

   - correct anatomical placement and alignment for axial and locomotor work,

   - technical proficiency in dance,

   - technical experience in and understanding of at least four dance styles,

   - proficiency in ballet or modern dance,

   - a keen understanding of dance as an aesthetic discipline in the performing arts, and

   - the ability to model best practices in both teaching and performance.

3. Certified K-12 dance specialists articulate

   - an extensive dance vocabulary—both conceptual and kinetic,

   - all the various tools of dance composition, and

   - choreographic principles of design in dance as art.

In Dance Education

Dance education courses focus on the content, instructional strategies, and assessments appropriate to teaching dance as an activity and blending it with the academic side of dance (see chapter 12). Although some delivery strategies are similar to those used in physical education and arts education, most strategies are particular to dance education. For example, there are specific dance education facilitation skills, such as facilitating movement exploration for dance making and improvisation, drumming to direct and modulate movement, and structuring activity-based learning in the artistic processes. In addition:

- Dance education studies child development from preschool to high school as it affects teaching dance.

- Dance education shows how content and instruction interact to build contextual coherence in dance.

- Dance education shows how to create performance-based assessments particular to dance education at different ages and stages.

- Dance education shows the way to structure a learning environment for artistry, safety, and performance.

- Dance education shows how to structure and deliver a curriculum in dance that achieves multiple objectives and accountability standards.

- Most teaching competencies in dance education also rely on your expertise in dancing, performing, creating, critiquing, and specialized skills about various dance styles and development of the expressive body. Bring them to your study of dance education theory and methods.

To approach learning from a synergistic **bodymindspirit** perspective is a unique pedagogical approach. Dance education helps you integrate learning from an arts education perspective and acquire a standards-based view of curricular expectations. Dance education addresses the construction and structural aspects of your teaching facility, as well as how to integrate the different aspects of dance into one unit to further aesthetic education.

Study modern dance technique (dance) and also modern dance pedagogy (dance education) to prepare yourself to teach modern dance. Also acquire an understanding of dance science and somatics.

Here you learn the fundamentals of teaching dance as art in education as well as how to facilitate inquiry in movement exploration, dance making, critiquing, and responding. Dance education is where you learn studio pedagogy for ballet, modern, and different dance styles and where you learn to analyze movement to better convey dance technique.

Get a strong background in dance before going into dance education. The more dance content knowledge you acquire and the more dance studies you complete before beginning dance education, the better. To teach dance as art requires you to have the spectrum of dance at your command as you design comprehensive curriculum. You need these dance education competencies.

DANCE EDUCATION COMPETENCIES

1. Certified K-12 dance specialists use
   - motor development principles;
   - aesthetic development principles;
   - theory and pedagogy of teaching different dance styles;
   - safe body mechanics, warming up, cooling down, and strength training;
   - guest artists as pedagogical extensions in the classroom; and
   - ways to accomplish external dance standards and internal objectives.

2. Certified K-12 dance specialists demonstrate the ability to
   - teach composition and choreographic craft;
   - lead movement exploration and creative dance for children;
   - teach technique in at least one classical dance style;
   - design a comprehensive, sequential, and substantive dance curriculum, using effective instructional strategies, according to age level;
   - organize growth experiences from the disciplines of dance and from diverse cultures; and
   - sequence age-appropriate dance instruction across a 13-year span.

3. Certified K-12 dance specialists articulate
   - characteristics of vernacular as well as concert forms of dance,
   - knowledge of safe dance surfaces and floor construction for dance facilities as well as height specifications and minimum size requirements for age level, and
   - the reasons dance is contributory to aesthetic education and overall student education.

From reading this list it becomes obvious that one dance education course isn't enough to develop the skills you need.

In Education

The study of education gives you a grasp of various learning modalities, methods and materials, class-room organization, and management. Such study helps you design units and lesson plans, identify goals and objectives, and acquire an array of instructional strategies, including inquiry techniques. It shows you ways to adapt lessons to special needs students. You learn the latest in educational theory and practices as well as sound pedagogical practice to round out your teaching skills.

EDUCATION COMPETENCIES

1. Certified K-12 dance specialists use
   - child development and readiness skills,
   - social development to judge the practicality of group constructs (such as when to use partners and when to work solo), and
   - Bloom's taxonomy of thinking.

2. Certified K-12 dance specialists demonstrate the ability to
   - build concepts from simple to complex;
   - sequence age-appropriate general instruction across a 13-year span;
   - assess students and evaluate programs according to national, state, and district standards; and
   - facilitate learning and establish stimulating, well-managed learning environments.

3. Certified K-12 dance specialists adapt activities to stimulate
   - physically and sensory challenged students,
   - emotionally challenged students, and
   - gifted and talented students.

Acquire breadth and depth of professional skills during undergraduate preparation so your students are the beneficiaries. Assess your strengths and accumulate skills you lack. Master all skills so they do not become the concern of accrediting agencies or program evaluators! Acquire strong professional skills in dance, education, and dance education so you can work miracles with students. (Further information is found in chapters 11 and 12.)

 Can you see why dance educators mature during the last 2 years of college? How many dance courses have you completed in preparation for dance education?

Preparation You Need

Being a dance specialist is an awesome responsibility! The profession demands qualified professionals in the classroom. Adequate knowledge and skills (i.e., what the dance specialist should know and know how to do) underlie your ability to deliver a complete educational dance program using the 6DC Cornerstone Model.

- Parents expect you to impart worthwhile knowledge and skills to their children.
- School boards expect your credentials to be the highest and your teaching ability exemplary.
- Principals expect standards to be met when measured from within the school and from outside accrediting agencies.
- Taxpayers expect you to live up to the certification given by your state.

Select your undergraduate program because it gives you the strongest professional array of current information and skills.

Although most colleges still use the 4-year model, increased licensure standards for credentialing professionals (and for accrediting higher education institutions with teaching degrees in dance, such as **BA** and **BFA**) stretch schools' limits in all three areas (dance, education, and dance education). Your institution must certify your competence to teach dance to preschoolers through high schoolers. What an enormous diversity of skills that takes! One option is 5-year licensure, which makes possible a more content-rich study in dance as well as more time to apprentice and intern.

Advantages of a 5-Year Certification Program

Five years permit time to acquire breadth and depth in the dance discipline, to develop proficiency in either modern or ballet technique, to learn non-Western dance styles, and to spend summers studying dance in different parts of the world. There is more time to master the art of dance—to create, improvise, and perform—as well as learn how to decode dances into a vocabulary of time, space, and energy and dynamics. A 5-year program gives you a chance to add more dance courses. Having time to focus on and discuss dances of different times and places (i.e., from a historical, critical viewpoint) connects you to the great works that are the lexicon of dance. A packed, rigorous 5-year dance-intensive program prepares you to teach for all ages.

Five years allow you to "have your cake and eat it too"—to construct your own double major with a BFA in dance and a BA in dance education (or a BFA in dance education).

Five years can perfect specialized professional skills needed to deliver dance artfully and articulately to others. Challenging course work in dance, professional education, and dance education—as well as general education—is prerequisite to transforming a dancer into a teacher who effectively teaches dance and links to other academic subjects. Unfortunately, there are few 5-year programs, and the 5-year models vary. In some instances, the fifth year is focused on education and dance education as the capstone to build on the strong study of dance during the first 4 years. Some offer graduate credit for the fifth year. But generally the 5-year program is just that—5 years for all the course work to fully prepare you to be a highly qualified teacher.

Advantages of a 4-Year Certification Program

Compact, intense 4-year programs—with summer study devoted to in-depth enrichment in dance (such as studying dances in different parts of the world)—help you achieve your primary goals for teaching in a shorter time. Take an inquiring attitude about dance and dance education. Spend summers at 6-week intensives such as American Dance Festival (North Carolina), Bates College (Lewiston, Maine), or the Ailey School (New York City). Why not study classical legong in Bali? How about native dances in Hawaii or American Samoa during the summer? Travel and study are natural companions.

Fill your course schedule with challenging and engaging courses to grow into the gifted professional you can become. Take in-depth professional education summer courses. Use every opportunity to increase your experience and world view for living and for teaching. An interesting person makes the best teacher. For example, Nicki thought astronomy would be a waste of time. But she discovered choreography in the stars: spatial designs in the solar system, motion, change, patterns, negative and positive space, shooting star accents. Not only did it inspire a beautiful piece of choreography, it developed into lesson plans that beautifully merged dance and science to serve the learning goals of both.

More universities offer 4-year programs, but it is hoped that as the field progresses a trend will develop for more 5-year programs. A 5-year program that is content-rich in dance and dance education would be ideal to develop the needed substantive understanding of dance's artistic and academic processes and to study dance education and education to help one teach dance in a developmentally appropriate way. Get as much supervised clinical experience in K-12 as possible.

In any case, with your first courses start your teaching file, to which you can refer during your student teaching internship. See the "Sample Teaching File Checklist" in appendix B for the kinds of items you should keep in your file. The better you organize it now, the more readily the materials will be accessible for you. Keep all your dance, dance education, education, and related textbooks (e.g., anatomy, theatre, music) there.

See appendix B for "Sample Course Requirements for BA in Dance Education" to see how general education, professional education (including education and dance education), and dance might break out in a 4- or 5-year dance specialist preparation program.

National Teacher Licensure Standards in the Arts

Teacher licensure standards in the arts followed the *National Standards for Arts Education* (1994) and the *NAEP Arts Education Assessment Framework* (NAGB 1994). The committee that drafted the standards used NAEP's "create/perform/respond framework," as it is called, because that framework comes out of the consensus project that gave us the national standards and assessments. Teacher licensure standards move states toward more uniform teacher education standards across the United States.

Entrance: INTASC Arts Standards

Because there are world-class K-12 standards for what all children are to know and be able to do in dance, of course there are standards for higher education that say what dance specialists should know and be able to do. In 2002, the Council of Chief State School Officers (CCSSO) published licensing standards in the arts—dance, music, theatre, and visual arts. These standards do two things:

1. Describe the in-depth professional dance education teaching standards for dance specialists.

2. Describe what all teachers—including dance specialists—should know and do in all the arts. That is, the music, theatre, and visual

arts expectations are general for you but dance is in-depth.

The professional criteria for all arts specialists and for classroom teachers (i.e., certified in all subjects) require general competence in each of the arts, including dance. That means that everyone who teaches will need basic dance skills. Likewise, all arts specialists require general competence in the other arts as well as specific competence in their own art discipline. The criteria for each arts specialist are rigorous: comprehensive, in-depth knowledge and use of the art form as well as skills of teaching it.

The CCSSO is a consortium of 33 states interested in reforming their teacher licensing systems using performance-based standards and assessments that relate to the national standards for K-12. The Interstate New Teacher Assessment and Support Consortium (INTASC), a program of CCSSO, published recommended licensing standards for all beginning teachers in all core subjects. In 2002, INTASC published the arts standards for teacher preparation in higher education. The INTASC standards are a model that states can use to develop their own state standards. If your university is NCATE accredited, it likely uses INTASC standards for teacher credentialing.

Download the INTASC art standards document, "Model Standards for Licensing Classroom Teachers and Specialists in the Arts: A Resource for State Dialogue 2002," for free from www.ccsso.org. These arts standards tell you exactly what is expected of you when you student teach as well as in your first year of teaching. It shows you not only what is expected in dance but also in the other arts. It endorses collaboration between specialists and classroom teachers to share arts expertise and skills for students.

INTASC's 10 Core Principles

INTASC's standards in all subject areas adhere to the same 10 core principles of teaching. These principles appear in teacher portfolio assessments. Principle 1 relates to your knowledge and skill in dance as art. Principles 2 through 10 relate to your broader teaching skills. You will be measured by these principles. Expect to demonstrate proficiency in each and to document them in a portfolio for certification purposes. In chapter 16, you will build your portfolio around these principles.

Although these and other national arts standards are voluntary, they are regarded as official quality markers and are taken seriously. In many ways

Outline of INTASC's 10 Core Principles

Principle #1: The teacher understands the central concepts, tools of inquiry, and structures of the discipline(s) he or she teaches and can create learning experiences that make these aspects of subject matter meaningful for students. (Subject Matter Knowledge)

Principle #2: The teacher understands how children learn and develop, and can provide learning opportunities that support their intellectual, social, and personal development. (Child Development)

Principle #3: The teacher understands how students differ in their approaches to learning and creates instructional opportunities that are adapted to diverse learners. (Diversity of Learners)

Principle #4: The teacher understands and uses a variety of instructional strategies to encourage students' development of critical thinking, problem solving, and performance skills. (Instructional Strategies)

Principle #5: The teacher uses an understanding of individual and group motivation and behavior to create a learning environment that encourages positive social interaction, active engagement in learning, and self-motivation. (Learning Environment)

Principle #6: The teacher uses knowledge of effective verbal, nonverbal, and media communication

techniques to foster active inquiry, collaboration, and supportive interaction in the classroom. (Communication Techniques)

Principle #7: The teacher plans instruction based upon knowledge of subject matter, students, the community, and curriculum goals. (Plans/Integrates Instruction)

Principle #8: The teacher understands and uses formal and informal assessment strategies to evaluate and ensure the continuous intellectual, social, and physical development of the learner. (Assessment)

Principle #9: The teacher is a reflective practitioner who continually evaluates the effects of his/her choices and actions on others (students, parents, and other professionals in the learning community) and who actively seeks out opportunities to grow professionally. (Self-Reflection/Professional Development)

Principle #10: The teacher fosters relationships with school colleagues, parents, and agencies in the larger community to support students' learning and well-being. (Community Involvement)

....

 What impact will the 10 core principles have on public schools after all teachers master basic arts skills, including dance?

they drive dance and arts specialist certification. Once they are adopted by a state, they become mandatory. INTASC arts standards will directly or indirectly affect you. You can find out at their Web site (www.ccsso.org) whether your state has already adopted these standards.

National Board Certification

After you are certified and hired to teach dance as art in education, ask your principal how long you need to teach before you are eligible to apply for full national board certification as an outstanding educator through the National Board for Professional Teaching Standards (NBPTS). Both INTASC and NBPTS espouse performance-based assessment and outcome-oriented competencies and dispositions for teachers. Whereas INTASC addresses new

teacher licensing standards, NBPTS espouses professional standards of the highest caliber for experienced teachers. With the No Child Left Behind Act and the emphasis on highly qualified teachers, it is to everyone's advantage for dance specialists to seek national board certification. Pursue generic national certification for two reasons: (1) validation (personal) and (2) visibility for dance (corporate). Not only does national certification reflect positively on your skills, it also demonstrates that dance educators have brains as well as brawn! It is a mark of professional excellence both ways. When administrators and other educators see such bright, dedicated, achievement-oriented professionals, it raises the stature of both the individual educator and dance education as a whole. We're counting on you. (Because the NBPTS does not yet have a board certification in dance, you may apply as a generalist teacher, not in a subject area.) You apply to NBPTS through your school to be a highly qualified teacher and have to be recommended by your principal to do so.

In appendix B find "Considerations For Hiring a Qualified Dance Specialist," which you can share with principals who are seeking dance educators for their schools so that they know what to look for.

Notebook/Portfolio:
Perspectives Notebook

Write a two-page essay titled "My Roles and Responsibilities as a Dance Specialist." Save it for your Perspectives Notebook (see chapter 16).

Reflect and Respond

Which of these four descriptions best fits you? What will you incorporate into your Statements of Belief (as explained in the Introduction)?

Example 1

I am enthusiastic about my subject and about teaching. Because I am a dance performer and choreographer as well as a teacher, I am committed to teaching dance as artistic expression to all ages, using movement to enhance holistic learning.

My teaching philosophy and practice rely on higher-order thinking. Therefore, I encourage students to analyze, synthesize, and evaluate experiences and information in dance in order to be actively invested in their learning. I ask myself, "Where are my students now (the point of departure), what do they need to know (new learning), and what strategies will best get them to this desired outcome (matching instruction to student needs)?"

My students are pushed to grapple with issues by reading, reflecting, discussing, journaling, problem solving, and experiencing dance, in addition to developing solid ballet and modern technique and performance skills. I try to support their journey on the sidelines to guide their growth in as many ways as possible. I take particular joy in seeing them create.

Example 2

My goal is to help students become deeply connected to the dance discipline and solidly grounded in the principles of the discipline. My goal is to expand their breadth of knowledge in dance, their diverse experiences in dance techniques, their ability to think critically, and their increasing problem-solving skills. My students must be inspired to achieve success. It is my role to ensure that they are inspired as well as empowered to be successful. They must take the responsibility for growth in their artistic and creative processes as well as seek useful knowledge and skills related spe-

cifically to dance. I help students enlarge their dance vocabulary about space, time, energy, and dynamics to increase their ability to describe to others what they see in dance.

My goals are to give them creative challenges and depth of content.

Example 3

My professionally active background enhances what I do in my classroom. The national and international perspectives I bring to students broaden their awareness of the world and of their own professional opportunities.

I work often with the other arts specialists in crossing arts disciplines, and I nurture an interdisciplinary perspective in students. I value and seek collaboration, joining with other teachers to design interdisciplinary instruction around a theme that we have in common.

Because I relish different cultures and art expressions, I live out my beliefs by studying authentic non-Western dance arts to share firsthand with students. I believe that it is important to stay inquisitive, be energetic, and hold high standards.

Example 4

I value the mentorship of others as well as being a mentor. By taking student teachers into my classroom, I am helping the profession grow and develop. I also like to advise my students about dance careers. I invite them to seek additional high-quality dance instruction in some of the excellent private studios in town.

My long-range plan keeps me on target. I refer often to the goals and objectives I have set to be sure each class is where it should be in both dance skills and knowledge. I believe in emphasizing content rooted in the dance disciplines, varying my methods of instruction to keep students on their toes, assessing student progress daily through organized record keeping and evaluation on how well my content and instruction achieve their desired outcomes.

Questions to Ponder

1. What are your primary roles as a dance specialist? Are you committed to this profession because of what you can do for dance or because of what dance can do for you? Do you like working with people and enjoy the successes of others so much that you like to shine the spotlight more on them than on yourself?

2. If the field of educational dance had a creed, what would it say?

3. How do you work with the local studio to enhance both programs? How do you build bridges rather than fences?

4. What are the major questions you have about the profession?

5. What reasons compel you to be certified as a K-12 dance specialist? Are there serious reasons you should list for not making this a career choice? What personal attributes do you bring to teaching?

6. Do you consider yourself a teacher first and a dance specialist second, or vice versa? Why?

7. If you take stock of the strengths of your professional preparation, are the courses mostly in dance, in education, in general education, or in dance education? How will your dance studies in undergraduate school prepare you to teach K-12? Which is best for you: a 5-year or a 4-year certification? Why?

8. How do national teacher licensure standards affect you (directly or indirectly)?

Rich Resources

RESOURCES

- The Research in Dance Education Database (RDE db). The U.S. Department of Education funded the development of RDE db, which comprises more than 2,700 studies and articles from 1926 to the present. It is housed at the Center for Research in Dance Education at Temple University in partnership with the National Dance Education Organization (NDEO). Membership in NDEO gets you a membership in the RDE db. There are also institutional memberships for such entities as universities and school districts. Access it at www.ndeo.org.

WEB SITES

- www.ccsso.org/intasc gets you the INTASC standards for initial teacher certification in the arts. These National Teacher Licensure Standards in the Arts include a dance section. CCSSO also publishes "Issues" papers, including one on NAEP.

- www.ncpublicschools.org/docs/curriculum/balancedcurriculum.pdf gets you to *Balanced Curriculum,* a document that justifies why the arts must be part of the basic curriculum during the K-5 school day. Especially relevant are pages 11-18, 52-55, and 170-172.

Emphasizing Aspects of Student-Centered Learning

"Aesthetic experience is required for high level tasks. All thinking and thoughtful action, as experienced moment to moment, are emotionally qualified."

—John Dewey

This chapter looks at your responsibility to deliver a student-centered curriculum driven internally by the needs of your students. This chapter presents the other side of a balanced curriculum, which keeps the curriculum from becoming standards driven. The chapter details the developmental stages of children pre-K to 12th grade in the four aspects most critical to teaching and learning dance: kinesthetic–motor, aesthetic–artistic, cognitive–intellectual, and psychological–social. The chapter helps you move students forward in all four aspects. This is necessary information to teach a developmentally appropriate child-centered curriculum. Use it to tailor all instruction.

Taking a Child-Centered Perspective

Children are the reason dance is so important to education. Educational dance is a means to help them reach their full potential. However, in an era dominated by standards and accountability, we must balance externals by attending to the personal as well as the collective needs of children that should drive curriculum and instruction from the inside. Student-centered learning—depicted in figure 4.1—maintains that children, as recipients, are at the center of the learning process and all else exists for that purpose, including standards and assessments.

Dancing involves the whole child—the intellectual, artistic, physical, and social child. Therefore, when you teach dance from a student-centered perspective, you incorporate all four aspects. They are all ways to perceive and interact with the environment, with information, and with others. Students vary in ability in each aspect. Your job is to focus on expanding individuals intellectually and socially through educational dance as well as kinesthetically and aesthetically.

Do not build a curriculum based on national standards alone—build a curriculum based on developing human perspective in the arts through dance. To reiterate, the purpose of school-based dance is to educate broadly by

Three National Assessment of Educational Progress (NAEP) dance assessment guidelines call for holistic learning:

"Dance assessment shall

1. Affirm dance as a way of knowing with a unique capacity to integrate the intellect, the emotions, and physical skills.

2. Honor dance as a discreet art form, but also encourage students to see the artistic experience as a unified whole.

3. Connect with the students' real-life experiences of dance."

—NCES (U.S. Department of Education Office of Educational Research and Improvement 1998b, p. 2)

stretching the body and the mind through dance. Use a holistic approach to teaching and learning that serves and stretches each student. To start, let's examine each vital aspect of student learning in educational dance (ED):

1. Kinesthetic–motor (moving and learning)
2. Aesthetic–artistic growth
3. Cognitive–intellectual (thinking, perceiving, and processing)
4. Psychological–social (feeling and interacting)

You must know the needs and abilities of each individual for the instruction to fit. It will not work to use the same instructional approach for everybody. In dance, you assess the child (age and readiness) and the instruction (the five stages of progression) to begin to fit the two well.

Stages. In each aspect of student learning discussed previously, there are either **stages of progression** or levels of complexity. Know these progressions so you can assess where students are and identify the next stage (or level) to which they should advance. Your grasp and use

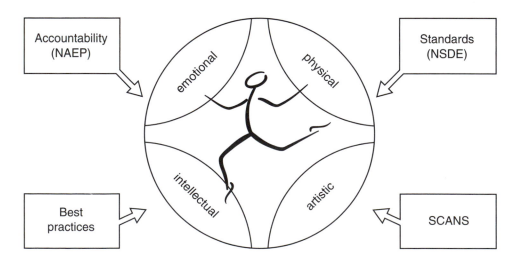

FIGURE 4.1   To teach the whole child, students are the focus of the dance curriculum.

of stages are essential to consistent student growth in dance. Examine how children advance from the underskilled stages to advanced skill stages along a learning continuum so you can lead them where they need to go.

There are five-point continuums (figure 4.2) for each of these aspects starting from and going to the following:

- Kinesthetic–motor development: from pre-functional to advanced performance
- Aesthetic–artistic development: from naive to sophisticated
- Cognitive–intellectual development: from basic to higher order
- Psychological–social development: from pre-social to prosocial

Make student needs paramount when making instructional decisions, because each group brings different needs. Make content age appropriate and rigorously engaging. Adapt content to meet learners where they are and take them where they need to go.

Ages. To learn realistic expectations about how far you can take dance students at each age, see the General Readiness Profile (presented later) of what to expect at different ages: 4 to 5, 6 to 7, 8 to 9, 10 to 11, preadolescent, and adolescent. Know readiness factors so you can concentrate on what is productive and avoid what is nonproductive at different grade levels (ages). This knowledge enables you to have realistic expectations of different ages to increase your effectiveness. For example, know the ages when boys and girls resist holding hands so you don't plan mixed-gender hand-holding in circle or partner dances then. Realize, too, that the

profiles describe what you can generally expect at that age, but making this determination is not an exact science. Expect some deviations because individual maturation varies. You will find some students ahead and others behind their age-mates. Analyze both age and stage and give equal weight to both as you plan so you design appropriate learning activities and tailor instruction to best serve your classes and individual students.

These are the skills you need to acquire by the end of this chapter.

1. Understand each five-point stage of progression (or level of complexity).
2. Have a mental picture of what different ages are capable of and ready for.
3. Tailor instruction to meet students where they are and to move them to the next stage of progression.
4. See how the SCANS Report recommendations from chapter 2 fit.

Keep realistic expectations about how far children can move in 1 year. By knowing where they are and where they need to go, you can give helpful, specific feedback that is neither too advanced nor problematic. Stages are more fluid than ages. It is a whole year before age changes, but they can advance more than one stage during that year.

The 6DC Cornerstone Model of Inquiry-Based Educational Dance advances a child's cognitive, kinesthetic, psychological–social, and aesthetic growth. The next sections focus on each of the four aspects to illuminate where students are and how dance takes them forward. By the end, synthesize them to see how their interplay develops the whole child in dance.

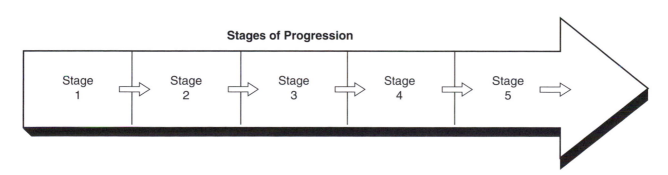

Stages of Progression

Stage 1   Stage 2   Stage 3   Stage 4   Stage 5

FIGURE 4.2   Your ongoing duty is to identify where learners are on this five-point continuum so that you provide the means for them to advance to the next stage.

Kinesthetic–Motor Development (Moving and Learning)

It is essential that you see individuals in motion—not just a group of children moving. As you learn how to zero in on an individual's moves, you also must learn to interpret what you see. By astute observation you can discern a child's present stage so as to determine the appropriate steps to take. Plan movement activities to challenge and extend the individual's kinesthetic abilities. That is the way students progress in dance. To teach movement skills and concepts that students already know doesn't move them forward to the next stage.

Here we identify stages of kinesthetic progression and then note general movement readiness profiles for different ages.

Kinesthetic–Motor Stages of Progression

Let's focus just on kinesthetic–motor stages of progression to see how students move through unsophisticated movement patterns to become more proficient performers. There are five progressive stages you should move students through from kindergarten to 12th grade. The five stages, similar to George Graham's four-stage motor skill proficiency for kindergarten through grade 5,

Plan dance activities to challenge and extend each child's kinesthetic–motor ability.

cover K-12. They incorporate motor development; however, the refined movement called for in dance as art goes beyond basic motor development into more proficient techniques and advanced skill development.

Each student falls somewhere on this continuum at any given time. Use these general characteristics at each stage of skill progression to help you assess where students are so you can tailor dance instruction:

Stage 1: Prefunctional (Beginning)

Descriptor: Lacks motor coordination for dance.

Students are unable to consciously control all movement or replicate particular movements.

Stage 2: Functional (Basic)

Descriptor: Becoming an adept mover, although not yet a dancer.

The body appears to respond more accurately to one's intention. Movements become increasingly similar to the desired response.

Stage 3: Preperformance (Developing)

Descriptor: Adept at moving and beginning to develop isolated performance skills.

Movements are even more autonomic and reflexive as students become able to move in a variety of contexts. Performance is informal and process oriented.

Stage 4: Proficient Performance (Mastery)

Descriptor: Increased coordination and fine motor skills for dance and performance.

The child exhibits controlled movement and is challenged by repeating movements exactly and by using movement in unpredictable and creative ways. The child has the ability to perform dance creations for peers in class but a somewhat limited ability to perform for an audience.

Stage 5: Advanced Performance (Sophisticated)

Descriptor: Sophisticated, high-level performance of dance.

Student intentions are translated into movement with ease. There is balance as well as neuromuscular coordination to enable complex movement and motor patterns. There is rhythmic accuracy and the ability to elevate, land, and turn. Performance for an audience is appropriate. Older students at this stage refine their performance skills, and some display an aesthetic sense of themselves in motion.

The five stages are not age specific: There is individual variation as to when students reach the stages. Stage 4 (proficient performance) is unlikely to be achieved below grade 2 and Stage 5 (advanced performance) unlikely below grade 4. Table 4.1 shows specific characteristics that learners exhibit as they progress from naive to sophisticated. Use this table to assess students, design dance experiences, and give students targeted, constructive feedback based on realistic expectations of where they are and where they need to be.

Tailoring Movement Instruction for Different Ages

A child's physical maturation, background, and prior movement experiences combine to determine movement readiness. Not all children automatically progress to a high level of movement and control unless you design meaningful movement techniques for them to master. Within each age group, individuals move differently depending on their physical makeup, fitness level, coordination, attributes, and limitations. To be certified across a span of 13 grade levels, you need to know what to expect when.

Here are profiles of typical movement abilities at different ages. Although profiling students is not an exact science, use the profiles to help you improve the quality of movement instruction. Readiness factors help you know what to generally expect at different ages in order to plan sequential units and instructional strategies to maximize learning. The stages of progression further help you adjust up or down depending on student ability and sophistication.

Primary and Elementary School

The General Readiness Profiles for ages 4 to 11 follow. You will learn what students are like and what they need during pre-K through grade 5.

Four- and Five-Year-Old Profile Four and five-year-olds need to move! They make sense of their world and themselves through motion. Allow them to be successful by encouraging them to move safely, with purpose, with increasing motor coordination, and with increasing expression. Teach them to move without making noise and without running into others or objects and to isolate different body parts.

Four- and five-year-olds are learning to control their own bodies. Teach stopping and starting on cue to increase self-governance and aid coordination of the moving body. Give them whole-body activities that emphasize large muscle groups, especially the torso and legs. Structure lessons to increase motor coordination, traveling skills, weight transfer, and balance. Teach children how to move while they move. Don't overexplain. They need to move to gain mastery of the body instrument. They grow by **exploring** all dance elements, especially the body elements. Emphasize body and space much more than time, energy and dynamics, and relationship at this age.

Four-year-olds like to discover what their bodies can do. They delight in isolating body parts, changing directions and levels, exploring each part's range of motion, and increasing their abilities. They love gross motor (large) movements such as jumping but tire easily. Fours start to balance on tiptoe while they move.

Kindergarteners are crucibles of energy. Movements are often energetic blurs with the body going all over the place. First, teach dance elements from the body category to help them gain mastery over their moving body. Next, relate body to space by emphasizing shape so that they get a fuller sense of how to design the body in their personal space before going into general space concepts (e.g., traveling, directions, pathways). Improvisational dance making usually gets exuberant and lively results. Teach children to improvise dances using simple structures (e.g., beginning, middle, and end). Use their raw energy as a natural resource. Channel their desire to move into ways to help them increase motor skills to be used for dance.

Realize physical limitations of this age group and be realistic. All the prodding and insistence in the world won't produce a classical pirouette! Instead develop balance, coordination, and gross motor skills. Because children tire easily, alternate between big movements and smaller, less energetic ones.

Review and repetition are important at this age. Students gain confidence and stamina by reviewing and repeating what they know how to do. Although they are not ready for leg stretches or coordinated jumping and landing techniques, give them simple, big torso stretches before and after large movements, locomotors, and jumping. Have them march, knee bend, and clap high and low to warm up for going into the air.

Following are some of what children at this age need to do:

- Work on static balance, coordination, and stop and go cues
- Work on gross motor movement and simple locomotors

Table 4.1 Movement Stages of Progression in Dance

	Prefunctional	Functional	Preperformance	Proficient performance	Advanced performance
General technique	-Has undeveloped ability to demonstrate qualities of movement most of the time -Lacks physical skill and control in executing movements	-Achieves limited quality of movement -Achieves some physical skill or control in executing technique	-Demonstrates some use of expressive quality of movement -Demonstrates some use of physical skill and control in executing technique	-Demonstrates expressive qualities of movement most of the time -Demonstrates physical skill and control in executing technique	-Clearly and consistently demonstrates expressive qualities of movement -Demonstrates high level of physical skill and control in executing technique
Dance elements	-Does not use these particular dance elements: space, time, and energy -Lacks rhythmic accuracy during most exercises -Lacks dynamic range	-Uses some dance elements -Developing rhythmic accuracy -Developing use of dynamics in movement	-Uses the dance elements -Demonstrates rhythmic accuracy most of the time -Demonstrates use of dynamics in selected movements	-Efficiently uses the dance elements -Demonstrates rhythmic accuracy consistently -Uses a range of dynamics	-Artfully uses the dance elements -Clearly and consistently demonstrates rhythmic acuity -Clearly and consistently demonstrates appropriate use of a range of dynamics
Sequencing	-Does not yet grasp logic for sequencing movements and connecting them	-Grasps logic in movement sequences and understands concepts of phrasing	-Uses phrasing when performing sequences	-Phrases movements so they flow into coherent units and statements	-Consistently uses coherent movement sequences with attention to phrasing
Alignment	-Lacks alignment or is yet unaware of static or dynamic alignment	-Begins to exhibit static and dynamic alignment	-Maintains ankle, knee, hip, and torso alignment some of the time	-Maintains ankle, knee, hip, and torso alignment throughout most technique exercises and sequences	-Maintains proper total body alignment during technique exercises and sequences
Static balance	-Holds on-center static balance with a wide base of support -Balances on different body parts -Holds flat foot balance on both legs	-Holds on-center static balance on a narrow base of support -Balances on different body parts -Balances on one leg, flat foot	-Holds static balance positions in two-foot relevé -Balances on different body parts	-Performs relevé balanced on one leg at the barre	-Consistently maintains static balance in dynamic movement sequences and can land with balance after jumping and leaping
Dynamic balancing	-Inconsistent balancing in motion	-Maintains balance most of the time	-Moves from on-center balance to off-center balance and can sequence balance moves	-Balances with on- and off-center directional changes -Performs relevé balanced in the center with quarter turns	-Maintains balance in dynamic movement sequences and can land with balance after jumping and leaping -Performs turns on half toe that require balance (e.g., pirouette) and regains equilibrium after turns in order to balance

68

	Not ready for partner work	Ready for partner work	Can share weight with a partner and maintain balance	Can consistently share weight with a partner and maintain balance	Can share support and balances during lifts and perform with ease
Partner balances					
Shaping	-Makes unbalanced, wobbly shapes; is unable to link shapes (shaping)	-Begins to hold static shapes and to link shapes (shaping); uses both symmetrical and asymmetrical shapes	-Holds shapes and controls body shaping in one place; begins to perform traveling shapes	-Confidently uses body shaping that is more complex in design and steady in control; travels into off-centered shapes with weight on different body parts; travels with changing shapes that are continuous and controlled	-Changes complex shapes that flow from one to another whether in place or traveling through space; performs with a sense of shapes and shaping
Weight transfer	-Transfers weight on feet when traveling in simple locomotion -Transfers weight from feet to other body parts without traveling; travels on various body parts -Transfers weight using even rhythms	-Moves between points of contact using twists, curls, and stretches -Transfers weight from feet to hands -Transfers weight on a steady beat changing directions -Transfers weight to uneven rhythms going forward and sideways	-Transfers weight to a partner -Begins to lift and center torso weight between both legs in first and second positions, parallel and turned out -Transfers weight using syncopated rhythms; transfers weight rhythmically and in appropriate dance style	-Transfers weight throughout a sequence -Increases vertical and horizontal distances of weight transfer in leaps and jumps -Lifts the torso weight out of the hips so as not to "sit down into the hip"; supports and lifts from the center -Transfers weight with rhythmic and stylistic accuracy most of the time -Transfers weight with rhythmic complexity	-Transfers weight from feet to different body parts and to increasingly complex supports; transfers weight to one leg, supports and balances weight on one foot or body part -Makes weight transfers with complex changes in level, shaping, and dynamic qualities
Traveling	-Travels in even rhythms: rhythmic walk, march, run, jump -Travels solo -Travels at the same tempo with limited ability to change directions -Is unable to execute some steps -Lacks some gross motor skills	-Travels in even rhythms adding the ability to leap and hop; travels in uneven rhythms: galloping -Travels in relation to obstacles and others in space -Travels in different directions, speeds, and levels -Executes a simple two-step with rhythmic and step accuracy -Demonstrates gross motor development	-Travels in even rhythms: combinations of basic steps; travels in uneven rhythms: skipping, sliding, and chassés -Travels in relation to obstacles and people; travels in relation to a partner -Combines locomotor patterns to rhythm -Executes complex two-step with direction changes; uses various stepping patterns: hopping, leaping, schottische -Uses gross motor skills and is beginning to use fine motor coordination	-Executes even and uneven rhythms and knows the difference -Travels in varying environments with ease -Contrasts traveling and nonlocomotor movements; changes directions with all locomotors without losing rhythmic accuracy -Executes triplets -Executes fine and gross motor skills	-Memorizes and performs rhythmic as well as nonmetered sequences, timing them accurately -Travels in solo, duet, and group dances with the ability to relate to the environment -Performs complex locomotor sequences and ably mixes locomotors with nonlocomotors -Executes turning triplets, polka, and mazurka -Performs both fine and gross motor movements

Header descriptors (Partner balances row):
-Not ready for partner work | -Ready for partner work | -Can share weight with a partner and maintain balance | -Can consistently share weight with a partner and maintain balance | -Can share support and balances during lifts and perform with ease

(continued)

Table 4.1 *(continued)*

	Prefunctional	Functional	Preperformance	Proficient performance	Advanced performance
Elevations	-Precedes a jump with a run -Precedes a leap with a run -Jumps in different directions -Leaps in different directions -Jumps from one to two feet -Jumps from two feet to two feet	-Executes jumping sequences -Jumps and leaps with rhythmic and spatial accuracy -Forms body shapes in the air -Begins to change facings when landing -Lands with plié most of the time	-Combines jumping and leaping -Combines jumps and leaps with other locomotor patterns -Mirrors partner jumps -Is consistently able to change direction of landings -Lands with plié consistently	-Jumps for increased elevation -Leaps for height -Leaps for distance -Uses elevation in expressive ways -Uses elevation for expressive purposes -Varies rhythm and timing in elevations -Uses consistent preparations and soft landings -Lands with plié and with foot articulation	-Performs refined elevations and landings -Flexes through the joints when landing and maintains balance and muscle control throughout -Uses plié to begin and end elevations -Articulates the foot to demonstrate landings that are soft and move sequentially through the joints -Executes complex air work with varied timing challenges -Prepares and lands consistently with high-quality joint articulation -Lands with accurate joint articulation
Turning	-Unable to turn with control of center	-Performs quarter turns with ease and begins to execute half turns -Turns and rolls at different speeds -Executes three-step turn and simple turns	-Combines turns and rolls with preparatory or follow-up moves, like rolling to stand and turning into a shape -Executes a turn balance, turn sequence -Executes two-step turns, chaînés turns, and quarter pirouette turns on flat foot -Finds center and is able to turn around an axis in isolated exercises	-Rolls, recovers, and continues with another action -Turns for direction changes -Executes a turn–balance–turn sequence at different speeds -Executes continuous 360-degree turn, piqué turns, and quarter pirouette turns with relevé -Turns around a center axis across the floor in sequences	-Can roll into one-leg balances and other narrow base supports and balances in performance -Is able to control turns -Turns into static and dynamic transitions and makes inventive direction and level changes -Performs varied-axis turns -Performs 360-degree turns, half to full pirouette turns, and early fouetté turns

- Identify the spine and its relation to designing torso shapes
- Isolate body parts
- Increase strength of major muscle groups
- Increase ability to self-govern in movement—move in control on cue
- Learn the use and function of their bodies
- Use arms oppositional to feet in locomotor movements
- Do simple circle dances
- Change directions and levels
- Be versatile in the use of hands and feet
- March to a steady beat at different tempos

Six- and Seven-Year-Old Profile   Fine motor skills become steadier at this age. Small muscle coordination develops faster in girls than in boys, but fine muscle coordination is increasing in both. Start exploring all the dance elements, still emphasizing body and space. Contrast extremes in timing (fast and slow) and dynamics (sharp and smooth). Children at this age learn by being challenged, not by repeating what they already know how to do.

Here are some of what children at this age need to do:

- Increase their repertory of even steps and locomotor patterns
- Increase the length of time they hold a static balance
- Work to increase dynamic balance (while moving)
- Work on cadence, steady beat, and moving in simple rhythmic patterns
- Isolate joints (internal) and body parts (external)
- Do simple circle and line dances with unison movement
- Use the spine to design torso shapes
- Explore the BSTER elements, emphasizing the body in space
- Work on laterality (right and left)
- Explore divergent activities such as creative dance
- Perform group dances with unison movement rather than coordinating steps with a partner
- Have opportunities to increase ability to self-govern

Eight- and Nine-Year-Old Profile   Here you'll find a wide range of physical and motor maturity. There is usually large and small muscle control, because fine muscle coordination has been developed. Loco-motor skills and balance as well as strength, speed, and endurance increase. Children of this age prefer large muscle movements, and they like to move in extremes. Although fine motor skills are improved, these children tire of too much small, isolated, controlled movement. However, they do show interest in developing refined movement skills. They also show interest in learning about the world through world dance and folk and social dances.

Emphasize all the dance elements. Move from contrasts of extremes to modulations between extremes so children can learn the full range of each element (e.g., enlarging and shrinking in space). Now the artistry of gradation between extremes will be their challenge (e.g., not just contrasting quick and slow, but acceleration and deceleration to speed up and slow down the timing).

Following are some of what children this age need to do:

- Perform traveling patterns
- Control static and dynamic balance
- Use all the dance elements
- Explore creative activities such as movement exploration and creative dance making
- Learn basic compositional skills and different structures in which to make dances
- Learn the dynamic qualities of movement
- Take responsibility to work in small groups to make dances
- Design and refine dances based on the dance elements; respond to performed works
- Learn origins and style along with step patterns in folk dances
- Take on challenging balances and shapes (such as upside-down shapes)
- Show works to peers for feedback and refine their dance creations

Ten- and Eleven-Year-Old Profile   At this age children have increased motor skills and stamina. Challenge them to use fine motor skills with more complex step patterns and dance techniques (balance, elevation, turning). They are adept at the body element but need to further refine the other BSTERs. Emphasize refining space (pathways) and relationship (meeting and parting, small group compositions). These children need to be challenged with dynamic and time variations. They are ready to experiment with all the Laban effort qualities.

Following are some of what children at this age need to do:

- Learn to perform complex coordination and locomotor patterns
- Learn to turn on center
- Balance on half toe
- Work on one-leg balance with hip rotation

Middle School

The General Readiness Profiles for ages 12 to 14 follow. In middle school, fine muscle coordination is possible when students are not in extreme growth spurts, because balance and coordination are adversely affected during these times. Expect a certain amount of awkwardness and clumsiness in general. Learning ways to master specific movements and techniques becomes appealing. Because these students are more interested in peer alikeness than uniqueness, creative work can be somewhat threatening. These students often find more security in learning predesigned movement patterns and perfecting them than in creating their own.

Following are some of what students this age need to do:

- Expand all aspects of their movement vocabulary
- Learn balance, coordination, and fine motor skills
- Develop kinesthetic awareness of what their new bodies can do and strive to improve physical skills
- Develop kinesthetic awareness by feeling a body position without visual feedback from a mirror
- Perform locomotor movements requiring strength more than agility

"Children use the arts unselfconsciously, with joy and intensity, with obvious delight in their discoveries and achievements. They have no doubt that the pictures made, the songs sung, the dances danced, and the stories told and enacted are as important as anything else they do."

—Arts Education Partnership Working Group (1993, p. 4)

Reprinted, by permission, from The Arts Education Partnership Working Group, *The Power of the Arts to Transform Education*, The Kennedy Center for the Performing Arts and the J. Paul Getty Trust, 1993.

- Learn axial movements of flexion, extension, rotation, and design of body parts
- Gain experience performing

High School

The General Readiness Profiles for ages 15 to 18 follow. This age group is able to execute challenging physical and rhythmic patterns. Provide differentiated movement for males and females when possible to give males the opportunity to develop strength moves as well as coordinated rhythmic patterns. Some may be ready to partner in the advanced classes. Peer pressure exerts an enormous influence, so take care that all students are able to perform their best, or at least to an acceptable level, before putting them in front of an audience. (High school peer audiences can be very cruel.)

Following are some of what students this age need to do:

- Practice challenging coordination and fine muscle work
- Increase balancing and turning skills
- Perform locomotor movements requiring strength and agility
- Learn technique for turnout
- Learn to coordinate arms and legs
- Master two varied dance styles
- Develop artistic expression and stylistic nuance
- Develop rhythmic timing and musicality
- Allow for individuality and find ways to encourage it within the group structure

Aesthetic–Artistic Development

Aesthetics relates to quality, value, and meaning. It reaches into more areas than just the artistic. As we respond to something particularly beautiful, something that touches us, we have an aesthetic reaction or a feeling response. Encourage an aesthetic feeling response in dance to help learners savor life's best opportunities and experiences. Help them acquire a direct link to themselves through dance to know what it is to be human, to be alive, to live deeply, and to participate fully.

Aesthetics involve both cognitive (thinking) and affective (feeling) domains. Therefore, aesthetic experiences in the arts connect reason with emotion. Some aesthetic exploration and experiences actually yield reactions that are preconscious or precognitive. As we aesthetically respond to dance, we seem to be moved more emotionally than mentally, yet dance work should also be looked at, analyzed, and talked about (using left brain cognition). So the aesthetic–artistic dimension crosses domains. In dancing and performing, aesthetics are an avenue to bring together the kinesthetic, cognitive, and affective domains in a bodymindspirit experience.

Aesthetic education should develop both expressive skills and cognitive, academic ones. Use it to raise the level of artistic judgment and appreciation. Students who only see rudimentary peer works do not move forward aesthetically. They must see dance products of aesthetic value to raise their level of aesthetic awareness. They must see the powerfully rendered dances on subjects of humanity to be able to grasp the communicative power of dance and to understand what this art form encompasses. That is why unpacking great dance works (see chapter 9) is a necessary part of an aesthetically driven curriculum. Students need a diet of dances from mature choreographers as well as student choreographers to stretch aesthetically in dance.

How can you lead aesthetic growth? Ask learners to make critical judgments about specific works they encounter and to critically think about what they do and see. Be concerned less with what is done (quantity) and more with *how* it is done and *how well* (quality). Help students of all ages see cause-and-effect relationships, which can drive them to create new solutions and find unique responses to movement problems. Teach all ages to take responsibility for the artistic quality of their work. Inspire excellence.

Aesthetic education in dance incorporates meaningful dance criticism. Dance criticism is one place in which aesthetics are applied. Dance criticism gets all ages to describe, analyze, interpret, and evaluate professional quality dance as well as student works (see chapter 9). To build an aesthetic eye, show works of aesthetic quality; to build an aesthetic vocabulary, critique works of aesthetic quality; to build aesthetic appreciation, create and choreograph original works.

Aesthetic–Artistic Stages of Progression

Determine where students are aesthetically by listening to the verbal and kinesthetic responses they give as they encounter dance works, as they create dances, and as they perform them. Notice how, as students create, perform, and respond to dance, they reveal their stage of artistic development. Artistic stages of progression range on a continuum from naive to sophisticated. Each student falls somewhere on this continuum at any given time. Use these five recognizable stages to identify where students are artistically so you can effect individual aesthetic growth in dance.

Being artistically gifted and talented (AG/T) is not a developmental issue. It's an "inborn trait and capability" issue. AG/T students develop from one stage to another, but they often achieve at a higher stage earlier than their age mates. Move AG/T children along the stages of progression in order to give them appropriate challenges.

Your job is to move individuals to as high an aesthetic–artistic level as possible at all grade levels. An arts education perspective recognizes that aesthetic awareness in the other arts—especially visual arts—transfers to aesthetic awareness in dance. Therefore, those with arts education backgrounds should more quickly comprehend our shared

- artistic principles and processes (c/p/r),
- terminology, and
- foundation disciplines (i.e., composition, techniques, history, and criticism).

Stress arts commonalities as much to bolster artistic principles in dance as to reinforce them in the other arts (see chapter 10). Here we build on Michael Parsons' descriptions of aesthetic awareness in visual art and extend them to dance—the other visual art.

Stage 1: Preoperational (the Favorite Stage)

Descriptors: Naive, unsophisticated, unschooled

At Stage 1, students will respond to their attraction to the subject of a dance work. They will make an association between the dance and something else they liked or an intuitive interest in something about the dance.

- "I liked the costumes."
- "I liked its story."
- "I liked it because it was funny and reminded me of a cartoon."
- "I liked it because the music was by the Backstreet Boys."

Stage 2: Operational (the Beautiful Stage)

Descriptors: Naive, unsophisticated, unschooled

At Stage 2, student response is based on how an idea is represented. A dance work is more attractive if the representation is realistic or easily identifiable. Straightforward themes and story ballets are generally enjoyed. Appreciation of complexity does not enter in.

- "It is pretty."
- "It tells a story all the way through so I could follow it."
- "The costumes were really beautiful under the lights."
- "I thought it was ugly that a dancer was on her knees scrubbing the floor in the dance."

Note: There is an important teacher-facilitated step to move students from Stage 2 to 3. It is discussed later in this chapter after all five stages are presented.

Stage 3: Connectional (the Expressive Stage)

Descriptors: Growing awareness, connection on an emotional level

Students respond at Stage 3 to a dance's expressiveness. They look at dance for the quality of experience it produces. The more intense and the more interesting the experience, the better the dance.

- "I had a strong connection to the dance."
- "It pulled me into it and made me want to see what was going to happen next."
- "I was surprised when the whole stage seemed to turn upside down which drew me into the work even more."
- "I liked the pas de deux because it was so beautiful and so tenderly danced."

Stage 4: Insightful (the Style and Form Stage)

Descriptors: Aware; connection is cognitive and emotional.

Students develop insight about the significance of the dance work. They recognize that dance exists within a tradition that includes many dancers and choreographers across time. Here students see the relationship between different works and styles. Historical perspective adds to the interpretation of style and form. Complexity begins to be appreciated.

- "The use of exquisite lifts makes this dance athletic and aesthetic."
- "This dance fits into a style that comes out of the modern dance tradition."
- "The way the white cloth was used throughout the dance to represent multiple situations was something that held the dance together and created visual interest. It also added an element of inventiveness to the dance."
- "The dance holds interest because of the playful way the movements and music interact."

Stage 5: Advanced (the Independent Artistic Stage)

Descriptors: Sophisticated, advanced; sees symbols; connects on mental, emotional level

Stage 5 is where students realize that each individual must judge the dance based on the criteria, concepts, and values by which the society constructs meaning. Students realize that these societal artistic values change with history and must be continually readjusted to fit contemporary circumstances. Students develop a personal aesthetic viewpoint that comes into play as it differs from (or coincides with) that of society. Choreographic complexity and performance refinement are noticed and valued. For example, students might respond as follows:

- "In the end the dance work is too loose and self indulgent. I don't like that; I want more self control in the dance."
- "It seems that the choreographer drives home the point that everyday movement can be transformed into dance movement."
- "This dance appeals to me more than the previous one because its message is universal and transcends cultural differences."
- "This dance breaks out of the restrictions of early modern dance and truly finds a place in dance history by its discriminating juxtaposition of movement qualities not heretofore seen in dance."

Adapted, by permission, from M.J. Parsons, 1987, *How we understand art* (Cambridge: Cambridge University Press).

Building a Bridge Between Stages 2 and 3: A Teacher-Led Transition

A big shift in sophistication is required for students to go from Stage 2 to Stage 3. You, as a specialist, play a critical role in getting them from Stage 2 to 3. Students at this juncture must acquire—if they haven't already—a thorough background and vocabulary in the dance elements. They need to be able to use the BSTER elements to express in words and in movement the dance concept they want to convey. Without these vocabularies, students simply cannot progress sufficiently to the next stages. Unless you intentionally teach the language of body, space, time, energy and dynamics, and relationship (BSTER), students will not learn it. (Chapter 6 deals with the specifics of teaching BSTER.)

This transition step, or "bridge," is critical to the ability to qualitatively analyze dance. If a student has a background in dance elements, the transition can happen as early as second grade, but it is more common by third grade. This transition can happen at any subsequent age, depending on when students begin their study of dance, but the transition depends on the following:

- Students have had consistent, high-quality creative dance lessons in which they explored and experimented with each of the BSTERs.
- They have developed a strong BSTER vocabulary (movement and conceptual).
- They have created and composed dances using the BSTERs.

As soon as primary-age students develop a working BSTER vocabulary and get lots of experience moving and creating with them, students can be taught to review and unpack dance works. Get students to apply BSTERs by dancing them, creating with them, and responding with them. Daily critiquing in early childhood with the BSTERs builds all dance skills: seeing, talking about, making, and doing dance.

Keep dance makers goal oriented. Students do best when they are consistently given simple compositional criteria and review criteria at the start of a creative problem. They know at the outset what to do and what the audience will look for. They can then create the dance study or structured improv knowing they will get and give artistic feedback.

> **"Art is communication spoken by man for humanity in a language raised above the everyday happening."**
>
> —Mary Wigman (Stewart and Armitage 1970, p. 21)

Students who can consistently compose dances with the clear choreographic criteria you give them are ready to evaluate each other's work with those same criteria. Turn the criteria into critiquing questions. Use the questions to pinpoint exactly what is the most important part of that lesson. Thus, day by day you ask students to closely observe each other's dances and respond in quality terms, such as these:

- A dance's use of space
- Use of high-quality movements based on the criteria
- Effectiveness of shapes
- Dancer–creator's movement quality
- Quality of the beginning and ending
- Moves that are memorable
- Moves that are "dynamite" or "killer" moves (like balances and turns)

Even young children can rate overall artistic quality on a three-point scale (such as top quality, 3; good or OK, 2; or needs work, 1) and do so rather astutely.

Specialists who have not seen this type of critiquing in action may be skeptical that it can happen at so early an age. But by engaging youngsters in analysis and aesthetic evaluation (i.e., critical thinking), you can jump-start their overall aesthetic perception. Then you can lead them to make discriminating choices and increase the quality of their own artistic output. Make this an intentional transition to Stage 3, where students learn to discuss a work's expressive qualities. Stage 3 presupposes a BSTER vocabulary with which to articulate about dance. The bridge is pivotal to further developing that vocabulary. To be clear, the bridge is a teacher-facilitated rather than an automatic step. Children don't just learn this on their own. It depends on you.

If we were to list descriptors of the bridge, they would look like this:

Descriptors: Beginning awareness of dance as an expressive art, ability to discern the qualitative use of the dancing elements, and ability to respond to specific review criteria regarding artistic quality in performance and design. The bridge is teacher facilitated rather than innate and is a critical step to getting students to Stages 3 and beyond.

Three Artistic Processes: Creating, Performing, and Responding (c/p/r)

To teach dance as art in education is to create a sense of aesthetic awareness at all ages. Aesthetic development does not happen on its own: You must make it happen. Infuse aesthetics into all three artistic processes to ensure that the dance curriculum is aesthetically driven.

Parsons emphasized that people can get to Stage 3 on their own. But many people stay at Stage 2 for life unless someone—usually a teacher—helps them progress. Parsons contended that individuals really do not get to Stage 4 or 5 on their own; they must be taught, must acquire a vocabulary, and must be led to see beyond Stages 1 and 2. One reward of arts teaching is to get students to upper levels of aesthetic perception. Although first graders typically do not attain Stage 4 or 5 because of limited vocabulary, you should begin aesthetic development around age 7 (Parsons 1987).

Although the aesthetic–artistic stages are not classified by age, they are commonly achieved by the ages listed in figure 4.3. That said, don't hesitate to take students as far as they will and can go. Don't underestimate the levels of artistry of which young children are capable. Teach "up" to them—not artistically "down." Second and third graders, even those new to dance, can astound you in the level of artistry they exhibit in creative dance—exploring, improvising, and dance making. They often achieve this artistry more easily than they express it in words, but your instruction and their practice help them learn how to use the words. Emphasize the BSTERs in creative dance early on. Once students connect BSTER understanding to words that express what they see and do in dance, their aesthetic perception grows by leaps and bounds. Their ability to analyze dance also takes a big jump once they have made dances with all the BSTERs. Therefore, use creative dance to

- boost artistic expression in movement and
- develop students' dance vocabulary to verbalize about this artistic expression. (You learn how to accomplish this for young ones in chapter 6.)

Increase aesthetic–artistic practice in all three artistic processes (c/p/r). Consider how the art of moving itself (performing) is primary to creating and responding to the dance movement one views.

Performing

A performance aesthetic resides in the core of each body. Students can find it around grade 3 if led to do so. It involves **bodythinking.** *Bodythinking* is a term I use that means using the entire nervous system to integrate one's total expressive instrument to communicate an idea or concept through motion. Bodythinking engages the full nervous system, from brain to nerve endings, while moving. For example, Murray Louis asks students to scatter their brain cells throughout their bodies so that they think with every cell of the body while dancing. Performers need this kind of body sensitivity in order to project. Such an alert dancer is fully aware; is hyper-attuned to space, time, and energy; and communicates something specific to others. The dancer is fully sentient and fully present in this kind of dancing moment. Lead students to form such an aesthetic sense about the performing body as early as possible. I have had second graders rise to this level with the utmost integrity and consummate embodiment of an idea.

Other noted dance artists have described this superhuman quality in other ways. For example, as a dancer, Isadora Duncan believed the solar plexus in the center of the body was the bodily location of the soul because this part of the torso is both the visual and motor center of dance movement. Torso-centered dance shows the performer fully of the body and nature more than of the spirit (Arnheim 1971). Bodythinking is fully human and driven by the nervous system.

Insist that dancers refine how a movement is performed as they perform it. Total awareness and intention are important. Ask all ages to create, explore, and improvise with simultaneous body and mind integration. Bodythinking invites children to think out aesthetic choices in dance while they move. Bodythinking increases artistic integration of body–mind so they learn to bodyspeak. **Bodyspeaking** describes their ability to express themselves nonverbally with intention and clarity,

Grades K-1	Stages 1 and 2
Grades 3-5	Stages 1, 2, and 3
Middle school	Stages 1, 2, 3, and 4
High school	All stages

FIGURE 4.3 Realistic ages for aesthetic growth.

to speak through their movement. Bodyspeaking and bodythinking are the ultimate in dance communication. If started young, by adolescence these abilities can be transformed into increased somatic awareness in dance.

Creating

Lead children in creative dance so they learn to make dances. This is how children apply their understanding of the dancing elements and how they make dances that communicate meaning. Creative dance is in effect improvisation and choreography for kids. Lead them to experience the art of movement and to refine their expressive bodies from a perspective of bodythinking and bodyspeaking. Enrich their creative process with generous amounts of movement exploring, dance making, and critiquing their own and peer works.

Make creative dance the core of the primary and elementary school dance curriculum (see chapter 7). In elementary school, teach the simple compositional structures to help them make monumentally important dances. At this time they need to learn how to sharpen their aesthetic eye and refine their compositions to express exactly what they want to say in dance (i.e., bodyspeak). Your job is to facilitate this well.

Creative work with middle and high school students builds on basic compositional skills they learned in earlier grades. Here you nurture their creative voices and cultivate their growing aesthetic and compositional skills. Such aesthetic growth enables them to select, edit, refine, and choreograph works to show. The same aesthetic viewpoint expressed in performing also permeates creating. Aim for bodythinking and bodyspeaking as an outcome of creative dance.

Responding

Knowing about dance is essential to valuing it. Introduce the great works of dance at the outset so that students know what dance all over the world looks like, feels like, is! Students' richness of response comes from the richness of knowing dance as art and as human expression (see chapter 9). First you have to increase their eye for dance by building their

To bodyspeak, one must fully embody a concept and perform it with conviction and artistic clarity.

dance elements vocabulary so they can describe what they see and can talk about dance. Then you have to move them through each aesthetic stage so they discriminate between what is effective and ineffective in a dance. Get them beyond the "I liked it," so they can talk about a dance's expressive qualities and what it means to them—and what its value is to the world.

Routinely evaluate quality in each lesson so everyone learns to expect it. State exactly what they are to look for by giving review criteria. Thus, students will expect to account to a panel of peer experts who are critical friends as well as fellow choreographers! For example, second and third graders adeptly respond to three critiquing questions (that come directly from their dance-making assignment) placed on a chart and prominently displayed as part of the lesson, such as, "Where did you see these emphasized?"

1. Jumping shapes in the air
2. Directional changes
3. Dynamite stillness

In addition to critiquing their peers, first and second graders should also critique excerpts of major works. They should transfer the same peer critique skills (using review criteria) and process to large-screen video choreographies. Third graders who have consistently given peer critique since kindergarten can be expected to observe closely and critique slices of such works. First graders can be expected to identify examples of bodyspeaking and bodythinking and be inspired to model performance qualities brought to their attention.

Cognitive–Intellectual Development (Thinking, Perceiving, and Processing)

Perceptual processing refers to the myriad ways we take in information and use it. In particular, perceiving is the way we take in information, and information processing or ordering includes how we think, recall, problem frame, problem solve, and adapt information. In dance it is apparent that thinking is just one way to perceive and to process, because the nervous system processes information taken in through the body as well as the mind. The advancement of the theory of multiple intelligences (MI) validates that humans perceive in many different ways and, as such, process information quite differently. Let's look at how MI serves arts education and how systems of complex thinking operate in the classroom.

Multiple Intelligences Theory and the Arts

Multiple intelligences are different ways of knowing and expressing, many of which are vital to arts knowing and expression.

Harvard developmental psychologist Howard Gardner advanced the theory of **multiple intelligences (MIs)** in the 1980s. The implications of MIs for art, creativity, and education revolutionize the way we teach and measure student progress. MI theory acknowledges that there are different ways of being intelligent—different perceptual modes. It challenges old beliefs about what "smart" is. MI theory affirms modes of thinking and processing important to the arts—beyond verbal and logical thinking.

Intelligence is not just the ability to do well in school; it comprises different **aptitudes** for living and learning. It crosses cultures. It is not fixed at birth; it is fluid. Intelligences seem to reside in the physiology of the brain. They are the ways we are smart. People with these aptitudes function well in arts professions like the following.

HOWARD GARDNER'S SEVEN INTELLIGENCES
- Linguistic–verbal intelligence (poets, journalists, writers, dance critics)
- Logical–mathematical intelligence (dance notators, composers, architects)
- Musical intelligence (composers, musicians, performers)
- Spatial intelligence (painters, architects, choreographers)
- Bodily–kinesthetic intelligence (dancers, choreographers, mimes, actors, athletes)
- Interpersonal intelligence—understanding others (teachers, actors, therapists)
- Intrapersonal intelligence—understanding oneself (journal writers, writers)

Other aptitudes have been added since, such as a naturalist with extreme taxonomic capacities (e.g., biologists).

Before MI, valid academic learning was considered either verbal or mathematical—what could be tested on paper. Even IQ tests measured how "smart" an individual was, although these tests narrowly measured left-brain function on short-answer test instruments. But Gardner's message focuses us on how kids are smart, not how smart they are. Arts-smarts are seen as valid in this theory. As brain research disclosed how differently the two lobes of the brain process information and functions, MI theory legitimized other ways of knowing found in the arts. *Dance not only relies on but also develops these aptitudes.* For example: The MIs show different ways you should engage students: to heighten body–mind connections, spatial intelligence, bodily kinesthetic skills, and musical skills. Even underperformers in math and language often excel in one or more of the arts, and these students need a place to succeed. Dance is often that place. Gardner observed that even prodigies are not good at everything and often have uneven cognitive profiles.

Gardner's definition of *intelligence* serves the arts: "an ability to solve problems or to fashion a product, to make something that is valued in at least one culture"

(Gardner 1990, p. 16). Gardner calls *intelligence* the ability to make something—create a work of art, write a poem, compose a symphony, run an organization, or teach a class. He calls *aptitudes* neither inherently artistic nor nonartistic but "intelligences singularly or in combination that can be put to artistic uses. They can be used to create or to understand artistic works, to work with artistic symbol systems, to create artistic meanings" (Gardner 1990, p. 20). Applied to dance, this theory affirms that the dances kids create and refine into polished works are acts of intelligence and value.

Use each intelligence to nourish creativity. Gardner says, "Creativity has . . . to do with getting to know the subject in great detail, and then being willing to take that knowledge and use it in new kinds of ways" (Gardner 1990, p. 21). Applied to dance, this theory means that students need to learn foundation knowledge in dance and then be given opportunities and structures to synthesize what they understand into their own dances.

The theory of MI helps dance and the arts gain educational respect. Traditional education embraces MIs as different avenues to increase skill mastery, attention, comprehension, and retention. Traditional educators agree that students with different aptitudes need to be reached in different ways to succeed in school (e.g., more bodily–kinesthetic or spatial). These educators see potential dropouts reclaimed by arts programs that use students' aptitudes or ways of knowing to grasp the same content they'd miss in traditional classrooms.

Look at MIs more as "pathways" to achieve different areas than ways to prescribe individual interests. Those strong in bodily–kinesthetic aptitudes may or may not choose to channel that ability into dance or sport, but that aptitude gives them a chance to succeed if they do. Identify students whose profiles indicate bodily–kinesthetic as a preferred learning modality and invite them into dance. This is a way to be a student advocate.

> **"Different modes of thinking provide the most productive ways ahead, not the least of which is analogical, as opposed to deductive, reasoning. Diplomacy and statecraft, leadership, politics, persuasion, negotiation, entrepreneurship, envisioning alternatives, and a host of other 'unscientific' activities all depend on imagination and creativity and are all essential to the human enterprise."**
>
> —Consortium of National Arts Education Associations (1994, p. 7)

Certainly civilization's highest accomplishments are not seen in scoring rubrics and standardized test scores! What we value and pass down through generations are our great art works, scientific discoveries, legends and literature, music and myths, folk and classical dances—not numbers and statistics. The theory of MI also names what different cultures value as intelligent behavior, such as mapping systems and astrologic navigational charts prized in some island cultures (spatial), tracking abilities in the Himalayas (spatial and interpersonal), and musical genius in European cultures.

Thus, a revolution that started in education benefits arts education. As educators and administrators recognize the importance of the arts to learning, the arts become more legitimate in schools. You have a responsibility to demonstrate how broadly educational dance teaches what other subjects cannot by appealing to different forms of artistic intelligences and aptitudes.

Just as creativity can be nurtured in all of the intelligences, so can levels of thinking. Let's investigate levels of thinking, perceiving, and processing information. Meanwhile, let's do so in the context of MI theory's different ways of knowing in the arts, especially in dance.

Levels of Complex Thinking, Perceiving, and Processing

Unlike the stages of progression in the kinesthetic–motor and aesthetic–artistic aspects, each level of thinking complexity serves students at every age. You have to cultivate higher-order thinking, however. The teenage couch potato with an MP3 player glued to his head usually does not engage in a full range of systematic, complex thinking on his own. Too many children mentally zone out, passively observing the world. Too few learn to think beyond basic levels unless taught how to do so, and few are consistently engaged at upper levels. Your job as an educator is to teach thinking skills and as a dance specialist to give engaging content and experiences that stimulate complex thinking and inquiry in dance.

One of the most valuable educational products you offer in arts education is teaching individuals how to critically think and problem solve, how to use what they know in different ways. Arts education relies on complex thinking and processing to create, perform, and respond. Indeed, NSDE 4 (applying and demonstrating critical and creative thinking skills in dance) champions critical and creative thinking in dance from K through 12. So does the SCANS Report. Cognitive skills must increase through dance experiences.

 What is complex thinking and how do you use it?

Let's identify six levels of thinking, perceiving, and processing for teaching and learning, then learn to use them. You will need a thorough grasp of these levels to facilitate dance criticism (see chapter 9) and to write goals and objectives (see chapter 12).

Bloom's Taxonomy of Thinking: Six Levels of Complexity

Thinking, perceiving, and processing levels of complexity range on a continuum from basic (recalling basic facts) to higher order (creative and critical thinking). Bloom identified six levels of progressive cognitive functioning on this continuum: knowledge, comprehension, application, analysis, **synthesis,** and evaluation. Beginning with knowledge, one by one each level increases the functional cognitive complexity, with evaluation being the most complex level of cognition and perception, as pictured in figure 4.4.

Reaching the evaluation level is like ascending a staircase. You go up one step at a time, and to get to any given step you must have gone up those that precede it. You can go down the stairs at any time, but to get to the top, you have to go up all of the steps. Likewise, when one level of cognition is mastered, rather than discarding it for a higher level, the student retains the ability to move back down when necessary. A student engaged at the evaluation level relies on the information and thought processes from all of the other five levels of thinking.

Your job is to see that learners acquire and *know* basic facts, *comprehend* information, *apply* what they learn, *analyze* aspects of dance, *synthesize* individual parts into a new whole, and *evaluate* performance. You are the one who operationalizes Bloom's taxonomy in your classroom to stretch boundaries, diversify instruction, and optimize thinking ability. Then your students can move with ease up or down the staircase. As you get to chapter 9 you will learn specifically how to conduct student inquiry in all six levels in dance.

Levels 1, 2, and 3 of Bloom's taxonomy identify the more basic thinking skills. Levels 4, 5, and 6 identify higher-order thinking skills (HOTS). Your mandate is to engage students at the upper levels to teach them how to think through problems and make well-informed decisions. Levels 4, 5, and 6 call on critical thinking—analysis, synthesis, and

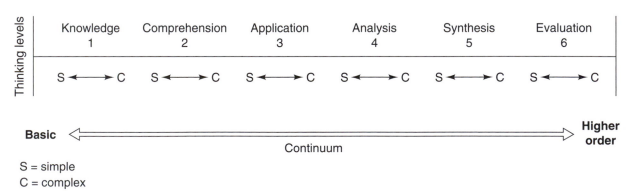

Thinking, Perceiving, and Processing Levels of Complexity

(Bloom's taxonomy)

Thinking levels						
Knowledge 1	Comprehension 2	Application 3	Analysis 4	Synthesis 5	Evaluation 6
S ←→ C	S ←→ C	S ←→ C	S ←→ C	S ←→ C	S ←→ C

Basic ⟵――――――――――――――――――――――――――――⟶ Higher order

Continuum

S = simple
C = complex

FIGURE 4.4   Bloom's taxonomy describes six levels of thinking from basic to higher order. The type of thinking required at each level becomes more complex as one moves from basic to higher order. Within each level there are also degrees of complexity ranging from simple to complex, so teachers engage students at every thinking level according to their cognitive maturation.

evaluation. In educational dance, we rely on critical thinking

- to create dances,
- to make judgments about one's own creative expression as well as works of choreographers and peers, and
- to analyze quality of movement and to refine if necessary.

It is up to the teacher to fashion experiences that force students to function at that level. Students have to learn to think for themselves in dance and to make split-second decisions about what is best—in straight thinking or in bodythinking (detailed in chapter 9).

This does not mean we reserve the upper levels for older students. You should stimulate higher-order thinking at all ages. However, there are also degrees of sophistication, difficulty, or complexity within each thinking level (figure 4.4), from simple to complex, depending on the age and cognitive maturation of the child. For example: At level 1 (knowledge), you'll teach simple facts to the young child, whereas you teach far more intricate or sophisticated (complex) facts to high school students. Likewise, a child's maturation determines the degree of complexity possible (from simple to complex). Each of the six levels contains a wide spectrum of sophistication and complexity that you can tap. For example, whereas kindergartners analyze whether a movement is getting faster (i.e., accelerating) or staying the same (simple), a high school student observes a slice of choreography to analyze its timing, rhythmic structure, and time changes (complex). Both are processing at level 4 (analysis), and both are working at appropriate levels of sophistication or degrees of complexity. (See "Correlating Dancing Activity to Brain Function" later in this chapter.)

Here is a breakdown of Bloom's taxonomy for dance:

LEVEL 1: KNOWLEDGE

- *Synopsis:* Recalling specific information
- *Key words:* Know, describe
- *Descriptors:* Fact based (who, what, when, where), basic information, acquiring details
- *Process:* Recall from memory, simplistic mental processing, remembering facts and information (e.g., remembering a combination, recalling facts about a choreographer)
- *Verbs to use at Level 1:* List, name, observe, memorize, remember, recall

LEVEL 2: COMPREHENSION

- *Synopsis:* Understanding information without relating it to other information
- *Key words:* Understand, explain, describe
- *Descriptors:* Recognize, identify, describe material
- *Process:* Grasping the meaning of material (e.g., understanding the concept of levels)
- *Verbs to use:* Identify, summarize, describe

LEVEL 3: APPLICATION

- *Synopsis:* Using information in a new situation
- *Key words:* Demonstrate, use
- *Descriptors:* Explaining, showing, demonstrating
- *Process:* Applying what one knows to what one does; using acquired information or skills to demonstrate a skill or comprehension (e.g., applying choreographic form to dance making)
- *Verbs to use:* Explain, apply, show, use, sequence, organize, imagine

LEVEL 4: ANALYSIS

- *Synopsis:* Breaking down information into its constituent parts
- *Key words:* Examine, analyze
- *Descriptors:* Categorize, identify, describe
- *Process:* Breaking down material into parts to be more easily understood (e.g., breaking down a sequence or choreography into sections, observing a work and describing its use of space)
- *Verbs to use:* Characterize, categorize, examine, distinguish between, describe, analyze

LEVEL 5: SYNTHESIS

- *Synopsis:* Putting parts together to make a new whole
- *Key words:* Compose, create
- *Descriptors:* Combining, composing, creating
- *Process:* Putting together material to form a new creation
- *Verbs to use:* Create, choreograph, relate, invent, plan, compose, construct, design, improve, edit, refine

LEVEL 6: EVALUATION

- *Synopsis:* Making and defending judgments
- *Key words:* Critique, judge
- *Descriptors:* Judge merit, assess quality
- *Process:* Judging artistic merit, critiquing a dance composition or performance quality; judging validity of information or relevance to a dance work or the creative process
- *Verbs to use:* Evaluate, critique, judge, value, conclude, rate, solve

Levels of Complexity for All Ages

You might think Bloom's taxonomy is about isolated thinking levels or even about isolating levels, when in fact it is a system. By using this system, you are able to move students from basic to higher-order thought—just by the way you frame questions and set up inquiry. (In chapter 9 you learn how to facilitate each level so it is educationally and aesthetically valuable.) When functionalized as a teaching approach, inquiry becomes an educationally profound way to fully involve students. It is also your responsibility to lay the foundation facts so you can stimulate students from those facts all the way to the upper levels of cognition. By engaging all six levels, you teach students how to think, problem solve, and make well-informed decisions—all of which are useful in life as well as in dance. These skills lead students to make discriminating artistic choices so vital to educational dance. You can transform a classroom simply by intentionally interacting with students this way and expecting complex thinking, processing, and responses.

Dance specialists embed higher-order thinking skills into the artistic processes to address NSDE 4 (applying and demonstrating critical and creative thinking skills in dance). By functioning at all six levels, students begin to develop and sharpen critical judgment. Then students outgrow responding to dance in naive ways (such as "I like it, it was pretty," or "I don't like it, they had ugly costumes") and learn to judge artistic quality. Following is an example that uses the element category "space" at progressive levels of thinking complexity:

Space can be perceived and processed in numerous ways to use different thinking levels from basic to higher order. You will notice that each step builds on the thought processes and information acquired in previous levels. For example:

- Knowledge: Students know and list the different aspects of space.

- Comprehension: Students recognize how space is the element of dance that dancers use and move through and how the dancing body relates to space.
- Application: Students apply this information by moving and dancing at different levels, in different directions, in place, and through space.
- Analysis: Students look at a dance and break it down into its constituent parts so that they can determine how levels are used and analyze how they were applied to the movement idea.
- Synthesis: Students create their own dances that use levels in new ways and create new patterns.
- Evaluation: Students judge how well space was used in their own dance so that they can edit and refine their work. They critique others and give them feedback to refine their work.

At evaluation, students call on all of the previous five levels. They must

- have fact-based knowledge on the element of space,
- understand this knowledge,
- apply it,
- analyze it in a different application, and
- synthesize the material into their own creative work.

Relationship of Inquiry to Higher-Order Thinking

One of the six defining characteristics (6DC) is inquiry based, which can be made a higher-order critical thinking process. To do so, you lead students to inquire so that they apply and analyze information instead of merely regurgitating facts from memory. You can use an inquiry approach to move students to all levels above knowledge. Your questions should check to see if students comprehend. You should ask them to apply what they understand to their creative and re-creative work. Ask students questions that urge them to think analytically, and then use what they analyzed to create or synthesize as the next step. Ask complex inquiry questions based on the previous five steps that enable students to evaluate what they perceive and process (see chapter 5).

Beware: Students want to skip steps and jump from level 2, the ability to apply information, straight to level 6, evaluation. Obviously they don't have enough information to use. They stumble up the steps by believing that they can make value judgments based on incomplete data or unfounded conceptual understanding. Critical judgments are invalid unless students have a solid knowledge base and the ability to apply it, analyze it, and use it. Keep them on solid footing by systematically leading them up the stairs so that they use all six steps. One of the important steps to emphasize in this process is Level 3, application, which gets students to take an idea or concept and put it into immediate practice.

Aesthetic inquiry is built on the six levels of thinking and perceiving. Parsons' stages of aesthetic–artistic growth parallel Bloom's taxonomy. To get to upper stages of aesthetic sophistication requires the ability to go further than merely knowing facts and applying them. Critical and abstract thinking in the artistic processes (c/p/r) rely on the ability to analyze, synthesize, and evaluate.

To teach the four dance curriculum cornerstones, you must call on all six levels of perceiving and processing. Students must acquire a facts-based knowledge of dance (i.e., Levels 1, 2, and 3—knowledge, comprehension, and application). They must also create, perform, and respond (application, analysis, synthesis, evaluation). Critical thinking, creating, and critiquing all require upper levels of thinking. Reflection usually requires critical thinking.

Correlating Dancing Activity to Brain Function

Eric Jensen explores how dance advances learning, especially its value as a universal language, a symbol system, and a vital form of human expression. He describes how highly complex movements such as dance increase brain function close to 100 percent. Dance has indirect benefits that facilitate the maturation of the brain's cortical systems according to research Jensen cites. It is the activity of dance that speeds up the process, which makes the brain move faster and more efficiently because dance activity includes challenge, novelty, feedback, coherence, and time. Dance improvisation seems to prime the brain with new ideas and develop the will to carry them out. Jensen even asserts, "There are some correlations with movement art and higher college entrance scores" (Jensen 2001, p. 76). Jensen's book, *Arts With the Brain in Mind,* is for all serious students of dance education. See Rich Resources for more information.

Brain research shows that the brain changes and develops through every experience it processes over time. Particular educational and artistic tasks are best processed during a child's "optimal window of learning" particular tasks. Canadian brain researcher Dr. Bruce Perry refers to it as a developmental "hot zone"; others such as Russian psychologist Lev Vygotsky call it the "zone of proximal development (ZPD)." This zone is the time when a child's learning and problem-solving abilities are primed for particular challenges. At this time, challenging tasks promote the maximum cognitive growth for that individual. Therefore, the teacher's selection of tasks and her timing are critical to a child's optimal cognitive development. Perry states:

> Learning starts in the safety of the previously learned and familiar—our comfort zone. In order to learn, however, we must enter the developmental hot zone. This is where a child, reaching from the familiar, can grasp at new facts, concepts and skills. And with practice, the previously unknown becomes known and is added to our comfort zone. Spending time in this developmental hot zone adds new skills, concepts, and behaviors in a sequential and cumulative way. (Perry 2005c)

As you aim for this hot zone, you also risk that the child is not yet ready for the experience or fails at the task, which has the unintended consequences of diminishing his pleasure of learning and increasing his unwillingness to take on new challenges.

> There is for each child . . . a set of *presently* impossible-to-master facts, concepts, and skills. . . . When we push children too far beyond their comfort zone, they will not meet with success. . . . As you spend your days guiding children into their hot zone, keep the following in mind:
>
> - Children need to be introduced to new tasks gently. Too much, too soon is overwhelming. . . . [S]tart with the known and familiar and then move on, in small steps, to a new content.
> - Learning requires focus, sustained attention and the capacity to tolerate frustration. All of these are *very* energy-consuming activities. During the most active phases of learning, children fatigue quickly. Remember that "new" translates into "stressful." Allow a child to work with a new challenge long enough to explore and practice, but not so long that she becomes fatigued and discouraged. The further a child gets from her comfort zone, the more difficult it becomes to maintain focused attention.
> - Most children develop faster in one domain (motor, emotional, cognitive, social) than others.
> - Mastery in one domain can't be generalized to others. (Perry 2005c)

Age-Related Cognitive Development

Cognitive (mental) development hinges on both inherited and environmental factors (nature and nurture). Experiences help shape the size and the synaptic complexity of the brains of young children. In fact, studies show that the earlier children engage in stimulating experiences such as dance, the longer-term benefit they seem to reap. Studies show that

> stimulation from the environment (experience) can shape the trillions of finer connections that complete the architecture of the brain. Scientists now believe that to achieve the precision of the mature brain, stimulation during the early developing years is necessary. (Gabbard 1998, p. 54)

Educational dance is intent on developing the mind along with the body. Alonzo King, renowned African American ballet choreographer and teacher, said:

> The most essential thing I can say about teaching is that things have to proceed from within. Steps and shapes, like arabesque, tendu, must originate in idea and should be expressed as ideas before they are merely imitated physically. It is the mind that does the dancing: the body is the instrument. So, it is the mind that we are really addressing as teachers, more than the body. (Gdula 2001, p. 58)

Other noted educators have weighed in on the subject of cognitive development; for example, Jean Piaget described the development of different ages rather than stages. This reminds us that there are ages at which certain aptitudes predominate. Before we look at the General Readiness Profiles, let's consider Piaget's perspective:

PREOPERATIONAL STAGE (EARLY CHILDHOOD)
- Egocentric thinking predominates.
- Memory and imagination develop.
- Use of symbols and language matures.

CONCRETE OPERATIONAL STAGE (EARLY CHILDHOOD THROUGH PREADOLESCENCE)
- Egocentric thought diminishes.
- Thoughts are logical and can be manipulated.
- Concrete symbols are used.

FORMAL OPERATIONAL STAGE (ADOLESCENCE)
- The child logically uses symbols related to abstract concepts.

Information adapted from Educational Psychology Interactive: April 9, 2003

Study the following profiles for a broad picture of what you can expect.

Elementary School
The General Readiness Profiles for ages 4 to 11 follow. You will learn what these students are like and what they need.

Four- and Five-Year-Old Profile These students follow directions and specific movement instructions. They enjoy and benefit from imaginative, creative work. Moving like an animal is fun and allows them to make connections between their own bodies and the bodies of other creatures. They enjoy imitating movement, but that is neither the extent of their ability nor the emphasis you should give. They more need to understand what their body parts are and to learn how their body is put together in order to move, which helps them develop awareness of muscle control. They can bodythink to show with the body clearly what they think and know—clarifying intent of movement. Identify body parts and increase descriptive vocabulary using the dance elements. Connecting movement and words is enormously important. Personal expression is important at this age, which eventually leads to aesthetic expression. Attention span is very limited and activities should be alternated regularly.

Some of what students at this age need to do:

- Learn a dance elements vocabulary
- Engage in concrete more than abstract thought
- Focus movement skills on bodythinking (learning movement concepts in motion)
- Grasp all the dance elements in the body category
- View and respond to short dance works
- Learn about major choreographers and see some of their works to critique and build vocabulary
- Explore movement possibilities within a repetitive structure
- Engage in creative activities that ask for them to elaborate on a movement idea
- Practice spontaneous creative problem solving with movement

Six- and Seven-Year-Old Profile This age group is beginning to develop concentration. Therefore, 6-year-olds cannot be expected to pay attention to one task for long periods of time—15 to 20 minutes at the most. Refocus the class periodically around the same topic, but use new activity in all dance activities. (See chapter 7 for ways to refocus creative dance classes.) For example, when teaching folk dances, change activities from learning basic movement patterns to watching a short video of the dance being performed by indigenous performers and talk about the style of movement. Then work on performing with attention to stylistic concepts.

These students' vocabulary and understanding of concepts are expanding rapidly. Children at this age like to use their newly developed abilities in reading, math, and the arts. Some are still not yet planning dances and are better at spontaneous, more improvisational dances around a set structure. They are developing the ability to symbolize experiences and act out situations. They are unable to deal yet with complex or abstract ideas.

Some of what students at this age need to do:

- Increase dance elements vocabulary
- Participate in class structures that change activities and refocus attention around one main idea (see previous example)
- Analyze simple concepts in time, space, and dynamics such as extremes—high and low, fast and slow, sharp and smooth—to develop an eye for dance and a way to describe it
- Structure movements into short improvisational compositions with beginning, middle, and end
- Learn simple **forms** such as AB, ABA, and **cinquains**
- Begin to unpack dance works (see chapter 9)
- Interpret concepts and translate them into movement
- Become aware of dance as nonverbal expressive movement
- Develop a sense of discrimination and selection of movement
- Engage in complex and critical thinking
- Experience creative dance

Kindergarten through grade 1 students draw on the affective domain when they create with their bodies. They seem to create spontaneously, almost from impulse. Whatever is inside of them gets expressed. This makes sense considering that this age group tends to be self-centered and not

concerned with others unless others directly affect them. The key is to give these children enough cognitive structure and movement understanding to enhance their learning without hindering the wonderful freedom of expression they naturally have (Jan Scott, personal correspondence through e-mail, May 15, 2003).

Adapted by permission of Jan Scott.

Eight- and Nine-Year-Old Profile   These students concentrate on selected activities for indefinite periods. They mentally project themselves into places and situations that they have not actually experienced. Judgments and decisions about problems are given more thought than at earlier ages. These students find dance history and cultural studies interesting, and they enjoy rhythmic experiences.

Some of what students at this age need to do:

- Mentally map out a movement composition to express an idea
- Tap their imagination for creative inspiration and ideas
- Engage in complex, challenging stimulation and problem solving in dance
- Immerse themselves in dances from around the world to see how others express themselves in movement
- Learn compositional forms such as call and response, theme and variation
- Consider abstract concepts
- Participate in activities that increase concentration
- Engage in reflective thinking
- Engage in critical thinking

Ten- and Eleven-Year Old Profile   Students are developing the ability to plan ahead and take on larger assignments. They can analyze problems and create possible solutions. They can focus attention on dance works with topical interest and relevance to them and study these works for inspiration for their own creative expressions. These students are attentive to details. They need challenging higher-order thinking and production. They like to perfect and refine one thing at a time. Assessment of themselves and their performance is possible.

Some of what students at this age need to do:

- Learn formal dance forms
- Learn historic dance works

- Reconstruct dance works of the past (like through the American Dance Legacy Institute)
- Learn dances and have time to perfect movement patterns for performance
- Analyze dance works
- Engage in critical thinking and production activities in dance
- Learn compositional structures and ways to organize dance
- Begin to understand dance in different historical, social, and cultural contexts
- Write and reflect about dance and its meaning in their lives and in a broader social context
- Participate in spontaneous dance experiences that are nonthreatening
- Explore abstract thoughts and inquiry
- Participate in activities that increase concentration
- Engage in reflective thinking
- Engage in critical thinking

In grades 3 to 5, students become so concerned about others' opinions that their "self" becomes stifled. These students need the opposite approach from that of the kindergartners and first graders. They need you to teach to the cognitive in a safe, positive, accepting, and nurturing environment so that they can create movement freely. Structure is very important at this age, and students actually like to be told what to do. They are afraid of making a mistake and looking silly, so if you begin by appealing to their brains with more dance instruction, they often have a more positive, enjoyable learning experience. Thus, you give them courage to take risks and express themselves creatively through movement. That way, the affective goals are attained by way of the cognitive (Jan Scott, personal correspondence through e-mail, May 15, 2003).

Adapted by permission of Jan Scott.

Middle School

The General Readiness Profiles for ages 12 to 14 follow. Middle school students begin to examine the social and cultural components of dance more closely as they expand their perception of themselves as dancers and creators. Their vocabulary expands greatly as does their ability to analyze dance.

Some of what students at this age need to do:

- Analyze dance movement both kinetically and aesthetically
- Analyze dance movement from a variety of cultures
- Learn dance terminology such as ballet and technical terms
- Work with AB, ABA, canon, call and response, and narrative choreographic structures
- Work with reordering and chance in choreography
- Construct multiple solutions to a movement problem
- Explore the difference between pantomiming and abstracting gestures
- Compare dance with other art forms
- Compare dance with non-arts disciplines
- Learn abstract concepts

High School

The General Readiness Profiles for ages 15 to 18 follow. Dance careers should be discussed in high school. Higher-order thinking should be highly developed (analysis, synthesis, evaluation, interpretation, critiquing). These students can learn to effectively evaluate and refine their own work and evaluate the work of others.

Some of what students at this age need to do:

- Work to understand advanced choreographic forms and structures
- Work to understand the meanings that abstract movement can communicate
- Evaluate their own work and the work of others based on aesthetic criteria
- Create and revise dances and articulate the reasons for the revisions made
- Compare dance with other art forms
- Compare dance with non-arts disciplines
- Analyze dance styles from other cultures and select aspects of that style to synthesize into new choreography
- Engage in abstract and evaluative thinking
- Have multiple foci

Advanced students who are enrolled 3 to 4 years in school-based programs after grade 8 are expected to exceed NSDE's proficiency standard by achieving advanced standard.

Psychological–Social Development (Feeling and Interacting)

The fourth aspect of student-centered learning connects to individual psychological development and the ability to relate to others. We can't ignore how a child feels, because it will determine his ability to concentrate and his willingness to participate in dance class. We want to increase social skills through dance. We want to promote a sense of well-being and ensure that students feel good about themselves as movers and dancers. It's counterproductive to ask for opposite-gender partner work at certain social stages. Focus your attention on psychological–social development to maximize student participation and interaction and to avoid emotional upheavals.

Jeanne Ellis Ormrod explained Nancy Eisenberg's prosocial theory:

> In most cultures, one intended outcome of children's socialization is the development of such prosocial actions as sharing, helping, cooperating, and comforting—behaviors that promote the well-being of other individuals. People will be more productive adult citizens if, as children, they learn the advantages and good feelings associated with occasionally putting the needs of others before their own. (Ormrod 2000, p. 106)

Eisenberg's research shows that as a general rule, children act in more prosocial ways as they grow older.

You need to first look at stages of social interaction to see where your students are. Then move them to the next stage as soon as possible.

Psychological–Social Stages of Progression

Nancy Eisenberg identified levels of social behavior that children move through as they go from being self-centered (presocial) to being socially responsible and responsive (prosocial). She describes this process as a continuum through the stages: self-centered, allowing, other oriented, empathetic, and prosocial. We use Eisenberg's descriptions for stages of prosocial behavior and adapt this information to describe what to expect at different ages that affects learning dance. For example, one big social question is, "At what age can I take students from working individually to productively working with others in small groups or in pairs?" Can you find the answer? These stages help you determine levels

By high school, help students refine the choreographic forms they have learned earlier as structures for their dance expression.

of interpersonal and intrapersonal maturity. There is some give and take in each stage. For example, a child at an upper stage occasionally exhibits less mature characteristics like self-centeredness. But we all do this. When you assess these stages, select the one where the student generally functions most of the time.

Stage 1: Self-Centered

Descriptors: Selfish and self-centered orientation.

Students show little interest in helping others apart from serving their own interests. They exhibit social behavior primarily to benefit themselves. They are unable to empathize; thus, the stage is sometimes called "pre-empathetic." Students work best as individuals rather than in groups. They respond well to movement exploration in creative dance classes. This stage applies to any age, but you can expect it to predominate in most preschoolers and a few elementary children.

Stage 2: Allowing

Descriptors: Superficial "needs of others" orientation.

Students show some concern for another's physical and emotional needs, but their concern is simplistic and lacks true understanding of the other's situation. They are able to work on tasks in groups. This stage applies to all ages, but you can expect it to predominate in many elementary school students and even some preschoolers.

Stage 3: Other-Oriented

Descriptors: Approval and stereotypic good boy or girl orientation.

Students show prosocial behavior because it seems the right thing to do and because they will be liked or appreciated if they help. They hold stereotypical views of what "good" and "bad" boys and girls do. They can work in groups or with individual partners. You can foster this stage at all ages but will have more success after grade 2.

Stage 4: Empathetic

Descriptors: Empathic orientation.

Students have true empathy for another's situation and a desire to help a person in need. They seem genuinely concerned with the well-being of others. They are willing to produce in groups and with partners. You can expect this stage at all ages but will have more success after grade 3. Many secondary and a few elementary students exhibit these qualities.

Stage 5: Prosocial

Descriptors: Internalized values orientation.

Some high school adolescents have internalized values about helping other people—values that reflect a belief in the dignity, rights, and equality of all human beings. These students express a strong desire to help those in need and to improve the conditions of society as a whole. This is most successful with secondary students.

Ormrod, Jeanne E., *Educational Psychology: Developing Learners*, 3rd Edition, © 2005, p. 105. Adapted by permission of Pearson Education, Inc., Upper Saddle River, NJ.

Occasionally children need to just dance to directly express their feelings through the body without having to process these feelings with word symbols and without having to structure their movements and then refine them to show and critique. Encourage direct expression from the inside out from time to time when the need appears—especially with small children because they are less inhibited, they are emotionally freer, and their linguistic vocabulary is limited. Recognize times when some students need to express what is going on with them personally through dance as a catharsis. Find appropriate ways for them to do so. Help students find an expressive voice through dance. If you feel that a certain dance is mostly cathartic, be sensitive to whether it should be shared with classmates.

It is vital for children to transform feeling into movement as part of their expressive development in art and dance. Help them. Many works of great artistic worth have been created from the depths of the soul of feeling by both old and young.

Emotional Safety and Inquiry

An inquiry approach to teaching and learning aims to pique curiosity and increase investment in learning. Unless the child's self-confidence has been eroded, his sense of curiosity is what enables him to explore, discover, and learn. However, depending on the child's previous experiences and age, some children will have become less curious and less easy to motivate. Bruce Perry tells us this:

> There are three common ways adults constrain . . . the enthusiastic exploration of the curious child: 1) fear, 2) disapproval, and 3) absence.
>
> 1) Fear: Fear kills curiosity. When a child's world is chaotic or when he is afraid, he will not like novelty. He will seek the familiar, staying in his comfort zone, unwilling to leave and explore new things.
>
> 2) Disapproval: "Don't touch. Don't climb. . . . Don't. Don't. Don't." Children sense and respond to our fears, biases, and attitudes. . . .
>
> 3) Absence: . . . the lack of a caring, invested adult to provide two things essential for optimal explorations:
> - A sense of safety from which to discover
> - The opportunity to share the discovery and . . . get the pleasure and reinforcement from that discovery. (Perry 2005a)

From "Curiosity" by Bruce Perry, from Scholastic.com. Copyright © 2005 by Scholastic Inc. Adapted by permission of Scholastic Inc.

Thus, a vital part of the inquiry approach is to create a safe place for students to explore and create, to share their excitement at what they discover with them, and to inspire them to share their discovery with others. You also must provide a safe learning environment in which peers are receptive to each other's discovery and support the creative process.

Why is it important to determine where students are psychologically and socially before planning lessons? What are ways to encourage students to move from one psychological–social stage to the next? Should students be encouraged to work outside of their current psychological–social stage in order to grow socially?

Student Dispositions at Different Ages

To profile how children change on the way from kindergarten to high school, let's consider some of their pre- to prosocial characteristics at different ages. This is not an exact science, and no individual fits a mold. Variations occur based on an individual's cultural and family values, social experiences, and unique personality. Let's see generally how emotional and social maturity develops to help you maximize arts learning in dance.

Elementary School

The General Readiness Profiles for ages 4 through 11 follow. You will learn about these students' social and emotional readiness in this section.

Four- and Five-Year-Old Profile   These students are just learning to cooperate in group activity, so cooperation is sporadic. They become concerned when things affect them personally. They are impulsive. They respond to situations affecting them (positively and negatively) with a range of emotions, and emotions vary drastically within a short time period. These students' emotional state tends to determine how they perceive their own competence. They are innately so creative at this age that they just need to be guided to express themselves. You don't have to coax feeling out of students at this age.

At this age students have strong peer interactions, enjoy follow the leader, and will take turns. They like to explore and create and are good with individual and group explorations and improvisations. They show increasing self-confidence. They are not yet equipped to work unsupervised in groups.

Some of what students at this age need:

- Time to experiment with body parts and test their own physical possibilities
- Individual work and group tasks
- Improvisational dance making (not set and repeated dances)

- Divergent movement activities and explorations
- Supervised movement exploration and critical thinking questions

Six- and Seven-Year-Old Profile   These students take turns during group work. They want things to be fair. They tend to please adults to receive attention. If they don't receive attention for actions that usually warrant compliments, 6- and 7-year-olds will find other ways to receive attention (e.g., stories that are irrelevant to the task at hand, talking out of turn, saying "look at me"). It is very important for students at this age to receive genuine, individualized compliments throughout the class. They want to achieve and demonstrate their personal capabilities. They talk about their strengths and weaknesses but tend to get embarrassed and frustrated when they don't do things right. They are beginning to respond empathically to each others' feelings.

At this age students are becoming more competitive. They are ready for small group activities and improvisation. Girls particularly seek teacher approval. Both boys and girls begin to move cooperatively with each other. They tend to be cautious.

Some of what students at this age need:

- Both individual and cooperative work
- Opportunities to take turns
- Positive feedback
- Encouragement for individual efforts
- Close guidance to stay on task

Eight- and Nine-Year-Old Profile   These children can be reasoned with. They are aware of social rules and can uphold them. They can resolve differences with peers on their own and can work together for a common goal. They experience many emotions and are increasingly able to express them. You can use their social reactions to increase their understanding of social expectations in a class setting. Boys and girls do not like to work together in partners but are OK in small groups. They feel pretty safe with creative work, but they are generally satisfied with the first draft of a dance. If left on their own, they usually won't refine a dance. They must be taught how to refine work; with encouragement they will produce very good work. They can concentrate on viewing works with specific viewing questions and criteria. They are developing their expressive vocabulary and like to use it.

Some of what students at this age need:

- Supported opportunities for problem solving and creative expression
- Prodding to continue creative activity
- Reinforcement and support for all their work
- Patience
- Gender-alike partners

Ten- and Eleven-Year-Old Profile These students desire recognition and greater independence, yet they like to work with others better than alone. Many of them have a genuine interest in being helpful. They feel safer with conformity than with creativity. They ask for directions and are reticent to use their own judgment. They are highly capable of creative activity but need prodding to finish and constant reinforcement. They collaborate during group work if a strong enough structure is established and expectations are clear. They are highly observant of each other. They are increasingly concerned with what others, especially peers, think and do. They form exclusive groups at this age. Boys tend to single people out to make fun of them, so teachers have to stay tuned to what is going on to interrupt such behavior.

Some of what students at this age need:

- Group and cooperative work
- Teacher supervision
- Gender-alike partners rather than same-gender partners
- A mix of boys and girls in group work
- Opportunity to analyze and decode dance works
- Infiltration of their exclusive groups

These students also need encouragement and prodding when given creative work. They need specific expectations, with clear criteria about what they are to do and when they get it right. Getting it right is very important at this age. These students tend to perfect one thing rather than to create many new ones. There is a narrow spectrum of what is safe and OK. The creative task has to be safe and nonthreatening.

Middle School

The General Readiness Profiles for ages 12 through 14 follow. Preadolescents are inhibited. They rely on teachers to create an atmosphere of trust. They need to feel accepted as they learn techniques and movement skills. They are self-conscious about their changing bodies and at times frustrated by their lack of coordination. Do not laugh at students. Try to turn their frustrations into successes whenever possible to encourage their growing satisfaction with themselves and with their dancing bodies. Capitalize on their natural enthusiasm at this age and minimize their anxiety about their insecurities and self-consciousness. They work well in groups or alone but prefer to perform in groups. Performing in front of a class can cause extreme stress. Ensure that the venue is emotionally safe and supportive before putting these students before any kind of audience.

Peer pressure rules. These students are self-conscious about learning new skills and don't want to stand out. They are unsure of relationships (peer and authority) and are thus insecure. Thirteen-year-olds often want to observe more than participate and have to be encouraged to participate. Antagonism for the opposite gender has been replaced by interest. Some girls have difficulty making friends.

Some of what students at this age need:

- A safe learning environment
- Individual and group work
- Same-gender partners
- Assigned groups or partners to encourage interaction with a variety of students
- Positive reinforcement
- Performance in small groups of five or six, for each other rather than for the whole class, until a comfort level is reached in that venue (gradually increase the size of the audience)
- Constructive feedback during the creative process
- Opportunities to create dances with personal significance
- Opportunities to work on appropriate audience behavior
- Time to analyze and decode dance works
- Practice communicating opinions about dance to peers in a supportive and constructive manner
- Contracts to set their own personal goals for improvement

High School

The General Readiness Profiles for ages 15 through 18 follow. At this age, social growth is inconsistent, and some high school students exhibit the same characteristics as preadolescents. Even as these students are developing confidence, they are plagued by insecurities. Help them build a positive self-image through dance.

Many high school students seem embarrassed or lack confidence when attempting new dance skills. They often prefer to sit on the sidelines and observe rather than participate. Make a supportive environment and encourage full participation through genuine, specific positive feedback. Encourage students to participate in dance by finding out and tapping into their interests. Students at this age are less comfortable experimenting with big body movement in front of others.

In early adolescence, antagonism for the opposite gender turns into interest. This period of identity formation may not find students consistent in attitude or appearance. Be patient and understand their need for personal experimentation. Girls can have trouble making friends, so be vigilant when they are working on small group projects that require close interaction, such as performing and creating. Students are well equipped to work in groups and by themselves, with same- and opposite-gender partners in dance.

> **"Experience is the chief architect of the brain."**
>
> —Bruce Perry (MD, PhD)

Minorities become more aware of their minority status during high school and seem to have trouble fitting into the whole group. Find ways to ensure cultural studies in dance to celebrate diversity. Encourage friendships between students of all backgrounds.

Some of what students at this age need:

- Genuine support and encouragement
- A safe learning environment
- Caring and nurturing, not coddling
- Structured ways to branch out and work within teams and groups
- Assigned partners to promote interaction with a wide variety of peers
- Opportunities to demonstrate their strength skills (males)
- Opportunities to design their assignments
- Encouragement to reflect on their personal growth over time

Teaching the Whole Child

Student-centered learning means putting students at the forefront—even ahead of the curriculum content that is to be mastered. Do not ignore the content, but instead use standards-oriented dance instruction to touch students directly and speak to their needs. Dance experiences should help them integrate different aspects of themselves—the moving self, the thinking self, the artistic self, the emotional and social self, and the spirited self. Because dance is a metaphor for life, our aim should be to bring dance to students—and students to dance—in such a way that each student lives fully in the moment and acquires an artistic perspective of the world.

If dance is integrative for all of us, it is even more so for the young child. Keith Donahue (1997) emphasized the vital holistic benefits of dance for this age. This perspective reminds us that dance's intrinsic value cannot, and must not, be overshadowed by undue emphasis on standards or assessments.

For young children, dance offers avenues for exploration, discovery and the development of natural instincts for movement. Dance activities offer many benefits for children, encouraging mental and emotional development as well as obviously enhancing motor skills.

Dancing gives the young child a chance to experience and understand both personal and social perspectives in a stimulating situation. Dancing offers opportunities to express thoughts and feelings and to understand others' thoughts and feelings.

The dynamic balance of dance's physical, mental, and emotional aspects should be present in dance education, regardless of whether the child plans to pursue a career in dance. (Donahue 1997, pp. 16-17)

Student-centered learning, then, is about teaching the whole child. It's about holistically cultivating children's kinesthetic, aesthetic, cognitive, and psychological–social growth. These aspects overlap and interact; children come prepackaged with them. It is up to you to ensure that students consistently advance all of these aspects through dance. To ignore any aspect risks student inattention, imbalance, and loss of self-confidence. Use student readiness markers to purposefully target general instruction to everyone in a class while at the same time you give specific feedback to individuals.

Maximizing Learning

As if there is not enough to think about regarding student growth and development, there is another aspect to teaching dance: working with diverse learners who have different learning styles and sets of preferred **modalities.** Purposely advance all

Dance Engages the Whole Person

"Although dance can be great exercise, it is primarily an art form and an aesthetic expression of mind and body. As an art form, dance has three dimensions:

- "Learning: Like other art forms, dance helps us to perceive and communicate who we are.
- "Knowledge: Dance has its own body of knowledge, which can be shared, passed on, and enlarged.
- "Experience: The very nature of dance is best discovered through experiencing it. In this, it is almost unique as an art form, and very special as part of a child's education.

"By combining these three dimensions, dance engages the whole person in simultaneously moving, thinking, and feeling. Thus, dance education can enhance [a] child's physical, mental and emotional development." (Donahue 1997, p. 16)

---

facets of dance. Capitalize on the fact that dance is a kinetic art when you're the doer and a kinetically based visual art when you're the audience.

Preferred Learning Styles and Modalities

The Gregorc model of learning styles is useful for dance educators. It describes the way we take in information (perception) and how we organize and use the information we take in (ordering). The variables of perception and ordering help you unlock some of the mystery of why we learn differently from one another.

According to Gregorc, each mind possesses two perceptual qualities: **concrete,** which brings in information directly through the five senses, and **abstract,** which allows us to visualize and conceive ideas. Although people use both qualities (concrete and abstract perception), each person is normally more comfortable using one over the other. This is referred to as the person's *dominant ability.* For example, one who prefers concrete wants specific, literal, and direct information. One who prefers abstract will pick up on subtle cues and use intuition and imagination (Tobias 1994, pp. 14-15).

In addition, Gregorc's ordering qualities provide the means to classify the information we take in. Two ways of ordering or organizing the informa-

tion we take in (or perceive) are sequential and random. Sequential ordering is linear, step-by-step organization, "in order." Random ordering organizes information by chunks without needing a particular sequence. Those whose random qualities are dominant comfortably start in the middle or at the end and work backward, for example. These four styles—concrete, abstract, sequential, and random—cluster in different ways for different people to create their particular *dominant learning style* (such as concrete-sequential, abstract-sequential, concrete-random, or abstract-random). By understanding the profiles of these four, you realize how to alter learning experiences to increase student success. You also see that no individual exhibits just one profile (Tobias 1994, pp. 16-20). Learn what to use and what to avoid with each dominant style cluster in your classroom.

This Gregorc model helps you approach children in varied ways to increase their ability to understand and retain what is important. This is where sensory modalities come in. Look for modality checklists and inventories that help determine whether a child learns best through hearing, seeing, or doing. Each person has preferred modalities (or ways) of perceiving and processing information:

- Kinesthetic (by moving)
- Tactile (by touching, feeling)
- Visual (by seeing)
- Auditory (by hearing)

Because all students don't learn the same way, don't expect to teach all students the same way. Some actually require information to be presented in a particular way to grasp it. For example, kinesthetic learners need to physically experience something to learn and remember it. Plan dance activities with these differences in mind:

- Visual learners learn best by watching someone else demonstrate.
- Kinesthetic–tactile learners want to experience the movement and to feel it.
- Auditory learners listen for verbal descriptions and focus on rhythms and sounds to learn movement patterns.

Note: This text aligns kinesthetic and tactile into one heading because dance often combines the two at once.

Applying Sensory Learning Modalities

Kids use their senses to gather and process information all the time. Give information so that it has to be absorbed through the senses, especially touch, sight, hearing, and movement. Naturally dance relies on moving, touching, hearing, and seeing. They go together. But your instructional strategies must also consciously involve learners through their senses for them to fully assimilate their dance experiences and information. Further, these modalities determine the way they remember and retain information. For example, some will retain what they heard, while others retain what they saw or did. We will examine three modalities: kinesthetic–tactile, visual, and auditory.

Apply sensory modalities in two ways:

- *Teach to each person's dominant (i.e., preferred) modalities.* Present information and experiences to capitalize on a student's learning strengths and to maximize information processing and real engagement.
- *Take individuals outside their dominant comfort zones* by using other modes so as to push them toward well-roundedness and stimulate peak performance. (See appendix B for a "Learning Modalities Inventory.")

Those who rely more on one sense than others exhibit specific characteristics. Approach students who have difficulty learning one way with the same material another way. To decode learner types, let's identify their trademark characteristics and find what dance teaching strategies get best results. Then you can adapt sensory instructional strategies in dance for the tactile–kinesthetic learner, the visual learner, and the auditory learner.

Tactile–Kinesthetic Learner Profile

Tactile Learners   Descriptor: Hands on.

- Touch objects to learn about them and want to explore the environment
- Like to be hugged or touched
- Want concrete objects used as learning aids

Kinesthetic Learners   Descriptor: Movers.

PREFERS

- Think better on their feet and while moving
- Rely on hand gestures and body language when conversing

- Are fascinated by movement
- Are usually well coordinated, not clumsy
- Talk fast, chatter, chew gum
- Always seem to be in a hurry and have high energy
- Are always ready to move, have good energy supply, and get out of their seats and walk around frequently

DISLIKES

- Need kinetic stimulation for optimum output
- Need to practice skills rather than read or see a video about them
- Are impatient and may interrupt others
- May be underachievers in academics
- Might be wrongly considered hyperactive

TEACHING STRATEGIES

1. Present all significant data so that it is perceived and processed through the body.
2. Have students move not only to learn to dance but also to learn about movement and the body.
3. Use manipulative, movable, **three-dimensional** teaching aids and resources.
4. Give hands-on, tactile feedback. Keep students in motion as often as possible.
5. Give instructions in dance while students are moving and teach as they move.
6. Give kinesthetic learners additional movement tasks to do inside and outside the classroom.
7. Help them with personal organization skills, which are often lacking.
8. Assess students on what they can do and show in movement.

Visual Learner Profile

Descriptor: Lookers.

PREFERS

- Enjoys pictures, charts, and visuals along with lectures, examples, and movement demonstrations
- May draw pictures or doodle while listening to instructions
- Makes lists, takes notes
- Communicates with gesturing, nodding of the head, making facial expressions

- Notices small changes in environment; especially recalls costumes, sets, and movement sequences viewed in dance works
- Looks to see what others do when given only verbal directions
- Needs time to think about answering
- Watches lips and facial expression of speaker and body language
- Expects eye contact
- Is noticeably picturing things while listening

DISLIKES

- Wishes people would not talk so much
- Doesn't like long conversations
- Can't pay attention to audiotapes for very long
- May be slow to get started
- May ignore verbal input or summaries because they're hard to follow

TEACHING STRATEGIES

1. Present all significant data so that they can be processed through the eyes.
2. Teach so student can watch your mouth.
3. Give concepts and learning material visually (video clips, maps, word cards, charts, pictures, transparencies, diagrams, posters).
4. Use gestures as visual cues, especially when guiding movement exploration and giving oral instructions.
5. Write instructions on the board or charts and use a bright, light-filled learning environment.
6. Encourage note taking and list making when appropriate to convert auditory assignments into visual form. (These students need to make note taking and list making lifelong habits. Expect them not to remember auditory and memory assignments. Replace these assignments with organizational assignments that students can input into electronic devices or calendars to jog their memory.)
7. Allow students to draw pictures during listening assignments.
8. When describing movement, ask them to picture something in their minds.
9. Assess what they draw or write.

Auditory Learner Profiles

Descriptor: Listeners.

PREFERS

- Loves to talk to self or others
- Loves to listen to others talk
- Loves to read aloud, move lips, or subvocalize
- Comprehends oral reading better than silent reading
- Needs word cues and timing cues for learning movement phrases
- Remembers what people say as well as the sound of their voice, music scores, and rhythmic patterns
- Prefers word explanations to visual cues and drawings
- Learns dance by focusing on timing cues, rhythmic phrases, musical cues, or word phrases

DISLIKES

- Inattentive to visual tasks and may have trouble picking up sequences if predominantly visual
- Does not recall how movement phrases look, people's faces or details of looks, costumes, sets
- May have trouble attending to details of performance observation
- May get lost easily and have trouble with visual movement details
- Usually has weak visual memory (therefore won't remember details of viewed choreography)

TEACHING STRATEGIES

1. Present all significant data and instruction so that they can be processed through the ear.
2. Present concepts and information verbally: count out phrases, give pulses, use word cues for movement sequences.
3. Give guided viewing questions before observing video clips of dance works. Follow up viewing activities with discussion (see chapter 9).
4. Use songs, rhymes, and chants to increase memory.

5. Include some small group discussion to give more chances to verbally interact about dance.

6. Use verbal classroom critique, discussion, reflection, and journal writing (because many readers sound the words they write).

7. Repeat written instructions orally.

8. Assess them more on their verbal explanations than how they move and what they write.

Planning for Multisensory Integration

Intentionally include different intelligences (MI) such as spatial or bodily–kinesthetic to capitalize on an individual's perceptual strengths. Then use learning modalities to address diverse perceptual and processing needs as you plan instruction. Involve the senses. Insightfully adapt instructional strategies so that all learners excel.

Stacking the Learning Deck If the learning environment becomes electric when charged by the senses, it becomes sheer dynamite when you engage all four at once. Learn to facilitate multisensory integration. Your mantra will be, "Show it, tell it, do it"—all at the same time, all in the same lesson. To maximize the learning experience, "stack the deck" for learning by stacking the sensory modalities one on top of the other. Thus, you reach all children at one time and utilize everyone's dominant modalities at once while also developing their least preferred modalities. This charged learning environment is perfect for the arts teacher, even more so than for the classroom teacher, because you have all avenues so readily available to you. Once you see how effective this approach is, you'll be hooked.

Using multiple senses at once increases the chance for success for those wired with different learning preferences and perceptual needs. Not only can dance increase aesthetic and kinetic development, but moving actually also helps kinetic learners think and process information. For example, refer to the vocabulary word *plié* on the board as you demonstrate with students who do a plié as you explain it (i.e., show it, tell it, do it).

By integrating a child's senses, body, mind, and personality, you are able to

- increase comprehension and retention,
- promote performance artistry, and
- promote creative development appropriate for each age.

How would you incorporate multiple sensory modalities into a dance lesson to stack the learning deck? It seems pretty clear that dance uses them all:

- Dancing is naturally physical, *kinesthetic*.
- You use *tactile* feedback to help with placement, alignment, and body awareness.
- You give instructions, *auditory* movement cues, and phrase counts.
- You view dance as a *visual* art.

So, how can you take it further? *It is critical to stack sensory cues.* For example:

- Add visual cues to verbal instructions.
- Show pictures and words, and demonstrate to increase attention while you explain.
- Show a clip of a dance work to demonstrate the concept you are teaching.
- Find appropriate ways to incorporate touch (tactile) using props, manipulatives, and partners.
- Use the floor and walls to give tactile placement and alignment feedback.
- Display key vocabulary words and refer to them often during class.
- Prepare charts of written reflection questions to use at the end of class so you can visually focus students who need to see the questions to enhance the auditory.
- Dramatically post the lesson's main topic as well as the day's objectives to remind everyone what they are about.
- Keep students moving while you talk them through the concepts and describe what success would look like.

The more senses you involve at once, the more alive your classes are and the more engaged and successful students are. Why not join with other teachers to give students learning styles inventories at the beginning of the year to identify your new students' preferred learning profiles? Age-appropriate inventories are available in your school's guidance office and are administered there. They are multiple choice, and the results are a printout of each child's profile. With these profiles you can factor in acute perception differences among individuals as you plan instruction.

Finding Your Modality Preference

Perhaps you'd find it instructive to take a learning styles inventory, too, to learn your preferred modality. Be aware that we tend to teach others in the ways we ourselves learn best, so your tendency toward one modality means you may rely on it more than the others. That is important to recognize. See Rich Resources for more information and appendix B for a "Learning Modalities Inventory."

Reflect and Respond

Part I

Bloom's taxonomy of complex thinking and cognition identifies how we process information at different levels. *Learning styles* identify the way we perceive and order information. *Modalities* are sensory ways we perceive best. The *theory of multiple intelligences* identifies different ways of knowing. Mix them to accommodate the learner's modal strengths as often as possible to facilitate learning in ways each student learns best. Therefore, consider these questions:

1. How does dance engage or relate to all seven of the intelligences that Gardner identified?

2. How does Gardner's musical intelligence compare with the characteristics of auditory learners?

3. How do those with bodily–kinesthetic aptitudes compare with kinesthetic–tactile learners?

4. How do those with spatial intelligence aptitudes compare with visual learners?

Part II

Should Gardner add "artistic intelligence" to his original list? If so, how would you describe it? Would "artistic intelligence" be singular or plural? If plural, how do artistic intelligences apply to products of poetry, literature, painting, sculpture, dance, music, and drama? If singular, does it apply to art as a generic process. . . ? (Eisner 1990, p. 31)

Mentoring

Your students bring an amalgam of kinesthetic, artistic, cognitive, and psychological–social characteristics. They have learning preferences. All forms of intelligence reside in each one, so as you teach the whole child your effectiveness depends on how you reach—as much as how you teach—students. Reach them in as many ways as possible to engage and stretch them.

In addition, adapt these two teaching strategies to reach the whole child: **scaffolding** and apprenticing.

Scaffolding

Scaffolding describes the way teachers support students until they are able to perform tasks that are in their readiness level on their own. By scaffolding you assign appropriately timed dance tasks so students succeed with support from you or others until they learn the skill well enough to succeed independently. Jeanne Ormrod explains:

> To understand this concept, let's first think about how scaffolding is used in the construction of a new building. The *scaffold* is an external structure that supplies support for the workers (a place where they can stand) until the building itself is strong enough to support them. As the building gains stability, the scaffold becomes less necessary and is gradually removed. In much the same way, an adult guiding a child through a new task may provide an initial scaffold to support the child's early efforts. (Ormrod 2000, p. 46)

Therefore, as students become gradually more confident and able, carefully remove the support to allow them to succeed without aid. Anytime you sense a lack of readiness—either cognitive, aesthetic, or psychological–social—support with a scaffold so you guide children to move, explore, create, and respond in ways they are still incapable of doing by or for themselves. For instance, you ask questions that either provide clues or narrow their options of possible answers. You divide a complex task into several simpler tasks. You give frequent feedback for novices so they know whether or not they are on the right track (Ormrod 2000, p. 46). Eventually they are able to find their artistic voices in dance.

To scaffold you need to know stages of progression in each aspect of dance and how students move through them. Understand readiness factors so you are tuned in to when additional support is needed. This way you can tailor instruction most productively for children by giving them the support they need while they build skills.

Apprenticing

Advanced high school performers and artistically gifted student choreographers and critics benefit from apprenticeships. This is where they work intensely with a mentor to master specific artistic skills and gain insights into some of the inner workings of the profession. Students who aspire to choreograph as a career need to apprentice with experts who can coach them to explore, reflect, inquire, and articulate about their choreographic processes and products. Help students find mentors who can teach them things you cannot. Find mentors who present students with opportunities that increase in difficulty and sophistication as the students advance. Be sure mentors are willing to provide the artistic scaffold to support students throughout the process until they reach an advanced skill level. Consider apprenticeships also for younger artistically gifted and talented dance students prior to high school (Ormrod 2000). If your state has a Governor's School of the Arts, recommend your most gifted students to this program. There they'll get intense preprofessional dance training of the highest caliber. Most of these programs are summer programs, but some states have year-round schools.

Reflect and Respond

What should I do? A high school beauty pageant and prom are coming up. Girls in my dance class want me to take time to prepare them for both during class. Why is this or why is this not a good idea?

Expecting Jagged Educational Profiles

Mentoring is individualistic and student focused. Just as in nature, nothing grows straight; individuals are so unique it is hard to describe a norm. Most have special needs or a "jagged educational profile." For example, one person is high in one area and low in another, moves rapidly ahead in one area and not another, and thinks, perceives, and processes differently than other students. However, because dance relies on both movement and thinking, you can mentor individuals within your classes by attending to individual progress in specific areas. Challenge all students—most especially the academically and the artistically gifted. Stimulate the physically challenged as well as the gifted mover. Adapt teaching strategies to address uneven needs so that you enhance the student first and her dance skills second, thereby making students the focus of a standards-oriented arts education in dance.

Teaching Gifted and Talented

The gifted are not obvious. They come in all shapes and sizes. There are people who are gifted in different areas of intelligence. They require differentiated learning that challenges and speaks to their areas

of giftedness—academic or artistic giftedness (or both). Consider Renzulli's definition of giftedness to identify a cluster of traits that are present:

- above average ability
- a high task commitment
- highly creative

Some students are both gifted and talented, while some are talented or gifted. "Talented" is the ability to display a skill. "Gifted" refers to superior conceptualizing capacity. Within the gifted and talented group, only a small majority are actually superior at conceptualizing (gifted).

Both the gifted and the talented have a propensity toward creative thinking and production, which should be stimulated and developed. In the United States, approximately 5 percent of the population will be truly gifted. It is they who take civilization forward because they are able to see what is not yet, but what should be. Use inquiry to keep the gifted challenged at their own levels of proficiency and to encourage their curiosity in dance.

Combining Kinesthetics and Aesthetics Into Kin-Aesthetics

Aesthetic aspects should permeate all experiences in an aesthetically driven, student-centered educational dance (ED) curriculum. Keep aesthetic aspects integrated so as to be inseparable. For example:

- In critiquing, ask students to make qualitative artistic judgments about what they see.
- In creating, ask them to apply aesthetic principles.
- In dancing and performing, ask them to color how they dance.

Persistently and consistently emphasize the motional alliance between the aesthetic and kinesthetic so your students dance well, perform well, express themselves artistically well through movement, and secure their ability to communicate in and about dance.

One vital contribution dance makes to education is its ability to merge the aesthetic with the kinesthetic. Inspire student performance to be more **kin-aesthetic** than *kinesthetic* to emphasize the artistic quality of dancing. You, as a dance specialist, point the young beyond merely moving and take them into the realm of artful bodyspeaking and bodythinking. (See chapter 6 for details.)

Reflect and Respond

Betty A. Block's article "Literacy Through Movement: An Organizational Approach" (2001) theorized a multilevel perception system that integrates motor learning with the reading process. She used five "levels of complexity" to show how, before they are able to read (preliterate), young children are able to use word symbols that actually prepare them to compose and later to read. This important area of research explores how word sequences can be translated into movement sequences and eventually into choreography.

Should the dance educator try to build reading readiness through dance composition? Dance and linguistics both rely on symbols to communicate. There are numerous connections between dance and reading. One of the most useful is translating word sequences into a choreographic structure (e.g., stretch, run, jump, turn, and twist). Can you make a case for using dance to support linguistic development in the young?

Questions to Ponder

1. How does dance engage and relate to all seven of the intelligences that Gardner identified?

2. How does musical intelligence compare with the characteristics of auditory learners? How do bodily kinesthetic aptitudes influence tactile–kinesthetic learners? How do spatial intelligence aptitudes influence visual learners?

3. How can you effectively teach a class with students at many different movement stages? Is it appropriate to have a class in which students are not at similar levels?

4. When planning lessons, how might you integrate the six levels of complex thinking from Bloom's taxonomy with Gardner's seven intelligences?

5. Why is it important to determine where students are psychologically and socially before planning lessons?

6. What are some ways you can encourage students to progress from one psychological–social stage to the next?

7. In what ways should you incorporate your students' preferred learning styles into your tests of their knowledge and skills?

8. Why is it a good idea to use higher-order thinking skills in teaching dance?

For dance students to excel you must create a holistic learning environment where you keep students growing in all ways. They must mix kinaesthetics with thinking and feeling. They must invest totally (physically, artistically, cognitively, psychosocially) when they create, perform, and respond to dance. Monitor continually where they are so you take realistic steps to move them to the next level. Use your understanding of student readiness to select content and instruction to fit learner needs. Assess authentically. Use higher-order thinking. Increase kin-aesthetic perception. Thus create a consistent, coherent, student-centered program that ensures accomplished, well-balanced dance students.

Rich Resources

RESOURCES

- Jensen, Eric. *Arts With the Brain in Mind.* Alexandria, VA: Association for Supervision and Curriculum Development, 2001. This book deals with how the arts stack up as a major discipline; what their effect is on the brain, learning, and human development; and how schools can best implement and assess an arts program such as dance.

- Tobias, Cynthia U. *The Way They Learn.* Wheaton, IL: Tyndale House Publishers, 1994. Cynthia Tobias makes the Gregorc learning styles model easy to grasp. She shows how individuals receive and use information. She

Notebook/Portfolio: Perspectives Notebook

Write an article for your Perspectives Notebook. Title it "What I Believe About Student-Centered Learning."

focuses you on the dominant aspects of learning styles and how they cluster to affect the way individuals learn. Unpack the four clusters so you can approach children in multiple ways to increase their probability of understanding and retaining what is important.

- Graham, George, Shirley Anne Holt/Hale, Tim McEwen, Melissa Parker. *Children Moving: A Reflective Approach to Teaching Physical Education,* 6th ed., New York: McGraw-Hill, 2004.

- Gilbert, Anne Green. *Brain-Compatible Dance Education,* AAHPERD, 2005. This text incorporates current brain research into planning and presenting dance lessons that stimulate the brain through dance. Order it through NDA at www.aahperd.org/NDA.

WEB SITES

- Learning Styles Inventory: www.learnativity.com/learningstyles.html
- New England Complex Systems Institute: http://necsi.org
- www.howtolearn.com
- www.scholastic.com

Identifying the Cornerstones of Dance as Art in Education

"What
we call
'curriculum'
is too often more
a cafeteria line of
subjects, a hodgepodge
that lacks a clear vision of
what constitutes an educated
person."

—Will H. Willimon (1995, p. 57)

This chapter identifies dance's four indispensable content areas, called cornerstones. You will investigate why they are the core curriculum in dance and how they relate to the standards to which you are accountable (see chapter 3). You will learn about the pivotal role of inquiry and its use in each cornerstone to further the artistic processes (c/p/r). You will understand the relationship of the cornerstones to the NSDEs and both of them to writing goals and objectives for learning. This chapter prepares you for part II, the cornerstone chapters, by giving you an overview of what you need to do in those chapters.

Four Cornerstones

Four foundation cornerstones of the dance discipline are foundations of the educational dance curriculum. They contain the substance of dance essential to aesthetic education.

Too often dance instruction is a mixture of isolated events. Dance teachers tend to overemphasize one aspect of dance at the expense of another. We forget to relate the different facets of the dance discipline to each other so students grasp the total effect of what dance is and can be. It's time to change old habits—like forgetting to place our dance lesson's main topic into a broader dance context. We must hold in our mind's eye the ideal of what an arts-educated person in dance should look like, be like, think like, and do, so all our efforts move students toward that ideal. This means activating each of the four dance cornerstones to achieve desired outcomes.

Dance's core content comes from dance's foundation disciplines: dance performance, choreography, dance history, and dance criticism. They comprise the cornerstones for the dance curriculum. You find rigorous content as well as all the artistic processes there. The four educational dance cornerstones are as follows:

- Cornerstone 1 (C1): Dancing and Performing (Performing)
- Cornerstone 2 (C2): Creating and Composing (Creating)
- Cornerstone 3 (C3): Knowing History, Culture, and Context (Knowing about)
- Cornerstone 4 (C4): Analyzing and Critiquing (Responding)

Each cornerstone contains the content and the skills that all students *must* know in dance. The cornerstones contain the treasures of the discipline that all students *should* know. Out of the cornerstones come the mega-ideas and concepts that promote enduring understanding in dance.

Taught well, the cornerstones individually and collectively ensure that dance education is comprehensive, substantive, and contextual.

- Incorporate all the cornerstones to bring *comprehensiveness* to your program.
- Include the depth of each one to bring *substance* to your program.
- Relate them to each other to create a *dance context* that supports dance as a multifaceted art form and keeps dance study coherent.

Inattention to any cornerstone results in unevenly educating students in and about dance. To omit one undermines the integrity of the entire curriculum. A complete (i.e., comprehensive, substantive, sequential, aesthetically driven, contextually coherent, and inquiry-based) dance curriculum requires that you effectively incorporate all four cornerstones. They

help you create well-rounded achievers who have a substantive dance experience from the time they start to the time they graduate.

All four cornerstones (the 4Cs) are vital to aesthetic education in dance. Each contributes different aspects of dance. Each develops skills and knowledge through a different artistic process (c/p/r). Those who experience all four know and respond to dance through the choreographic works of others and themselves and through their own dancing bodies. Figure 5.1 shows us each distinct cornerstone and how the cornerstones overlap to support each other.

- C1 (Dancing and Performing) includes the basic dance technique, participation, dancing skills, motor skills, techniques in many different styles, mastery of an articulate body, and all kin-aesthetic skills (see chapter 4). It is grounded in the dance elements and uses them as dance and conceptual vocabularies. Here are learned cognitive aspects of dance as well as knowledge and use of anatomy, kinesiology, injury prevention, diagnosis and treatment, safety, proper nutrition, and rest.
- C2 (Creating and Composing) includes improvisation, creating, composing, exploring, problem solving in movement, and experimenta-

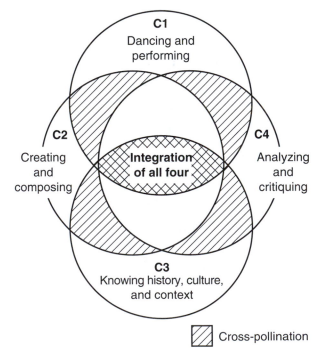

FIGURE 5.1 To teach dance fully, teach and integrate each cornerstone.

Table 5.1 Cornerstone Actions

Viewpoint	Cornerstone	Action
1. Dancer	C1	Articulate!
2. Choreographer	C2	Create!
3. Dance historian and anthropologist	C3	Relate!
4. Dance critic	C4	Evaluate!

tion with and **elaboration** in movement. It includes inquiry into movement ideas, creative design based on a stimulus, and study and use of the choreographic principles of design.

- C3 (Knowing History, Culture, and Context) includes classical, traditional, multicultural, folk, vernacular, broad topics, and many styles. It is culturally inclusive. It looks at famous dancers, significant choreographers and critics, and major choreographic works across time and place. It includes dance past and present.

- C4 (Analyzing and Critiquing) includes aesthetic scanning, aesthetics, critical thinking, analyzing, and synthesizing. It is about seeing and valuing dance, using higher-order and reflective thinking, assessing and evaluating, and refining one's work.

Dance's four foundation disciplines—the cornerstones—do not change. Every 8 to 10 years, national standards change. NAEP assessments change over time. State dance frameworks change. Achievement standards change. *But the four cornerstone disciplines in the art of dance are constant.* They are solid no matter what headings the assessments and standards use. Content and instructional strategies that derive from these four disciplines comprise the breadth of dance knowledge and skills your students need.

The dance cornerstones bring together the national standards and assessments (see chapter 2) and the artistic processes that keep the content personal and student centered (see chapter 4). A 6DC comprehensive, substantive, sequential, aesthetically driven, contextually coherent, and inquiry-based curriculum derives from the four cornerstones.

Viewpoints

The cornerstones provide dance experiences from four artistic viewpoints. Each viewpoint is associated with an action and method of inquiry (table 5.1).

Any cornerstone may be the starting place to develop a **unit of study,** for there are as many avenues into dance as there are aspects of dance. They all become points of entry over time as you see in figure 5.2. It doesn't matter where you begin. It only matters that overall you include aspects of all cornerstones in each unit so they support each other and create a learning matrix in which to put the dance experience.

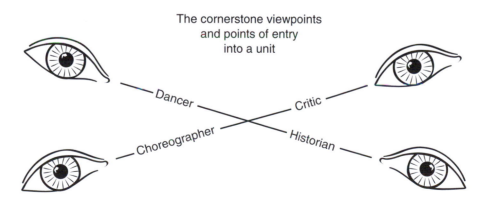

The cornerstone viewpoints and points of entry into a unit

Dancer

Choreographer

Critic

Historian

FIGURE 5.2   Entry points and viewpoints.

Organize dance instruction into cohesive units of study. Group related lessons around a concept, theme, dance style, or dance work for educational connectivity and so the cornerstones interact and support each other (see chapters 13 and 14).

One cornerstone may take the foreground in a particular unit or lesson and the supporting aspect of another. Integrate them when educationally beneficial to relate concepts to each other and to give balance to the curriculum. Some lessons blend all four seamlessly, but often you need more than one lesson to interrelate all cornerstones. That said, use them to varying degrees of emphasis in each unit. Not all units need to place equal emphasis (i.e., 25 percent) on each cornerstone. Use as much of one as is helpful to achieve the objectives of each unit. By the end of each unit—as well as each semester—to ensure overall curricular balance, see that each cornerstone is equitably represented and that students consistently grow in all four viewpoints. Each unit typically incorporates at least one noteworthy choreographic work as either a prime example of, a connecting point to, or the aesthetic support of the unit's main theme or concept.

Mega-Ideas and Concepts

Mega-ideas and concepts are those that promote enduring understanding in dance. They come out of the cornerstones and from the broadest reaches of dance as art and expression. Although national standards identify what students should know and be able to do in dance, these understandings go beyond that. You are expected to surpass *knowing* so you get to *understanding based on knowing*. The key difference between knowing and understanding based on knowing is that the latter remains fluid so it can transfer to new contexts and transform into new theories. Knowledge is more like correct beliefs and understanding is more akin to insight (McTighe and Wiggins 1999). Aesthetic education seeks genuine understanding and applied insights more than correct answers.

It is up to you to identify—and help students identify—the **enduring understandings** in dance that they absorb more than recall. The enduring understandings are the recurring themes that endure. What are these fundamental precepts of the dance discipline that all your dance instruction supports—the "mega-ideas" in dance? List exactly what you believe are the most important concepts to grasp in and about dance. Add this list to your

perspectives notebook in chapter 16. Following are some examples:

- In dance the body is the instrument and movement is the medium of expression.
- Great dancers and choreographers leave an indelible imprint on the art of dance through time.
- Dance is a universal language of human expression.
- Principles of design support the art of choreography.

Thus, the enduring understandings underlie what you teach. They reinforce understanding of dance. Bring the mega-ideas to life in different ways to reinforce them in varied contexts. Make them recurring themes in your classroom year to year.

A Place for All Styles

Make a place to study all kinds of dance in the fine arts curriculum. To focus too much on one dance style—no matter how important a style—weakens your program and keeps it from being standards oriented. Draw from the major dance works in different styles to increase broad-based understanding of dance as a phenomenon of human expression. The integrity of a dance art program requires stylistic accuracy and high performance standards for all forms of dance.

Include traditional participation styles such as social and folk dance. Make a place for them to convey history and culture and thus create context. For example, think broader than just a unit of folk dance. Instead, tie specific folk dances to other units. Ask yourself, "Which folk (or world or social) dance contributes particular substance to this unit?" to achieve one or more of the following:

- Compare what is being studied in another dance genre yet on the same theme or topic
- Add cultural breadth
- Stimulate choreographic and creative activities
- Increase step mastery
- Emphasize pattern
- Reinforce rhythmic accuracy in technique
- Increase contextual learning

Aside from stressing high performance quality, use the intricate figures and footwork from

Make movement the medium for learning as often as possible so concepts are embodied and practiced.

participation styles to diversify step vocabulary and performance skills and to show how group dances are constructed. Stylistic variety increases one's personal dance repertory. Even urban social dances like hip-hop give opportunities to analyze and critique, to compare and contrast. Social and folk styles are living dance history and culture just as much as they are legend. Being literate in such a rich dance legacy contributes to better understanding the world. Ask learners to use this information in non-dance settings and as bridges to other subjects. Different dance styles launch us into new realms of education and dance—either as art or as participation—and propel us bodily into the authentic cultural traditions of dance (see chapter 8).

Integration of the Cornerstones

To teach dance fully you must not only teach each cornerstone but also relate one to the other. Although we isolate the cornerstones for instruction,

we also cross-reference and integrate them. There are good reasons to do both.

Each one brings students closer to grasping the full effect of dance as art and as cultural phenomenon. To go deeply into the facets of one cornerstone builds precise skills that are vitally important. But also to cross-pollinate among the cornerstones makes dance study richly related and builds context. The integration enlivens learning and keeps content and methods interactive and meaningful for all but the very young. Use both ways to develop students with the dynamics to express themselves as dancers, choreographers, historians, and critics. Such study focuses fully on the dance discipline and applies it to students' overall aesthetic education and to their lives (refer to appendix A for NSDEs 1-5).

ISOLATE AND FOCUS ON EACH CORNERSTONE SO STUDENTS

- grow in each viewpoint;
- develop aesthetic and kinesthetic clarity;
- expand their creative problem-solving skills;
- grasp pertinent information about great works, their time, place, and purpose;
- examine works of others to give feedback and critique; and
- learn specific skills in each content area.

INTEGRATE THE CORNERSTONES SO STUDENTS

- relate the artistic processes organically to each other,
- understand dance as an art form and a means of cultural expression,
- reflect on their own works to evaluate quality,
- know important choreographers and about their creative process and major works,
- reflect on the value of dance as an art form,
- acquire a global context for learning various aspects of dance, and
- critique both composition and performance quality of dance works.

Make movement the learning medium as often as possible because so many concepts are best grasped while moving. Ask students to locate where they are supporting their turnout as they execute a rond de jambe. Ask them to bodythink and to discriminate in motion. What good is knowledge about movement if it can't be applied in motion? You can also relate relevant bits of dance history as students dance.

Pivotal Role of Inquiry

Students retain more knowledge and skills when they are at the center of the learning process rather than at its periphery. Dance inquiry changes the way learners learn. Inquiry is both active and interactive. It puts students in the center of the learning experiences and asks them to take different dance roles and to examine different viewpoints in dance. It leads to understanding dance. Dance inquiry is accomplished through active investigation, questioning, and problem solving in all four cornerstones, as shown in figure 5.3.

Inquiry is both an active learning process and an approach to teaching. This text differentiates two different processes related to inquiry: *Dance inquiry* is the learning process—what students do. An *inquiry approach* is a teacher-conducted instructional strategy to facilitate and promote personal investigation.

Dance inquiry activates creative and critical thinking that are very personal. The child is the agent of his own learning:

- Dancing inquiry—how does my body work? (C1)
- Technique inquiry—how can I do that better? (C1)

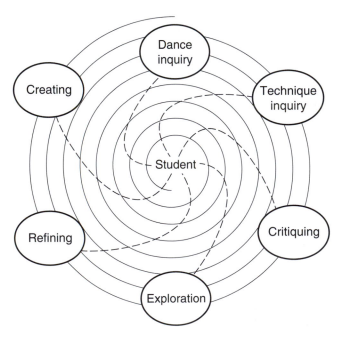

FIGURE 5.3 Inquiry puts each student in the center of the learning experience and asks them to take different dance roles and to examine different viewpoints in dance. Inquiry makes dance personal for each learner.

- Exploration—what can I do with shaping in space? (C2)
- Creating—how can I best express my idea? (C2)
- Critiquing—how well is this working? (C4)
- Refining—how might I do this better? (C4)

Other forms of inquiry are these:

- Analyzing great dance works (C3 and C4)
- Seeking historical roots of a dance (C3)
- Investigating multicultural dances (C1 and C3)
- Comparing dance styles (C1 and C3)
- Performing diverse styles (C1 and C3)

Each Cornerstone—A Method of Inquiry

Each cornerstone approaches dance a different way. To think of cornerstones only as content limits their value and use and makes them remote and disjointed. Although cornerstones are content, they are more importantly active **methods of inquiry.** As such, they keep students actively at the center of learning and personalize each student's experience with dance. For example, teachers' roles have changed. Instead of being a fountain of knowledge, a teacher is more a facilitator of learning through inquiry. Instead of dispensing dance information to students, as much as possible ask questions that help them find answers themselves. This way students learn to integrate experiences and invest more of themselves into what they learn. This method keeps the student at the center of learning rather than the teacher.

Four methods of inquiry are necessary for personal artistic growth. Inquire from distinct yet related viewpoints, as described in table 5.2.

Dance inquiry leads learners to ask what they are doing and why. Make inquiry an active and personal investigation for each person:

- *To personally inquire as a dancer* (C1) is to investigate how you move; how the dance elements interact; how you turn, balance, travel, and shape; and how you express yourself through dance. It is to dance from different perspectives.
- *To personally inquire as a choreographer* (C2) is to explore movement options, improvise,

Table 5.2 Cornerstone Methods of Inquiry

Cornerstone	Viewpoint	Type of inquiry	Method of inquiry
C1	As a dancer	Physical—discovering about the body and how to dance: dancing, performing, learning the dance elements, discovering the workings of the body, perfecting dance technique, learning stylistic skills	With neurosensory and muscle receptors
C2	As a choreographer	Creative—discovering how: exploring the creative process, expressing through dance, exploring movement, improvising, composing, dance making, learning the tools of the craft, learning design principles	With imagination and creative self
C3	As a dance historian or anthropologist	Intellectual—discovering who, what, when, where: notable dancers, choreographers, choreographic works, multicultural dance, social impact of dance, context for dance	With the mind and heart
C4	As a dance critic	Aesthetic—discovering why and how well: looking into the inner workings of dance, responding to dance performance, appreciating dance, analyzing, critiquing, editing and refining one's work	With critical discernment

create dance phrases, and investigate the structures of composition; it is to inquire into the art and craft of making dances.

- *To personally inquire as a dance historian and anthropologist* (C3) is to uncover what other dancers do and what other choreographers make, investigate varied dance styles and cultural expressions, and explore dance through time and place; it is to discover the amazing intricacies of dance and how dance affects you.

- *To personally inquire as a dance critic* (C4) is to analyze a dance work, investigate its artistic integrity and its ability to communicate; to give and receive feedback; to inquire into the quality of a dance and sharpen one's perception of the choreographic principles.

As you facilitate inquiry, ask questions that indicate what is important to look for. Your questions should penetrate to the heart of the art and show how to take an inquiring attitude about the subject of dance. Your questions should expand everyone's understanding of dance. How do you do that? Let's look at specific examples to get you started. Use

them to increase your understanding of how to lead inquiry in each cornerstone.

Inquiry From the Viewpoint of a Dancer (C1): Dancing and Performing (Chapter 6)

C1 is about the art of movement or the aesthetics of human movement (i.e., kin-aesthetics). Dancing, moving, acquiring technique, performing, and approaching dancing with an aesthetic sensitivity are all necessary to one's kin-aesthetic growth. Hereby students develop aesthetic perception by performing and cohesively connecting movements. Such flow transcends mere movement and becomes dance. A direct experience with dancing develops the dancing body and the motion vocabulary—both of which are necessary. Inquiry into skill development in movement, technique, and performance increases body awareness. It activates full use of the dance elements. It moves students beyond mundane movement. It moves them to express themselves artistically through the art of motion. Learning the safe use of the body instrument opens the door to developing a somatically aware dancer.

How do you get students to inquire about their dancing body during a movement class? What kinds of questions turn actual moving experience into personal kin-aesthetic investigation? Here are some examples with different degrees of complexity:

- "How can you go into the air and land softly?"
- "How does that focus help your turning? Your balance?"
- "Where do you feel that impulse coming from? Is it from the hamstrings or the quadriceps?"
- "Can you initiate your battement from the gluteal muscles and hamstrings rather than from the quadriceps? Can you engage your quads like a parachute on the release (the return to place) so the leg softly lands in place?"
- "Can your foot brush the floor to return to first position?"
- "What does this cross-lateral movement teach you about balancing?"
- "How does learning to perform phrases from this master work help you comprehend the full expressive power of that movement? What specifically does performing this work teach you that just observing does not (timing counts, musicality, strength required)? What details do you pick up while performing it that you would have missed otherwise?"
- "Are you performing these phrases with the proper dynamics? Correct rhythmic timing? Exact focus?"
- "How does maintaining your strong center support your arm and leg extensions? How does that affect the way you are able to dance this phrase?"

Inquiry From the Viewpoint of a Choreographer (C2): Creating and Composing (Chapter 7)

Creative expression is another important component of educational dance. Give students ample opportunities to experiment with movement, explore, improvise, and move spontaneously. Movement exploration broadens students' movement repertory. Give them progressively challenging structures in which to compose short dance studies to learn how to shape and design ideas in dance. Develop their compositional skills—starting with the building blocks—and as skills are acquired, move students to longer works.

Teach them to compose and shape movement into coherent dance studies or dances. This way you help them acquire an intimate understanding of the creative process of dance along with the craft and principles of dance making.

How do you facilitate inquiry into the creative process? What kinds of questions turn the actual experience into a personal investigation? Here are some examples:

- "How can you show this is a dance about opposites of 'slow' and 'fast'?"
- "How can you emphasize different levels in space?"
- "Can you rebuild the middle section of the dance to emphasize body part isolations more than full body movements? How might that make your point more clear?"
- "Can you design a dance sentence (i.e., with a beginning, middle, and end) that transforms an activity you do every day into an abstract spatial pattern?"
- "Can you create a dance environment with found objects? Can you place them in space so that they interrupt the dancers' pathways and become an integral design element in the dance?"
- "Can you choreograph this prop as a link between the two dancers? How will you introduce it, develop it, and end so the prop remains as vital to the dance as the dancers?"

Inquiry From the Viewpoint of a Dance Historian and Cultural Anthropologist (C3): Knowing History, Culture, and Context (Chapter 8)

Educational dance has a strong historical, social, and cultural component. Such contexts contribute to a better understanding of why particular dance works were choreographed. By questioning students about the main ideas of a dance, acquaint students with such features as the time period, the beliefs of the artist who created the work, and the choreographer's influences at the time it was created. Look into the role and stature of the choreographer's works in society, movement choices available to the choreographer, descriptions of background issues involving the composition of the work, and, when applicable, the community impact of the work.

> **"The arts are the key to a sense of what is not yet."**
>
> —Gordon Ambach

The scope of dance heritage is broad. Our heritage is the dance legacy that must be passed from generation to generation through educational dance. Both viewing and doing dance offer our students unique insights into the world and ultimately about themselves.

How might you facilitate inquiry to lead students into a personal investigation about history and world cultures? Here are some examples:

- "Who was the choreographer? When and where did she live and in what kind of artistic environment?"

- "What aspects of his personal background influenced his professional dance life?"

- "Of what artistic and cultural significance was this choreographer to her time? To us now as we look back into history? What are her main contributions to dance?"

- "How do you think the choreographer found and refined the movements to convey the idea he wanted?"

- "What other dance works compare to this one?"

- "What other major choreographic works were being made at this time? In this place? Was there a relationship between the works? The choreographers? Who are the choreographer's dance contemporaries?"

- "Who are her visual artist contemporaries? Composers? Playwrights?"

Inquiry From the Viewpoint of a Dance Critic (C4): Analyzing and Critiquing (Chapter 9)

Educational dance uses analysis and critique. Criticism (i.e., making personal judgments about dance works based on aesthetic criteria) is informed by synthesizing information about the historical context, the aesthetics, the production activities, and the actual performance of the work. This kind of scrutiny divulges the meaning, artistic value, and significance of the piece more completely as students observe and participate. Familiarity lets students individually own the dance, thus enabling them to move forward with intellectual ease and independence. Invite students to delve into each dance work by guiding their viewing experience before and discussing it after with questions such as those that follow.

This cornerstone is about responding to dance and to all the other cornerstones and artistic processes. It is where you inquire about all aspects of dance and build a vocabulary for seeing, making, and doing dance. In many ways C4 synthesizes the entire dance experience. It is not more important than the other cornerstones; it just encompasses all of dance. Look at the diverse ways to inquire, analyze, and critique.

How do you invite analysis and critique in class? What kinds of higher-order and critical questions generate critical thinking? Which questions make students look deeper? Compare? Evaluate? Reflect? Describe? Which questions keep students investigating on their own? Here are some examples:

- "What do you see in this work? How is it structured? How does the beginning of this dance relate to its ending?"

- "Describe the grouping of the dancers. Describe the soloists in relation to the group. Who is 'background' and who is 'foreground'? Is there any difference?"

- "What is this piece really about? How do we know?"

- "What descriptive action words (verbs) best describe the dance? Adjectives?"

- "Does conflict take place in this dance? If so, where? How?"

- "What are the strongest movement images the work creates for you? What are the strongest visual images in this dance for you?"

- "Can you relate these movement images to everyday life? How are they different in dance?"

- "How does the accompaniment affect the piece? How do the costumes complement or support the dance idea?"

- "Does this piece effectively develop from beginning (through middle) to the end? Describe it."

- "How does this piece compare with other works by the choreographer? In what way is it similar? Different?"

- "Can dance affect attitudes of people in a country? How do we know? What are examples?"

- "Would we know what this piece was about if we didn't know its title? How?"

- "Is the dance long enough to be satisfying? How so?"

- "What do we really need to know to understand this work?"

- "Did the choreographer accomplish what she/he intended? Explain."
- "Is this an effective work?"

Inquiry Approach

An inquiry approach is a questioning approach to dance content and experiences. It is how you take individuals beyond their dancing selves to the larger world of dance and back again to relate that world to themselves. It is how you challenge everyone simultaneously at their own degree of ability, for it holds back none. Inquiry changes the way teachers teach. It doesn't ask you to do more but rather just do it better.

There are two main approaches. Use both.

First, ask direct questions, such as the preceding examples (direct questioning techniques are found in chapter 12).

Second, adopt a questioning attitude about each lesson's content and experiences. For example,

create an exploratory atmosphere in your room by encouraging students to search the Web for areas of dance interest or for information about a choreographer or dancer they particularly like. Not all are graded assignments but might encourage interested students to choreograph or to look into dance careers as an option. A questioning attitude helps students find dance doors they can open themselves. Thus you create a continuous exchange about what dance is (outer world) and how it affects each one personally (inner world). This approach keeps learning "first person." It is how you encourage individuals to unlock their limitless, innate creativity. It shows them that you value the personal talents each brings to the table (see chapter 4). This process smoothly takes experiences from one cornerstone to the other to cross-pollinate them. Make places in each unit to relate the parts to the whole and tie aspects together—especially at the end of the unit. Design questions so students critically think about what they experience and relate it to the whole study (see chapter 12).

The exponential nature of inquiry is that your questioning attitude is like tossing stones in a pond, causing an exponential ripple effect: Inquiry generates personal interest. Interest leads to further inquiry. Secondary inquiry often generates further interests.

How do you foster a spirit of substantive inquiry in dance? Not only do you facilitate an attitude of discovery—you can also join in. Make units opportunities to investigate all manner of things: performance skills, choreographic structures, new ways to use the dance elements, rhythmic variations, partnering skills, creative expression. You have much to include: How will you personalize aesthetic inquiry, technique inquiry, and historical inquiry? How will you facilitate critical inquiry, compositional inquiry, and cultural inquiry? As you choose the main topic for your units, remember that you can start at any entry point in the cornerstones.

Develop an acute sense of body in space at all times, whether students are dancing (C1), choreographing (C2), or viewing (C3) and critiquing (C4) professional dancers such as this.

- You identify the mega-ideas that the topic promotes.
- You design where the unit starts, how it develops, and where it goes.
- You incorporate all artistic processes and cornerstone methods of inquiry.

Start with a main idea or topic. Choose one that helps students achieve several national achievement standards and also takes forward one or more mega-ideas and concepts that promote enduring understanding in dance. Decide the entry point into the unit and then plan ways to spiral outward to connect useful aspects of other cornerstones. Incorporate several objectives and standards. Vary methods of inquiry in a unit by starting with one cornerstone and going to another, like a chain reaction.

For example, the unit's main topic may be a particular school of technique such as Vaganova, or a dance style such as Bharata Natyam. Or the main topic may investigate performance techniques such as better ways to turn, balance, leap, and hang in the air. In either case, decide how you will introduce the topic. That is, will you move first (C1), begin with a creative activity (C2), first look at a sample (C3), or critique a sample (C4)? (Unit planning is explained further in chapter 12.)

Extended Example of Unit Planning

In this example, the main idea is to introduce a new dance style, such as modern dance.

In pre-unit planning, select a good performance sample of a choreographic work in that style (such as Alvin Ailey's "I Been 'Buked" from *Revelations*). Use deductive reasoning to "unwrap" or "decode" the work's creative impetus. Decide on your entry point (ours is C2). Facilitate a chain reaction of inquiry in the unit:

1. C1 and C2: Launch the investigation with a creative idea you take straight out of the work's performance sample (such as the opening section with all dancers in center stage, close together before they move apart into space). Before you show the dance, explore the prominent dance elements (such as level changes and the contrast between curved and straight body shapes). Then go from exploring into a dance-making activity (such as contrasting curved and straight shapes with the torso and arms with level changes high, middle, and low).

2. C3 and C4: Show the performance sample to demonstrate how this work uses the same concepts, and ask viewers to describe stylistic particulars of the technique that they see.

3. C1: Work on techniques and sequences using that style now that students have seen it modeled and described it.

4. C2, C3, C4: Look at a slice of the dance work. Ask students what they notice about the creative ideas behind the dance work. Apply their responses to the dance-making project or the technique class.

5. C2, C3, C4: Inquire into the larger dance work more closely and respond by critiquing its structure and form, its use of motif, and its performance quality. You might apply aspects of the discussion to student creations as well.

6. C3: Explore the choreographer's process and role in making the work. What was his motivation for making the work?

7. C1, C3, C4: Compare a different work in the same style (modern dance).

8. C3: Select a visual art work of the same period that uses similar techniques and compare. Use as a stimulus to move.

9. Tie it to a mega-idea like, "Dance as a performing art requires an articulate body." Or perhaps, "Dance is a universal language of human expression."

10. Reflect on the learning experiences at the end of the unit. Ask, "What did you learn?"

To be well-prepared you must gather all materials for the unit and write learning objectives at the outset. Intrigue learners and make them think; add a little suspense to hold interest rather than dole out disconnected information for them to memorize. Construct the unit so that by the end multiple objectives have been achieved and students have invested themselves in learning.

Reflect and Respond

Of what educational benefit is dance inquiry? Could comprehensive, substantive dance education for all students give us a populace who

- can dance and think of dance as an expressive art,
- appreciate dances of diverse cultures and are aware of dance and the arts around them,
- recognize notable dance works and their creators as part of their cultural literacy, and
- value the creative process in dance and make informed judgments about dance works?

Main Rules for In-Class Inquiry

1. Keep an attitude of inquiry alive in your classroom.
2. Tailor instruction to fit individuals.
3. Ask questions after students possess enough knowledge and experiences to think deeply and respond insightfully.
4. Be a teacher–facilitator—more of a "scribe on the side" than a "sage on the stage."

What an Inquiry Approach *Is*

- An invitation to explore dance
- A way to make students responsible for their own learning
- A way to make students accountable to teacher-specified outcomes
- A collaborative venture for you and your students, because discovery fuels all involved

What an Inquiry Approach *Does*

- Allows students to learn at their own rate
- Makes dance accessible to everyone, not just to dancers
- Applies to all dance styles
- Involves students in their own creative work
- Fosters active thinking while actively moving

What an Inquiry Approach *Uses*

- Rubrics to keep students on task and within the parameters of the inquiry
- Open-ended questions to stimulate thought and discussion
- Multiple outcomes within a given structure so learning is not always the same for all students
- Student research
- Varied types and extent of investigation at different ages
- Natural links to other aspects of dance as well as other arts and subjects
- Cogent questions to ask students

What an Inquiry Approach *Needs*

- Active participants
- Higher-order thinking and action
- Criteria for success (assessment standards) and authentic ways to measure them

What an Inquiry Approach *Relies On*

- Positive direction, motivation, and supervision from a teacher
- Background of facts-based knowledge
- Student energy and motivation to achieve results

What an Inquiry Approach Is *Not*

- Centered on rote learning
- Chaotically conducted or weakly constructed
- Resistant to facts-based learning
- 100 percent creative exploration
- Focused entirely on research and questioning
- Focused only on product
- Spent teaching dances choreographed by an adult and performed by students
- Dependent on teacher lecture to communicate most information

Using an Inquiry Approach Is *Not*

- For teachers who are looking for the easiest way to teach
- For teachers who seek the same, simultaneous outcomes for all students
- For teachers who expect one right answer per question
- For teachers who want to control every aspect of learning
- For teachers who mostly want to test with objective instruments (such as multiple choice and true–false)

Professional Works as a Basis for Inquiry

Major dance works model what this art form can do and must create sources for worthwhile inquiry and creative stimulation. Dance—the "other visual art"—has to be seen as well as done. Show a professional example to generate aesthetic inquiry during a unit. Most units include at least one dance work—or with younger learners, a section of work viewed in smaller bites called slices—to demonstrate specifically what is to be learned. The work opens the door for aesthetic inquiry. If you think showing an example takes too much time away from dancing activity, think again. For example, you can pop in a cued video or DVD for 3 minutes during a lesson and accomplish all this and more:

- Use and expand dance vocabulary
- Draw students in to the work
- Increase ability to read dance
- Identify dance elements
- See professionals demonstrate fundamentals of performing and model technique
- Introduce a choreographer
- Introduce a great work of dance
- Respond to the aesthetics of the work
- Inquire into what the dancer is expressing and how well
- Relate the work to what students are learning about dancing and performing
- Build a context for what is being studied
- Show what dance in all its many facets is and communicates across cultures

Model for students what performance dance looks like. That gives them a standard of excellence to strive for. If your students only see dance on MTV, that's what they think dance is. How will they know dance is art unless you feed them a slice of professional dance along with their regular movement activities in dance?

You have an opportunity to deepen aesthetic perception and help students achieve many national dance standards by inquiring into professional work. You can use the work to provide the unit's main focal point, to serve as context for another aspect of the unit, to establish a unit's theme, to demonstrate a dance style, or to unify several unit goals—or all of these. Showing professional work is how you introduce the stars of our discipline and its prime movers (the dancers, choreographers, dance critics, dance historians, composers for dance, set designers, and aestheticians).

Reasons to Adopt an Inquiry Approach

Personal investigation is more intrinsically satisfying than being told what to do or think, and inquiry is the key to personal investigation.

Inquiry is adaptable to all dance topics. It suits contemporary choreography and historical master works alike. Inquiry gives you significant interaction between content and instruction but also significant personal interaction between student and content. Students often uncover content that you don't know. Such active inquiry is important to arts education because

- there are far more facts and information than you can teach in a limited school day,
- learning how to learn is vitally important to academic and artistic growth,
- students need to learn how to recognize what is worth pursuing and what is not,
- different modes of inquiry diversify learning skills,
- inquiry neither holds back the gifted learner nor penalizes a methodical learner,
- memorizing isolated facts is of little educational value (as are tests that measure them), and
- "telling" is not "teaching."

To facilitate inquiry is one way you can shine the spotlight on others. See page 112 to find the "Main Rules for In-Class Inquiry" and frequently asked questions on inquiry.

Reflect and Respond

How do you react to this quotation?

"Winning students over to the idea that they must be responsible for their own learning is not always easy. Students often see the teacher's authority as absolute and think that their role in life and learning is to comply passively with authority. It is all the harder when parents believe that it is the responsibility of teachers to tell students what to do. In fact, life is easier for both teachers and students when higher-ups do the thinking." (Peterson 1992, p. 121)

Excerpts adapted, by permission, from *Life in a crowded place: Making a learning community*, by Ralph Peterson. Published by Heineman, a division of Reed Elsevier, Inc., Portsmouth, NH, 1992.

Overview of the Dance Cornerstone Curriculum Framework

A curriculum exists to meet the needs of children. A sequential framework for educational dance shows how to organize a comprehensive and substantive cornerstone curriculum to that end. It takes all of what students should know and do and breaks it out so that you may implement various parts in a systematic, sequential fashion. It enables you to minimize gaps and maximize instructed learning for children. A framework gives you perspectives, rather than being prescriptive, by showing you a structure of the whole.

Frameworks encapsulate what is to be accomplished in dance to inform the development of units of study. They start with goals and objectives to identify the big picture. They also help you determine

- what to include in dance,
- how one concept or skill develops over time,
- the scope and the sequence of a full curriculum,
- which skills come before and after the ones you are to teach, and
- significant experiences that enable students to meet national standards.

Whereas standards give desired student achievement levels, a framework describes the incremental development of content, concepts, and skills that get students to that level. Taken in total, a framework reveals the scope; in increments, it reveals the sequence. A framework identifies the significant content and concepts in dance. It breaks down a concept to show how you develop each aspect of dance over time. A framework lists the significant content, which you then weigh against student readiness (chapter 4) and achievement standards (chapter 2). It's up to you to correlate all of these elements for the educational benefit of the child.

A framework doesn't tell you how to teach or exact particulars to teach—these are left to your judgment. A framework shows what to teach to keep students growing and achieving.

Outline of the Dance Cornerstone Curriculum Framework

The dance framework in part II helps you plan content from the four dance cornerstones (4Cs). It guides a complete standards-oriented dance curriculum. The "Overall Outline of the DCC Framework" (following) shows a thumbnail sketch of what a cornerstone curriculum includes. It parallels the layout of the main headings of the **Dance Cornerstone Curriculum (DCC) Framework,** which is detailed in chapters 6 through 9.

Show dance works so your students see what performance quality and performed dance works look like.

Overall Outline of the DCC Framework

I. Dancing and Performing
    > Understanding and using the dancing elements
    > Using dance vocabularies

II. Creating and Composing
    > Experimenting
    > Using composition and choreography
    > Polishing and sharing creations

III. Knowing History, Culture, and Context
    > Experiencing dance as universal expression
    > Understanding the significance of dance
    > Preserving dance for future generations

IV. Analyzing and Critiquing
    > Responding to dance
    > Critiquing dance

Adapted from Lunt and McCutchen, 1995, with permission of the South Carolina Department of Education.

Organization and Use of the Dance Cornerstone Curriculum Framework

The DCC Framework is in three parts. The first part (goals and objectives) identifies the desired outcomes. The second part (content outline) breaks goals and objectives into an outline. The third part breaks the outline into a suggested developmental sequence detailed later in the chapter for K-2, 3-5, 6-8, and 9-12.

Look at the dance framework in each of the cornerstone chapters (chapters 6-9). The framework is printed in four sections—one per cornerstone, thus one per chapter. Put them together to get the whole DCC Framework. Keep in mind the relatedness of all cornerstones even as you emphasize one cornerstone. Rarely do you teach an entire dance unit with material or experiences from one lone cornerstone—even a unit emphasizing technique. Much is said about the cornerstones as interrelated and symbiotic.

The DCC Framework—like dance education itself—fuses kinesthetic learning with cognitive. So the framework's content and skills often are inseparable. All cornerstones in some way address the kin-aesthetic moving art of dance—by dancing it, creating it, learning about it, or responding to it.

You may wonder why the sequential framework breaks elementary out into kindergarten through grade 2 (primary), grades 3 through 5 (elementary), grades 6 through 8 (middle school), and grades 9 through 12 (high school) instead of the grade clusters like the national standards (K-4, 5-8, and 9-12). There are several reasons.

1. K-2, 3-5, 6-8, and 9-12 more closely parallel the grade levels you are likely to teach.

2. Child development changes rapidly between K and 4, therefore what is appropriate for elementary is too advanced for primary ages.

3. It is more instructive to you as you plan curriculum to see the developmental breakout in four increments rather than three.

Also, remember that NSDEs and NAEP inform curriculum but are not a curriculum. Their primary purpose is to ensure student accountability (tests and measurements of achievement) in seven broad categories. They keep the curriculum on target, but their purpose is not to present a systematic, sequential curriculum design. Also, NSDEs are grouped as they are to coincide with NAEP's national assessment of all academic subjects in the United States.

Chapters 6 through 9 each present one-fourth of the total framework, so you can do the following:

- Look down each vertical graded column of each cornerstone to find the depth of experience that makes your content substantive.

- Follow each concept horizontally across the page to see how it increases in complexity so as to be sequential.

- Look among cornerstones to find their relationships.

- Follow one age group through all cornerstones to see what students are to learn and do.

Design your own dance units to accomplish as many of the items as possible. Construct lessons to emphasize aesthetics and to build context and relationships (i.e., aesthetically driven and contextually coherent). Also remember that each cornerstone is a method of inquiry into dance. Part II of this book zeros in on the content and concepts of each cornerstone. See figure 1.1 (page 16) to be reminded of the six defining characteristics of educational dance so you can see how the 6DCs are all carried forward in the DCC Framework. Also see in figure 5.4 the schematic for teaching the cornerstones.

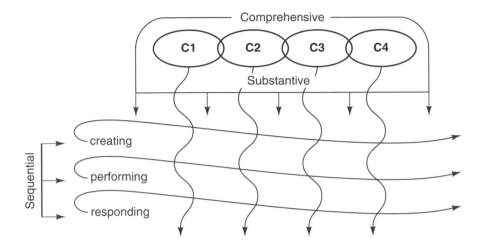

FIGURE 5.4 Comprehensive content is broad and includes all four cornerstones. Substantive content is deep, delving into important details in each cornerstone. Sequential content progresses uninterrupted year by year, moving students through a complete program in all four cornerstones. Complete content is all of the above delivered in a way that is aesthetically driven, contextually coherent, and inquiry based.

How the Cornerstones Lay the Foundation for Accountability

NSDEs hold dance specialists accountable for student achievement. OTLS hold school districts accountable to provide quality dance programs so that students can achieve to standard.

To optimize aesthetic education in dance, you have to teach more than standards. You need more content depth than standards can address or assess. Immersion in goals and objectives from the cornerstone's methods of inquiry prepares students to meet and exceed national standards as well as to acquire an aesthetic education in dance (above the national measure). For example, to operate a class on standards alone is one-sided. Without goals and objectives, you don't know where your class is going or how to get your students there. Standards only tell you what students have to know and be able to do at the end of grades 4, 8, and 12.

Comparing Cornerstones and Standards

The cornerstones are the basis for constructing curriculum. Standards are the basis for keeping the curriculum on track and measuring student achievement.

Thus, a quality educational dance curriculum is more standards *oriented* than standards *driven*.

Reflect and Respond

Why is it essential to use a written, sequential curriculum? Apply Dobbs' description of visual art curriculum to dance from chapter 1.

> "A written, sequential curriculum facilitates competent instruction and cumulative learning. As youngsters move through their school years they require an art program that reinforces and builds rather than merely repeats the previous lessons. . . . Students encounter art in a progressively more complex and sophisticated manner. Its goal is for youngsters to experience 12 years of art education, not to have 1 year of art education 12 times." (Dobbs 1989, p. 10)

Do you think a written sequential curriculum is too structured and too closely resembles the way other subject areas are organized? Or do you believe well-designed curricula can be used as blueprints and resources to be mediated by informed teaching? Do you believe that within a comprehensive curriculum blueprint, endless possibilities exist to expand children's imaginations and develop their divergent problem-solving skills? Do you believe that a written sequential curriculum can stretch the teacher's instructional technique as well as expand student learning (Dobbs 1989)?

Without a sequential curriculum, a student gets an incomplete and incoherent dance education from grade to grade. Learning smatterings of dance is not enough. You need cornerstones and standards to write dance curriculum. You also need their combined synergy to get students to where they need to be in dance. Make instruction more complex year to year, and keep students on track measuring student achievement by the standards. Notice how the cornerstones parallel the national standards. A complete cornerstone curriculum, however, exceeds standards. The two measures coexist compatibly.

You must respond to internally driven student needs while your students achieve desired outcomes based on external criteria (i.e., national and state standards). Standards keep arts education on track, but professionals like you operationalize the standards in the classroom so they meet student needs.

Standards are isolated measurements. If standards were to drive curriculum it would be like teaching for a short-answer test rather than teaching for understanding in context. Curriculum needs to be progressive and systematically link new skills to previous ones. It should be designed so that student objectives build one on another. To design a substantive aesthetic education curriculum in dance requires overlaying content and methods of inquiry from all cornerstones, as shown in figure 5.5.

Using Goals and Objectives

Your cornerstone goals and objectives lay out what is necessary for students to achieve in a quality aesthetic education in dance. Cornerstone goals and objectives keep you focused on the ends, on the desired outcomes. Studies show the most important strategy for student achievement is to emphasize goals and objectives so students know where they are going and what is expected of them (Wong and Wong 1998). All goals and objectives combine to educate students broadly and deeply in dance while ensuring they achieve national standards.

Goals and content standards are the abstract vision statements, the big picture. On the other hand, objectives and achievement standards turn the big picture into a concrete, working, action plan for the student. You mobilize all four. Goals drive the boat, whereas objectives tell you where you are going, and the NSDEs are the rudder that keeps students on course.

Write goals based on what you deem important for your students to know (such as the concepts

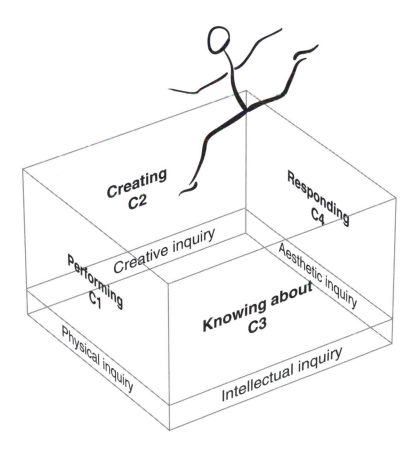

FIGURE 5.5 Cornerstones are the foundation of an aesthetic education in dance. Although national standards are revised and changed periodically, the cornerstones are a constant foundation for the dance discipline.

117

listed in the DCC Framework and enduring understandings). Write goals that incorporate NSDE content standards to ensure that you are going in the right direction. Then at specific grade levels, you design the concrete experiences to get students moving toward the goals by way of the objectives. Because your goals point the way, your objectives become the actual pathways to get students to their goals. But never lose sight of the NSDE achievement standards to make sure your students achieve what they need and according to expectations.

Thus, whereas goals and objectives derive from best practices (from the cornerstones, and from the six defining characteristics), the NSDEs keep them on course. Be sure to incorporate all NSDE achievement standards into learning objectives. And as you put learning objectives into practice, design units that best serve your own students and their needs (see chapter 4).

Information in the frameworks in the next four chapters suggests what students should learn in primary, elementary, middle, and high school. This information will help you identify, select, and develop content and then write long-range plans with cornerstone goals and objectives, which you later use for ongoing assessment (see chapter 12).

Before you enter the world of goals, objectives, and national standards, you should know their general differences and similarities (also see figure 5.6).

Objectives (internal) and NSDE achievement standards (external) are personal and measurable. Meeting several objectives moves students toward achieving a larger goal (internal). Meeting several NSDE achievement standards moves students toward achieving an NSDE content standard (external).

Goals statements follow a student all the way through school in K-12. Goals are broad outcomes, and they are for all grades. An example of a goal is, "To use the body as an instrument of expression." This goal applies to kindergartners as well as high school students, so it follows a child through school.

Objectives break goals down into specific student outcomes. Objectives start with a verb—a Bloom's verb as you will see in chapter 9. An example of an objective for high school is, "Students are expected to *demonstrate (verb)* the ability to land safely and softly with an articulated foot." (Of course, this is one aspect of our goal, "To use the body as an instrument of expression.")

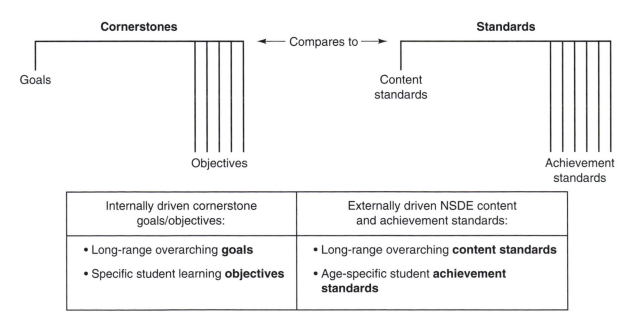

FIGURE 5.6 Similarities of goals and content standards: They encompass all grades, K-12. They identify long-range vision, overall destination, and the desired outcomes. Incorporate content standards into your goals rather than rely on national content standards. Similarities of objectives and achievement standards: They describe what students are to accomplish. Incorporate achievement standards into learning objectives rather than rely solely on them.

118

Objectives drive curriculum. Objectives require you to list the acceptable evidence that demonstrates a student achieved. Therefore, they list criteria by which you measure students' achievement. For example, eighth grade criteria for the previous objective might be as follows:

- Criteria 1: Landing is through the ball of the foot to the heel with both heels on the floor.
- Criteria 2: The torso is vertical, is erect, and does not collapse on landing.
- Criteria 3: There is plié at the end of the landing with heels on the floor.

In the upcoming framework, look for these specifics:

- Each cornerstone states its main goals and objectives.
- There are more cornerstone goals than national content standards.
- The cornerstone goals take the artistic discipline of dance forward.
- The goals incorporate the NSDEs and carry them forward.
- The objectives are similar to the national achievement standards and carry them forward.

- The objectives are general so you can adapt them as appropriate for differing ages and stages of development.

Notice the real difference, which is the substance of the framework itself. As methods of inquiry, the four cornerstones ensure that standards-oriented educational dance is

- comprehensive,
- substantive,
- sequential,
- aesthetically driven,
- contextually coherent, and
- inquiry based.

National Standards

The cornerstones parallel the national standards and assessments, as shown in table 5.3.

NSDEs 1 through 5 include the substantive dance content from the cornerstones, whereas 6 and 7 relate to dance across the curriculum and to healthy living. All are vital, but the main substance of the dance discipline is mostly in the first five NSDEs.

 How does each cornerstone carry out the national standards and prepare students for the upcoming NAEP assessments?

Table 5.3 Cornerstones Parallel the National Standards and Assessments

Systems	National Standards for Dance Education (NSDEs)	National assessment of the NSDEs by National Assessment of Educational Progress (NAEP)	The four dance cornerstones	General divisions: dancing dance making dance appreciating
Dance content	1. Dance elements and movement skills	Performing (with creating, responding)	Cornerstone 1 (as dancer)	Dancing
	2. Choreographic principles and processes	Creating (with performing, responding)	Cornerstone 2 (as choreographer)	Dance making
	3. Creative and critical thinking	Creating, responding (with performing)	Cornerstones 2 and 4 (all)	Appreciating, dance making
	4. Expressing and communicating	Creating, performing, responding	Cornerstones 2 and 4 (as dance critic)	Appreciating
	5. History and cultures	Responding (with performing)	Cornerstone 3 (as dance historian and anthropologist)	Appreciating
Related issues	6. Healthy lifestyle 7. Crossing curriculum	Links to all	Links to Cornerstone 1 Links to all four cornerstones	

C1: DANCING AND PERFORMING (CHAPTER 6)

- Relation to NAEP: "Performing"
- Relation to NSDEs: 1 and 6
  > 1. "Identifying and demonstrating movement elements and skills in performing."
  > 6. "Making connections between dance and healthful living."

C2: CREATING AND COMPOSING (CHAPTER 7)

- Relation to NAEP: "Creating"
- Relation to NSDEs: 2, 3, and 4
  > 2. "Understanding choreographic principles, processes, and structures."
  > 3. "Understanding dance as a way to create and communicate meaning."
  > 4. "Applying and demonstrating critical and creative thinking skills in dance."

C3: KNOWING HISTORY, CULTURE, AND CONTEXT (CHAPTER 8)

- Relation to NAEP: "Responding"
- Relation to NSDEs: 5 and 7
  > 5. "Demonstrating and understanding dance in various cultures and historical periods."
  > 7. "Making connections between dance and other disciplines."

C4: ANALYZING AND CRITIQUING (CHAPTER 9)

- Relation to NAEP: "Responding"
- Relation to NSDEs: 3, 4, 5, 6, and 7
  > 3. "Understanding dance as a way to create and communicate meaning."
  > 4. "Applying and demonstrating critical and creative thinking skills in dance."
  > 5. "Demonstrating and understanding dance in various cultures and historical periods."
  > 6. "Making connections between dance and healthful living."
  > 7. "Making connections between dance and other disciplines."

This material is reprinted from the *National Standards for Dance Education and the Opportunity-to-Learn Standards in Dance Education* with permission of the National Dance Association (NDA). The original source may be purchased from: National Dance Association, 1900 Association Drive, Reston, VA 20191-1599.

The Dance Standards were completed as part of the Arts Standards, a project developed by the Consortium of National Arts Education Associations (American Alliance for Theatre & Education, Music Educators National Conference, National Arts Education Association & National Dance Association). This project was under the guidance of the National Committee for Standards in the Arts, & prepared under a grant from the U.S. Dept. of Education, the National Endowment for the Arts and the National Endowment for the Humanities.

NDA is an association of the American Alliance for Health, Physical Education, Recreation & Dance (AAHPERD).

The national standards expect world-class instruction in the arts. NSDEs authenticate what must happen for satisfactory student accomplishment in educational dance. Its writers envisioned an aesthetically driven program that is comprehensive, substantive, and sequential. Table 5.3 is a grid by which to cross-reference the NSDEs, the NAEP, and the cornerstones. Even though word headings differ, note the compatible intent. This chart points out the main parallels. You will discover others the longer you work with it. As you study the chart, keep the following in mind:

- State standards are legislative law (mandated), but national standards are voluntary at this time.
- NAEP assessments measure the national world-class standards (sample in chapter 12).
- If state standards are more stringent than national, *always use the higher standards.*

Achieving Five National Dance Standards With Four Cornerstones

The first five national content standards describe specific dance mastery in creating, performing, knowing about, and responding to dance. A cornerstone curriculum prepares students at all grade levels to meet or exceed them (NSDEs 1-5).

Best practice expects that dance be on equal footing with the other arts. That means students achieve a complete education in dance:

1. The full dance discipline (history, criticism, dance making, dancing)
2. All the arts processes (creating, performing, and responding)
3. Connections to all arts disciplines (art, music, and theatre)

Achieving Two National Dance Standards With Teaching Strategies

The last two content standards, 6 and 7, connect and extend dance to other areas:

6. "Making connections between dance and healthful living."
7. "Making connections between dance and other disciplines."

To put dance in a context of healthy living personalizes it even more as you relate dance to daily living, injury prevention, care of the body, nutrition, and rest. Let dance meet students where they live to affect both health and artistic choices they make every day. Encourage lifelong learners who are personally comfortable with dance as well as literate in dance.

Students achieve the last standard differently—by relating dance to other areas. Ask them to relate dance to other arts and academics, to technology, and to contemporary issues and ideas to bring dance into other worlds. You don't have to compromise artistic standards in dance by including standards or content from other disciplines. Use them to enhance dance (see chapter 10 for details). Especially pursue interdisciplinary collaborations across the arts.

Reflect and Respond

What Would You Advise?

A high school curriculum was designed strictly from NSDEs. It was sparse and disjointed. There was not enough continuity to build coherence or enough sequence to hold the curriculum together. Instruction was divided into isolated areas so dance happened with mostly unrelated lessons: dance history as one unit, composition as another, and technique in jazz and ballet. Although the curriculum addressed the standards, it lacked grade-by-grade development for experiences or concepts. This curriculum fell short of a quality aesthetic education for the students.

If you were hired as the teacher, how would you revise the dance curriculum to achieve the learning goals and objectives of a 6DC cornerstone curriculum?

Questions to Ponder

1. Do you have to be experienced to facilitate dance inquiry?
2. Are students always seated (and not moving) when inquiring?
3. How do the four cornerstones become both content and method of inquiry?
4. Why should a curriculum exhibit the six characteristics to be complete?
5. Why are the national standards sometimes used to build curriculum? Why is a cornerstone approach more systematic, more student centered, and more contextually coherent?
6. Of what benefit are the four cornerstones to a child's education?
7. How does "chain reactioning" organically integrate learning and help build context?
8. How does this information add to or reshape your Statements of Belief (as explained in the Introduction)?
9. An inquiry approach activates higher-order thinking skills that involve the senses and the self. How can you use this approach to increase creative work? Re-creative work?

Rich Resources

Go to your State Department of Education Web site and download its Fine Arts Standards and Curriculum Framework. Compare it with the Dance Cornerstone Curriculum Framework and the 6DC Cornerstone Model. Always teach to the higher standard and cover everything mandated by your state's arts education legislative law.

Clarifying the Content of K-12 Educational Dance

The Cornerstones

Dancing and Performing

 Cornerstone 1

"Art is communication spoken by man for humanity in a language raised above the everyday happening."

—Mary Wigman (Sorell 1975, p. 17)

This chapter features Cornerstone 1—one of the four educational dance cornerstones. The chapter focuses on all key aspects of dancing and performing. It integrates the kinesthetic and aesthetic skills of dancing with the cognitive aspects of perceiving, thinking, and processing of dancing. The dancing and performing cornerstone makes artistic use of the dance elements—space, time, energy and dynamics, relationship—and applies them to the element of body as it becomes the instrument of expression in dance. The substance of this cornerstone aligns with national standards. Cornerstone 1 is outlined in detail to help you build curriculum, write goals and objectives, and design assessments. It may be the starting place for, the main focus of, or one part of a unit of study, but it is a necessary part of each unit. A sequential K-12 curriculum framework is presented. Cornerstone 1 enrolls the learner as dancer and performer.

Relation to National Standards and Beyond

Cornerstone 1 brings dance into a child's life. By dancing and performing, children integrate body, mind, and spirit in a vital form of human expression. Dancing is not merely an activity; it is a language learned. This language, based on centuries of human expression, is refined to an art of personal expression in educational dance. As we examine the main aspects of dancing and performing, let's not lose sight of how important this kinesthetic dimension is to children's development. It brings so much of the world alive to them: whether it's structured dance, like folk dance, or creative dance, like improvisation. Dancing is a very personal and integral way to learn. As you increase students' movement vocabulary and begin to emphasize technique, recall how important dance is to your life and strive to find dynamic ways to bring it to life for others.

This cornerstone features the "performing" aspect of NAEP's report card. It fleshes out NSDE 1: *Identifying and demonstrating movement elements and skills in performing dance.* It also addresses part of NSDE 3: *Understand dance as a way to . . . communicate meaning.* Before going further, read all the NSDE's achievement standards listed for Content Standard 1 (i.e., grades K-4, 5-8, and 9-12).

Dance study and courses that prepare you to teach this cornerstone: Technique, Dance Company, Diversity in Dance, Repertory, Labanalysis, Creative Dance, Anatomy and Kinesiology for the Dancer, and Dance Injuries furnish you the actual content and knowledge base from which to teach this cornerstone, as well as to dance and perform.

Overview of This Cornerstone

The main foci of Cornerstone 1 are the dance elements, the many dance vocabularies, dance technique, and performance skills.

The elements of body, space, time, energy and dynamics, and relationship (BSTERs) are basic to dance—all dance, all styles. The body is the instrument of expression; space, time, energy and dynamics, and relationships are the context in which the body instrument moves. These five categories of dance elements comprise dance, as surely as the chemical elements in the physical world comprise

all matter. And all domains interact simultaneously while dancing: the cognitive, affective, and psychomotor.

Indeed, dance itself requires all elements: *body* movement and motion in *space* for a certain *time,* modulating *energy and dynamics,* and in *relationship* to something or to someone. Although all elements are called on when we dance, to teach them you must bring them to awareness so students learn to use each one. Their artful use totally depends on how you convey them and how thoroughly they permeate your teaching.

C1 must be included in all units. Specific units of study may begin from C1: the point of entry, the inspiration for, or the emphasis of the unit. C1 inquires into technique and also uses visual samples of some of professional dance works. It enriches a unit whether it is the focus of the unit's content or the support for its experiences.

A student's artful use of each dance element depends on how you convey them and how thoroughly they permeate your teaching.

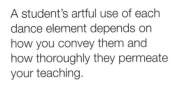

Some mega-ideas and concepts from this cornerstone follow:

1. The body is the instrument and movement is the medium of expression in dance.

2. The dance elements (BSTERs) are the basis of all dance and dancing.

3. Dance technique develops specialized skills for dance performers.

4. Dance technique merges anatomically sound movement principles with dance artistry.

5. Professional dancers are proficient athletes and consummate artists.

6. There are numerous languages of dance, such as kinetic, aesthetic, linguistic, and notational.

7. Gestures, postures, and steps are vitally important in dance.

8. Dance can be read and written using notation.

Goals and Objectives of Cornerstone 1

C1's portion of the Dance Cornerstone Curriculum (DCC) Framework is presented in three parts in this chapter: The first part (goals and objectives) shows the big picture. The second part (content outline) breaks goals and objectives into an outline. The third part extends the outline into a developmental sequence detailed at the end of the chapter for K-2, 3-5, 6-8, and 9-12. Parts 1 and 2 are both comprehensive and substantive. Part 3 is comprehensive, substantive, and sequential.

These suggested K-12 goals and objectives help you fully convey Cornerstone 1. See the many ways they prepare students to meet or exceed the NSDE achievement standards—especially for content standard 1.

Goal 1: To activate the dance elements and the body as an instrument of expression

1.0 Desired outcomes: To show kinesthetic awareness of the body in motion and in stillness. To master dance concepts and techniques through a multisensory integration of the dance elements.

Learning objectives: The student will

1.1 Demonstrate use of the body as an instrument of artistic expression (one BSTER).

> Demonstrate knowledge and use of anatomically and kinesiologically sound movement principles for safety, efficiency, and longevity as a dancer.

> Demonstrate increasing levels of coordination, balance, stamina, elevation, and technique appropriate to age and development.

1.2 Use the key elements related to space (one BSTER).

1.3 Use the key elements of time and timing in dance (one BSTER).

1.4 Use the key elements of energy, dynamic qualities, and force (one BSTER).

1.5 Use the key elements of dance relationships (one BSTER).

Goal 2: To use universally accepted dance vocabulary, terminology, and symbols of dance

2.0 Desired outcomes: To understand dance terms and vocabularies by moving (kinetic) and speaking (conceptual) dance languages.

Learning objectives: The student will

2.1 Use BSTER vocabulary.

> Demonstrate increased ability to kinaesthetically articulate the BSTER vocabulary and also use it as a universal dance vocabulary (with which to communicate about dance).

> Demonstrate developmentally appropriate movement and use a conceptual vocabulary based on the dance elements.

> Use general dance terms and specific dance terminology appropriate to the dance style.

2.2 Use anatomical vocabulary to identify parts of human anatomy.

2.3 Use aesthetic principles of design as vocabulary and in practice.

2.4 Use Laban-based symbols in movement such as Language of Dance, Labanotation, or motif writing.

Adapted from Lunt and McCutchen, 1995, with permission of the South Carolina Department of Education.

Content Outline

Use this framework outline to guide comprehensive long-term curriculum planning. The outline headings are developed into a framework at the end of the chapter (page 156).

Teach so students learn to dance efficiently, safely, and with awareness of themselves and others. The desired outcome is to develop a body instrument that can communicate meaning at all ages and develop an articulate body in advanced work in high school.

Goal 1.0 Understanding and Using the Dance Elements

Objective 1.1 The Body as Instrument of Expression

1.1a Body awareness (body parts, alignment, placement)

1.1b Body actions and moves (swing, sway, curl, twist, turn, vibrate, shake, extend)

1.1c Body shape (curved, twisted, angular, combination)

1.1d Traveling and locomotor movements

1.1e Body relationships

1.1f Moving in control (control of speed, weight, transfer, balance, motor coordination, efficiency)

1.1g Body and self-image

1.1h Safe use of the body

1.1i Balance

1.1j Mobility and stability

1.1k Core muscle strength and awareness of center

1.1l Development of main technique areas

1.1m Turning

1.1n Functional anatomy and kinesiology

1.1o Body conditioning

1.1p Gestures and postures

1.1q Transfers into movement

Objective 1.2 Space

1.2a General–personal, negative–positive

1.2b Level (high, middle, low)

1.2c Direction (forward, backward, diagonal, sideways)

1.2d Pathway (air–floor, indirect–direct, straight–curved, other)

1.2e Focus (inward, outward)

1.2f Range (amplitude, size, distance)

1.2g Body design (symmetrical, asymmetrical, organic, geometric)

1.2h Shaping (still, axial, locomotor)

1.2i Combinations of space components (level, direction, focus, facing)

1.2j Elevation

1.2k Circling (centrifugal, centripetal)

Objective 1.3 Time

1.3a Accurate rhythmic response (pulse, underlying beat, accent, downbeat, 3/4 and 4/4 meter, syncopation)

1.3b Meter

1.3c Tempo (sudden–sustained, rate of speed)

1.3d Form (sequence, beginning–middle–ending, AB, ABA, round, rondo)

1.3e Phrase (metric movement phrases, breath, kinetic)

1.3f Duration

1.3g Polyrhythms and resultant rhythms

1.3h Nonmetered music and soundscape

1.3i Accompaniment for movement

1.3j Immediacy

Objective 1.4 Energy and Dynamics

1.4a Laban's effort actions

1.4b Flow (bound, free)

1.4c Dynamic accent

1.4d Motivation (peripheral, central)

1.4e Qualities (vibratory, swinging, collapsing, suspension, percussive, sustained)

1.4f Graining

1.4g Expressivity

Objective 1.5 Relationship

1.5a Relationship of one body part to another

1.5b Relationship to other dancers

1.5c Relationship to an object or prop

1.5d Relationship to the other dance elements

1.5e Relationship to accompaniment

Goal 2.0 Dance Vocabularies

Objective 2.1 Movement Vocabulary

2.1a   Step vocabulary (locomotor steps)

2.1b   Universal dance vocabulary (UDV, the dance elements)

2.1c   Classical ballet terminology

2.1d   Stylistic vocabulary

Objective 2.2 Anatomical Terms

2.2a   Bones and joints

2.2b   Muscles

Objective 2.3 Aesthetic Vocabulary

2.3a   Artistic principles of design (choreography)

2.3b   Artistic performance qualities

Objective 2.4 Laban-Based Vocabulary

2.4a   Motif writing and Language of Dance (LOD)

2.4b   Labanotation

2.4c   Labanalysis (LMA)

2.4d   Laban terminology

Adapted from Lunt and McCutchen, 1995, with permission of the South Carolina Department of Education.

Cornerstone 1 Thumbprint (C1)

Students gain dancing proficiency and performance skills. They learn to use the element categories of the body in space with varying time, dynamics, and relationships. They learn to dance safely and with artistic integrity. They continually refine movement quality to increase performance skills.

- **K-2:** Students in kindergarten through grade 2 gain control of their movements in such a way as to dance. They learn the basic skills and use the dance elements. They become confident about dancing. They bring kinetic, visual, auditory, and tactile experiences into dance.

- **3-5:** Students in grades 3 through 5 refine basic skills and increase range of motion in the element categories of space and time. Dynamic range is extended. They start developing technical skills. They learn to remember and refine sequences.

- **6-8:** Students in grades 6 through 8 refine dance technique skills with increased kinesthetic and aesthetic awareness.

- **9-12:** Students in grades 9 through 12 refine dance technique and skills through increasing kinesthetic and aesthetic awareness. They apply principles of kinesiology to moving. They learn to dance confidently and safely.

Adapted with permission of the South Carolina Department of Education, © 1993.

See the details in the sequential framework at the end of the chapter.

Artful Use of the Dance Elements

As a dance specialist, you are also a movement educator who teaches students to move, think, process, and perceive with the body in space. You teach the art of motion. But first you create a strong BSTER matrix to support all the artistic processes in educational dance (ED). You convey the dance elements as the basic building blocks for dance technique and the superstructure of all kinesthetically based dance lessons. You see that students acquire an elements movement vocabulary in dance and that it becomes the linguistic and conceptual vocabulary with which to communicate about dance.

Dance Motion and Movement

Dance is movement, but not all movement is dance. You need to convey the difference so students distinguish between movement and dance. Not all dance teachers know how to do this.

A main aesthetic question is, "When does movement become dance?" or "What must happen to transform movement into dance?" What important questions. The answer is partly a matter of intention and partly a matter of aesthetics. First, a moving body must *intend* to make dance movement instead of a functional, utilitarian movement. This intent to communicate something through dance is part of what transforms regular movement into dance. There must also be a conscious effort to link movements together rhythmically, spatially, bodily, dynamically, and artfully so they connect and flow together in order for the movement to transform into dance.

Alwin Nikolais taught students to transform raw movement into expressions of motion in order to be dance. Whereas movement calls attention to itself, motion calls attention to its results. He differentiated that one *does* movement but one *creates* motion as an artful expression according to how movement is done.

Lay the groundwork for recognizing motion in elementary school. Then by middle and high school, students will be able to differentiate between the movement and motion. Show how motion intensifies movement to communicate why a movement is done. For example, when you stir a pot, the *motion* (effect) is stirring but the *movement* (cause) is arm circles. Try both. See the difference between stirring and arm circles. See how motion expresses an intent out of the raw material of movement.

From there, go on to demonstrate how dance motion expresses an artistic intent. For example, repeat a movement sequence of the right arm going from place-low to forward-middle to side-middle and stopping there. First, show how the arm can merely move to the side with no point of view or expressive intention. Then, the same movement can be transformed into motion if it conveys the intention of opening space and communicating that to an audience. Therefore, motional intent does more to communicate than plain movement. Movement causes motion. Motion is the result of movement intentionally used to communicate. *This is part of the kin-aesthetics of dance.* Start this level of aesthetic differentiation in upper middle school and refine it in high school.

- Perform the right arm sequence as *movement:* Go from place-low to end side-middle.

- Perform the action as *motion 1:* Use the arm with the intent to stir up the space as it goes and see the space it disrupts along the way.

- Perform the action as *motion 2:* Emphasize the fingertips drawing a curved peripheral **line** in space.

- Perform the action as *motion 3:* Use the arm as though the hand pushes back a curtain to open up a space to look into.

Do you show the arm itself moving (movement) or do you show the motion the arm creates as it moves? In each case, the emphasis of the motion changes. This is the artistic **transformation** that undergirds dance. Yet this subtle distinction must be first taught and then emphasized. This is how one learns to artfully distinguish and express a variety of intentions within the same basic movement. See figure 6.1.

Dance Motion as Kin-Aesthetics

You have already met the term "kin-aesthetics" in chapter 5. Let's further define it. Three concepts play into the art of dancing and are the root words of *kin-aesthetics:*

- *Kinetic* is moving.
- *Kinesthetic* is the way one perceives or feels movement in one's body.
- *Aesthetics* is the philosophy of beauty and rarity.

By merging these three concepts (and words), we pinpoint the kind of aesthetic motion that we must create to transform mere movement into expressive dance movement. This is the art of dance. Kin-aesthetics merge all three: kinetic + kinesthetic + aesthetics. Dancing and performing, or Cornerstone 1 (C1), is all kin-aesthetics. Kin-aesthetic movement is about dancing with attention to the qualitative aesthetic choices one makes. Kin-aesthetic education helps dancers and performers integrate the aesthetics of **intentional motion** into their dancing.

Elevate the commonplace to the aesthetic by emphasizing intent and dynamics of movement. It is up to you to give students clear guidance about how to achieve kin-aesthetic motion and then expect them to rise to that level. This is not just for the big kids. All ages can respond kin-aesthetically at their level of progression within realistic limits (see chapter 4). Ensure that all students get the intrinsic satisfaction of achieving their best. High-quality performance brings much satisfaction to someone who is learning to dance. *You only get the quality you teach and expect.*

Set aesthetic standards and then consistently show students samples of professional kin-aesthetic quality (video or live) to motivate them. Use samples to inspire students to better articulate and express themselves and to set higher expectations. Demonstrate high standards yourself. Your students' success depends on having these models, standards, and your expertise. For example, if the only music you hear in primary school is the music you make, you don't know what fine music quality sounds like. Likewise, if you only see your own peer dances, you don't yet envision what quality dance is. Therefore, use major works as exemplars.

130

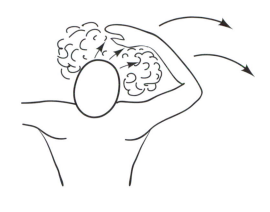

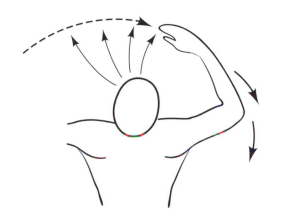

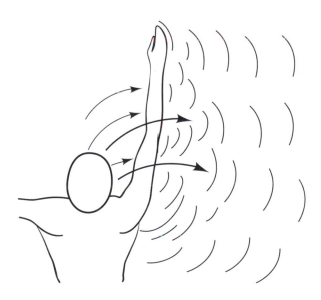

FIGURE 6.1   Dance kinesthetics: One movement can have many meanings depending on how the mover intends to communicate with it. Motion 1 stirs up the space; motion 2 draws a line in space; motion 3 opens up a space to look into.

Dance Elements: The Basis of All Dance

Dance is about a body in motion that takes place in space, in time, with an expenditure of energy and dynamics and that happens in relationship to dancers, objects, space, and time. These five dance element categories are the basis for all dance learning and instruction.

What Are the Basic Dance Elements?

The dance elements are not body, space, time, energy and dynamics, and relationship (BSTER). The dance elements are the subcategories of the BSTERs. Although some books call the main categories the elements, this book refers to the BSTER subcategories as the "dance elements." See figure 6.2 to find the dance elements under their main categories:

- The study of the dancing body is the study of how the body moves, what moves, what its actions are, and how it balances, aligns, supports itself, elevates, and travels. **These are the body elements.**

- The study of the body in space is the study of shape, direction, level, size, place, focus, pathway, elevation, and distance. **These are the space elements.**

- The study of the body in time includes tempo and duration, rhythms and accents, patterns, and metered and nonmetered approaches to movement. **These are the time elements.**

- The study of body dynamics delineates the way energy is expended and directed through the body in dance: Body dynamics expose the level of exertion, the weight of the movement, and the muscular strength used. Body dynamics are about the sheer physicality of the movement. Body dynamics modulate the intensity of the move and the quality and texture of the motion (such as its smoothness or percussiveness). Body dynamics adjust how much effort is expended and how the directional flow of energy is released (i.e., energy that streams out of the body or energy that is pulled in toward the center of the torso). **These are the energy elements.**

- The study of relationship makes dancers conscious of the dance environment and what or who shares their space. Learners attune to being near to and moving in relation to something (e.g., another dancer, a group of dancers, a prop, an inanimate object, a set, an audience, or the open stage or space itself). In solos, relationships are different; they may take the form of one body part to another, oneself in space, oneself in time or to accompaniment, or oneself and the mood of the work. **These are the relationship elements.**

Use of the Dance Elements

The body, space, time, energy and dynamics, and relationship are present in every movement. You can't move without them. The artistic challenges are to

- master each one independently in dance,
- emphasize different ones at different times, and
- relate one to another for total performance integration.

The dance elements are basic content and vocabulary for every dance class—whether technique, criticism, analysis, composition, improvisation, world concert dance, folk dance, creative dance, notation, somatics, or kinesiology. Purposefully relate the body elements to all other elements so learners are able to dance and perform with

- a more aware body and a more alert mind,
- a more perceptive, integrated self,
- a conceptual vocabulary with which to communicate about dance, and
- a versatile movement vocabulary.

Educational dance totally depends on the understanding and use of the dance elements. They are the alphabet of dance movements, which when mastered, help us to dance and to speak of dance. They are at once our movement vocabulary and our conceptual vocabulary (i.e., we "move" the elements and we "think" with the elements). Teach students to embody the elements so they do both simultaneously (i.e., bodythink). Also see that learners use this vocabulary to describe dance as they respond thoughtfully to dance works. BSTER is our educational dance vocabulary.

Feature the dance elements as either the main focus of or auxiliary helper for all dance units. In this way the elements are always part of the vocabulary and content. By fourth grade, start shaping the elements into some dance techniques. Make the elements analytical tools of dance and the basic vocabulary of dance (see chapter 9).

Figure 6.2 identifies the dance elements. Study them. Teach them. Make them clear so students apply the elements as both linguistic vocabulary and movement concept. Refer to this chart throughout the book. Aim to teach all elements by the end of third grade so students can spend the remaining years refining and integrating them.

Relationship—The Fifth Element

Dancers practice relationship by moving with others, relating to another dancer onstage, or sometimes relating to the space itself (as in a solo dancer leaping across the space or someone pushing to seemingly compress the space). Here, teach how the body relates to something broader than its own self dancing. Emphasize relatedness to keep dance from becoming too "me" oriented in the classroom.

Relationship is not always listed as a separate element because it can be part of all the other element categories—body, space, time, and energy and dynamics. Yet it deserves emphasis to

- ensure that relationships are not overlooked,
- stress ways that relationship should be artfully used in dance as art,
- remind us to foster psychosocial growth through dance,
- underscore the important role of relationship in dance, and
- lay groundwork for duets, trios, and groups.

Relationships are perceptions. The dancing body perceives

- through space (in a spatial relationship to something),
- through time (in rhythmic or time relationships, in call and response relationship, or one after another as in a canon or a round), and
- through dynamics and energy (in amount of force exerted on another dancer, matching movement qualities, contrasting textures and qualities).

Relationships between academic disciplines and dance should always enlarge the study of dance as well as bring other academic studies new life (see chapter 10).

Dance Intention

For dance to be expressive, it must have something to express: a point of view, an intent. Otherwise, it

Categories	Elements	Descriptions
Body	Body parts	Inner: muscles, bones, joints, heart, lungs (breath) Outer: head, shoulders, arms, hands, fingers, back, rib cage, hips, legs, feet, toes, face
	Body moves	Stretch, bend, twist, circle, rise, collapse, swing, sway, turn
	Body actions	Action verbs, such as expanding, twirling, slithering, spinning, skimming, lifting, extending, melting. Note: There are more than this, but this is a start.
	Steps	Walk, run, leap, hop, jump, gallop, skip, slide
	Balance	Stability, especially with limited supports
	Supports	Parts of the body in contact with the floor
	Turns	Axial turns, turns through space, full and partial turns
	Body shaping	An internal focus on shaping the body from the core more than the distal, but including the distal in the total shape and focusing on the use of the whole spine
	Stasis	Dynamic stillness by which the body enlivens time, space, and energy
Space	Shape	Body design in space, positive and negative space
	Level	High, middle, low, rising, sinking
	Direction	Forward, backward, up, diagonal, down, sideways, turning; direct–indirect
	Size (range)	Large–small, growing–shrinking
	Place	In one place, on the spot, through space
	Focus	Direction of gaze, object of eye contact
	Pathway	Curved, straight, zigzag, irregular, circular
	Elevation	Degree of height achieved; going into the air and landing
	Distance	Amount of space covered
Energy	Textures	Sharp–smooth, rigid–soft, bumpy, malleable, squishy, fluffy, prickly; other adjectives and adverbs
	Force	Amount of energy expended in any movement, exertion
	Dynamics	Modulation of energy so that certain moves are emphasized more than others
	Weight	Heavy–light, indulging–fighting, yield–resist, fine touch–firm touch
	Strength	Tight–loose, strong–weak
	Flow	Free-flowing, bound, balanced, the way energy is released, firm, fine
	Attack	Dynamics of the way a phrase begins
	Qualities	Swinging, suspending, collapsing, vibrating, percussive, sustained
	Laban's Basic Effort Actions	Combining the efforts in space, time, and weight: Punch, float, glide, slash, wring, dab, flick, press

FIGURE 6.2 The dance elements.

FIGURE 6.2   [**continued**]

Categories	Elements	Descriptions
Time	Accent	Dynamic point of emphasis
	Beat	Underlying pulse
	Duration	Long, short, sudden, sustained; length of time overall
	Tempo	Speed: quickness or slowness
	Rhythms	Time signature; varying pulses and patterns in time
	Metered or nonmetered	Metered: measured; organized around time signatures, patterns of timing Nonmetered: not according to a set timing pattern; organic
	Accelerate–decelerate	Speeding up and slowing down
	Phrasing	The way movements are grouped together for coherence
	Pattern	Combinations, sequences
Relationship	A body part to another A person to another A person to an object A person to a group One group to another A person to stage and properties A person to performance space A person to production elements (sets, music, lights, costume, mood) Across the curriculum	

has little value to others; it is just for self. Although there is value in the sheer personal enjoyment of dance and for dance as a purely self-indulgent activity, the stage is not the place for that. Educational dance performance should take students beyond pure self-indulgence to craft. Here they learn to craft an expression to share with others. Educational dance intends to communicate to others. It has an intent, a purpose, an expressive aim.

Help students learn to share dance with others: Teach them how to shape an idea into body movement, how to put it in space, how to extend it out in time and with dynamic changes. Teach this when they explore, improvise, and compose. Help them find suitable concepts to perform (i.e., not too lofty, grandiose, trite, or esoteric, and not just shaking their "booty" to look sexy). Then help your students conceptualize what they want to convey with the dance. Show them how to translate that intent into

a decipherable movement expression to share. Help them in three ways:

- Give them simple, manageable topics for composition
- Give them critical feedback so they grow increasingly articulate and expressive
- Show them enough dance works that they get a sense of what dance can communicate

Before students learn the craft of movement composition—which is to shape and express a coherent concept—they mostly dance from the heart. This is good! Dancing should be from the heart. That's where our aesthetic sense lives. In these pure heartfelt dance expressions you find all the seeds that students also need to eventually make clear statements and compositions. Not all dance must be shaped, but you are in the business of teaching

How Do You Define Dance?

Try using the dance elements to create your own defining statements about dance.

For example, "Dance is motion created by the body in space with the intent to dance, by consciously using time and energy and dynamics to create motion. The body instrument builds relationships to itself, to others, and to objects in space."

through of the head from the line of the spine; not the ability to place the arms and legs in opposition, but the understanding of the torque of the body. The way in which the energy of the body is used is important, the way in which the contraction and release of muscles are used to stretch, bend, twist, circle, lift, fall, and step in time and space. Such uses of the body in relation to the physical laws of motion on earth, inertia, momentum, gravity, and reaction, are the basics that are clarified for children and by children in a technique class. (1984, p. 2)

Extending the Elements

The dance elements are the basis of dance, so make the dance elements basic to your teaching of all four dance cornerstones. Embody each element to get a well-rounded grasp of human movement possibilities. Fully conceptualize each dance element by experiencing it in the body. Explore with the elements, create and critique with them, write about them, discuss them, and reflect on their use.

The BSTER elements also translate across disciplines. Look back to figure 6.2 at "Body actions." There are actually thousands of words we could list if there were space. Why don't you supply a list of action verbs in addition to the elements listed? Ask students to move in a manner suggested by the meaning of these additional verbs to extend the use of body actions. Discover how full of dynamic action words (i.e., verbs) on grade-level word lists are. Get students to explore these words in movement and then structure them into dances. Kids may not realize they are actually building linguistic vocabulary and expanding cognitively because of the **organic** way the body and mind simultaneously experience these word concepts. To learn words with the entire nervous system (which includes the brain) strengthens word-meaning comprehension for most students. Indeed, those strong in kinesthetic intelligence (one of the MIs) need to embody some word concepts to fully comprehend them. For example, distinguishing between the earth's rotation (on its axis) and its revolution (around the sun) may be too abstract to grasp until students physically do the movements to see how they differ according to their space and relationship (turn vs. circle). Embodiment is shown to improve reading comprehension, a goal of all education. Note: Write these danceable words where they can be seen by all and refer to them often to reinforce visual learners (see chapter 4).

compositional skills to help students clearly convey intent. Sometimes that intent is moving in space. Sometimes it is relationship to an object or an idea. Sometimes it is showing the virtuosity of the human body. There are many intentions and thus many points of view to take in dance (see chapter 7).

Teach performers to emphasize what they want the audience to see. It is similar to voice inflection when one speaks. Speak clearly. Dance clearly. Accent the important points. Draw attention to a relationship by focusing full attention and intention on it (the relationship). Teach them to articulate what they intend. For example, is the dance emphasizing a body part in space, the total body in space, or a featured body part in contrast to another one? Is it none of those? Is it meant to contrast time or rhythm? What is its intent? If intent is unclear, the performer isn't yet communicating. Show all ages how to place emphasis so what they "say" in dance can be "read" by an audience.

By third grade, teach how body focus clarifies intent. Distinguish between internal body focus or **graining** (which heightens performer awareness of intent and enhances communication) and external visual focus such as on a part of the body or a place in space (which calls audience attention there).

Compare focus with the way visual artists use line, color, and shape to draw the eye to certain places in a painting or sculpture. Because dance requires an intention to be dance, it must be clear and not muddled. Teach students to project a point of view by their dynamic emphases, the relationships they show, and their clear focus on communicating it.

Mary Joyce reminds us:

What matters is not how high the leg will go, but how the leg goes; not the pointed toe, but the stretch from the center; not a specific use of the head, but the follow-

Explore the myriad ways dancers use stillness (the element, **stasis**). Explore stillness that is so alive it seemingly explodes in all directions and stillness that holds energized shapes in space; stillness that drops a curtain so the dancer is detached and unnoticed (focus is inward) and stillness that stays connected to what is going on around him (focus is purposeful and outwardly directed). Find small stillness between phrases in some dances, still moments that occur during call and response, and stillness as counterpoint to action that can build suspense.

Adverbs and prepositions dance well. Students learn in Language Arts that adverbs describe how one moves (e.g., sharply, quickly, largely). To explore these words in dance helps dancers find movement qualities (of how they do an action) and increase subtlety and variety. Use adverbs to increase dance texturing. Improvising with adverbs is a favorite of all ages.

Prepositions clarify how one thing relates to another (e.g., with, between, around, beside, over, near, under, through, toward). Prepositions help pre-K students sense relationships of their own body parts to each other. To move with prepositions also helps students relate to the world. Prepositions are satisfying for all ages to explore—even adults.

"Word dances" are staples in the dance diet. Elementary students also like to make up their own words for composition, like "whooshey" and "upping and downing." Occasionally brainstorm new words for creating dances.

Another way to extend the dance elements is to select word pairs that relate to space, time, and energy. Such word pairs extend the palette of movement ideas into infinity. Figures 6.3, 6.4, and 6.5 give examples. Select pairs for the ages you teach.

Space

To move concepts in space, such as the contrasting word pairs in figure 6.3, help realize general educational goals as well as dance goals. Processing these concepts by moving enables learners to transfer and apply understanding across disciplines.

Time

Concepts of time and timing, such as those in figure 6.4, help learners transfer timing concepts to music and math as well as comprehend essential relationships to the world.

Energy and Dynamics

Dynamics—the lifeblood of dance—are sometimes overlooked in teaching. Dynamics bring texture to

Vertical–horizontal	Enormous–minuscule
Short–tall	Gigantic–little
Narrow–wide	Gather–scatter
Constricted–extended	Enlarge–decrease
Up–down	Earth oriented–airborne
Here–there	In place–through space
Curved–straight	Ascending–descending
Circular–linear	Positive–negative
Direct–indirect	General–personal
Symmetry–asymmetry	Ebb–flow
Round–flat	Meet–part
Expand–contract	Forward–backward

FIGURE 6.3 Space word pairs.

Sudden–sustained	Enduring–transient
Quickly–slowly	All at once–gradually
Late–early	Accelerate–decelerate
Fast–slow	Metered–nonmetered
Long–short	Rhythmic–arrhythmic
Swift–prolonged	Staccato–largo or smooth
Stop–go	Then–now
Pause–continue	Short–long
Now–later	Broken–continuous
Currently–subsequently	Interrupted–uninterrupted
Past–future	Rapidamente–lentamente (Spanish)
Suddenly–slowly	Rapidement–lentement (French)
Allegro–andante	
Presto–largo	

FIGURE 6.4 Time word pairs.

movement. Choreographers and performers who overlook dynamics have dances that are flat and uninteresting. Bodies (i.e., dancers as well as everyday bodies) need to modulate energy and feel its flow so energy is channeled and expended purposefully. Introduce dynamics to first graders, and then keep it active in artistic work through high school. Use figure 6.5 to explore the gradations of dynamics within each pair as well as the stark opposites.

Contrast word pairs at all ages. Incorporate words from K-12 grade-level vocabulary lists. Continue to develop dynamics by seeking additional sophisticated word pairs that high school students will find

Heavy–light	**Lively**–inactive
Strong–soft	**Vigorous**–inert
Sharp–smooth	**Bound**–free
Accented–unaccented	**Tension**–relaxation
Emphasize–minimize	**Contract**–release
Powerful–weak	**Press**–release
Energetic–sluggish	**Fortissimo**–pianissimo
Vibrant–dull	**Agudo**–liso (Spanish)
Active–passive	**Push**–hold
Spirited–lethargic	**Pull**–push
Intense–subdued	

FIGURE 6.5   Dynamics word pairs. Boldfaced words show learners the stronger qualities.

challenging. Add word pairs related to energy and science (e.g., anatomy and astronomy). Encourage students to create textural dynamic words of their own imagination, like *squiggly, squooshed,* or *squeezy.* Create word pairs on charts appropriate to your age level. Also create word pairs on flash cards. Let students create with word pairs (and choose the word pairs used).

Vocabulary Systems Used in Dance

Use the BSTER elements to teach dance languages. The elements—basic to all dancing—are also basic to understanding dance, creating dances, and responding to dance. These languages are both kinesthetic and cognitive: learned in motion and used linguistically to put dance into words for thinking and speaking.

Dance specialists benefit from knowing Laban Movement Analysis (LMA), which translates actions into describable concepts related specifically to body, shape, space, and effort.

Teach the dance elements (figure 6.2), which include Laban terminology, as basic dance vocabulary. They apply to all dance styles. Whereas other dance terminology identifies specific moves (such as a rond de jambe en l'air or a chaînés turn), it does not describe how a movement is performed—only what is performed. Therefore, the qualitative and expressive explanations still must come from the BSTER–Laban vocabulary. The Laban vocabulary particularly helps you explain the quality of a move, its spacing and timing attributes, its dynamic range,

its expressive quality, and its relationship to something (such as music, partner, space, dynamics).

Movement Vocabulary

It would seem obvious that humans learn to dance by moving. Reading books or visiting Web sites about dance won't do it. Experiencing dancing is the only way to learn dance. Yet too often teachers stop movement to overexplain a movement concept when what is actually needed is more opportunity to apply it, to get the concept into the body, so learners practice motional skills and concepts. Each concept takes time to work itself into the body. It also takes time to work itself into the bodymind. To keep students moving and improving, "coach on the side" (sometimes "*coax* on the side"). There are only a few instances where you must stop a group to clarify a concept: when they totally misunderstood or did not grasp it, or for a management or safety issue. Instead, get students to apply the concept as you explain. Help them acquire a movement vocabulary! Aim to make movement the main mode of learning for the greatest percentage of time possible in studio classes. Thereby get students directly into purposeful, on-task skills development and concept practice. Get them dancing.

If you can do the following while you are dancing, you know that it is the act of dancing (instead of listening) that integrates the cognitive, **affective,** and psychomotor domains.

- Assimilate information and be cognitively engaged
- Make sense of time and space
- Understand and find your full dynamic range
- Make strategic, discriminating choices
- Express ideas nonverbally and communicate feelings

Become adept at assessing students' skill to dance the language and clearly communicate while they move. Then you won't lose time assessing skills. Also use your observations to remediate and refine their movement vocabulary while they move (see chapter 12).

Universal Dance Vocabulary

Educational dance requires dance specialists to use a universally understood dance vocabulary that transcends styles and transfers across grade levels. The dance elements furnish such a universal dance vocabulary (UDV). Think of the dance elements as a **taxonomy** that classifies the main structural elements of dance. Use this taxonomy so all ages can classify and describe dance to better understand its parts (BSTER) and their relationship to each other. Stay consistent with terms because you are teaching an unfamiliar language. Once learned, language transfers with students from grade to grade as they change dance specialists, relocate, or take NAEP assessments.

The way you convey the vocabulary of dance also determines how learners perceive their own dancing bodies. Start the elements (UDV) concepts early so they are integrated into the bodymind early on. Call on the UDV to express concepts in movement terms, to refine technique, to explain dance sequences, and to give movement exploration cues. Because the UDV is the underlying movement language of dance technique, one's dancing skill either directly or indirectly depends on how well each person applies the dance elements vocabulary. Again, consistency

is key, and in schools with more than one dance specialist, take time at the beginning of the year to codify how all of you use the terms.

Eventually use all UDV terms, but introduce them as the concept matches the child's ability to comprehend and apply it (Bloom's second and third levels). Incorporate Laban terms into the UDV so all of dance's taxonomic terms (elements) coexist in your teaching as easily as they do in the dance elements chart (figure 6.2) and the framework. If your background in Laban is insufficient to allow you to use all Laban terms throughout K-12, at least find a way to introduce them by high school. For example, consider the dance element "shape." To a first grader, the element of shape is simply body shape and shaping. As he advances grade levels his use of shape evolves with greater complexity (e.g., symmetrical and asymmetrical shape). By high school he is ready to grasp some of the different shadings of the Laban concepts of shape.

Step Vocabulary (Locomotor Steps)

Make locomotor steps part of the UDV. Teach them so everyone has basic traveling skills as well as a common language by which to understand them. Use the understanding of the basic locomotor steps to decode step patterns and rhythms as well as to understand movement directions and weight placement. Build on these foundations to develop advanced dance technique and footwork skills.

Teach the five basic locomotor steps, which are basic to all other steps. They are usually executed with an even rhythm.

- Walk: transfer of one's weight from one foot to another with a constant support by the floor
- Run: transfer of one's weight from one foot to another with a brief moment of nonsupport
- Leap: transfer of one's weight from one foot to another with a longer time of nonsupport
- Jump: movement from both feet into the air (nonsupport) and landing
- Hop: movement from support on only one foot into the air and landing (same foot)

These steps are basic skills for all students. Note that a hop requires more balance and coordination than the others.

Next teach the three compound locomotor steps, which are created out of the five basic steps. They go into the air (nonsupported) and are executed in a syncopated, uneven rhythm.

Relationship elements create a context for eventually relating to and collaborating with partners in performance.

- Skip: a walk (step) and hop in a dotted rhythmic pattern alternating leading sides
- Slide: a walk (step) and close going sideward (actually a leap by definition but not by familiarity) in a dotted rhythmic pattern with the same foot leading and the other chasing
- Gallop: a walk (step) and close going forward (actually a leap by definition but not by familiarity) in a dotted rhythmic pattern with the same foot leading and the other chasing

Next build up to other complex locomotor steps that combine the original five even-rhythm steps in various ways:

- Grapevine: step sideways, alternating the crossing forward and back of the trailing foot (walking, running, leaping)
- Schottische: step together, step, hop (walking or running)
- Triplets: 123, 123, 123, 123, which alternates leading foot
- Two-step: step-together-step-hold timed in a quick, quick, slow pattern

Classical Ballet Terminology

In addition to the UDV, classical ballet terminology is internationally codified. Using ballet terms greatly simplifies giving direction as well as writing lesson plans and choreographic notations. Sandra Noll Hammond (1984) said, "Because ballet was first nurtured in the royal courts and academies of France, French became the language of the art. All ballet exercises, steps, body positions, and movement directions have French names. These names are in use in every ballet studio the world over, although such wide diffusion has led to certain differences, even corruption in specific terminology" (p. 54).

Using correct ballet terms and precise movements is mandatory to developing students who know ballet basics and speak correct ballet terminology. Although you don't need advanced performance proficiency to teach beginning ballet, you must execute the technique correctly and use all terms accurately.

Stylistic Vocabulary

Each style of dance has specific terminology. In addition to teaching the UDV, teach every age some of the stylistic vocabulary to identify specific movements. For example, *jatis, adavus,* and *mudras* are part of Bharata Natyam terms; *layouts* and *jazz squares* are basic to jazz; *contract–release* and *fall–recovery* are part of modern terminology. But also remember, in educational dance, style vocabulary is secondary to the dance elements vocabulary (UDV). It is more beneficial to learn the basics of movement and descriptive language than it is to learn stylistic terminology. Stylistic vocabulary becomes more important to advanced classes, gifted and talented dance students, and those seeking professional careers in dance than it is to students studying dance in the basic curriculum. (See chapter 12 for discussions of the three levels of educational priority.)

Anatomy Terms and Vocabulary

Begin using some of the major anatomical terms with kindergartners. Develop grade by grade. Lay the groundwork in elementary school for what is to follow. This is the age when language is easily assimilated. Incorporate kinesiology and the correct use of anatomical terms by middle and high school. Apply body science to movement concepts in real, personal ways related to placement, movement initiations, and using support from different body systems (e.g., muscular, skeletal, nervous, circulatory, respiratory).

Incorporate **somatics** into technique class to develop a feel for muscle engagement and joint initiation. Teach efficient use of the working, dancing body to ensure correct technique without strain and to reduce risk of injury. Teach students how to apply anatomy and some kinesiology to prevent dance injuries and support rehabilitation of injuries.

Learn about kinesiology—specifically *dance kinesiology*—so you can use dance to teach anatomy and kinesiology, and use anatomy and kinesiology to teach dance. And be sure to get it right! For example, there is no anatomical waist or waist muscle. Waist is a clothing term for the place we wear a belt or sash. Alexander Technique says, "To teach about a waist is a waste!" Instead, ask students to activate muscles according to the movements being executed. For example, a dance contraction doesn't activate stomach muscles. Stomach muscles are part of the internal digestive system that involuntarily contract and expand to digest food in the stomach organ. Abdominal muscles or abs are those which you voluntarily engage and contract to round the spine in dance—but they are not stomach muscles.

Teach the body as a moving anatomical organism. Name the body system or muscle group you are working and what initiates movement—is it the bones, muscles, joints, organs, circulatory system, or nervous system? Help students learn about the body and how to move it, and increase their perception of the way the body functions as an organism as well as an instrument of expression. Help students differentiate the body systems that support particular movement qualities.

Use an anatomical chart as a teaching aid at all grade levels. Teach students that anatomy is vital to learning about the dancing body. For example, at Halloween, I introduce bones and joints to kindergarteners through a goofy-looking skeleton called George who is hinged and moveable in some of the right places. Kids like to see him move and learn to hinge in two dimensions like he does. Then they gleefully learn how some of their joints move three dimensionally, different from George's. He whimsically introduces 4- and 5-year-olds to moving joints before they get to first grade, where I use a smaller three-dimensional skeletal model. By third grade we refer to anatomical charts to identify large muscles we are engaging. Anatomy study becomes more complex through middle school so that in high school advanced classes we use anatomical charts and flexible-ligament models of knees and ankle joints to refine somatic awareness of distal and core or central initiations in technique class.

Aesthetic Vocabulary

Although the UDV helps you describe, analyze, interpret, and evaluate the movement in dance elements terms, you must also use the **principles of design (PODs)** to evaluate and create aesthetically cohesive choreography. Create and critique with the same principles of design vocabulary that the other fine arts use (i.e., the literary arts, the visual arts, the performing arts, and the design arts). The 10 principles of design are unity, variety, repetition, contrast, sequence, balance, transition, harmony, climax, and proportion (see chapter 7 for details). Teach them as your main aesthetic vocabulary to judge artistic quality.

Make this aesthetic vocabulary central to your aesthetically driven curriculum. Understanding the principles of design moves students through the stages of progression in their aesthetic–artistic growth (see chapter 4). Apply the PODs so students perceive and articulate aesthetic–artistic quality in choreography. The more thoroughly upper elementary through high school students grasp the concepts behind this aesthetic vocabulary (PODs), the more astute they become at critiquing and choreographing (i.e., responding and creating).

To fully operationalize the aesthetic vocabulary, you must also call on the BSTERs (UDV). A functional aesthetic vocabulary requires both. Teach the principles of design to increase perception of artistic quality; teach the BSTER elements to describe, analyze, and explain how the principles of design function in a work. That is, the language of body, space, time, energy and dynamics, and relationship describes how to apply the principles of design. For example:

- "The way he changes *levels* (BSTER) all the way through creates a motif for the dance. The level changes add *variety* (PODs) to the *shapes in space* (BSTER) and hold the dance together (*unity*—a POD term)."
- "The way she uses *isolated body parts* (BSTER) adds interest to the middle section. It's effective because it *contrasts* to what comes before and after it (PODs)."

Laban Terminology

Labanotation symbols are basic codes to analyze and identify movement. Teach Labanotation as a basic form of dance literacy. Visually reinforce the study of the dance elements and bring them alive by using the "direction," "duration," and "level" symbols (the three most basic notation symbols) on a large movement notation scale drawn on a chart and laid directly on the floor or projected on the wall. Use these symbols to teach pathways, step patterns, weight placement, and time duration. One enduring understanding is that dance can be read and written using dance notation. So teach that there is a notation system (just as for music), and movement scores can be read, much like music scores. Use Labanotation symbols both ways in your classroom: to write your own dance patterns and to read and reconstruct dance patterns from a score.

A specific shorthand emanates from Labanotation that has broad application in education as an introduction to Labanotation literacy as well as for its own value: **motif writing,** also called Language of Dance (LOD). LOD uses the same symbol system (although not *all* the same symbols) as Labanotation. But LOD stimulates the creative process by suggesting movement concepts. Labanotation symbols, on the other hand, help one to analyze movements in time and space and to record dance moves with more specificity. Although motif writing–LOD is quite useful to the creative process and an option for learning about notation, don't discount the benefit of also teaching the basic

Labanotation symbols themselves so learners learn to place them on a movement scale. If students learn to recognize these symbols from an early age, then by middle school they will be able to read and write basic phrases from the two center columns (the weight columns and arm columns). LabanWriter software is available for the middle and high school classroom. (Refer to chapter 10's section on math for figures of Labanotation scores.)

The symbol languages (i.e., notation systems) offer the student a different lens through which to observe, discuss, interpret, understand, and communicate about movement. By using LOD symbols (see figure 6.6), you offer a common base of information that can inspire various creative responses from warm-up to dance making. Labanotation enables dance to be written for reconstruction in complete detail with accuracy in the reproduction. Both LOD and Labanotation give us another common dance vocabulary. Mix them according to what is best suited for age-level comprehension and application.

The Language of Dance Center publishes resources to assist you in knowing and using LOD with students. They even publish a series, *The Adventures of Klig and Gop,* to introduce an alphabet symbol language to primary age children. Learn to use these notation symbols to accompany studio work in order to reinforce your concepts as well as to help students analyze types of movement. This symbol language develops a concrete way to code and analyze movement. Keep it an ongoing part of your classroom work so that students evolve an effective way to read and write basic movement concepts.

Use Laban Movement Analysis (LMA) in dance. The terms *spoking, arcing,* and *carving* have become basic language for body actions in space. LMA brings a richness to dance, especially at the secondary level (middle and high school). Laban terminology is both basic and descriptive, therefore it is extremely important to know and use. This text incorporates it into the taxonomy of the dance elements (see figure 6.2).

Dance Technique and Skill Development

Technique means *skill*. Skill is secondary only to joy in dance. Both Mary Joyce and Elizabeth Hayes, two stellar dance educators, emphatically remind us that each dance lesson must have as one of its goals to enable students to experience the joy of dancing. Remember this, especially as you teach technique. Everyone needs to know what it feels like to dance fully. Mary Joyce shares an example:

> All great teachers inspire their students to reach the feeling state. I watched an exciting and inspirational teacher aim at the feeling state directly. She was presenting a series of high-energy movements across the floor with quick changes of direction and a spin. She exhorted her students to let go in order to go farther, to take a risk, to increase their range. She wanted them to find the delight inherent in the flow of movement. She kept repeating with great force, "I want you to know what dancing *feels* like." Such "feeling" is sometimes called "pure dance." It has nothing to do with overlaid emotional feeling. The feeling is caused by the action.
>
> Children instinctively know the joy that exists when movement uses their total selves. They must find this totality each time they come to class. They must know it is there for them to seek and find in each exercise. (Joyce 1984, p. 14)

Dance technique (i.e., skill) starts around grade 4 and develops through grade 12. (Review chapter 4's stages of progression.) Teach technique as a way for dancers to find inner motivation for movement. Start techniques at the age when children are able to internally connect with themselves. Internal technique is what manifests externally, not vice versa.

Joyce (1984) surveyed dancers between ages 10 and 16 to learn at what age they were first aware of feeling their muscles working correctly or incorrectly. She found without exception that at age 8 or 9, fourth grade students understand for the first time what teachers mean by instructions such as "turning out from the hips" or "elongating the back." The children said that before that, they imitated the teacher and did what they thought was right, but they did not move from an internally motivated intention. When Joyce asked students what helped them best learn to move from their own internal motivation, she found it to be a combination of several factors. Among the factors was having the teacher give them direct tactile feedback to show them how to move correctly. Another factor was to be given enough time to repeat a movement until they were able to feel it themselves. Other factors included being shown a movement instead of merely being told how to do it and having teachers create word pictures to describe desired movement. They indicated it also helped to have a mirror to see how a movement or shape looked and to get tactile feedback from a hard surface (such as a wall or floor) to sense the use of their backs.

The prime actions and concepts of which movement is comprised are as follows:

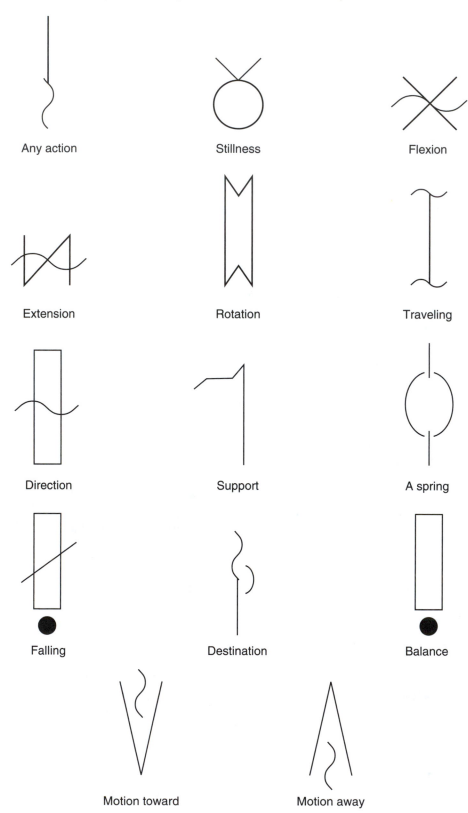

FIGURE 6.6 The movement alphabet of the Language of Dance (LOD) is applicable to all ages.

Emphasis Points for Teaching Dance Technique

Make movement vital to each unit of study in dance. Even if a student practices long and tries hard, she will not develop good dance habits and strong technique on her own. It is your duty to instill the right habits that increase dance technique. In general, emphasize first anatomically correct body alignment and somatically sound movement principles so that after years of good foundations students begin to correctly place themselves. Then add the artistic elements. Whether students are static or moving, ensure that they develop early movement habits that grow into sound techniques. Emphasize safety, aesthetics, and joy at all ages.

As a prelude to teaching dance technique, make sure students use all BSTER elements and are thoroughly rooted in the creative processes. Teach dance as a way to make significant expressive statements. Promote the body as an instrument of expression more than of show. Rely less on repetitive drills and sequences so that students do more than merely memorize sequences and dance routines. Take seriously your students' need to feel a solid sense of center as well as skeletal alignment and functionality. Your goal is to get students to use their developing sense of somatics and aesthetics soon after they gain their sense of center, alignment, muscular strength, and skeletal–joint functionality.

Somatic Awareness

Foster somatic (internally felt) awareness, whether one is mobile or stable, by using appropriate anatomical images (of internal spatial relationships), which depend on your thorough knowledge of anatomy and kinesiology and your understanding of somatic work (e.g., Body-Mind Centering, Bartenieff Fundamentals, Feldenkrais, Alexander technique). Also use gentle tactile reinforcement. Let's look at ways to develop somatic awareness to increase kin-aesthetic technique for the sake of both mobility and stability in dance for all ages.

Mobility and Stability   Mobility and stability are hallmarks of good dance technique. **Mobility** is about articulating the body, increasing its range of movement in the joints, and moving in and through space. **Stability** is about alignment, finding one's center, balancing on different support bases, and using bilateral and cross-lateral support to maintain body equilibrium. Develop an acute awareness of the body instrument in motion and in stillness. Both are aspects of somatic awareness. (Principles for stability support principles for mobility.)

Always ensure that somatic (physical) development emphasizes the aesthetic (see chapter 4). Articulate the body and increase its range of movement to clarify expression. Teach technique for the purpose of improving the art of dance. Emphasize the artistic integration of body and mind while dancing (mobile and stable) by

- increasing somatic awareness in the joints and musculature,
- establishing the core–distal relationships that increase mobility and stability,
- using the nervous system to sharpen quick response,
- increasing joint articulation and overall flexibility, and
- using the physics of movement to maintain center and balance for stability.

Keep attentive to the aesthetics of motion (mobility) by

- refining dancers' timing, use of spatial dimensions, and texturing movement;
- modulating dynamic range and attack of movement;
- clarifying movement qualities, focus, and accent to add artistic quality; and
- strengthening leg muscles for the power and endurance needed for elevations, lifts, and strength moves.

Diligently give aesthetic feedback. Assess what students grasp internally by what shows up externally. For example, notice how an insight, image, or correction is internalized and embodied or articulated in motion. Constantly look for evidence that students are incorporating aesthetic feedback across the floor, at the barre, and during creative dance exploration. Notice how full-out they improvise. Look for nuance—slight adjustments to the way they execute a plié or maintain center. Rudolf Laban says, "Don't think of back bending but think, 'Your head leads into a backward arc towards the floor. . . !' Space imagination (intent) and spatial power (spatial initiation) enliven the muscle, transmit the intent to move skeletal parts" (Bartenieff and Lewis 1980, p. 229).

Use **Bartenieff Fundamentals** to develop core body awareness. (Bartenieff Fundamentals are a series of preparatory exercises developed by Laban's protégé, Irmgard Bartenieff, to stress the diagonal connection between the upper and lower body as well as spatial motivation to initiate movements.) Use them to increase core–distal relationships that support and maximize mobility and stability of the upper and lower body. Help students organically connect through **homologous, homolateral,** and **cross-lateral** patterns of movement supported on the floor and upright. (For more information, see the work of Bonnie Bainbridge Cohen cited in Rich Resources.)

Somatic Inquiry Emphasize personal somatic awareness as a natural part of inquiry. Also foster it by the corrections you give middle and high school students. Correct gently but insistently. Some corrections avert injury, whereas others create beauty of form. Consistently reinforce desirable dance technique and explain why. Prepare learners to habituate these skills and to take ownership for their own technique development. Perpetuate artistic inquiry in dance. Also motivate your students to direct their own inquiry to make positive self-corrections by asking themselves questions such as these:

- "What am I doing with my arms?"
- "How is this accomplished most successfully *for me?*"

Lightness and lift are aesthetic aspects to acquire, as are extensions of the torso and limbs.

- "What is leading?"
- "Is my weight centered?"
- "Are my knees over my toes?"
- "How is this comment related to what I already know?"
- "What initiates this battement?"
- "How long can I hold this balance? Where is the center point for me?"

Tactile Reinforcement Aids Somatic Awareness We as humans, and we as dancers, need to sense our own body boundaries. It is through the skin surface that we tactilely experience who we are. Our skin surface, our volume, and our depth and dimensions all become clearer in relation to certain objects, a wall, the floor, or someone else's touch. Somatic hands-on work is so helpful because of the tactile feedback. It is a way for the body to get direct information that is available no other way.

In technique class, making postural alignment and placement corrections by tactile reinforcement (i.e., gentle touch with clear instructional intent) communicates directly and nonverbally to the student. We know this direct feedback to be extremely beneficial. No other method promotes such acute somatic and kinesthetic awareness of placement and spatial alignment. In fact, most students need that kind of feedback to feel their bodies in space. Many cultures teach dance directly from teacher to student—body to body—without relying on words (e.g., Balinese dance). However, in many cultures, including American, don't assume you can give hands-on tactile feedback. Ask official permission through the school from parents to touch students for corrective technical purposes. Follow all district policies related to touching and tactile teaching. Also be personally respectful of your students so as to correct gently and appropriately. It is best to ask students' permission individually before you touch them. Ask, "May I give you tactile feedback?" When you touch someone, be aware that they touch you equally.

Artful Movement Flow Somatic movement flow is the felt sensation of inner connections as movement runs in and out of the body instrument. Emphasize movement flow for mobility. Teachers such as Ruth Solomon remind us that "motivating forces of movement flow [are] deep within the body." She says, "The technique

144

I teach in class is intended to bring the student to a kinesthetic understanding of *how* movement is produced. The emphasis is on the cause of the movement—how it is motivated, rather than on the effect—how it is perceived. . . . This is the common denominator of virtually all intelligent dance teaching" (Solomon 1980, p. 62).

Adapted, by permission, from R. Solomon, 1980, "It's getting harder to teach, isn't it?," *Journal of Physical Education, Recreation and Dance* (March 1980): 62-71.

Main Technique Areas

Let's name all the main technique areas to develop in a dancer. No matter what level of middle and high school you teach (from basic to AG/T), these apply and you can make your own decisions about the most appropriate level for your students. Use the following list as you make long-range plans to be sure all areas of technique are developing concurrently. (This checklist will also appear in appendix A for you to refer to later.)

The list applies to all ages; however, as you will see later in this chapter, kindergartners start with just the merest hint of technique work (e.g., muscular strength, balancing, use of multiple body supports, shaping). As a child develops, you increase the level of sophistication. Use the developmental information in chapter 4 and the information in this chapter along with the dance framework to inform your choices about what is age appropriate in each category.

A checklist of main technique areas follows:

- A strong sense of center
- Muscular strength: core muscle strength (central torso)
- Muscular strength: limbs
- Use and articulation of the feet
- Body alignment (lower body, torso, shoulder girdle, arms, neck, and head)
- Hip rotation (turned out and parallel)*
- Placement of arms and legs in relation to the torso
- Placement of weight between feet
- Flexibility and stretch (extension)
- Balance
- Joint articulation and movement flow
- Turning (axial and locomotor, and on different axes)
- Elevation (lift, lengthening torso)
- Elevation (jumps, leaps, air work)*

- Landing (safely articulating through each joint)*
- Breath support
- Coordination of movements
- Use of multiple body supports
- Shaping (torso and limbs)
- Accurate rhythm, beat, and timing
- Steps (basic to complex)
- Focus
- Muscular endurance
- Cardiovascular endurance for performance
- A range of movement qualities
- Full range of dynamics*

Areas marked with an asterisk are developed further in this chapter under the heading "Technique in Middle and High School." Also see appendix B for "Sample Rubric for Technique Areas" that you can adapt to suit your needs.

Explain Your Technique Points of View

Think about it: Shouldn't you start building skills with the very first warm-up activity of the lesson—be it a unison warm-up or improvisationally guided warm-up? Shouldn't you impress the same skills in warm-up as in the center and across the floor to focus the body and mind on the main topics or artistic emphasis of the technique class?

Tell students above fourth grade how to focus their energy and attention in each class. Show them how to project a particular point of view to maximize their expressive intent in performing. Explain why you are teaching a "combination" or what skills you are asking them to develop that day and why. What is your purpose? For example, is it to increase memorization skills or improve fine muscle coordination? Is it to work on technical skills like rapid weight shifts, or on turning, or on upper leg strength by changing levels? Is it to work on balance or on elevation skills with an intent to improve landing mechanics? While teaching you must express your artistic point of view (i.e., your objective for movement); otherwise over time you will wonder why your students' dancing is muddled, incoherent, and lacks ability to communicate. So what if dancers can get through a combination? If they can't make their artistic point, or if technique is awful while they do the combination, how could you be advancing them educationally or artistically?

The actual movement sequence (i.e., combination) that you use for middle and high school students is not important—although many teachers spend more time dreaming up cool combinations than they do thinking about what they're teaching through those combinations. Remember this: *It is technique you are teaching—not combinations.* All students need to know how to strengthen and articulate the foot. They need flexibility in the joints of the leg and hip. They need to practice landing and takeoff for safety as well as for elevation. To do so they must be well placed and properly aligned. They must also be able to articulate each series of joints in sequence to move fluidly.

Be specific as to what you want students to address. For example, tendues in first position to the front could teach several things. Instead of merely teaching tendues, tell students which concepts and artistic points you are working on. What are you emphasizing today as you teach tendues?

- How the foot articulates through each joint, from the ball to the point, as the working foot goes out to extension and returns to place, with the little toe leading back to place
- How the heel leads through space while the little toe stays on the floor to work the hip rotators on the stretch
- How to spiral out the upper thigh to establish the habit of turning out properly from the hip socket
- How to strengthen the foot muscles through resistance against the floor

Technique should systematically and incrementally build a dancer's body by the way dancers learn to apply correct movement principles. While you emphasize their internal somatic motivations and increase rhythmic and movement quality, remember to grow both a skilled and a joyful dancer. Technique is more than work.

Technique in Primary and Elementary School

For the young child, kindergarten through grade 3, creative dance provides the building blocks that will eventually develop into both technique and choreography. It is where kids learn and master all the dance elements. (This mastery is required at whatever age students are introduced to dance.) Creative dance inspires young students to come up with their own movement—which is long on divergent movement activities. Creative movement also teaches young children how to move well. Creative dance provides pretechnique work by exploring such things as

- balancing (centering),
- turning (centering),
- elevating and landing,
- bodyshaping,
- extending the torso and the limbs,
- strengthening and lifting the center, and
- articulating body and joints.

Creative dance is still vital to fourth and fifth graders. But they also need to increase some convergent skills through simple full-body techniques. By fourth grade, children are ready to challenge themselves to find counterbalances in their bodies that increase their stability and balance. They like to challenge themselves to turn without becoming dizzy or disoriented, to leap and hang in the air. Their attempts at bodyshaping enable them to engage the spine and the skeletal–muscular system and to integrate them with the body core. By fourth grade, children learn to extend the torso and the limbs all the way through the toes so that extensions are full and complete. They are ready to understand alignment and how a strong body center (abdominal muscles) supports leg movement, bodyshaping, static support, balance, turning, and articulation

---

Reflect and Respond: Case Study

You and Toni are having coffee one Saturday morning when Toni confides, "I hate to admit that during my first year of dance teaching—long before dance certification—I reworked and retaught combinations I'd learned from my teachers to my students. Classes were more random experiences than part of a systematic long-range plan to get students to reach specific goals. There were no scope and sequence books to follow. I had no cohesive concept of teaching technique. I still am not sure what I'm teaching in technique. And I still find myself recycling dance combinations I've learned in master classes without a clear sense of what I'm teaching. Do you ever do this? How do you know what it is you're supposed to teach in technique?"

How would you respond to Toni?

of the total body. Techniques begun at the earlier grade levels (balancing, turning, elevation) are no longer challenging and must be made to require more skill and concentration.

After a thorough grounding in movement exploration, start teaching fourth graders to develop technique skills from a felt perspective—a somatic awareness—instead of mimicking what they externally perceive a movement to be. At this age, focus on getting fourth graders to increase their inner perception in six main areas: centering, balance, extension, turnout, foot articulation, and abdominal control. These areas, as Mary Joyce (1984) noted, are age appropriate for children.

Joyce's *Dance Technique for Children* (1984) is helpful. Her humanistic approach to dance and her vast teaching experience and knowledge of dance are valuable to dance specialists teaching children, or for that matter, any ages.

Technique in Middle and High School

Technique in middle and high school is about learning to articulate the body clearly, safely, and aesthetically from different points of view. We will focus on several from the longer list earlier in this chapter marked with an asterisk.

Technique: Dynamics and Flow

To teach movement qualities and a variety of dynamics is vital. Avoid the sameness of dynamic range too often found in particular dance styles—hard pumping for jazz or smooth and even for ballet. Add dynamic contrasts to all styles. It's not about how dancers look in the mirror—their external appearance. It is about what is going on inside the body instrument. If the music keeps on pumping out a beat at a steady dynamic and the dancers keep the same dynamic monotone as the accompaniment, where is the interest? Where are the variations and subtleties? What is the point?

Carefully select music accompaniment for technique class. Choose music that doesn't negate the movement qualities and the range of dynamics and textures you want to develop in students (or make your own accompaniment with percussion instruments). Energy and dynamics are one of the five categories of dance elements. Dynamics are the lifeblood of the dance. Whereas time is dance's heartbeat, dynamics are its vibrancy, its quality, its energy, its strength. Artful use of dynamics

transforms choreographing as well as performing. Dynamics are the means by which we emphasize certain moves in contrast to what is merely the transition and the glue. It is a shame to see dancers with potential who have not been taught how to modulate qualitative differences in dynamics. They stay in one single wide-open dynamic of projecting each movement to its extreme. Ruth Solomon describes them as having

> no sense of subtlety or flow, or transition—of any of those things that the trained observer immediately recognizes as having a sense of integrity. The single dynamic dancer asks only "which foot goes where?" And "how high is my leg going?" And "how do I look doing this?" There is little if any insight into the motivating factors involved in producing movement; the focus is on the shape one is making, rather than the energy flow making that shape. Most of the students of whom I speak seem never to have been asked the "how" of movement. (1980, p. 62)

Adapted, by permission, from R. Solomon, 1980, "It's getting harder to teach, isn't it?," *Journal of Physical Education, Recreation and Dance* (March 1980): 62-71.

Your charge is to make technique mechanics secondary to quality of motion. Cultivate a vision that transcends the teaching of mechanics and emphasizes dynamic range. One strategy is to involve students regularly in improvisation around dynamic qualities to develop a spectrum of its range. "Somehow incorporate into the teaching of dance a sense of aesthetics which goes beyond just training the dancer in the essential skills" (Solomon 1980, p. 71).

Adapted, by permission, from R. Solomon, 1980, "It's getting harder to teach, isn't it?," *Journal of Physical Education, Recreation and Dance* (March 1980): 62-71.

Technique: Turnout

Turnout is another hallmark of technique. The term *hip rotation* is a little more accurate, because turnout comes from a rotation action that initiates deep in the femoral joints of the pelvis (i.e., hip socket). Indeed, all turnout begins in the hip, although it is apparent in the line of legs and placement of the feet. Turnout is used in most dance forms for mobility and stability. It is a strong part of technical training in performance styles besides classical ballet, such as south Indian Bharata Natyam and Kathakali, Balinese legong and baris, and jazz and musical theatre.

Turnout gives the ballet dancer specific advantages:

- Turnout displays the dancer's line at maximum. The line of the leg is more aesthetically pleasing to the eye than when seen straight on.

147

- Turnout increases traveling mobility, especially to the side.
- Turnout aids turning.
- Turnout facilitates direction changes. If your feet are parallel and side by side—normal position—you have no "back foot." Moving sideways or backward is much more difficult in parallel than when turned out.
- Turnout allows leg extensions to go higher than when in parallel.
- Turnout gives a wider stance for balance. When a dancer is supported on one leg, there is greater stability because of the wider base of support when rotated.

Adapted from www.criticaldance.com: TURNOUT—A Ballet Basic.

However, biomechanical considerations must supersede the sheer artistic if they are in conflict. It would be unethical and immoral to injure students, and you can if you force turnout, especially at certain ages. Read orthopedic surgeon James Sammarco's definitive article, "The Hip in Dancers," (see Rich Resources). His comments about teaching children who are serious students of dance also apply to teaching school dance. He states,

> [Turnout] occurs entirely at the hips. The entire lower extremity is rotated externally beginning at the hip, with the knee and leg following after. Turnout develops the aesthetic line of the lower extremity. . . .

> Children beginning to dance . . . between the ages of six and 12, have the benefit of maintaining a turnout through a stretching process by externally rotating the hips and holding them in that position, as during a dance class. After the age of 11 the femoral neck can no longer be altered to the molding process of continual pressure. Subsequent development and maintenance of external rotation must be achieved by [at the expense of] stretching the soft tissues about the hip. . . .

> To increase turnout the dancer can create problems, both at the hip and elsewhere. If the hips are forced into abduction [rotation] for several hours a day, stretching at the hip capsule causes chronic strain resulting in calcification at the acetabular attachment of the capsule. . . .

> In addition to damaging the hip, forcing external rotation may cause problems in the medial ligaments of the knee and in the medial foot. (Sammarco 1987, pp. 5-6)

Technique: Elevation

Elevation is part of the space element "levels." It includes mechanics of going into the air and landing. It is about aesthetics, safety, mobility, and resiliency. It is also about lift and learning to hang in the air.

To establish correct habits of going into the air and landing, first strengthen the muscles that control the action. Teach preparatory pliés and relevés with proper alignment of toes, ankle, knee, and pelvis. Connect relevés and pliés as the initial preparation of jumping and landing, and ensure alignment of foot and ankle as you observe students executing this motion. Stress foot articulation through the ball to the point. Strengthening the takeoff and landing muscles of the foot and leg comes through repeating the action to develop the muscles as well as to instill the feel of correct alignment and resilience. Give students more than enough practice to develop

- strong ankle and foot muscles,
- correct alignment of the ankle and knee,
- the deepest demi-plié possible (with heels on the floor) in proper alignment with knees over toes,
- correct alignment of the pelvis and low back, and
- rotation from hip rotators felt deep in the musculature (when working in turnout).

When an individual leaves the floor, there are always two safety concerns: floor construction and student readiness.

Floor construction: Avoid jumps and leaps on floors with little or no resiliency, such as tile or wood laid directly over cement. Because such floors lack give, the students' lower joints absorb all the shock during landing, causing unnecessary joint stress and often shin splints (see chapter 11).

Student readiness: Assuming the floor is resilient, prepare students by warming them up (sending blood supply to large muscle groups) before engaging in large jumps and leaps. Adequate flexing and extension of the foot and pliés help prepare the shin for landings.

Lightness and lift are aesthetic aspects to acquire. Coordinate the use of breath: Inhale on the rise, exhale on the descent. Inhale at the height of a leap. Use aesthetic images like someone lifting you into the air as you engage the abdominals to execute jumps and leaps.

- Plié deeply and spring from the coiled tension created using the legs and feet to power the jump.
- Emphasize lightness of movement and body lift while going into the air.
- Inhale to gain height on the ascent; exhale on the landing.

Reflect and Respond: Case Study

I thought I taught rather good modern dance technique classes to college students. The classes were aesthetically based, and students grew and loved learning to dance. This happened before the days of dance teacher certification and dance education degrees. Several years later one of my former students invited me to observe a dance class she was teaching to help her select children who showed potential as performers. That was the day the need for systematic dance teacher preparation hit home with me.

This wonderful dancer and beloved student—neither a dance major nor dance education major—had opened a private dance studio. To my utter dismay, she was teaching 7-year-olds the same movement combinations and warm-up activities I had taught her in the university class. She was teaching them by using center combinations meant for young-adult college students! These 7-year-olds were clearly not ready for such combinations, but even more important, they had not yet acquired any body alignment—so the plié combinations were an anatomical mess. Besides that, their feet were sickled as their attempted tendues were lifted into a point rather than brushed against the floor to strengthen the metatarsals.

She gave them the same combinations and movement I had used in the university's technique class, but she gave no instruction on how to physically accomplish an action or its intent. She forgot to use an artistic point of view—which I had stressed with the university classes. These movements were clearly inappropriate for children who did not have the basics of alignment. Therefore, they were not learning anything of technical value, only to mimic movements.

What would you have said in this situation to your former student whom you cherished and cared about and who clearly did not know she was not teaching well?

- Keep the head lifted and the focus up and out toward the audience.
- Energize the arms to prevent them from dangling in space.
- Create a moment of suspension at the top of the leap or jump. Along with breath, also defy gravity by contracting the abdominal muscles to lift the pelvis as though a partner lifted you in midair (grades 6-12).

Body Systems Approach

Bonnie Bainbridge Cohen, founder of **Body-Mind Centering** (**BMC;** one of the noted body therapies and somatic systems in practice), shows us how to use the different body systems for dance warm-up to fully tap the body's sources of movement potential. The systems she uses for warm-up and for expressive purposes are the skeletal–muscular, organ–endocrine, autonomic nervous, somatic nervous, and fluid systems. Use the different systems to access the different movement qualities because each system contributes something unique to one's dancing quality. Use each of the systems to expand technical skills and movement vocabulary so students learn to dance with all bodily resources available to them.

Introduce each system separately before weaving them into a regular technique class in order to distinguish the salient qualities of each one. Following are examples:

- Moving from the skeletal system emphasizes stability and mobility (i.e., bones for stability and joints for mobility)
- Moving from the nervous system is about timing and quickness.
- Moving from the muscular system is about strength and power.
- Moving from the circulatory system is about energy quality and flow as the energy of the lifeblood moves through the body (it supports stillness and action).
- Moving from the respiratory system is about expansion and contraction, rising and falling, suspension and collapse.

Advanced high school classes delve into further somatic technicalities. For example, teach dancers to activate the autonomic nervous system to achieve full-bodied alertness toward space and environment. This focus enables dancers to act and react to what is around them. The somatic nervous system enervates movement, sparking the nerves to fire the muscles to move. In reverse, the somatic nervous system receives sensory feedback from our moving muscles to increase our own internal somatic awareness. So the somatic nervous system is important to the quickness and responsiveness of our own internal impulses.

It is artistically useful to work from each body system. Use each one at different times for technique warm-up, center work, and work across the floor. Use each one to increase kin-aesthetic awareness so that dancers tap their inner resources to fine-tune their body instruments. Use each body system to aesthetically enhance creating and improvising dance. There is much to work with. For example, see what Bonnie Bainbridge Cohen says about the different aspects of the skeletal–muscular system:

SKELETAL–MUSCULAR SYSTEM:

- Moving the distal bone (the bone more distant from the center of the body) at any joint moves the distal limb (head, hands, feet, and tail) through space. This increases the articulation and intent of the movement.

- Moving the proximal bone (the bone closer to the center of the body) at any joint moves the body through space. This has two aspects:
  > Proximal bones act as levers for propelling the body through space. This increases the efficiency and range of the movement and carries the movement through the whole body.
  > The weight of the body being moved through space becomes the resistive force that increases the strength and support of the larger, more powerful muscles.

- Matching the range of movement of the distal bones with that of the proximal bones balances the muscular forces passing over the joints.

- Initiating and expressing movement through the skeletal system bring out the inherent qualities of clarity, effortlessness, and form.

- Initiating and expressing movement through the muscular system bring out the inherent qualities of vitality and power as well as the dynamics of meeting, overcoming, yielding to, and balancing resistance.

- Initiating and expressing movement by actively lengthening and shortening the ligaments increase range, clarity, and focus.

Reprinted, by permission, from B. Bainbridge Cohen, 1988, "The dancer's warm-up through body-mind centering," *Contact Quarterly Dance Journal: A Vehicle for Moving Ideas* 13(3): 28-29, 32-33. www.contactquarterly.com

Other Emphasis Points

Technique class exists to emphasize artful performing. Depending on the abilities and experiences of your students, technique study starts around the middle school grades. It depends on a level of fitness.

Performance Quality In an aesthetically driven curriculum, what one does is not as important as *how* it is done—how the bodymindspirit unifies to fully realize movement. To accept less is to fall short of the goals of teaching all ages, and especially so for technique in middle and high school. For example, how are middle and high school students to project? How do their timing and rhythm help project the musicality of this sequence? How does their somatic awareness motivate their joint articulation and breath quality of their movement? How are the movements linked together to show us that the flow is felt internally? Emphasize body focus externally by gaze and internally by graining. Technique teaches artistry. We are not training mechanical dolls but rather showing students how to tap their inner resources and body systems to move expressively within the fullest range possible. To achieve performance quality is to dance fully and be fully aware.

Teach dancers to emphasize the body's aesthetic center. Rudolf Arnheim reminded us that audiences view performers on a stage differently than they view people every day. In the everyday world, people attune to a person's head as they interact. But audiences attune to a dancer's torso as the aesthetic center during performance, barely noticing the head (Arnheim 1971). Therefore, teach performers to focus energy in—and call aesthetic attention to—the torso and limbs instead of the head to achieve their artistic goals.

He makes a related point about audience perception of the dancer:

> The audience sees the performer create motion, in time and space. However, we react in a felt kinesthetic, visual, and auditory way with feeling and awareness of its artistic presence. We judge the aesthetic quality of the movement, not the machine-like function of its efficiency. We perceive the dancer displacing space as an expression of art, not function. (Arnheim 1971, pp. 389-391)

Adapted, by permission, from R. Arnheim, 1971, *Art and visual perception: A psychology of the creative eye* (Berkeley, CA: University of California Press).

Fitness In addition to teaching artistic qualities in technique class, incorporate fitness at this age. Sacrifice none of the three main fitness goals: endurance, strength, and flexibility. Work on muscle strength, muscle–joint flexibility, balance, coordination, muscle endurance, cardiovascular endurance, and postural alignment. Stress technical artistry as an objective for a fit body.

Ask your physical educator colleague to set up a resistance weight training program for dance students to increase muscle strength and tone. Use pedometers in activity classes, especially folk dancing, to emphasize the link between dance and fitness.

Build long-range fitness goals into dance warm-ups. Dancers need muscular strength and flexibility. Flexibility without strength is dangerous. Studies show **ballistic stretching** to be potentially dangerous. **Static stretches** achieve more beneficial results with relaxed rather than taut muscles. Static stretches of the hamstrings for middle and high school students are best done near the end of class or after a thorough warm-up. Because most of your students are not going to be professional performers, avoiding long-term injury is more important in a school-based program than how high the leg goes.

Warm-Ups   Students must warm up before they move. Warming up helps prevent both injury and muscle strain. Warm-ups should not start with stretches but rather should start by getting blood circulating to the large muscle groups in the legs and torso. Full body swings, pliés, brushes, leg swings, and foot articulations are all good starting places. Warm-ups should include flexions and extensions.

Warm-ups also prepare the mind for what the body is to do. In fact, use the warm-up to help the body and mind transition from everyday movement to the art of movement using the **bodymind.** Use warm-up time to introduce each lesson's main topic—be it technical emphasis or creative concept. Even if you use a standard warm-up every day, state the day's points of emphasis so students are clear where to focus their attention as they warm up.

Flexibility and Stretching   Stretches that are used consistently over time can increase range of motion and flexibility; it takes about 6 weeks to increase range of motion in any muscle group. Stretches should not hurt. Dancers should stretch only until they feel a light pull as they lengthen the muscle, but a muscle must be relaxed to stretch. To stretch a taut muscle is to risk tearing the muscle. Overstretching is far worse than understretching. Dancers should warm up a minimum of 5 to 8 minutes before stretching to maximize the effect of the stretch. Make flexibility both a fitness and an artistic goal in dance.

Strength   Develop torso strength in two ways: with a weight training program and floor work. Use deep breathing in strengthening exercises—slow inhales and exhales—to bring dancers in touch with the gentle rise and fall of their inner organs, which increases their mobility as the muscles contract and release. Pilates mat exercises and floor work are good as well as artistic techniques such as Graham floor work. Keep students connected to how the movement feels so as not build strength at the expense of movement quality.

In advanced high school classes, use standing extensions at the barre to develop torso strength. Develop leg strength through resistance work such as pliés, level changes that move the pelvis close to and away from the floor, and elevations such as jumps. Also cultivate strength without rigidity by emphasizing awareness of breath and body systems to support movement quality.

Spatial Work   Technique class goes beyond working the body to include its relation to space. Focus, projection, shape, spatial relationships, and the performer's artistic points of view toward space are necessary to refine the use of the space elements. Incorporate aspects of Labanalysis to increase spatial orientation. For example, include Laban space–shape with spoking, arcing, and carving for two- and three-dimensional work.

Timing   Connect students with rhythm. Teach them to accurately count phrases. Emphasize timing and rhythm with and without accompaniment. Begin in elementary school to teach children how to use transitions between movements. Teach the children how to phrase movements to hold them together for continuity. Teach secondary-age students to refine dance as a "time art" and modulate time to set the tone of a piece as well as hold coherent thoughts together. Teach students how the pulse of dance is felt through the way it is timed or extended into time. Include the extremes of timing to demonstrate the full spectrum of fastest to slowest. Use acceleration and deceleration—concepts that in turn have practical application to physical science. Use self-accompaniment as often as you use metered accompaniment so timing is not overly dependent on music.

Levels of Technical Mastery   One issue you will likely face is whether to put students en pointe in ballet. Generally a K-12 program does not include pointe work. However, if you teach artistically gifted or talented (AG/T) ninth through twelfth graders, you may have to consider the viability of pointe work. If so, adhere to specific technical criteria for placement en pointe. The criteria serve a dual purpose: for artistic reasons but even more for safety and liability. Present the criteria to students well before their audition so they know what they must have mastered before they can proceed. Safety and liability require you to hold firm to strict criteria.

Figure 6.7 shows sample criteria used as a placement form for AG/T students matriculating from middle to high school. Because both schools are urban gifted dance programs (with some students from private studios who take pointe), the middle school teacher assesses the readiness for pointe work of the graduating eighth graders who are moving to high school. The middle school teacher completes the checklist and gives it to the student and parent to communicate strengths and weaknesses as well as the justification for placing the student. The student must present this signed sheet to the high school dance specialist with adequate ratings documented before being considered for or placed en pointe.

Reflect and Respond: Case Study

Which and Why?

Teacher A uses a standard 18-minute warm-up for every class. What are the advantages and disadvantages?

Teacher B designs warm-ups integrated into each lesson and uses them to get the body moving immediately (and gently) in the spirit of the day's lesson concepts. Example: For a lesson focusing on body part isolation, the warm-up also focuses on individual body parts leading and moving independently and some total body movement that uses body parts together to warm up the large muscle groups. What are the advantages and disadvantages?

Which teacher uses instructional time best? Why?

Dance Cornerstone Curriculum (DCC) Framework

Cornerstone 1 (C1) integrates cognitive content with kin-aesthetic skills.

This part of the DCC Framework (following Rich Resources) shows what students should know and be able to do to achieve aspects of the NSDEs, particularly 1 and 3. It shows how concepts develop from kindergarten through 12th grade to help you

break them down into teachable chunks. They are not isolated tasks but merely broken out so you can see the progression of each concept. The chart is divided into four sequential parts: primary (K-2), elementary (3-5), middle (6-8), and high school (9-12). The developmental continuum goes from simple to complex to adapt to your learners.

- Look across the chart for sequence as to how each concept builds as students learn.
- Look down the chart for substance as to the scope, what is essential to include.
- For older beginners, spiral back to the first column to pick up the basic skills rather than start at their age level.

Questions to Ponder

1. Why is "kin-aesthetic" a good term to express the artful skill of motion and dance?

2. How would you describe marking a sequence versus dancing a sequence? What does the dancer do to perform full-out in dance that she doesn't when marking or rehearsing a dance? When does movement become dance?

3. How are the dance elements a universal dance vocabulary? Under the BSTER subcategories, which elements are most appropriate to introduce at primary level? At elementary (grades 3-5)? Are there some that are best saved for middle and high school students?

4. What are the basic elements of the other arts? How are dance elements similar to them?

5. Considering the vocabulary systems we use in dance, what are the developing vocabularies and languages brought to us through technology? Have you learned to use LabanWriter to increase dance vocabulary?

6. Why are the principles of design important to teaching dance as art? How can you use them to improve dance compositions?

7. Why is a warm-up for body and mind needed before a technique class? How does technique in elementary school differ from technique in middle and high school? At what age is it appropriate to introduce ballet basics in elementary school?

8. What can you add to your Statements of Belief (as explained in the Introduction)?

Sample Criteria: "Technical Aspects to Master Before Beginning Pointe Work in Classical Ballet"

1. Correct Skeletal Alignment

- ___ Pelvis, rib cage, and spine are properly aligned at all times.

TEST: Standing on flat and relevé in first and fifth positions.

2. Correct Placement of Weight

- ___ "Pull-up" in pelvis and legs—weight should be lifted away from feet at all times with stretched knees via use of abdominals.

- ___ Weight should be centered over one or both feet, not over heels.

TEST: See #1 and tendu devant, à la seconde, and à derriére.

3. Articulation of Feet

- ___ No clenching or gripping toes in tendu.

- ___ In tendu, foot articulates sequentially through the joints.

TEST: Flex to point and battement tendu.

4. Perfect Balance (2 legs)

- ___ Balance while holding equal rotation (turnout) in the hips, with no faltering and with perfect alignment and placement (45 seconds).

TEST: Balance on demi-pointe in first, second, and sous-sus positions.

5. Perfect Demi-Pointe

- ___ Demi-pointe on 1 and 2 legs with no evidence of sickling or tendency of toes to curl or clutch (fully extended ankles).

TEST: See #4 and demi-pointe in relevé for 45 seconds on each leg.

6. Torso Strength and Control

- ___ Use of rectus abdominus and external obliques (not soft, mobile, or floppy).

TEST: Grand rond de jambe with both legs.

7. Strength of Back Muscles

- ___ Ability to hold up back in arabesque position.

TEST: 90-degree arabesque hold for 45 seconds on each side.

8. Overall Strength, Alignment, Placement, Turnout, and Control

- ___ Grand plié in center (without wobbling or altering position of feet).

TEST: Grand plié in fifth position in center.

Ballet students must score at least 4 out of a possible 5 points in each task category to qualify for pointe work in the high school advanced technique class.

FIGURE 6.7 Sample checklist (rubric) of skills to master before being eligible to audition for a pointe class.

Adapted by A. Wrenn Cook from *The Pointe Book* by Janice Barringer and Sarah Schlesinger.

THREE-ACT REFLECTION: WRITE–ASSESS–REFINE (C1)

Act I: Write

Prepare a three- to four-page typed paper for your Perspectives Notebook that expresses what Cornerstone 1 contributes to educational dance. Address the specific criteria without using them for an outline. Use them first for Act I as composition criteria and for Act II as review criteria.

C1 Composition Criteria (and Review Criteria)

___ Explains the various facets of dancing and performing

___ Clarifies the goals of Cornerstone 1

___ Explains the dance elements and their value

   a. ___ Clearly identifies what they are

   b. ___ Tells the ways they are used

   c. ___ Says why they are critical to teaching and learning

   d. ___ Explains what they contribute to learners' kinetic and conceptual growth

___ Tells how learning in the elements must progress from simple to complex as students sequence through primary, elementary, middle, and high school

___ Explains the various languages of dance and how they are used

___ Explains teaching and learning process in K-12

___ Explains how national standards address the elements

___ Integrates content and achievement standards from national standards

___ Relates kin-aesthetic vocabulary to critical and creative thinking

___ Makes overall case for valuing the elements in dance and their emphasis in dance education and using them to promote learning at all ages

Act II: Assess (25 minutes)

The most successful papers will amalgamate the criteria to build context rather than address criteria as individual points.

Formal In-Class Peer Assessment

Step 1: On the date your class submits these papers to your professor, engage in a formal, in-class peer evaluation. Attach a rating sheet (the review criteria in Act I) to your paper, and do a cooperative peer review. Swap papers so three peers evaluate your paper and make comments while you do the same for others. Rate 1, 2, or 3 on each criterion based on correctness of information, thoroughness of coverage, and clarity of expression. (Successful coverage of all three rates a 3.)

Step 2: After evaluating peer papers and getting yours evaluated, return papers to the owners to check ratings and comments before giving them to your professor to grade.

Step 3: Your professor grades your paper and adds comments.

Act III: Refine

After your professor returns your paper—with all comment sheets attached—synthesize all comments and refine your paper (out of class) to earn 3s on all items. Incorporate concepts and information from peer papers that make your paper better. Place your reworked paper into the Perspectives Notebook.

Four benefits of the three-step assessment: You grade papers using criteria with which you are familiar. You deepen understanding of the topic. You are able to articulate it to others. You end up with a first-rate paper for your professional portfolio.

You will find a similar reflection exercise in each cornerstone chapter (chapters 6-9). Use the same three-act format. It is also found in appendix A.

Rich Resources

RESOURCES

- Mary Joyce's *First Steps in Teaching Creative Dance to Children* (1994) focuses on the dance elements for K-5 creative dance lessons. Her *Dance Technique for Children* (1984) shows how to start technique with upper elementary students.

- Anne Green Gilbert's *Creative Dance for All Ages,* another helpful book, cites numerous ways to effectively teach the dance elements.

- *Move! Learn! Dance! A K-6 Dance Teaching Resource Guide* outlines in a scope and sequence graded lesson plans for pre-K through grade 5 that emphasize the dance elements. Order it from Children's Dance Theatre, Mary Ann Lee, Artistic Director, 1215 Annex Bldg., Salt Lake City, Utah 84111. Phone: 801-581-7374.

- Familiarize yourself with *Contact Quarterly* journal, particularly early editions in which Bonnie Bainbridge Cohen explains the seminal work of Body–Mind Centering in developmental movement. Read "The Dancer's Warm-Up Through Body-Mind Centering" before you teach middle and high school students (*Contact Quarterly Dance Journal: A Vehicle for Moving Ideas* 13(3): 28-29, 32-33, 1988).

- *The Nikolais/Louis Dance technique—A Philosophy and Method of Modern Dance* (2005) prepares you to teach modern dance technique from a contextual and artistic point of view. The book–DVD combination describes and demonstrates the artistry that drives each concept and each lesson plan. This model advances the artistic use of the dance elements. It integrates the physical, artistic, psychological, and cognitive aspects of teaching and learning (see chapter 4). This teaching model is a complete, contextually coherent way of teaching and learning modern dance. Highly recommended.

- Also study the definitive work on turnout (by an orthopedic surgeon) published in the arts medicine journal *Medical Problems of Performing Artists:* "The Hip in Dancers," by G. James Sammarco, MD, FACS, pp. 5-14, March 1987.

WEB SITES

- www.invisionguide.com and www.anatomicaltravel.com: For Alexander Tsiaras' four-dimensional medical scans with artistic vision. His fluoroscopic images of dancers show both the anatomical and artistic beauty of dancers in motion.

- www.lodc.org: For LOD and motif writing, Motif-at-a-Glance, mini-flipcharts, and other resources compiled by the Language of Dance Center, New York City.

- http://aweb.bham.ac.uk/calaban/frame.htm: For more about CALABAN, a Windows®-based computer solution for various aspects of your work with Labanotation. It is a full-featured graphics editing software capable of producing just about every variation on drafting Labanotation scores: These range from producing a single page of notation for your homework, project, or assignment to publishing an entire article or book, including text—perhaps photographs and Labanotation graphics.

- www.bodymindcentering.com: For information on Body-Mind Centering and its founder, Bonnie Bainbridge Cohen.

1.0   Understanding and Using the Dance Elements

Grades K-2	Grades 3-5	Grades 6-8	Grades 9-12
1.1 The body as instrument of expression			
1.1a *Body awareness*			
Explores and identifies body parts and learns to move them with variety in isolation.	Experiences total body movement and isolated body and body part movement (as it relates to dance). Refines articulation of body instrument.	Develops technique to warm up the body to promote flexibility and strength and to give attention to body part placement. Articulates the body instrument and all parts clearly.	Deepens involvement with dance technique based on the principles of anatomy and kinesiology. Develops an articulate, expressive body instrument.
Learns basic joint actions.	Learns joint actions, articulations, and basic anatomical terms (muscles and bones).	Learns basic anatomy and relates it to dance. Learns basic kinesiology principles and applies them to dance. Increases articulation.	Learns basic anatomy and relates it to dance. Learns basic kinesiology principles and applies them to dance. Learns Bartenieff Fundamentals or basic somatic work to increase articulation.
Focuses attention on how it feels to move in contrasting extremes.	Focuses attention on the kin-aesthetic sensations of movement.	Discovers kin-aesthetic sensations in movement. Relates them to balancing, turning, and jumping.	Finds inner "feelings" of the kin-aesthetic sensation of dancing and performing.
———	———	Finds movements to artfully express mood and feeling; extends a movement to make it clearer and more emphatic.	Finds movements to artfully express mood and feeling; extends a movement to make it clearer and more emphatic. Performs and projects with confidence using the entire body. Demonstrates full commitment and involvement to the performance.
Learns good posture; begins to articulate the spine.	Learns to center the body through specifically designed exercises to locate, strengthen, and improve abdominal control. Maintains body alignment while performing basic movement sequences.	Learns proper body alignment for the dance instrument in parallel and turned out positions (static and dynamic). Maintains alignment appropriate to the dance form while performing.	Uses the body instrument efficiently in varying dance styles with keen awareness of center and body alignment. Uses vertical, off-center, and non-vertical alignment. Maintains body alignment appropriate to the dance style performed. Articulates all parts of the body while performing complex movement sequences and self-corrects while performing complex movement sequences.
———	Identifies the difference between movement that is centered and off-centered.	Works both in centered and off-centered movement.	Works both in centered and off-centered movement.
1.1b *Body actions and moves*			
Learns nonlocomotor body actions that are different and varied: bend, stretch, shake, twist, turn.	Expands nonlocomotor vocabulary to include bending, stretching, shaking, twisting, turning, collapsing, suspending, rising, falling. Performs with artistic awareness.	Expands nonlocomotor vocabulary to refine previously mentioned body actions and modulate them. Performs them with artistic awareness.	Sensitively approaches texture in dance and finds movement potential in adjectives, adverbs, and verbs to increase the subtlety of nonlocomotor body actions. Performs with artistic awareness.

Dance Cornerstone Curriculum Framework—C1: Dancing and Performing from *Teaching Dance as Art in Education* by Brenda Pugh McCutchen, 2006, Champaign IL: Human Kinetics

Grades K-2	Grades 3-5	Grades 6-8	Grades 9-12
1.1c Body shape			
Explores making a variety of created body shapes that emphasize shaping the spine (static and dynamic).	Makes body shapes that link together in time and with continuous movement flow. Focuses attention on making shapes, such as round, straight, angular, twisted, three-dimensional. Refines static shapes. Learns to use the spine to sculpt the body from the inside: bodyshape with "immediacy."	Focuses attention on bodyshaping to deepen the performing experience and to commit to quality artistic movement design. Clarifies bodyshaping as an intentional core body action that emphasizes shape of the spine and body core.	Refines the sense of shaping to clarify intent and increase design interest. Increases performing skills with an emphasis on shaping and sculpting the body.
1.1d Traveling and locomotor movements			
Learns to travel using simple steps: walk, run, hop, jump, gallop, and leap.	Expands movement vocabulary using complex locomotor movements: skip and slide.	Combines simple and complex locomotor movements in challenging sequences. Articulates the foot and lower extremities.	Travels with locomotor movements in skillful and challenging combinations. Improves technique and articulation of combinations and step sequences in broad dynamic range.
Learns to differentiate between simple rhythms (steady beat) and complex rhythms (dotted rhythms).	Differentiates between and performs simple rhythms (steady beat) and complex rhythms (dotted rhythms).	Increases not only technique but artistic use of traveling through space with rhythmic accuracy as appropriate to selected dance styles.	Increases not only technique but artistic use of traveling through space with rhythmic accuracy as appropriate to selected dance styles.
Learns to perform locomotor and nonlocomotor movements with confidence.	Accurately reproduces locomotor movements in space with proper time and dynamic modulation.	Accurately reproduces and performs locomotor and nonlocomotor movements in space, accurately modulating time and dynamics. Performs movements with confidence and engages the entire body when traveling.	Accurately reproduces and performs locomotor and nonlocomotor movements in space, accurately modulating time and dynamics. Performs movements with confidence and engages the entire body when traveling.
1.1e Body relationships			
Explores moving body parts alone and in a variety of combinations.	Learns to perform "one body part" dances. Relates the featured part to other parts of the body.	Becomes articulate in the use of whole-body movement in which all body parts function as a unit. Learns to feature one body part at a time and relate body parts to each other.	Becomes articulate in the use of whole-body movement in which all body parts function as a unit. Learns to feature one body part as a "soloist."
Incorporates left-sided and right-sided movements (laterality).	Recognizes body connections—upper to lower, lateral and cross-lateral—and how they contribute to performance quality.	Demonstrates body connections—upper to lower, lateral and cross-lateral—and how they contribute to performance quality.	Uses body connections—upper to lower, lateral and cross-lateral—and how they contribute to performance quality.
1.1f Moving in control			
Experiences group movement exploration and learns to move the body in space without touching others. Stops and starts on cue.	Experiences creative movement in groups to self-direct the body in general and personal space with the ability to stop and start on cue and respond to movement cues.	Experiences self-management while moving. Develops self-awareness through dancing sequences and dance works.	Uses the body as an instrument of expression. Increases coordination and concentration when moving and performing.

Dance Cornerstone Curriculum Framework—C1: Dancing and Performing from *Teaching Dance as Art in Education* by Brenda Pugh McCutchen, 2006, Champaign IL: Human Kinetics

157

1.0 Understanding and Using the Dance Elements

Grades K-2	Grades 3-5	Grades 6-8	Grades 9-12
1.1f Moving in control (continued)			
Learns to control the body as it moves through space so as to be capable of stopping suddenly, traveling quickly or slowly, and using quiet movement successfully.	Recognizes how control of the body instrument requires muscular control and power in energy bursts as well as quiet moments.	Refines body control by practicing movements that require muscle strength, power, and sustained energy, especially for the legs and trunk.	Refines movements that require muscle strength, power, and gradation of power for parts of the body. Recognizes how executing movements and coordination of different body parts contribute to quality performance.
1.1g Body and self-image			
Experiences movement activities that build self-esteem. (Students with impediments to movement are given challenges within their range of motion.)	Experiences movement activities that build self-esteem and positive attitudes toward self and others in dance.	Exercises self-management in movement to develop positive feelings about exploration and communication through movement and dance.	Develops a positive self-image as a performer, dancer, and creator. (Works within range if disabling conditions prevail.)
1.1h Safe use of the body			
Begins movement experiences gently and gradually. (Take care not to overexert the young child.)	Begins movement slowly and gradually in order to increase blood flow to muscles.	Engages in incremental warm-up activity before technique.	Applies principles of anatomy and kinesiology to initiate movement and ensure safe use of the body. Begins to learn about somatics and use body therapies such as Alexander, Feldenkrais, and Bartenieff Fundamentals.
————	Learns to articulate the foot and plié when landing.	Uses efficient landing techniques with safe alignment of lower limbs and lower spine.	Uses efficient landing techniques with full spinal and limb alignment.
Learns important safety factors related to moving the body and to dancing.	Relates anatomical knowledge to dance for safety and deep internal awareness.	Relates kinesiology to dance in an internal way to ensure safety and to deepen bodily awareness.	Dances with internal awareness of kinesiology for artistry, to ensure safety, and to maximize movement.
Knows that special shoes are used for some dance styles and bare feet for others.	Dances in bare feet and special dance shoes, and concentrates to control the body on various surfaces.	Controls body in motion in both bare feet and dance shoes.	Uses dance footwear appropriate to the dance style and in relation to the floor surface for safety and body control.
1.1i Balance			
Increases balance with wide base of support in both static positions and traveling.	Increases balance on one foot and other narrow bases of support.	Increases balance in turning, shaping, and using innovative bases of support.	Increases balance in technique on flat foot as well as half toe. Executes more sophisticated turns such as pirouettes and chaînés while working on balance.
1.1j Mobility and stability			
Works on stability while stationary and traveling. Increases mobility with locomotor and nonlocomotor movements such as rolling, changing levels, and moving through space.	Increases overall stability and mobility as they relate to dance technique. Increases ability to turn and to travel.	Increases overall stability and mobility as they relate to dance technique. Uses somatic awareness to increase mobility and stability in complex movement patterns.	Increases overall stability and mobility as they relate to dance technique. Uses somatic awareness to increase mobility and stability in complex movement patterns.

Dance Cornerstone Curriculum Framework—C1: Dancing and Performing from Teaching Dance as Art in Education by Brenda Pugh McCutchen, 2006, Champaign IL: Human Kinetics

Grades K-2	Grades 3-5	Grades 6-8	Grades 9-12
1.1k Core muscle strength and awareness of center			
Practices ascending from the floor and descending to the floor slowly through shaping the body and using muscle control.	Increases muscle strength, flexibility, and coordination. Finds multiple ways to shape while changing levels and keeping the body center elevated rather than collapsed on the floor.	Begins techniques to strengthen the core (abdominal strengthening).	Uses core muscle strength in technique and bodyshaping.
1.1l Development of main technique areas			
Explores turning, elevation, landing, jumping, supporting oneself, balancing, joint actions, shaping, and traveling.	Uses techniques with multiple body supports, accurate rhythm and timing, accurate placement, and articulation of the feet, identifying a sense of center. Develops strength, balance, and coordination and increases flexibility.	Uses body alignment, hip rotation, placement, flexibility and stretch, and locomotor turning, turning on different axes. Increases use of all technique areas.	Refines all main technique areas and masters specific dance vocabulary related to the efficient and artful use of the body instrument.
1.1m Turning			
Learns turning as a central axis concept. Turns to face different directions. Creates patterns that call for various turning movements, although not formal turns.	Learns formal turns: three-step turn, quarter and half turns. Learns how to turn on the ground and in the air.	Masters formal turns: half and full turns, chaînés. Learns how to turn in the air and on the floor, such as triplet turn en l'air and à terre.	Masters formal turns: tour jetés, pirouettes. Refines turning en l'air and à terre. Increases turning techniques to include off-center turns.
1.1n Functional anatomy and kinesiology			
Understands and uses joint actions: ball and socket and hinge.	Learns basic anatomy as it applies to movement and mobility.	Learns basic anatomy and kinesiology as they apply to movement and dance.	Learns anatomy and kinesiology and is able to use proper terminology for muscles, bones, and joints when referring to dance movement.
1.1o Body conditioning			
Learns to move in ways that increase conditioning aspects, such as cardiovascular endurance, muscular strength, and muscular endurance appropriate to age level.	Learns to condition as a part of increasing body function: strength, flexibility, and endurance. Works with overall body conditioning and upper torso and limbs.	Engages in body conditioning that strengthens the total body. Uses conditioning practices such as Pilates.	Engages in body conditioning that strengthens the total body. Uses body conditioning to increase range of motion and strength of the artful body. Works with such conditioning models as Pilates or Gyrokinesis and somatic work such as Body–Mind Centering, Feldenkrais, or Alexander.
1.1p Gestures and postures			
Learns how gestures communicate. Emphasizes gestures of the hands, arms, head, and face. Studies everyday postures to see how they communicate meaning. Explores gestures and postures.	Increases awareness of gesture as it relates to expression and communication. Becomes able to abstract gesture for dance purposes. Uses postures associated with dance and those derived from everyday movement expressions.	Abstracts everyday gestures and postures into dance works. Becomes adept at using dance postures appropriate to the movement style.	Refines specific dance gestures and postures in styles such as classical ballet, Bharata Natyam, jazz, tap, and modern dance. Uses postures to communicate meaning. Performs expressively through literal and abstract gesture and movement to communicate an idea.

Dance Cornerstone Curriculum Framework—C1: Dancing and Performing from *Teaching Dance as Art in Education* by Brenda Pugh McCutchen, 2006, Champaign IL: Human Kinetics

1.0   Understanding and Using the Dance Elements

Grades K-2	Grades 3-5	Grades 6-8	Grades 9-12
1.1q Transfers into movement			
Transfers shapes, sounds, and stories into kinesthetic responses.	Transfers visual designs into movements and dance patterns. Matches sounds with movement qualities.	Transfers visual and auditory cues and patterns into the kinesthetic. Accurately memorizes and reproduces movement sequences.	Transfers visual and auditory cues and patterns into the kinesthetic. Accurately memorizes and reproduces movement sequences.
1.2 Space			
1.2a General–personal, negative–positive			
Defines, maintains, and explores personal and general space. Learns to respect others' personal space.	Develops controlled use of space when moving alone or in groups.	Develops sense of personal performing space and relationship to others.	Uses general and personal space.
Shows ability to move freely, yet safely, within personal and general space.	Shows ability to use direction, levels, and pathway within general and personal space.	Increases mastery of body design, pathway, and overall stage space as a performance skill.	Shows sensitivity in using performance space with groups and individuals, pathways, focus, and design.
Moves through space and prevents collisions.	Anticipates timing and spatial relationships when dancing with others.	Refines skills in the ability to meet, part, and work in time and space with others.	Dances with others in space, at a given moment in a dance, to accomplish such things as balances and turns and to change group designs in space.
————	Understands negative and positive space.	Demonstrates spatial awareness regarding own negative and positive space.	Demonstrates spatial awareness regarding own negative and positive space. Uses space in compositions: both negative and positive space as design elements.
1.2b Level			
Discriminates between high, middle, and low shapes and movements.	Discriminates between high-, middle-, and low-level movement and consciously makes movement transitions between levels.	Develops skill in using a variety of levels in dance exploration, composition, and technique.	Develops technical skill with level changes. Uses level changes as a design element in compositions. Develops partnering skills that enable contrast of level changes through lifts, balances, or other means.
1.2c Direction			
Discriminates between moving upward and downward.	Creates intentionally focused upward and downward movement.	Develops skill designing rising and sinking movements with upward–downward focus.	Develops technical skills in rapid direction changes. Develops "going up and down" as useful intentional directions in space. Uses them to increase range of motion and artistry.
Moves sideways and backward. Learns to dance in directions other than forward.	Moves backward, sideways, diagonally, turning, circling, upward, and downward.	Moves efficiently in all directions with appropriate balance and weight shifts.	Uses direction as a design element in composition and improvisation. Uses inwardly and outwardly directed material.
1.2d Pathway			
Distinguishes between curved, straight, and zigzag pathways.	Uses floor and air pathways such as straight, zigzag, and curved pathways.	Uses complex floor and air patterns as well as direct and indirect pathways. Creates lines in space that travel as pathways.	Executes floor and air patterns with increasing complexity. Combines pathways and other design elements to create visually interesting floor and air pathways.

Dance Cornerstone Curriculum Framework—C1: Dancing and Performing from *Teaching Dance as Art in Education* by Brenda Pugh McCutchen, 2006, Champaign IL: Human Kinetics

Grades K-2	Grades 3-5	Grades 6-8	Grades 9-12
1.2e Focus			
Understands the concept of focus.	Learns to use focus of eyes and other body parts. Uses eye and body focus as ways to clarify intent.	Develops and uses body graining to clarify intent and extend focus to the full body.	Develops the use of inward and outward focus, as well as graining. Projects while performing. Uses focus to clarify movement and intent.
1.2f Range			
Contrasts large and small movements related to the body and to the space used.	Varies the range or size of movements.	Uses different-sized shapes and movements for variety and contrast.	Modulates and uses the broadest range of movement in space for artistic and expressive clarity.
Grasps the concept of distance or amount of space traveled. Increases ability to judge distance when moving.	Understands and uses space in relation to distance traveled or distance between objects or persons.	Uses distance as an artistic choice as it relates to dancing with other people or distance traveled through space.	Uses distance as an expressive tool to communicate intent.
1.2g Body design			
Discovers shapes that are matched and those that are not matched. Identifies symmetry and asymmetry.	Uses symmetrical and asymmetrical body designs.	Incorporates body designs from different dance styles such as attitude (ballet) and aramandi (Bharata Natyam).	Designs the body in space and relates to space as if it were a partner.
1.2h Shaping			
Explores a variety of shapes in space: (1) still and frozen (2) moving and axial (3) traveling and locomotor movement	Develops the use of negative and positive space within static and dynamic shapes. Demonstrates the ability to use space and shape as rich design tools.	Designs body shapes related to space itself, objects in space, and other dancers in space. Acquires a sense of sculpting the body in space.	Designs static and dynamic shapes in space. Sculpts the body in space.
1.2i Combinations of space components			
	Experiences changing directions and levels kinesthetically as well as cognitively.	Explores air pathways and floor pathways in space.	Uses varied facing, focus, direction change, level change, and pathways in challenging personal coordination and technique.
1.2j Elevation			
Practices takeoffs and landings. Creates "jump shapes" in the air. Learns to land safely and softly from elevations, including jumps.	Perfects "jump shapes" and adds turns in the air. Learns how to plié as preparation for coming off and returning to the floor. Learns to articulate the foot in landings. Acquires other elevation skills in hopping and leaping both for distance and for height.	Perfects alignment, preparation, and landing for jumps and leaps. Strengthens and articulates the foot for safety and precision.	Refines techniques related to aerial work. Perfects alignment, preparation, and landing for jumps and leaps. Strengthens and articulates the foot for safety and precision.
1.2k Circling			
Learns the difference between circling (moving in a circular pathway) and turning (around one's own central axis).	Differentiates between circling and turning as two separate ways of continuous directional change.	Differentiates between circling and turning as two separate ways of continuous directional change. Increases the use of floor patterns, which include circling, zigzag, angular, and straight.	Differentiates between circling and turning as two separate ways of continuous directional change. Increases the use of floor patterns, which include circling, zigzag, angular, and straight.
		Contrasts centripetal and centrifugal circling concepts.	Contrasts centripetal and centrifugal circling concepts.

Dance Cornerstone Curriculum Framework—C1: Dancing and Performing from *Teaching Dance as Art in Education* by Brenda Pugh McCutchen, 2006, Champaign IL: Human Kinetics

1.0 Understanding and Using the Dance Elements

Grades K-2	Grades 3-5	Grades 6-8	Grades 9-12
1.3 Time			
1.3a Accurate rhythmic response			
Recognizes steady beat and moves to varying tempi of steady beats.	Responds in movement to even (steady) and uneven (dotted) rhythms.	Responds in movement to rhythmic variations within a phrase, as well as to the underlying beat.	Masters working with and against rhythm of accompaniment in dance.
Moves to varied rhythmic sounds at different tempi.	Dances to a variety of rhythms generated from internal and external sources.	Dances to a variety of rhythms generated from internal and external sources.	Performs to a variety of rhythms generated from internal and external sources.
Identifies and moves on the downbeat (heavy accent).	Recognizes 3/4 and 4/4 meter by correctly distinguishing the downbeat of both and moving accurately to that beat.	Accurately uses accented and unaccented beats in 3/4 and 4/4 meter.	Explains and uses syncopation to add variety to time. Uses accented movement related to different tempi.
————	————	Uses timing accents and variations within a phrase to add interest kinesthetically, rhythmically, and visually.	Uses timing accents and variations within a phrase to add interest kinesthetically, rhythmically, and visually.
————	Distinguishes between steady beat and general melodic rhythm.	Distinguishes between steady beat, melodic rhythm, and the inherent rhythm of lyrics.	Takes rhythm cues from different aspects of accompaniment.
————	Moves rhythmically.	Shows awareness of complex rhythms used in various dance styles.	Uses complex rhythmic patterns when choreographing specific dance styles.
1.3b Meter			
Experiences the kinesthetic feeling of moving to both duple and triple meter.	Differentiates between duple and triple meters and performs accurate movement to each meter.	Performs movement phrases with more complex metric structure than duple and triple.	Creates and performs with multiple and contrasting metric structures.
1.3c Tempo			
Identifies speed of dance as fast or slow, getting faster, or getting slower.	Recognizes and responds to tempo changes as they occur in dance and music. Experiences getting faster (accelerating) and getting slower (decelerating) in dance.	Expands dance vocabulary related to tempo. Increases skill in performing the full spectrum of tempo changes.	Expands dance vocabulary as well as performance skill in using the full spectrum of tempo.
Identifies tempo contrasts both conceptually and kinesthetically: long–short sudden–sustained, fast–slow.	Identifies tempo contrasts both conceptually and kinesthetically: long–short, sudden–sustained, fast–slow, long–short (duration). Performs movement phrases that show the ability to manipulate time concepts.	Shows different tempi with different body parts at the same time (e.g., arms slow, feet fast). Performs movement phrases that show the ability to manipulate time concepts.	Performs dance studies and compositions that use time and tempo in unpredictable ways. Modulates time factors for artistic interest and expressive acuity.
1.3d Form			
Performs a series of improvised movements in a simple sequence.	Structures and performs phrases that have an identifiable beginning, middle, and end. Sequences phrases logically to create a dance study in two-part form (AB, verse and chorus).	Develops dance studies, alone or with a small group, for at least three of the following forms: two part (AB, verse and chorus), three part (ABA or ABC), canon, theme and variation.	Uses several different structural forms according to needs of the work.

Dance Cornerstone Curriculum Framework—C1: Dancing and Performing from *Teaching Dance as Art in Education* by Brenda Pugh McCutchen, 2006, Champaign IL: Human Kinetics

Grades K-2	Grades 3-5	Grades 6-8	Grades 9-12
Recognizes a round in music and in dance.	Learns to dance a round in three groups.	Learns to dance a round in solo or duet groupings.	Dances canons and rounds.
Identifies sections in a dance as same or different from each other.	Identifies and uses simple dance and music forms: AB, ABA, round.	Identifies and uses more complex dance and music forms: theme and variations, rondo.	Identifies and uses all major dance and music forms, including canon and call–response.
———	Recognizes and repeats sequences of movements that fall into patterns called phrases.	Recognizes sequences of phrases linked by transitions; recognizes the way they create order and continuity in composition.	Uses phrasing and transitions to build effective sequences and dance forms.

1.3e Phrase

Grades K-2	Grades 3-5	Grades 6-8	Grades 9-12
Uses internal rhythms of the body through pulse. Identifies phrasing of sounds and movements.	Uses internal body rhythms through various gaits and nonmetered motions. Learns phrasing.	Uses internal body rhythms through breath, gait, and nonmetered motions. Uses phrasing.	Uses internal body rhythms and kinetics as phrasing tools. Becomes adept at phrasing with and without music.
Uses metric phrasing.	Uses metric and kinetic phrasing.	Uses metric, kinetic, and breath phrasing.	Uses metric, kinetic, and breath phrasing in performing as well as in creating studies and compositions. Uses nonmetered and metered (musical) phrasing in dancing.
———	Uses asymmetrical phrases. Creates phrases of different lengths within the same section to avoid predictability (e.g., two to the right, two to the left).	Uses asymmetrical phrases. Creates phrases of different lengths within the same section to avoid predictability (e.g., two to the right, two to the left).	Uses asymmetrical phrases. Creates phrases of different lengths within the same section to avoid predictability (e.g., two to the right, two to the left).
Knows how to concentrate and to be inside oneself to start and stop movement phrases effectively.	Anticipates ahead of music so movement can begin on cue with the music phrase.	Anticipates ahead of music so movement can begin on cue with the music phrase.	Anticipates timing to start on musical cue. Uses timing for effective transitions in movement with and without accompaniment.

1.3f Duration

Grades K-2	Grades 3-5	Grades 6-8	Grades 9-12
Experiences quick and slow movement.	Contrasts sudden and sustained in movement sequences.	Combines use of sudden and sustained timing as it relates to both the time and the dynamics of a phrase or dance work.	Consciously uses sudden and sustained as contrasts within phrases and dance works.
Identifies the length of time a move or dance takes, whether it is long or short.	Creates dance phrases of different lengths. Is aware of duration and length of dance.	Learns to determine the appropriate length of a dance one is creating.	Uses awareness of appropriate length needed for dance making so that a dance is neither too long nor too short to make its point. Stops a dance after it has finished saying what it needs to say. Avoids using music that is too long for accompaniment.

1.3g Polyrhythms and resultant rhythms

Grades K-2	Grades 3-5	Grades 6-8	Grades 9-12
———	Claps and stamps two rhythms at the same time.	Learns to use multiple rhythms at the same time. Analyzes and accurately performs resultant rhythm patterns previously created.	Uses multiple rhythms at the same time. Performs and designs resultant rhythm in choreography.

Dance Cornerstone Curriculum Framework—C1: Dancing and Performing from *Teaching Dance as Art in Education* by Brenda Pugh McCutchen, 2006, Champaign IL: Human Kinetics

1.0   Understanding and Using the Dance Elements

Grades K-2	Grades 3-5	Grades 6-8	Grades 9-12
1.3h Nonmetered music and soundscape			
————	————	Creates nonmetered phrases that do not rely on accompaniment.	Creates dance studies that are not reliant on accompaniment. Also creates dances with non-metered accompaniment as an independent soundscape.
1.3i Accompaniment for movement			
————	Learns to create percussion scores for peer and personal works.	Creates percussion scores for peer and personal works. Selects both metered and nonmetered music for accompaniment that does not have words and is not on the top-10 hit list of current songs.	Creates percussion scores and designs accompaniment that underscores peer and personal works. Becomes non-reliant on music to stimulate dance composition. Creates soundscapes for accompaniment and "found sound" (musique concrète) scores.
1.3j Immediacy			
————	Differentiates between "in time" and "out of time."	Learns to be "in the moment." Demonstrates ability to become "one with movement" during technique and performance.	Is "in the moment." Demonstrates ability to become "one with movement" during technique and performance.

1.4   Energy and dynamics

Grades K-2	Grades 3-5	Grades 6-8	Grades 9-12
1.4a Laban's effort actions			
Learns to contrast strong–firm and light in movement.	Contrasts strong–firm and light force in movement phrases.	Combines and modulates the use of strong–firm and light dynamics within movement phrases.	Expresses intent through the artful use of energy and dynamics appropriate to a dance. Modulates effort to give variety within the sequence, the phrase, or the study.
————	Becomes familiar with Laban's eight basic efforts: flick, dab, float, punch, wring, press, slash, glide.	Works with the Laban efforts to develop a range of dynamics and effort possibilities. Learns at least one Laban effort scale.	Works within the Laban effort vocabulary to develop a wide repertory of dynamics and effort movements.
————	————	Explores the use of internal body force created by varying tensions within one's physical structure.	Demonstrates awareness of internal force and intensity required to execute movements, whether original phrases or set sequences.
1.4b Flow			
Uses tight and loose movements to contrast each kinesthetic feeling and to conceptually clarify the two concepts.	Distinguishes between bound and free-flowing movements and contrasts them in technique.	Contrasts bound and free-flowing movements and contrasts them to discover their communicative potential.	Performs bound and free-flowing movements and contrasts them. Experiences energy flow as an important dynamic tool in technique.
————	————	Executes energy flowing out and energy streaming in during technique class to direct intent.	Uses flow as a compositional and performance tool.

Dance Cornerstone Curriculum Framework—C1: Dancing and Performing from *Teaching Dance as Art in Education* by Brenda Pugh McCutchen, 2006, Champaign IL: Human Kinetics

Grades K-2	Grades 3-5	Grades 6-8	Grades 9-12
1.4c Dynamic accent			
————	Changes dynamic qualities within movement phrases. Develops ability—and sensitivity to the need—to add forceful accent as a compositional tool.	Modulates movement phrases according to amount of force and energy to ensure that rises and falls of dynamics can be seen and felt and that dynamic accents are used efficiently.	Artfully uses dynamic accents for counterpoint and climax (within dance sections and full dances) to clarify intent and make points of emphasis.
1.4d Motivation			
Explores different body parts that can initiate movement.	Uses body parts leading. Uses motor impulse motivation to initiate movement phrases.	Motivates movement from both central initiation (torso) and peripheral initiation (distal).	Articulates movement initiations in technique and in performance.
1.4e Qualities			
Experiences some of the movement qualities, especially vibrate, swing, and percussive.	Experiences the six qualities: vibrate, swing, percussive, sustained, collapse, suspend.	Develops skill in using the six qualities as dynamic tools.	Masters the six dynamic qualities by interweaving them skillfully throughout compositions, technique, and performance.
————	————	————	Modulates appropriate dynamic qualities to clarify the intent of a study or dance work.
1.4f Graining			
————	————	Senses movement flow through the body and from one part to another. Develops total body awareness and directs dynamic energy flow in such a way that movement is immediate and textured.	Senses movement flow in and through all parts of the body, using flow to connect movements. Develops total body awareness and directs dynamic energy flow in such a way that movement is immediate and textured.
1.4g Expressivity			
Uses energy to express an idea through movement and dance.	Directs movement flow and effort to fully express an idea or concept. Performs movement sequences expressively through abstract gestures and postures.	Modulates dynamics in a way that makes a clear expression of intent. Performs movement sequences expressively.	Modulates dynamics in a way that makes a clear expression of intent. Performs movement sequences expressively. Projects dynamic range.

1.5   Relationship

Grades K-2	Grades 3-5	Grades 6-8	Grades 9-12
1.5a Relationship of one body part to another			
Isolates body parts. Can show dances with one part in conversation with others (e.g., hands, elbows, and knees).	Isolates body parts as an emphasis or embellishment to dance studies. Relates one body part to another in a "duet" of body parts.	Relates body parts to each other in shaping and for developmental movement patterns. Begins to use body isolations as both emphasis and interest in dance studies.	Coordinates relationships of different body parts such as use of limbs to artfully relate to other parts of the body.
————	————	Relates body parts to each other in shaping, gestures, and postures related to technique development (such as ballet port de bras and épaulement).	Relates body parts to each other in shaping, gestures, and postures related to technique development (such as ballet port de bras and épaulement).

Dance Cornerstone Curriculum Framework—C1: Dancing and Performing from *Teaching Dance as Art in Education* by Brenda Pugh McCutchen, 2006, Champaign IL: Human Kinetics

1.0 Understanding and Using the Dance Elements

Grades K-2	Grades 3-5	Grades 6-8	Grades 9-12
1.5b Relationship to other dancers			
Relates to others in small groups. Learns to dance together, to mirror, and to dance one after another.	Relates to others in small groups. Effectively mirrors, shadows, and dances using juxtaposition with a partner. Uses space concepts such as meeting–parting, near–far, unison, contrast.	Performs in small groups and relates to others in the dancing space. Performs in large groups using peripheral vision to see others. Communicates concepts such as meeting–parting and structures such as call and response and canon.	Refines ability to perform with others to express clear intent. Relates to others in multiple ways including lifts, supports, and contact improvisation (where appropriate).
Dances prepositions such as *over, under,* and *around* to embody the concepts and learn to relate to others through dance.	Dances prepositions to show relationships such as *with, against, on, away from, through, beside, toward, between, near,* and *far.*	Dances word dances and improvisations with a partner. Makes partner dances using verbs and prepositions.	Performs group dances that use complex groupings such as juxtaposition, canon, solo to group or chorus, and call–response.
1.5c Relationship to an object or prop			
Relates in space to stationary objects and eventually to moving objects.	Creates duets with inanimate objects or props. Creates individual dances in which a prop is a partner.	Creates solos with inanimate objects as props used in creative and unpredictable ways. Partners with a prop to perform a duet with the prop used as though it were a different object.	Creates dances based on a relationship between animate and inanimate objects. Makes an artistic statement about either object or dancers or about their relationship. Designs props in such a way that they are integral to the dance used as major focal points.
1.5d Relationship to the other dance elements			
Relates the body to space and time.	Creates and performs dances that relate the body to space, time, and dynamics.	Creates and performs dances that relate the body to space, time, and energy and dynamics.	Creates and performs dances that relate the body to space, time, and energy and dynamics.
1.5e Relationship to accompaniment			
Moves in time to accompaniment as appropriate: folk dance, learning locomotor steps and steady beat.	Performs selected dance styles in sync with accompaniment regarding time and movement quality.	Relates dance to the musical quality and timing of the accompaniment.	Relates to rather than relies on musical accompaniment in time and dynamic quality. Uses sound to coexist with movement.

2.0 Dance Vocabularies

Grades K-2	Grades 3-5	Grades 6-8	Grades 9-12
2.1 Movement vocabulary			
2.1a Step vocabulary (locomotor steps)			
Uses all five simple locomotor steps that are basic to all others: walk, run, leap, jump, hop. Performs some simple folk dances and learns to use basic even steps with rhythmic accuracy.	Perfects simple locomotor steps and complex locomotor steps done in uneven rhythms such as skip, slide, and gallop. Learns to execute even rhythm steps such as grapevine, schottische, and two-step. Performs folk dances that use a variety of steps. Learns to perform the step vocabulary with different rhythms and stylistic variations.	Increases step vocabulary to include ballet terminology for locomotors such as glissade, chassé, pas de bourrée. Performs folk and vernacular dances that use steps and furthers the ability to apply them to various rhythms and styles, such as Irish step dance or hip-hop.	Increases the ability to perform basic and complex steps with rhythmic accuracy and stylistic variation. Increases performance skills with step dancing, such as flamenco or Scottish step dances (strathspey, sword dance).

Dance Cornerstone Curriculum Framework—C1: Dancing and Performing from *Teaching Dance as Art in Education* by Brenda Pugh McCutchen, 2006, Champaign IL: Human Kinetics

Grades K-2	Grades 3-5	Grades 6-8	Grades 9-12
2.1b Universal dance vocabulary (UDV, the dance elements)			
Systematically builds concepts and skills in dancing and analyzing dance movement with the dance elements vocabulary (UDV).	Systematically builds concepts and skills in dancing and analyzing dance movement with the dance elements vocabulary (UDV).	Systematically builds concepts and skills in dancing and analyzing dance movement with the dance elements vocabulary (UDV).	Systematically builds concepts and skills in dancing and analyzing dance movement with the dance elements vocabulary (UDV).
2.1c Classical ballet terminology			
_____	(5th grade) Learns to initiate rotation and execute plié and relevé in first and second positions facing the barre. Is introduced to terms and proper use of tendues, dégagés, and battements at the barre, facing the barre. Acquires the technique to execute these aspects of ballet.	Reviews previous work and learns to describe and execute additional limited barre and center work from first position, such as rond de jambe à terre, attitudes, attitude leg swings, passé, développé. Adds third position (no fourth unless a gifted class). Uses en croix in first position, *always facing the barre*.	Reviews previous work and learns to describe and execute additional limited barre and center work from first and third positions only (no fourth and fifth), such as rond de jambe en l'air, piqué turns, and grand jeté. Executes barre work in first and second (and third *facing the barre* and possibly one hand on the barre).
_____	Emphasizes proper execution of movements with the terms.	Emphasizes proper execution of movements with the terms.	Emphasizes proper execution of movements with the terms.
2.1d Stylistic vocabulary			
Learns some stylistic vocabulary related to dances around the world.	Learns stylistic vocabulary related to folk dances and modern dance. Develops basic use of some steps, positions, and motions.	Adds stylistic vocabulary related to ballet and modern dance. Develops basic use of steps, positions, and motions in different styles.	Adds stylistic vocabulary related to performance styles such as Bharata Natyam (mudras, jatis), Japanese Kabuki (mie), and jazz dance (break, layout, switchkick).

2.2 Anatomical terms

2.2a Bones and joints			
Through dancing, identifies major bony landmarks such as the patella and major bones such as the femur. Compares hinge and ball-and-socket joints.	Identifies bones and joints as part of the techniques being studied. Uses hinge and ball-and-socket joint action with ease.	Identifies joints for mobility. Knows there is no anatomical waist. Uses anatomy to relate to and describe movement. Is successful on performance-based tests of functional anatomy.	Identifies joints for mobility. Relates skeletal anatomy to movement. Is successful on performance-based tests of applying anatomy.
2.2b Muscles			
Identifies major muscles such as abdominals, quadriceps, triceps, and biceps.	Engages muscles that are used in developing early technique such as abdominals, gastrocnemius (calf), and hamstrings.	Learns deeper muscles that serve acute balance flexion and extension of the body such as psoas, obliques, latissimus dorsi, and erector spinae.	Learns and engages muscles such as the gluteals, trapezius, pectoralis major and minor, and deltoids.

2.3 Aesthetic vocabulary

2.3a Artistic principles of design (choreography)			
Understands the concept and use of unity and sequence.	Knows and applies the basic artistic principles of design: unity, repetition, and contrast.	Knows and applies principles of design: unity, variety, contrast, sequence, and climax.	Knows and uses all 10 principles of design: unity, harmony, variety, contrast, repetition, balance, climax, proportion, sequence, and transition.

Dance Cornerstone Curriculum Framework—C1: Dancing and Performing from *Teaching Dance as Art in Education* by Brenda Pugh McCutchen, 2006, Champaign IL: Human Kinetics

2.0 Dance Vocabularies

Grades K-2	Grades 3-5	Grades 6-8	Grades 9-12
2.3b Artistic performance qualities			
Learns to bodythink and body-speak.	Articulates through bodythinking and bodyspeaking.	Increases aesthetic vocabulary to include projection, musicality, quality, articulation, and timing related to performing. Refines kinaesthetic bodyspeaking.	Increases aesthetic vocabulary for performance to include projection, dynamics, musicality, somatic awareness, breath support, articulation, and timing. Refines kinaesthetic motion.
2.4 Laban-based vocabulary			
2.4a Motif writing and Language of Dance (LOD)			
Learns and uses some of the LOD symbols.	Learns LOD symbols and vocabulary. Recognizes them and translates them into movement.	Applies LOD both to writing movement in symbols and to decoding simple LOD patterns; constructs phrases using LOD.	Applies LOD both to writing movement in symbols and to decoding LOD patterns; constructs phrases using LOD.
2.4b Labanotation			
Learns level and direction symbols in Labanotation.	Applies and uses Labanotation symbols for level, direction, and duration on the center of the movement scale (weight placement, step patterns).	Reads and writes introductory level Labanotation scores on the center of the movement scale with accurate level, direction, and duration symbols; reconstructs basic traveling patterns.	Reproduces traveling movement sequences from short Labanotation scores. Where possible, learns to use LabanWriter for choreographing and notating dance. (Advanced: adds arms.)
2.4c Labanalysis (LMA)			
————	Learns and uses several Laban effort actions within a unit's context.	Learns and uses Laban effort actions within a unit's context. Uses two-dimensional concepts of spoking and arcing.	Uses Laban vocabulary to identify, describe, and perform effort actions within a unit's context. Uses two-dimensional concepts of spoking and arcing and three-dimensional carving.
————	————	Acquires, classifies, and describes movement according to basic effort actions (Laban).	Acquires, classifies, and describes movement according to basic effort actions.
2.4d Laban terminology			
Learns and uses relevant Laban terminology, such as *kinesphere*.	Acquires and uses relevant Laban terminology related to body and space, including the three-dimensional planes, direct and indirect (space) within a unit's context.	Builds on and increases application of Laban terminology; adds time, including flow, sudden and sustained (time) within a unit's context.	Builds on and increases use and application of Laban terminology; adds effort, including bound and free, firm and fine (flow) within a unit's context.

Dance Cornerstone Curriculum Framework—C1: Dancing and Performing from *Teaching Dance as Art in Education* by Brenda Pugh McCutchen, 2006, Champaign IL: Human Kinetics

Creating and Composing

 Cornerstone 2

This chapter features Cornerstone 2—one of the four educational dance cornerstones. Cornerstone 2 focuses on the key aspects of creating and composing dance as art. It features both creative process and product. It encompasses creative dance, **divergent thinking,** improvising, composing, and choreographing. The substance of this cornerstone aligns with national standards. It is outlined in detail to help you build curriculum, write goals and objectives, and design assessments accordingly. Cornerstone 2 may be the starting place for, the main focus of, or one part of a unit of study, but it is a necessary part of each unit. A sequential K-12 curriculum framework for Cornerstone 2 is presented in this chapter. Cornerstone 2 enrolls the learner as choreographer.

Relation to National Standards and Beyond

The creative side of dance comes out of each child differently. Creativity in dancing involves reaching into the soul and bringing out what is there in the forms of movement and creative thinking. It is the place to celebrate each child's unique self. It is the place where each one learns his own language of dance and finds his own creative movement voice. Whether a child is working with a thematic structure, a narrative content, or abstract ideas, individuals create their own personal meaning as they make dances to communicate their perspectives. "Creativity cannot be taught. . . . We can only set conditions for it and insure its reappearance through re-enforcement" (Smith 1970, pp. 5-6).

This cornerstone features the creating aspect of NAEP's report card. Cornerstone 2 fleshes out NSDE 2, *Understanding choreographic principles, processes, and structures;* NSDE 3, *Understanding dance as a way to create and communicate meaning;* and NSDE 4, *Applying and demonstrating critical and creative thinking skills in dance.* Before going further, read the NSDE Achievement Standards 2, 3, and 4 in grades 4, 8, and 12.

Dance study and courses that prepare you to teach this cornerstone: Creative courses in dance such as Improvisation, Creative Dance, Dance Composition, and Solo and Group Choreography furnish you content and skills with which to create, perform, and teach.

Overview of This Cornerstone

The focus of Cornerstone 2 is creating. It emphasizes the creative process that yields creative products. Educational dance thrives when it has a strong creative problem-solving component.

The creative process is about experimenting with movement, movement exploration, and improvisation. Its hallmarks are creative dance for children, composition for all ages, and choreography; it involves performing one's creations for feedback, editing, refining, and performing again. It progresses from composition basics (K-5) to choreography.

The creative process is about experimenting with movement, movement exploration, and improvisation. Give creative problems to solve that increase artistic use of movement as well as expand one's movement options.

To increase awareness of movement and to build compositional skills, create movement problems that feature the dance elements (i.e., the use of the body in space and time, with energy and dynamic clarity, and in relation to a variety of factors). Give students the kinds of creative problems to solve that increase artistic use of movement as well as expand their movement options. Base these problems on students' prior knowledge, skill level, and artistic readiness. Give creative criteria not only to guide the process but also to shape quality and build compositional skills. Let your students know that productive creativity is more than doing your own thing without any guidance. Productive creativity depends on the parameters specific to the composition goals.

Ensure that the creative products evolve out of the creative process. Don't make them isolated events. Bring creative products forth from the skills students are acquiring about thematic material, form and structure, and the principles of design. Show students how to refine and polish their creations to show others. Artful creation depends on how the teacher conveys the tools of composition.

Specific units of study may begin from C2: the point of entry, the inspiration for, or the emphasis of the unit. C2 enriches a unit whether it is the focus of the unit's content or the support for its experiences. Incorporate creative work in each unit, because this personalizes and artistically enriches each unit.

Some mega-ideas and concepts from this cornerstone follow:

1. Choreographers create movement to communicate meaning and intent.
2. Choreographers are the creative artists of the dance discipline—just as composers are in music, playwrights are in theatre, and visual artists are in art and design.
3. The creative process is as important as the creative product in education.
4. Creative and critical thinking in the arts use and develop complex skills of application, analysis, synthesis, evaluation, and interpretation.
5. Artistic principles of design apply uniformly across all the arts.
6. The creative process relies on divergent as well as **convergent thinking** and action.

Goals and Objectives of Cornerstone 2

The Dance Cornerstone Curriculum (DCC) Framework is in three parts. The first part (goals and objectives) shows the big picture. The second part (content outline) breaks goals and objectives into an outline. The third part breaks into a suggested developmental sequence detailed later in the chapter for K-2, 3-5, 6-8, and 9-12.

These suggested K-12 goals and objectives help you fully convey Cornerstone 2. See the many ways these goals prepare students to meet or exceed the NSDEs—especially 2, 3, and 4.

 Goal 1: To communicate ideas, feelings, and images through movement in dance

1.0 Desired outcomes: To fully explore the dance elements for their expressive potential in order to use dance as a personal language of expression.

Learning objectives: The student will

1.1 Explore and experiment with movement as part of the creative process.

> Use originality and develop individual style.

1.2 Improvise to find expressive movement with which to make dances.

> Improvise to sharpen perception.

> Use the dance elements, abstract imagery, and environmental and sensory stimuli as the impetus for composing dances.

> Problem solve in dance through spontaneous movement.

1.3 Problem solve in dance before designing dances.

 Goal 2: To apply compositional tools and choreographic principles

2.0 Desired outcomes: To create and compose dances.

Learning objectives: The student will

2.1 Perform original movement motifs, phrases, and dance compositions for others in informal and performance settings.

> Apply compositional tools to structuring dances.

2.2 Use the tools of dance making and refine the craft of choreography.

> Organize movement into dances with specific form and structure.

> Select and organize movement into coherent phrases and compositions.

> Use selected choreographic forms and structures.

2.3 Create and evaluate one's own dance works with form and structure.

> Apply aesthetic criteria and the principles of design (PODs) to compositions and criteria.

2.4 Choreograph using choreographic criteria.

> Apply choreographic criteria to shaping one's work in progress.

Goal 3: To edit and polish creative works for performance

3.0 Desired outcomes: To show one's works for critical feedback and to refine them for performance.

Learning objectives: The student will

3.1 Polish and show works in progress for editorial feedback and critique (formal and informal).

> Self-evaluate and edit one's own works to improve artistic integrity.

> Use review criteria for peer and self-critique.

> Polish compositions to clarify intent and to communicate meaning.

> Polish and perform works for peers or others.

3.2 Show work for feedback based on review criteria.

> Show work for summative critique.

> Show work for in-process (formative) feedback.

Adapted from Lunt and McCutchen, 1995, with permission of the South Carolina Department of Education.

Content Outline

Use this framework outline to guide comprehensive long-term curriculum planning. The outline headings are developed into a framework at the end of the chapter (page 195).

Teach so students learn to freely explore dance. Teach them to create and compose dances individually and with others. The desired outcome is to make dances that communicate meaning at all ages and develop choreographic skills in high school.

Goal 1.0 Experimentation

Objective 1.1 Movement Exploration

1.1a Exploring the dance elements (body—body part isolations and full body, space, time, energy and dynamics, relationship)

1.1b Exploring stimuli (tactile, visual, auditory–verbal)

1.1c Exploring gestures and postures

1.1d Exploring mobility and stability

1.1e Exploring imagery (concrete and abstract)

1.1f Experiments with movement concepts

Objective 1.2 Improvisation

1.2a Qualities (textures, body systems approach, dynamic range)

1.2b Spatial designing (near–far, meeting–parting, opening–closing, negative–positive)

1.2c Body relationships (self and others, props, support and contact-improvisation)

1.2d Timing (tempo, accelerating, decelerating)

1.2e Themes and relevant topics (conflict–resolution, together–apart, isolation–community, and topics related to other studies)

Goal 2.0 Composition and Choreography (Shaping Movement Into Dance)

Objective 2.1 Basic Skills of Composing

2.1a Beginning–middle–end

2.1b Selecting movement and motifs

2.1c Phrasing

2.1d Stating a theme

2.1e Extending and manipulating movement

2.1f Clarifying and refining to communicate intent and meaning

2.1g Parallels to written composition

Objective 2.2 Form and Structure

2.2a Basic forms: phrase or sentence, study, composition, choreography

2.2b Structural forms: two-part, three-part, theme and variation, theme and development

2.2c Choosing a structure (to communicate intent and meaning)

2.2d Grouping: solo, duet, trio, group (small and large)

2.2e Structured improvisation

2.2f Organic and kinetic structures

2.2g Structures based on accompaniment

Objective 2.3 Aesthetic Principles of Design

2.3a Sequencing

2.3b Repetition

2.3c Contrast

2.3d Variety

2.3e Unity

2.3f Climax (crescendo)

2.3g Advanced design principles: proportion, harmony, transition, balance

2.3h Overall aesthetic quality

Objective 2.4 Choreographing

2.4a Choreographic criteria

2.4b Aesthetic choices

2.4c Technology: software

 ## Goal 3.0 Polishing and Sharing Creations

Objective 3.1 Polishing Compositions

3.1a Making aesthetic decisions

3.1b Editorial feedback: showing works in progress

3.1c Self-evaluation and editing

Objective 3.2 Performing for Critique

3.2a Performing: using review criteria for critique

3.2b Performance quality

Adapted from Lunt and McCutchen, 1995, with permission of the South Carolina Department of Education.

Cornerstone Thumbprint (C2)

Students gain proficiency in creating and composing. They experience the gamut of creative activities—from the spontaneity of improvisation and exploration to the formal structuring of movements into a dance. They experience the interplay between creative process and creative products. They learn to value exploration and improvisation as valid creative expression as well as an organic way to start composing dances. Students learn form, structure, and aesthetic design principles as part of learning to choreograph.

- **K-2:** Students in grades K through 2 explore the dance elements systematically to become thoroughly familiar with the language of motion. They create phrases with simple structures. They make mostly individual responses and develop an elements movement vocabulary. Emphasize creative movement and problem solving.

- **3-5:** Students in grades 3 through 5 extend their range of movement through improvising, creating short dance studies, and structuring dance into two- and three-part forms using solo, duet, and some small group work. Most creative work is unaccompanied. They work both individually and in groups. Creative processes and products emphasize the dance elements.

- **6-8:** Students in grades 6 through 8 continue to explore and improvise. They create more complex dance studies on their bodies and in small groups, applying criteria for three-part form, rondo, theme and variation, and other compositional structures. They learn to apply the aesthetic principles of design to increase the compositional quality and clarify intent.

- **9-12:** Students in grades 9 through 12 refine improvisational and compositional skills. They choreograph with and without accompaniment. They edit, refine, and rework compositions to improve the clarity and the aesthetic quality by applying the principles of design.

Adapted with permission of the South Carolina Department of Education, © 1993.

Creative Process and Products

Creative work includes the spontaneous, unplanned skills of exploring, experimenting, and improvising. It also includes planned, structured skills of composing, dance making, and choreography. The first is divergent (i.e., open ended, extends into multiple directions, explodes outward). The second is convergent (i.e., selective, comes together, focuses on a product, collecting, specific).

Dance's creative process is about exploring, improvising, and creating multiple responses to stimuli. It is student centered. Unique expressions emerge and dissolve. Its aim is to find and use movement to clearly express an idea, thought, feeling, or concept in dance. The process takes many forms. It is sometimes spontaneous and improvisational;

it is sometimes set and planned. Either way, the overarching goal is to increase the creator's ability to use the body in time, in space, with dynamic power and relational skill.

The raw material of dance is simply movement and motivation. The dance elements are at the same time part of the raw material and the tools for manipulating movement. Although everyone has the same space and time to work with, everyone has a unique body instrument with a different energy flow and ability to shift dynamics. To shape this raw material into artistic expression requires tools such as the aesthetic principles of design.

Creative Process

Creative process can either "drive" or "ride with" a unit. In either case, it needs to be there. The creative process starts in a void, with a blank slate. There comes a spark of an idea or a motivation from the teacher or from a student. Something is envisioned where nothing previously existed, and it starts to become structured so something new is generated. Creating is divergent with almost unlimited possibilities. That doesn't mean that creative structures are not needed in educational dance. Not only are they needed: They are required.

Dance making around one dance element will yield different dances as unique as the individuals making the dances. Such personal responses to creative stimuli and their simultaneous translation into expressive movement present young choreographers with many options:

"The game of a future idea comes suddenly and unexpectedly."

—Tchaikowsky

- To create a dance abstracting everyday movement associated with the subject
- To find movement to reflect ideas or feelings about the subject
- To design space, dynamics, and time in a way that emphasizes aspects of the topic
- To find an inventive take on the subject
- To explore and express the kinetic possibilities inherent in the subject

During this creative, evolutionary process, the dance emerges. It merges aspects of the topic with each person's unique perspective. It is no wonder that choreographic works are so subjective. They reveal much about the creator. Their sources of inspiration are myriad:

- To express personal feelings
- To make social and political commentary
- To express the joy of dancing
- To tell a story or represent a concrete idea
- To take an idea and abstract it
- To use combinations of these approaches

You are there to guide the process so the composer–choreographer's creation contains perceptible interpretations of the subject without reproducing exact imitation or pantomime. You are to help students discover how their creations use abstraction and creative invention. You show them how to find movement elements that best translate the subject into action. You teach them to identify the dynamics inherent in the topic and translate them into motion to communicate its essence.

Elizabeth Hayes expresses it best by comparing creating with the elements to a kaleidoscope of variable colors.

Art expression, like form created by a shifting kaleidoscope, is forever changing, forever new. The myriad of geometric designs that one sees in the kaleidoscope are all made from the same elements, variously shaped pieces of colored glass, but as the relationships of these colored objects to each other are changed, new forms ensue. Although all forms of art are derived from materials inherent in human experience, each work of art varies according to the particular patterning of these materials. As is the case in the kaleidoscope, the possibilities for structural variation are incalculable.

In art, however, an additional variable factor lies in the substance of *individual* human experience. No two persons undergo exactly the same experiences. Not only do the events or circumstances in their lives vary, but even when individuals are subjected to similar experiences, their perceptions of these experiences differ according to the fabric of their particular backgrounds and personalities. (Hayes 1993, p. 1)

Creativity requires several things from learners:

- Rational thinking
- **Originality**
- High levels of emotional development
- High levels of feeling sensitivity
- High levels of consciousness, use of imagery, imagination, and fantasy
- High levels of physical development and sensing with the body and mind

Creative and Critical Thinking

Higher-order thinking and processing are called on to create and critically evaluate dances.

- Creative thinking is elaborative, inventive, and open ended.
- Critical thinking is analytical, interpretive, and evaluative. Both dwell in Bloom's thinking–processing ranges of application, analysis, and synthesis (Bloom's taxonomy).

Problem Solving and Movement Exploration Problem solving in dance requires creative thinking and processing. Movement exploration is one of the first uses of problem solving. For example, you might ask your students, "How many ways can you jump and land?" With age, experience, and stamina, students can solve creative problems that are more complex. There are three kinds of spontaneous, divergent exploratory work in the dance curriculum:

- *Exploring* seeks all options (movement exploration).
- *Experimenting* tries out an idea or a concept and focuses on it (experimentation).
- *Improvising* is a way to spontaneously create—alone or in a group (improvisation). It is created spontaneously around a theme or in response to someone or something (e.g., music, poetry), sometimes as part of informal performances.

Solve artistic problems with the BSTER elements during movement exploration to develop students' language for dance and dancing. Thoroughly work the concepts from the BSTERs so all students know the dance elements language in concept (conceptually) and in movement (kinetically). After students master this vocabulary, extend movement exploration to a wider selection of words, especially the body actions (figure 6.2), which include many movement concepts. For example, try assigning action words (verbs) from students' spelling and vocabulary lists to explore. You can't run out of verbs! Some examples worth exploring are in figure 7.1. Guide students to elaborate on a verb by varying movement response as the word is spoken aloud (e.g., moving one verb in multiple, exploratory ways such as using different body parts; changing the tempo from fast to slow, then accelerating and decelerating; changing the space used from high to low, large amount to small, direct to indirect, different path-

Melt	Cling
Wiggle	Flip
Bounce	Slink
Jiggle	Skip
Ooze	Shrink
Collapse	Sway
Soar	Stretch
Snatch	Flop

FIGURE 7.1 Students can explore numerous verbs through dance.

ways, shapes, place, directions). But stick to each verb's inherent dynamic quality or other defining characteristics.

Experimenting and Improvising Spontaneously creating movement is just as important as learning dance techniques. Both **experimentation** and **improvisation** exist for their own sake. They are quite valid on their own. They take an inquiring, evolutionary, loosely structured approach. They are also vital forerunners to composition. They are an important source of natural, unaffected, fresh movement material that enlivens a composition, keeping the resulting dances from being too much from the mind so they're grounded in the organic wellspring of motion and kinetics.

Whereas experimenting is intentional stop–start kinetic problem solving, improvisation is in-the-moment streaming. **Improvising** puts the mover in touch with the creative flow of the present. It enables young people to get inside their movement and learn to trust themselves and the creative process. Improvising is often observed by others much like a jam session. As long as the classroom improvisation has boundaries and is structured around a point of emphasis, students can create. But if students are asked to move any way they feel, there is not enough for them to work with and there is little to learn (except how self-conscious this can make them!). Always define the parameters of an improvisation in the classroom to focus students' efforts in a way that makes room for their creativity and invites it within a structure. (Refer to Nikolais-Louis' book in chapter 6's Rich Resources for myriad ideas.)

Improv is a dynamic in-the-moment experience. It ranges in sophistication from beginner level to proficient enough to be performed live for others. Those observing get the chance to read and respond to the movement invention—to watch what serendipitously happens. Improv is about spontaneity and serendipity.

An effective way to begin movement experimentation with children is to work with contrasts, or antonyms. Experiment by contrasting the extremes with the full body. Then add other elements. For example, if contrasting "sharp" and "smooth," experiment using different body parts, levels, and shaping. Experiment by taking the movement into space, traveling in motions that are smooth or explosively sharp. Alter the timing of movements, and emphasize dynamic differences between the two extremes. Use experimentation to simultaneously build dance and conceptual vocabularies.

For more experienced dancers, use word pairs to stimulate improvisations. Emphasize not only the exaggerated extremes but also all the gradations in between. See figure 7.2 for word pairs to get you started. Invite students to brainstorm all the antonyms they can think of to use for experimentation. At the appropriate time, use these words as the theme for an AB dance composition.

To enhance the creative process, keep creative materials on hand to stimulate experimentation. Keep on the lookout for materials to motivate dance composition and improvisation. Some ideas include these:

- Prop box
- Colorful fabric strips and ribbons
- Textured fabric
- Stretchy body socks
- Stretching balls and stretchy elastic bands
- Recipes and cookbooks
- Magazines and news articles
- Sports articles and descriptions

- Textured objects from nature
- Feather boas, masks, and streamers

Composing The creative process leads into dance making. All ages need to learn and refine dance composition skills (just as they do written composition skills). Composition skills are the building blocks of choreography. Begin when children are young so they acquire a sense of order and sequence and understand basic structures for composing. Build compositional skills one at a time until students acquire all the skills they need to eventually choreograph. That is, compose with one dance element at a time to ensure that students use it fully. Then progress from short studies about easily grasped, concrete concepts to more complex or abstract concepts.

Composing is no less an art than choreography. Composition is just less complex. Compositional tools are specific and give parameters to dance making. Herein lies the craft of composing dances. By the time students are in advanced high school classes, they might even take liberties with some compositional rules and create some new structures. Compositions and dance studies are like lead-up games in sports.

BSTER elements are the alphabet (materials) of dance making. Composing involves using the body in space, designing timing and dynamic contrasts, and building relationships that convey the message of the dance. Therefore, to re-emphasize, BSTERs are both the kinetic and conceptual language of composing dances and dance studies.

Composing is different from choreographing: Composing is about organizing movement. Skill in composition builds skill in choreography. The difference between a composition and a piece of choreography is that a composition is a shorter work with a more limited topic or scope. For example, the dance composition may be about fully using one prop or taking a theme such as meeting and parting. Choreography requires students to have many such compositional building blocks in their repertory before they tackle a full dance work. Otherwise the product (dance work) is either limited or unclear and unable to communicate.

Compositions are often works in progress. But for students to improve at composing, their works need to be performed for qualitative feedback (informal or formal) and then edited and refined.

Editing and Refining You've heard the saying, "The devil is in the details." *Editing is the "details."*

Improvise, exaggerating the extremes between the word pairs.

Large–small	Straight–curved
High–low	Still–active
Loud–soft	Smooth–sharp
Quick–slow	Flat (2-D)–spiral (3-D)
Sticky–fluffy	Bound–free
Tight–loose	

FIGURE 7.2 Antonym word pairs.

The artistry of composition happens in the editing and refining stages. Editing requires acute critical thinking. Composition from third grade on is not complete until it has had a thoughtful evaluation either through self-reflection, through critical feedback from others, or both (see chapter 9). Use feedback and critique to move the creative process toward an artistic product.

Creative Applications to Folk Dance

Even **codified dances,** such as folk dance, may involve creativity without compromising integrity. Here are some ways to turn folk dancing concepts into a creative process.

Simple Rearrange movements from a set movement sequence.

For example, the Russian dance of three horses, Troika, contains three figures danced by groups of three. After the dance is taught entirely, ask each trio to rearrange the figures into a different order. Rearranging known step patterns is the simplest form of making creative choices.

Easy Add movement patterns to an existing folk dance that contrast yet complement the learned dance. Keep the movement within the thematic range and the same stylistic and rhythmic structures. Add a new section to the dance based on a concept that adds one more feature to the dance. For example, add a fourth figure to Troika. Design a floor pattern that has not yet been used (e.g., something different from zigzag, arching, and circles). Use prancing (running steps). Substitute the new figure for one of the sections.

Complex Create a dance in the style of a folk dance you have learned that adheres to one aspect of the dance. For example, the new dance could take the original dance's motivation, its rhythmic style and meter, its cultural style, its structure, its floor pattern, or a combination to create a new dance inspired by the original folk dance.

Artistic Creative Process and the Scientific Process

The creative process (i.e., aesthetic–artistic inquiry) is not unlike the scientific process where a hypothesis is researched and explored through guided questions. Both processes gather information, identify potential problems, seek solutions, and conclude the investigation. Both processes usually go step by step, but not always are the steps linear; sometimes they spiral back through to pick up previous steps. By the end of each process—which is educational in and of itself—the investigator has used higher-order thinking along with inductive and deductive reasoning. The product that results either will be a new creation or will resolve a question that was unanswered before the process began. Look at the scientific process alongside the creative process in figure 7.3 to see where they parallel and where they differ.

Facilitating the creative process with students furthers their artistic growth. Notice that Steps 5 and 6 are artistic steps to improve the results or products. Step 5 (refinement and reflection) shapes the drafts so they communicate clearly and expressively. Older students use the aesthetic principles of design (PODs). Step 6 (performance) yields a refined artistic product.

Safety in the Artistic Creative Process

Students must feel emotionally safe and physically comfortable to take creative risks. They must trust you to guide them to satisfying conclusions. They must know you will not make them look foolish or stupid or laugh at them. This means you should praise on-task, on-target efforts; redirect what is not. Do not praise unproductive work. Over time, lead students beyond trusting you to trust themselves and each other. Thus set the stage for them to trust their dancing bodies and build confidence.

Guide students to create studies that integrate mind and body so the mind no longer dominates but supports self-directed exploring, creating, and performing. In nondancers, the mind tends to dominate and overpower the body in the first stages of creating. Frequently, the mind grasps the concept but the body is unsure how to respond. (After all, the body is made up of a full orchestra of complex body parts and joints—"Which ones do I use?" it asks!) Inexperienced movers, conditioned to trust the mind more than the body, need time to get over this hurdle. By anticipating this you can guide explorations that help them bodythink to integrate body and mind so mind and body complement rather than work against each other. For example, ask students to bodythink a series of still shapes around one concept. Then link the shapes together. Your encouragement and leadership at this point can increase student comfort and eventually lead students to succeed in exploring, problem solving, creating, and dance making. Encourage them to explore options, make increasingly creative choices, and take more creative risks over time.

Give learners many opportunities to explore and improvise. But also be sure they observe others

Scientific process	Creative process

• **Step 1:** Gather data.
  -Observe and gather information and data.
  -Identify any problems to resolve.
	• **Step 1:** Preparation
	  -Observe and gather information and data.
	  -Identify a problem to be solved.

• **Step 2:** Use inductive reasoning to formulate a hypothesis.	• **Step 2:** Incubation
	  -Sense the relationship of all aspects of the problem.
	  -Hold concepts.
	  -Suspend judgment.
	  -Allow lots of different ideas (fluency and flexibility).
	  -Elaborate (extend and extrapolate ideas).
	  -Foster original, nonlinear, chaotic thought.
	  -Brainstorm.

• **Step 3:** Observe and experiment using deductive reasoning.	• **Step 3:** Illumination
	  -Gain clarity
	  -Appearance of the "a-ha" thought

• **Step 4:** Gather new data.	• **Step 4:** Verification
	  -Manifest an idea or concept through externalization of the inner process.
	  -Bring order out of chaos.
	  -Make, do, write, choreograph a draft.

• **Step 5:** Draw a conclusion based on whether the new data support your hypothesis.	• **Step 5:** Refinement and reflection
	  -Edit and refine first draft.
	  -Reflect on its strengths and weaknesses and make improvements.
	  -Evaluate and polish the draft.

• **Step 6:** Report your findings.	• **Step 6:** Performance

FIGURE 7.3 Comparing the scientific process and the creative process.

dancing (peers and professionals) so they can objectify dance, to externalize and visualize the effect of their own work. This subjectivity helps them make increasingly astute artistic and aesthetic choices and to realize how movement looks from an audience's perspective.

Creative Products

Not all creative activity results in a tangible product. When it does, the creative process will have incubated and worked itself around to some tangible product, but it will have been creative long before it is translated into final form.

Dance's creative products are so closely aligned with its creative process, it is sometimes unclear when the products emerge. Creative products are sometimes spontaneous and loosely structured,

sometimes codified. Creative products range in length from short (such as dance phrases, dance sentences, dance paragraphs, and dance studies or études) to longer compositions and choreographies. The artistic creative process yields dances that communicate meaning or intent, that are refined for performance, and that emphasize principles of choreographic design factored in one at a time as soon as it is age and stage appropriate.

Any old creative product is not good enough. Creative products are the result of students having learned basic compositional building blocks at an early age, having made simple dances based on the building blocks, and over time refining dances into the craft of choreography. In kindergarten through grade 2, place more emphasis on the creative process than on the product. By third grade, help students begin to refine their creative products.

Creative products give focus to the process and bring it to resolution. Show products so that students can analyze and evaluate the works of others and get feedback themselves. Through reading each other's dances and giving feedback and critique, both creator and critic become more able to make dances.

Use compositional criteria to guide dance making and to give the parameters for reviewing it. Compositional criteria double the chances that compositional skills will be applied and that critics will better evaluate the work. A good rule when creating compositional criteria is to emphasize a main point through several criteria. Also include criteria on the BSTER elements regarding the effective use of particular aspects of time, space, force and energy, dynamics, body shapes, and rhythm. Always be sure that

- the work has an effective beginning, middle, and end; and
- the work clearly communicates the main idea.

Whether the created product is generated from an individual or a small group of students, insist on clarity and refinement until the product is able to successfully communicate its intended idea.

Creative Dance for Children

Make creative dance the core of the kindergarten through grade 5 dance-as-art curriculum. Creative dance builds a child's understanding of movement as a form of human expression. It lays the foundation for all that is to come in dance. Creative dance invites all cornerstones to interact by immersing kids in the artistic processes (c/p/r). It begins students' aesthetic education at the same time that it develops their creative problem-solving skills. To merely explore movement does not go far enough. In addition, see that kids in first grade take a structured improvisational approach to dance making. Teaching creative dance is to do all of the following:

- Promote a thinking body (bodythink) as a personal instrument of expression.

- Foster a kinetic approach (rather than just a mental approach) to creating and composing.
- Teach basic structures by which to organize dances.
- Emphasize the artful use of the dance elements.
- Teach students to analyze dances.
- Promote thoughtful, insightful critique.

Creative dance downplays teacher-made dances and instead features kids creating and composing. It calls up unique movement responses. It personalizes dance.

Creative dance lays the foundation for all educational dance experiences that follow. Ideally, creative dance starts in preschool and builds through elementary school. It relies on open-ended divergent thinking (exploring, brainstorming, and problem solving) and delimited convergent thinking (learning compositional tools and the craft of choreography). Creative dance becomes modern dance, choreography, improvisation, and performance in middle and high school.

Creative dance mobilizes the dance elements so students thoroughly learn to manipulate them. It contains all the seeds that later bloom into choreographing: exploring, structuring, refining, critiquing, and reflection. Think of creative dance as teaching "choreography for kids." It starts simple and increases in complexity through upper elementary by adding new structures and forms. Introduce some principles of design (PODs) in creative dance: contrast, variety, unity, and repetition.

Creative dance emphasizes all the artistic processes:

CREATING

- Ample exploration of one element at a time to increase young children's working understanding of each element
- Opportunity to compose dance studies of appropriate length based on cognitive development

PERFORMING

- Time to show their creations and perform for each other

> **"Dance's most neurotic moments historically . . . have come when technique dictates content."**
>
> —Wendall Beavers

RESPONDING

- Giving and receiving critical feedback to and from an audience of peers and teachers
- Critiquing peer works with the dance elements vocabulary

Help students take command of the moving medium and translate it into their personal artistic expressions. Help them refine their ability to express themselves by designing dances, writing, and speaking about dance with the dance elements' kinetic and linguistic vocabulary (see chapter 6).

Teaching Creative Dance

Facilitating creative dance requires skills that are not usually a part of a dancer's own experience. For that reason creative dance facilitation is discussed at different points in this book. Because creative dance is the starting point for educational dance, the successful facilitation of creative dance is vital. Here is where

students learn to move with integrity and intent. Here is where they acquire their movement and dance vocabulary. Here is where they experiment, explore, and improvise in ways that feed their artistic sense of expression. Here is where they learn to make dances and critique works. Here is where they learn the language of dance. Find the "Developmental Indicators" in appendix B to see the psychological–social and the kinesthetic–motor progressions that advance students from a beginner stage toward a more self-controlled use of movement.

Creative dance is not just movement exploration; it starts out with movement exploration. Teaching dance as art in education requires going from exploration to structuring dances, refining them for informal performance, and making evaluative judgments about them through critique.

All dance movement derives from the elements. We will look at how to emphasize BSTERs as the source of creating, performing, and responding to dance (NSDE 1), which expands the motional and linguistic repertory of students in kindergarten through fifth grade. Make creative dance experiences that reach kids physically, artistically, cognitively, and socially. Build such a deep connection with dance that it affects the artistic development of students at a young age (see chapter 4).

Emphasize the Dance Elements

In primary grades (or any age beginners), feature one BSTER element (not BSTER category) as the main topic for each creative dance lesson (see figure 6.2).

- Fully explore one dance element per lesson (the featured element, such as levels). Explore this featured element (e.g., levels) by way of the other elements to give a three-dimensional understanding of the featured element, such as making shapes at different levels and traveling at different levels (ref., Bloom's knowledge and comprehension).

  - After a full exploration, ask students to share what they learned about this element.

  - Ask students to immediately apply what they learned. Give them a simple structure so they transfer what they learned into a dance. Investigate how the element works in a dance structure (ref., Bloom's application).

Explore one element at a time to increase young children's working understanding and use of each element, such as levels (space element).

- Make dances about one topic to help students learn to clearly express that element.

Over time, this depth of experience with each element produces dancers with a breadth of movement understanding. Complexity increases as experience compounds. By upper elementary grades, you can encourage more integration of the elements if students have had continuous dance experiences since kindergarten and have advanced to that point.

Introducing the Elements   As you learned in chapter 4, young children are self-centric, so a good place to introduce the BSTERs is with the body elements (figure 6.2). Isolate body parts in motion, progress to full body, and then combine body parts. Get students to realize they have choices about different body parts they feature when exploring and composing. A follow-up lesson could feature body moves (such as twisting, bending, stretching, shaking, collapsing, and swinging).

Eventually bring in steps (weight-bearing movements of the feet and legs used to move from one place to another) but not too early in the process. Steps tend to get kids lodged in the brain more than the body. Steps require specific coordination and timing, so when they are taught too early steps tend to frustrate nondancers. Save steps until there is great comfort with body moves and coordinated traveling through space with changes in directions and levels. It is more important to learn to move the body through space than to make step patterns. For example, not every child can get footwork exact. Attempting to teach the steps of dance too early can backfire. It is one reason so many adults believe they can't dance. They equate dancing with doing steps correctly.

Developing the Elements   Subdivide the category of space into various studies such as shape, directions, level, focus, pathway, and place. Use space elements to teach simple dance concepts as well as complex ones. Teach shape and shaping as necessary to bodyspeaking. Also teach direction and levels to orient them to space. For example, for second graders, teach over, under, around, and through by setting up a dance environment of stretchy elastics. Use space for complex concepts such as centrifugal and centripetal motion for secondary level students. For example, use centrifugal and centripetal center sequences in which one draws lines with the fingertips in the horizontal plane while traveling in a small circular floor pattern leaning away from the center of the circle (centrifugal). Then transition the outwardly directed centrifugal circles in toward the center as the floor pattern gets smaller and smaller. Gradually bring fingertips into the body core with a body contraction to pull the energy into the center of the circle and the self (centripetal).

Energy and dynamics are the way one uses muscular tension in the body to command strength. They include the way movement flows in the body; its weight (Laban terms for amount of firmness or lightness); the movement qualities, textures, accents, attack, and phrasing; and the time factors of movement. Grades 3 and 4 relish this work because they have the fine muscle coordination and intellectual ability to comprehend and apply these subtleties of movement.

Time is subdivided into many parts: rhythmic beat (a structure of time), tempo (how fast or slow), duration (length of a movement, section, or an entire dance), accent in timing or with sound, and accelerating or decelerating (speeding up or slowing down). Timing in the context of musical accompaniment is appropriate to consider with secondary-age students, such as whether their choice of music is to be randomly selected or intentional, counted out in beats, or worked with as a coexisting background wash. (Accompaniment—metered or unmetered—is a different issue!)

Relationship ties dance to its environment. It may be a relationship between one's body parts to the whole body, the dancer to an object or another dancer, or the dancer to a group. Relationship includes relating to the accompaniment and the performing space. It also includes the awareness that a performer develops in relation to safe movement, to kinesiology, and over time to technique development, centering, and placement. Start developing these concepts as students develop a movement vocabulary and kinesthetic work in creative dance.

Creative dance relies on the artful use of the elements to make dances of artistic integrity using the PODs.

Extend Artistic Learning

Some creative dance classes stop prematurely after movement exploration and others after dance making. There is more! Maximize aesthetic learning in creative dance by incorporating additional aspects.

Guiding Exploration   During guided movement exploration, develop keen listeners. Give cues only once. Shoot rapid-fire cues, one at a time, that require students to pay attention with every fiber and nerve. Guide exploration so students must listen, hear the cue, and immediately translate it into action knowing another cue is coming right behind it. Have no lag time. Get students wired into their bodies so they bodythink—a skill so critical in dance.

Remember to lead the class as though you were also a student in your own class (see chapter 3). Then you know when it's time to go into the air, to turn, or to reshape the spine. Your classes are more organic when you are involved in the movement or are shadowing each step of its exploration. Link cues so one organically follows the other to make transitions smooth. (This is easier when you are moving, too.) Keep movements connected and flowing and keep bodies exploring the skills that lead to achieving the objectives.

Guided movement exploration is a fertile process for students. Here they find their movement options. They master their moving bodies in a way that is unique to them yet part of the group's experience. They turn the elements into their own actions. Real kin-aesthetic progress occurs (see chapter 5). Students clarify many concepts under a skilled teacher's direction. Don't cut this process short! Technique development is important, but it is not the only educational dance goal. Feed the creative spirit while you feed the moving body at each age and stage. Here is where students first grasp dance as movement art. It is where you also plant and nurture the seeds of improvisation.

Seeing Professional Performance   Creative dancers must see dances performed by accomplished dancers to know what dance performance looks like. Use short dance clips as models. Most students will never have seen dance or how it is composed until they encounter the movement concepts you teach them. How can they possibly fully identify aesthetic concepts—such as body control, qualities and textures of movement, bodyshaping, extension, balance for dance—until they see these concepts transformed into actual dance performance?

Dance Making   Out of movement exploration and improvisation comes the fresh movement material around a theme that movers organize and shape into short compositions. Here children learn to organize movement around a concept to communicate meaning. Provide a clear structure with specific criteria for a dance composition such as that in figure 9.1

(page 262). Stress the need for a beginning, a middle, and an end for all beginners (and reinforce it as needed with everyone from kindergarten through fourth grade). Be specific: "Do (this), then (that), and end in a still shape."

Showing Work   Insist that students start and end a dance in stillness to signify when the dance study starts and ends. Children who blur either the start or end of a dance lose their peers' attention. How can an audience distinguish between movement that is pedestrian and movement that is dance if the dancers don't make a clear start and stop, entrance, or exit? Stress the need for full concentration before, during, and at the end of their showing.

Extend Impact

Two more factors affect the quality of your efforts in teaching creative dance: scheduling and facilitation skills.

Ensuring Closely Sequenced Learning   Consecutive-day classes for a nine-week quarter are more productive than twice-a-week classes for a semester. Closely sequenced learning

- builds continuity and increases carryover;
- strengthens focus and concentration;
- increases body conditioning;
- intensifies momentum for creating, editing, and refining; and
- promotes integrated learning.

Tell the principal how scheduling affects the quality of your creative dance classes as schedules are made. Inform the principal that creative work suffers, standards are weakened, and continuity is compromised when dance experiences are spread too far apart. Closely sequenced learning helps students retain concepts and refine their work far better than with time lapses (see chapter 12). This is true at all ages but particularly so with young learners.

Directing Your Comments in Creative Dance   To generate effective responses, give clear directions. Nonspecific, indirect cueing is the cause of vague movement responses in creative dance and undermines all aspects of creative dance: guided exploration, dance making, and critiquing. See figure 7.4 for ways to turn ineffective prompts into specific directions and coaching during exploration. Your guided directions cue students' exploration and movement

Change ineffective indirect comments . . .	. . . to effective direct directions:
"Move while the drum sounds, OK?"	"Move while the drum sounds."
"Make a shape." "Move."	"Make an upside-down shape. A spiky upside-down shape. A one-legged upside-down shape. Shake that shape. Change its facing. Make it smaller . . . larger."
"Nice." (to the class)	"That's a good balance example, Joey."
"Move through the room making shapes."	"Show the difference between a moving shape (in place) and a traveling shape."
"Move through the room making shapes."	"Show how you design different levels in one place . . . and then through space."

FIGURE 7.4   Ineffective and effective directions.

response. Your phrases shape the specificity—thus the quality—of the kin-aesthetic results. How will students know to explore all options unless you guide them to?

Structure a Creative Dance Class

The five steps of creative dance class are the first five steps of the Eight-Step Plan (8SP), referred to as the Five-Step Plan (5SP). All five steps are active learning phases in addition to the lesson's introduction and its closure activities—which are also vital to each lesson. See figure 13.3 (page 412) for the 5SP and 8SP.

After you introduce the lesson's main element and learning objectives, the five steps are these:

1. Guided exploration (Explore It)
2. Viewing (View It)
3. Dance making (Compose It)
4. Performing (Show It)
5. Critique (Analyze It)

At the end of the lesson, you set aside time to close the lesson with a reflective thinking activity. More is explained about this structure in chapter 13.

Benefits of Creative Dance

To teach dance as art accomplishes multiple objectives through creative dance. It furthers educational dance goals and it furthers general education as well. Consider the direct and the indirect educa-tional benefits of using creative dance instead of rote teaching.

Dance Benefits (Direct)

The direct benefits to students are legion. Following are several important benefits that advance dance:

1. **National dance standards.** Creative dance helps advance all seven national content standards in kindergarten through fifth grade. (It can also be used for beginners who are in grades 6-8.) Creative dance easily incorporates all cornerstones. It is already exploratory and inquiry based. If you make it aesthetically driven and contextual, you have all 6DCs!

2. **Choreographic models.** Creative dance provides students firsthand knowledge of a choreographer's creative process. To incorporate a great work into creative dance (view it) as an example exposes that choreographer's creative process and how it is similar to students' own processes (i.e., professional choreographers also explore movement, shape it into dances, critique it, and refine it for performance). Professional choreographers use similar creative stimuli. Ask students to compare their creative process with those of the choreographer. This affords kids the opportunity to see how an aesthetically driven choreographic process can yield a unique artistic work with lasting value. Students also get the chance to put their own creative dance experiences into the context of the work. Thus inspire children to see where their creative

expressions could lead—even to lasting professional performance works. Give them a vision of the dance masterpiece that is within themselves.

3. **Expressivity.** Experimenting and improvising enhance students' expressivity. Students are able to explore their full potential as moving humans so they experience the full range of motion and dynamics available to them. As students explore the world through movement, for kinetic ideas, they also organize, structure, and compose movement that communicates just as written composition communicates. As they read dances with the UDV (dance elements), they increase their expressive vocabulary—both kin-aesthetically and linguistically.

4. **Personal growth.** Creating dance is personal—it is about the uniqueness and individuality of the mover. It tends to increase students' involvement with dance because they can be successful (move their own way) rather than fail to move like everyone else. When you align creative dance experiences with what is going on in students' lives and other academic classes, you enhance both and you aid student growth and development. Refer to appendix A for the list of stages of progression in the four developmental areas.

> "Learning to teach creative dance to young children is as a journey that is never completed because you keep learning just as children do."
>
> —National Dance Association (1990, p. 17)

Global Benefits (Indirect)

In addition to artistic and dance growth, creative dance contributes broader, more global skills. These skills also indirectly increase dance's artistic outcomes and productivity in dance.

1. **Listening skills.** Expect learners to move on cue while the drum sounds and stop when it stops. They must listen astutely to each instruction and cue in the silences between drum sounds. Try not to repeat cues. Any who do not listen well—and consequently sit out a while—seem to be better listeners on their return. Dancers have to be able to pick up auditory cues. Those who can't are not able to perform, so it directly affects performance.

2. **Concentration.** Creative dance requires concentration. Because it is fast paced, learners must pay total attention so as to quickly respond with the body from cue to cue. They must integrate body and mind when creating and performing to respond with concentrated energy and focus.

3. **Better ability to articulate.** As body–mind articulation increases, students are better able to verbally articulate. Refined skills (i.e., creative problem solving, analysis, and synthesis) transfer to other academics. Movement articulation increases brain functioning. Learn—and teach—Anne Green Gilbert's "BrainDance" (see Rich Resources).

4. **Divergent thinking.** Movement exploration increases divergent thinking through problem solving. Students seek all options as they explore and brainstorm with the bodymind. Press them to find multiple solutions to one problem and to not give up until they have stretched their perceived limits. Divergent thinking skills transfer from the movement class to the classroom, to the stage, to life.

5. **Organization.** Organizing and sequencing movement enable students to compose and convey coherent dances. The opposite side of creative thinking (divergent) is convergent thinking, which organizes, sequences, outlines, and structures. These skills transfer broadly to all academics. Dancers apply critical feedback to increase their ability to organize dances—a valuable skill mentioned in the SCANS Report and Skills for the 21st Century (see chapter 2).

6. **Ability to embody a concept.** To embody a concept is to apply it and understand it (e.g., symmetrical and asymmetrical). One step further, as students communicate a concept to an audience in performance, the dancers really understand the concept. Performing it connects it to the entire nervous system—rather than just to one part of the nervous system, the brain.

7. **Self-management.** Dancing requires self-governance. Incorporate principles of good citizenship as students move cooperatively around the room. Have them practice moving without making sounds, without touching anyone or anything, and on cue (i.e., at appropriate times). Help them pick up movement cues and respond to others in the moving space to attune them to their environment. This helps them also live within prescribed boundaries.

Choreography

Choreography is a complex kind of composition that expresses an idea, a thought, or a concept in a mostly nonverbal movement medium. Its purpose is to communicate meaning and to be performed. To teach choreography is to teach the craft of composition, organization, and structure and, beyond that, to use one's command of the dance elements to express a point of view. These tools of the craft enable individuals to take on the challenge of being "meaning makers" and creators of dance. Choreography literally means "to dance *(choreo)* write *(graph)*."

Choreography is creative, not imitative. It invents new movement to convey ideas. Emphasize that the realm of choreography is the realm of movement invention, creating innovative actions, shapes, and designs that have not been used before. Rearranging familiar steps is an extremely limited form of choreography. That is why improvisation is so vital. It is also why basic compositional skills are necessary. They increase the choreographer's ability to say what she wants to communicate.

Feature dance making and choreography in some way all the way through K-12. But emphasize composition in kindergarten through sixth grade to build the specific skills for more complex choreography in later middle school and high school.

The ability to choreograph full dances comes out of knowing some of the craft of choreography centered in compositional skills. Choreography isn't just a bunch of movements thrown together. However, learning to choreograph is a skill that develops in a nonlinear way. That is OK. Compositional skills accumulate. Over time, through application, they become part of each person's creative skills package. As students learn a particular choreographic skill, ensure that they practice using it in different choreographic contexts. There is no one logical order. Build skills on skills, and trust your intuitive judgment to sense where students are and to identify what is missing. Whatever skill is missing is sometimes the next best skill to develop.

Choreography requires conceptualization and organization. It depends on both sides of the brain: the right brain globalizes and the left brain organizes. Whereas the right brain goes after the whole issue or concept to grasp all the possibilities, the left brain has to sort out what is most important, select from it, and order it into a coherent compositional sequence.

Of course, choreography in step-based styles (e.g., Irish step dancing, musical theatre, jazz, ballroom) is more about rearranging known steps than creating all new movement. The choreographic principles you teach in dance as art also apply to dance as entertainment and musical theatre.

This text uses the term *dance making activities* to mean creating, designing, or organizing movement into patterns within a structure. Dance making, a generic term for making dances, can be as simple as early dance-making activities such as a dance sentence, phrase, or one-concept cinquain. Dance making can be as complex as the most advanced choreographic endeavor. Anything that involves intentionally designing movement to dance is dance making. Now we look into kinds of dance making from early dance-making activities to composition and choreography.

Early Dance Making

Dance-making activities start in kindergarten. Use simple structures so movements can be freely improvised within those structures. Call them "dance sentences" and repeat the same conceptual pattern while children improvise different movement patterns. (These dance-making activities set the stage for later composition.)

A kindergarten example would be, "Reaching high, going low, shaking fast, moving slowly." Kindergartners need to be free in movement. There is no need to belabor setting or codifying movement with kindergarten and first-grade students. It is more beneficial to improvise the sequence in different ways than it is to set the exact movement into a repeatable movement sequence. That is, have the sequence established in a rhythmic word cadence that is repeatable in different ways (e.g., an 8-count phrase with each syllable of the word on one beat: "*bo-dy-shap-ing* [4 counts], turn, and hold shape"; or "go through space, go high and low, then stay in place, move fast, then s-l-o-w").

For a third grade example, "Jump shape, jump shape, jump turn shape, travel (backward) into a **safe space.** Open and close, open and close, turn to a new place." (Repeatable patterns like these reinforce the math concept of pattern.)

One way to start is by making "one-concept dance": either body-part dances, traveling dances, dances that go into the air, fast dances, or slow dances. Another one-concept dance is a cinquain such as the one in figure 7.5. Its concept is "shape." It may be improvised (as described previously) on each repeat

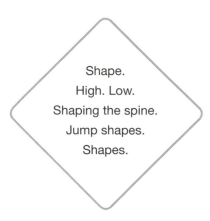

Shape.
High. Low.
Shaping the spine.
Jump shapes.
Shapes.

FIGURE 7.5 Elaborate on this cinquain. Start and end in still shapes. Create more than one movement for each line.

(elaboration) or set to be repeated exactly, depending on the student's age and stage. After students are familiar with making dance cinquains, they can collaborate to write their own using a dance element—and then make a dance with it.

"Two-concept dances" that contrast opposites teach students the fundamental PODs of contrast. Use word pairs that are antonyms, like those in figure 7.2 as well as figures 6.3, 6.4, and 6.5 (pages 136 and 137). For example, contrast A (quick) with B (slow).

Composition's Relationship to Choreography

The difference between composing and choreographing is a matter of degree. Compositional skills are the basic building blocks of choreography. Students learn compositional skills one at a time. First they learn to construct a sequence with a beginning, middle, and end. Early compositions use one or two concepts at most. Then one by one add new composing skills to what students know. By gradually accruing a number of different compositional skills, budding choreographers can begin to incorporate these skills in varied ways to prepare them to tackle longer works.

Composing tasks are lead-up activities to choreography. For example, before playing basketball, students learn dribbling, passing, and shooting skills. Just as such sports lead-up activities are taught before playing a complex sport, so compositional skills are learned before composing a larger dance work.

Practice compositional skills all the way through elementary and middle school. Compositional

concepts are not just for the mind. To learn them, students must apply and translate them into movement. It takes a lot of practice before students acquire sufficient compositional skills (conceptual and practical) to tackle the complexities of a long, set choreographic work. Skill improves through qualitative critique (self, peer, and teacher). Eventually students have enough compositional skills to begin to design what could be called choreography.

Choreography calls on a variety of compositional skills. The following are just a few. They are in addition to the composition building blocks discussed in "Composition Building Blocks for Choreography". Notice how some reinforce a POD:

- Shaping movements within an overall structure (unity)
- Paying attention to spatial design
- Using groupings (contrast and variety)
- Including entrances and exits (transition)
- Using level changes (variety)
- Creating variety within a work
- Restating thematic material for unity
- Repeating and developing a motif or theme for coherence
- Phrasing to hold movement thoughts together (unity)
- Changing dynamics to keep the piece modulating (contrast)
- Using timing and dynamic climaxes and high points for emphasis
- Including transitions between sections
- Using enough contrast to add counterpoint and interest

Help your students hone the craft of organizing movement into dance studies by first learning to put movements into phrases, sentences, paragraphs, and longer studies, like writing does.

Composition Building Blocks for Choreography

Composition teaches the underlying structures on which choreography is built. By using the basic principles of design, individuals learn to design dances to clearly express intent (NSDE 3). Use these basic building blocks.

Phrase

A phrase or dance sentence expresses a complete thought in dance—like a written sentence does. A phrase is a basic compositional structure with a beginning, middle, and end—like a written sentence. Phrases are composed with movements—usually built on dance elements concepts—just as sentences are composed with words. Longer dance studies have numbers of phrases that relate to each other—just as paragraphs and stories have numbers of sentences that further the topic. Short dance studies (or études) use a series of phrases with transitions between them. Start short.

Phrasing, a basic compositional tool, is both a structural form (functional) and an artistic form (aesthetic). Teach students how to use phrasing in different contexts. Phrasing is also basic to the forms that follow.

Statement of Theme

Just as paragraphs build around a theme or topic sentence, dances build around a theme, an idea, or a movement motif. Teach students to stay true to their idea, theme, or motif in composition just as they do in written composition. For example, a paragraph doesn't talk about everything in the world. It states its topic sentence and then develops it. Likewise, a dance theme can be stated at the outset and developed and elaborated on in the dance paragraph or composition.

To use a theme doesn't mean the dance has to be tight or constricted. The theme becomes the clarifying point that allows for the real creativity in movement to occur. It is the way movement holds together for coherence in order to communicate meaning (NSDE 3). As in music, the first phrase can be an **antecedent phrase** (introductory phrase) and the second a **consequent phrase** (resulting phrase). Eventually, advanced high school students extend and elaborate on such structures once they have mastered the basics of composition, much as creative writers adapt language skills they have learned when they write poetry, plays, and other creative writing. Teaching the structure has carryover (or transfer) value to other subjects.

Motifs are identifiable characteristics that are used in dance to state and restate. They function as part of a movement theme. Motifs return during the piece, developed in new ways. Themes are to be varied, but motifs help hold a work together and bring unity to a work. For example, both hands clasped together could be a motif that is developed during a study. The hands are taken apart and rejoined in different ways, with timing variations, as the study progresses. One motif can also be the subject of a dance. Viewers notice highlighted motifs, such as the recurring hand-flutter in "Fix Me Jesus," one of the dances from Alvin Ailey's *Revelations*.

Beginning–Middle–End

Just as a written word sentence begins with a capital letter and ends with a period or other end punctuation, so a dance sentence (or phrase) starts and ends in stillness. Consistently reinforce the underlying principle of beginning–middle–end (**B–M–E**) throughout all grade levels as the basic foundation of composition. Early primary grades compose three-part dance sentences:

1. Beginning: Still shape (predance)
2. Middle: Movement (featuring a dancing element)
3. End: Still shape (ending)

Dance Elements Approach

Feature the dance elements in composition and choreography assignments all the way through K-12—and into adulthood. If you approach composition and choreography from an exploratory, experimental perspective, students will be inventive and creative with their dances. Students will find ways to express their unique perspectives on space, time, dynamics, and body moves, and they will understand how the elements interact. This is what professional choreographers still do with exciting results—it's simply a matter of degree of complexity as students move from kindergarten through twelfth grade. The more practice students get in K-12 in designing dances based on the elements, the more sophisticated choreographers and astute audience members they are sure to become.

Process-Oriented Composition

Almost never is it productive to assign a composition without having some movement exploration and experimentation first. Otherwise the results will be stiff and cerebral—instead of movement based and organic—which diminishes the aesthetic impact of the dance. Dances that come from the head without consulting the moving body look like they came out of the head! They are usually step oriented. They rely on static poses and technique combinations. When learners formulate and compose through **process-oriented composition,** they use what they know and have discovered themselves. For example, if they only know steps, or a style like jazz, that is what the composition will consist of. Ensure that students get a wide variety of styles as part of their dance feast and know the full range of movement options from the BSTER elements as they begin to formulate their own creations.

Organically take students from exploration (exploring) to dance making (designing) so that students select from the explored, spontaneous movement inventions they found and put them into dance. Just as you clearly guided their exploration, now give clear compositional criteria so movers learn to formulate and compose. Base the criteria on the topic of exploration (which is from the lesson or unit objective). Give concrete criteria that specify which concepts to include. This opens up an array of movement options from which to choose within your stated parameters.

Form and Structure

Personally armed with all the compositional forms you have mastered in choreography class, you will have an array of structures to teach. Now let's focus on ones especially useful as introductions to choreography. The list starts simply and increases in complexity. Thus, all dance forms and structures are not addressed here. Ease students into dance-making structures that build sequentially.

Simple Forms

The simplest forms are succinct and uncomplicated:

- One-part form: Beginning–middle–end; cinquain.
- Two-part form (AB form): Contrasting opposites—one idea is expressed in A and the contrasting, yet related, idea is expressed in B.
- Three-part form (ABA form): Still contrasting two related ideas of AB but returning to the original idea (A) at the end.
- Round and canon: Repeat at a designated point, one after another. It is a way to extend movement material (which is the same or slightly varied) in time, to design for more than one dancer in space, and to link one dancer to another (relationship).
- Call and response: Relating one dancer to another or one group to another. One issues a "call" and the other echoes a "response"—back and forth. The responses may be the same as or different from the call.

Make the simple forms more and more challenging by increasing the complexity of the choreographic criteria.

Intermediate Forms: Theme-Based

The earliest intermediate forms for young people are theme based. There are different ways to teach theme. One emerges out of the one-concept dance, which takes either one dance element (e.g., a body part such as feet) or one translatable concept (e.g., verticality) to work with. Fourth and fifth graders who have had dance since kindergarten are ready to create thematic dances.

Teaching Basic Theme   *Create*. Get students to build a dance sentence or phrase. Make the phrase repeatable (i.e., design the end so it is ready to start again from the same body position—not necessarily from the same spatial place). Do a sample process. Then give students several criteria for making this phrase (e.g., length, 8 counts; emphasis, feet; space, in place, it is repeatable). Monitor students to keep the themes simple enough to later be developed.

Analyze. Analyze the theme by breaking it down into its constituent parts (i.e., types of movements, motifs, elements). Spend time with this step to make clear what movement words are in the dance sentence. Show students how the theme compares to their topic sentence in writing a paragraph. But realize that they need your help to decipher the dance words they use because the words are in symbol form rather than in actual words. This is an important step in learning to decode dance as a language of expression. Decode the dance words with the BSTERs. (After you provide several examples for the middle and high school students, get them to work with partners to analyze each other's themes.)

Develop. After analysis, instruction, time, and practice have clarified what "theme" is, teach the two fundamental theme-based forms: theme and development, and theme and variation. Use these forms to shed light on different ways to write a dance paragraph. (You can make these as basic or as complex as your students need.)

Theme and Development   Students extend the movement material from their original repeatable theme (phrase) by developing the material and coming back to reuse parts of it to hold the dance work together for unity. Show them how the thematic material becomes the identifiable part of the dance. When a choreographer goes so far away from what she started out with, the dance loses its way and an audience cannot follow it. If we are to teach students how to communicate meaning (NDSE 3), we must teach them about compositional clarity—not to make a dance stiff but to keep it within its realm of intent. Everything but the kitchen sink randomly strung together is not choreography. Extraneous movement only communicates naivete. Why would choreography be considered a serious art if it were just about rearranging the same steps over and over (boring) or putting any movement someone likes in a dance work (incoherent)? What if music compositions did that? What if visual arts did that? Of course, the fabulous artists of our time throw away the rules and create new ones. That is fine for professional artists but not while they are still in educational dance in K-12 as part of the basic arts curriculum.

Introduce theme and development in elementary school, but save it as a full choreographic structure for middle school and older. It is more abstract a concept than theme and variation, although the latter is more complex to pull off. Start with a very simple theme and variation to introduce theme-based forms, because theme and variation is concrete and highly structured. After students understand theme in that form, they are better prepared to develop themes in all theme-based forms.

From time to time spiral back to one of the theme forms to reinforce it. For example, why not build a dance unit around an accessible dance work such as David Parsons' *Sleep Study*? A commercially available video shows Parsons as he creates the initial theme using sleep positions. Then he codifies (or sets) them. Parsons takes you with him as he goes through the experimental compositional process of putting the dance together. He uses a series of sleep positions as the theme and varies them: in time, in space, in dynamics, in relationship, in sequence. His demonstration shows how theme holds a work together and how interesting the results are.

Going through a similar creative process gets students to experiment with different ways to extend a theme into a full dance. Although young students are not ready to make a long dance work, they can nonetheless create shorter studies that use the same creative process based on other topics such as one familiar daily routine or a sports gesture. This demonstration presents the perfect opportunity to show the different ways theme can be artistically developed—by extending it, manipulating it, and

> **"Choreographers do not make dances out of words. They compose them in the vocabulary of movement."**
>
> —Eleanor Metheny

varying it. (See chapter 15 for more information on *Sleep Study*.)

Complex Forms: Theme and Variation

Theme and variation is fun as a class experimentation. It is more concrete and tightly structured than other theme-based forms. You can vary the complexity of this form to make it simple to start out, but because it is more exacting than the other forms, it is actually more complex. Ask the music specialist to help you find a musical theme and variation that works well with your grade levels. Let the music help you teach the concept of theme and variation. First the theme is purely stated. Thereafter, each time it repeats it is adorned in a new way so it takes on a different quality each time.

For example, there is a sassy electronic music score that uses the familiar theme of "Twinkle, Twinkle, Little Star." Each time it repeats (variation), the theme sounds completely different in style and quality. At one school, fourth graders collaborated to design a short dance theme (phrase) the same length as the music theme. Everyone learned to perform the dance theme in unison. Then they listened to the score together to count the number of repeats (variations) as well as how many ways the music varied. Next the dance specialist and children brainstormed all the possible ways to vary the original movement theme and listed them on a chart. In small groups, students secretly determined the variation they would create. (Mystery adds to the process.) They prepared it to show, using these structural criteria:

- All group members state the dance theme in unison with the music theme as accompaniment.
- With each music variation, one small group of dancers at a time performs their variation while the others hold still shapes.
- To end, all return to restate the unison theme.

Half the class performed while half observed, and then they switched roles and repeated the process. When giving feedback, the peer audience identified how the other half varied the theme. The whole class discussed the best order for small groups to show variations—whether two groups with similar variations should be featured together or separated in time and place. They made aesthetic decisions to add variety and unity. They decided to keep two performing halves as before. Both halves incorporated the feedback and set a sequence for their dance. Each half made a different decision about their ending, about restating the original theme: One group faced different directions for the unison theme and the other used it as a way to exit the stage. Each group critiqued the other in the final showings and offered choreographic and artistic fine-tuning.

This process helped them conceptualize how theme and variation extends movement material. They had so enjoyed doing their own variation that they asked to learn each other's variations, too. Occasionally after that experience they would ask to do another theme and variation. By keeping a spirit of inventiveness, you can keep the form fresh. At all costs, avoid being too academic about teaching this form. Figure 7.6 provides some ideas for variations.

Use theme and variation from fourth grade on, especially for light or comic dances. Theme and variation is a good form to poke fun at something—whatever is stated in the theme as absolutely serious can go awry in the variations. Hilarious variations can happen with a prim and proper beginning

theme where everyone dances in unison and then one at a time goes off into wild variations, finally restoring some semblance of order by restating the theme at the end.

Solo, Duet, Trio, and Group Constructs

Early dance-making activities are usually through creative dance as each individual creates his own movement response within the large group. This is not solo work, although it is individualized within the group. As you move away from creative dance and begin to teach basic composition, you also need to decide whether it is best done as solo work or with partners. Much of that choice depends on the students' stage of development—particularly their psychosocial stage. Whereas solo choreography can be mastered most easily psychosocially, it is harder to pull off because of the lack of other developmental areas—often one's underdeveloped artistic development and maturity (aesthetic–artistic). There is no hard and fast rule. You must judge based on the four developmental stages of progression (refer to chapter 4). For example, you decide whether students are ready to express themselves alone, with a partner, or in a group based on all of the following factors:

- Kinesthetic–motor development (Are their movement skills ready for this?)
- Aesthetic–artistic development (Does the idea translate best to solo, partner, or group?)
- Cognitive–intellectual development (Will they understand the concept in terms of dance elements, and have they acquired the compositional skills?)
- Psychological–social development (Is it better for them to work alone or with a partner?)

Solo   Solos are tricky. Solo work is easiest to start out with at any age, especially in elementary school, but it can also be the most complex by the time a student is in an advanced high school class. Solos are good starting places, however, because

- they evolve out of individual exploration,
- they are quicker to put together and show than group work,
- everyone can work on the same concept at the same time,
- students maximize time on task, and
- each person works at his own stage of development (child-centered).

- Traveling variation
- Jumping or hopping variation
- Sharp, angular variation
- Leaning variation (off center)
- Isolated body parts variation
- Shaking and shaky variation
- Turning variation
- Disjointed (stopping and starting) variation
- Bound, stiff, robotic variation
- Very slow variation, followed by a very fast one
- Change of rhythm variation (e.g., from 3/4 to 4/4 time)

FIGURE 7.6   Variation treatments apply to the duration of each variation you are working on—not just to one part. Try variations such as these.

Show first-grade solos several at a time in class. That way each student does a dance but it is viewed as a group "chance" choreography. (By fourth grade you can teach how to design dances using chance as **juxtaposition** and adjusting time and space when necessary to enhance the viewing impact.)

Duet Mirroring movement is a simple duet. Show several mirror duets simultaneously. Give observation criteria, such as whether the partners exactly stay together, concentrate, or change levels. Consult chapter 4 to determine when students should work with partners or are best alone. Second graders pick up this mirroring concept, but fourth graders have better concentration for performing it.

Trio Wait to use trios until students work in small groups well. Watch out for group dynamics in trios, because in a triangle someone can be left out and have hurt feelings.

Composing is a basic skill in dance as art. Start students early to think structurally in dance. The forms and structures are elementary enough to use with all ages. Introduce forms in elementary school so students compose with movement at the time they learn to compose in writing. Once they learn forms and structures, increase the amount and complexity of the choreographic criteria. This chapter's framework will help.

Group Group compositions are more artfully mastered after students are successful with solo, duo, and trio work because group dances use all three. That said, there are also psychosocial developmental issues that play into deciding when group work is useful. For example, middle school students seek validation from group collaboration because most prefer the anonymity of a group and the safety of being one of the group rather than taking the creative lead. Also, AG/T dance students will be ready for group work because of superior conceptualization ability at a younger age than regular students.

Choreographic Criteria

Choreographic criteria are teacher generated all the way through K-12. (Self-generated criteria are useful for advanced high school students who have had lots of experience with choreography and who need the chance to develop their own with your supervision.) It is better to err on the side of too much teacher-generated criteria than not enough. There are two forms of compositional or choreographic criteria to use: structural criteria (quantitative) and aesthetic criteria (qualitative).

Structural Criteria

Structural criteria is quantitative and names what goes into the work and how it is to be organized. It names the basic material for the dance. (For example, "Use an AB form. Show development from beginning–middle–end in both the A and the B. The A theme is Quick and the B theme is Slow.")

Compose in trios after students work well in small groups. Watch out for group dynamics in trios so that all relate and no one is left out.

Beginners can handle three criteria. Don't add more until it is obvious that three aren't enough. It is better to use three criteria and increase their complexity than to give too many criteria (which is too much for students to keep up with). Here is an example of structural criteria for first grade:

- The dance starts and ends in a still spiky shape.
- The dance uses at least one low level and one jump shape in the air.
- The dancer reshapes the spine while traveling through the space.

Aesthetic Criteria

Aesthetic criteria are qualitative and address how well the dance is put together. Aesthetic criteria address two aspects: the quality of the dance design and the quality of the performance. The first evaluates choreography; the second evaluates the performer. Aesthetic criteria set up an expectation that what is composed will be designed with quality (aesthetic design criteria) and that the work will be performed with integrity (performance criteria). See figure 9.1 (and chapter 9) for examples of choreographic criteria and performance criteria.

Base the aesthetic criteria on the unit goals and objectives and on what you want to emphasize. Also base it on the age and stage of progression of your students. Use these criteria to advance students to a higher level of both choreography (design) and performance quality. Thereby emphasize not only what is done but also how it is done.

For middle and high school students who have acquired sufficient technique and performance skills, include technique execution as part of the performance criteria. Here is an example of a technique criterion for jumping, leaping, and landing: "Execute a plié after landing through the ball of the foot to the heel." Before students develop technique, when they show work in class (perform) ask instead for quality of concentration, energy, and focus as well as muscle engagement. Then critique those qualities. Examples of review criteria for a novice's performance technique are "maintained focus throughout performance" and "maintained energy and muscle engagement throughout."

Chapter 9 gives more details on how review criteria correlate with the choreographic criteria.

Principles of Design

The principles of design (figure 7.7) are the basic aesthetic criteria that guide and evaluate choreography.

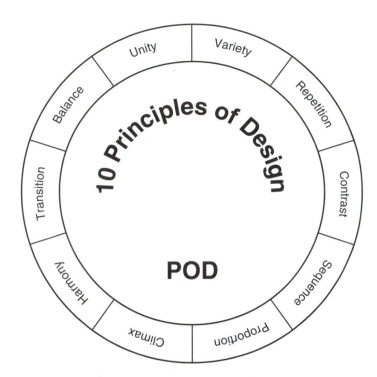

FIGURE 7.7 Principles of design kaleidoscope for grades 4-12 choreography and dance criticism.

Use them to compose and to critique. They are necessary to an aesthetically driven dance curriculum.

The aesthetic principles of design (PODs) are vital criteria. Sometimes called "artistic principles of form and composition," they apply to all art forms. They inform the creative process in the arts and measure the quality of the creation (product). An artist who uses these choreographic principles as benchmarks while choreographing is more likely to be artistically successful than one who does not.

You see the design principles crop up everywhere in the arts. You may find slight variations in the names. This book follows those described by Elizabeth Hayes (1993) in *Dance Composition and Production:* **unity, variety, repetition, contrast, sequence, climax, proportion, harmony, balance,** and **transition.** For descriptive, detailed information on the design principles, refer to Hayes' work and also to Schrader's *A Sense of Dance* (2004).

These indispensable principles mark well-crafted choreography. The works hold your interest. They draw you in and capture your imagination or your curiosity. They start at some place and go forward—not round in circles or off on an incoherent tangent. These are how the PODs translate to the real world.

- The work holds together. (unity)
- It doesn't repeat the same thing over and over. (variety)

- There is enough repetition to make the work coherent (but variety in the repetition). (repetition)

- There is contrast within the overall dance to keep the dance from being too flat. (contrast)

- The sections are in a logical sequence rather than random. (sequence)

- There are dynamic shifts so overall the work reaches one or more high points. (climax)

- The relationship of one section to another is effective, so the work maintains an overall consistency of theme and development. (proportion)

- There is a pleasing quality about how the work evolves and how it works as a product. (harmony)

- One section is not too short and another too long, so proper emphasis is maintained and one section doesn't dominate to weaken the others. (balance)

- There are not jarring transitions that disrupt the sequence or the flow of the dance as it progresses. (transition)

The craft of choreography is based in the PODs. Use them as artistic guides for student compositions. Works that achieve the PODs are artistically strong. Not only do they guide our creating, but also they give us eyes to evaluate our own dance compositions and those of our peers as well as a vocabulary to express our perceptions of quality in them. Choose the PODs according to age appropriateness (see the DCC Framework later in the chapter). Use the PODs in both the choreographic and review criteria. The same criteria apply to both processes (choreographing and critiquing) during one assignment (see chapter 9). To evaluate a dance design—even with such criteria—is still subjective, however. (That is why it is beneficial to have more than one person evaluate.) Ask for precise evaluation because more than one critic giving precise feedback helps the choreographic process even when the feedback differs.

Notebook/Portfolio:
Perspectives Notebook

THREE-ACT REFLECTION: WRITE–ASSESS–REFINE (C2)

Act I: Write

Prepare a three- to four-page typed paper for your Perspectives Notebook that expresses what Cornerstone 2 contributes to educational dance. Address the specific criteria without using them for an outline. Use them first for Act I as composition criteria and then for Act II as review criteria.

C2 Composition Criteria (and Review Criteria)

____ Explains the various facets of creating and composing

____ Clarifies the goals of this cornerstone

____ Explains the creative process and problem solving in dance

____ Explains how critical thinking and evaluation are tied in

____ Discusses by grade group (primary, elementary, middle, and high school) what shape creative work takes

____ Makes clear the importance of creative work in dance

____ Tells how the creator uses reflection, analysis, synthesis, and evaluation in creating work

____ Tells how the observer uses reflection, analysis, synthesis, and evaluation in observation

____ Meaningfully integrates content and achievement standards of NSDEs

Use the structure for the Three-Act Reflection: Write–Assess–Refine in appendix A for Acts II and III (the same structural format and directions as the one in chapter 6).

Dance Cornerstone Curriculum (DCC) Framework

Cornerstone 2 (C2) integrates cognitive content with kin-aesthetic skills.

This part of the DCC Framework (following Rich Resources) shows what students should know and be able to do to achieve NDSEs 2 and 3. It shows how the creative concepts mentioned develop from kindergarten through twelfth grade and breaks them down into teachable chunks. C2 is divided into four sequential parts: primary (K-2), elementary (3-5), middle (6-8), and high school (9-12). Its developmental continuum goes from simple to complex to adapt to your learners.

- Look across the chart for sequence as to how each concept builds as students learn.

- Look down the chart for substance as to the scope, what is essential to include.

- For older beginners, spiral back to the first column to pick up basic skills rather than start at their age level.

Questions to Ponder

1. What word is the antonym (opposite) of *creation* or *creating*?

2. How does our desire to overcome destructiveness in schools find solutions through the creative arts?

3. What compositional skills should one know by fourth grade? By eighth grade?

4. What role does spontaneous movement creation (movement exploration, experimentation, improvisation) have in educational dance? How does it contribute to one's movement vocabulary? One's ability to communicate with movement? One's ability to compose and choreograph?

5. How does this information add to or reshape your Statements of Belief (as explained in the Introduction)?

6. Why are the principles of design so necessary to teaching dance as art in education? Why is it important to learn and apply them to dance-making activities as early as elementary school?

Rich Resources

- Hayes' *Dance Composition and Production* contains vital information about composing with the artistic principles of design.

- Minton's *Choreography* (1997, 2nd ed., Champaign, IL: Human Kinetics).

- McGreevy-Nichols, Scheff, and Sprague's *Building Dances* (2nd ed., 2005, Champaign, IL: Human Kinetics) and *Building More Dances* (2001, Champaign, IL: Human Kinetics).

- Schrader's A *Sense of Dance* (2004, Champaign, IL: Human Kinetics) includes principles of design.

- Anne Green Gilbert's *Brain-Compatible Dance Education,* accessed on her Web site at www.creativedance.org. Order her *Brain-Compatible Dance Education* from www.aahperd.org/nda.

- "Chance-A-Dance" cards are word cards for dance making. Order from Foster Educational Systems, Lanie Keystone at L.keystone@netzero.com.

- National Dance Association's *Guide to Creative Dance for the Young Child* (1991, Reston, VA: AAHPERD) is an informative and helpful set of guidelines for creative dance.

Dance Cornerstone Curriculum Framework—C2: Creating and Composing

1.0 Experimentation

Grades K-2	Grades 3-5	Grades 6-8	Grades 9-12
1.1 Movement exploration			
1.1a Exploring the dance elements			
Explores simple aspects of all the BSTER elements. Emphasizes the body elements.	Explores all the dance elements (BSTER).	Fully explores and experiments with concepts that relate to all the BSTER elements.	Experiments with the movement elements individually and together. Develops a wide repertory of movement with the body in space with the conscious use of time, dynamics, and relationships.
———	Finds multiple ways to solve a movement problem, incorporating a variety of movement elements such as time, space, energy and dynamics, and relationships.	Finds multiple ways to solve a brief movement challenge, choosing the most effective solution and articulating the reasons for the selection. Performs it with clarity of intent.	Explores various dance elements improvisationally to generate new material for dance.
Explores body parts in isolation and in various combinations.	Explores the movement potential with isolated body parts and joints. Creates body part dance studies. Uses body parts in combinations with all other dance elements.	Becomes articulate at using the full body and isolated body parts and joint actions when moving. Increases range of motion within all body parts and joints.	Articulates the body in such a way that it is a tool for inventive design and improvisation.
———	Explores straight, zigzag, and curved pathways. Fully explores earth and air pathways. Learns floor patterns related to folk dance and creative dance.	Creates pathways. Explores floor patterns and how the use of floor patterns alone creates scenario. Learns floor patterns as a means of remembering the spatial design of a sequence.	Explores pathways in the air and on the earth as they relate to floor pattern and overall movement design. Experiments with pathway as a nonverbal story element.
Focuses on organic shapes within one's body and relates them to organic shapes in nature. Differentiates between still shapes and moving shapes.	Focuses on organic shapes within one's body and relates them to organic shapes in nature. Contrasts organic shapes with geometric shapes. Distinguishes between still shapes, moving shapes, and traveling shapes.	Explores the full range of organic shapes as they relate to shapes that are off balance and on balance, that are spiral, and that fully involve the fluidity of the spinal column. Differentiates between two- and three-dimensional shapes.	Refines body shaping so that it is organic and motivated from within the body more than externally motivated. Explores shapes that are intricately balanced, in the air, and supported with different body parts. Explores transitions that link shapes for full artistic affect.
Explores space as it relates to general and personal space.	Explores space as it relates to manipulating it: push–pull, carve, spoke, arc, spiral.	Explores space fully and experiments with its communicative value in composition.	Explores space fully and experiments with its communicative value in composition. Finds artistic viewpoints that relate to space, such as dancing with space as a partner. Creates scaffolds, harnesses, or other spatial structures to generate wider spatial options for dance. Engages in site-specific choreography and takes an artistic viewpoint toward space.

1.0 Experimentation

Grades K-2	Grades 3-5	Grades 6-8	Grades 9-12
1.1a Exploring the dance elements (continued)			
————	Responds to concepts, such as force, and extends range of movement and dynamics.	Explores movement concepts such as linear, curvilinear, and spiral. Gives these ideas visual form.	Uses abstract ideas acquired from discussion, reading, and observation of the world to stimulate movement exploration with BSTERs.
Explores movement qualities. Emphasizes the difference between percussive and smooth.	Explores movement qualities. Emphasizes the difference between percussive, sustained, swing, and sway.	Explores movement qualities. Emphasizes a full range of movement qualities. Includes suspend and collapse.	Explores movement qualities. Emphasizes a full range of movement qualities. Includes suspend and collapse.
1.1b Exploring stimuli			
Responds to a variety of everyday sounds and musical instruments as auditory stimuli.	Uses percussion, computer-generated sound, strings, and other auditory stimuli for movement exploration. Uses poetry, vocalization, and "found sound" to motivate exploration.	Makes sounds on and with the body (clap, tap, slide on the floor) as stimuli for rhythms and dynamics to stimulate movement exploration.	Creates sound score, uses "found sound" (musique concrète), and creates own auditory stimuli for movement and accompaniment to movement.
————	Responds to verbal stimuli with movement that is non-imitative and based on the BSTER elements.	Extends the range of movement while responding to visual, auditory, tactile, and verbal stimuli.	Explores movement possibilities by combining stimuli (verbal, auditory, visual, tactile).
Responds to tactile stimuli (such as fuzzy and prickly) and translates these textures directly to movement feeling and textures.	Responds to tactile stimuli (such as fuzzy and prickly) and translates these textures directly to movement feeling and textures.	Explores everyday objects as props to stimulate movement ideas. Incorporates these objects as an integral part of the dance.	Explores a wide variety of props, tactile stimuli, and multisensory experiences to motivate movement phrases and studies. Integrates textures from stimuli into dynamics in a dance.
————	Uses an art work (such as Ansel Adams' landscapes with contrasting light and dark, shapes and textures) to stimulate movement. Points out its visual use of shape, textures, pattern repetition, value, and linear design to motivate movement and translates these elements to pathways, body shapes, dynamic qualities, and timing devices.	Uses an art work (such as M.C. Escher's tessellated patterns) to stimulate movement. Points out its visual use of shape, textures, pattern repetition, value, and linear design to motivate movement and translates these elements to pathways, body shapes, dynamic qualities, and timing devices.	Uses an art work (such as *The Scream* by E. Munch) to stimulate movement. Points out its visual use of shape, textures, pattern repetition, value, and linear design to motivate movement and translates these elements to pathways, body shapes, dynamic qualities, and timing devices.
Responds in movement to action words (dart, melt, wriggle, explode).	Responds to verbal stimuli by moving the same as the word and opposite the word. Contrasts two words to create opposites in movement.	Explores in movement the textures and qualities within words. Combines several words to create movement sentences and studies.	Uses poetry or short stories to stimulate movement exploration about the images, shapes, and textures.
Responds to one stimulus.	Responds to more complex stimuli, such as two contrasting elements.	Transforms stimuli into appropriate actions.	Transforms stimuli into appropriate actions.
Translates an external stimulus into movement.	Uses experimentation as a part of dance making and a tool for composition.	Experiments with various stimuli to extend the range of movement before selecting material for compositions.	Applies improvisation, experimentation, use of various stimuli, and manipulation tools as preliminary to or integrated with the choreographic process.

Dance Cornerstone Curriculum Framework—C2: Creating and Composing from *Teaching Dance as Art in Education* by Brenda Pugh McCutchen, 2006, Champaign IL: Human Kinetics

Grades K-2	Grades 3-5	Grades 6-8	Grades 9-12
1.1c *Exploring gestures and postures*			
Experiments with everyday gestures of the hands and arms that communicate. Experiments with transposing an arm or hand gesture to the total body.	Experiments with everyday gestures of the hands and arms that communicate. Experiments with transposing an arm or hand gesture to the total body. Creates dance studies based on transposing gestures to different body parts.	Explores gestures of the legs, feet, arms, and head. Takes them from expressive gesture to abstract gesture and develops them in time, space, and with dynamic changes.	Creates dance studies based on gestures. Extends everyday gestures into abstract dance movement. Uses movement motifs that incorporate the original gestures and provide a sense of continuity within the study. Experiments with gestures found in different dance styles (jazz, mudras of south Indian dance, gestures commonly found in ritual dances in certain Native American or West African cultures).
——————	Explores how postures communicate a personal feeling state in dance. Explores postures such as upright, off center, off balance, precarious, asymmetrical, closed, and curved downward.	Explores postures as they relate to communication and translates feelings. Uses postures for design purposes to communicate feelings. Explores using abstract postures for design interest.	Experiments with postures used in dances around the world: earth-oriented postures such as Native American, West African, Balinese, Javanese, and Australian Aboriginal and air-oriented postures such as ballet (including en pointe) and American musical theatre.
1.1d *Exploring mobility and stability*			
Explores the mobility of the young body and its low center of gravity. Explores a wide base of support for stability when supported by different body parts and moving through space.	Explores the full range of mobility of the body. Explores ways to maintain stability when balanced on one leg or small base of support. Uses principles of mobility and stability in performance and in creative work.	Explores the full range of mobility of the body. Explores ways to maintain stability when balanced on one leg or small base of support. Explores ways that stability helps enhance mobility. Uses findings in performing and dance making.	Explores the full range of mobility of the body. Explores ways to maintain stability when balanced on one leg or small base of support. Explores ways that stability helps enhance mobility. Experiments with mobility punctuated by still points of refined balance. Experiments with how long one can hold a balance before it gives way to mobility and generates other movement phrases. Uses findings for performance and composition.
1.1e *Exploring imagery*			
Explores imagery in such a way that translates into body movement in time and space, with energy and dynamics, or in relationships.	Explores imagery that is concrete and specific in concept but abstract in movement.	Explores imagery that is concrete and specific in concept but abstract in movement. Explores imagery as a way to increase technique (such as Franklin describes in *Dance Imagery*).	Explores imagery that is concrete and specific in concept but abstract in movement. Explores imagery as a way to increase technique (such as Franklin describes in *Dance Imagery*).
——————	Goes beyond the purely imitative when responding to imagery or stories in dance.	Moves away from concrete gesture and pantomime into abstract expressive movement.	Moves away from concrete gesture and pantomime into abstract expressive movement.

Dance Cornerstone Curriculum Framework—C2: Creating and Composing from *Teaching Dance as Art in Education* by Brenda Pugh McCutchen, 2006, Champaign IL: Human Kinetics

197

1.0 Experimentation

Grades K-2	Grades 3-5	Grades 6-8	Grades 9-12
1.1f Experiments with movement concepts			
Experiments with movements in place or through space, movements that occur one after another, and the difference between moving and traveling.	Experiments with motion and stillness as expressive tools. Learns to follow the leader, initiate as leader, follow timing and movement cues, and make entrances and exits.	Experiments with unison, canon, juxtaposition, and other timing concepts.	Experiments with differentiating between movement and motion as artistic concepts in dance.

1.2 Improvisation

Grades K-2	Grades 3-5	Grades 6-8	Grades 9-12
1.2a Qualities			
———	Improvises using contrasts of dynamics (such as sharp–smooth, bumpy–slick, hard–soft) to refine the student's ability to communicate clearly the extremes within the range.	Emphasizes opposites to increase clarity of expression. Moves to the full range of going from one extreme to the other to show transition and gradual change.	Contrasts extremes and all gradations in between. Improvises with increasing awareness of energy flow as it relates to the felt sensation of movement as well as to its expressive quality.
———	———	Improvises with a body-systems approach to movement. Differentiates between movement that is inspired by the bones, the joints, the muscles, the fluid systems, and the nervous system.	Improvises with a body-systems approach to movement. Differentiates between movement that is inspired by the bones, the joints, the muscles, the fluid systems, and the nervous system. Refines improvisational ability to shift dynamic quality and range.
———	Uses extremes in dynamic range and movement quality.	Increases dynamic range and ability to add texture to movement.	Increases dynamic range and ability to add texture to movement.
1.2b Spatial designing			
———	Improvises with spatial concepts such as near–far, meeting–parting, advancing–retreating, gathering–scattering.	Improvises with spatial concepts such as near–far, meeting–parting, advancing–retreating, gathering–scattering. Also explores opening–closing and negative–positive space.	Improvises with spatial concepts such as near–far, meeting–parting, advancing–retreating, gathering–scattering. Also explores opening–closing and negative–positive space.
1.2c Body relationships			
Improvises by relating oneself to the duration of a movement (how long it can last), its size or dimension (range: how big or small), and its relationship to the self (how near or far away from the body).	Improvises with another person using stimuli such as over and under, around and through, balance, stillness and action, and dynamics or effort contrasts.	Improvises with increasing sensitivity to the movement of others in response to verbal, visual, tactile, and auditory stimuli.	Improvises while paying attention to group shaping and designs, dynamics, and available space.
———	Improvises with self-accompaniment (body sounds, voice, instrument).	Improvises with self-accompaniment (body sounds, voice, instrument).	Improvises with self-accompaniment (body sounds, voice, instrument). Improvises with others to tactile, auditory, visual, or verbal stimuli. Also responds to the movement of others.

Dance Cornerstone Curriculum Framework—C2: Creating and Composing from Teaching Dance as Art in Education by Brenda Pugh McCutchen, 2006, Champaign IL: Human Kinetics

Grades K-2	Grades 3-5	Grades 6-8	Grades 9-12
1.2c Body relationships (continued)			
———	Improvises alone to create body relationships. Uses focus to communicate intent.	Improvises alone to create body relationships. Uses focus and graining to help communicate intent.	Improvises alone to create body relationships. Uses focus and graining to help communicate intent.
———	———	Explores everyday objects as props such as chairs, umbrellas, hoops, mops, and fabrics to find their movement potential.	Explores a wide variety of props as motivation for movement improvisations and eventual compositions.
———	———	Improvises ways to support oneself and dance partners. Works on spatial relationships and timing. Works with others to extend movement options, including mobility and stability.	Improvises push, pull, reach, and roll concepts with others. Works with others to extend movement options in time and space and with dynamic variety. Increases ability to spontaneously respond to others and relate to them. (Advanced classes: If appropriate, mature and responsible students experiment with supporting weight and contact improvisation.)
1.2d Timing			
Experiments with timing and tempo changes.	Improvises at different speeds (nonmetered) and tempi (metered).	Moves beyond the extremes of fast–slow timing to include accelerating and decelerating. Learns to be sensitive to timing and duration of improvisation.	Moves beyond the extremes of fast–slow timing to modulate tempo. Uses accelerating and decelerating to communicate sensitivity to timing change. Learns to be sensitive to timing and duration of improvisation to determine when to bring it to a close.
1.2e Themes and relevant topics			
(Grade 2) Improvises with a partner to convey simple concepts such as cooperation and working together.	Incorporates themes such as meeting and parting to improvise variations for what happens after the meeting and before the parting.	Takes relevant topics (related to dance or other studies) to incorporate into movement improvisations.	Turns schoolwide themes into movement improvisations (such as conflict resolution, loyalty, or transformations). Takes relevant topics (related to dance or other studies) to incorporate into movement improvisations.

2.0   Composition and Choreography

Grades K-2	Grades 3-5	Grades 6-8	Grades 9-12
2.1 Basic skills of composing			
2.1a Beginning–middle–end			
Learns to compose with beginning, middle, and end. Learns to make dances that have still shapes at the beginning and end of the movement.	Creates compositions that have a definite beginning, middle, and end. Features beginnings and ends that are still shapes on stage and that are entrances and exits.	Takes beginning–middle–end into creating dance studies. Evaluates the effectiveness of the beginning and the end and the relationship between the beginning and the end.	Creates short studies that have unique, captivating beginnings that develop through to a logical conclusion.

Dance Cornerstone Curriculum Framework—C2: Creating and Composing from *Teaching Dance as Art in Education* by Brenda Pugh McCutchen, 2006, Champaign IL: Human Kinetics

Dance Cornerstone Curriculum Framework—C2: Creating and Composing

2.0 Composition and Choreography

Grades K-2	Grades 3-5	Grades 6-8	Grades 9-12
2.1a Beginning–middle–end (continued)			
———	Creates, repeats, and performs a dance that has a clear beginning, middle, and end; makes effective use of time, space, and energy and dynamics throughout.	Creates, repeats, and performs dance studies that demonstrate effective use of time, space, energy and dynamics, body shapes, and rhythm and have a beginning, middle development, and ending.	Creates, repeats, and performs dance studies that demonstrate effective use of time, space, energy and dynamics, body shapes, and rhythm; have a beginning, middle, and end; and use choreographic principles such as theme and variation, canon, and call and response.
2.1b Selecting movement and motifs			
(Grade 2) After exploring one dance element related to the body (such as body parts or body moves), selects only a few of the movements that were the most delightful and puts them in a short dance sequence with a beginning, middle, and end.	Through exploring one of the dance elements fully, selects the unique and interesting movements to sequence into a dance sentence. Selects the most effective order from beginning, through middle, to end.	Through improvisation, experimentation, and exploration, selects movements that best serve one area. Sequences them into artfully designed movement études or studies.	Explores and improvises around a dance concept keeping the movements that communicate most clearly and discarding the others. Sequences and organizes movement statements and phrases.
———	Creates, repeats, and performs a dance that communicates an idea. Selects movement that communicates the meaning and intent of the dance.	Creates, repeats, and performs a dance that deals with an issue of personal significance. Selects movement that communicates the meaning and intent of the dance.	Creates, repeats, and performs a dance that deals with a contemporary social issue. Selects movement that communicates the meaning and intent of the dance.
2.1c Phrasing			
———	Joins like movements together into dance phrases. Learns how breath phrasing holds together movement in time.	Works with breath phrasing and kinetic phrasing to connect movement in time into visually digestible morsels.	Uses phrasing to help communicate intent and to keep some movements together in sequence. Learns to make phrases of different length to keep a dance composition from being too predictable or too choppy.
2.1d Stating a theme			
Composes cinquains on one theme.	Understands the concept of and is able to create a movement theme. Compares it to a "topic sentence" from which a dance develops and movement will be extended.	Uses movement themes and at least one theme-based form to create dance studies. Develops and varies movement theme and motif to communicate intent.	Learns to develop movement within a thematic context. Uses movement themes and theme-based forms to create dance studies and dances. Develops and varies movement theme and motif to communicate intent.

Dance Cornerstone Curriculum Framework—C2: Creating and Composing from Teaching Dance as Art in Education by Brenda Pugh McCutchen, 2006, Champaign IL: Human Kinetics

Grades K-2	Grades 3-5	Grades 6-8	Grades 9-12
2.1e Extending and manipulating movement			
Learns to transpose movement to different body parts.	Manipulates movement material. Transposes movement to different body parts as a way to extend movement. Learns fragmentation of a movement theme to break it into parts and put it back together in different ways.	Manipulates movement material. Learns to extend a movement theme through manipulation tools, such as augmentation, diminution, fragmentation, retrograde, and transposing to different body parts.	Manipulates movement material. In groups, learns ways to extend movement themes and develop them using manipulation tools such as a round, a canon, inversion going one after another, or juxtaposition of one group against another. Selects and manipulates original movement material to make a dance.
Makes an improvisational dance that contrasts two concepts. Learns how all dances need contrasts to be interesting.	Learns to extend original movement by adding contrasts and finding ways to repeat with variation, thus creating interest by developing the original movement.	Incorporates contrasts, repetition, and variation to develop a movement concept and take it from the original statement to a new place.	Incorporates contrasts, repetition, and variation to develop a movement concept and take it from the original statement to a new place.
2.1f Clarifying and refining to communicate intent and meaning			
———	Learns how to edit movement once it has been selected to remove extraneous movement. Edits to clarify and refine work.	Learns how to edit movement once it has been selected to remove extraneous movement. Edits to clarify and refine work.	Edits to remove extraneous movement and clarify and refine work.
2.1g Parallels to written composition			
Translates word concepts into movement in word dances. Translates the word concept into movement so the intent is accurate and clear. Emphasizes verbs (actions) and prepositions (relationship words).	Learns to make dance sentences that join separate movements together into phrases. Notes that dance sentences have a beginning, middle, and end similar to a sentence and are punctuated like a sentence (sentences begin with a capital letter, state their idea or theme, and end with a period). Learns to move dance compositions forward rather than restating material repetitively.	Works on composing clear sentences and paragraphs (dance studies). Sees how composing dance parallels writing paragraphs: Presents topic sentence (movement theme) and makes sure all else in that section relates to that theme to either clarify or extend it. Learns to move dance compositions forward rather than restating material.	Compares composition in dance to writing descriptive narratives to which various paragraphs contribute. Sees the way both have a sense of development so that the beginning sets up the middle and the end brings resolution. Moves dance compositions forward rather than restating material.
———	———	Relates dance composition to poetry. Uses only the essence of the movement that is needed to convey the idea. Learns to eliminate extraneous movement to clarify intent.	Relates dance composition to poetry. Uses only the essence of the movement that is needed to convey the idea. Learns to pare down movement to convey a maximum of intent.

Dance Cornerstone Curriculum Framework—C2: Creating and Composing from *Teaching Dance as Art in Education* by Brenda Pugh McCutchen, 2006, Champaign IL: Human Kinetics

2.0 Composition and Choreography

Grades K-2	Grades 3-5	Grades 6-8	Grades 9-12
2.2 Form and structure			
2.2a Basic forms: phrase or sentence, study, composition, choreography			
Learns the basic form of structuring dance movement: beginning, middle, and end.	Learns basic forms: phrase, sentence, and dance study.	Learns to use the building blocks for organizing movement: phrase, sentence, study. Masters composition basics.	Uses phrases to compose theme-based dances. Applies principles of composition to choreography.
———	Shapes phrases or studies so that they develop through beginning, middle, and end.	Consciously shapes phrases into studies, works in progress, and finished pieces that have clear overall form and develop from start through to a conclusion.	Sensitively and consciously uses choreographic skills with phrasing that develops the beginning, middle, and ending effectively within the overall form of the final dance (study, work in progress, completed dance work).
2.2b Structural forms: two-part, three-part, theme and variation, theme and development			
Experiences simple two-part improvised dances that contrast opposites (e.g., fast–slow, high–low, in one place–through space).	Creates short studies in two-part form (AB) emphasizing contrasts. Creates studies in three parts (ABA) that restate the original theme at the end for continuity and emphasis. Works alone and in pairs to complete studies in two- and three-part form. Creates around structural and aesthetic criteria.	Shows the relationship of theme to parts by working with theme-based works alone and in small groups to create dances with structural and aesthetic criteria.	Creates dances in such forms as narrative and call and response. Uses a variety of tools to extend movement compositions using theme and variation. Works alone and in small groups to create dances with structural and aesthetic criteria. (Advanced students experiment with formal structures such as pre-classic dance suites [pre-ballet] to inspire composition based on the style of each part of the dance and music suite.)
Uses literary structures such as cinquain for creating dances.	Uses literary structures such as haiku and cinquain for creating dances.	Uses haiku, cinquain, limerick, and other selected literary forms for creating dances.	Uses haiku, cinquain, limerick, and other selected literary forms for creating dances.
———	Uses criteria for two- and three-part form with compositional and performance clarity.	Analyzes compositional assignments for self and peers to select and effectively execute dance forms such as AB, ABA, and theme and variation.	Develops and manipulates movement material to meet criteria for specific dance forms, such as theme and development.
2.2c Choosing a structure (to communicate intent and meaning)			
Uses teacher-selected structures such as cinquain, beginning–middle–end, and dance sentences to communicate one idea clearly.	Uses teacher-selected structures such as cinquain, beginning–middle–end, and dance sentences to communicate one idea clearly. After mastering these structural forms, self-selects different structures to communicate the intent of dance studies.	After mastering structural forms, selects a structure to communicate the intent of a dance study.	After experimenting with structural forms, selects a structure to communicate the intent of a dance work. Chooses the most effective structure to clearly convey the intent or meaning of one's dance composition.

Dance Cornerstone Curriculum Framework—C2: Creating and Composing from *Teaching Dance as Art in Education* by Brenda Pugh McCutchen, 2006, Champaign IL: Human Kinetics

Grades K-2	Grades 3-5	Grades 6-8	Grades 9-12
2.2d Grouping: solo, duet, trio, group			
_____	Uses a minimum number in a group to best communicate the intent of the dance study. Experiences positive group interaction in preparing for and performing dances.	Uses a minimum number in a group to best communicate the intent of the dance study. Creates and performs solo, duet, and small group works with the focus on the intent of the product itself (movement clarity, spatial and effort clarity, aesthetics).	Recognizes the communicative impact that can be achieved by solo, duet, and trio dances. Uses a minimum number in a group to best communicate the intent of the dance study. Works on solo and duet choreography on a specified topic and choreographs sensitively to achieve the intended artistic and thematic impact. Discovers how much more intricate the solo and duet work is than group work and how much more precise the movement has to be to communicate meaning.
_____	Works cooperatively with a partner or group of students to create dances that successfully communicate a shared idea.	Works cooperatively with a partner or group of students to create dances that successfully communicate a shared idea.	Works cooperatively with a partner or group of students to create dances that successfully communicate a shared idea.
2.2e Structured improvisation			
Learns how some dances do not have set movements but are improvised within a structure.	Creates structured improvisations on movement topics stressing beginning, middle, and end, with the middle being improvised around a theme or idea.	Uses structured improv as a movement form.	Uses structured improv as a movement form.
2.2f Organic and kinetic structures			
_____	_____	Uses an open structure for organic and/or kinetic movements to develop on their own and be presented.	Uses an open structure for organic and/or kinetic movements to develop on their own and be presented.
2.2g Structures based on accompaniment			
_____	Given several music selections from which to choose, selects accompaniment that best meets the intent of the dance study, factoring in tempo, duration, and instrumentation.	Selects accompaniment without lyrics and consciously (1) parallels the music, (2) uses music visualization, and (3) dances in contrast to the accompaniment.	Selects accompaniment appropriate to the intent or meaning of the dance: instrumental, percussion, metered, or nonmetered.
_____	Analyzes the overall form of selected metered accompaniment and consciously relates the composition to that form.	Analyzes the overall form of selected metered and nonmetered accompaniment and consciously relates the composition to that form.	Uses accompaniment as a soundscape that underlies a dance but does not dictate its form or structure. Discusses the limitations of composing a dance to a musical work or score.

Dance Cornerstone Curriculum Framework—C2: Creating and Composing from _Teaching Dance as Art in Education_ by Brenda Pugh McCutchen, 2006, Champaign IL: Human Kinetics

2.0 Composition and Choreography

Grades K-2	Grades 3-5	Grades 6-8	Grades 9-12
2.2g Structures based on accompaniment (continued)			
———	———	———	Recognizes the pitfalls inherent in any of the following practices: (1) paralleling accompaniment or lyrics exactly throughout a composition, (2) willfully negating overall form and fundamental meter of rhythmic accompaniment, or (3) paralleling or totally negating the dynamics of the accompaniment.
Responds to percussion accompaniment by the teacher when creating dances.	Makes dances without accompaniment.	Refines skills in moving without music, and establishes a distinct rhythm within oneself.	Refines skills in moving without music, and establishes a distinct rhythm within oneself.
2.3 Aesthetic principles of design			
2.3a Sequencing			
Develops a sense of sequence as an outgrowth of understanding beginning, middle, and end. Relates sequencing to math, science, arts, and language arts concepts.	Refines a sense of sequence and sequencing. Relates sequencing to math, science, arts, and language arts concepts.	When designing compositions and choreography, attends to the sequence of its various parts chronologically and logically. Relates sequencing to math, science, arts, and language arts concepts.	When designing compositions and choreography, attends to the sequence of its various parts chronologically and logically. Relates sequencing to math, science, arts, and language arts concepts.
2.3b Repetition			
Repeats patterns in folk dances. Can also repeat structured phrases, such as "jump-shape, jump-shape, turn and travel."	Learns to make patterns in dance by repeating rhythms, movements, and sequences. Learns how repetition contributes to unifying a dance work and emphasizing certain parts.	Learns to make patterns in dance by repeating rhythms, movements, and sequences. Learns how repetition contributes to unifying a dance work and emphasizing certain parts.	Learns how all art forms rely on visual and auditory repetition to help make dances coherent. Investigates repetition as emphasis, motif, ground bass, and unifier. Investigates how other art forms use repetition for emphasis and unifying a work.
2.3c Contrast			
Experiences contrasts through antonyms.	Learns to use contrast as a way to increase interest in a dance work. Learns how the relationship between one object and something different clarifies each one.	Experiments with contrasts and counterpoint to add interest to compositions.	Experiments with contrasts and counterpoint to add interest and clarity to compositions. Investigates how other art forms use contrast.
2.3d Variety			
Learns the concept of variety through changes of level, body part, direction, shaping, timing, and other elements.	Uses variety to increase interest and enrich the composition.	Uses variety to extend movement themes to make them interesting and to keep them from being monotonous. Adds variety without jeopardizing unity.	Restates significant movements in the theme but varies them to add interest according to the intent of the composition. Uses elements from space, time, dynamics, and relationships to vary a theme. Adds variety without jeopardizing unity.

Dance Cornerstone Curriculum Framework—C2: Creating and Composing from *Teaching Dance as Art in Education* by Brenda Pugh McCutchen, 2006, Champaign IL: Human Kinetics

Grades K-2	Grades 3-5	Grades 6-8	Grades 9-12
2.3e Unity			
Works with one idea or theme and develops a sense of clarity about one topic.	Prepares works with one single motivating idea. Learns how to make a clear statement in dance around a theme. Edits to remove extraneous movement that does not contribute to its clarity.	Understands that the most fundamental premise in all the arts is that a work should hold together in a way that creates a sense of unity.	Understands that the most fundamental premise in all the arts is that a work should hold together in a way that creates a sense of unity. Removes extraneous material that does not add aesthetic value to the dance.
2.3f Climax (crescendo)			
(Grades 1 and 2) Learns to make big moves like exclamation points.	To communicate meaning, learns how to build to a high point and learns the concepts of crescendo and decrescendo.	Learns to use climax and crescendo and decrescendo to keep compositions from being flat. Learns to use these for primary emphasis in time, in space, or with dynamics. Investigates how other art works use this principle.	Learns to use climax and crescendo and decrescendo to keep compositions from being flat. Learns to use these for primary emphasis in time, in space, or with dynamics. Investigates how other art works use this principle.
2.3g Advanced design principles: proportion, harmony, transition, balance			
———	———	Works on transitions between sections of dance.	Works on transitions between sections of dance. Works for a sense of balance, harmony, and proportion in dance creations.
2.3h Overall aesthetic quality			
———	Begins to consider the aesthetic quality of one's movement design when composing.	Considers the aesthetic quality of one's movement design.	Uses the principles of design (PODs) and other aesthetic criteria when creating and critiquing dances.

2.4 Choreographing

Grades K-2	Grades 3-5	Grades 6-8	Grades 9-12
2.4a Choreographic criteria			
Works from established criteria provided by the teacher.	Works from established criteria provided by the teacher.	Works from established criteria provided by the teacher. Learns to create own choreographic criteria.	Works from established criteria provided by the teacher. Works from both externally motivated and self-generated criteria.
———	Uses choreographic criteria for composing. Specifies criteria according to structure and aesthetics. Uses choreographic criteria as review criteria to evaluate the effectiveness of dance creations (structure and aesthetics).	Uses choreographic criteria when making dance studies and compositions. Specifies criteria according to structure and aesthetics. Uses gradual increase in complexity of criteria. Turns choreographic criteria into review criteria to evaluate the effectiveness of dance creations (structure and aesthetics).	Choreographs both from established choreographic criteria and by creating own choreographic criteria for dance making. Turns choreographic criteria into review criteria to evaluate the effectiveness of dance creations (structure and aesthetics).

Dance Cornerstone Curriculum Framework—C2: Creating and Composing from *Teaching Dance as Art in Education* by Brenda Pugh McCutchen, 2006, Champaign IL: Human Kinetics

2.0   Composition and Choreography

Grades K-2	Grades 3-5	Grades 6-8	Grades 9-12
2.4b Aesthetic choices			
_____	Makes aesthetic choices when selecting movement material and editing and refining it. Develops artistic eyes to make discriminating choices.	Makes aesthetic choices when selecting movement material and editing and refining it. Develops artistic eyes to make discriminating choices. Makes aesthetic choices based on the PODs to increase the artistic integrity of the work.	Makes aesthetic choices when selecting movement material and editing and refining it. Develops artistic eyes to make discriminating choices. Makes aesthetic choices based on the PODs to increase the artistic integrity of the work.
_____	Develops the artistic perspective in dance making that less is more. Chooses the smallest number of dancers needed to convey an idea.	Develops the artistic perspective in dance making that less is more. Chooses the smallest number of dancers needed to convey an idea. Avoids "casts of thousands" and "including all of your friends."	Develops the artistic perspective in dance making that less is more. Chooses the smallest number of dancers needed to convey an idea. Avoids "casts of thousands" and "including all of your friends."
_____	_____	_____	When available, uses technology such as CD-ROMs of Wild Child (choreography software) and Motifs for a Solo Dancer to increase understanding of how choreography is aesthetically driven and to learn choreographic skills.
2.4c Technology: software			
_____	_____	Is introduced to DanceForms software (if available, or current choreography software like Motifs for a Solo Dancer). Increases artistic quality of movement design and choreographic interest through these tools. Learns the terminology used in DanceForms.	Uses DanceForms software (if available, or current choreography software like Choreographic Outcomes). Increases artistic quality of movement design and choreographic interest through these tools. Learns the terminology used in DanceForms.

3.0   Polishing and Sharing Creations

Grades K-2	Grades 3-5	Grades 6-8	Grades 9-12
3.1 Polishing compositions			
3.1a Making aesthetic decisions			
Refines one's movements by assimilating aspects of viewing samples of great works.	Edits to improve the clarity of intent or meaning.	Makes aesthetic decisions based on evaluating one's own dance's communicative clarity. Edits to improve the clarity of intent or meaning.	Makes aesthetic decisions based on evaluating one's own dance's communicative clarity. Edits to improve the clarity of intent or meaning.
_____	Polishes compositions for performance quality.	Polishes compositions for performance quality.	Polishes compositions for performance quality.

Dance Cornerstone Curriculum Framework—C2: Creating and Composing from *Teaching Dance as Art in Education* by Brenda Pugh McCutchen, 2006, Champaign IL: Human Kinetics

Grades K-2	Grades 3-5	Grades 6-8	Grades 9-12
3.1b Editorial feedback: showing works in progress			
Incorporates peer and teacher feedback by refining movements for performance.	Serves as an informal peer evaluator, clearly relating to the criteria (time, space) provided by or for the choreographers.	As a peer evaluator, cultivates a sensitive way to identify both the effective and weak factors of a dance work in light of given criteria. Is introduced to the Liz Lerman's Critical Response Process as a model for choreographic critique.	Responsibly evaluates the choreography of others in their use of space, time, and energy and dynamics; the clarity of the dance idea; and other appropriate facts. Uses the Liz Lerman's Critical Response Process as a model for choreographic critique.
Shows dances to peers with pride.	Shows works in progress to one or two peers for editorial feedback. Shares group studies with at least one other group during class with emphasis on overall design.	Performs works in progress for peers in an informal setting for editorial feedback.	Performs solo, duet, and small-group works in progress for editorial comment about the clarity of intent and quality of performance.
Gives and receives peer feedback.	Engages in external or peer evaluation to increase clarity of intent and artistry. Recognizes that a dance piece is necessarily subject to both internal and external evaluation to become the clearest possible performance product.	Engages in external or peer evaluation to increase clarity of intent and artistry. As a peer evaluator, understands all criteria in the assignment as well as the choreographer's stated intent.	Engages in external or peer evaluation to increase clarity of intent and artistry. Grasps the choreographer's intent before offering comments as to the strengths and weaknesses and making suggestions for improvement of the dance study or completed work.
3.1c Self-evaluation and editing			
Reflects on own work to make it better.	Evaluates own dance works according to artistic use of the body (shaping, use of body parts in isolation, use of total body) in time (timing, rhythmic shifts, appropriate length) and in space (levels, direction, spatial interest), and the modulation of energy and dynamics. Edits for a clearer product.	Analyzes the use of the BSTER elements in own dance works. Evaluates the artistic integrity of the work. Applies design principles to improve a product.	Analyzes the use of the BSTER elements in own dance works. Edits according to the aesthetic principles of design to increase the artistic integrity of the works.
————	Reworks parts of dances that are not yet clear.	Refines in-process drafts into polished products.	Refines in-process drafts into polished products.
3.2 Performing for critique			
3.2a Performing: using review criteria for critique			
Shows works in class.	Performs works in class for analysis and critique.	Performs completed works in a setting where the audience is composed of class peers and possibly others of varying age range (i.e., culminating performance on completion of a particular unit of work by all dance students). Uses review criteria based on the choreographic criteria for peer critique of the finished product.	Following appropriately organized rehearsals, performs completed works in a formal or informal setting with personal pride and joy. Uses review criteria based on the choreographic criteria for peer critique of the finished product.

Dance Cornerstone Curriculum Framework—C2: Creating and Composing from *Teaching Dance as Art in Education* by Brenda Pugh McCutchen, 2006, Champaign IL: Human Kinetics

3.0 Polishing and Sharing Creations

Grades K-2	Grades 3-5	Grades 6-8	Grades 9-12
3.2a Performing: using review criteria for critique (continued)			
Increases concentration and clarity of peer performances.	Performs with concentration and commitment to quality. Engages in peer critique.	Performs with concentration and commitment to communicate meaning and build self-esteem and confidence through quality performing.	Performs with concentration and commitment to communicate meaning and build self-esteem and confidence through quality performing.
3.2b Performance quality			
———	Gives attention to performance quality before and during performance.	Refines performance quality before and during performance.	Refines performance quality before and during performance.
Learns to bodythink and bodyspeak.	Acquires performance skills through bodyspeaking.	Applies acquired performance skills.	Applies refined performance skills.
Gives peer critique.	Assimilates peer and teacher critique.	Uses critique to improve performance.	Uses critique to improve performance.

Dance Cornerstone Curriculum Framework—C2: Creating and Composing from *Teaching Dance as Art in Education* by Brenda Pugh McCutchen, 2006, Champaign IL: Human Kinetics

Knowing History, Culture, and Context

 Cornerstone 3

"The best way to understand and appreciate another culture is to study, discover and experience its people and the role that the arts play in its society."

—Ferne Yangyeitie Caulker, "African Dance: Divine Motion" (Nadel and Strauss 2003, p. 18)

This chapter features Cornerstone 3 (C3)—one of the four educational dance cornerstones. This cornerstone focuses on the historical, social, and cultural components of a comprehensive dance curriculum. It advocates the study of dances across cultures, dances through time, and significant dance works of the past and present. C3 encompasses dance as art and as human phenomenon. It builds a broad context from which to study dance as art. C3 promotes preserving dance as well as reconstructing and reclaiming lost works. The substance of this cornerstone is aligned with national standards. C3 is outlined in detail in this chapter to help you build curriculum, write goals and objectives, and design assessments. Cornerstone 3 may be the starting place for, the main focus of, or one part of a unit of study, but it is a necessary part of each unit. A sequential K-12 curriculum framework is presented, which relates to all the artistic processes in dance and emphasizes knowing dance as an art form. This cornerstone enrolls the learner as dance historian and dance anthropologist.

Dance has the unique power of bringing to life and giving energy to experiences of other people, at other times, at other places. This cornerstone contains the enormous body of work that has sprung forth from the creative imagination of men and women around the world since the beginning of time. Study of Cornerstone 3 exposes dance as a human phenomenon that shows learners how groups as well as individuals have expressed themselves rhythmically, kinetically, and artistically since before recorded time. By reconstructing dances of the past, you make them part of the present. These dances broaden a child's world by increasing his experiences. They give unique insights into dance, the world, the self. Great choreographers from the past communicate their thoughts and feelings directly to those who delve into their works.

Think about the incredibly rich dance legacy we inherit that is ours to pass on—the stunning ballets, fabulous folk dances, mesmerizing modern dances, exotically beautiful classical dance forms from Asia, dynamically spirited dances from Africa. The list is truly endless. Dance heritage encompasses all the roots and styles of dance throughout time and place, history, and cultures.

Our growing appreciation for this emphatic system of human expression called dance unfolds as we peel away our own ignorance of dance to discover notable works from the creative imagination of humankind. The full significance of dance, dancing, and dancers becomes apparent to us, not all at once, but bit by bit. So we inquire into diverse contemporary and historic dance works to assemble a full appreciation of dance. Maybe we learn through choreographers' stories or their artistic design, hearing about the motivation to create a particular work, seeing how choreographers transferred an idea into movement and how they embodied a concept. This is how we take on a new appreciation for their human perspective and experiences. These insights stoke our own creative fires. This is how we gain confidence and inspiration to create our own works.

Choreographers of the past share their perspectives and artistry with us through their creations. Their works bring them back to life to be explored by educators, scholars, and students. Their artistic expressions thrill audiences of the present. In their lifetimes, these choreographers experienced the same kind of emotional highs and lows that all humans experience. The difference is they were

Seeing how choreographers transferred an idea into movement often ignites our own creative fires and inspires us to create our own dances.

compelled to embody their ideas and put their perspective of the experience into organized movement. They designed spectacular dances ranging across all human emotion—from lust, fear, anger, dread, and frustration to beauty, joy, ecstasy, and love. Our understanding of dance as art expression comes from experiencing these great works. We expand dance by bringing these works to life for our students and illuminating what it is to be fully human. And we sense the necessity of document-

ing and preserving dances of the past, present, and future to leave a legacy of dance for generations.

Exciting units of study can be generated from this cornerstone. Units of study motivated by other cornerstones integrate history and cultural diversity in ways that draw on and promote our rich dance heritage.

Relation to National Standards and Beyond

This chapter features "knowing" and "responding" aspects of NAEP's report card. It fleshes out NSDE 5, *Demonstrating and understanding dance in various cultures and historical periods,* and NSDE 3, *Understand dance as a way to create and communicate meaning.* Before going further, read NSDE Achievement Standards 3 and 5 for grades 4, 8, and 12.

Dance study and courses that prepare you to teach this cornerstone: Take as many courses in cultural study and dance anthropology as possible. Information, concepts, and experiences come from such diverse courses as Dance History, Dance Anthropology, World Dance Techniques, Diversity in Dance, Folk Dance, Non-Western Rituals in the Arts, and other cultural studies and art history courses that shed light on the arts across time and place. Keep your notes organized with your textbooks for teaching reference.

Overview of This Cornerstone

The focus of Cornerstone 3 is to bring the whole world of dance to us: dance through history, multicultural forms, and study of famous contributors to dance and their works. They make up the lexicon of dance.

Specific units of study may begin from C3: the point of entry, the inspiration for, or the emphasis of the unit. C3 enriches a unit whether it is the focus of the unit's content or the support for its experiences.

Some mega-ideas and concepts from this cornerstone follow:

1. Dance is a product of its time and place.
2. Dance has a long and significant role throughout history.

3. Universal themes recur in dances all around the world.
4. Different cultures have unique styles of dance based on their cultural influences.
5. Traditional dances reveal important human values.
6. Dance's major works evaporate unless preserved, documented, and performed.
7. Dance should be valued as art and preserved for future generations.
8. Dance is both a participation and a performance art.
9. Major works of dance should be studied—just like major works in the other arts.
10. Major works of dance demonstrate performance techniques and choreographic skills at their best and introduce us to the outstanding artists of our discipline.
11. World-class choreographers should be as well known as world-class composers, playwrights, and artists.
12. Great dancers and choreographers leave an indelible imprint on the art of dance.

Goals and Objectives of Cornerstone 3

C3's portion of the Dance Cornerstone Curriculum (DCC) Framework is presented in three parts in this chapter. The first part (goals and objectives) shows the big picture. The second part (content outline) breaks goals and objectives into an outline. The third part breaks the outline into a suggested developmental sequence detailed later in the chapter for K-2, 3-5, 6-8, and 9-12.

These suggested K-12 goals and objectives help you fully convey Cornerstone 3. See the many ways these goals prepare students to meet or exceed the NSDEs—especially 5.

 Goal 1: To understand dance as universal expression across time and place

1.0 Desired outcome: To discover how broadly dance exists in the world.

Learning objectives: The student will

1.1 Explain how dance reflects, records, and shapes history and plays a role in every culture as a universal language.

> Demonstrate how dance takes many forms, is a valid form of expression for males and females, and communicates ideas in different ways.

> Recognize the human need to communicate through dance.

1.2 Explain or demonstrate cultural and historical similarities and differences among dance styles.

> Identify a variety of dance styles and have proficiency in executing more than one style.

1.3 Relate dance to its place, time, and purpose.

> Relate dance's purposes and functions in different cultures.

> Place dance in context.

1.4 Recount the impact external factors make on dance.

 Goal 2: To recognize the significance of dance in society, notable contributors to dance, and a body of significant dance works

2.0 Desired outcomes: To experience the diversity of dance and know its key players.

Learning objectives: The student will

2.1 Recognize dance as an artistic form of communication.

> Explain the role of the dancer in society as an expressive artist or entertainer, who helps create artistic values and accomplishments of civilization.

> Explain the role of the choreographer in making dance as art.

> Explain the artistic role of dances and choreographers of the past and present.

2.2 Explain the roles dance plays in society.

> Reveal the roles dance plays in diverse cultures.

2.3 Identify important dance innovators in past and contemporary cultures.

> Explain the artistic role of dancers and choreographers of the past and present.

> Identify notable dance performers from selected time periods, styles, or cultures who made an impact on the world of dance.

> Illustrate the contributions of diverse choreographers, past and present.

> Identify patrons and promoters of individuals and collectives who moved dance forward through history and made an impact on it.

> Identify leading teachers who increased our understanding of dance technique and artistry.

> Identify dance historians and anthropologists who give us a broader appreciation of dance as an art form across different cultures.

> Identify important dance critics who recorded dance and called attention to dance trends throughout history.

> Perform dances from around the world (folk, classical, social).

2.4 Identify important dance works and their choreographers from different time periods, styles, and cultures.

> Examine how significant dance works relate to those of history or other cultures.

> Know one or more examples of European works from the 17th century to the present.

> Be able to describe significant non-Western dance works.

 Goal 3: To acquire skills in documenting and preserving dance works

3.0 Desired outcome: To take a personal role in carrying on the traditions of dance.

Learning objectives: The student will

3.1 Demonstrate the ability to record, retrieve, and archive dance works.

> Access or retrieve historical works from archiving facilities or access Web sites that assist with archiving and retrieving works.

3.2 Identify opportunities for lifetime involvement in dance and dance careers.

3.3 Reconstruct parts of études or full dance works from noted choreographers.

Adapted from Lunt and McCutchen, 1995, with permission of the South Carolina Department of Education.

Content Outline

Use this framework outline to guide comprehensive long-term curriculum planning. The outline headings are developed into a framework at the end of the chapter (page 237).

This outline identifies multiple ways that dance is rooted in the past and present. It names the facets that help you make dance instruction contextually coherent and aesthetically driven. Teach to build a global perspective of the world's important dance works to see how dance develops over time throughout the world.

 ### Goal 1.0 Dance as Universal Expression

Objective 1.1 Purposes and Functions

1.1a Universal themes
1.1b Rites of passage and ritual
1.1c Entertainment
1.1d Religious
1.1e Human expression
1.1f Artistic expression

Objective 1.2 Diverse Styles and Genres

1.2a Folk arts and square dance
1.2b Classical ballet
1.2c Non-Western classical dance (Asian, African, Indian, Middle Eastern)
1.2d Non-Western participation dance
1.2e Modern and postmodern dance
1.2f Experimental and creative dance
1.2g Jazz, tap, and musical theatre
1.2h Fad dance, dance mania, street dance, pop culture, special trends
1.2i Social dance
1.2j Africanist elements

Objective 1.3 Dance Heritage in Context and in Relationship

1.3a Historic context
1.3b Social context
1.3c Cultural context
1.3d Relationship between music and dance
1.3e Geographic origins (cultural roots, climate)
1.3f Education
1.3g Recreation

Objective 1.4 Other Aspects of Dance

1.4a Participants (number, group, composition, age)
1.4b Groupings and formations for participation dances (circle, line, square, couple, free form)
1.4c Groupings and formations for performance dances
1.4d Impact of architecture on dance
1.4e Impact of costume and dress on dance

 ### Goal 2.0 Significance of Dance in Society

Objective 2.1 Artistic Roles

2.1a Creator and choreographer
2.1b Skilled performers

Objective 2.2 Societal Roles

2.2a Roles in society
2.2b Dance in the world
2.2c Dance for healing

Objective 2.3 Notable Contributors to Dance

2.3a Notable performers of dance
2.3b Choreographers
2.3c Patrons and promoters
2.3d Teachers
2.3e Dance historians and anthropologists
2.3f Dance critics

Objective 2.4 Significant Dance Works

2.4a Earliest known works
2.4b 17th and 18th centuries
2.4c 19th century
2.4d 20th century
2.4e 21st century

 ### Goal 3.0 Preserving Dance for Future Generations

Objective 3.1 Documentation

3.1a Preserving dance for the future
3.1b Transitory nature of dance
3.1c Recording and notating

3.1d Motor memory and dance legacy

3.1e Kinesthetic teaching

Objective 3.2 Lifetime Involvement

3.2a Recreation and fitness

3.2b Avocational dance

3.2c Dance careers

Objective 3.3 Repertory

3.3a Reconstruct and perform significant dance works

3.3b Personalize historic dances by dancing them

Adapted from Lunt and McCutchen, 1995, with permission of the South Carolina Department of Education.

Cornerstone Thumbprint (C3)

By participating in a variety of dance styles and inquiring into their roots, students experience dance's universal themes, gain exposure to cultural styles different from their own, and grasp the significance of dance to people other than themselves.

- **K-2:** Students in grades K through 2 recognize different dance styles and purposes of dance. Viewing dance works from around the world broadens their perspective on dance.

- **3-5:** Students in grades 3 through 5 increase technical skills by learning varied cultural dance forms and basic skills in square and folk dance, jazz, and tap; demonstrate the ability to perform authentic cultural dance styles different from their own; and identify dance traditions in various societies. These students are able to talk about dances from other cultures as well as their own and identify several great dance works.

- **6-8:** Students in grades 6 through 8 know repertory works in cultural and classical styles and develop increased skill in participation and performance styles. They increase skills in modern, ballet, square and folk dance, jazz, and tap; they recognize characteristics of different cultural dance styles. These students grasp the significance of traditional dance in world cultures and the role dance has played in politics throughout history. Students increase

familiarity with icons of dance and major dance works. They begin to document their dances.

- **9-12:** Students in grades 9 through 12 gain proficiency in performing and critiquing folk dance and concert dance forms; apply historical and universal themes in creative work; and know some of the great works, choreographers, and performers who created dance and shaped its history. They preserve their finished works.

Adapted with permission of the South Carolina Department of Education, © 1993.

Dance Across Cultures: Cultural Diversity

The essence of America is diversity. We are a nation of immigrants. We have been called a melting pot. Our clothes, our music, our food, our idols, and our habits demonstrate that we are cosmopolitan and sophisticated consumers of world culture.

However, we are more than a melting pot. We are a smorgasbord, a conglomerate of cultures, a patchwork of rich and varied descriptions. There are intact language groups (such as Gullah, Creole, Hmong, and Cajun), religious groups (such as Greek Orthodox, American Protestant, and Russian Jewish), and ethnic groups (such as Scots-Irish, Samoan, Japanese). When you look around, who do you find?

At different times throughout history, smaller cultures struggled to keep from being wiped out by predominant cultures. Native Americans tenaciously held their traditions despite attempts to "civilize" them by those who would have destroyed their cultures. Their dances, once outlawed, are being revived. Enslaved Africans of the rural South in earlier centuries were prevented from dancing by slaveholders to suppress uprisings, to discourage community, and to repress African cultural and aesthetic ties. But dances survived. We have in the United States a multitude of cultures, nationalities, and language groups whose dances and languages are intact. The list is long: the Portuguese in New England; the Irish and Italians in New York; the Hmong in Minnesota; the Ukrainians in New York; Alpine Germans in northern Georgia; the Basques in rural Oregon, Idaho, and Montana; the Gullah in the Sea Islands of Georgia. Wherever you live, you can find pockets of identifiable cultural groups who

Aim to reflect cultures as authentically as possible, learning that there are differing perspectives to consider and variations within cultural groups to explore.

have rich dance, music, arts, crafts, and folk traditions. We have so much to learn.

In our communities we find beautifully woven tapestries of cultures waiting to enrich our dance study. Living in proximity to each other, we have discovered compelling dance forms about which we previously knew little, such as the classical Balinese legong and the Brazilian capoeira.

Multiple sets of cultural values exist within the world community, and dance draws from them. We use such terms as *multiethnic, multiracial, multicultural,* and *cross-cultural* to capture the scope of cultural diversity in the arts. In the midst of society's cultural pluralism, let's distinguish between them:

- **Culture** is an ever-changing system of shared beliefs, values, traditions, customs, learned behaviors, and artifacts that are transmitted from one generation to another.
- **Ethnicity** refers to expressions and manifestations of attitudes, values, and behaviors that are based on a specific tradition, ancestry, history, and cultural heritage.
- **Multicultural education** is concerned with increasing educational equity for a wide range of cultural groups.
- **Multiethnic education** modifies the total educational environment to reflect the ethnic

diversity within American schools. That environment includes school policy and institutional norms, attitudes and expectations of faculty and staff, counseling programs, courses of study, teaching methods, assessment strategies, and instructional materials.

- **Ethnocentric education** asserts the idea that people of diverse ethnic origins must be seen as subjects of history and of human experience. It takes the perspectives of the culture being studied to affirm both the struggles and achievements of different ethnic groups.

Adapted with permission of the South Carolina Department of Education.

Diversity in the Curriculum

Dance specialists must insist that our educational system include a smorgasbord of cultural forms instead of finding exclusivity in Western–European culture. All people have culture to celebrate. We must not separate people or look on their work as strange, unapproachable, or less artistic than our own. It is just as educationally important to be able to distinguish between contemporary Afro-Caribbean rhythmic dance forms as to know the differences between language groups in Western Europe. Build bridges across cultures so Americans with European heritage acknowledge the beauty of diverse populations here and abroad and non-Europeans accept European traditions.

Demographic changes in America give us access to new dance flavors. Foster cultural acceptance by introducing different dancing communities. Teach important classical, folk, and social dance forms of the world.

Schools have a trust to acknowledge the cultural and ethnic diversity of their students. Students need to see themselves reflected in the curriculum to make their instructional experiences relevant. Teachers who value diversity rather than merely accept it find teaching examples, materials, and instruction sensitive to their particular students. Diverse educational material of global proportions abound. By valuing diversity, you value your students. Give each student a place to be proud of his or her heritage—which increases self-esteem and builds cultural bridges.

 What traditions are celebrated in your community?

Diverse Perspectives

Aim to reflect cultures as authentically as possible, knowing that there are differing perspectives to consider and variations within cultural groups. Above all, show respect for cultural diversity. Avoid promoting cultural stereotypes. Show sensitivity when cultures are discussed and mixed. Take care not to offend by misrepresentation. Ask yourself these questions:

- What is the objective of multicultural education, and how do we embrace other world cultures while preserving their (and our own) identity?
- How do we create methods and materials suited to the cultures of the students who are a part of our classroom?
- Where do we start; where do we stop?

- How do we also present subgroups within larger cultural populations like "Hispanic" that encompass a variety of distinct cultures (e.g., Dominican, Columbian, Puerto Rican, Cuban, Mexican)?
- Can choreography class yield strategies for conflict resolution and problem solving?

Use the arts as a vibrant way to initiate open, non-threatening communication between cultures. Invite diverse people to your long-range planning table, find indigenous peoples to share information and skills with you, and experience the cultures around you. Seek those whose opinions you trust. Present authentic performance, discussion, and technique classes. Invite diverse groups to help you identify appropriate ways to celebrate this tapestry. Enrich your students' worlds by whom and what you bring to your classroom and by what you assign students to do outside class. Encourage efforts to expand, to grow, to inquire, and to seek out new dance worlds close by and on the Web.

Americans can no longer teach from an exclusively Eurocentric perspective. Unless we take an **Africanist** perspective when teaching dances of Africa and an **Asianist** perspective when teaching dances of Asia, we can't convey the true aesthetics of these dances or proper appreciation for them. Remember, diverse cultures must not be judged by the aesthetic criteria of the predominant culture. To do so, or to judge other art forms unfairly, misinforms students and does not provide a complete artistic educational experience.

Many world cultures belong in your dance program. Include more than just token folk dances from diverse cultures. Celebrating World Dance Week in June or teaching the Dance of Welcome (Ghana)

"We consistently have denied the traditions of our many non-European citizens, and have excluded their cultural heritages from our programs. This has left deep scars. Even among non-European ethnic groups that have already achieved a high degree of success in this country such as the Chinese and the Japanese; support for European-based arts is not proportional to their size in the population. If we continue as we have, there is nothing to suggest that even larger ethnic groups, once they achieve stability, will be great supporters of the established arts in America."

—Robert Garfias
(1989, p. 25)

and the Tinikling (Philippines) is not enough! A substantive, diverse program includes dancing yet also investigates the dance's stylistic qualities, techniques used, and background. An inclusive program also looks into the artistic contributions of the dance, the significance of the dance to society, and its star dancers, costumes, props, and music. Whether a dance is ritual or secular, ask the five Ws: who, where, when, what, why. This is educational dance at its best. No later than middle school students should compare and investigate similar kinds of dances from other regions, other dances of the same place, the arts of that culture, the role of dance in that society, and the aesthetics of that dance from an authentic (i.e., non-Eurocentric) perspective.

Look at the dance roots of today's dances. For example, find out where hip-hop dances come from and how the rhythmic structures so important to these dances echo traditional African dances that mixed drumming and song. Learn how there was a time when these dances were disallowed in this country, but although hidden or disguised, dance among the enslaved Africans did not die. Despite efforts to do away with African dance, aspects of the Africanist aesthetic survived in vernacular forms that continue to define American jazz dance, music, and popular culture. Investigate the African aesthetic that includes unrestricted posture, articulate spines, isolatory movement, polyrhythmic movement, syncopation, improvisation, interplay with accompaniment, competitive spirit, unabashed sensual joy in movement, and earthy get-down movement.

Trust the cultural environment around you. Because you can't travel to all countries or know all world dance forms of native cultures, rely on regional artists and artists-in-residence to bring diverse dimensions to your classroom. As guest artists teach your students, they also teach you—so you acquire new knowledge and skills.

 How can this shape your teaching and your belief statements?

Codified Dances

Teaching set dances in the curriculum is good if students learn to perform them with stylistic and expressive authenticity. Use codified dances to teach technique and stylistic variations as well as to expand repertory. They are part of the dance fabric. Use them to generate stylistic inquiry and increase kin-aesthetic experiences in technique and performance.

It is paramount to capture style and movement quality when learning codified dances such as folk dance and classical dances of the world. Teaching dance as art requires you either to have a firsthand knowledge of cultural style or to cross-reference written descriptions with videos of authentic performance. Rarely do all these materials come prepackaged, except in the case of the JVC Video Anthology of World Music and Dance, which has videos and descriptions of authentic dance. Look for other cultural documentaries. Part of teaching dance as art is to prepare students to perform cultural dances with authentic stylistic and expressive qualities.

Occasionally use a reverse-technique lesson. For example, teach an unembellished, core movement pattern—purposefully using no stylistic information—and then have students research (through video, Internet, written descriptions) the stylistic qualities they should overlay on the movement pattern to make it stylistically accurate. With oversight by you, this can be a way to bring discovery into a project, but you must ensure stylistic accuracy and ensure that the dance can also be performed to its authentic music accompaniment.

Even social dances from different periods in American history and Broadway musicals give a wealth of dance material to enrich and extend your curriculum. These round out appreciation for the multiple roles that dance plays. Repertory studies from these dance styles often interest middle and high school students, enticing them to join dance class by creating interest in vernacular styles.

Travel Study

Why not travel to study dance firsthand? Bring the world to your students by having the firsthand experience of being there and dancing. When you're in a new country, set up pen pals for your students.

Travel is one of the best ways to collect authentic dance materials for your dance diversity classroom. While traveling, visit toy stores, bookstores, record stores, arts shops, museum stores, video stores, and street markets. Bring back music instruments, pieces of fabric, and distinctive costume parts for your students. Don't overlook the interest that you can generate around an unusual candy wrapper, fans, menus, coins, ticket stubs, hats, and masks. To study dance in another country is an experience you owe yourself. The added bonus is the extent to which it enriches your teaching perspective.

If you can't travel, correspond with an English-speaking teacher in another country. Exchange materials and ideas on e-mail without great expense. Get free posters and brochures from travel agencies, international airlines, multinational businesses, Washington-based embassies, and consulates and visitor's bureaus in major cities around America. Ask for embassy video catalogs and use their dance resources at little or no cost. Internet technology places the world at your fingertips. Bring the world to your students and encourage them to explore it.

Aiming for Diversity

What specific guidelines help you achieve cultural diversity in your class? What builds culturally rich dance programs in your classroom? Find the answers in these items, which later become criteria for evaluating your skills.

SUCCESS FACTORS FOR TEACHING DIVERSITY

To be an effective dance specialist, you should do the following:

1. ____ Expose students to dance experiences beyond the predominant culture of their community.

2. ____ Increase their knowledge of diversity in areas such as facts, food, festivals, and fashion.

3. ____ Include a variety of concepts, issues, events, and themes from multicultural perspectives to effectively broaden students' world view and to stimulate creative activities in dance.

4. ____ Seek multicultural educational opportunities to share with others across the curriculum.

5. ____ Enrich the cultural environment for all students, in addition to those in dance classes.

6. ____ Seek authenticity—a 100 percent authentic, person-to-person experience is worth more than 20 Web sites.

7. ____ Bring ethnic diversity in dance from the community to your classroom or studio and share the experience with all your classes and with other disciplines.

8. ____ Find systematic ways to assess the quality of multicultural content and methodology in the dance curriculum and in the instruction materials available.

9. ____ Educate for diversity by helping students develop a cross-cultural aesthetic.

10. ____ Show students how to appreciate the creative expression of those unlike themselves.

11. ____ Develop in students cross-cultural social skills, such as conflict resolution, team building, effective communication practice, tolerance and appreciation, and suspension of judgment.

12. ____ Use dance to increase social justice awareness and thereby help students see and rectify inequities and injustices around them regarding race, age, sex, and ability.

13. ____ Strive to use culturally balanced instruction and content.

Notebook/Portfolio:
Perspectives Notebook

PEER AND SELF-ASSESSMENT: HOW EFFECTIVE IS MY TEACHING?

How effectively do you integrate cultural diversity into your teaching? As with Success Factor checklists you'll find in upcoming chapters, turn these 13 criteria into performance indicators. Use them for self-reflection and mentor evaluation.

1. Use a rating scale: 1 = needs improvement, 2 = OK, 3 = very successful

2. Ask mentors to critique your teaching one or more lessons to children and assess your ability to effectively deliver diverse content at that grade level.

3. Ask mentors to rate each item and then give you feedback for any item rated 1. Continue mentor evaluations until you consistently get 3s on every criterion.

4. After mentors have critiqued you and you have practiced and polished your skills to earn all 3s, add the signed and dated evaluations to the Teaching and Skills section of your Perspectives Notebook.

What else can build student knowledge or skills and also affect their attitudes about diversity?

Dance Through Time: Dance History

This section on dance history incorporates aspects of cultural diversity, because history encompasses dances from around the world and crosses all time periods.

Inquiry into dance history and dance anthropology brings much to the academic table. The older the learner, the more depth is possible and the more abstract thinking is generated.

USE HISTORICAL INQUIRY TO INVESTIGATE CONCRETE ASPECTS:

- Who choreographed this work?
- Why was it choreographed; what motivated it?
- What was the social climate at the time this work was created and first performed?
- How does it compare with other dances of its time? To other dances by the same choreographer?

USE INQUIRY TO INVESTIGATE ABSTRACT CONCEPTS:

- What qualifies this work as a major choreographic work?
- How well does it convey meaning to other cultures or other time periods such as today?

Apply all six levels of Bloom's taxonomy to dance history (as explained in chapter 4). Inquiry into dance history should leave students with a perspective of dance through time and place, with a sense of the social context of dance. Dance history should put us in touch with contemporary works and relate them to what has gone before. Overall, dance history should give a sense of the significance of dance through time and a basis for comparing works from prehistory through today.

Inquiry Into Dance History

An anthropological study of dance gives the underpinnings for knowing about dance. Before humans had words, they relied on movement to convey meaning. Movement is still a natural part of human

expression, although we are increasingly dependent on the written and spoken language (and even computer emoticons) to convey our thoughts, feelings, and ideas. To discover why humans dance is basic to understanding dance. Through dance, primitive people communicated with unseen forces of nature and the spirit world to live successfully. It was as necessary to life as food and water. The power of dance to convey meaning and create magic was life sustaining. It still is life sustaining, only in a different way.

Reflect and Respond

Reflect on these belief statements. Check all with which you agree.

___ The arts tell us who we are and who we were.

___ Moral and aesthetic reasons compel us to educate about diversity.

___ Teachers can embrace students both as individuals and as extensions of their cultures.

___ Teachers can help students use their own experiences as resources for personal growth and development in dance.

___ Dance can become a vehicle for greater fulfillment and self-realization for all.

___ You can present cultural dance in community performances to reinforce and affirm the heritage of diverse audiences.

___ Art works of each culture are self-validating and of equal worth.

___ As you emphasize tolerance, respect, and sharing, you can also promote and nurture authentic traditions from a variety of sources.

___ By sharing our cultures, we neither compromise them nor threaten to lose them to a synthesized, homogeneous, or pastel world.

___ Unless people are familiar with multiple cultures, they can't effectively compete in a global marketplace.

___ If we value diversity, we will model it to those in our sphere of influence—our family, friends, coworkers, students, and community.

___ To be leaders of social change, we not only believe everyone deserves to be acknowledged, valued, and included in the tapestry, but we take steps to bring diverse people together when we see the opportunity. One of the best avenues is to celebrate through the arts.

___ We can build interest by showcasing some of the cultures represented by class members.

Shouldn't students investigate gestures and body postures, our nonverbal language that transcends time, place, language, and culture? Shouldn't they ask, "What is the difference between a utilitarian gesture and a dance gesture? They both communicate meaning, don't they?" Shouldn't students discover the difference found in the intent of the gesture and the movement quality and dynamics with which the movement is done? (One is functional; the other is for expression.) Dance history helps us find the roots of expressive movement and transform daily gesture into the rhythmic, patterned movement called dance—which is set apart from everyday, pedestrian movement.

Isn't it fascinating to learn the roots of dance? Don't you want to open the door for students to chronicle the development of dance over the course of human history, to learn how it was perceived at a particular time, who danced and why? Do you enjoy seeing how dance transformed over time in the same location and discovering how universal themes continue to be found all over the world? Does it distress you that so many important dances are lost and many important dancers will never be heard of? Does that make you cherish all the more the important dances and dancers we do know, whose contributions have made a difference to the art of dance? That's reason enough to bring dance history alive in your classroom.

Notable Persons: Our Creative Fires

History is full of prominent creative geniuses and pioneers who took risks to take dance to a new level. Who are these people who made such an impact on this career you have chosen (figure 8.1)? Whom from the past would you add to this list? From the present? Whom would you like to meet if you could? Whom will you introduce to students first?

These are only a few contributors who made, or continue to make, an impact on the world of dance: heroes and heroines whose significance students should investigate. Most were dancers but others had such a passion for dance that they affected it for generations.

- Consider Rudolf Laban, who gave us a notation system and a way to analyze movement that continues to redefine and refine itself even today in computer programs such as LabanWriter and notation systems such as Language of Dance.

- Consider *New York Times* critic John Martin, who accurately described choreographic works

and artists, information that could have vanished without a critic present to chronicle in descriptive language the powerful dances of the golden age of modern dance.

- Consider the south Indian Pillai Brothers and Balasaraswathi, who saved the highly refined, classical temple dance style Bharata Natyam from near extinction. After it fell into disgrace and was banned, these artists not only revived the dance form but restored it as a vibrant, living, technically challenging world dance form that now thrives.

- Consider Liz Lerman, who pioneered a multigenerational dance company with ages ranging from 8 to 80 to confirm that expressivity is not limited to youthful agility but is the province of all who will dance.

Historic Dance Places

When you make travel plans, consider including places of dance interest on your itinerary. There are intriguing places to visit in dance history: Hopi sacred dance grounds in the midwestern United States, the site of the original Olympics in Greece, Covent Garden in London, Lincoln Center in New York City, Kennedy Center for the Performing Arts in Washington, DC, school auditoriums, college campuses, fiddling conventions in the Appalachian mountains, contra dance halls, gatherings of the Scottish clans across the world, Greek weddings, temple courtyards, festivals, churches such as Riverside Church in New York City, and the New York Public Library Dance Collection.

- Consider the outdoor Javanese court pavilions in Jogjakarta where you can watch rehearsals for the masked dance-dramas that are to be presented and hear the magical shimmer of the Javanese **gamelan** music that transports you to another world.

- Consider the Dionysian theater in Greece. Also consider the oldest playhouse ever known, which is on the island of Crete, where in 2000 b.c.e., Dionysian court theaters that could seat 500 people were built at Phaestus and at Cnossus. See the "dancing floor" that Homer spoke of as the place where "youths and seductive maidens join hands in the dance . . . and a divine bard sets the time to the sound of the lyre."

- Consider visiting the caves of Les Trois Frères at Arriège, France, where you can experience

How Many of These Pioneers Can You Identify?

Alvin Ailey	Michael Flatley	Donald McKayle
Alicia Alonso	Michel Fokine	Arthur Murray
Fred Astaire	Margot Fonteyn	Ruth Lovell Murray
George Balanchine	Bob Fosse	Martha Myers
Balasaraswathi	Loie Fuller	The Nicholas Brothers
Irmgard Bartenieff	Gus Giordano	Bronislava Nijinska
Mikhail Baryshnikov	Savion Glover	Vaslav Nijinsky
"Peg Leg" Bates	Joe Goode	Alwin Nikolais
Maurice Bejart	Matteo and Carola Goya	Anna Pavlova
Auguste Bournonville	Martha Graham	Marius Petipa
Enrico Cecchetti	Jose Greco	Joseph Pilates
Marian Chace	Margaret H'Doubler	The Pillai Brothers
Alison Chase	Arthur Hall	Pearl Primus
Martha Clark	Anna Halprin	Shanta Rao
Bonnie Bainbridge Cohen	Hanya Holm	Jerome Robbins
Honi Coles	Lester Horton	Bill "Bojangles" Robinson
Merce Cunningham	Doris Humphrey	Bessie Schonberg
Asadata Dafora	Judith Jamison	Ted Shawn
Chuck Davis	Bill T. Jones	Marcia Siegel
Catherine de Medici	Gene Kelly	Nancy Stark Smith
Agnes de Mille	Nakamura Kichiemon	Ruth St. Denis
Serge Diaghilev	Jiří Kylián	Lulu Sweigard
David Dorfman	Rudolf Laban	Marie Taglioni
Isadora Duncan	Liz Lerman	Paul Taylor
Katherine Dunham	José Limón	Twyla Tharp
Eiko and Komo	Louis XIV	Utaemon
Suzanne Farrell	'Iolani Luahine	Edward Villella
	Luigi	Mary Whitehouse
	John Martin	Mary Wigman

FIGURE 8.1   Learn about the movers and shakers of your chosen field.

prehistoric dance drawings made by the hands of ancestors so ancient no one knows who they were.

- Visit the magnificent old Théâtre du Chatelet, where the Ballet Russe de Monte Carlo made its Paris debut in 1909 and where Diaghilev brought Fokine to present his dance works with such stars as Nijinsky, Pavlova, and Kar-

savina performing in the elaborate costumes of famous visual artists of the day, such as Benois and Bakst.

- Visit the Paris Opera and the Sun King's Court at Versailles to see where ballet got its foothold with the establishment of the Académie Royale de Danse in the court of Louis XIV and the places of the early extravagant ballets of

Catherine de Medici. Even find the Neolithic painted dancing figures (from the Sahara) at the Musée de l'Homme.

Bringing dance history alive for yourself enables you to bring it alive to others. Dance history should not become dusty or moldy, something that once was and has no relevance to today's dance. It is our legacy waiting to be uncovered and waiting to whisper all the important truths of what dance can do and has done in times we shall never otherwise know.

Travel and research are two dynamic ways to uncover the mysteries of the past and present in dance. (Refer to chapter 3, "Be a Dance Scholar.")

Types of Historical Inquiry

Dance heritage must involve students in topics of depth that hold their interest. When you effectively motivate student interest and pique curiosity in dance topics, the inquiry process yields many benefits:

- Promotes independent and group research
- Invites students to make comparisons and contrasts
- Encourages reflection to relate new information to that previously learned
- Involves higher-order thinking to develop these skills

- Invites students to take the initiative to learn
- Encourages students to delve deeply into the subject

Facilitate eight distinct types of dance history inquiry (adapted from visual arts) as shown in figure 8.2.

How will you use these ideas to design curriculum?

History in the Curriculum

Use dance history to broaden perspective about dance and create a context for learning about it. History is current as well as past; it is continually constructed and reconstructed as perspectives shift, experiences broaden, and people live. See how different cultures often take different perspectives on historical facts. Everyone holds an individual perspective and a cultural perspective, which may or may not be the same. History reflects the cultural biases at the time (e.g., the supremacy of ballet over modern dance in the mid-20th century).

 Where is this useful to teaching?

Universal Themes

Analyze world dance by looking for recurring themes that are universal to dance. Since prehistory, humans

Attribution	Identify where, when, why, by whom a particular dance work was made: to whom it is attributed
Authentication	Investigate the way(s) the work was documented, its authenticity
Iconography	Examine the meaning of the motifs, symbols, sets, costumes used
Provenance	Survey the companies that performed the work or have it in their repertory
Function	Examine the original purpose of the work, why it was created
Style	Analyze its distinguishing characteristics, establish its genre, relate it to other works within the same genre
Psychology	Explore what influenced the choreographer—especially his/her social, political, or cultural surroundings, personality, artistic community, and family
Connoisseurship	Explore the work with depth, determine its place in the lexicon of dance works through time, judge its artistic merit and worth—to the individual observer and to the dance world

FIGURE 8.2 Types of historical inquiry to enrich and diversify learning.

have danced for much the same reasons: to heal, to communicate, to express emotion, to celebrate, to effect magic, and to court or mate.

But notice how every culture dances differently, creating identifiable, unique dances to express a common theme. Dances on a theme in one culture vary considerably from those of the same theme in another (e.g., their motions, costumes, accompaniment, style, rhythms)—for these are specific to each culture. For example, a fertility dance in Ghana, West Africa, uses specific moves different from a fertility dance in Hawaii. Teach these dances as cultural variations on the universal themes. To analyze differences in universally alike dances across cultures, focus on three aspects:

- **Gestures** (extremities—mostly arms, legs, knees, hands, feet, head, face, and sometimes shoulders and hips)
- **Postures** (torso—especially use of the spine)
- Step patterns (basic steps, weight shifts, rhythmic use of footwork)

Call on dance anthropology's wealth of information about how and why humans dance all over the world. Dance anthropologists (like Alan Lomax and others) shed light on obscure dance practices and provide data and recorded documentaries for your classroom. Authentic dance films with commentary shed the kind of insights worth knowing in educational dance.

Dance Categories

The simplest, most common way to categorize world dance is to make three groups: those that are performed for an audience (performance), those in which everyone dances and joins in (participatory), and those reserved for sacred purposes (ritual). Dance from all categories contributes to a comprehensive dance curriculum.

 How will you use them?

- Performance dances have a separation between dancer and audience. Usually the dancer has trained to be highly skilled in the style (e.g., Irish step dancing, exhibition ballroom dance, Kabuki, a ballet concert, break dancers).
- Participation dances may be for one or many, but people engage in the dance activity (e.g., communal dances, folk and social dances,

buck dance and clogging, spontaneously inspired dance, movement choirs, popular dance).

- Ritual dances involve designated persons who are responsible to dance for the benefit and well-being of the collective (group). The purpose is to communicate with unseen forces, often sacred. Highly specialized dancers, such as shamans, train for a precisely regimented ritual observance. Sometimes the rituals are participatory, but ritual dances fall outside the first two categories above because of its specific intent.

 What unique dance forms other than ballet, tap, jazz, and modern have you studied and know how to perform?

Performance Dances

The human drama is forever told in dance works. The sheer volume of dance works, significant choreographers, and famous dancers throughout history creates numerous opportunities to stimulate students academically and artistically. Use these opportunities to compare styles, to identify universal themes, to learn societal values, and to understand more about dance so students uncover human values worth learning.

To teach dance as art in education is to use the essence of varied dance styles to increase understanding of dance. Use varied dance styles to introduce new ways of moving and creating dance as art. Avoid emphasizing any one style to the exclusion of others so students gain broad dancing skills and perspectives (which are needed to meet standards).

Study the gamut of performance styles between kindergarten and twelfth grade. Go from modern to ballet, from musical theatre to jazz, from tap to toe, from folk to classical, from the dramatic to the abstract, from the ancient to the modern, from the postmodern to hip-hop, from island to mainland dances, from upland to lowland dances, from Irish step dancing to opera–ballet, from the fiery to the frosty, from the pithy to the silly, from sacred to profane, from the rhythmic to the uncountable, from the stunningly crafted works of small companies to world-class dance concerts.

General Considerations for Teaching Study a variety of performance types (genres). Increase dance literacy by responding to works of many types. Distinguish between those that are art and those that are entertainment. Meet the artists who create and perform these works. Build units around different genres for older students. For example, there are heavy psychological dance-dramas of Martha Graham's like Medea in *Cave of the Heart.* There are Mark Morris' fanciful, witty dances, and Alwin Nikolais' abstract dance–theatre works like *Sanctum.* Look at Donald McKayle's strong social commentaries like *Rainbow Round My Shoulder,* Fokine's tragic *Petrouchka,* Cunningham's "chance" dances, Momix's quirky site-specific works. Find riveting stories performed in Japanese Kabuki, ghost plays in Noh, myths and legends enacted in opera–ballets. Absorb the ethereal, stylized gestures and postures in Balinese dance—the feminine classical legong keraton as well as the tense postures and quick jerks of the male baris dancer preparing for battle. There are hypnotic dances like the undulating solo Damballah snake dance of Ghana and the snake trance dances from India. There are animal and bird dances like one of the Mexican deer dances and the Cherokee eagle dance. We can experience the elegance of Petipa's *Swan Lake* and Balanchine's *Jewels* as well as some of the hard-pumping, earthy jazz and hip-hop on MTV.

Even within a single choreographer's repertory, there is a broad range. For example, compare Alvin Ailey's emotion-filled *Cry,* to his uplifting *Revelations,* to the slinky *The Mooche.* Students need to see these works. The more you uncover, the more you find: World dance repertory is exciting as well as infinite. Bring it alive.

Inventory Yourself

1. Which of the following have you seen performed? Some are styles; others are dances.

2. Which do you know something about (i.e., motivations, setting, significance, techniques used, or repertory works)?

3. Which ones do you dance (or have you danced)?
   - Japanese Noh and Kabuki
   - Russian Korobushka
   - Indian Kuchipudi and Bharata Natyam
   - Irish step dancing
   - Balinese legong, kebyar, and baris
   - Dahomean Yanvalou
   - Brazilian capoeira
   - Mali Kanaga
   - Israeli Hora

There are many ways to access these works. The JVC Video Anthology of World Music and Dance provides an amazing array of authentic, indigenous dance footage filmed on site. Start your own video library. Fill it with resources to teach world dance.

Rate yourself: Give 1 point for each dance listed in answer to question 1, 2 points for each dance listed in answer to question 2, and 3 points for each dance listed in answer to question 3. (The highest possible score is 42.)

 How do you rate?

Be a resource to social studies teachers. There is hardly a social studies topic that doesn't have an aesthetically viable choreography that compellingly relates to it. For example, studies of other countries, famous people, important places, innovators, cultures, transformations, or the triumph of the human spirit—all play out in dance. Offer to conduct a facilitated inquiry into such a dance work for both classes together (dance and social studies). Share "outside your walls and down the hall" the expressive depth of major world choreographers. Go cross-discipline to get more dance into your school building.

Survey how many students or colleagues have attended a live dance performance. *The Nutcracker* may be the only live ballet people have seen. Outside metropolitan areas, live performance is rare. Therefore, public education is obliged to introduce noteworthy dances to those in their reach. Why shouldn't famous choreographers be as well known as famous playwrights, composers, and visual artists? References to significant world dance forms abound in literature, in films, and in media of all kinds. To be an educated world citizen, one should know about dance.

Use dance on the screen. PBS specials like "Dancing" and "Great Performances" reached wider audiences for dance; MTV, *Stomp,* and *River Dance* brought world dance into the mainstream. Still schools should also increase dance literacy in the population. Make quality dance works accessible (even on a large screen TV) to students, and invite parents, too. Use Raymond Strauss' chapter, "Dance on the Screen," as a resource (see Rich Resources).

Classical Dances of the World   Can you believe many Americans still think ballet is the only classical dance form! They aren't aware that other significant non-Western classical styles are every bit as structured, exacting, and precise as ballet and that these styles are as aesthetically governed as those from Western traditions.

Dancing diverse classical styles increases technique while expanding perspective. Lead students to compare and contrast diverse dance styles and find inspiration for their own choreography. Each classical style's repertory contains as wide a range of themes and topics as does ballet's repertory.

Classic dances stand the critical test of time and exhibit a high degree of excellence in design or delivery. They transcend century and place to convey a timeless message to different generations. There are classic dances that date back as far as early Mediterranean cultures. *Classical* dances are highly stylized and have turned into a performance art through refinement of techniques. Following are classical dances that are also rooted in classic dance. They are models of artistic integrity and refinement. Study their craftsmanship. Give them a place in a K-12 curriculum:

ASIA:

- Bugaku
- Noh
- Kabuki
- Classical Chinese opera

INDIA:

- Bharata Natyam (SE)
- Kathak (NW)
- Kathakali (SW)
- Manipuri (NE)

INDONESIA:

- Legong (Bali)
- Kebyar (Bali)
- Baris (Bali)
- Masked Javanese court dance (Java)

 Can you name some titles of repertory works in these styles? Which other cultures do you know well enough to recognize or to dance their classical dance forms?

Show how choreographic ideas get translated into motion symbols. All the arts—including dance—use repetition as an aesthetic design element.

Anthropological Considerations for Teaching   As you consult dance history books, take note that many are written from a Eurocentric perspective, calling anything other than Western dance forms "ethnic." Before the world became so small, early to mid-20th century American and European dance historians were either uninformed about or unaware of the distinctions between non-Western dance forms and considered anything non-European as ethnic.

Joann Kealiinohomoku's article titled "An Anthropologist Looks at Ballet as a Form of Ethnic Dance" was a lightning bolt felt around the world. It is required reading for all who teach dance. She helps us see through her dance anthropologist eyes when she states: "By ethnic dance, anthropologists mean to convey the idea that all forms of dance reflect the cultural traditions within which they developed" (Kealiinohomoku 1983, p. 533).

This one article marks a turning point in how the dance community uses the term "ethnic." It demands we acknowledge how dances in each culture develop out of that particular culture and that each one is therefore ethnic, including ballet, modern dance, and other Western dance forms. How vital to hear from anthropologists such as Kealiinohomoku and ethnomusicologists such as Gertrude Kurath to keep us broad in our thinking so that we don't inadvertently mislabel or incorrectly categorize dance styles.

Kealiinohomoku points out that so many of our greatly esteemed dance historians, whose books give us so much valuable information and on whose work we depend, were actually not in tune with an anthropological view. Many books, such as those of Sir James Frazier, Curt Sachs, Agnes DeMille, Walter Sorell, John Martin, Franz Boas, Walter Terry, and others, inadvertently misrepresent non-Western forms of dance. They tend to stereotype dance styles as "primitive," "ethnic," and "folk" dance and even worse, ascribe generic (and naive) characteristics to them. Kealiinohomoku explains that there are no generic dances. Neither are there generic Native American dances, for example. There are, however, Hopi dances or Cherokee dances. Some of these dance historians minimized the uniqueness of dances based on their lack of familiarity with the different customs and cultures represented. "No wonder that balletomanes reject the idea that ballet is a form of ethnic dance! But Africans, North and South Amerindians and Pacific peoples would be just as horrified to be called ethnic under the terms of the stereotype" (Kealiinohomoku 1983, p. 536).

Find more appropriate ways to categorize dances. One way is to categorize the dances of the world (as this textbook does): "performance" (those danced for an audience), "participation" (those in which everybody dances), and "ritual" (those done expressly for spiritual or healing purposes, which can be either performance or participation).

Participation Dances   Many people love to dance. Even those who think they can't, can. The sheer variety and number of significant participant forms—folk, social, fad, round, square—remind us how vital a role dance plays in the lives of so many people, especially in homogeneous cultures. Participating, besides being fun, promotes healthful living. Ask how many colleagues regularly participate in social dance groups like square dance guilds, African dance and drumming ensembles, salsa groups, or Scottish country dancing guilds. How many of your students do? Include those dances.

Introduce folk dances that embody traditions of a group of people. The movements of these dances are often less elaborate than concert styles, although there are exceptions. Homogeneous cultures blend gestures, postures, steps, movement qualities, rhythmic patterns, costumes, and accompaniments that contribute to their cultural identity. These people pass the dances from generation to generation without written notes, yet the dances survive (unless oppressors ban them). People naturally dance traditional dances at festivals, celebrations, rites of passage, and other community occasions. These dances bring generations together to embody their heritage, affirm their community, and relive significant ancestral moments. These dances reinforce the roles of young and old in the culture and value to the community. Reliving such dances codifies the culture and affirms its identity to the rest of the world. Teach them.

Also find a place for social dances to show how people interact and socialize. Some social dances provide vital cultural context to units of study. Some give us intricate footwork and varied rhythms. Some have come and gone but still make up the significant historical dance repertory—like the Charleston, the lindy hop, the tarantella, the Cha Cha Kofi Sa. Social dances sometimes have a short life span, fall out of favor, and disappear completely because of lack of documentation. Although dance crazes come and go, the dances are part of the fabric of people's lives and memory, and for many they retain significance for a lifetime.

 What is today's dance fad? Which did your grandparents most enjoy? Your parents? (Ask them!)

To inquire into participatory forms is to uncover a multitude of reasons humans dance. These dances bring new rhythms and movement vocabularies with them. Use them to teach composition.

Dancelike forms such as dance therapy and aerobic dance are participatory, but their purpose is to promote physical and mental health rather than artistic expression. Although the ancient Chinese martial and exercise art, t'ai chi, retains aesthetic aspects and exact techniques, it is considered exercise rather than dance.

Ritual Dances

Religious rituals across the globe contain potent movement and dance. Neither performance art nor participation style, rituals exist in the realm of ceremony ordained for certain events or circumstances. Some are considered magic. Often performed on behalf of others in the community, dance rituals are executed in a designated sacred or auspicious place. Their real significance and power are usually only known by the believers. Movements are customarily predetermined, are exact, and are solemnly carried out without elaboration. They are appropriate to bring into most high school settings (unless there is a strong conservative presence).

Shamans are intermediaries between the natural world and the spirit world. The dancer–shaman's job is to balance good and evil so evil doesn't get the upper hand. In the process, the dancer–shaman rights bad situations, puts a spiritual blessing on someone, or cures a crisis—personal or communal. The Balinese call this spirit world *sekala* (seen world) and *niskala* (unseen world). People in many world religions—especially animist traditions—act out mythological, historical, and religious beliefs through dance ceremony and rituals. Some enact stories from myths and sacred texts. Numerous indigenous religions use dance to entice, invoke, worship, and entertain their deities. West African language groups such as the Yoruba (Nigeria), the Dogon (Mali), and the Ashanti (Ghana) enact different aspects of their divinities through a blend of dance and the other arts (drumming, singing, masks, storytelling). "[O]ne of the major cognitive activities among early humans was a grappling with . . . existential issues. . . . [M]uch early art, dance, myth, and drama dealt implicitly or explicitly with cosmic themes" (Gardner 1999, p. 62).

To teach world dance, one has to acknowledge the ritual influences. For example, many sacred temple dances of south India, Southeast Asia, and Indonesia—highly refined dance forms of great aesthetic value—are being taken out of the temples and performed on secular stages for paying audiences. Once sacred, Bharata Natyam and legong are now viewed as the elegant classical dance forms they also are, outside their prescribed ritual temple settings. When this happens, ritual aspects are stripped away to allow the dance to become secular spectacle. We all need to consider the long-term effects of stripping the sacred significance from these beautiful ritual dances. Some may argue that the dance's integrity is not compromised (i.e., its religious significance is not diminished) by taking on a second life as performance art. Some may wonder if the power and magic that the dance effects in its authentic ritual home become less pure, less potent, or confused and contaminated. Some may believe you can't have it both ways.

Universal themes drive rituals across all cultures and are reasons to study rituals. As with other dance forms, although the ritual is for a similar purpose in different cultures, its manifestation is different in each culture. The unique movement style of each culture changes the way a dance is presented and perceived. Ask older students the five Ws: who, where, when, why, what. Then ask, "How?" By teaching the significant aspects of varied dance expressions, help students see how others express traditional beliefs in ways unlike or like their own. For example, as mentioned earlier in this chapter, there are interesting examples of footage in the JVC Video Anthology of World Music and Dance that document authentic ritual dances. Use these resources with high school students to add context to a theme. The video of Jiří Kylián's "Road to the Stamping Ground" is an interesting way to see a choreographer's process at the same time you understand his reverence for the Aborigine rituals he observes (see Rich Resources).

Documentaries that shed light on such ritual topics as these are available:

- Propitiating evil and good spirits
- Intervening on behalf of someone to heal
- Restoring well-being or giving blessing
- Foretelling the future
- Marking rites of passage (births, weddings, deaths)

As older students understand the underlying purposes of ritual dances, they can compare them to their own rituals and beliefs to

- appreciate the consistencies across all religious expression,
- acknowledge the variety of ways to express similar beliefs and values,
- become more tolerant of those who believe differently, and
- appreciate the significance and beauty of time-honored rituals and traditions across all cultures.

A word of caution: Religious rituals and practices should be taken seriously. Leave objects of religious significance out of the classroom. Sensibilities could be offended. For example, a well-meaning art teacher had children make kachina (katsina) dolls, not realizing that authentic ones were Pueblo ritual objects of great significance that held sacred power. This offended Hopi and Zuni families in the school community. To avoid such cultural trespassing, check with indigenous community leaders or the churches serving the culture in question to learn whether an activity or object is acceptable to bring into the classroom and for which kind of education purpose(s).

Significant Dance Works in the Curriculum

This section calls on the preceding sections about dance history and cultural diversity, because repertory works come from all times and places. Great works are our inheritance, our dance legacy.

Significant repertory works include the vast body of artistic work that helps define what dance is and has been across the centuries and the world. Dance is identifiable as an art form through these collective works. They unveil dance's cultural impact and help determine its overall artistic value. Studying them helps us understand dance's role in different circumstances. We can translate past works into the present and see what they say to us today. Being acquainted with a diverse repertoire gives you valuable resources on which to draw for teaching.

Can you add to this list compelling reasons your students must study significant dance works?

- To see how different works are constructed
- To delve into how and why a work was made
- To determine why a work has enduring value
- To decide the extent of a work's aesthetic contribution
- To see how a work speaks to us today

Great works of dance comprise the canon (or body) of our art as much as great works of literature, poetry, and drama do in their disciplines. Is not the creative, expressive genius of major choreographers as significant as the creative genius of

composers, playwrights, poets, and visual artists who are studied? Leading choreographers are the Shakespeares of our discipline. Their masterpieces must be shared with the world. Compare Graham's output to Ibsen's or Picasso's; compare Petipa's works to Shakespeare's or Ravel's. Appreciating enduring work underscores its aesthetic value to the world. Student inquiry into great works builds insight into the craft of choreography and also into the mind of a great choreographer. Notable choreographers have searched for and found ideas of depth, passion, cruelty, novelty, humor, pathos, tragedy, worship, joy, grandeur, and all the emotional states known to humans. Out of these ideas they crafted a composition, a statement that expresses more than words can convey. Bring their major works and the choreographic process to students to stimulate creative ideas, spawn technique lessons, build context and a historical perspective, open the door to other worlds, and deepen appreciation for the art of dance.

Can students fully engage in a meaningful critique of the work before they gain background information about it? Shouldn't they examine its context, the creator, the selection of movement motifs, the decisions about accompaniment, the movements and rhythms, and the choreographic structure itself to fully appreciate it before critiquing it? Learning about works and making critical judgments are cognitive and affective processes, but both require comprehension of information to inform student analysis.

Great Works for Study

How do you go about selecting and incorporating works to build a context for your units?

Great works are far more than a "rainy day" activity. Learn to integrate these works organically into study. Find works that model the very aesthetic concepts you are after. Select varied styles. Find works that give glimpses of the sociological issues of the time. Find works that should be taught "because they carry ideas, themes, expressive qualities, knowledge, and subjects of art which should be requisite for educated individuals" (Wilson 1992, p. 107). Find dance works to demonstrate the best in choreography, performance, and aesthetic principles.

Use these criteria to help you select works:

1. Their significance and artistic merit
    > Works should be universally important.

> Master works from world cultures should be included.

> Works should be relevant to North America in general.

> There should be works that are also important to your community or region.

> Works should be selected for their artistic merit.

> Master works as well as minor works should be included.

2. Their time

> Works should include contemporary as well as traditional.

> Works should include currently produced choreography.

> Works should be from many historical periods.

3. Their availability

> There should be access to as many live performance works as possible.

From B. Wilson, 1992, Postmodernism and the challenge of content: Teaching teachers of art for the twenty-first century. In *The future: Challenge of change,* edited by N.C. Yakel (Reston, VA: National Arts Education Association), 99-113. Adapted with permission from the National Arts Education Association, © 1992.

Use newly created pieces. Choreographers make great new dance works every day. Identify choreographers with something to say and skills to share. Bring their works to your students. Show them how a choreographer's idea has been effectively translated into motion symbols to represent that intent and clearly communicate. Show students an example of creative process at its best or in a unique form. Show notable dance works from the great canon of dance past and present to demonstrate what is of educational value in dance:

- Ideas or themes inherent in the work
- Ways the dance ties the past to the present
- Social or political conditions that affected the dance style
- Ways a dance work evolves and changes over time as well as how it was perceived differently through time

It is valuable for you to know how dance historians, critics, and dance anthropologists have interpreted the works. To these interpretations, you can add your own interpretation and elicit student interpretations.

Dance works create a context for learning to dance, to choreograph, and to critique. Units of study should contain at least one major work as a contextual anchor. Learn to use works as springboards to

- teach technique,
- teach repertory,
- create dances on the same theme,
- bridge disciplines,
- increase linguistic skills and vocabulary (in dance and in other subjects),
- critique performance by world-class dancers, and
- investigate what technical elements (lighting, staging) contribute to performance.

Show newly created dance works. Identify choreographers with something to say and bring their works to your students.

229

This creates the contextual coherence your students need. It enables them to know firsthand what dance in all its diversity is and gives them something of value to take with them (cf., the list of Mega-Ideas and Concepts earlier in this chapter [page 211]).

Guided Viewing of Great Works

Try to learn the piece by performing it yourself, studying a videotaped version, or, ideally, both. The better you know the work, the more ideas you can generate from it. Guide students into the work with inquiry questions. Refer to the section in chapter 5 titled "Pivotal Role of Inquiry" (page 106), which lists many questions you could ask as springboards into a work. Let the viewing spawn ideas for teaching technique, teaching sequences based on the style of the work, stimulating compositional problems to be solved, making dances about certain themes, and sharpening critical thinking by analyzing the dance work (the subject of chapter 9).

Check copyright laws for dance broadcasts. For example, when you show a video of a PBS program copied from a broadcast within 10 days of the broadcast date, you fall safely within the fair use guidelines for educational purposes.

Embody the Work by Reconstructing It   One dynamic way to study a dance is to embody it. Reconstruct it. The Dance Notation Bureau provides notators who reconstruct major works that they have documented at the bureau in New York. The New York Public Library also has accessible documentation samples to use so long as the works are not performed for an audience for a fee and are used only in an educational setting. To actually learn and perform Doris Humphrey's *Water Study* is vastly different from watching a video of it or reading about it. Embodying the work increases its lasting impact. Reconstructing brings works back to life that might have been lost—a worthy goal itself.

Embody the Work Through Études   Later in this chapter you will learn about people and programs who endeavor to document and preserve our dance heritage before it is lost. Leading American choreographers create short sketches from their larger works and turn them into movement studies (called études). The American Dance Legacy Institute at Brown University has an études project through which for a nominal fee your students can learn and perform selected choreographic études.

Catalog Dances to Study

Keep a file of reference sheets to catalog works and record ideas for teaching. As you encounter dance works in courses such as dance criticism and dance history, create thumbnail sketches of them. List aspects of the work that would help you get certain points across to students: BSTERs, artistic aspects, technique, performance, and choreographic style. For example, does a work show exemplary technique and performance? Does the work use a particular structure or dance style? Is the work highly rhythmic or arrhythmic? What points do you want to make about the design, form, or subject matter of the work? How does it connect with literature or music? Is there something unique about the dance company? Does the work stimulate a dance-making project?

Use figure 8.3's blank form: Thumbnail Sketch of Dance Works for Teaching. Keep copies to catalog dance works. Promptly complete the forms as you encounter a new work while it's fresh. Put the forms in plastic sleeves in a notebook for quick reference.

Preservation and Documentation

This section on preservation and documentation calls on the preceding sections—cultural diversity, dance history, and significant dance works—to emphasize preserving our world dance heritage.

Dances, being ephemeral, are so easily lost over time, so hard to find record of, and so soon forgotten. We must diligently preserve the significant dances we encounter. It is so easy to lose a dance as we put it aside for a new creation. We must remind ourselves constantly of the necessity of videotaping the works we make to preserve them for our own use as well as for the world of dance as art. It is never clear to a choreographer exactly when he or she will want to revive a work in some way—to edit it, to revisit it, or to restore it. Retrospectives of our dances are as important as retrospectives of visual art. By the end of your career, do you want all your creative work to have evaporated? It's the same as a visual artist losing her major works in a fire. Unfortunately, few choreographers keep good documentation of their works: who danced them, where and when, and other important details.

Another way to preserve dances is by embodying them—learning dances to perform informally. Performing dances brings them alive for students. Students feel how the movement communicates and how it's structured. Also teach students to preserve and record their own dances and keep dance notes as they create dances. Videotape student works and help students start portfolios for later auditions and scholarships.

Another way to preserve repertory is to keep dances alive in dancers' bodies. Run old dances from time to time to keep them current with the hope that understudies will get to perform them at another time. Pull dances back for lecture–demonstrations, and keep a repertory current at all times in advanced high school classes.

External Preservation Efforts

The dance world has finally realized that too many of our significant dance works are lost. There are now at least four national preservation projects that help support documentation: National Initiative to Preserve American Dance (NIPAD), Dance Heritage Coalition (DHC), American Dance Legacy Institute (ADLI), and American Dance Festival (ADF).

National Initiative to Preserve American Dance

NIPAD provides a sizeable grant program for documentation efforts to solidify the cultural contributions made by dance artists and scholars in the United States. It is administered by the Kennedy Center for the Performing Arts, Washington, DC.

Dance Heritage Coalition

DHC is a leading organization that strengthens the national dance documentation and preservation network. Founded in 1993, DHC promotes documentation, gives grants, and acts as a clearinghouse for the extensive array of dance resources on the Internet at www.danceheritage.org. This site provides information, tools, training resources, and services for dance research and documentation, along with searchable, full-text finding aids to more than 50 collections of primary resources at DHC member libraries online. DHC member institutions include American Dance Festival; the Dance Collection at New York Public Library for the Performing Arts; the Harvard Theatre Collection, Houghton Library, Harvard University; Jacob's Pillow Dance Festival; the Library of Congress Music Division; Ohio State University; and the San Francisco Performing Arts Library and Museum. You may link to library catalogs and national databases that include dance materials, where you can download outlines and documents focused on dance documentation and preservation.

American Dance Legacy Institute

ADLI provides the opportunity to practice and participate in contemporary and historic masterworks of dance. Its motto is, "That which is saved is that which is valued. That which is valued is that which is known and shared." It is located at Brown University, Providence, Rhode Island (see Rich Resources). ADLI commissions from selected choreographers an ongoing series of short studies or études extracted from their dance masterpieces and makes them available to serious dance students, teachers, and professional dancers. These studies are recreated by either the choreographer or a representative who is commissioned by the ADLI. The Repertory Études Collection includes more than a dozen dance works from diverse American choreographers. This list of performance études provides much-needed access to important works of dance—resources taken for granted in the other arts, which have other means of preserving their body of material. This collection makes masterworks accessible to dancers for purposes of reflection, study, and performance, which directly increase dancers' dance literacy and appreciation.

> Prior to this ground-breaking initiative, the dance field had not actively addressed the importance of individual kinesthetic knowledge as one essential aspect of dance preservation, nor did there exist a mechanism through which great American dance artists could shape their own legacy by personally presenting to the next generation, a jewel-like distillation of kinesthetic and emotional information. Most importantly, the Repertory Études™ connect the dancers of the 21st century to the roots of American dance. Each Repertory Étude™ is based on a signature work by a noted American dance choreographer and contains the essential elements of the larger work from which it was derived. (American Dance Legacy Institute 2000)

From American Dance Legacy Institute, 2000. www.adli.us/index.html.

American Dance Festival

The ADF at Duke University, Durham, North Carolina, has collections documenting the history of the festival, the history of American modern dance, and its influence around the world. The collections provide both still and moving images.

Make a reference book of dance works you know about.

Dance title: _____   Choreographer: _____

Length of work: _____   Number of dancers: _____

Part of a longer work? _____   Performers: _____

Title of video: _____   Theme or topic: _____

File location: _____   Number of video: _____

Appropriate for young children?   Yes / No

Appropriate for grades 3-8?   Yes / No

Style: _____

Useful when teaching (circle all that apply)

Body articulation	Isolated body parts
Performance quality	Shaping (still and moving)
Spatial design	Use of a props
Thematic material	Dramatic story line
Movement motif	Levels
Symmetry	Asymmetry
Use of chorus and soloist	Accent
Polyrhythms	Steady beat
Nonmetered accompaniment	Use of percussion for accompaniment
Music concrete, found sound	Unison vs. nonunison movement
Partnering	Lifts
Elevations (jumping, leaping)	Contact work (as in contact improv)
Pedestrian, everyday gestures	Use of focus for clarity
Abstraction	Translation of subject matter into dance
Costume enhances movement	Masks or masklike makeup
Non-Western or ethnic folk dance	Non-Western or ethnic classical dance
Locomotor, traveling	Somatic awareness
Solo or duet	Group work
Minimal movement	Principles of design:_____

Additional: _____

_____

_____

[continued]

FIGURE 8.3   Thumbnail sketch of dance works for teaching.

From *Teaching Dance as Art in Education* by Brenda Pugh McCutchen, 2006, Champaign, IL: Human Kinetics.

Useful for teaching compositional form and structure:

ABA	Theme and variation	Canon
Rondo	AB	Other: _____

Example of a particular style within the genre:

Mega-ideas and concepts

1.

2.

3.

4.

Inquiry: essential questions

1.

2.

3.

4.

Inquiry: aesthetic scanning and critiquing questions

1.

2.

3.

4.

Overall aesthetic impact of the work:

From *Teaching Dance as Art in Education* by Brenda Pugh McCutchen, 2006, Champaign, IL: Human Kinetics.

Preserving Your Own Dances

Video your own choreography so your works will be available to you as well as others. Compile a video portfolio documenting your professional contributions and a record of your works so you have your collective works later to reconstruct, to rework, or to use in preparing a choreographer's retrospective. Start now, and keep this collection as part of your Professional Teaching Portfolio.

Document and archive your dance works to be added to the canon of dance works for posterity and for the good of the field. Record them so they exist beyond the present. Prepare scrapbooks, take photos, keep programs and news clippings to document dates, record places of performances, and list performers. Write or voice-record anecdotes, comments, and quotations from the creative process, from rehearsals, and from the performance. Preserve the dances you make so they are available to future generations and to researchers.

Dance Cornerstone Curriculum (DCC) Framework

Cornerstone 3 (C3) integrates cognitive content with kin-aesthetic skills.

This part of the DCC Framework (following Rich Resources) shows what students should know and be able to do to achieve NDSEs 5 and 3. It shows how concepts of dance history develop from kindergarten through twelfth grade and breaks dance history down into teachable chunks. C3 is divided into four sequential parts: primary (K-2), elementary (3-5), middle (6-8), and high school (9-12). The developmental continuum of C3 goes from simple to complex to adapt to your learners.

- Look across the chart for sequence as to how each concept builds as students learn.

- Look down the chart for substance as to the scope, what is essential to include.

- For older beginners, spiral back to the first column to pick up basic skills rather than start at their age level.

THREE-ACT REFLECTION: WRITE–ASSESS–REFINE (C3)

Act I: Write

Prepare a three- to four-page typed paper for your Perspectives Notebook that expresses what Cornerstone 3 contributes to educational dance. Address the specific criteria without using them for an outline. Use them first for Act I as composition criteria and for Act II as review criteria.

C3 Composition Criteria (and Review Criteria)

____ Identifies the different components of this cornerstone

____ Identifies the goals of Cornerstone 3

____ Explains universal reasons why humans dance

____ Makes a strong case for studying historical dance periods and notable dance works

____ Explains the value of learning diverse styles and techniques

____ Demonstrates understanding of and ability to integrate this cornerstone with other core dance cornerstones to deepen and extend learning at various age levels

____ Adds personal beliefs about or experiences with this cornerstone

____ Integrates content and achievement standards from national dance standards

____ Names and explains resources that enrich study in this cornerstone

Use the structure for the Three-Act Reflection: Write–Assess–Refine in appendix A for Acts II and III (the same structural format and directions as the one in chapter 6).

Questions to Ponder

1. What impact do this chapter and NSDE 5 have on your comprehensive dance curriculum? On your Statements of Belief (as explained in the Introduction)?

2. What cultures are near your community that would enrich study in dance heritage? How can arts specialists in your school or district collaborate for cross-cultural exchanges?

3. Are we going to become a unitary world culture in this millennium where separate cultures no longer have their own artistic identity? Should we? Why? Why not? What role will dance play? Are you morally obligated to affect student attitudes about diversity? How?

4. What do you know about your state arts council's artist-in-residence program? How might a week with an artist, dancer, storyteller, or craftsperson bring authentic heritage to all students? To the community? How might you use this experience as a springboard for a creative project? How can you collaborate with other arts teachers to make good use of an artist-in-residence?

5. What études are available from the American Dance Legacy Institute to reconstruct with your students? Would one of these études coordinate well with another discipline (such as "The Moor's Pavane" to the middle school literature class on Shakespeare)?

6. What repertory works have you learned? Which ones have you refined to performance level? Where can you reconstruct major dance works from notable choreographers past and present?

7. How will you model the importance of dance preservation and documentation to your students? What equipment and resources do you need in your classroom to preserve our dances? Might you plan a retrospective of your dance works in 10 years? Your students' works?

Rich Resources

CULTURAL DANCES

- Find out about World Dance Week each year at www.worlddanceweek.com.

- www.nrityanjali.org: This site describes a touring group that brings the culture and dances of Andhra Pradesh, India, to people around the world.

- www.pbs.org/wnet/freetodance/index.html: This is an awesome Web site on African American dance that is the companion Web site for the "Free to Dance" PBS series. The site has a comprehensive timeline from 1619 to 2002, essays written by dance historians, biographies of African American dance artists, lesson plans, and rich resources.

- Dances of the World Society (9258 Sugar Run Road, Copper Hill, VA 24079) rescues and preserves traditional dances in danger of extinction.

- "Road to the Stamping Ground" video shows choreographer Jiří Kylián as he attends a gathering on Groote Island, Australia, to which various Aboriginal tribes from around Australia bring ceremonial dances. Filmed over a period of several days at a sacred ceremonial stamping ground, the video shows authentic ceremonial dances yet also documents the care with which Kylián approaches the experience. He shows us how the stamping ground inspires his choreography and his avoidance of anything that would try to imitate it. Order from Princeton Books at www.princetonbooks.org or from Kultur Video at www.kultur.com.

- The JVC Anthology of World Music and Dance: This series of 30 videos has authentic, documentary footage of indigenous dances worldwide. Videos are accompanied by descriptive notes as well as teaching suggestions. They are available at www.multiculturalmedia.com, www.lyrichord.com, and www.worldmusicstore.com.

- Insight Media offers excellent video of dances from around the world. Many focus on one culture, but some are anthologies (or collections from different cultures). Contact Insight Media at 800-233-9910 or at P.O. Box 621, New York, NY 10024-0621.

- Locate obscure folk dance music at Great Activities Publishing Company (e.g., Lloyd Shaw Foundation folk dance tapes; 800-927-0682); Wagon Wheel Records and Books (e.g., World of Fun: Around the World in Folk Dance); Education Record Center (ERC) at www.erc.com or 888-372-4543; Educational Activities, Inc., at 800-645-3739; Kimbo Educational at 800-631-2187; and www.lloydshaw.org.

DANCE HISTORY

- *Studies in Dance History,* a semi-annual publication of the Society of Dance History Scholars, disseminates scholarly research on dance history. Each issue contains either an extended monograph or a collection of articles on one topic, out-of-print articles, and references (from A-R Editions, Inc., 801 Deming Way, Madison, WI 53717).

- www.artslynx.org/dance/index.htm: The dance section of the Artslynx Web site includes a "This Month in Dance History" calendar, video resources with direct links, a ballet history resource list arranged by ballet title, and more.

- *Dance a While: Handbook for Folk, Square, Contra, and Social Dance, Eighth Edition,* is packaged with a folk dance music CD from Allyn & Bacon, Department 894, 160 Gould St., Needham Heights, MA 02494-2315; Web address www.abacon.com; phone 800-852-8024.

- *Dancing Through the Curriculum* (1997): American Dance Legacy Institute published a teacher's guide to videotapes and resources to enrich curriculum for dance specialists and classroom teachers.

- *The Dance Experience* by Nadel and Strauss (2002) contains a chapter, "Dance on the Screen," to help you track down dance films and videos as it also keeps you aware of the limitations of dance in media presentations.

DANCE DOCUMENTATION AND PRESERVATION

- American Dance Legacy Institute at www.adli.us/index.html and P.O. Box 1897, Providence, RI 02912

- www.annaswebart.com/culture/dancehistory/index.html

- NIPAD: www.danceusa.org/programs_publications/nipad.htm

- Dance Heritage Coalition: www.danceheritage.org

- American Dance Festival (ADF): www.americandancefestival.org

PRINT RESOURCES FOR DOCUMENTATION AND PRESERVATION

These print documents help you document and preserve dance:

- Preserve, Inc., Jacob's Pillow, P.O. Box 28, New York, NY 10113-0028, published an informative manual: *Dance Archives: A Practical Manual for Documentation and Preservation of the Ephemeral Art* (ISBN 0-9646606-0-1). It includes topics such as conducting oral history interviews and using concert playbills as useful research documents. Access their instructional video on how to archive and preserve dance materials.

- *Afterimages: The Newsletter of Performing Arts Documentation and Preservation* has ongoing articles about preserving works, grants, and projects involved in documenting dance. It is published at Preserve, Inc., Jacob's Pillow, P.O. Box 28, New York, NY 10113-0028, and may be subscribed to for $10 a year at www.jacobspillow.org.

- *Beyond Memory: Preserving the Documents of our Dance Heritage* is a workbook published by Dance Heritage Coalition and Dance/USA showing how to document, label, and organize videotapes and other important archival information.

- Dance on the Internet is available with access to a computer, a modem, communications software, an Internet service provider, and a membership to a dance organization. Subscribe to listservs of organizations you belong to like the National Dance Education Organization and the National Dance Association to receive current information on a variety of topics from conferences to classes, from job postings to new publications and resources. When you become a member, you will be asked to provide your e-mail address for the listserv. There are generic Internet newsgroups you can log onto for dance information without an organizational membership, such as these: alt.arts.ballet, rec.arts.dance, and rec.folk-dancing.

1.0 Dance as Universal Expression

Grades K-2	Grades 3-5	Grades 6-8	Grades 9-12
1.1 Purposes and functions			
1.1a Universal themes			
Recognizes dance as one way people express themselves for different reasons and to commemorate occasions.	Identifies dance as a means of communication throughout history and learns specific world dances (classical and folk).	Identifies dance as a means of communication throughout time (history) and place (various world cultures including our own).	Investigates why humans dance.
Recognizes that dances differ from each other and are about different topics. Examines dances with universal themes: animal dances, imitation of nature, dances based on stories.	Identifies many reasons that cause humans to dance. Investigates dance themes that relate to individuals and to groups. Identifies universal dance themes found throughout the world: such themes as work, war and weapons, hunting, astral and planetary themes. Emphasizes dance as communication.	Investigates the universal themes, purposes, and functions of dance through time and across cultures. Examines universal dance themes around the world, including initiation, worship, healing rituals, and communion with unseen forces of nature. Emphasizes participation dances to build community and performance dances that express ideas of individuals.	Examines universal dance themes around the world. Includes dances with themes of courtship and marriage, fertility, worship, and death. Examines social issues expressed through dance. Emphasizes dances that express universal human themes.
Recognizes that dance communicates across cultures.	Recognizes the importance of dance through history and its ability to communicate across cultures.	Recognizes the importance of dance through history and its ability to communicate across cultures.	Recognizes the importance of dance through history and its ability to communicate across cultures.
1.1b Rites of passage and ritual			
Uses dance to express special events and occasions (e.g., creating a birthday dance).	Uses dance to express special events and occasions. Examines common subjects, recurring themes, and commemorative dances from around the world.	Uses dance to express special events and occasions. Identifies rites of passage, and uses them to increase cultural understanding.	Uses dance to express special individual and communal events and occasions. Studies dance rituals across cultures and rites of passage that use dance (such as the Tyi Wara of the Bambara people of Mali, the hunting dance of the Krachi people called Abafoo). Uses dance rituals to deepen understanding of the use of ceremonial dance as art, worship, and celebration. Uses ceremony to stimulate dance making (personal or communal).
1.1c Entertainment			
Notices dance on television programs and sees dance performances.	Notices how dance appears as entertainment on stage, in television programs, and in commercials.	Differentiates between dance as artistic expression and dance as entertainment.	Differentiates between dance as artistic expression and dance as entertainment.
1.1d Religious			
_____	_____	Studies dance as religious ritual to see the many forms it takes from the earliest times to the present (i.e., selected Native American, West African, Southeast Asian, Pacific Islander, and Australian Aborigine).	Investigates dance as religious ritual in lineage-based societies to see the many forms it takes throughout history and cultures.

Dance Cornerstone Curriculum Framework—C3: Knowing History, Culture, and Context from *Teaching Dance as Art in Education* by Brenda Pugh McCutchen, 2006, Champaign IL: Human Kinetics

1.0 Dance as Universal Expression

Grades K-2	Grades 3-5	Grades 6-8	Grades 9-12
1.1d Religious (continued)			
——————	——————	——————	Discovers dance as a healing art, past and present. Compares dance to related forms such as t'ai chi, Qigong, or body therapies.
1.1e Human expression			
Creates dance improvisations based on familiar gestures.	Identifies the difference between gestures and postures as part of human expression in dance. Uses gesture to stimulate creative dance making. Studies different postures and how they communicate meaning.	Explores similarities and differences in gestures and postures throughout selected cultures and different times as basic to human expression.	Learns to read the language of dance through gestures and postures across cultures and through history. Uses gestures and postures as a way to decode dance works and decipher meaning in dances of our own culture and cultures unlike ours.
Identifies topics and ideas that are easily communicated in dance. Learns how dance communicates nonverbally.	Examines the human need to communicate individual ideas through movement and dance. Compares and contrasts dances with similar themes.	Examines the human need to communicate individual ideas through movement and dance. Compares and contrasts dances with similar themes.	Examines the human need to communicate individual ideas through movement and dance. Compares and contrasts dances with similar themes.
Learns simple folk dances that communicate an idea to learn how people express ideas through group dances.	Learns dances from around the world that communicate something unique about specific cultures (e.g., Ghanaian Dance of Welcome).	Examines and learns dances from around the world that communicate something unique about specific cultures (e.g., Hawaiian hula as welcome, Tanko Bushi as a Japanese coal miners' dance, Philippine Singkal).	Examines and learns dances from around the world that communicate unique aspects about specific cultures (e.g., Tinikling, which uses two poles to catch the tikling bird in the marsh).
1.1f Artistic expression			
Learns about dance as an art form.	Interacts with dance as artistic expression from professional performers around the world. Views dance as art.	Examines dance as artistic expression. Includes different dance styles and dances across other cultures that are elevated to an art form (such as Scottish sword dance).	Examines dance as artistic expression. Includes different dance styles and dances across other cultures that are elevated to an art form (such as Kathakali).
1.2 Diverse styles and genres			
1.2a Folk arts and square dance			
Becomes aware of different folk dance styles.	Acquires beginning skills in style, technique, and step combinations for square and folk dance.	Refines skills in selected folk art dance forms. Traces the evolution of square dance.	Masters a diversity of stylistic repertory in folk art forms. Learns the evolution of several folk forms. Investigates folk styles that have been refined into a performance art.
————	Views authentic folk and square dance live or on video to identify stylistic qualities.	Views authentic folk and square dance live or on video to identify stylistic accuracies.	Views authentic folk and square dance live or on video to identify stylistic accuracies. Uses stylistic aspects to stimulate dance making.

Dance Cornerstone Curriculum Framework—C3: Knowing History, Culture, and Context from *Teaching Dance as Art in Education* by Brenda Pugh McCutchen, 2006, Champaign IL: Human Kinetics

Grades K-2	Grades 3-5	Grades 6-8	Grades 9-12
1.2b Classical ballet			
Views excerpts from at least one classical ballet besides *The Nutcracker.*	Executes basic ballet movements and learns some basic terminology.	Traces the evolution of ballet. Learns stylistic differences. Increases ballet vocabulary and terminology. Views significant footage of ballet.	Traces the evolution of ballet. Learns stylistic differences and terminology. Demonstrates stylistic skills in ballet technique. Recognizes and knows about at least two notable ballets besides *The Nutcracker*.
_____	Views slices of ballet.	Views ballet excerpts to acquire stylistic variations.	Views ballet excerpts to acquire stylistic variations.
1.2c Non-Western classical dance (Asian, African, Indian, Middle Eastern)			
Sees dances from around the world. Learns that some, but not all dances, relate to stories. Watches dances that tell stories—like Balinese legong and baris (children's dances).	Learns basic postures and gestures from non-Western dance forms. Learns their distinguishing characteristics. Learns some south Indian mudras.	Refines the use of postures and gestures from non-Western dance styles such as Bharata Natyam (India), Kabuki (Japan), and other classical forms. Learns to execute non-Western classical dance forms using their distinguishing characteristics.	Learns to execute techniques of at least one non-Western classical dance style.
1.2d Non-Western participation dance			
Learns children's dances from other cultures, such as Cha Cha Kofi Sa (West Africa).	Learns about selected non-Western dance and its roots, such as Tanko Bushi (Japan).	Learns roots of selected non-Western dance. Learns basic postures and gestures from participation styles (folk and social). Compares participation dances of selected groups, such as Nigerian, Mexican, Argentine, south Indian, Australian Aborigine, Native American.	Learns roots of selected non-Western dance. Follows its evolution into the 20th century. Learns social and folk dances found in selected non-Western cultures. Compares and contrasts their techniques, postures, and gestures. Examines origins to see if they have evolved or stayed intact.
1.2e Modern and postmodern dance			
_____	Recognizes examples of modern dance.	Demonstrates developing technique and stylistic skills in modern dance.	Demonstrates developing technique and stylistic skills in modern dance. Studies some of the major technique styles of modern dance (Graham, Cunningham, Humphrey, Dunham).
1.2f Experimental and creative dance			
Engages in creative dance and movement exploration.	Engages in creative dance and movement exploration that lead to experimenting with how to express ideas through movement.	Engages in improvisation to develop skills in spontaneous movement expression.	Engages in improvisation to develop skills in spontaneous movement expression.
Relates one's own creative dances to those of professional choreographers.	Compares one's own creative dance-making process to that of noted choreographers.	Compares one's own creative process and products to those of noted choreographers' works.	Compares one's own creative output to that of noted choreographers. Uses great works to stimulate dance making.
Experiments with using body parts and total body movement similar to that seen in a great work.	Experiments with space, time, energy and dynamics, or relationships as stimulated by a great work.	Experiments with the dance elements in ways stimulated by a great work.	Experiments with the dance elements in ways stimulated by a great work.
Experiments with ideas found in a major dance work.	Experiments with ideas found in a major dance work.	Experiments with ideas found in a major dance work.	Experiments with ideas found in a major dance work.

Dance Cornerstone Curriculum Framework—C3: Knowing History, Culture, and Context from *Teaching Dance as Art in Education* by Brenda Pugh McCutchen, 2006, Champaign IL: Human Kinetics

1.0 Dance as Universal Expression

Grades K-2	Grades 3-5	Grades 6-8	Grades 9-12
1.2g Jazz, tap, and musical theatre			
Becomes aware of different dance styles such as tap, jazz, and creative dance.	Executes basic jazz moves and tap steps. Traces the origins to African dance.	Demonstrates stylistic skills in tap and jazz. Connects these forms to vernacular dance and to African dance.	Demonstrates stylistic skills in jazz moves and tap steps. Sees how jazz, ballet, modern, and tap are used in musical theatre, both past and present.
1.2h Fad dance, dance mania, street dance, pop culture, special trends			
Realizes dance is often a part of everyday life and looks for it in the world.	Becomes aware that popular dance is different from concert dance. Looks for popular dance trends.	Studies fad dances for the short impact they have in dance history. Looks for dance trends of the past and perhaps predicts trends for the future.	Studies the dance manias (such as the tarantella and Dance Macabre) as unusual phenomena associated with dance and the surrounding circumstances of their development. Looks for developing dance trends.
1.2i Social dance			
Learns to dance cooperatively with others.	Examines group social dances. Emphasizes step patterns for social dances such as the cha-cha, the two-step, and the Charleston.	Examines social dances. Emphasizes step patterns for social dances such as the waltz, the swing, and the salsa.	Examines group social dances. Emphasizes step patterns for social dances such as rumba, samba, foxtrot, tango, and the calinda from Dahomey as the grandfather of the French sarabande.
1.2j Africanist elements			
Learns to isolate body parts and to move to drum accompaniment.	Articulates body in space using Africanist elements with the limbs and spine, torso inclined forward, lower center of gravity, and circular formations with improvisations in the center to express the uniqueness of the individual within the group.	Learns rhythmic Africanist elements: isolated body parts working in polyrhythms (syncopated), pushing the rhythm, and exchange of rhythm between drummer and dancer.	Focuses on Africanist elements and their adaptation in various forms of dance from jazz to hip-hop. Uses the elements mentioned and adds vocalizations while moving, the "get down" quality in the "aesthetic of the cool."

1.3 Dance heritage in context and in relationship

Grades K-2	Grades 3-5	Grades 6-8	Grades 9-12
1.3a Historic context			
Recognizes that dance belongs to different times and places and is found in all countries in the world.	Examines the richness of the dance world with its varied forms of expression and styles. Learns what motivated dance and what continues to motivate it.	Examines the richness of the dance world with its varied forms of expression and styles. Learns what motivated dance and what continues to motivate it.	Examines the richness of the dance world with its varied forms of expression and styles. Learns what motivated dance and what continues to motivate it.
Learns the origins of the dances studied.	Inquires into the origins of dances that one studies.	Inquires into the origins of selected dances throughout history and traces their development and evolution through time.	Inquires into the origins of selected dances throughout history and traces their development and evolution through time.

From *Teaching Dance as Art in Education* by Brenda Pugh McCutchen, 2006, Champaign IL: Human Kinetics

Grades K-2	Grades 3-5	Grades 6-8	Grades 9-12
1.3b Social context			
———————	Understands how dance can promote social unity within certain cultures (such as the highlife from Ghana).	Studies social and courtship dances from different time periods and parts of the world. Compares them with current American social dance trends.	Inquires into social dances of the past. Performs a preclassic dance suite or other selected social dances from past times. Discusses how the movements relate to the mores of the culture and period.
1.3c Cultural context			
———————	Examines the dance art heritage by focusing on specific dances.	Examines the dance art heritage by focusing on specific choreographers and their dances.	Examines the dance art heritage by focusing on specific choreographers and their dances.
1.3d Relationship between music and dance			
Dances to folk dance music with various tempi. Discovers how music inspires movement and influences style.	Recognizes the symbiosis of music and dance when learning dances from around the world. Analyzes tempo, rhythmic patterns, style, structure, and form as they coexist.	Examines dance forms that developed along with musical forms or in response to musical forms (e.g., Appalachian clog dances and fiddle music, drumming patterns with Nigerian and Dahomean dances).	Examines dance forms that developed along with musical forms or in response to musical forms (e.g., waltzes, preclassic dances, polkas, reggae music and dance, zydeco music and Cajun dance).
1.3e Geographic origins (cultural roots, climate)			
Realizes that dances come from all countries in the world.	Learns the cultural and geographic origins of dances. Learns step vocabularies of selected regional dances (such as south Indian, Balkan, Scandinavian, Spanish).	Recognizes the impact of culture and geographic origins on the characteristics, costumes, and styles of dances (e.g., mountainous, cold climate, flat terrain). Learns to differentiate styles and apply stylistic performance skills. Accurately performs dances from a variety of styles and traditions. Acquires specific skills (such as the Scottish sword dance and strathspey).	Acquires the use of movement subtleties caused by geographic origin, climate, and specific cultural roots. Acquires a vocabulary of dance steps, styles, rhythms, and rhythmic variations. Understands the role played by costumes, the number of performers, the use of partners or group formations, and the composition of the group (e.g., partners, all male).
1.3f Education			
Examines how dance is used for education in all places of the world (past and present).	Examines how dance is used for education. Emphasizes dance education in America.	Examines how dance is used for education in all places. Emphasizes dance education in Western cultures.	Examines how dance is used for education in all places of the world (past and present). Emphasizes dance education in non-Western cultures.
1.3g Recreation			
Sees how dance is used recreationally in all cultures.	Sees how dance is used recreationally in all cultures. Sees how recreational dance has changed over time in our culture.	Sees how dance is used recreationally in all cultures. Sees how recreational dance has changed over time in our culture. Examines its relationship to dance as art and sees how one affects the other.	Sees how dance is used recreationally in all cultures. Sees how recreational dance has changed over time in our culture. Examines its relationship to dance as art and sees how one affects the other.

Dance Cornerstone Curriculum Framework—C3: Knowing History, Culture, and Context from *Teaching Dance as Art in Education* by Brenda Pugh McCutchen, 2006, Champaign IL: Human Kinetics

1.0 Dance as Universal Expression

Grades K-2	Grades 3-5	Grades 6-8	Grades 9-12
1.4 Other aspects of dance			
1.4a Participants (number, group, composition, age)			
————	Participates in dances for groups of boys, girls, or boys and girls together, and in groups of varying sizes.	Realizes that historically, dances from the folk tradition are designed for a specific number of dancers, a specific age group, and groups composed just of women, men, or the two together.	Enjoys performing in groups of the same sex or mixed gender.
————	————	Creates large group dances for mass movement choruses that rely on simple movement phrases that communicate a specific idea. Learns how participation dances for large groups require simplicity.	Creates large group dances for mass movement choruses that rely on simple movement phrases that communicate a specific idea. Learns how participation dances for large groups require simplicity.
————	————	Creates performance dances as art, learning to use a minimum number of dancers. Sees how fewer dancers can convey a stronger message using more complex movement.	Emphasizes how dance as art astutely selects groupings and numbers of dancers. Contrasts that with dance as entertainment or spectacle where large numbers of dancers perform.
1.4b Groupings and formations for participation dances (circle, line, square, couple, free form)			
Recognizes how participation dances are designed in circles, lines, and free formation. (Emphasize individualized work for K-1 and introduce circle dances in grades 1 and 2. Include circles, lines, and squares.)	Participates in dances of different historic and cultural origins that use a variety of formations. Emphasizes the use of space and relationship. Emphasizes group and partner formations in grades 3 and 4. Learns dance formation vocabulary.	Participates in dances of different historic and cultural origins that use a variety of formations. Sees how specific formations convey symbolic meaning. Uses the broadest spectrum of formations and partner work as is age appropriate.	Learns to connect dance formation, style, geographic origin, and cultural roots to gain greater appreciation of a dance's intent and meaning. Incorporates a spectrum of formations in dance works.
————	————	Grows in ability to relate to other dancers.	Grows in ability to relate to other dancers. Increases understanding of the element of relationship in dance. Increases the artistic use of group formations in intricate dance patterns and partner exchanges.
1.4c Groupings and formations for performance dances			
Identifies which performance dance styles predominantly use dancers in circles and lines and which use less structured spatial groupings.	Describes dances seen in terms of spatial groupings and formations.	Describes dances seen in terms of spatial groupings and formations.	Describes dances seen in terms of spatial groupings and formations.
1.4d Impact of architecture on dance			
————	————	Learns how dance spaces and places influence dance (e.g., theater in the round, proscenium arch with frontal facing, medieval castles with long halls and fireplaces at either end).	Learns how dance spaces and places influence dance (e.g., stamping ground, open communal spaces, amphitheaters).

Dance Cornerstone Curriculum Framework—C3: Knowing History, Culture, and Context from *Teaching Dance as Art in Education* by Brenda Pugh McCutchen, 2006, Champaign IL: Human Kinetics

Grades K-2	Grades 3-5	Grades 6-8	Grades 9-12
1.4e Impact of costume and dress on dance			
Learns that different dance styles use different kinds of costumes, masks, and head pieces.	Investigates dance masks and costumes and how they impact certain dances.	Focuses on costumes that inhibit movement (such as Balinese sarongs, head-pieces of south India such as the Yakshagana, masks in Japanese Noh, Serige and kanaga masks of Mali).	Focuses on costumes that enhance movement (such as Russian boots with heels for men, Scottish kilts for men, African kaftans in such dances as the Nigerian Taki dance, ankle bells in north Indian Kathak, brocaded kimonos and head-pieces in Japanese Bugaku).

2.0 Significance of Dance in Society

Grades K-2	Grades 3-5	Grades 6-8	Grades 9-12
2.1 Artistic roles			
2.1a Creator and choreographer			
Realizes that those who create dances are not always the ones who perform them. Learns vocabulary words. Meets a choreographer (live or on video).	Sees how dance creators contribute to society and how each creator evolves a unique product to communicate to the world. Becomes acquainted with notable choreographers.	Articulates how creator–dancers give the art world unique dances that may become part of the dance tradition and heritage. Becomes acquainted with notable choreographers.	Understands (through personal and observed experience) how creators conceptualize ideas and transform them into unique dance expressions. Articulates their distinct contributions. Becomes acquainted with notable choreographers.
2.1b Skilled performers			
Views dance excerpts and talks about quality of dance performance. Learns to distinguish between performance quality and rehearsal.	Distinguishes reasons why some performers are more exciting to watch than others (projection, dance styles, dance technique, musicality, movement flow).	Distinguishes reasons why some performers are more exciting to watch than others (projection, dance styles, dance technique, musicality, movement flow). Recognizes how strong performers give clear visual pictures that become part of the audience's visual memory of dance works and repertory.	Analyzes and discusses the characteristics of noted dance performers through history and up to the present. Realizes how their style, strong technique, quality of movement, and performance projection have distinguished them and made a mark on the development of dance.
2.2 Societal roles			
2.2a Roles in society			
Learns about how dance contributes to each society and community.	Learns how dance is used to promote community spirit, further a political agenda, or reinforce values in communities.	Emphasizes dance for the broad impact it makes on society as a whole. Investigates dances that go along with other dance studies for contextual relevance.	Emphasizes dance for the broad impact it makes on society as a whole. Examines dance as an art form and how it contributes to the arts environment of our country. Compares cultures where dance maintains a strong presence (e.g., Australian Aborigines, Native American, Polynesian, and Caribbean).
2.2b Dance in the world			
Discovers how they relate to dance.	Examines dance's relationship to theatre, music, and art.	Examines dance's relationship to government in countries such as the United States, Russia, Romania, Mexico, Indonesia, and India.	Examines dance's relationship to religion in countries such as the United States, Indonesia, India, Japan, Mexico, Bolivia, and Polynesia.

Dance Cornerstone Curriculum Framework—C3: Knowing History, Culture, and Context from *Teaching Dance as Art in Education* by Brenda Pugh McCutchen, 2006, Champaign IL: Human Kinetics

2.0 Significance of Dance in Society

Grades K-2	Grades 3-5	Grades 6-8	Grades 9-12
2.2c Dance for healing			
———	———	Examines the roles where shamans are present and involved in dance-healing activities. Examines the society's relationship to this dance performer and healer.	Examines the roles where shamans are present and involved in dance-healing activities. Examines the society's relationship to this dance performer and healer. Investigates examples of healing dances.

2.3 Notable contributors to dance

Grades K-2	Grades 3-5	Grades 6-8	Grades 9-12
2.3a Notable performers of dance			
Is acquainted with noted dancers, emphasizing those alive today. Studies outstanding dancers from different cultures.	Is acquainted with noted dancers (such as Baryshnikov, Savion Glover, Bill "Bojangles" Robinson, and "Peg Leg" Bates). Studies outstanding dancers from different cultures.	Knows about noted dancers (such as Nijinsky, Mario [Balinese dancer], Isadora Duncan, Marie Taglioni, and other romantic ballerinas). Studies outstanding dancers from different cultures.	Knows about noted dancers (such as Louis XIV, Utaemon [Kabuki], Anna Pavlova, Denishawn dancers). Studies outstanding dancers past and present and from different cultures.
2.3b Choreographers			
Learns at least three notable American choreographers per year (such as Alvin Ailey, David Parsons, and Twyla Tharp).	Learns at least three notable American choreographers per year (such as Pilobolus, Alwin Nikolais, and George Balanchine).	Learns the important contributions of different choreographers in selected dance styles and cultures. Sees dance history come alive through the works of the important artists of our time and times past (such as Jiři Kylián, Marius Petipa, and Michel Fokine).	Learns the important contributions of different choreographers in selected dance styles and cultures. Sees dance history come alive through the works of the important artists of our time and times past.
2.3c Patrons and promoters			
———	Learns of the importance of patrons of dance as art throughout history.	Learns the importance of patrons of dance as art throughout history (such as Louis XIV, who established the Royal Academy of Music and Dance; the court patronage in Italy, France, Russia, and Belgium; and Lucia Chase, a patron of American Ballet Theatre).	Learns the importance of patrons of dance as art throughout history (such as Diaghilev as an impresario; Catherine de Medici in the 16th century; individual benefactors for major ballet companies). Examines the role that the National Endowment for the Arts—through federal funding—plays in supporting dance in the United States. Recognizes corporate sponsorship.
———	———	Learns how to become a patron and promoter of dance as art.	Learns how to become a patron and promoter of dance as art.

Dance Cornerstone Curriculum Framework—C3: Knowing History, Culture, and Context from *Teaching Dance as Art in Education* by Brenda Pugh McCutchen, 2006, Champaign IL: Human Kinetics

Grades K-2	Grades 3-5	Grades 6-8	Grades 9-12
2.3d Teachers			
————	————	Notes teachers who have contributed to and changed dance by their presence (such as Lully's contribution to the Royal Academy of Music and Dance in France; Arthur Murray's presence in ballroom dance; Rudolf Laban's movement analysis in Labanalysis, Labanotation, and motif writing; Margaret H'Doubler's educational dance pioneer work; and Noverre's ballet d'action).	Traces noted teachers and choreographers who have left a lineage. For example, the lineage from Mary Wigman to Hanya Holm, to Alwin Nikolais, to Ririe–Woodbury, and others. Another lineage from Delsarte to Laban to Denishawn. Investigates the importance of teaching choreographers who have emphasized the artistic aspects of dance and created an artistic heritage for us (such as Michel Fokine, Enrico Cecchetti, Carlo Blasis, Auguste Bournonville, Alwin Nikolais, Hanya Holm, and Jean-Baptiste Lully at the Royal Academy of Music and Dance in France).
2.3e Dance historians and anthropologists			
————	————	Investigates the contributions of dance historians and anthropologists (such as Walter Sorell, Margaret Mead, and Pearl Primus).	Investigates the contributions of dance historians and anthropologists (such as Curt Sachs, Alan Lomax, Lincoln Kirstein, and Katherine Dunham).
2.3f Dance critics			
————	————	Investigates dance critics and their contributions to preserving records and influencing the quality of dance as art. Investigates how critics provide us with descriptive words to describe and evaluate dance. Investigates critiques by critics such as John Martin and Marcia Siegel.	Investigates dance critics and their contributions to preserving records and influencing the quality of dance as art. Investigates how critics provide us with descriptive words to describe and evaluate dance. Investigates critiques by critics such as Deborah Jowitt, Walter Terry, and Martha Swope.

2.4 Significant dance works

Grades K-2	Grades 3-5	Grades 6-8	Grades 9-12
2.4a Earliest known works			
————	Investigates why humans dance in circles in prehistoric times. Investigates the 3-day performance of *Ballet Comique de la Reine* and the equestrian spectacles. Studies contemporary dances inspired by ancient dances such as Isadora Duncan's dances and Charles Moore's depiction of Awassa Astrige, replicating ancient ostrich dances from the African continent.	Investigates the earliest known classical dance works such as the Balinese legong, the south Indian Bharata Natyam, and the West African ritual dances passed through generations.	Investigates the earliest known works, such as those of the Japanese Noh and the figure of the shaman in both prehistoric times and today in other cultures.

Dance Cornerstone Curriculum Framework—C3: Knowing History, Culture, and Context from *Teaching Dance as Art in Education* by Brenda Pugh Pugh McCutchen, 2006, Champaign IL: Human Kinetics

2.0 Significance of Dance in Society

Grades K-2	Grades 3-5	Grades 6-8	Grades 9-12
2.4b 17th and 18th centuries			
	Learns about significant dance works of the 17th and 18th centuries (such as the tarantella).	Creates a timeline for important works of these centuries. Uses video study to bring them to life and to acquire details of style and significance. Studies dances such as Kabuki stylistic posturing (mie) and Balinese legong and baris.	Creates a timeline for important works of these centuries. Uses video study to bring them to life and to acquire details of style and significance. Studies such dances as Bharata Natyam and kathakali (India).
2.4c 19th century			
Learns about significant dance works of the 19th century (such as *The Nutcracker*).	Learns about significant dance works of the 19th century (such as Fokine's *Petrouchka*).	Learns about significant dance works of the 19th century (such as Petipa's dance works, Michel Fokine's works, and such works as *Swan Lake, Giselle,* and *Sleeping Beauty*).	Learns about significant dance works of the 19th century (such as Petipa's and Fokine's works and Chinese opera).
2.4d 20th century			
Learns about significant dance works of the 20th century (such as Alvin Ailey's "I've Been 'Buked" *[Revelations]*).	Learns about significant dance works of the 20th century (such as Balanchine's *Jewels;* Arthur Mitchell's *John Henry;* Merce Cunningham's *Suite by Chance* and *How to Pass, Kick, Fall, and Run;* Agnes De Mille's *Rodeo;* Eugene Loring's *Billy the Kid;* and David Parsons' sleep postures in *Sleep Study*).	Learns about significant dance works of the 20th century (such as selected Denishawn works; Martha Graham works such as *Frontier, Appalachian Spring,* and *Errand into the Maze;* Nikolais' works such as *Crucible, Tensile Involvement,* and *Tent;* Doris Humphrey's *Soaring;* the Bolshoi's *Sleeping Beauty* and *Don Quixote;* Donald McKayle's *Rainbow 'Round My Shoulder* and *Games;* Pearl Primus' *Buschasche;* Twyla Tharp's *Push Comes to Shove*). Works with shaping and strength moves such as Ailey's "Didn't My Lord Deliver Daniel" *(Revelations)*.	Learns about significant dance works of the 20th century (such as Alvin Ailey's *Cry;* Paul Taylor's *Aureole;* Ailey's "Wading in the Water" *[Revelations];* Doris Humphrey's *Water Study;* art fusion works by Meredith Monk; Japanese butoh; south Indian kathakali dance and drummers; dances of Asadata Dafora, Mexican Ballet Folklorico). Connects dance to cross-curricular studies in literature such as Agnes de Mille's *Fall River Legend,* Limón's *The Moor's Pavane,* John Butler's *Othello,* Valerie Bettis' *A Streetcar Named Desire,* and *Romeo and Juliette.*
	Sees dance through video documentaries for contextual relevance (such as the "Dancing" video series).	Sees dance through video documentaries for contextual relevance (such as the "Dancing" video series and JVC Video Anthology of World Music and Dance documentary series).	Makes contextual relationships through video documentaries such as the "Dancing" video series and JVC Video Anthology of World Music and Dance documentary series.
2.4e 21st century			
Notices dance in the media.	Knows current forms of dance.	Keeps abreast of current significant works.	Keeps abreast of current significant works.

Dance Cornerstone Curriculum Framework—C3: Knowing History, Culture, and Context from *Teaching Dance as Art in Education* by Brenda Pugh McCutchen, 2006, Champaign IL: Human Kinetics

3.0 Preserving Dance for Future Generations

Grades K-2	Grades 3-5	Grades 6-8	Grades 9-12
3.1 Documentation			
3.1a Preserving dance for the future			
Recognizes the difference between dances present and dances past. Understands different ways of passing dances to others (learning dances, filming, performing).	Recognizes the difference between dances present and dances past. Understands different ways of passing dances through generations (learning dances, filming, performing, notating).	Discovers how dance heritage is passed down through generations in each culture. Investigates one's own dance heritage and ways to transmit it to others.	Learns to preserve dances by teaching them to others, using notation symbols, and writing descriptions of dances.
Learns of the need to preserve dances for others.	Learns ways to preserve dance for future generations.	Uses filming and motif writing to document and preserve own dances.	Learns to make video documentaries of own work and make artistic portfolios.
3.1b Transitory nature of dance			
————	Notices how memory fades when trying to recapture dances learned in the past. Uses repetition and concentration to help remember dance moves from one day to the next.	Finds ways to recall dances when observing, and relies on visual-kinesthetic memory.	Values the uniqueness of each live dance performance. Learns to capture visual images of fleeting moments in performances to store in memory.
3.1c Recording and notating			
————	Views videotapes and dance films to learn how dance is documented. Learns motif writing and basic Labanotation (directions, levels, steps, time duration).	Applies comprehension of basic Labanotation symbols on a staff to reconstruct simple dance steps in sequence with proper time and space.	Learns basic dance notation and is able to reconstruct simple dances from a score from the center column.
Notices how different dance looks on video and in live performance.	Notices how three-dimensionality is lost in filmed dance works.	Reconstructs dance phrases from video performances of master works.	Reconstructs dance phrases from video performances of master works.
Sees photographic essays of dance and dance posters.	Collects photographic essays of dance and dance posters.	Creates photographic essays based on original dance works.	Becomes familiar with a range of dance literature from periodicals, texts, photographic essays, and poster art. Creates photographic essays of original dances and posters to promote performances.
3.1d Motor memory and dance legacy			
————	Learns how motor memory helps us recall dance sequences and dance works.	Experiences firsthand how repertory dances are remembered and passed on to other generations of performers by those who have danced roles. Sees examples of older performers mentoring and coaching new generations of dancers to pass on the legacy of dance.	Sees old film clips of special dancers from earlier time periods as a way to identify style. Discovers how oral traditions of preserving dance are subject to subtle shifting caused by each person's role interpretation and own motor memory of the part through time.

Dance Cornerstone Curriculum Framework—C3: Knowing History, Culture, and Context from *Teaching Dance as Art in Education* by Brenda Pugh McCutchen, 2006, Champaign IL: Human Kinetics

3.0 Preserving Dance for Future Generations

Grades K-2	Grades 3-5	Grades 6-8	Grades 9-12
3.1e Kinesthetic teaching			
————	————	Views examples of kinesthetic teaching where dance is transferred directly from one body to another (such as Balinese baris and legong, where the teacher actually moves the student's body).	Views examples of kinesthetic teaching where dance is transferred directly from one body to another (such as contact improvisation, teacher's corrections, somatic work, and teaching partnering skills through hands-on work).
3.2 Lifetime involvement			
3.2a Recreation and fitness			
————	————	Pursues dance as recreation or fitness and conditioning outside of class. Identifies local studios offering dance classes.	Pursues dance as recreation or fitness and conditioning outside of class. Identifies local studios offering dance classes, Pilates, Gyrokinesis, yoga, and other movement classes.
3.2b Avocational dance			
————	Pursues avocational dance such as participating in community dance events.	Pursues avocational dance. Looks for opportunities in musical theatre and stage productions that provide performing opportunities. Researches available community dance classes to extend skills in diverse dance styles. Researches sites to pursue after graduation.	Pursues avocational dance. Looks for opportunities in musical theatre and stage productions that provide dance opportunities. Researches available community dance classes to extend skills in diverse dance styles. Researches sites to pursue after graduation.
3.2c Dance careers			
Identifies and comprehends the primary dance roles: teacher, performer, choreographer, and observer.	Examines the dance careers: choreographer, dance critic, performer, teacher.	Examines personal preferences about participating in dance as a recreational pursuit or as a professional career.	Seeks relevant information concerning discipline, knowledge, and skills required for career preparation in dance. Explores a variety of dance careers: choreographer, dancer–performer, dance critic, dance historian–anthropologist, and teacher.
————	Identifies leaders in dance and examines their contributions, lifestyles, career goals, and impact.	Selects role models in dance. Examines those with whom student personally identifies.	Selects role models in dance. Examines those with whom student personally identifies.
————	————	Explores diverse career options in dance through discussion, reading, and demonstrations by a variety of professionals (production designer, performer, dance therapist, notator).	Explores diverse career options in dance through discussion, reading, and demonstrations by a variety of professionals (production designer, performer, dance therapist, notator).

Dance Cornerstone Curriculum Framework—C3: Knowing History, Culture, and Context from *Teaching Dance as Art in Education* by Brenda Pugh McCutchen, 2006, Champaign IL: Human Kinetics

Grades K-2	Grades 3-5	Grades 6-8	Grades 9-12
————	————	————	Identifies summer programs such as American Dance Festival, Bates, Jacob's Pillow, the Alvin Ailey School, Joffrey, American Ballet Theatre, New York City Ballet, Pittsburgh Ballet. Identifies NASD-accredited colleges and schools that offer further dance study.

3.3 Repertory

3.3a Reconstruct and perform significant dance works

Grades K-2	Grades 3-5	Grades 6-8	Grades 9-12
————	Views major dance works on video and learns movement phrases from them. Increases use of the dance elements vocabulary by discussing these dances.	Recognizes how traditions in dance are a source of dance repertory. Reconstructs contemporary or historic dance works available through such sources as the American Dance Legacy Institute.	Sees how traditional dance works stimulate ideas to evolve new dance works. Establishes relationships of past to present by recreating and reconstructing a major dance work.
Develops dance literacy by observing digestible chunks of selected dance works and being able to recognize significant works.	Increases dance literacy by reconstructing and performing dance studies from sections of significant dance works.	Increases dance literacy by reconstructing and performing études of dance works.	Increases dance literacy and understanding by reconstructing and performing a significant dance work.

3.3b Personalize historic dances by dancing them

Grades K-2	Grades 3-5	Grades 6-8	Grades 9-12
————	————	Learns at least one repertory work or an étude during middle school.	Learns at least part of a repertory work or an étude each year during high school.
————	Acquires skills in folk and square dance. Learns about at least three world dance styles danced by children (age-mates). Demonstrates skills in at least one dance style.	Acquires motor and stylistic skills for both folk and classical forms around the world. Demonstrates skills in at least one non-Western dance form.	Acquires a repertory of folk dances from other cultures. Proficient: Accurately recalls and performs a variety of dance styles and traditions using accurate steps, positions, and patterns. Advanced: Demonstrates proficiency in at least two dance styles: one Western and one non-Western.
Performs simple folk dances from around the world.	Performs folk and social dance in the context of other dance studies.	Performs folk and social dance in the context of other dance studies.	Performs different dance styles from around the world in class.

Dance Cornerstone Curriculum Framework—C3: Knowing History, Culture, and Context from *Teaching Dance as Art in Education* by Brenda Pugh McCutchen, 2006, Champaign IL: Human Kinetics

Analyzing and Critiquing

👁E Cornerstone 4

"Most curriculums pay no attention at all to aesthetics, a branch of philosophy that deals with questions, What is art?, Must all art be beautiful?, Does art provide knowledge? . . . Somewhere between kindergarten and twelfth grade students ought to be introduced to such questions in order to participate in an intellectual dialogue that has been going on for two thousand years."

—Elliot Eisner (quoted in Ron Brandt 1987-1988, p. 7)

This chapter features Cornerstone 4—one of the four educational dance cornerstones. Cornerstone 4 focuses on key aspects of analyzing, responding to, and critiquing dance from an aesthetic perspective. This cornerstone relies on the dance elements vocabulary to analyze dance. It calls forth critical and reflective thinking, and it incorporates responding to dances of others and self. Here we increase our aesthetic awareness and apply it to the other cornerstones. The substance of Cornerstone 4 is aligned with national standards. It is outlined in detail to help you build curriculum, write goals and objectives, and design assessments. Cornerstone 4 may be the starting place for, the main focus of, or one part of a unit of study, but it is a necessary part of each unit. A sequential K-12 curriculum framework is presented. It emphasizes all three of the NAEP categories of creating, performing, and responding. Cornerstone 4 enrolls the learner as dance critic.

Relation to National Standards and Beyond

Dance criticism is where individuals take their understanding of movement and the vocabulary they have developed for it and express their aesthetic perceptions about dance. This is where they learn to analyze and talk about all aspects of dance. They learn to take—and speak from—different points of view: a choreographer's perspective, a dance historian's perspective, a dance performer's perspective, and a critic's perspective. This analytical process, when used on one's own dances, encourages reflective and critical thinking, evaluation, and refinement of work. All of the artistic processes—creating, performing, and responding—personalize dance and bring aesthetic issues to the educational table. Cornerstone 4 ensures that we create an aesthetically driven curriculum (one of the six characteristics of educational dance). Cornerstone 4 interacts with all other cornerstones to apply aesthetics to them.

Attending to artistic and aesthetic aspects brings dance literacy full circle: Individuals learn to dance, they learn to create dances, they learn about dance, they learn to evaluate and talk about dance, and they learn to read and write dance—total dance literacy.

Cornerstone 4 enables students to better make artistic value judgments about dance. Here they analyze the other cornerstones from an artistic perspective. They ask how they are dancing, how effectively they've created a dance, and what needs to be reshaped and refined to make the dance communicate more clearly. They ask how historical works and dances from different cultures increase understanding of dance as art. In an aesthetically driven curriculum in educational dance, aesthetics are at the heart of it all.

An aesthetic sense is the feeling of deep satisfaction we get from doing something well and beautifully—like balancing exactly on center or turning in the air, like experiencing flow of movement through the body and having movements connect. It's like taking a mental image and giving it motional form by creating your own movements in a dance. It's like leaping really high for the first time. This kind of personal aesthetic has meaning and value to the individual.

This chapter mixes theory and application and turns attention to the lifeblood of educational dance: how you apply aesthetics to all aspects of dance.

- You need to know aesthetics to apply aesthetics.
- You need to know how to draw out levels of complex thinking.
- You need to understand dance criticism to help students unpack a dance work.
- You need to facilitate reflective thinking.

Aesthetic education in dance furthers what we believe is its artistic best. We arrive at this artistic best by what we think are the best-crafted choreography and the best performance techniques available. Aethetic education applies aesthetics to all parts of the dance curriculum: performing, creating, knowing, and responding. It uses the dance elements as the descriptive vocabulary with which to think and talk about dance. It incorporates higher-order and evaluative thinking as part of inquiry. This means you now must acquire skills to facilitate critical thinking, aesthetic scanning, aesthetic valuing, and dance criticism—all valuable ways for students to respond aesthetically to dance.

Even as this chapter features the responding cornerstone, it includes all aspects assessed on the nation's arts report card (c/p/r). The chapter fleshes out NSDE 3, *Understanding dance as a way to create and communicate meaning,* and NSDE 4, *Applying and demonstrating critical and creative thinking skills in dance.* In addition, it builds on NSDEs 1 and 2. Before going further, read the NSDE Achievement Standards 3 and 4 for grades K-4, 5-8, and 9-12.

Dance study and courses that prepare you to teach this cornerstone: Modern and Ballet Technique, Dance Analysis, Composition, Dance History, Labanotation, Laban Movement Analysis, Performance, Choreography, Aesthetics, Dance Criticism, and all other courses that involve critical thinking and evaluative response enable you to analyze and respond to dance and to facilitate criticism.

"Inspire. Inquire. Acquire." In a child-centered curriculum, you inspire children to create as well as acquire skills. Therefore, you nurture creativity with one hand and raise the aesthetic bar with the other.

Overview of This Cornerstone

The focus of Cornerstone 4 is critical thinking and critiquing artistic quality. That involves analyzing dance works, interpreting what you see, using the principles of design (PODs) as benchmarks, and evaluating a dance's artistic effectiveness. Artistic choices made by critical and creative thinking (NSDE 4) hit the three highest levels of thinking in Bloom's taxonomy—analysis, synthesis, and evaluation (see chapter 4 for details). (Refer to appendix A for a list of Bloom's taxonomy as well as the PODs.)

This cornerstone evaluates quality: quality of performance, quality of creative work, and at times even the quality of the critical response itself. All artistic processes (c/p/r) call on this cornerstone in aesthetic education. Response goes two ways: being responded to and being a responder (critic role). It is vital for adults and peers to evaluate student work in order to see and say what works and what needs improving. Not only do performers need critical input to improve their performance skills, but composers also need it to edit and refine their work.

Put aesthetics to work during the creative process without reserving them just for creative products.

Realize that the creative process produces several rough drafts. Each draft is not the ultimate finished product! Take each draft as a concrete way to show learners where and how to make a work stronger. The student—who is at once dancer, choreographer, and audience–observer for peers—needs to grow critical and aesthetic discrimination to produce good quality and recognize it.

Show students how to break down existing dance works into parts (analysis) to see how they are put together. This will expose compositional tools available to students and increase their grasp of the craft and their descriptive vocabulary about dance. Analyze to increase their dance elements vocabulary as you talk in terms of space, time, and energy. As you teach each element, see that students apply it as choreographic criteria in a creation. Then use the choreographic criteria as review criteria so as to artistically evaluate what students have done.

Give evaluative feedback during student compositions to show what needs to be edited and reworked. Be specific about what is needed where so students can focus their energies when they edit. Then give them opportunity to refine their work. Critique their finished dances to demonstrate what to look for in a work. Over time this increases a class's artistic expectations and augments their collective ability to compose and refine as well as critique.

Peer critique sharpens analytical and critiquing skills. The more chances students get to analyze dance works according to choreographic criteria, the better they get at critiquing. Peer critique increases perception and raises awareness of details and refinements. Peer work is accessible because everyone is creating and critiquing with the same criteria at the same time in the same unit. Thus, each student gains confidence in seeing and speaking about dance.

Peer critiquing sharpens choreographic skills, too. As students switch roles between choreographer and critic, they learn both skills. One artistic process feeds the other (i.e., creating feeds critiquing and vice versa). The same aesthetic criteria are both the choreographic criteria and the review criteria. Peer critiquing forces students to take an **objective** outside view of the choreography. By making suggestions to others about what works best and how to improve their dances, the critic learns firsthand what works. The critic immediately incorporates this new insight into his or her own creative work. Thus, close observation of others' work as a critic gives additional ideas and insights to a choreographer as well.

Maximize the aesthetic processes in a comprehensive, substantive, aesthetically driven curriculum. Apply critical thinking in analysis, applied aesthetics, critiquing, and reflective thinking.

- **Analysis** breaks dance down into identifiable concepts. It opens the observer's eyes to detail. For example, "What do you see here?"

- **Applied aesthetics** put aesthetic criteria to practical use. For example, "As you refine your dance, decide whether it is more effective to enter from offstage or be onstage to begin." "How many dancers will you select to best convey this dance idea, two or three?" "Consider whether that section would be better later in the dance than at the beginning."

- **Critiquing** involves judging artistic quality of what is seen or done. For example, critiquing is about a specific work: "How is contrast used effectively in this dance?" "How satisfactorily is the motif repeated in this dance?" "Where did you see impressive examples of level changes?" "Where did you see two people moving exactly alike or in unison? How effective was it?"

- **Reflective thinking** relates new learning to what has gone before to put the experience into a broader context. For example, "How is this like the one you learned last week?"

The aesthetic outcome of your program depends on how well you convey these four aspects of this cornerstone. You need a background in aesthetics to help others make discriminating choices. Much depends on your teaching of aesthetics: others' ability to refine their work for artistic integrity, their ability to analyze and evaluate dance using aesthetic criteria, and their ability to understand dance as an art form in relation to the world of dance.

Specific units of study may begin from C4: the point of entry for, the inspiration for, or the emphasis of the unit. Most often C4 is the support that integrates the artistic aspects of the other three cornerstones. This cornerstone invites aesthetic inquiry and criticism by asking learners to scan and unpack professional dance works. C4 is most often integrated into C1, C2, and C3 by critiquing technique, choreography, and aspects of dance history. C4 enriches a unit of study whether it is the focus of the unit's content or the support for its experiences.

Some mega-ideas and concepts from this cornerstone follow:

1. Dance is an aesthetically driven art.
2. Dance has both personal and cultural significance.
3. The aesthetic principles of design are the basis of judging artistic quality across the arts.
4. Critiquing judges artistic quality to improve performance across the arts.
5. Critiquing is used in all aspects of the dance discipline.
6. Dance is a powerful mode of human expression.

Goals and Objectives of Cornerstone 4

C4's portion of the Dance Cornerstone Curriculum (DCC) Framework is presented in three parts in this chapter: The first part (goals and objectives) shows the big picture. The second part (content outline) breaks goals and objectives into an outline. The third part extends the outline into a developmental sequence detailed at the end of the chapter for K-2, 3-5, 6-8, and 9-12. (For older beginners, start with the K-2 column. Move AG/T students ahead of grade level as needed.)

These suggested K-12 goals and objectives help you fully convey Cornerstone 4. See the many ways they prepare students to meet or exceed the NSDEs—especially 2, 3, and 4.

Goal 1: To purposefully respond to dance

1.0 Desired outcomes: To appreciate dance as a communication art and respond to its personal and cultural significance.

Learning objectives: The student will

1.1 Apply the languages of dance to respond to dances.
> Use BSTER dance elements vocabulary to respond to dance.
> Use accurate stylistic and design vocabulary.
> Expand and use technical theatre terms, dance terminology, symbol systems, and reference points (historical and cultural) to describe dance.

1.2 Value dance from the dual perspectives of observer and participant.
> Experience the joy of seeing and responding to dance.
> Give thoughtful attention to dance works.
> Appreciate the universality of dance and other art forms.
> Recognize the value of great works of dance as creative and artistic milestones.

1.3 Use review criteria to respond to works in progress and finished works.
> Apply criteria from the principles of design to review dance.
> Apply aesthetic criteria when creating, performing, and responding to dance.
> Create review criteria from choreographic criteria.

1.4 Use critical thinking to respond to dance.
> Use higher-order thinking.
> Use reflective thinking.

Goal 2: To judge artistic quality

2.0 Desired outcome: To astutely critique dance works.

Learning objectives: The student will

2.1 Apply artistic discrimination when judging artistic quality of the choreography as well as the performance of it.
> Use aesthetic criteria when analyzing and evaluating dances.
> Apply principles of design as criteria to judge choreographic quality.
> Judge the quality of peer dance works as well as professional dance works.
> Establish criteria to judge performance quality.
> Use review criteria to evaluate how performance skill contributes to the clarity and effectiveness of performance.

2.2 Unpack professional dance works.
> Know great works of dance from having interacted significantly with them.
> Use the Four-Step Critique.
> Analyze and critique professional dance works.
> Respond to diverse world dance forms and evaluate diverse dance styles from different aesthetic perspectives.
> Develop artistic judgment for critique.

2.3 Critique own works and those of others in the classroom.
> Provide feedback to others and accept feedback as part of the artistic processes in dance.
> Refine work based on feedback and critique.
> Use steps of the Lerman Critical Response Process to give feedback to peers.
> Critique works in progress as well as finished works.
> Aesthetically evaluate choreographic process and products.

Liberally adapted from Lunt and McCutchen, 1995, with permission of the South Carolina Department of Education.

Content Outline

Use this framework outline to guide comprehensive long-term curriculum planning. The outline headings are developed into a framework at the end of the chapter (page 285).

The desired outcome is for students to think critically about artful communication in dance. Teach so that students acquire an aesthetic understanding of dance. Teach so that all ages become able to decode dance and use its languages to analyze and critique dances.

 *Goal 1.0 General response to dance*

Objective 1.1 Using Dance Vocabulary to Respond

1.1a BSTER vocabulary

1.1b Stylistic vocabulary

1.1c Design vocabulary

1.1d Laban and Language of Dance (LOD) vocabulary

1.1e Technical theatre terms

Objective 1.2 Appreciating Dance

1.2a Communication

1.2b Enjoys dance

1.2c Values the dance discipline

Objective 1.3 Using Review Criteria

1.3a Uses review criteria based on choreographic criteria

1.3b Uses review criteria based on principles of design (PODs)

1.3c Uses review criteria based on performance quality

Objective 1.4 Critical Thinking

1.4a Analysis

1.4b Synthesis

1.4c Evaluation

1.4d Reflection

 *Goal 2.0 Dance criticism*

Objective 2.1 Artistic Discrimination (or Applied Aesthetics)

2.1a Applies discrimination

2.1b Applies aesthetic principles of design

2.1c Assesses choreographer's aesthetic choices

2.1d Assesses production elements

2.1e Evaluates dancer's performance quality (professional and peer)

2.1f Communicates meaning (clarity of intent)

Objective 2.2 Unpacks Professional Dance Works (Four-Step Critique)

2.2a Uses Four-Step Critique to describe, analyze, interpret, and evaluate great works

2.2b Evaluates work's overall effectiveness

2.2c Responds to great works past and present (professionally choreographed)

2.2d Compares great works

2.2e Responds to diverse world dance forms

2.2f Uses overall artistic judgment

Objective 2.3 Personal Critiques

2.3a Critiques peer works

2.3b Critiques own works

2.3c Uses Lerman's Critical Response Process

2.3d Incorporates peer feedback to refine own compositions

Liberally adapted from Lunt and McCutchen, 1995, with permission of the South Carolina Department of Education.

Cornerstone Thumbprint (C4)

Students aesthetically respond to and evaluate dance from the dual perspectives of dancer and observer. As observer they respond to the performance products and the creative process of peers and professionals. As dancer they evaluate themselves both as creator–choreographer and as performer of the work. Emphasis is on using aesthetic judgment to refine one's work. This is the place in the curriculum where students sharpen their perspective on artistic quality.

- **K-2:** Students in kindergarten through grade 2 learn to be dance observers and dance critics. They recognize the basic differences between these roles and apply simple aesthetic criteria to observing the work of others.

- **3-5:** Students in grades 3 through 5 critique the work of their own and peers as well as great works. They learn to assess quality by using the principles of design and the dance elements vocabulary.

- **6-8:** Students in grades 6 through 8 analyze aesthetic factors for dances (solo, duet, trio, and group). They formulate constructive suggestions and feedback to peers. They give meaningful critique based on choreographic and aesthetic criteria. They distinguish between compositional criteria (structural considerations) and artistic (aesthetic choices).

- **9-12:** Students in grades 9 through 12 integrate as many aesthetic principles and factors as possible when reviewing and critiquing dance. They make succinct written and oral aesthetic judgments.

Adapted with permission of the South Carolina Department of Education, © 1993.

Aesthetic Valuing

Chapter 1 introduced you to aesthetics and chapter 4 to aesthetic stages of progression. This chapter determines what aesthetics are and how you use them to elevate student perception about the dance's artistic integrity and value.

> **"Quantity is competitive whereas, quality is complementary."**
>
> —Detriech Bonhoffer

Defining Aesthetics

Aesthetic experiences elevate us from the ordinary to the extraordinary, from the usual to the rare, from the mundane to the special. Artistic encounters register in our minds (i.e., cognitively), but when an art work actually strikes its mark aesthetically it resonates in the heart. Aesthetic perception includes seeing with the eyes of the heart. Such experiences touch us deeply. Many aesthetic experiences are born from our own or someone else's inspiration (*spirit,* root word) and are capable of transforming the way we (the viewers) see, think,

and feel. Dance as art can inspire because it speaks to the bodymindspirit of the doer and viewer.

What reaches the emotions in dance is aesthetics. Dance transcends mundane movement. Engaging the aesthetic self calls on the highest order of critical thinking (cognitive), the highest level of physical refinement in motion (kin-aesthetic), and the fullest use of psychosocial skills, while incorporating ways of knowing (multiple intelligences). Aesthetic process calls up a child's best in the way of performing, creating, and dance responses. Because the aesthetic process personally affects the learner's bodymindspirit, such a process can be the ultimate in student-centered experience. The aesthetic self qualitatively integrates experience and information. It is unthinkable to leave aesthetics out of a child's life. Many would say it's reason enough to have dance in school. Thus engaged, students have reason to be legitimately satisfied with what they do. That alone keeps some students from dropping out of school.

Two Types of Aesthetics

Aesthetics deal with two main questions: "What is the significance of dance?" (communal) and "How do I respond to it?" (personal).

In education you bring two sets of aesthetic standards together—one personal and the other cultural. Aesthetic valuing covers both:

- How individuals perceive and determine what has artistic merit for us (personal)
  - The broad scope of what a culture values as artistically significant (communal)

Personal Aesthetics When we respond to dance, we use our personal aesthetics. Individuals also develop a personal sense of taste about what we do and see. One thing satisfies, whereas another does not. For example, we have personal preferences for dance styles and for particular dances. Each person's unique personal aesthetic determines what pleases (and displeases) him or her. However, personal taste changes with experiences and education.

Communal Aesthetics Civilization has also evolved artistic criteria or standards for what is aesthetically sound and of artistic value. Some communal aesthetics use design criteria. Much of the world's art, including dance, is valued according to respected artistic principles of design that apply to all the arts. For example, even though a particular art work or dance work may please us personally, it may not have lasting value or be of artistic significance as measured by design standards, and vice versa.

To bring aesthetics into educational dance is to advance students' aesthetic–artistic development (i.e., move them along the stages of progression—see chapter 4). This chapter looks at how educational dance uses design criteria to inform and develop one's personal aesthetic perception.

Broad Applications of Aesthetics

Your dual responsibility is to teach students how to inquire into what is personally meaningful to them and why, as they react to dance works. You need to bring significant dance works to them to broaden their world view and increase their personal and cultural aesthetic experiences. They must apply artistic standards to all artistic processes to infuse aesthetics into all kin-aesthetic activity, creative activity, and cognitive response activities.

Aesthetic valuing is broad enough to incorporate different cultural perspectives. Because various world cultures have different aesthetic criteria for what pleases the eye and ear, students should be familiar with those of their own culture as well as those that apply to diverse world dance forms.

Philosophical aesthetics inquire into the nature and meaning of dance as art and investigate what is of lasting value. Art critics in all arts disciplines help to determine general standards and then to evaluate specific arts works in that context. Likewise, we must ask students to think deeply about what dance is and what its meaning is for society. Asking students to reflect about the nature of dance is necessary to an aesthetically driven curriculum. "When does pedestrian movement become dance?"

> **"The term *aesthetic* itself has been variously defined as 'of or pertaining to the beautiful, as distinguished from the merely pleasing, the moral, or the useful,' as 'the science of cognition through the senses,' and as being 'responsive to the beautiful in art or nature.' In some definitions, it deals with standards of beauty, correct form, and good taste. Similarly, the word *aesthetics* refers to the branch of philosophy dealing with beauty and the beautiful and ways of judging them, especially in the fine arts."**
>
> —Kraus et al. (1991, p. 14)

and "What is beauty in dance?" These questions are effective with middle grades and older students with experience in the artistic processes. If students began in early grades to apply aesthetic principles to what they create, they are primed by middle grades to reflect on aesthetic quality. Apply aesthetics in grades 1 through 5 to prepare these students to deal with dance's philosophical issues by grades 6 through 12.

Here are some examples of broad philosophical aesthetic issues (also essential questions in dance):

- What is the impact of dance on society?
- What aesthetic functions does dance serve in our world?

The following are practical aesthetic questions that apply to specific works (critiquing questions):

- How effectively did the dynamics in that section convey the idea?
- How was the transition between the two sections accomplished? How well?

Applying Aesthetics

Dance appreciation has to happen alongside dancing and creating; otherwise, learners never grasp the power of dance. Applying aesthetics means putting them to work in the classroom:

- *Creating:* Using the aesthetic principles to make and refine dances
- *Performing:* Demonstrating high-quality performing skills
- *Responding:* Critiquing specific dance material in a particular dance work or one in process

Start even the youngest children with short viewing experiences and ask for their responses. Talk about the work. Ask students to describe what they see. Help them talk about the dance elements and how they are involved in the work. Point to the use of space, the timing, and the body shapes and designs. For example, look at one short dance clip several times through different "lenses." Look once for its use of space, another for its use of time, and another for its use of relationships. For all students, apply aesthetics to improve awareness of what is good quality work. Point out what is especially effective. Ask questions like those in chapter 5's "Each Cornerstone—A Method of Inquiry." Get students to critique, inquire, judge, and draw conclusions about specific dances. Help them develop aesthetic eyes. Through **formal analysis** of dance works, break down dances according to the dance elements and choreographic principles of design. Include aesthetic norms from other cultures and point out aesthetic variations across dance styles like jazz and ballet. Increase their stage of aesthetic–artistic growth by applying principles of design (PODs) to what they see and do. For example, call attention to examples that use repetition for the sake of unity yet contrast to get better artistic results. Compare similar qualities in two-dimensional and three-dimensional art works. In so doing you prime the child to apply his own aesthetic choices to creating and composing.

Doing Aesthetics

Valuing dance and dance processes comes from being involved. Lay aesthetic groundwork in all the artistic processes. Students can't fully appreciate dance without creating original dances and performing existing dance works. Through critiquing their own and peer creations, students gain a perpective on their own creative output and that of others. This is where you invite students to also apply aesthetic criteria and the principles of design. Give them this base on which to expand their personal aesthetics

> **"The ability to make qualitative judgments depends on the quality of one's perception and the ability to apply a set of qualitative criteria. This criteria, developed personally or held commonly by any culture, constitute a belief system or philosophy. Participation in a range of artistic experiences enables students to develop an understanding of different cultural philosophies or belief systems and differing criteria used in considering and making judgments about the quality of works of art. These experiences are crucial to the development of a personal philosophy of art and aesthetic sensitivity about the nature, meaning, and value of the arts as a human activity."**
>
> —National Council of State Arts Education Consultants (1992, p. 9)

as they apply aesthetics to their work and the work of others.

Do aesthetics. Aesthetic education creates dancers who make artistic, qualitative choices when performing, creating, and critiquing dance. Increase aesthetic education by incorporating learning objectives that expect students to

- remove extraneous movements from dances;
- design dances that go beyond front-facing unison movement;
- improve the quality of performance skills for a production;
- make discerning choices when creating and composing dances;
- sharpen their use of space, time, and dynamics;
- view historic dance works with an analytic artistic eye to compare with similar works;
- use cultural criteria from a broad perspective; and
- use the universal dance vocabulary to describe dances.

Apply aesthetics in each dance cornerstone. Be sure students see aesthetics in action, use them in process and product, and are inspired by being given specific aesthetic criteria. Also expect students to unpack professional dance works to see

- how they are put together,
- what motivates them,
- how effectively a concept or feeling is conveyed, and
- how the dance work compares with their creative process.

Keep aesthetics at the forefront of all dance learning. Let them drive instruction. Help kids discriminate between what is effective and what is not. It would be unethical to tell students what they must think, but you are to show them how to think so they make good aesthetic decisions. All the discussions in the world about aesthetics probably won't affect someone's dancing or choreographing. It is far better to do aesthetics. For example, teach students how to

- choose one specific movement over another to express an idea in composition,

- refine a movement phrase in class,

- rework choreography to make it clearer and to the point,

- use dance vocabulary to describe and discuss specific choices, and

- discriminate about the appropriate length and the number of dancers to cast to best convey the intent.

 How can you build aesthetic awareness and discrimination so students can put these skills into practice as they make artistic choices? To affect the artistic quality of their responses?

Developing Personal Aesthetics

Aesthetics are subjective. There are shades of gray in aesthetics—not always exact answers. Aesthetic inquiry leads one to elaborate, to diverge in thought, to brainstorm, to think about related things, to investigate. Aesthetic inquiry is a process that can't be measured on a multiple-choice test. It is best assessed by seeing how students respond in practice as they apply aesthetics. What good is it for them to know about aesthetics to write on a facts-based test if they can't use aesthetics?

Some of the first things to ask yourself as a teacher are whether your students apply aesthetics to their viewing and doing. See how you can help them apply aesthetics to ensure different kinds of aesthetic responses. For example, see that your secondary students ask themselves the following questions:

- How does the work connect with me? Is it satisfying? (aesthetic response)

- How effective is the work? What particularly makes it effective or ineffective? (criticism)

- How effective is the work and how does it connect with me personally? (aesthetic criticism)

All aesthetic response is personal—from the most naive to the most sophisticated (see chapter 4). As you educate even the youngest child about design criteria, also validate his or her own aesthetic perceptions. In fact, nurture personal preference but expand its boundaries by introducing quality in the world of the arts. Give students enough experiences with the art of dance that they develop a sophisticated artistic perspective and personally value dance.

In addition, aesthetic valuing enables children to learn to appreciate their own creative work and that of others, which can be a first step toward valuing others who are different from themselves. To see how differently each person solves the very same movement problem shows that each is an individual with unique ways of seeing the world and responding to it. By sensitively analyzing and critiquing each other's works, we learn to appreciate each other's unique creations. This can be an avenue to also value the person and thus contribute to one's own psychosocial development (see chapter 4).

> "...there is a tendency not to notice that for which we have no language. Where there are no words, training is needed to enable the perceiver to see."
>
> —Jacqueline Smith-Autard (2002, p. 34)

Using Aesthetic Criteria

Now we focus on aesthetic criteria. Criteria break big artistic goals down into measurable artistic objectives. Criteria show exactly what needs to be included and what is specifically desired. To use aesthetic criteria is a major step in translating the principles of design into personal practice. Specify clear artistic criteria based on standards of excellence. Use artistic criteria to create (C2) and then to evaluate (C4) what is created. Cornerstone 4 looks at the evaluation side of the process so that students

- inquire into particular qualities of a dance,

- give specific feedback according to the criteria,

- understand exactly what they are looking for in a dance,

- identify what is important to a dance work, and

- over time learn what specifics to look for in dances.

It is relatively simple to turn choreographic criteria into review criteria. For example, consider the following choreographic criteria:

1. Shows contrast between sharp and smooth.
2. Creates unity through the intentional use of repetition.
3. Incorporates entrances and exits into the dance.

The review criteria would be these:

1. Contrast between sharp and smooth is effective and consistent.
2. There is enough repetition to create unity, and variety to create interest.
3. Entrances and exits are well-timed.

Notice the POD words—*contrast, variety, repetition, unity.* These principles of design find their way into the choreographic criteria and the review criteria for upper elementary school students and beyond.

Aesthetic criteria—in this case used as review criteria—are very instructive to students. Aesthetic criteria show students exactly what to critique (and are normally the same criteria used to create the work). Make sure your aesthetic criteria are aligned with your desired outcomes so that you help train the eye about what to look for. It is a good indication that students have internalized the use of criteria when they call on previously used criteria from weeks or months before to make additional judgments about a work.

Include aesthetic criteria from other cornerstones when you critique compositional design. Work that is randomly put together probably will not be good enough. Good work needs to achieve certain criteria (i.e., according to aesthetic–artistic standards). For example, use criteria that clarify the expected artistic quality of the

- use of the dance elements (C1) and
- use of particular compositional elements (C2).

On-target review criteria by themselves instruct learners about what is considered good and what to look for in a work. List aesthetic review criteria at the outset of the lesson and unit to increase aesthetic awareness. To do so moves students further along

than they would go on their own (see chapter 4). As students start seeing and hearing review criteria—and applying them—the artistic bar raises.

Critique Using Artistic Principles of Design

The principles of design (PODs) apply to all art forms. They are the underlying principles that hold a work together (listed in appendix A). In dance, they are benchmarks to measure the design quality of a dance work when you compose and when you critique. The PODs are concepts that promote enduring aesthetic understanding in dance. Use the PODs as evaluative lenses to unpack professional dance works. Use them to apply aesthetics when critiquing. For example, "Did this work hold together or was it disjointed and hard to follow (unity and repetition)?" "Were there enough contrasts to keep you interested?" "Was any one section too long for the other parts of the dance (balance)?" Such analysis and evaluation sharpen the critic's eye and the choreographer's skills. To thus assess strengths and weaknesses of professional dance works gives learners confidence when they respond to peer works

We are not born knowing how to critique. We must be shown. Show students how to use the PODs to analyze and evaluate dance works. This advances students to higher stages of cognition and aesthetic–artistic progression (see chapter 4). Introduce design principles early. The dance framework in this chapter suggests when to introduce certain principles because some are easy to apply. For example, kindergarteners can and should identify repetition.

Use the choreographic principles of design to self-evaluate and to critique works of others. Applying certain of the principles to short compositions prepares students to apply the principles to longer choreographies. The longer and more complex their work, the more design principles you will use. List the PODs as part of the aesthetic criteria. For example, see how a creative dance class could apply aesthetic design criteria using the principles (italicized) to evaluate fourth grade peer works in the design column of figure 9.1. Notice how figure 9.1 incorporates the BSTERs.

Using Review Criteria

Review criteria, such as those in figure 9.1, focus attention on what is aesthetically imperative in the lesson. Review criteria hold students accountable for quality. Take criteria directly from a unit's goals and objectives. Criteria should also come from several other sources: the principles of design, national

Review criteria (1-5 points each, with 3 being average)

Design criteria:

___ *Contrast* between sharp and smooth is effective.

___ There is enough *repetition* to create unity.

___ Entrances and exits are well timed.

___ Groupings added spatial interest.

___ Unison movement is used rarely—only enough to emphasize—without being predictable.

___ *Transitions* effectively connect phrases and sections.

___ There is enough *variety* in the dance to hold the audience's interest.

___ Movements are in a logical order or *sequence*.

Performance criteria:

___ Focus conveys intent.

___ Muscles are engaged throughout.

___ Statement is expressively clear.

___ Performer holds still shapes strongly.

___ Performer is spatially involved.

___ Performer achieves high aesthetic performance quality.

___ Group work is cohesive.

FIGURE 9.1 An example of the two kinds of review criteria: design criteria and performance criteria. Where do you see the choreographic principles of design incorporated?

standards, broad aesthetic standards, effective use of the BSTERs, and—when appropriate—diverse cultural and stylistic standards.

There are two kinds of qualitative aesthetic criteria for critiquing: the quality of the dance design and the quality of the performance. The first evaluates the choreography; the second evaluates the performer (see figure 9.1).

Principles of design apply only to dance design—not to performance quality. Performance criteria apply to how well the dancers execute or realize the dance. For example, in kindergarten through third or fourth grade use general rather than technique-based performance criteria. By grade 7, increase the technical expectations. Examples of performance criteria for grade 2 might be these:

1. Holds a still shape at the beginning and the end of the dance.

2. Keeps a performance focus throughout.

3. Emphasizes the use of *(the dance element topic, such as level changes)* in the dance.

These relate to performance quality rather than compositional skills.

Review criteria state desired outcomes concretely—in black and white. They enable students to assess each other. They help you assess students. They test how well persons apply the concepts, elements, or principles (but you don't need to tell your students that!).

To teach without review criteria is an incomplete process. Embed the lesson objectives as criteria (e.g., use of the dance elements, the design principles, techniques) into the learning process at many points to reinforce the ability to create, to see, and to evaluate. List the review criteria and use them in class. Use rubrics to make criteria concrete. Rubrics help students see what can increase the quality of what they do (see chapter 12). (For more examples, see figures 12.10, 12.15, and 12.16 on pages 383-385, 395, and 396, respectively.)

Teacher-generated review criteria are important at all age levels. High school seniors with years of experience using teacher-generated criteria can eventually create their own criteria. If you can teach students to do this, they are on their way to being lifetime audience members who seek quality.

Make criteria concrete and specific for viewing assignments. Prominently display review criteria visually as you give them verbally. Put criteria on a chart for class reference and call everyone's attention to the chart just as they are about to critique a work and again as soon as they finish viewing the work. It is also helpful for grades 5 and older to have scoring rubrics in their hands with a grid that allows them to mark criteria for each work (see chapter 12). Both charts and rubrics present criteria in visual form, which all learners need so they can refer to criteria as they watch a dance.

> **"Good questions outrank easy answers."**
>
> —Paul A. Samuelson

Reflect and Respond

In the following, Erick Hawkins describes the kinds of dance he finds satisfying to view. Which of his statements paint the clearest word pictures for you? How do they sharpen your eyes to analyze and add to your vocabulary for critiquing dance? How do they relate to the choreographic principles of design?

Hawkins' aesthetics embrace:

> Dance that is violent clarity. Dance that is effortless. Dance that lets itself happen.
>
> Dance that uses technique that is an organic whole, not a grab bag of eclecticism. Dance that loves gravity rather than fights gravity. Dance that senses itself instant-by-instant like the prick of a pin. Dance that does not try to explode the same bubble twice.
>
> Dance that reveals the dance AND the dancer. Dance that knows that the art is more than the personality of the dancer. Dance that knows dance can be, should be, and is a way of saying now.

From the poem "What Is the Most Beautiful Dance?" by Erick Hawkins. Used with permission of Chicago Review Press.

Critical Thinking and Processing

Critical thinking is a way of thinking more than an isolated thinking event. Criticism is responding to something specific.

Critical thinking is generally analytical and evaluative. It makes judgments based on solid thinking.

Critical thinking uses the higher-order thinking processes—analysis, synthesis, and evaluation—described in Bloom's taxonomy (see chapter 4). These three processes are the most involved cognitive levels for processing information and have a national standard devoted to them (NSDE 4). Critical thinking doesn't always produce a concrete outcome. It can stay in the mind. But in dance it often has an outcome: an action or an application. Its outcome may or may not be aesthetically driven.

Criticism is the act of responding to a particular dance work through critique. Criticism uses judgment and perception. Critiquing is a qualitative artistic value judgment we make at the highest thinking level: evaluation. To critique we use information, understanding, and the ability to analyze. Critiquing responds to something concrete (e.g., a dance, an art work, one's performance quality). The outcome is aesthetically driven.

Mobilizing Higher-Order Thinking in the Arts (Analysis, Synthesis, Evaluation)

Critical thinking is higher-order thinking. Bloom's taxonomy is the best source for understanding and intentionally using higher-order thinking skills (HOTS, chapter 4). Dance HOTS translate to action: They get students to apply what they know, analyze information and ideas, and problem solve. Higher-order thinking thus fuels dancing and creating as well as thinking about and responding to dance. The most complex critical thinking is that which creates, synthesizes, reflects, assesses, interprets, evaluates, and makes informed judgments.

Lower-order thinking skills are the basic skills that underpin critical thinking. They deal with comprehending facts, ideas, and basic information. They use memorization and recall: Students apply what they know and demonstrate that they understand. Lower-order thinking provides the important facts-based information that critical thinking uses. One must have concrete specifics to work with. General education relies on lower-order comprehension of facts and application of information. The arts include but go beyond lower-order thinking so everyone works with substantive information and processes.

Artistic principles of design promote the use of repetition for the sake of unity. Where are horizontal, diagonal, and vertical lines repeated in this design?

Stimulate students to inquire at higher levels by asking them how and why they are doing what they are doing. Expect them to set artistic goals and to assess their own performance. Expect them to focus on the aesthetic quality of their movement.

Varying Levels of Complex Thinking

All ages use all six levels of thinking. But not all ages are ready to process difficult and challenging subject matter. (Obviously, young children need easier subject matter to process than older ones; mentally challenged students require less complex material.) At each higher-order thinking (HOT) level, select subject matter with the appropriate degree of informational sophistication and difficulty according to the age (figure 9.2).

Facilitate and question at each level. Keep the verb and concept list in figure 9.3 handy. Use the verbs to ask targeted questions (and to write clear goals and objectives as you see in chapter 12).

The question you pose governs the level of response. The way students respond to HOT questions reveals the level to which they understand and can process the information or activity (i.e., the ability to explain how or why demonstrates that they can analyze). Therefore, responses help you find out three things: (1) what students know, (2) what levels of cognitive complexity they can use, and (3) what level of artistic sophistication they have achieved. Being able to assess where they are helps you get them to the next level.

Facilitating Different Higher-Order Levels of Thinking

Here we see how the highest levels of Bloom's taxonomy mobilize critical thinking—the three HOTS levels.

Teaching with higher-order thinking puts you in the category of a "super teacher." Learn all you can about Bloom's taxonomy. It is necessary for successful educational dance facilitation. Use Bloom's taxonomy specifically to

- stimulate student thinking (lower and higher order),
- learn how to ask questions and how to evaluate responses,
- prompt students to analyze dance works (i.e., break them apart),
- get refined work and focused critique from students,
- plan units and lessons,
- teach lessons,
- construct written tests,
- develop rubrics and set choreographic criteria for students, and
- influence the kinds of projects, research, and tasks you assign.

Learn to ask effective, targeted questions. That is the crux of effective inquiry-based dance education. The level of cognition you generate in students depends on the skills with which you pose questions. Preparing cogent inquiry questions is one of the most challenging teaching skills. It requires practice, patience, and action verbs.

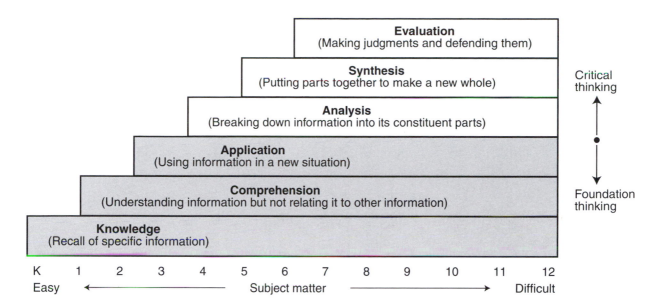

FIGURE 9.2   Bloom's taxonomy of thinking.

Verbs drive questions. For example, *list, describe, categorize, combine.* The response totally depends on the kind of question you ask. The verb is the key that cranks up thinking. The verb determines how the brain responds and which level or gear it jumps to as it begins to process a response to the question. You have to know which verb drives which level of thinking—whether your questions are discussion questions, reflection questions, guided movement exploration questions, guided viewing questions, or test questions. Match the levels of thinking to the verb and concept chart in figure 9.3 so you ask cogent questions to stimulate inquiry. Use these imperative verbs to write clear behavioral objectives for students (e.g., "The student will *[verb].* . . ."). Then practice your questions on students. Also ask the 5Ws: who, what, where, when (lower order), and why (higher order).

Writing Goals and Objectives for Critical Thinking

Critical thinking objectives in dance require basic foundation thinking (i.e., knowledge of dance, comprehension of the cornerstone content, and application of the artistic processes [c/p/r]). But by definition, critical thinking in dance is analyzing and interpreting, synthesizing and composing, evaluating and critiquing. These are Bloom's HOTS.

Lessons and units should include critical thinking goals and objectives (NSDE 4). Think of goals and objectives like to-do lists. Each list starts with a verb:

Wash the car. *Go* to the store. The difference is that goals and objectives are not for you. They are student achievement to-do lists. National achievement standards drive goals and objectives, for students must achieve them. But students must achieve more than just the standards to have a full experience with dance. The four cornerstones methods contain the significant content for critical thinking. Write cornerstone content into goals and objectives. Also use the standards to begin your to-do list for what needs to be learned and achieved. Then go to the dance frameworks to add significant, well-rounded content. The goals determine what you teach and how you teach it, so include critical thinking as a goal (see chapter 12).

Go to the verb and concept chart in figure 9.3. Learn how to target the HOTS (i.e., use the three highest levels of thinking—analysis, synthesis, and evaluation). Start each critical thinking objective with these verbs. For example, look at the following practice objectives to see how the underlined verbs drive the objectives (e.g., compose, measure, discriminate). With which critical thinking level does each objective correspond? (Hint: The underlined verb will tell you.)

PRACTICE OBJECTIVES FOR STUDENTS

- "Discriminate between (this and that)."

- "Compose a dance study using contrasting timing following exploration of timing tools in dance."

To get different levels of thinking . . .	. . . ask students (to):
KNOWLEDGE (basic skill, lowest level) • Recalling • Remembering previously learned material • Repeating from memory	Cluster, define, demonstrate, discover, experiment, explain, format, know, label, list, match, memorize, name, observe, outline, recall, recognize, record, recount, repeat, show, sort Ask facts: Who? What? When? Where?
COMPREHENSION • Translating • Grasping the meaning of material • Rephrasing, comparing information	Cite, compare, conclude, describe, explain, express, group, identify, locate, paraphrase, recognize, rephrase, report, restate, review, tell, translate, summarize, support Ask to explain facts: Who? What? When? Where?
APPLICATION • Generalizing • Using learned material in new and concrete situations • Problem solving in a new situation using appropriate principles, rules, and concepts	Apply, choose, classify, construct, demonstrate, group, illustrate, imagine (information known), imitate, list, manipulate, model, order, organize, perform (known movement), record, relate, report, select, sequence, show, solve, summarize, test out, use Ask: How to apply it?
ANALYSIS • Discovering • Breaking down material into its component parts so that it may be more easily understood • Identifying logical order of components	Analyze, associate, categorize, characterize, classify, compare and contrast, combine, create, debate, decide, defend, describe (method), differentiate, discriminate, distinguish, divide, draw (conclusions), examine, fill in, identify, imagine (information not known), infer, interpret, isolate, map, measure, note similarities and differences, order, pattern, put together, question, refute, relate to, research, respond (to parts), separate, support, survey, take apart, take away Ask: Why? How (analysis)?
SYNTHESIS • Composing • Putting material together to form a new whole • Combining known components into new ideas and plan	Add to, alter, assume, choreograph, combine, compare and contrast, compose, connect, construct, create, design, develop, devise, emulate, estimate, extend, formulate, hypothesize, imagine, improve upon, integrate, invent, maximize, minimize, modify, plan, predict, propose, reconstruct, regroup, reorganize, speculate, substitute, suppose, symbolize, synthesize, translate, vary Ask: What if . . . ?
EVALUATION (highest level) • Making general judgments • Judging the value of material for a given purpose • Forming a judgment or opinion based on specified criteria	Argue, assess the artistic merit of, choose, compare (strengths and weaknesses, pros and cons), conclude, convince, criticize, critique, decide, discuss, evaluate, give opinion, infer, interpret, judge, justify, persuade, predict, prioritize, recommend, rank, rate, select, solve, validate, value, verify Ask: How well . . . ?

FIGURE 9.3   Verb and concept chart for each level of thinking.

- "Integrate the knowledge of (this) with (that)."
- "Measure the worth of . . ."
- "Judge the quality of . . ."
- "Assess whether the peer work included all the choreographic criteria."

You will learn in chapter 12 that critical thinking assessments have to grow out of and be put into lesson goals and objectives. Performance assessment tasks in dance must measure exactly what is to be learned and how well it was learned according to the desired outcome of the objectives.

Choosing Critical and Creative Thinking Instruction (NSDE 4)

Target the HOTS when you design instruction for students of all ages.

Prompt critical and creative thinking in dance with a variety of experiences that use upper levels of thinking (Bloom's taxonomy):

- Movement exploration (Bloom's application, analysis, and synthesis)
- Problem solving (Bloom's application, analysis, and synthesis)
- Dance analysis (Bloom's analysis)
- Guided viewing of works (Bloom's analysis)
- Reflective thinking (Bloom's analysis and synthesis, often evaluation)
- Critiquing (Bloom's evaluation)
- Aesthetic scanning (all Bloom's levels)
- Inquiry (all Bloom's levels)
- Composing (all Bloom's levels)
- Improvising (all Bloom's levels)
- Brainstorming (all Bloom's levels)

Use key critical thinking task words from the chart in figure 9.3 to write essay questions. Ask students to do the following:

- *Analyze:* To divide something into its parts in order to understand it better, and then to see how the parts work together to produce the overall pattern. Analyzing a problem may require you to identify a number of smaller problems that are related to the overall problem.
- *Contrast:* To identify the differences between things.
- *Describe:* To give a general verbal sketch or account of something in narrative or other form.
- *Diagram:* To show the parts of something and their relationships in pictorial form, such as a chart. You are usually expected to label the diagram, and you may also be asked to explain it in words.
- *Explain:* To clarify and interpret something. Explanations generally focus on why or how something has to come about. Explanations often require you to discuss evidence that may seem contradictory and to tell how apparent differences in evidence can be reconciled.

- *Interpret:* To explain the meaning of something in your own words and discuss the significance.
- *Justify:* To argue in support of some decision or conclusion; to show sufficient evidence or reason in favor of something. Whenever possible, try to support your argument with both logical reasoning and concrete examples.
- *List:* To present information in a series of short, discrete points.
- *Outline:* To present information in a series of main points in appropriate order, omitting lesser details. Also present some information in the form of a series of short headings in which each major idea is followed by subheadings or smaller points or examples that fall under the heading.
- *Prove:* To give a convincing logical argument and evidence in support of the truth of a statement.
- *Relate:* To show the relationship between things. This can mean showing how they influence each other or how a change in one thing seems to depend on or accompany a change in the other.
- *Summarize:* To give information in brief form, omitting examples and details. A summary should be short yet cover all of the most important points.

This figure is reprinted with permission from the *Journal of Physical Education, Recreation & Dance*, January 2003, p. 43. *JOPERD* is a publication of the American Alliance for Health, Physical Education, Recreation and Dance, 1900 Association Dr., Reston, VA 20191.

Editing and Refining Work Based on Analysis and Evaluation

Critical thinking and aesthetic criticism intersect when it's time to edit and refine one's creative work. The creator benefits from this process. Facilitate the aesthetic dialogue between a student choreographer and a student critic who serves as a critical friend. After a critical friend analyzes and evaluates, she or he offers constructive feedback to the student choreographer. The quality of the student's output depends on this refined equation:

Aesthetic criteria + critical thinking = the informed ability to critique.

What would happen if you did not use critiquing to assist student choreographers? It would be like the language arts teacher not marking spelling and grammar errors in written work to show learners how to correct them. What if that teacher highly praised first writing attempts and did not expect students to correct or refine their written work? The student's compositional skills would suffer.

The same is true of dance. Movements strung together that are not yet coherent are to be validated as process. To say that incoherent work is superb is not only dishonest, but it robs students of the compositional skills they need. How else would they learn to compose or to critique? First give pointers, and then give opportunities to rework aspects of a dance to make it more coherent. Stay with the appropriate developmental stage of progression (see chapter 4) so students can achieve. At times stretch them to the next level so you can give them meaningful pointers. Students learn a lot by trial and error, but they learn more if their work receives astute critical feedback. Constructive feedback can build skills without damaging confidence or self-esteem. Demonstrate how to give helpful critical feedback to students to aid the process without undermining someone's self-confidence.

Reflect and Respond

Master Bloom's Taxonomy

After you learn Bloom's taxonomy, apply it to your own thinking.

1. Identify the six thinking levels described in Bloom's taxonomy, which describes a progressively complex system of thinking. This information is your knowledge.

2. Recognize that each thinking level becomes progressively more complex and is accessed through different tasks. Comprehend the different terms and descriptions. Know there will be different questions that will engage students at different levels. This shows your comprehension.

3. Apply what you know and understand to write or ask HOT questions that use verbs from all six levels. This is application.

4. Analyze student answers to see if they are on the targeted level.

5. Synthesize the taxonomy and facilitate complex higher-order thinking so students are facile at analyzing, synthesizing, and evaluating—in and about dance and across disciplines.

6. Evaluate student effectiveness through reflective thinking and by assessing students' ability to use all six levels of thinking.

Reflective Thinking

Reflective thinking is a particular kind of critical thinking that is needed in dance. **Reflection** takes place at the top by analysis, synthesis, and evaluation. Reflection aids understanding, and over time it cultivates human judgment.

To reflect is to recall, review, and relate. So as you ask students to recall what just happened, review information or experiences, and relate information or experiences to something else, you ask them to reflect. When you ask them to relate experience broadly, you ask them to reflect. Reflection is inquiry at its best. It ties together experience and concepts.

There's a difference between reflecting and critiquing. Although both can be evaluative, reflection evaluates over time. Critiquing is a qualitative assessment or evaluation of the artistic merits of a particular dance work or works. Reflection generally evaluates in a broader context than critiquing. Students need both: to evaluate (aesthetically critique) their own works and the works of others and to reflect on their artistic growth. Sometimes reflecting and critiquing overlap.

Why Reflective Thinking Is Needed in Education

Dance underuses reflection. You may be a product of that. Have you ever tried to explain what you do in dance or convey why dance education is important and found yourself searching for coherent phrases? Unless educational dance makes body learning conscious, most of the right-brain body stimuli bypass the analytical left side of the brain. Universally, dancers can't say what they do in class—much less what dance is about, how dancing is educational, and what of value happens in the studio. The most analytical part of technique class is usually when one is asked to break down a movement sequence. After technique class, we usually leave the experience in the body instead of inviting it into the mind to incubate and grow. If we ignore reflective inquiry, though, we fail to gain perspective or to mature the bodymind.

We owe it to students to help them integrate experience. Students seldom take the dancing experience further until we ask them to relate what they learned to something else (i.e., to say how the elements were applied or recall how the movement felt). The abstract needs to become concrete. We need to schedule reflection activity as a regular part of the lesson. If students leave class without stating what they learned, they may only retain general feelings and impressions. As soon as another feeling comes along to replace those impressions, the dance feeling or affect evaporates.

Feelings and impressions about a dance experience are legitimate. They're the affective part of the experience. Dancers remember general impressions: that something good or important, exhilarating, or stimulating happened during the kinesthetic experience. But public education must do more than entertain students with their own dancing skills. We must help students bring body experience to consciousness by giving it words. Two things have been chronically underdeveloped in dancers: an expressive dance vocabulary and a habit of reflecting on the content of dance and what it means to dance.

Educational dance uses reflection to enable students to say

- what they do in class,
- what of value happens there,
- how dance relates to the other arts,
- why dancing experiences are important to learning and to education, and
- what aesthetic education is in dance.

Reflection Helps Validate Learning   Reflecting validates for all—including the responder—what has been absorbed and processed. Use reflection in individual lessons, with each unit, and over an extended period of time to help students build perspective and relate present experience to a broader context. Reflection validates for the public school what learning took place. It helps individuals remember what they learned and relate it to past and future lessons. It enables them to answer when asked what they learned in dance. It provides a means of valuing the experience as worthwhile, not only as fun. Shared group reflections build a collage of what was learned in class to aid group memory.

Reflection Promotes Student-Centered Learning   Our culture works against reflection. Children are barraged with external stimulation (from television, radio, CDs, Internet, video games, handheld gadgets, DVDs), which sets up expectations for instant gratification and an obsession for more, faster, bigger, new, and different. Little time is devoted to connecting with others in meaningful

conversation, sharing ideas and values, building virtues we admire, engaging in group arts activities, and encouraging time to process what is going on. Of all the problems this seems to cause in children (and adults), social disconnection and values deprivation are the greatest.

Schools have an obligation to structure a time for reflection so students assimilate personally meaningful aspects of lessons and experiences into their aesthetic education and their overall experience. Reflecting puts the learned concept into personal terms so each individual owns it and applies it. This is student-centered learning at its best.

How Reflection Affects Learning

Reflection builds perspective. Over time, students need to reflect on their personal growth and progress in dance (NSDE 6). Scheduling day to day, regular question–response puts all on notice to be cognitively engaged in daily activities so they can articulate about them by the end of class. Students should come to expect to use the BSTERs to describe what they did in class. As students progress from grade to grade, questioning goes from simple to complex. General reflective questions are springboards to reflective aesthetic valuing questions.

Reflection Helps Memory   Reflection helps take an experience from short-term to long-term memory. By recalling and examining what has passed, students enable present reality to join past experience to give insight for the future. Webster says reflection is "an idea arising in the mind." To see your reflection in a mirror, you look past yourself into another place. So reflective thinking examines information previously stored to process now and to use in the future.

It is useful to revisit what was learned in class. The exhilaration of a dance class soon fades as a new experience takes its place. To maximize learning, help students acknowledge and articulate what they're learning while the impressions and experiences are still alive in their bodies. Add "to reflect about the dance experience" as a learning objective.

Reflection Contextualizes Learning   To reflect individually and in groups puts new experiences into context. Students acquire perspective by comparing new experiences with previous ones. Habitually compare one aspect to another to increase analytic and aesthetic discrimination.

Reflecting helps students relate information and experience to what is already known and to place isolated events and experiences into a broader educational context. Broad reflective inquiry asks these questions:

- What is important about this information?
- To what in the other arts does this relate?
- To what in history does this relate?
- Why do I need to know this?
- Why do I need to know how to do this?
- Of what educational value is this to me?
- Of what educational value is this to the world?

Journaling is a form of reflective learning in dance. Journaling is a writing activity to record what was experienced and how it affected the learner. Periodic journals are valuable for all students above the third grade. Vary journaling assignments to include

- reading assignments,
- experiences, and
- insights about what students have done and where they are in their growth.

Self-assessment journals open channels of honest intrapersonal dialogue. Whether writing is assigned by topic or is occasionally self-initiated free writing, journaling helps learners define themselves personally and artistically. Teachers who read and respond thoughtfully to journals build mutual trust and extend learning.

Reflection Aids Articulation   Both journaling and oral reflection increase articulation. Challenge, invite, and allow students to make meaningful connections with what they learn and find words to express what they are beginning to understand about dance. Use reflection to increase dance vocabulary and to express thoughts and feelings about dance. Encourage students to be articulate responders as well as articulate movers. Unless you make articulation a lesson goal (just as joint articulation is part of technique goals), students are too often unable to talk meaningfully about dance.

Incorporate reflective writing into students' high school dance portfolio. Encourage them to share insights about their artistic growth and their perspective on dance as art.

Reflection Furthers Aesthetic Growth   Aesthetic reflection and response help students evaluate qualitative aspects of dance and dancing. Some of their reflective responses play out in thought and others in action. Incorporate reflection to further aesthetic growth in the present (e.g., untangling a choreographic snag, improvising through a movement problem, self-assessing). Use reflection to build learner aesthetic perspective over time (e.g., having an "a-ha!" insight, comparing the quality of their choreography through several revisions, chronicling their improved technique, comparing what they did today with what they did previously). Use reflection to help decision making (e.g., making choices by weighing several artistic options available, considering all the options available before deciding). Use reflection to deepen students' ability to assess a situation (e.g., self-assessment of choreography and performance, assessment of the quality of work produced or needed, assessment of peers' work).

For the sake of artistic inquiry, pose thought-provoking questions that stay in the mind for a while. Send students home with these questions. Bring them back up from time to time. Keep several questions going as threads that weave through the year. Use them to generate thinking about concept relationships and artistry. Use questions so students acquire a perspective on their creative and artistic growth. Promote enduring understanding.

The richness of response depends on your ability to ask probing, thoughtful questions in a meaningful context. You set the stage for responses to be accepted in an open, nonjudgmental way. Help students to extend personal reflection to other academics and to think through problems or situations.

Facilitating Reflection

Reflection does not always call for response. Students don't have to respond aloud in order to reflect. Practice facilitating reflection around each of the six defining characteristics (6DCs) of educational dance. Use reflection in different ways so it is

- comprehensive (about many topics),
- substantive (about complex concepts),
- sequential (occurring over time),
- aesthetically driven (about artistic concepts),
- contextually coherent (linked to related and relevant concepts), and
- inquiry based (used as a form of personal, inner inquiry).

Vary the Use of Reflection Use reflection activities to draw attention to detail and nuance as well as to the big picture. Use reflection at different times:

- In class (integrated reflection)
- At the end of class (culminating reflection)
- In the long term (broad reflection)

Strategically use reflection with activity classes to enhance attention and to cultivate thoughtful actions. Let's consider some applications, particularly relating to the activity class in the studio.

Culminating reflection and response make a good closure to class—even while students quietly put on their shoes in the circle. In as little as 3 to 5 minutes, you can help kindergarten through fifth grade students synthesize what they learned, put it into words, and outline it for memory; this process codifies and deepens their original experience. Vary the length of time according to age and topic for middle and high school students. Otherwise, useful learning goes unprocessed. (See the Eight-Step Plan in chapter 13, which models how to culminate lessons with reflection questions.)

Here are sample culminating reflection questions for an activity lesson on negative and positive space:

1. "What did you learn about negative and positive space today?"

2. "What ways did you solve the movement problem of turning negative spaces into positive in your exploration today? In your choreography today?"

3. "What difficulties did you have today and how did you solve them?"

4. "How might you use negative and positive space consciously in daily living?"

5. "What folk dance did we learn recently that included negative and positive spaces in the spatial formations? Explain where and how."

6. "What were some choices you made today while designing your dance study that made it better?"

7. "How does negative and positive space apply to visual arts (like drawing, sculpting)?"

8. "How effective was your contrast of negative and positive space in your dance study or improvisation? What would have made it better?"

Culminating reflection works well for activity classes when integrated reflection can disrupt. Determine if stopping movement breaks the flow of energy or the lesson's dynamics. You can't build and sustain the energy level of a movement class if you stop too much. That said, there are valuable processing questions to ask while students are in motion to clarify and extend the material during movement, which keep it progressing dynamically. Such questions can raise bodymind awareness and add a spirit of inquiry about personally examining one's own dancing.

Over time your students can also be led to extend the culminating reflections to ponder larger issues based on their long-term rich experiences to broaden their perspective of dance. After midpoint in the year when your middle and high school students are ready for it, pose some broad reflections based on mega-ideas and concepts that promote enduring understanding in dance.

On occasion you might even vary your approach by starting class with an integrated reflection question that students respond to later in the lesson as is most useful. For example, "Why is it essential to warm up before we dance?" (No response is expected yet.) Then lead warm-up while including not only what is being done but why it is being done: for blood circulation, heart rate elevation, joint fluidity, joint articulation, movement flow, transition from pedestrian movement to dance movement. Later in the lesson ask students to respond to the initial question.

Vary the Kinds of Reflective Response How might you vary reflection activities? You could ask your grade 3 through 5 students to do the following:

1. Respond verbally to a partner while putting on shoes.

2. Share in small groups of three or four.

3. Write a journal entry.

4. Group write, where all write their answers on a board or chart paper at once.

5. Form a class circle to verbally share, one at a time.

6. Draw responses (pictures or symbols).

7. Think about it overnight and return with responses.

8. Write a short paper with responses to the question.

Take Time for Reflection Send students out of class with reflection questions from time to time. Substantive reflecting takes time, so occasionally create space and time between your question and their response. Older students especially need time to think through complex issues that will be discussed the next day. (Off-the-cuff questions usually get superficial answers.) Pique interest in an upcoming topic with, "Why do you think Diaghilev . . . ?" "How could the Denishawn dancers have . . . ?" Inquiry, aside from stimulating thought, personalizes the issues that will be raised.

Build Higher-Order Responding and Thinking Grow higher-order thinking and artistic thinking in students. Reflect at all levels. Move up Bloom's taxonomy from simple to complex by targeting questions at all six levels. Ask students to do the following:

- Remember what they did or what they learned (Knowledge)
- Understand what they learned (Comprehension)
- Apply what they learned (Application)
- Break their learning down into the individual steps or parts (Analysis)
- Put it together in new ways by relating and comparing with other learning (Synthesis)
- Make judgments and evaluations about their learning (Evaluation)

Use Reflection as Entree to Assessment Assess a lesson's general success by taking reflection questions from the lesson objectives. As you write your lesson plan, make a habit of immediately turning objectives into three reflection questions. Write them first—before you complete your full lesson plan—so they play into your instructional design and connect the lesson's start and conclusion. (The planning model in chapter 14 features reflection as a consistent part of the lesson and unit.)

Use reflection questions to spotlight what was featured and hear what students understood. Their insights convey enough for you to keep tabs on their artistic growth and provide a basis for notating quick daily grades for them (as described in chapter 11).

Reflect and Respond

Do you regularly reflect with your professors and peers? Journal?

Essential Reflection Question: "What Did You Learn?"

The most basic culminating reflection question is, "What did you learn today?" or **"WDYL?"** (as you write it in your lesson plan). This question asks students to recall specifics, mentally synopsize what happened during class, and say or journal what was learned. The responses (oral or written) validate to everyone what was learned by naming it. There is also value in processing it aloud to further validate, review, and synopsize key points so that everyone benefits from hearing what others learned, as in the example on page 273.

Create follow-up questions from the responses—similar to facilitating a conversation. This keeps questioning and responding student centered and student focused. For example:

- "Why is that important to you?"
- "What does that bring to mind?"
- "What does this mean to you?"
- "What would have happened if. . . ?"
- "What can you do as a result of this class that you couldn't do before?"
- "What do you know today that you didn't know yesterday about dance?"

WDYL springboards to individual journaling. The class discussion plants many ideas on which to elaborate, so individual journal writing afterward tends to be more focused and elaborative. This increases the comfort level for reflective journaling.

Dance Criticism

Dance criticism is a process to describe, analyze, interpret, and evaluate specific dance works. It uses aesthetic principles—mainly the choreographic principles of design (PODs)—to evaluate the artistic quality of a specific work. Its purpose is to offer insight into a choreographic work by illuminating its creative process and its choreographic components. The process lets an audience evaluate how well a work accomplishes its overall artistic goals or its intent. Thus criticism inquires into the quality of design as well as its delivery by the performers.

As you see in figure 9.4, performance requires the delivery of a dance design. You take the quality of the design and delivery into account to measure its total aesthetic value. A critique of both is needed to determine how the work stands up according to broadly accepted aesthetic criteria. Both are also

Sample Class Closure on Symmetry

One way to end activity class is in a circle where each person says what he or she learned. (No repeats are allowed, which keeps concepts flowing and sharpens listening skills.) There are general benefits to be had from WDYL as well as specifics.

Teacher Question: "What Did You Learn Today?"

Student Responses

- The first person might say, "I learned that **symmetry** is a shape that is the same on both sides."

- The second, "I learned that symmetry means balanced equally on each side."

- The third, "I learned that symmetry has a center line running through it in the middle so you could fold it over and each side would match."

- The fourth, "I learned that my body facing affects whether my symmetrical shape is seen as symmetrical or asymmetrical by an audience."

- The fifth, "I learned you can move in symmetrical shapes, but it takes a lot of concentration."

- The sixth, "I had already learned symmetry in math, so I learned to take it into space."

- The seventh, "I know about symmetry from art and architecture, and I think dance is like moving architecture."

Reflect on Students' Responses: Which of the Following Are True?

Specific to the Lesson's Topic

- __ The entire class gets a review of symmetry as well as what happened in class.

- __ Students who answer validate to themselves and others that they learned worthwhile information on symmetry.

Broader Than the Lesson's Topic

- __ Students must listen carefully to hear what is said in order to answer differently.

- __ Students without an initial response can get ideas from others' comments to elaborate on.

- __ Students leaving class can say what they learned to those who were not in the class.

- __ Students coming out of the class may be better dance advocates.

- __ You gain a sense of how well the content was learned.

- __ You gain a sense of who learned what.

- __ You have a better feel for assessing individual student's learning.

- __ You learn whether to go on to new material or to stay with this topic longer.

Add Aesthetic Reflections

Extend this closure activity into aesthetic valuing by asking valuing questions:

- "What of value did you learn today?" (Describe)

- "How can this increase your technical skill?" (Analyze)

- "How is that better than what you did last week?" (Analyze)

- "What is an aesthetic downside of using too much symmetry in a dance?" (Evaluate)

After students master WDYL, add extensions. For example:

- "How does that relate to what you learned yesterday (or last week)?"

- "How does that stretch you as an artist?"

- "Why do you need to know that?"

- "Can you use this in other subjects?"

- "How does this relate to science, social studies, or language arts?"

- "Does the art of dance depend on that?"

Teacher 1

A young teacher uses quarterly paper-and-pencil tests to nudge students to reflect on the significance of what they learned during the quarter. It is a way to help students make global connections among the individual parts that were taught day by day. He wants to know what sense students make of all the information and of what value it is to their education and to their aesthetic development. At the end of each test are three reflective thinking questions. Students choose one to respond to—and if time permits others. The students' reflective thinking is not built into classroom work or studio work or shared with peers through discussions in their class. The teacher believes that individual reflection is more meaningful than reflection shared with a group.

Teacher 2

This teacher takes an inquiry approach to technique class and imparts valuable technical knowledge that increases student skills. She does not start and stop the class to talk. She keeps the class moving and building and makes her comments while students move so they may immediately apply the corrections and the information. She uses cool-down stretches during the last 6 minutes of each class to bring bodies down and help minds focus through review and reflection. "What did you learn today that helps you be a better dancer?" she asks while they stretch. Students share their thoughts with her and the entire class. One person's response often triggers a related response in another, helping ideas to piggy-back and responses to easily flow. All answers are acceptable when answered in the context of the question—some serious, some light. Students expect to reflect aloud at the end of class, so they pay more attention during class to information and teacher feedback, to what they are doing, and to how they are assimilating the skills into their dancing. The responses tell the teacher what of the class experience was assimilated as well as what should be revisited during the next class with that group. Students believe there is continuous growth in the class and speak about it to their friends.

Teacher 3

This teacher believes that reflection is necessary for meaningful learning. She has students write reflection journals on what they learn in her class and how it affects their growth as dancers and choreographers. She receives these confidential journals on alternate Fridays to read and reflect on. She writes thoughtful, reflective comments back to the students, which helps develop great respect between teacher and student. Students believe they have a personal time with the teacher and can share what is going on in their own artistic development. Because the teacher is competent, experienced, and caring, she has much of value to share with students in individual journals. Journals give her the inside track to alert her to possible needs or to avert problems between students. She can offer guidance and target assistance in the journals as well as follow up with individuals after class quietly and efficiently.

Teacher 4

This teacher had problems with students not reading assigned chapters and articles. There are important articles he believes are necessary to student development that contain information worthy of serious classroom discussion. He does not assign meaningless reading but takes care to target reading assignments of specific value. He discovered that using reflection journals is the best way to ensure that students not only read the assignments but do so thoughtfully and attentively. He gives reflective thinking and guided reading questions along with every assignment. He lists what is expected from each article. Students then read and synopsize the article, write about its value to the field, and reflect on its value to them. On the day each assignment is due, they submit journals for peer review as a way to start discussion. Thereby discussions have been richer than if students had only read the articles without writing about them. The depth of discussions has surpassed the teacher's expectations.

Teacher 5

This teacher likes to put students in the hot seat. She has students do individual reflective thinking at a desk with paper and pencil, with time ticking away in a test setting, where students are nervous about a grade. She does not prepare them for reflection in the classroom but expects them to reflect under pressure of a grade. Sometimes students don't see the relevance of such thinking and write all around the question without saying much of depth or significance. The teacher often gives reflection questions as a part of open-book tests so students have access to basic information while being asked to write of its value to education or to the field of dance. Some students do well with this type of reflection, but some do not.

- Which of these teachers is insightful about the values of reflection? Why?
- Did any teacher assimilate all aspects of reflection into her or his teaching? Explain.
- Which reflective aspects from these five will you incorporate? Which will you abandon? Why?

REGULAR MODEL:

Design + delivery = performance

6DC CORNERSTONE MODEL:

Aesthetic design + artistic delivery = aesthetic value

FIGURE 9.4   Performance and aesthetic value formulas.

needed to hear how well the work satisfies the beholder (the dance critic).

Professional dance critics give us new windows into dance. They show us other perspectives. They peel off different layers of meaning that we would miss on our own. They make inferences that prompt us to make comparisons we'd have missed. They spark thoughtful debate about artistic issues. They teach us to relish the intellectual side of the art. They show by example how to analyze and unpack a work. They judge works and make interpretations that are supported by artistically defined and personally defined criteria. As professional critics illuminate the process of evaluating dance, they also extend our expressive language for dance. Critics from diverse cultures shed light on new forms and show us different aesthetic perspectives. They greatly broaden our view of dance. Bring their perspectives into the middle and high school curriculum.

Student dance critics use critical inquiry. They learn dance vocabularies to express their thoughts and feelings about a dance work (i.e., movement and the varied conceptual vocabularies). They analyze works from the viewpoints of dancer, choreographer, dance historian, and critic. Such diverse critical inquiry results in multidimensional aesthetic awareness of dance works.

Young creative dancers who explore the dance elements and shape them into dance studies understand the creative process. They can reflect on what they create and respond to peer works. Get them to describe and analyze dance using the BSTERs—the stepping-stones to criticism. Use creative dance to sharpen critic eyes and develop descriptive vocabulary.

Unpacking a Professional Dance Work: A Four-Step Critique

Unpack choreography by professional choreographers. Students are handicapped if all they see and evaluate is student choreography. Peer works won't move them forward aesthetically. Students have to see something of artistic depth and value to have their aesthetic awareness raised. That is why unpacking great dance works is vital to an aesthetically driven curriculum at all ages.

To critically inquire is to take a dance work apart piece by piece to see what is in it and how it is put together. Examine the tools the choreographer used to construct it. Analyze parts of the work as well as the whole. Look for clues under the surface to find out what makes it work. Investigate in depth how the choreographer used the craft of choreography. For example, examine specifics:

- Space—overall spatial interest; use of general and personal space, negative and positive space, and air pathways and floor pathways; use of levels, directions, range, and all the elements associated with space. Then determine whether space is part of the overall design or a major point of emphasis.

- Time—tempo, pulse, rhythmic interest, immediacy of performance in time, effectiveness of accompaniment. Then determine the degree of emphasis placed on this element—whether timing or rhythmic interest is emphasized or merely part of the design.

- Energy and dynamics—textures such as sharp and smooth, the weight of the movement, the flow, the amount of strength behind the movement, qualities and accents. Then determine whether the way energy is directed in dynamics is part of the overall rise and fall of movement or one of the major points of emphasis.

- Relationship—to space, to another person or object, to a group, to other elements of dance. Then determine the degree of emphasis placed on this element—whether the dance is about relationships, whether it emphasizes relationships of dancers in space or time, or whether the relationships are simply a part of the overall design without being emphasized.

- Production aspects—costumes, lights, accompaniment, selection of cast, technical strength of performers, number of dancers selected, overall performance quality.

- Design principles—how the work measures up to the aesthetic principles of design (PODs), which are the guiding aesthetic principles of form in choreography. The age and stage of the student determine which PODs are pertinent (for this information, see the DCC Framework in this chapter). After students have evaluated dance using the PODs through K-12, by graduation they are adept at unpacking dance works and critiquing. Two good rules are to

> use BSTERs for the main descriptive vocabulary for dance and

> use the PODs to evaluate and judge artistic quality of the composition.

Build viewing and responding skills year by year from first through twelfth grades (i.e., describing, interpreting, and critiquing skills). Start guided viewing and criticism with first graders. Help them read dances. Begin by asking beginners to respond to short slices or excerpts from video works by asking, "What did you see?" Soon they will be ready for specific criteria with which to observe slices of professional works and peer creative dances.

Review the aesthetic–artistic stages of progression in chapter 4. Let these stages guide the pace at which you try to advance students to the next level of awareness. Critiquing dance is necessary to advance aesthetic growth, just as are choreographing and performing.

Dance criticism evaluates the effectiveness of a dance choreography—its successful and unsuccessful parts. Dance criticism (i.e., critiquing) is an incremental process in four steps. Use them one after the other to uncover the artistic merits of a dance work. The four steps describe, analyze, interpret, and evaluate a dance work. This Four-Step Critique operationalizes earlier emphases:

- The dance elements (chapter 6)
- The artistic principles of design—PODs (chapter 7)

- All the dance vocabularies (chapter 6)
- Higher-order thinking skills—HOTS (chapter 4)

Critiquing Using the Feldman–Bloom Models

Dance's Four-Step Critique is based on a visual art criticism model developed by art professor Edmund Feldman and later adapted by Mac Arthur Goodwin. It generates critical and creative thinking (NSDE 4) by using all six levels of Bloom's taxonomy of higher-order thinking (see chapter 4). As you see in figure 9.5, each step in the Four-Step Critique incrementally advances aesthetic perception and awareness. It shows not only how Bloom's and Feldman's models independently support critical inquiry in dance but also, more important, how they combine to give dance an effective model for dance criticism. You ask the questions and facilitate, but let the students be the responders.

The Four-Step Critique teaches students to critically respond to full dance works. Emphasize Step 1 with beginners of any age to develop ability to see dance and use dance's vocabulary. Use Step 1 as a foundation (NSDE 4). As skill progresses, include more steps. Those who begin as kindergartners usually can handle all four steps by grade 4 or 5. The level of responses is more complex with older responders. The four steps also work with adults.

Step 1 is called "aesthetic scanning." When you facilitate a group scan, draw out everyone's descriptions. The better the scan, the better the rest of the process. Get off to a good start with a good scan. Invite the class to paint a remembered word collage of everything they noticed to

- increase focus and ability to see a dance,
- increase attention to details and expand perceptive skills,
- increase interest in the work,
- apply descriptive language,
- create a composite snapshot of the dance's memorable qualities,
- remediate those who may have missed details, and
- fully engage visual learners.

> ". . . the more I made public my own questions about my work, the more willing I was to hear other people's reactions to it."
>
> —Liz Lerman (Lerman and Borstel 2003, p. 6)

Bloom's general	Feldman visual art	Dance criticism: Four-Step Critique	Processes:
Know	Describe	Describe (aesthetic scanning)	Simple
Comprehend	Describe	Describe (aesthetic scanning)	↑
Apply	Describe/Analyze	Integrate (make inferences and connections)	
Analyze	Interpret/Analyze	Analyze	
Synthesize	Interpret	Interpret	↓
Evaluate	Evaluate/Judge	Evaluate	Complex

FIGURE 9.5 Here you see how the Four-Step Critique incorporates aspects of Bloom's taxonomy and how it compares to the Feldman art criticism model (Feldman 1967, p. 469).

Related Info

Following is the thumbprint of the Four-Step Critique for professional works.

Step 1: Describe (aesthetic scanning)

Step 2: Analyze

Step 3: Interpret

Step 4: Evaluate

Step 1—Describe (to Aesthetically Scan for Details)

Main question: "What do you see?"

During this step, invite students to recall all the details they can and to describe them. Notice the dance elements that are featured in the dance work. Observe as much detail as possible, including shapes, postures, gestures, movement patterns, use of space, use of timing, use of dynamics, and relationships. Describe the movement. Also ask students to describe other aspects of the dance such as costumes, lighting, stage set, period of dance, and dance style. Share remembered details orally to re-create a collective experience of the work and to start a conversation about it.

- Purpose: Step 1 paints a word collage of the collective experience for all viewers. This vital step helps all viewers recall the dance work and get in the habit of looking at dance, paying

attention to detail, and sharing their insights and observations. Appropriate for all age levels, it is a necessary preanalysis stage that increases students' ability to see movement and build vocabulary for dance.

- Age: In kindergarten and first grade, this may be as far as you want to proceed with criticism to get young learners to see and talk about dance (cf., using Bloom's knowledge and comprehension levels).

- Sample questions:
  > What is the feeling of the work?
  > Can you respond to the work with one word?
  > What is most noticeable about the work?
  > What is most memorable? What is a vivid detail?

Step 2—Analyze (to Look at Its Parts)

Main question: "How is the dance work organized?"

During this step, students collect facts. They notice how the choreographer used the dance elements in the dance. They notice whether the principles of design are effectively used in the choreography. They notice how the dancer executes the work.

- Purpose: This step breaks down the details and looks at the structure of a dance work.

277

- Age: It is an appropriate critical thinking step for students above grade 2. (This relates to analysis in Bloom's taxonomy.)
- Sample questions:
  > What type of lines, shapes, and patterns do you see in the work?
  > Are similar lines, shapes, or patterns repeated in the dance?
  > What movement motifs reappear throughout the work?
  > Is the dance work centered on a theme or a story, or is it abstract?
  > What is the most dominant feature of the dance?
  > How is the work organized? How many sections are there?
  > How competently do the dancers perform the work?
  > What does the choreographer emphasize in this dance?
  > How would you analyze the choreographic quality separately from the performance quality?

> How does the work flow dynamically? Through space?
> What are the points of highest and lowest interest?
> How are other art forms used in the production?
> How does the accompaniment support the movement?

Step 3—Interpret (to Decode Its Meaning)

Main questions: "What is happening?" "What does the choreographer want to say?"

Let the clues you collected in Step 1 (description and aesthetic scanning) and Step 2 (analysis) lead students to discover ways to interpret the meaning of the dance work.

- Purpose: This step invites students to relate what they see to what they know. They apply the details in Step 1 (description and aesthetic scanning) and Step 2 (analysis) to interpret what the choreographer is trying to say—to find the intent of the choreography.
- Age: This step is appropriate for all students above grade 2. (This relates to synthesis in Bloom's taxonomy.)
- Sample questions:
  > What is the mood of the work?
  > What is the expressive meaning of the shapes, movements, and relationships in the dance?
  > How does this choreographer use movement and music to create mood or tell a story?
  > What position has the choreographer taken about the situation portrayed in this work?
  > What does this dance mean? How does the movement convey intent and meaning?
  > How does the group analysis help you speculate about its meaning?
  > What is the choreographer wanting most to communicate?
  > Is there anything else you would have liked to see in this piece?

Use Step 2 (analyze) to focus on a dance's details. Ask questions such as these: "What types of lines, shapes, or patterns do you find in the work?" "Is it telling a story (representational) or abstract?" "What is the most dominant feature in the dance?"

Step 4—Evaluate (to Judge Its Artistic Value)

Main questions: "What do you think of the dance work?" "How effective is the dance work?"

During this step students evaluate how the dance is put together. They evaluate the degree to which the choreography succeeds or fails, and they assess the merits of the work. They make aesthetic judgments and artistic evaluations about the whole dance or its parts.

- Purpose: This step uses critical thinking to evaluate the level of effectiveness of a dance work.
- Age: This is important for all students above grade 3. (This relates to evaluation in Bloom's taxonomy.)
- Sample questions:
  > How does the work compare with other dances that you know as far as artistic worth?
  > How does it stack up with other great choreographies?
  > How does it measure up to other works by this choreographer?
  > How would you evaluate it according to the principles of design?
  > What is your personal opinion of the work?
    – Was it well-crafted?
    – Did it have a clear beginning, middle, and end?
    – Was the work meaningful to you? If so, how?
  > How effective is the dance work as an example of modern dance, ballet, or other dance style?
  > What place does this dance work have in dance history?
  > Do you see influences of other cultures in this dance work? If so, what?
  > Would you buy a ticket to see this work performed live?
  > Based on your close observation and the group discussion, how successful was this choreography?

Adapted, by permission, from Mac Arthur Goodwin.

Extending the Four-Step Critique

You can also extend the Four-Step Critique at any step as needed. Extensions do not replace a step: They take it further. They are not to be the emphasis. There are two ways to extend inquiry: by crossing disciplines and by personalizing.

Crossing Disciplines—"How Does This Relate To . . . ?" Investigate how topics or issues brought out during the four steps relate to topics and themes in other academic disciplines (e.g., regionalism in social studies, shapes in art, patterns in math). (This extension relates to application and analysis in Bloom's taxonomy.)

Personalizing—"How Does It Make You Feel?"

- How do you relate to this dance work?
- Is there an emotional reaction to it? If so, what kind?
- Does your emotional response add value to the dance above its own aesthetic worth?
- Does this dance satisfy you? In what ways?

(This extension relates to application and analysis in Bloom's taxonomy.)

Using Personal and Peer Critiques

Personal critiques are aesthetic responses to live choreographers. Personal critiques are another form of critical inquiry. They rely on the two main aesthetic questions:

1. How does it stack up to accepted aesthetic standards? (communal aesthetics)
2. How does it communicate to me or please and satisfy me? (personal aesthetics)

One main difference between critiquing a great work by a professional company and responding to peer works is that you are face to face with peers as you critique their work. Because our own creations are so personal, there is normally insecurity involved. To constructively point out what does and doesn't work requires a supportive, analytical approach built on mutual respect and trust. Although you lead peer critiques much the same as you do professional ones, you must

- keep a psychologically safe environment for the creator and
- be sure the critical friends have and use criteria by which to evaluate peer works.

Critical friends in grades 3 through 5 give insightful feedback to each other. As they reach middle and high school, they need a more in-depth process that is structured and nonthreatening. One of the best is by Liz Lerman. (Lerman is a professional contemporary dance choreographer who founded the Liz Lerman Dance Exchange in 1976. Not only does she take a collaborative approach to dance making, but she also often makes time at the end of performances for audiences to give facilitated feedback about what they saw. Her dance–theatre breaks boundaries between ages—some of her dancers are over 60 and not all members are professional dancers—and between stage and audience, and it takes dance into the community to bring people together. This multigenerational company resides near Washington, DC.) Lerman's process circumvents resentment or defensiveness about critique, for as Lerman pointed out, "When defensiveness starts, learning stops" (Lerman and Borstel 2003, p. 21).

Lerman's Critical Response Process gives a constructive step-by-step way to engage the choreographer and a group of critical friends in facilitated dialogue. It is one of the most effective face-to-face critiquing methods. Lerman created the process to gain useful feedback on her choreography, and the process evolved over time to address other forms of critical feedback in the arts and in the workplace. Its goal is to push the creator's thinking forward about his or her work. It is deliberate inquiry.

Not only is the process beneficial for the creator, but responders begin to realize the numerous ways people see art as they go further and further into the work. Such a group process encourages responders to be less opinionated and more inquiring when they look at dances. It creates helpful response; it can be used with all ages, but it is essential for gifted and advanced high school dance classes. Lerman explains how she came to it:

> . . . the more I saw of other peoples' work, the more it became clear to me that what I criticized in their work was that it wasn't like mine. If I didn't see my own ideas confirmed in the work of others I found myself being very critical—my critical comments told me more about myself than the nature of the work I was seeing.

> So, . . . I have been evolving a system of peer response. It is grounded first and foremost on my own experience as a choreographer. I discovered that the more I made public my own questions about the work, my work, the more eager I was to engage in a dialogue to "fix" the problem. (Lerman 1993, p. 4)

Related Info

Following is the thumbprint of Lerman's Critical Response Process for one-on-one (two-way) feedback.

Step 1: Statements of meaning

Step 2: Choreographer as questioner

Step 3: Neutral questions from responders

Step 4: Permissioned opinions

Adapted, by permission, from Liz Lerman's Critical Response Process℠.

Using Lerman's Critical Response Process as Inquiry for Peer Review

Lerman's structured process requires a choreographer and his or her completed choreography, critical friends as observers, and a facilitator (you or another teacher who is adept at the process).

The facilitator sensitively modulates critique and draws out the student choreographer—helping her form questions about her work—when needed. Young creators need to learn how to ask questions about their works. The facilitator sets the tone of the dialogue, to keep it moving and draw it to a conclusion.

- *Step 1—Statements of meaning:* In a positive way, observers tell the choreographer what communicated, what had meaning for them, and what was memorable, delightful, or unique. (Creators take time to let those comments soak in.)

- *Step 2—Choreographer as questioner:* Creators first say what they hope to achieve and then ask critical friends for feedback as to how well they achieved it. Specific questions are better than broad ones (e.g., "Should I have exited the stage at the end or held my pose while the lights dimmed?")

- *Step 3—Neutral questions from responders:* Observers ask neutral questions about the work. Questions must remain neutral to allow the responder (creator) to process reflectively and to be receptive to hearing what others are saying. Asking neutral questions tends to open dialogue with a creator whereas opinionated questions close it. You can get your point across with a neutral question, and it's not threatening or awkward for the creator (e.g., "What were you trying to accomplish in the last section?").

- *Step 4—Permissioned opinions:* Observers ask permission to offer an opinion on a certain aspect (e.g., "I have an opinion about the number of dancers. Do you want to hear it?").

Facilitating the Critical Response Process

Use as many of the steps as your students are ready for, but know them all so you can take the process as far as it can usefully go with a group. Adapt the process for younger creators to introduce them to the process. For example, I incorporate aspects of the first two steps with second graders—mostly adapted as affirmations—as soon as they have a dance elements vocabulary. It starts them looking for something they enjoyed or remembered. Although Lerman's Step 1 more correctly deals with meaning, it (Step 1) introduces the critiquing process to children and sets the tone for using it more fully in subsequent years. Because many young children are not yet ready for Step 2, I help them ask their questions (e.g., "Would you like to ask about your level changes?"), a form of scaffolding that introduces them to the process (see chapter 4).

By the time students are in middle school, they can use the full process as intended to critique. Occasionally the nature of a work intrigues upper-level students so much that they want to talk further about its background or its message. In the presence of the entire group—still with the facilitator—the choreographer may decide that he wishes to try some editorial changes for audience feedback. This is especially useful in middle and high school, where peer support is so important.

Before you take this process into a K-12 setting, learn the full process and bring it into one of your own choreography classes, using it with your own peers. Then you will know the process well enough to adapt it for young beginners. Find more detail and particular help with the process on Lerman's Web site, www.danceexchange.org, or in her handbook on the subject (see Rich Resources).

Developing Critical Inquiry Skills

The NSDE expects you to consciously stimulate critical thinking (NSDE 4) and engage students to discuss meanings in dance with competence and confidence (NSDE 3). Critical inquiry depends on how you apply the verbs in figure 9.3. Let's use them to practice inquiring into a great work.

A great work is valuable because it has so many aspects that can be highlighted as part of a lesson.

You can use one dance to teach choreography, technique, dance history or anthropology, and critiquing. It is unlikely you can exhaust a work's learning potential.

Do this exercise with other dance specialists or peers. In groups of three or four, practice writing substantive and challenging inquiries into a great work. Before you start, review the sample inquiry questions from the viewpoint of each cornerstone in chapter 5. Pick a solo work to practice on such as "I Want to Be Ready," Dudley Williams' memorable solo in Alvin Ailey's *Revelations*.

This process helps you unravel a dance work for the purpose of planning instruction and inquiry. It is how you find big ideas to teach in dance and see how the four cornerstones are integrated into a dance work. By repeat viewings to practice turning comments into questions for student inquiry, you are on the road to integrating instruction.

First Viewing

Watch a dancer perform the entire solo on video. (It is all right to be unfamiliar with the work.) Say aloud what you notice as you watch it. This is Step

---

Reflect and Respond

Most students are more familiar with watching television than live performances. With television they can get up and leave in the middle of a performance or carry on a conversation with others in the room during a program. Teach students that live performance audience responsibilities are different. When students attend performances and respond to them, remind them that dance is a two-way communication.

Anne Green Gilbert's "audience A's" give clues to remind audiences of their responsibilities during a performance:

- Attending
- Allowing
- Appreciating
- Applauding

Add two others after the performance:

- Analyzing
- Articulating

How do these six "A" words help you express to students the role they play as audience at live performances?

Reflect and Respond

How many of the following desired outcomes are accomplished by being a critical friend and observing peer works to offer qualitative feedback?

- Being a critical friend develops observational skills early, skills needed for dance appreciation at all ages.
- It gives a specific task to focus on, which increases attention span.
- It develops attention to detail.
- It gives a break from moving large muscles and a chance to observe closely.
- It helps students learn how to see and read dances using the elements vocabulary.
- It takes students outside their own movement long enough to see how the creative process produces other appropriate responses (from subjectivity to objectivity).
- It gives the critic ideas to elaborate on in her own work.
- It motivates the creator to complete the work and show it for others to value.
- It reinforces word recognition (and possibly reading skill and word comprehension).
- It holds students accountable for success.
- It rewards success from the performer and encourages students to try harder next time.
- It shows what success looks like.
- It sometimes raises the standard of excellence by virtue of seeing excellent performances.
- It stimulates more ideas and creativity from the viewer.

1: aesthetic scanning. For example: "What a difficult balance to hold. He must really have strong abs." When you finish, write some of them down.

Second Viewing

Examine the entire solo a second time with a pause remote. This time turn your comments around. Change each one from a comment to a question. Turn as many comments into questions as you can while you view this work, pausing to write them down. For example:

- "What do you notice about the way the dancer balances in this work?"
- "What kind of physical conditioning might a dancer need to perform this dance?"
- "How difficult would this dance be to perform? Why?"

Third Viewing

Closely observe the solo a third time to find additional, deeper questions. Use a remote control with a pause button. Ask questions about movement motifs, tempo, contrasts, unity, and variety in the movement. Ask about the work's dance elements. Ask about its relation to the rest of *Revelations*. Ask about its spatial design, use of full body and isolated gestures of small body parts, focus, and dynamics. Include questions about the music, costume, and sets. Write all your questions and pool them with the group. Prepare to use them with a group of students. Also discuss what ideas you see in the work to use as an example for technique class, for dance history, for creating and composing. See if you can now integrate the cornerstones in a unit around this work based on your inquiry questions.

Dance Cornerstone Curriculum (DCC) Framework

Cornerstone 4 (C4) integrates cognitive content with kin-aesthetic skills.

This part of the DCC Framework (following Rich Resources) shows what students should know and be able to do to achieve NDSEs 3 and 4. It shows how concepts develop from kindergarten through twelfth grade and breaks concepts down into teachable chunks. C4 is divided into four sequential parts: primary (K-2), elementary (3-5), middle (6-8), and high school (9-12). Its developmental continuum goes from simple to complex to adapt to your learners.

- Look across the chart for sequence as to how each concept builds as students learn.
- Look down the chart for substance as to the scope, what is essential to include.
- For older beginners, spiral back to the first column to pick up basic skills rather than start at their age level.

Questions to Ponder

1. How does developing a verbal and written vocabulary for dance contribute to aesthetic education?
2. Recall the list of words from Bloom's taxonomy that enable you to ask targeted ques-

Notebook/Portfolio: Perspectives Notebook

THREE-ACT REFLECTION:
WRITE–ASSESS–REFINE (C4)

Act I: Write

Prepare a three- to four-page typed paper for your Perspectives Notebook that expresses what Cornerstone 4 contributes to educational dance. Address the specific criteria without using them for an outline. Use them first for Act I as composition criteria and for Act II as review criteria.

C4 Composition Criteria (and Review Criteria)

___ Explains applied aesthetics and tells how they are used

___ Clarifies the difference between collective and personal aesthetics

___ Clarifies the difference between applied aesthetics and the philosophy of aesthetics

___ Identifies and explains all the major aspects of this cornerstone

___ Explains how applying the aesthetic cornerstone across the dance discipline increases a student's education in dance as art

___ Explains how the teacher accesses higher-order thinking (analysis, synthesis, and evaluation) by applied aesthetics

___ Explains the role of critical thinking in aesthetic education in dance

___ Identifies the steps of aesthetic scanning and dance criticism

___ Makes a case for editing, refining, and increasing the artistic integrity of one's work (i.e., technique, performance, somatics, choreography, composition, and response to dance)

___ Relates inquiry to aesthetics

___ Distinguishes between reflecting and critiquing

___ Integrates national dance content and achievement standards

Use the structure for the Three-Act Reflection: Write–Assess–Refine in appendix A for Acts II and III (the same structural format and directions as the one in chapter 6).

tions and initiate focused inquiry (verbs for different levels of thinking). How do these verbs enable you to target specific levels of student critical thinking?

3. Do you journal about dance experiences and concerts you see? Of what value is it?

4. Which teacher in the case studies on page 274 has the most useful views of reflection in the classroom? How can you foster reflective thinking in your classroom?

5. How does this information add to or reshape your Statements of Belief (as explained in the Introduction)?

Rich Resources

RESOURCES

- Lerman, Liz, and John Borstel. *The Critical Response Process—A Method for Getting Useful Feedback on Anything You Make, From Dance to Dessert.* Takoma Park, MD: Liz Lerman Dance Exchange, 2003. Important reading to grasp all the ramifications of the critical review process and how to facilitate it.

- Guest, Ann Hutchinson. *The Adventures of Klig and Gop.* Bethesda, MD: National Dance Education Organization, 2001. Introduces children to Language of Dance symbols (motif writing).

- Guest, Ann Hutchinson. *Your Move—A New Approach to the Study of Movement and Dance.* London: Language of Dance Center, 1995. Introduces you to motif writing and Language of Dance symbols for quickly notating and initiating movement.

- Lavender, Larry. *Dancers Talking Dance: Critical Evaluation in the Choreography Class.* Champaign, IL: Human Kinetics, 1996. Although geared to university classes, it introduces Lavender's ORDER approach to critiquing compositions, which has applications in advanced high school choreography classes.

WEB SITES

- www.danceexchange.org: For Liz Lerman's work and writing.
- www.lodc.org: For Language of Dance materials.

- www.criticaldance.com: Criticaldance.com is run by dancers and dance writers dedicated to all types of performance dance—especially ballet and modern. It includes a moderated bulletin board, newsletters, and interviews with dance celebrities. It encourages wide-ranging debate on dance issues.

1.0   General Response to Dance

Grades K-2	Grades 3-5	Grades 6-8	Grades 9-12
1.1 Using dance vocabulary to respond			
1.1a BSTER vocabulary			
Views dances that have clear messages and ideas and responds to them. Identifies the dance elements that are prominent in a work.	Describes the BSTER elements that are prominent in a work and explains how selected ones are used.	Describes dance using a BSTER vocabulary and describes how the dance elements are used in a particular dance.	Uses the BSTER vocabulary to respond to dance and describe and analyze how the dance elements interact in a dance.
Increases number of words to describe dance.	Increases vocabulary for describing dance.	Increases vocabulary for describing and evaluating dance.	Increases use of BSTER vocabulary to critique works.
Accurately uses basic BSTER terminology to describe aspects of space (level, direction, pathway, body parts), time (fast, slow), and energy and dynamics (sharp, smooth, heavy, light).	Uses BSTER vocabulary to accurately describe aspects of time, space, and energy and dynamics.	Uses BSTER vocabulary to accurately describe aspects of time, space, energy and dynamics, and relationships.	Uses complete BSTER vocabulary to accurately describe aspects of time, space, energy and dynamics, and relationships.
Begins to use some BSTER words to describe own dances.	Uses more BSTER words to analyze dances of self, peers, and professionals.	Increases BSTER vocabulary. Uses it to analyze dances of self, peers, and professionals.	Uses BSTER vocabulary to analyze professional works in depth and respond to peer works.
1.1b Stylistic vocabulary			
Responds to different dance styles. Learns and uses basic stylistic vocabulary.	Acquires stylistic vocabulary including names of steps and motions for different dance styles and uses it to respond to dance.	Uses stylistic terminology while responding to modern dance, ballet, and other major dance styles.	Uses stylistic terminology to respond to major dance styles. Identifies stylistic steps, positions, and motions (such as arabesque in ballet, layout in jazz, jatis and adavus in Bharata Natyam and Kuchipudi).
_____	Increases stylistic vocabulary.	Increases stylistic vocabulary to include non-Western dance.	Increases stylistic vocabulary to include non-Western dance. Shifts aesthetic perspective as needed.
_____	_____	Responds to major dance styles and begins to acquire a perspective on their evolution.	Responds to dance styles and discusses their ongoing evolution.
1.1c Design vocabulary			
_____	_____	Discusses aesthetic principles of design in relation to observed compositions. Begins to use the PODs as an aesthetic vocabulary.	Discusses effective use of aesthetic principles of design in observed compositions. Incorporates this vocabulary to write, speak about, and evaluate dance as art.
1.1d Laban and Language of Dance (LOD) vocabulary			
Responds to symbols such as those in *The Adventures of Klig and Gop* (Ann Hutchinson Guest), which introduces children to LOD symbols.	Describes and analyzes dance movement based on basic Laban and LOD concepts, symbols, and vocabulary.	Describes, analyzes, and uses Laban and LOD vocabulary to respond to dance, read, and record movement in symbols.	Describes, analyzes, and uses Laban and LOD vocabulary to read and respond to dance and to accurately record movement in symbols.
1.1e Technical theatre terms			
_____	Uses theatre terms *upstage, downstage, stage left,* and *stage right.*	Uses correct terminology for stage areas, stage directions, and aspects of technical theatre production.	Uses correct terminology for stage areas, lighting, and aspects of technical theatre production.

Dance Cornerstone Curriculum Framework—C4: Analyzing and Critiquing from *Teaching Dance as Art in Education* by Brenda Pugh McCutchen, 2006, Champaign IL: Human Kinetics

1.0 General Response to Dance

Grades K-2	Grades 3-5	Grades 6-8	Grades 9-12
1.2 Appreciating dance			
1.2a Communication			
Enjoys observing the creative and expressive work of others.	Appreciates opportunities to observe the creative and expressive work of others.	Appreciates the communicative aspect of dance when movement is organized and presented with clarity.	Appreciates the power of dance as both an expressive art and a creative outlet for ideas, feelings, dramatic themes, and social issues.
————	Knows dance is especially powerful as an art form because it uses the human form to communicate directly to an audience.	Notices that dance is especially powerful as an art form because of its interplay of visual, auditory, and kinesthetic aspects.	Perceives the aesthetic power of dance by its interplay of the visual, auditory, and kinesthetic. Grasps the role of aesthetics in dance's ability to communicate.
1.2b Enjoys dance			
Enjoys participating in and observing a variety of dance styles.	Enjoys participating in and observing a variety of dance styles including performance and participation styles.	Enjoys participating in and observing a variety of dance styles. Broadens areas of dance interest in both performance and participation styles.	Finds intrinsic satisfaction in creating, performing, and responding to dance.
Enjoys viewing dance. Contributes to group discussions about dance.	Contributes to group discussions about dance as human expression.	Enjoys being part of group discussions about dance as art and expression.	Enjoys discussing dance as art and human expression.
1.2c Values the dance discipline			
Appreciates dance as a form of human activity.	Appreciates dance as a form of human expression.	Appreciates dance as a form of human expression and as an art form.	Appreciates dance as a form of human expression, as an art form, and as a creative phenomenon.
————	Acquires a perspective on dance as an arts discipline.	Acquires a perspective on dance as art and as a discipline to master.	Acquires a perspective on dance and appreciates dance from different perspectives: performer, critic, historian, anthropologist, and choreographer.
Values originality and creativity in dance. Also values quality performance in dance.	Values originality and creativity in dance. Also values quality performance in dance.	Values originality and creativity in dance. Also values skilled performance in dance.	Values originality and creativity in dance. Also values highly skilled performance.
Notices when peers concentrate while dancing.	Recognizes how focus, time, and energy are required to create quality dances.	Realizes it takes a choreographer's time, energy, and mental commitment to make a high-quality dance.	Realizes that the entire choreographic process requires mental, emotional, and physical commitment from the creator.
1.3 Using review criteria			
1.3a Uses review criteria based on choreographic criteria			
————	————	Creates review criteria based on choreographic criteria given in a dance assignment.	Creates review criteria from choreographic criteria given in a dance assignment.
Learns to see professional dance works according to several teacher-named criteria. Gives responses based on the criteria.	Uses review criteria taken from choreographic criteria to observe and respond to peer dance works. Determines the extent to which the criteria are addressed.	Determines the extent to which the criteria are met and artistic goals are achieved. Uses scoring rubrics with these criteria to give in-process feedback to peers.	Discerns how effectively a dance realizes its choreographic criteria. Uses scoring rubrics to give in-process feedback and culminating aesthetic critique to peers.

Dance Cornerstone Curriculum Framework—C4: Analyzing and Critiquing from *Teaching Dance as Art in Education* by Brenda Pugh McCutchen, 2006, Champaign IL: Human Kinetics

Grades K-2	Grades 3-5	Grades 6-8	Grades 9-12
1.3b Uses review criteria based on principles of design (PODs)			
Uses "viewing questions" to view and examine dance works for clarity, contrast, and sequence.	Uses review criteria based on several PODs: sequence, unity, contrast, repetition.	Uses review criteria based on selected PODs: climax, unity, transition, variety, contrast, repetition, and sequence.	Creates and effectively uses review criteria based on all the aesthetic PODs.
———	———	Creates aesthetically based review criteria that include the PODs. Uses rubrics.	Creates aesthetically based review criteria that include the PODs. Creates and uses rubrics.
1.3c Uses review criteria based on performance quality			
Participates in viewing activities to assess quality of performance.	Assesses performance quality of dancers based on a set of review criteria.	Reviews performance quality based on criteria for technical skill. Uses rubrics.	Reviews performance quality based on criteria for technical excellence.
———	———	Creates review criteria to judge performance quality.	Creates review criteria to judge performance quality.

1.4 Critical thinking

Grades K-2	Grades 3-5	Grades 6-8	Grades 9-12
1.4a Analysis			
Analyzes short dance works that relate to the topics being studied in dance (e.g., folk dance and modern works that demonstrate an idea or concept).	Analyzes dance performances as part of a study unit. Analyzes how dance is different from other forms of human movement.	Analyzes dance performances as part of a study unit.	Analyzes dance performances as part of a study unit and as independent study.
1.4b Synthesis			
———	Compares and contrasts dance ideas.	Compares, contrasts, and interprets meaning of different dance works and of aspects of the same dance.	Compares, contrasts, and interprets a variety of dance works. Links ideas found in different dance works and relates concepts.
1.4c Evaluation			
———	Analyzes and evaluates the overall impact of a work.	Analyzes and evaluates dance based on originality and visual and emotional impact.	Analyzes and evaluates dance based on stylistic and cultural issues.
1.4d Reflection			
Recalls what is learned in class and relates it to what is already known.	Recalls what is learned in class and relates it to what is known and to other subjects.	Recalls what is learned in class and relates it to what is known and to other subjects.	Recalls what is learned in class and relates it to a broad context.
———	Engages in individual and shared group reflection.	Engages in journaling and in individual and shared group reflection.	Engages in journaling and in individual and shared group reflection. Uses reflection to aid memory and recall and to contextualize learning.
———	Reflects on own works in progress and finished works in order to refine them.	Reflects on own works in progress and finished works in order to aesthetically refine them.	Uses aesthetic reflection to enhance choreography and creative work, performance, and critique.

Dance Cornerstone Curriculum Framework—C4: Analyzing and Critiquing from *Teaching Dance as Art in Education* by Brenda Pugh McCutchen, 2006, Champaign IL: Human Kinetics

1.0 General Response to Dance

Grades K-2	Grades 3-5	Grades 6-8	Grades 9-12
1.4d Reflection (continued)			
———	Reflects on dance as an art form and as a dynamic form of human expression. Begins to build a context for dance through reflection.	Uses ongoing reflection to build a context for dance. Considers the significance of dance to the world.	Reflects on dance as art and as phenomenon. Continues to build a context for dance through ongoing reflection.
———	Reflects on the creative process and products in dance.	Reflects on the creative process and products in dance. Uses aesthetic judgment to increase the aesthetic quality of both.	Reflects on the creative process and products of dance to enhance both. Uses aesthetic reflection to refine works and to contemplate issues related to dance as art.

2.0 Dance Criticism

Grades K-2	Grades 3-5	Grades 6-8	Grades 9-12
2.1 Artistic discrimination (or applied aesthetics)			
2.1a Applies discrimination			
Learns to make discriminating choices in creating dance and in dancing.	Makes artistically discriminating choices in dance making and in dancing.	Uses artistic discrimination when creating, performing, and responding.	Uses artistic discrimination when creating, performing, and responding. Refines work to raise its aesthetic standards.
Becomes an observant dance critic.	Becomes an observant and informed dance critic.	Observes dance works in detail to absorb aspects related to space, time, and energy and dynamics as well as body use and relationships.	Observes dance and uses aesthetic criticism to make judgments about the worth of a dance.
2.1b Applies aesthetic principles of design			
Seeks unity and clarity when creating short phrases. Recognizes dances that hold together with an order (sequence) and structure.	Recognizes how the aesthetic design principles of sequence, contrast, repetition, and unity increase artistic clarity. Becomes able to use them in dance making and identify them in critiques.	Recognizes how climax, contrast, sequence, unity, and variety make a dance aesthetically work. Uses them to increase artistic integrity of their work and critiques.	Choreographs and critiques with judicious use of the aesthetic design principles: unity, harmony, contrast, continuity, variety, sequence, transition, climax, repetition, and proportion.
———	Sees how contrasts tend to hold one's attention while sequence, transition, and unity make viewing satisfying.	Sees how artistic quality relies on the effective use of aesthetic principles.	Interrelates aesthetic principles to evaluate the artistic quality of dance works.
2.1c Assesses choreographer's aesthetic choices			
Discerns how selected accompaniment fits the mood and idea of the dance.	Discerns how choice of instrumental accompaniment or percussive score fits the mood and intent of the dance. Assesses its suitability of tempo, sound quality, and length.	Discerns how instrumental accompaniment or percussive score supports the movement as far as coexisting. Evaluates whether the dance is too dependent on music. Evaluates the appropriateness of the choice.	Evaluates how the aesthetic quality of a dance work is affected by accompaniment. Analyzes how effectively the choreography coexists with its accompaniment. Uses aesthetic discrimination in selections of own accompaniment.

Dance Cornerstone Curriculum Framework—C4: Analyzing and Critiquing from *Teaching Dance as Art in Education* by Brenda Pugh McCutchen, 2006, Champaign IL: Human Kinetics

Grades K-2	Grades 3-5	Grades 6-8	Grades 9-12
2.1c Assesses choreographer's aesthetic choices (continued)			
————	Assesses the suitability of the movement, the number of dancers participating, and the length of dance works.	Realizes that some dance ideas require numbers of dancers, whereas other ideas are best danced by few. Is aware that the length of a dance affects its effectiveness and clarity.	Responds to the interplay between the length of a piece and its clarity. Responds to the effectiveness of the number of dancers used in a work. Assesses the effectiveness of the number regarding how clearly the idea or concept is carried forward and meaning is conveyed.
2.1d Assesses production elements			
————	Recognizes how production factors such as poor-quality sound and props may undermine the aesthetic effect of a performance.	Realizes that sound quality, sets and props, costumes, and stage management contribute to the aesthetics of a performance.	Realizes how the aesthetic integration of choreography, technique, lighting, design, execution, costuming, sound, and props and set creates an aesthetic product.
2.1e Evaluates dancer's performance quality (professional and peer)			
Discerns differences between peer and professional dance performances.	Discerns how effectively a dancer communicates concepts, ideas, and feelings.	Discerns how effectively a dancer communicates concepts, ideas, and feelings. Uses dance as a tool to convey concepts, ideas, feelings, and themes.	Discerns how effectively a dancer conveys ideas, feelings, themes, stories, social issues, and abstract concepts.
Evaluates the performer's use of space.	Evaluates the performer's personal spatial awareness. Evaluates use of general space as in pathways, levels, and directions.	Evaluates the spatial qualities of performance, particularly of body design, use of negative and positive space, and the overall use of stage space when performing.	Evaluates the degree of spatial sensitivity each dancer brings to a performance. Evaluates overall sense of spatial design. Evaluates how performers project in space and relate to others on stage.
Evaluates how effectively dancers use timing: being in time with music and being aware of time as a design element.	Evaluates how effectively dancers use timing: with duration of movement, with musical accompaniment, and with movement cues.	Evaluates how effectively dancers use timing: timing of entrances and exits, initiation of movement phrases, relation to accompaniment.	Evaluates how effectively dancers use timing: timing of entrances and exits, initiation of movement phrases, relation to accompaniment. Evaluates how timing contributes to transitions.
————	Evaluates how dancers relate to each other in time and space.	Evaluates how dancers relate to each other as they share spatial proximity (partnering, contact, group dynamics) and time.	Evaluates how dancers relate to each other in complex moves requiring timing and spatial designing, such as turning, lifts, and traveling phrases.
————	Recognizes when performers move precisely; notes if the dancers are careless with movement quality.	Judges the quality of a performance and how it contributes to choreographic intent and clarity.	Evaluates the quality of a performance and how it contributes to choreographic intent and clarity.
2.1f Communicates meaning (clarity of intent)			
Discerns whether dance intent is clear. Discusses reactions to dance.	Discerns overall clarity of work and its ability to communicate. Discusses reactions to dance.	Discerns specific factors that contribute to the clarity of intent. Evaluates performers based on these factors.	Discerns individual factors that contribute to the clarity of intent. Refines own works to increase clarity of intent.

Dance Cornerstone Curriculum Framework—C4: Analyzing and Critiquing from *Teaching Dance as Art in Education* by Brenda Pugh McCutchen, 2006, Champaign IL: Human Kinetics

2.0 Dance Criticism

Grades K-2	Grades 3-5	Grades 6-8	Grades 9-12
2.2 Unpacks professional dance works (Four-Step Critique)			
2.2a Uses Four-Step Critique to describe, analyze, interpret, and evaluate great works			
Describes professional dance works.	Describes and analyzes professional dance works.	Describes, analyzes, interprets, and evaluates professional dance works.	Becomes adept at using the Four-Step Critique to unpack works.
2.2b Evaluates work's overall effectiveness			
———	Discerns effectiveness of great works based on their use of the dance elements.	Discerns effectiveness of great works based on their use of the principles of design (PODs) and dance elements.	Discerns effectiveness of great works based on their use of the PODs and the dance elements.
2.2c Responds to great works past and present (professionally choreographed)			
Views and responds to great works using the BSTER vocabulary.	Views and responds to great works of the past and present.	Views and critiques great works according to the PODs and choreographic structure used.	Critiques great works according to PODs and choreographic structure used. Critiques by describing, analyzing, interpreting, and evaluating all aspects of dances past and present.
2.2d Compares great works			
———	Views several works by different choreographers. Unpacks each and compares and contrasts them.	Compares more than one work by a choreographer. Unpacks them and compares their artistic processes.	Compares great works of dance by theme, by genre, by generation, by period, and by choreographer.
2.2e Responds to diverse world dance forms			
Views and responds to dances around the world—with an emphasis on folk dances.	Views and responds to dances around the world: world folk dances and classical dances. Learns the Four-Step Critique to unpack dance works.	Describes, analyzes, and evaluates diverse world dance forms, both classical and folk. Uses the Four-Step Critique to unpack dance works.	Evaluates world dance forms using the Four-Step Critique. Acquires a broad perspective on world dance. Evidences both a Eurocentric and non-Eurocentric perspective.
2.2f Uses overall artistic judgment			
———	Shows developing artistic judgment when critiquing professional dance works.	Uses artistic judgment when critiquing professional dance works. Incorporates principles of design and takes an aesthetic viewpoint.	Shows artistic judgment about critiquing professional dance works. Uses principles of design to increase a sound aesthetic viewpoint.
2.3 Personal critiques			
2.3a Critiques peer works			
Becomes a critical friend to make suggestions for improvement in dance-making.	Becomes an observant critical friend and gives feedback to works in progress.	Is an observant critical friend who gives feedback to works in progress and suggests editorial revisions to improve a work.	Is a highly observant critical friend who gives feedback to works in progress and suggests editorial revisions to improve a work.
As observer, closely watches and describes steps and movement of peers.	As observer, analyzes dances for clear execution of locomotor patterns, body designs, shaping, and energy and dynamics.	As observer, focuses on the choreographic intent to determine how the movement visually and kinetically clarifies the intent.	As observer, recognizes that a visually clear performance aids in accomplishing the communicative intent of a dance. Analyzes the extent to which a peer work achieves such status.

Dance Cornerstone Curriculum Framework—C4: Analyzing and Critiquing from *Teaching Dance as Art in Education* by Brenda Pugh McCutchen, 2006, Champaign IL: Human Kinetics

2.3b	Critiques own works		
———	Reflects on the quality of own work to make it better.	Qualitatively reflects and critiques own work to make it better.	Critiques own work and refines it.

2.3c	Uses Lerman's Critical Response Process		
———	Learns and applies the first three steps of Liz Lerman's four-step Critical Response Process.	Learns and uses Lerman's four-step Critical Response Process to dialogue with others about their work and inquire into its origins and intent. Asks to give feedback.	Uses Lerman's Critical Response Process to evaluate the effectiveness of a work, to dialogue with the choreographer about it, and to give critical feedback.

2.3d	Incorporates peer feedback to refine own compositions		
———	Applies peer feedback to refine work and make clearer aesthetic choices to create a better aesthetic product.	Applies qualitative peer feedback to edit and refine original work. Makes clearer aesthetic choices to create a better aesthetic product.	Realizes aesthetic quality of a piece evolves as movements are selected, discarded, refined, and redesigned. Edits and refines work in light of qualitative feedback.

Dance Cornerstone Curriculum Framework—C4: Analyzing and Critiquing from *Teaching Dance as Art in Education* by Brenda Pugh McCutchon, 2006, Champaign IL: Human Kinetics

Presenting Dance as Art in Education

Chapter

10

Constructing Artistic Bridges to Other Disciplines

"Children's dance should be studied for its own sake as a discreet body of knowledge in the K-5 school context. Furthermore it should be integrated with, not studied in the service of, other academic and artistic subjects."

—Loren Bucek (1992, p. 39)

This chapter connects dance with other subjects. We investigate standards from seven core subjects, which include the arts, to see how their national standards connect to dance and to establish dance's broader role in education. Lesson ideas and plans are offered that accomplish multicurricular goals in the core subjects of language arts, math, science, social studies, the other arts, foreign languages, and geography; we also add physical education. This chapter invites you to explore dance as it imports and exports concepts across the curriculum.

Relation to National Standards and Beyond

In chapter 1 we said that the purpose of K-12 educational dance is to broadly educate all students in and through dance as an art form in all its facets. So your primary responsibility is to teach a substantive, sequential, and comprehensive curriculum in dance. In addition, you are to teach through the arts to use every available avenue for a child's education. See how you can use other core subjects to enrich the teaching of dance and use dance to teach pertinent aspects of other core subjects. You will call on your background in subjects like language arts, math, science, physical education, social studies, and all the arts to further enrich education.

Make no mistake: Student competence in dance comes first in dance class. You have national standards in dance to achieve. You cannot abdicate dance standards to achieve those in other disciplines. But dance incorporates general educational concepts by its very nature. It organically pulls from other disciplines, especially language arts, science, social studies, and the other arts. Yet you have to know dance to meaningfully import other concepts without weakening the dance experience.

Invite students to explore the difference between the concepts *revolve* (circle) and *rotate* (turn), and then perform them in a dance. The dancer here is turning off-center and will next travel a circular pathway.

This chapter illuminates these national dance content standards:

NSDE 6: Making connections between dance and healthful living.

NSDE 7: Making connections between dance and other disciplines.

This chapter also incorporates specific Council for Basic Education (CBE) National Content and Achievement Standards in math, science, social studies, English, the arts, foreign languages, and geography that have commonalities with dance.

Dance naturally imports ideas from many disciplines to express through movement. To embody a concept through dance is to wear it a new way. Dance also draws on the other arts: music for accompaniment; visual art and design for sets, lighting, costumes, props, and other visual effects; and theatrical art. As one of the core subjects in America's schools, dance has a necessary role to play. Let's think about how.

Dance's Role Across the Curriculum

Dance is one of the few places in the school curriculum where groups get the opportunity to work together as a team for a common goal. There are too few academic subjects in which students get the satisfaction of collaboration to polish skills except in sports and in the performing arts. Even so, most games and sports emphasize peer competitiveness, which is not the norm in dance. So the highly refined, noncompetitive ensemble work happens in the performing arts. Because dance requires such personal interaction, it helps develop social skills: taking turns, staying together, relying on someone else who is leading, depending on each other, sharing leadership roles, being on time, being cooperative, keeping commitments.

Grow in your thinking of how school-based dance contributes to the well-rounded education of each child—not only for the sake of dance but for the sake of a student-centered curriculum. Use your artistic strength and academic curiosity to bring dance into sharper focus by importing outside concepts and exporting dance to other settings. For example, clarify scientific concepts by embodying them. Fifth graders who choreograph and perform a volcano dance using the scientific facts about volcanic eruption and the aftermath retain the scientific concepts long after paper-and-pencil tests are gone. The applied concepts stay with them. As students critique peer work using choreographic review criteria (such as the specific volcanic actions to be incorporated into the dance), they also critique it using aesthetic criteria (which include quality of the dance design and the dancer's performance). This makes students more aware of the volcanic connections and the effectiveness of the dance. After considering which volcanic actions are effectively incorporated into the composition—and which seismic process was left out—students immediately use the science terms, which makes them more likely to be remembered.

Similar concepts and skills naturally link us to other disciplines. Embodiment of these concepts and skills is especially valuable for kinetic learners (as performers) and visual learners (as critics). Don't abandon aesthetics. Integrate them into the creative stimulation you take from seismic science's volcanic eruption. A lesson like this furthers many things: dance composition and structure, earth science facts, critical thinking in dance, critiquing skills, the BSTER vocabulary—all to the aesthetic education of the student. This is aesthetically driven, student-centered learning.

Connecting Academic and Arts Standards

Each core subject listed in the Goals 2000—Educate America Act has national standards that are assessed by NAEP (see chapter 2). Although we emphasize reaching the dance standards, we are obligated to make instruction relevant to the total education of the child. Dance plays an important role in overall educational success of children. Study carefully the accountability standards that dance could address in other academics so that you can build meaningful bridges to other core subjects. Aim to cover as many national standards as feasible (dance and the dance-related aspects of other core subjects). Let the standards guide you to make an educationally viable, student-centered curriculum.

Goals 2000 named the arts a core subject, basic to education. It was the first time the arts (as they are referred to in these documents) were nationally recognized as subjects of equal value to other academics. The CBE oversaw the implementation of the national standards for core subjects that are basic to education. Notice that they call their content standards "vision statements" and their achievement standards "accountability standards." As you peruse all these core subject standards, remember that the dance specialist needs to incorporate the vision for other core subjects where it fits with dance—just as other core subjects should do for the arts. That way core subjects collectively work for the good of the child. (Note: Just as the arts consist of separate disciplines, different documents refer to the core subjects by various headings; therefore, you may see some variation such as language arts vs. English and history vs. civics, government, or social studies.) You can access all core subject standards through the Alliance for Curriculum Reform (see Rich Resources)

Standards for All Core Subjects

To get the big picture of how dance education affects a child's total education, look at the CBE's Core Subject Vision Statements in table 10.1. Notice that these vision statements are the overarching goals for all grade levels equivalent to dance's K-12 content standards. Then view the selected Core Subject Accountability Standards in table 10.2. Notice that the accountability standards are the learning objectives students are expected to achieve by fourth, eighth, and twelfth grades, which are assessed by NAEP and are equivalent to dance's K-12 achievement standards. These are just a sample selected from the full list because they have a relationship to dance. From them you get an idea of what is expected in other subjects and disciplines that (1) parallel dance's artistic processes, (2) relate to the NDSE, and (3) enable you to achieve not only dance standards but also standards of other disciplines.

Notebook/Portfolio:
Perspectives Notebook

Using tables 10.1 and 10.2, create at least one document for your Perspectives Notebook:

- Assignment 1: Investigate the arts category in table 10.1. Explain dance's role in advancing all the arts.

- Assignment 2: Investigate the other six core subjects in table 10.2. Briefly describe how dance interfaces with each one. Explain how dance can benefit from incorporating other subjects without compromising dance learning. How can these standards generate cross-curricular ideas?

Table 10.1 A Sampling of Core Subject Vision Statements

Subject area	Vision statements: K-12 students will
The arts	• Communicate at a basic level in dance, music, theater, and the visual arts, using knowledge and skill in the vocabularies, materials, tools, techniques, and intellectual methods of each discipline. • Communicate proficiently in at least one art form; define and solve artistic problems in that form with insight, reason, and technical proficiency. • Develop and present basic analyses of works of art from structural, historical, and cultural perspectives and from combinations of those perspectives. • Know about exemplary works of art from a variety of cultures and historical periods and understand historical development in the arts disciplines, across the arts as a whole, and within cultures. • Relate various types of arts knowledge and skills within and among the arts disciplines.
English	• Read and listen interpretively and critically; find pleasure and satisfaction in reading and writing. • Write and speak English effectively and eloquently to various audiences for various purposes. • Understand literature as the written expression of the human imagination and as a transmitter of culture and values. • Analyze, classify, compare, and contrast language and literature; make inferences; and draw conclusions from a variety of oral and written texts.
Foreign languages	• Communicate across cultures. • Demonstrate insight into own language and culture. • Acquire new information and knowledge through the new language. • Participate fully in multicultural communities and in the worldwide marketplace. • Demonstrate knowledge of the artifacts, expressions, and traditions of the new language and culture.
Geography	• Understand that the relationships between people, places, and environments depend on an understanding of space. • Understand why people live in certain places because of climate and topography. • Understand the geographic background of local, national, and global events and conditions. • Perceive the factors surrounding environmental degradation, the rational use of ocean resources, and nuclear arms and energy.
History and civics	• Show evidence of critical attitudes and analytical perspectives appropriate to the study of history and civics. • Demonstrate a tolerance for ambiguity and an understanding that not all societal problems have solutions or a single correct answer. • Explain the sequence of and connections among events in world history. • Describe the development of the United States and its role in world history. • Offer specific examples of the interplay of change and continuity, and analyze the force of the nonrational, the irrational, and the accidental in history and human affairs. • Recognize the difference between fact and conjecture, between evidence and assertion; frame useful questions for further investigation. • Understand the economic problems and institutions of the United States and world and make reasoned decisions as citizens, workers, consumers, business owners and managers, and members of civic groups.
Mathematics	• Understand the connections among related mathematical concepts and apply these concepts to other content areas. • Understand mathematics as a science of patterns. • Think and reason mathematically and apply mathematics to various situations. • Understand the principles of algebra and geometry and know how and when to apply them. • Use the power of reasoning to explore, make conjectures, and validate solutions. • Read, hear, write, and speak about mathematics in both everyday and mathematical language.
Science	• Know when and how to use scientific knowledge and habits of mind. • Understand measurement and mathematics as essential components of the sciences. • Understand the growth of scientific ideas, the roles played by diverse investigators and commentators, and the interplay between evidence and theory over time. • Know how to use accurately and safely scientific equipment and materials.

Vision statements are the Goals Statements that apply across kindergarten through grade 12. They are similar to content standards (NSDEs).

Reprinted from the Council for Basic Education (CBE).

Table 10.2   A Sampling of Core Subject Accountability Standards

Subject	By grade 4 the student will	By grade 8 the student will	By grade 12 the student will
The arts	Dance: Identify and demonstrate basic movements, understand choreographic principles, create and communicate meaning, competently perform folk dances from various cultures.	Dance: Create dance in collaboration with others, perceive details of style and choreographic structure, reflect on what is communicated, integrate dance with other art forms.	Dance: Demonstrate technical expertise and artistic expression through reflective practice, study, and evaluation of own and others' work; demonstrate an ability to communicate through dance; improvise choreography; consistently and reliably perform technical skills.
English	Understand familiar oral or written texts by using prior knowledge. Read and listen critically and interpretively; respond personally to, and comprehend the literal messages of, a variety of texts, including poems, essays, stories, and exposition. Recognize and write in a variety of forms, including narratives, journals, stories, poetry, exposition, articles, and instructions, for many purposes and audiences. Make connections both within and among oral and written texts. Describe images, sounds, and cadences in written and oral texts.	Demonstrate the ability to analyze structure and construct the meaning of literary and nonliterary texts. Generate ideas for writing, select and arrange them, find appropriate modes for expressing them, and revise what has been written. Speak clearly and expressively about ideas and concerns; adapt words and strategies to situations and audiences.	Make connections within and among texts. Analyze the structures, languages, and content of oral discourse, including speeches, lectures, and discussions in other disciplines. Read critically nonliterary documents and articles associated with other disciplines. Communicate in a variety of forms, both literary and nonliterary, and closely analyze one's own writing and oral skills. Analyze and evaluate world literature, including ancient and significant works, using knowledge of historical eras and of the role of literature as a transmitter of culture and values.
Foreign language			Use language appropriate to the task and context and negotiate meaning successfully. Use the new language to obtain, reinforce, and further knowledge of other disciplines; to acquire knowledge primarily available through the new language or cultures; and to expand personal knowledge and experience. Describe and analyze the significance of the artifacts, expressions, and traditions of the new language and culture to the culture of origin and to the global community.
Geography	Discuss how regions are defined; compare and contrast regions on a state, national, or world basis using case studies environments.	Map the physical and cultural areas and regions in North America and explain how these regions were outlined.	Explore the origin and spread of cultures; environmental protection; the geography of settlement forms; and the human use of the habitat, its resources, and its impact on the ecology of the earth.

[continued]

Table 10.2 *[continued]*

Subject	By grade 4 the student will	By grade 8 the student will	By grade 12 the student will
History and civics		Perceive from a variety of perspectives past events and issues as they occurred at the time. Relate the tales of heroes and heroines and tell the stories of different peoples living under different conditions of work, geography, and tradition.	Present the story of the United States as the creation of a new nation. Grasp the essential events, individual contributions, and circumstances of the early history of Western and non-Western civilizations including the Near East and Africa and classic civilizations of India and China. Examine social, cultural, and technological changes during medieval and early modern times. Relate the study of history to biography, geography, other social sciences, and the arts and humanities.
Mathematics	Understand the properties of geometric figures and relationships. Collect and organize statistical data, begin to understand chance and probability, and recognize patterns. Solve and create real-world problems.	Make connections between related mathematical concepts and apply these concepts to other content areas. Demonstrate an understanding of geometric objects and relationships; use basic geometry to solve problems.	Construct and draw statistical inferences from charts, tables, and graphs that summarize data from real-world situations. Represent problem situations and their solutions using oral, written, and graphic forms, including finite graphs, matrixes, sequences, and recurrence relations.
Science		Collect, sort, catalogue, and classify; calculate; observe, take notes, and sketch; interview, poll, and survey; and use hand lenses, microscopes, thermometers, cameras, and other common instruments. Construct models for scale.	Draw conclusions and make inferences from data; select and apply mathematical relationships to describe results obtained by observation and experimentation; interpret, in nonmathematical language, relationships presented in mathematical form.

Accountability standards are the achievement standards in grades K-4, 5-8, and 9-12 that help dance draw parallels between objectives in the arts disciplines and the other core subjects.

 How can dance facilitate the goals of other subjects while advancing dance? Place a star beside all that directly relate to dance and a check beside those that indirectly relate.

Not only are the arts useful instructional strategies to teach aspects of other disciplines, but research also documents that the arts make for a vibrant learning environment and have a humanizing effect on students. Schools should use the arts to maximize both. School improvement councils and administrators can strategically use the arts to influence school climate as well as increase student cooperation, creativity, and civility.

Two popular educational terms are **arts infusion** and **arts integration.** Arts infusion, typically for academic classes, introduces arts into other subject areas. Infusion applies arts as learning modalities in classrooms just as naturally as books and blackboards (exporting dance). Arts integration typically means that the arts specialists comingle arts disciplines so as to reinforce the commonalities and artistic processes (importing and exporting dance).

Importing and Exporting

Sometimes it seems like public education wants to drill facts into kids' heads. However, allowing kids to use movement to embody concepts is a different approach that can get better results with quite a few kids. Concepts can be firmly grasped and used because they are understood through the whole nervous system, not just one part of it (the brain). You can remediate on the spot with performance-based assessments because they point out who doesn't yet understand. This keeps students from falling behind or being confused in silence.

Exporting Dance: Learning Through Dance

Collaborate with classroom teachers. Even those who first fail to see how vital movement is to learning convert after one good demonstration. Underachieving students with high spatial and kinesthetic intelligence actually need gross and fine movement to fully conceptualize some of math's and science's concepts. Invite classroom teachers to witness students who have trouble getting it in traditional ways successfully comprehending the concepts and expressing them in dance. Mentor other teachers so they can use movement-based instruction in their classes (see chapter 3).

Look for topics that have spatial pattern or movement in them. For example, one student in science is having trouble distinguishing between earth's movements of *rotate* and *revolve*. Use movement to demystify these terms: one turns, the other circles. You know they are motional and relational concepts, so by first moving each concept, the student sees, feels, and understands the difference. You could help the science teacher so she is comfortable using movement in such a way. Demonstrate how to assess understanding with performance assessment and remediate on the spot.

Importing Ideas Into Dance: Learning in Dance

Embodying such movement patterns makes an abstract cognitive process concrete. Everyone benefits when you bring such concepts into dance. For example, in dance we would make rotating and revolving the main dance concept. After exploring it and experimenting with the concept, we create a short dance study. Another related example: In a complex science lesson demonstrating the earth, moon, and sun's pathways in relationship to each other, one has to understand the specific relationships involved in space. If students move this lesson, it is obvious if they understand the clockwise and counterclockwise patterns by the way they apply them. If the moon takes the wrong orbit as it revolves around earth, a quick performance assessment catches it. You see who gets it and—even better—those involved give and receive peer feedback so they self-correct on the spot. Then, every child gets the concept.

Older students could add the variable of timing. Now they have to calculate the relationship of the moon revolving around the earth as it cycles around the sun to make accurate daylight and nighttime patterns so at least once in the dance the ratio of the cycle is carried out completely (then it can be varied). This very complex relationship is an excellent compositional problem to solve. Once students understand the relationship, it stays with them. Movement supports learning; dance supports science. However, once students understand the concept, you can abstract it and go further. For the concept to serve dance as art, it requires compositional integrity that takes this new awareness into aesthetic education. The next step is to take the concept and transfer it through abstraction and elaboration into a structured dance study. Use aesthetic criteria and critique to shape the ensuing work and make this process a useful dance experience so the movement no longer represents the actual orbits, but the composition becomes a study on pathways and relationships. Incorporate other aspects from the topic that enhance the dance composition.

Importing and Exporting in the Arts

The national arts standards (NSAEs) call for collaboration among the arts disciplines (see chapter 1). Each form of arts expression comes from the human need to express ideas, concepts, feelings, and images in powerful and concrete ways. Each one calls on different senses and sensibilities. Everyone needs each form of arts expression to express their differing creative urges:

- A sound medium (music)
- A visual medium (art or dance)
- A theatrical medium (theatre)
- A literary medium (literature)
- A design medium (design arts)
- A technological medium (media arts)
- A multidisciplinary medium (opera or music videos)
- A kinetic-movement medium (dance)
- Dynamic combinations of these

Aesthetically driven arts education highlights the parallels across the arts disciplines and arts processes, for they share similar cornerstone disciplines, as you see in figure 10.1.

Dance naturally incorporates aspects of the other arts because we share vocabulary and creative urges. Creative artists in all the arts know the principles of design (PODs) as artistic benchmarks and use them to critique works. The arts share common elements as well as a performance, exhibit, or production aspect. The times shape each art form just as surely as does its cultural milieu, so the arts share some cultural, aesthetic, and historical similarities. Many dance styles developed concurrently with artistic and musical styles of the day. It makes interesting inquiry.

Examine dance as a rhythmic art with close ties to music. Let literary arts furnish motivating ideas for choreographies by lending structure and substance to a choreographer's developing idea. Explore dance as a theatrical art found in musical theatre, opera, music videos, and some theatre and stage productions. Notice how architectural space surrounding dance's performance affects how dance is performed and perceived. Dance is itself a three-dimensional visual–design art. Dance audiences experience dance as a kinetic visual art (while dancers also feel dance in their bodies as a kinesthetic or sensed art of motion as they perform). Dance performance must be seen to be fully appreciated and wholly experienced. Although dance can happen without music (i.e., in silence) or without a story plot (i.e., drama), it can't be fully experienced by a viewer whose eyes are closed!

Different Models for Integrating the Arts in Education

How the arts are emphasized at any school determines not only student outcomes but also the way the whole school functions. It determines how the school is perceived by the community surrounding it as well as those within the school who are directly involved—the **community of learners.** It dictates the internal operations of the school: the kinds of instructional planning throughout the school and the structure of the school day so as to promote cross-curricular planning.

Different levels of commitment to the arts produce diverse school profiles and student outcomes. Three distinct school models emerge: **arts-centered schools,** arts integration schools, and arts-infused schools. The Arts in Basic Curriculum Project, which promotes five art forms instead of four, describes them this way:

Arts centered. The arts are used as a focal point for the identity and image of a school. An arts-focused school stresses competencies in all the arts (dance, music, theatre, visual arts and creative writing) and ensures that the arts are aligned with the general education core of the school. The arts are a hub of the main activities within a school and provide in-depth exposure of the arts for all students.

Arts integration. The arts are incorporated into the general education curriculum and are used to enhance the understanding of areas of study outside of the arts disciplines themselves, as well as in-depth learning in

Dance	Visual art	Theatre	Music
Dancing performance	Acting performance	Studio and exhibiting	Musical skills and performing
Choreography	Innovation	Playwriting	Composing
Dance history	Art history	Theatre history	Music history
Criticism	Criticism	Criticism	Criticism
Aesthetics	Aesthetics	Aesthetics	Aesthetics
Interdisciplinary arts	Interdisciplinary arts	Interdisciplinary arts	Interdisciplinary arts

FIGURE 10.1 An aesthetically driven dance curriculum parallels other arts curricula.

the arts (dance, music, theatre, visual arts and creative writing). Types of Arts integration (excerpts from Wiggins 2001):

- Thematic integration: A theme is chosen and then knowledge and skills that support this theme from different disciplines are sought.

- Topical integration: Specific topic from one discipline is determined where connective and interactive relationships among disciplines are explored.

- Teaching-tool integration: One discipline serves the other by providing a vehicle through which knowledge can be efficiently learned and remembered.

Arts infused. The arts enhance the education of every student and improve the general curriculum, as well as in-depth learning in the arts (dance, music, theatre, visual arts and creative writing). An arts-infused school disseminates and permeates the arts into the traditions and experiences that are at the core of every program within the school. Arts and non-arts disciplines mutually support and enhance each other through constant planning and collaboration.

Reprinted from C. Fisher and A. Svedlow, 2005, Arts in Basic Curriculum (ABC) Project, Rock Hill, SC: Winthrop University.

Teaching Other Academics Through Dance

To keep dance instruction student centered, relate dance to students' current academics. To keep dance coherent, connect it to bigger contexts explored elsewhere in the curriculum. In either case, keep instruction aesthetically driven. Reinforce the concepts and skills that your students learn in other subjects. Coordinate instruction with other teachers to assist each other. Promote interdisciplinary work when projects cross disciplinary lines; this improves the general curriculum. Make authentic connections that go further than acting out the life

"Encarta Encyclopedia (1997) defines poetry as 'a form of imaginative literacy expression that makes its effect by the sound and imagery of its language. It is essentially rhythmic and usually metrical and is frequently structured in stanzas.' Similarly, dance can be defined as a form of imaginative kinesthetic expression that makes its effect by the instrumental use of the body to create and relay meaning. It is essentially rhythmic and usually metrical and is frequently structured in spatial phrases."

—Betty Block (2001, p. 47)

cycle of a seed! Share unit goals between disciplines and create a broad instructional matrix to support learning. Dance education is more than an isolated dance event.

Let's look at two complete lesson plans (language arts and science) and several other ideas that are sketched out for you.

English and Language Arts

The links between language, literacy, and linguistic processing are legion. Many aspects of language adapt to movement, and many movement-based activities increase linguistic processing. As students embody word symbols, moving and thinking merge.

The rhythm of words and sentences in spoken language gives us meter, which translates into songs and dance. Both rhymes and dances use phrasing. From the youngest student who moves with rhythmic repetition to rhyming words, to the adolescent who translates a poetic concept into dance choreography, rhythm bridges the two disciplines.

Written composition and dance have much in common. In many respects dance is poetry. Both extract the essence of an idea and portray it with minimum of means. One favorite example is Carl Sandburg's *Fog*. Read it, and see what movement images dance in your head. It inspires a great dance study.

In literary arts, students analyze and critique significant works of world literature to study how (and how well) they are put together and how they transmit cultural values. Also notice how the literary composition's process of organizing thoughts and writing them in an ordered sequence parallels dance composition (see chapter 7). Dance's ordered composition unfolds in time just as composition does in music, literature, play writing, and screenplays.

Language Arts Lesson Plan: Word Dances From Haiku

A. Planning

Goal
To compose a dance based on a literary form. (NSDE 7)

Grade Level
3-5

Unit Title
Poetry in Motion

Lesson Title
Japanese Haiku

Duration
Two 50-minute classes

Task Description: Analysis of Haiku and Synthesis Into Choreography
After analyzing the words and concepts of the haiku as they relate to the dance elements, students will translate the haiku into abstract movement phrases and then into choreography.

National Dance Achievement Standards Grades K to 4

- 1b—Technique: Students will demonstrate basic locomotor movements.
- 2a—Choreography: Students will create a sequence with a beginning, middle, and end, both with and without rhythmic accompaniment; identify each of these parts of the sequence.

- 3b—Communication: Students will take an active role in a class discussion about interpretations of and reactions to a dance.
- 7a—Connections: Students will create a dance project that reveals understanding of a concept or idea from another discipline.

Instructional Objectives
The student will do the following:

- Analyze a haiku by underlining words that relate to movement.
- Select movements for a completed phrase with a beginning, middle, and end and follow the sequence of the haiku to create a repeatable movement pattern.
- Use selected words to inspire movement by comparing underlined words with the dance elements.
- Abstract the movement concepts from the selected work rather than literally portray the word concepts.
- Move with self-control for the entire class.
- Critique and respond to haiku dance using dance elements vocabulary.

Teacher Preparation and Materials

- Dance elements chart
- Blackboard or whiteboard
- Drum

Squads of frogs jumped in
When they heard the plunk-plash
Of a single frog.

   —Wakyu

Old snow is melting
Now the huts unfreezing to
Free all the children.

   —Issa

Softly folded fawn
Shivers, shaking off the butterfly . . .
And sleeps again.

   —Issa

Gliding river boat . . .
Rising skylarks . . . rippling sounds
To our right and left.

   —Ranko

Little silver fish
Pointing upstream, moving downstream
In clear quick water.

   —Unknown

FIGURE 10.2 Samples of haiku. Even though the rule is 17 syllables, some Japanese poets take license with that form. Likewise, dance takes license to abstract the concepts in movement.

Adapted with permission of Ellen Hollis Harrison.

- CD of Japanese shakahachi flute music; CD player
- Handouts of five Japanese haiku for the class (figure 10.2)

B. Teaching the Lesson

Introductory Statement

"Today we are going to create a dance based on the word concepts from haiku. Haiku is a form of poetry of Japanese origin. A Japanese haiku is a three-line, unrhymed verse traditionally written with 17 syllables distributed five, seven, and five. It indicates a moment, sensation, impression, or drama of a specific fact of nature. Haiku often suggests nature, color, seasons, contrasts, and surprises."

Procedures (Teacher Strategies)

Listen and Learn

1. Explain that a dance study is a series of moves with a beginning, middle, and ending. Explain how words can stimulate movement, ideas, and textures.

2. Instruct students to create a list of descriptive words and action words that can stimulate movements (e.g., *smooth, sharp, glide, soar, explode*).

3. Instruct students to listen to the drum as it accompanies them as they explore all of your words through movements as a warm-up (mental and physical).

4. Define *haiku* and read aloud one haiku that will later be used as an example.

5. Analyze the haiku for useful movement concepts. Use the following example by Ryuho.

   > I scooped up the moon
   >
   > In my water bucket . . . and
   >
   > Spilled it on the grass.

   Instruct students to underline words that can generate shapes and moves. Look for dance elements concepts to stimulate bodyshaping and movement. As students create and explore shapes, they are to find and remember the shapes they want to later use.

6. Demonstrate how one might analyze the haiku and use it to create movement. Model moving to the italicized haiku words after listing the words that stimulate movement:

   > Scooped
   > Moon (abstracted as "roundness")
   > Bucket (abstracted as "container")
   > Spilled

7. Practice creating movements to selected words—not to imitate the words but to use them for inspiration. Explore scooping motions that end in round, curved shapes with the arms and torso. Embellish the concept by repeating in different ways (PODs repetition and variety). Add turns to complete the roundness for *moon*. Take a concept of container (*bucket*) using gathering motions; then contrast *spilled* with scattering motions and showing how they can be elaborated on.

8. Have the groups show their work to each other for feedback; have them select words of the haiku to accompany their performance in some way (self-accompany).

9. Hand out five additional haiku from which to select for an in-class choreography assignment.

10. Creative process:

    > Divide the class into groups of four or five to work on a different haiku and select words.

    > Remind students to analyze the words of the haiku.

    > Instruct students to create a sequence with a beginning, middle, and ending, keeping the words in the same order. Assign 10 minutes to work in groups. Monitor the progress of each group.

    > Instruct students to show their group haiku dance to the class while you read the haiku aloud.

    > Challenge older students to memorize and recite the haiku as accompaniment (before, during, or after performance) for aesthetic effect.

    > Ask observers to describe, analyze, and evaluate each performance and facilitate discussion.

    > Instruct students on the use of the review criteria in the rubric and facilitate its use.

    > Ask students to aesthetically evaluate the process and products. Ask them to reflect on the creative experience.

(continued)

C. Learning Objectives: Conceptualize the Sequence for Creating a Dance

The student will do the following:

1. Select one haiku to stimulate a dance. Analyze the haiku and select words to abstract. List words that stimulate movement.

2. Create movements based on selected words.

3. Work in small groups to create haiku choreography. Practice movements with selected words of the haiku as accompaniment.

4. Show work (for feedback). Edit and refine the four-part sequence (of *scoop, moon, bucket, spilled*) as needed. Perform for peer critique.

5. Extend the choreography: Repeat with variations in space, timing, groupings. Add transi-

Rating Scale	0	1	2	3	Score
Content criteria					
Movement phrase (beginning, middle, and ending)	Dance does not have a clear beginning, middle, and ending.	Dance has two of the three.	Dance has a clear beginning, middle, and ending.	Dance has a strong beginning and end. It develops well in the middle.	
Application of haiku concepts	Students did not follow the haiku concepts to create their dance.	Created movements suggest use of haiku.	Haiku concepts motivate the dance.	Haiku motivates and concepts are inventive and artful.	
Verbal response to haiku dance (critique)	Student does not respond.	Student responds without using dance elements vocabulary.	Student responds using appropriate dance elements vocabulary.	Student responds with appropriate elements vocabulary to describe, analyze, interpret, and evaluate.	
Movement control	Student is not able to move with self-control.	Student is able to move in control for a portion of the class and creative process.	Student is able to move in control for the entire class and creative process.	Student moves in control and finds expressive ways to create and perform the haiku dance.	
Aesthetic criteria					
Composition: smooth transitions between each word concept	Movement concepts are disjointed.	Transitions are attempted.	Transitions are successful.	Transitions are smooth and connect the varied dance concepts.	
Performance: movement quality	Performance is not taken seriously.	Performance quality is partially maintained.	Performance quality is maintained throughout.	Performance quality and performance presence are excellent.	
Composition: sufficient variety and contrast to maintain interest	No contrasts are evident.	Contrasts are attempted but are unsuccessful.	Contrasts add interest to the work.	Variety adds interest and contrasts are used for maximum impact.	
Composition: abstracting word concepts from haiku	There is no evidence of abstracting.	There is evidence that words are used.	Concepts are brought out in appropriate movements.	Concepts are conveyed abstractly and with integrity.	

FIGURE 10.3   Haiku matrix rubric.

tions between the original sequence and the new variations.

6. Show the extended dance to compare with the original and to critique. (Possibly also combine several groups into a long work with transitions according to spacing, timing, entrances, and exits.)

D. Culminating Aspects

Summative Assessment

Assess students with a rubric with a maximum of 24 points as in figure 10.3. The rubric can score the whole group as well as individuals. Use three-pronged assessment (i.e., teacher observation, peer assessment, and self-assessment).

Reflection

Ask questions such as these:

1. What did you learn about the poetic form haiku?

2. How did the rhythmic structure of the haiku translate into your dance today?

3. How did the words and the concepts behind them translate into your dance today?

4. How do you explain the differences between abstracting an idea and imitating it?

5. Reflect on the creative experience.

E. Curricular Extensions

- In Lesson 2, students join with two other groups to create a longer work.

- In Lesson 3, students bring an original haiku to abstract into dance movement using the same process. Link this lesson with language arts as students compose haiku in creative writing, thus serving the goals of both. The students recite their own haiku as accompaniment before, during, or after the dance. Incorporate aspects of Japanese culture. Invite students to illustrate their haiku in visual art or compose music that expresses mood to further integrate the arts.

Advanced students create a dance with 17 beats to correspond to the 17 syllables of the haiku. Add complexity by listing criteria for taking the poetic structure to make three phrases of dance that correspond to the three lines of 5-7-5 beats.

Lesson by Ellen Hollis Harrison, Ridgeview High School, Columbia, SC.

Asking the high school English teachers to give you a syllabus of what students are reading can open the door to finding worthwhile choreographic subjects, whether poetry, novels, or short stories. See the language arts and dance lesson plan on haiku that dance specialist Ellen Hollis Harrison developed and used at Ridgeview High School, Richland District 2, Columbia, South Carolina.

There are numerous parallels between language and dance. Chapter 7 noted the parallel structures for composition and the use of basic building blocks for language arts (words) and dance (dance elements). Language arts use critiques much as dance does to describe, analyze, interpret, and evaluate both the process and the products.

Science

Science takes an investigative, inquiry approach to complex problems, as does dance. Thus science, too, relies on complex and higher-order thinking. The scientific process and the creative process in the arts are similar, as shown in figure 7.3 in chapter 7.

Link the body sciences (anatomy, kinesiology, somatics) to support dance instruction and performance refinement. Capitalize on the physical sciences as compositional stimuli and structure, for there are many systems that can be extrapolated into movement for beautiful dance works and for better understanding the earth's scientific phenomena as well. Of particular service is scientific inquiry into phenomena such as

- earthquakes (i.e., seismographic shifts in plate tectonics that result in tremors and quakes that lay an organic structure for dance development);

- weather systems and changing weather patterns (i.e., high and low pressure systems that move and collide to create changing weather systems, jet stream patterns, tidal waves, tornadoes);

- temperature effects on molecules (i.e., changes from solid to liquid to gas);

- plant growth cycles;

- chemical properties and reactions;

- life cycles from birth to death;

- gravity and weightlessness;

- oceanography;
- the law of natural proportion; and
- astronomy (e.g., lunar cycles, planetary movement, constellations, stars, comets, meteor showers).

Let's explore the concept of volcanic activity. On pages 309 to 313 is a dance lesson based on facts about volcanoes (which could be a collaborative project with the science teacher). Students analyze the facts, sequence the stages of eruption, and then abstract the scientific data on the volcanic process in movement (synthesize) by artfully using specific dance elements. Use this activity to develop vocabulary in both dance and science. In this sample lesson, students first read the assignment to comprehend the information and discuss it before they are asked to apply it to a dance composition. First, lead discussion to emphasize the main points.

The lesson can be adapted for grades 4 to 12. Although the factual information used here comes from *Microsoft Encarta Encyclopedia,* consider using grade-level science textbook material at your school for information and inquiry.

Social Studies

Talking about cooperation is not nearly as effective as cooperating. Learning to live together in social accord is better understood by having to live together in social accord. Teach democracy by modeling a democratic society. Striving for excellence is not at cross purposes with democracy. Promote this in dance by being the facilitator for learning rather than the autocratic voice of rigid conformity that hinders creative development. Everyone gets an equal chance to succeed through feedback, scaffolding, and safety nets.

Not only can you set up the classroom so students interact with each other and develop social skills in their dance making and doing, but you can also construct cooperative group dynamics through composing and critiquing. Keep competitiveness out of your classroom. Make sure holistic student-centered learning aids psychosocial development. When artistic processes become collaborative, they contribute a great deal to this development

- by asking critical friends to provide critique and feedback,

Folk dances can carry goals of social studies and dance forward. Students in grades 3 through 8 find folk dances particularly interesting.

- by composing and problem solving in a group, and
- by collaborating when performing.

Social studies and dance focus on the nature of human expression throughout history and in different cultures. Because dance universally expresses social, historical, cultural, and familial contexts, traditional dances naturally reveal insights into the people who made them. Folk dances can jointly carry goals of social studies and dance forward. Dances that have been passed through generations bring to life times and places other than our own (see chapter 8).

One way to retain vital information from a particular era is to embody dances of the era. World history can be taught just as easily in the context of the arts and culture as it is through military conquests and politics. In fact, the politics of the arts make interesting history study! Students in grades 3 through 8 find folk dances especially interesting. At the time they are learning to fit into the bigger world, they like to learn dances of the past and what motivated them—to learn about dances and to dance dances that other people made and danced

Science Lesson Plan—Volcanoes

A. Planning

Goal

To compose a dance using an organic form with beginning, middle, and end. (NSDE 7)

Grade Level

4-12

Unit Title

The World Around Us

Lesson Title

Volcanoes

Duration

Two 50-minute classes

Task Description: Analysis of Volcano and Synthesis Into Choreography

After analyzing movement and abstracting it, students compose an ABCDEF dance form (the kind of organic form that the subject inspires).

National Dance Standards Grades 4 through 12

- 1c—Students will transfer a spatial pattern from the visual to the kinesthetic.

- 1d—Students will create and perform combinations and variations in a broad dynamic range.

- 2a—Choreography: Students will create a dance with a beginning, middle, and end, without rhythmic accompaniment; they will identify each of these parts of the sequence.

- 3b—Communication: Students will take an active role in a class discussion before, during, and after the creative project. Students will serve as critical friends for peers. Students will answer questions about how movement choices communicate abstract ideas in dance.

- 4a—Creative thinking: Students will solve a movement problem and demonstrate multiple solutions; they will choose the most interesting solutions and discuss the reasons for their choice.

- 7a—Connections: Students will create a dance project that reveals understanding of a concept or idea from another discipline.

Instructional Objectives

The student will do the following:

- Comprehend basic facts about volcanoes and learn a vocabulary of terms related to the phenomenon.

- Examine photographs and depictions of preeruption through posteruption to visualize the concept.

- Analyze and write down the stages of development of an eruption in sequence.

- Select movements for each stage and create movement patterns that abstract the concept.

- Work collaboratively to determine the movements and the spacing, timing, and dynamics of each section.

- Build dynamics and timing into a fitting climax for the full dance composition.

- Abstract movement rather than literally portray the word concepts.

- Show work for critical feedback before editing.

- Critique and respond to others' work using dance elements and principles of design vocabulary.

- Create and perform an original group composition based on volcanic activity.

- Use a rubric to critique the aesthetic quality of the finished product (teacher, self, and peers).

Teacher Preparation and Materials

- Dance elements chart

- Whiteboard or blackboard for vocabulary words

- CD of nature sounds—thunderstorm; CD player

- Principles of design chart

- Handouts on volcanoes (from student research, science textbook, or *Encarta Encyclopedia*)

(continued)

B. *Teaching the Lesson*

Introductory Statement

"Today we are building on your science unit on volcanoes. We are exploring the sequence of events that lead to a volcanic eruption similar to the one you researched in Java, Indonesia—Mount Krakatoa. After we review these findings as a class, we are going to take a particular sequence from a short reading assignment (see figure 10.4). Based on this information we are going to launch several dance compositions in groups of five. It is a creative process with several steps that I will explain. As we begin our discussion, please be attuned to as many details as possible so there is interesting material to abstract into your creation."

Procedures (Teacher Strategies)

Read and Learn (Individually)

1. Distribute prepared handout (or project on a screen).

2. Have students read three paragraphs (figure 10.4) on volcanoes for comprehension (Bloom's Level 2).

3. Instruct students to immediately reread the paragraphs to analyze (Bloom's Level 4) their

   > spatial aspects (space),

   > temporal aspects (time), and

   > dynamic aspects (energy).

4. Point out the underlined word phrases that relate to space, time, and energy. These key phrases are to become the compositional material for the students' dance study on volcanoes.

5. Have students return to the text again for a sequence of events and write down the sequence.

Guide Student Practice (Group)

1. Randomly select five students to demo the process.

2. Facilitate a structured improv of the sequence, starting in low space.

Volcanoes are holes or vents in the earth crust created when molten material or *magma* under the crust is <u>forced upward</u> through the surface. Magma <u>collects</u> in a chamber beneath the crust. <u>Pressure increases</u>, <u>forcing it up</u> through cracks and fissures, and a <u>conduit</u> to the surface <u>is created</u>. Hot gases <u>try to escape but are trapped</u> in the magma. The surface begins <u>to bulge</u>. Finally the <u>pressure can no longer be contained</u>. Gasses and fragments of earth are <u>released in a violent explosion</u>.

A volcano <u>may erupt many times</u> during its lifetime of thousands of years. <u>Material expelled</u> during the eruptions <u>gradually builds</u> up a cone-shaped mountain. The throat of the volcano is called the "central vent." Usually there is a <u>bowl-shaped crater at the top</u> of the central vent.

Volcanic eruptions can be described as <u>"explosive" or "quiet."</u> When the magma is <u>sticky</u> and contains lots of gas then <u>eruptions tend to be explosive</u>. Hot debris particles, called *pyroclastics,* <u>are expelled</u> during <u>violent explosions</u>. <u>Heavier pieces land near the crater</u> and serve to <u>build the cone-shaped mountain</u>. <u>Lighter pieces can be carried by the wind</u> for hundreds of miles. When the <u>magma is more fluid and contains less gas, then eruptions are quiet</u>. Molten rock, called *lava,* <u>spills out</u> of the volcano and <u>cools on its slopes</u>. <u>Alternating eruptions</u> of pyroclastics and lava <u>build the mountain layer by layer</u>.

FIGURE 10.4 Volcanic eruptions handout. *Note:* Underlines show concepts to inspire choreography and are not part of the original *Encarta* quotation.

C. Learning Objectives: Conceptualize the Sequence for Creating a Dance

The student will do the following:

1. (Individuals) Work with this choreographic form: ABCDEF.

   > A. Stillness

   > B. Slow start of movement

   > C. Very gradual building of energy

   > D. Inevitable eruption (make it the high point)

   > E. Resolution and results of the eruption

   > F. Return to stillness

2. (Individuals) Visualize a group movement sequence that designs the spatial, temporal, and dynamic aspects of a pre- through post-volcanic eruption (i.e., space, time, dynamics and energy).

3. (Group) Select key phrases from the volcanic eruption handout and sequence them into this organic choreographic form. Collaboratively abstract the key phrases into nonliteral movement. Improvise. Then structure the movement material into a dance composition (A-F).

4. Show work in progress to peers for critical feedback. After students have edited and refined the work to performance level, they will perform for the class for critical response using the assessment rubric in figure 10.6.

D. Culminating Aspects

Summative Assessment

Assess students based on the criteria for a maximum of 30 points. Use the rubric for the group or for individuals. Assessment is three-pronged: teacher observation, peers, and self.

Reflection

Ask questions such as these:

1. How closely did you read the article for factual details to create an accurate sequence of events pertaining to a volcanic eruption?

2. What details did you use in your composition that you might have passed over or forgotten without such a dance project (if you had been given only a reading assignment)? What details did you recall? What details did others help you recall?

3. In what ways did having to compose a movement study reinforce your learning about volcanoes? About dance composition?

4. Do you think your long-term retention of details deepened from having to do something with the information immediately?

5. How memorable will this be as a movement study (composition)?

6. How memorable will the subject of volcanoes be as an earth science phenomenon?

7. Was your group able to go beyond just moving through the sequence to really performing it with integrity and conviction?

 What other topics in science lend themselves to spatial, temporal, and dynamic analysis?

E. Curricular Extensions

- (For older or advanced students) Inquire into other facts about volcanoes and incorporate them as aesthetic details to add artistic interest to your composition. See figure 10.5 for spatial and dynamic ideas to extend the composition further. How do these add texture and compositional interest without being literal portrayals?

- (For younger students) Inquire further into other science topics that have spatial, timing, and dynamic aspects (such as chemical reactions or tornadoes). Follow up on interests as time allows.

(continued)

Select at least three concepts from the following text and use aspects of them to add spatial, temporal, or dynamic variety to your original composition.

Craters

A volcano is a geological landform consisting of a fissure in the earth's crust, above which a cone of volcanic material has accumulated. At the top of the cone is a bowl-shaped vent called a *crater.* The cone is formed by the deposition of molten or solid matter that flows or is ejected through the vent from the interior of the earth. Most volcanoes are composite landforms built up partly of lava flows and partly of fragmental materials. In successive eruptions, the solid materials fall around the vent on the slopes of the cone, while lava streams issue from the vent and from fissures on the flanks of the cone. Thus, the cone is built up of layers of fragmental materials and flows of lava, all inclined outward away from the vent. Some enormous crater-like basins, called *calderas,* at the top of long-dormant or extinct volcanoes, are eventually occupied by deep lakes.

Eruption

In a violent eruption of a volcano, the lava is highly charged with steam and other gases . . . which continuously escape from the lava's surface with violent explosions and rise in a turbid cloud. This cloud frequently discharges showers of rain. Large and small portions of the lava are shot upward, forming a fiery fountain of incandescent drops and fragments. . . . These objects fall back in showers on the external slopes of the cone or into the crater, from which they are again and again ejected. Lightning often plays through the cloud. . . . Lava rises in the vent and finally flows over the rim of the crater or oozes, as a pasty mass, through a fissure in the cone's side. This may mark a *crisis,* or crucial point, of the eruption; after a final ejection of fragmental material, the volcano may then return to a quiescent state. The enormous energy expended during an explosive eruption is shown by the heights to which rocks and ash are projected.

Cooling Stage

For a long period after it has ceased to erupt either lava or fragmental materials, a volcano continues to emit acid gases and vapor in what is called the fumarolic stage. Eventually, the last traces of volcanic heat may disappear and springs of cold water may issue from the volcano and from the ground in its vicinity.

Inactive Periods

After becoming inactive, a volcano undergoes progressive reduction in size through erosion. . . . Finally the volcano may become completely obliterated, leaving only a volcanic pipe, that is, a chimney filled with lava or fragmental material and extending from the earth's surface to the former lava reservoir. The rich diamond mines of South Africa are found in volcanic pipes.

Theories of Volcanism

Geologists have succeeded in incorporating volcanism into the theory of plate tectonics. Wherever they occur, active volcanoes ultimately derive their energy from processes associated with movements of crustal plates. Volcanoes tend to occur near two different kinds of major plate boundaries:

1. Convergent plate boundaries, where one plate plunges . . . beneath the other, material on the upper surface of the subducted plate is dragged downward on an oblique path into the earth's crust until it reaches a depth where it becomes molten. It then rises along vertical fissures and is ejected at the surface through a volcanic vent.

2. Divergent plate boundaries, such as the Mid-Atlantic Ridge, where oceanic crust is being stretched and rifted apart, a linear zone of weakness (spreading center) forms; this serves as an outlet for eruption of magma (deep-lying molten rock material) brought upward by giant convection currents in the mantle.

FIGURE 10.5   Volcanic details handout.

Rating scale:

0 = makes no attempt to follow the criteria, does not meet standard

1 = attempts but is inconsistent, makes progress toward standard

2 = follows criteria, meets standard

3 = excels, exceeds standard

Content criteria

_____ Creates movement sequence that conveys all concepts from the underlined key phrases

_____ Effectively translates details from concept into movement

_____ Effectively incorporates timing changes to enhance the impact of performance

_____ Effectively modulates the dynamics of volcanism into a dance study

_____ Maintains overall group performance quality, concentration, performance integrity

_____ **Content total** (5-10 = edit further) (13-15 = ready to perform, excellent)

Aesthetic criteria

_____ Uses movement quality and texture that sustain audience interest throughout

_____ Uses timing in an artistic way that enhances the work and conveys the sequence of events

_____ Uses shapes and shaping in an artistic way that conveys intent of the piece and gives choreographic interest

_____ Shows performance integrity and conviction

_____ Shows choreographic integrity and quality

_____ **Aesthetic total** (5-10 = edit further) (13-15 = ready to perform, excellent)

FIGURE 10.6   Assessment rubric (for volcano lesson).

for centuries. Folk dance can rivet student attention in social studies or history. Performing folk dances is a cooperative activity as well as an opportunity to perfect unison movement patterns and refine stylistic quality.

Use historically based dance works such as *John Henry* by Arthur Mitchell to portray the story of the early 20th-century laying of the railroads across America. Or show the plight of the prisoners on a chain gang in Donald McKayle's *Rainbow 'Round My Shoulder* to raise social conscience. To investigate the times when dance was out of favor or in favor reveals the restrictiveness of the times. The times that certain dance forms were banned, such as the hula (Hawaii), the Bharata Natyam (south India), and the ring shout (southern United States), are keys to finding information about the times and the prevailing cultural values or political agendas. Kings who were dancers, such as Louis XIII and Louis XIV of France, brought dance into the courts and were the first examples of royal patrons of dance. Investigate them and others.

Foreign Language

Although dance may seem like a foreign language to beginners, they quickly learn it is a universal language that transcends linguistics. The language of dance accesses powerful nonverbal communication. Language, culture, and customs are inseparable in their origins, so why shouldn't they be explored together in education—especially arts education?

There are obvious links between dance and French. You can teach classical ballet terms, because many are dance action verbs that apply to everyday moves (e.g., dégagé, elevé, sauté, jeté). Parts of the body are used in ballet terminology as well, like port de bras (which means carriage of the arms) and rond de jambe (circle of the leg).

Also use verbs in other languages for word dances. Give compositional assignments that incorporate foreign words along with English words. Use languages represented in your class. When you make movement patterns or phrases such as "travel, turn, reach, and curl," explore them first in English. Then say the same words in another language as an accompaniment. For example, students say the word *traverse* as they travel and *tourne* as they turn. When students make dances in AB form (e.g., with contrasts such as sharp and smooth), translate the terms into a different language so students embody the words and concepts together and speak the words while performing them. Go after artful portrayal with word dances.

Compose a simple cinquain using English verbs, dance it, then translate it into Spanish and dance it again. (Cinquains are literary forms with five lines in a diamond shape and a specific number of syllables. See figure 7.5 in chapter 7.) The language changes but the concept and meaning behind the dance expression do not. Use the choreographed cinquain to underscore how dance as art communicates in a universal language—human movement—which doesn't change in the translation (from English to Spanish).

Geography

The study of dance cultures helps students understand how the relationships among people, places, and environments call on an understanding of space. Both geography and dance explore the climate's effect on people. Long-standing research has shown a propensity for people in cold climates to dance faster and more energetically than those in hot, humid, equatorial climates. Climate and temperature affect how humans move and how they express themselves in dance. Of course, climate also affects costume and, to a degree, culture, so the substance of the dance content is different between cold and hot climates.

To investigate dance from different cultures around the world requires that you use maps and globes as visual images to help students locate the country and the impact of its location and proximity to other continents as you compare and contrast dances in different world settings. You can look at migration patterns in Africa, for example, to see why dances in one area arrived at another. You can look at how dances of West Africa came through the West Indies and into the southern United States. Keep a world globe in your classroom to identify places in the world where specific dances are found. This helps you and the students keep a global perspective and increases awareness of the **universality** of dance.

Geography is a natural bridge that helps us increase dance understanding and global perspective. Many of CBE's standards for geography can be carried forward and enhanced through the study of cultural dance and human expression. Create lessons about place and space that meet achievement standards for both dance and geography. See how geography and dance together can explore the origins and movement of world cultures.

When your lesson calls for a folk dance, use a geographic point of entry. For example, when your unit of study focusing on Fokine's *Petroushka* calls for a Russian folk dance, use an inquiry approach such as, "What kind of dances could you expect to find in this climate?" (geography). "Listen to a piece of music from that region—how do you envision the dance movements?" (music). "What kind of costume is used for men? For women?" Then use the music to accompany a warm-up using several steps that will later appear in the folk dance you will teach. This gives you several options: to teach the dance next or to use the music to stimulate students' own creative work and step patterns. If you do both, after you finish you are ready to analyze the folk dance that is codified (i.e., set) and the one just created. This process could even produce some new movements to add to the original folk dance. And where did we start all this? All of it was stimulated from the question, "What kind of dances could you expect to find in this climate?"—a geography and dance question.

Physical Education

Physical educators in K-5 with experience and background in creative movement exploration teach the BSTERs (body, space, time, energy and dynamics, and relationships). Those teachers experienced in world folk dances, social, and line or circle dances teach rhythmic and locomotor skills in dance. Many use dancelike patterns for aerobics and Pilates mat classes for fitness. These all supplement dance education's goals of transferring movement skills into aesthetic performance.

How do you export dance as art to help meet physical education goals? Promote the use of the BSTERs as a universal movement and dance vocabulary (UDV). Collaborate, rather than compete, for instructional time. Acknowledge the differences and similarities in goals:

- Physical education—fitness, health, social, sport, and lifetime movement habits and skills
- Dance—less functional and more expressive goals, emphasizing the artistic processes and substantive knowledge in dance

Emphasize how both dance and physical education use higher-order thinking, critiquing, and technique enrichment. Work together to advocate for activity in the school day, because both dance and physical education bring an important kinesthetic dimension not found in other aspects of the curriculum.

Share Donald McKayle's *Games* to link to recreational-games-turned-choreography. Compare it to dance works inspired by the Olympics, such as *Troy Games*. Look at Momix's *Baseball*. Take sports themes as motivation for dance making in upper elementary and older. Boys and girls alike enjoy abstracting sports moves like tennis or golf swings and striking, throwing, kicking, and running patterns. For example, create a baseball dance. Use the baseball diamond as a floor pattern for a dance with five dancers—starting with one on each base and one in the center.

Math

Math emphasizes problem solving. Research shows that the positive tensions created in a learner through problem solving stimulate creative and critical thinking. Creative thinking is elaborative whereas critical thinking is evaluative. Although both involve decision making, critical thinking requires

it. Math is a good partner for dance because of the geometric shapes in space, patterns, symmetry and asymmetry, and counting of phrases. However, geometric shapes are mathematical constructs that can be difficult to translate into artful movement. Oftentimes they are too stiff and contrived. Geometrics can be more useful when the concepts are more organic and less contrived. See the example of organic versus geometric later in the chapter in "Integrating the Arts Through Dance Themes."

Counting the metered phrases of music accompaniment, figuring how many measures of accompaniment to use, and analyzing time signature in a complex music work are all mathematical processes. Reading and writing basic Labanotation scores use the same analytical skills as math. For example, a 4/4 score with eighth and quarter notes requires one to visualize how the fractions exist in time to fill each measure. See figure 10.7's depiction of different time signatures in dance script that uses fractions 2/4, 3/4, 4/4, 5/4, and 6/8. Post simple floor patterns in Labanotation to promote dance literacy in addition to reinforcing math (and music) skills. Labanotation also develops analytical skills (HOTS in chapter 4).

Creating repeating patterns (such as a ground base) is a mathematical process that requires measuring time (as do reading and writing notation). Sequence is one of the early concepts on which math builds. All of these can be reinforced by dance study.

Collaborating Across the Arts

Besides the tangible commonalities that the arts share—rhythm and timing, texture, the use of space, energy and dynamics, shape—we share artistic design principles (PODs). There's commonality in compositions: pattern, mood, and structure. Although we use different media, the arts share common artistic goals and processes. We are as process oriented as we are product oriented. We foster skill development in our disciplines, encourage creative expression and thought, celebrate heritage and history, and critique and refine our works for exhibits and performances. The intangible yet vastly important skills that we require include attentive listening, imagining, concentrating, problem solving, close observing, experimenting, differentiating, evaluating, describing, remembering, recognizing, selecting, and refining.

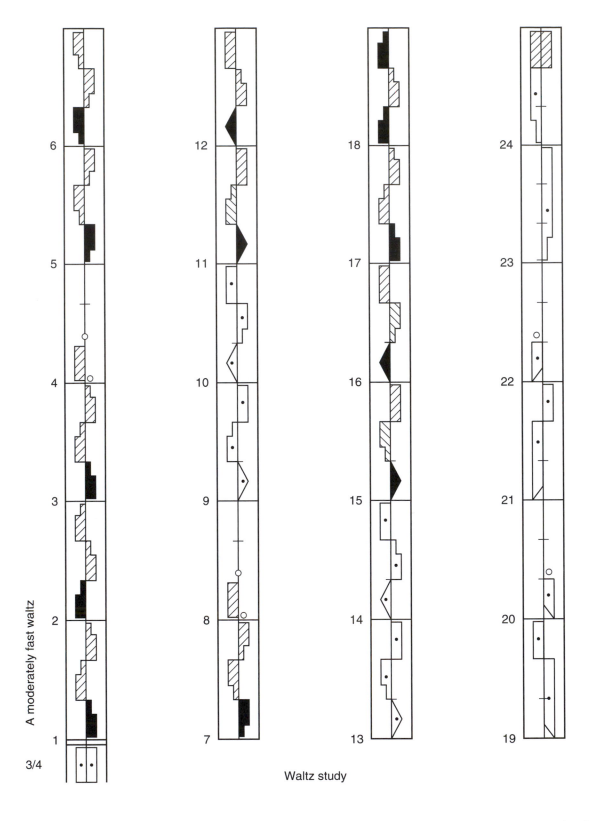

FIGURE 10.7   Labanotation scores.

Courtesy of the Dance Notation Bureau.

(continued)

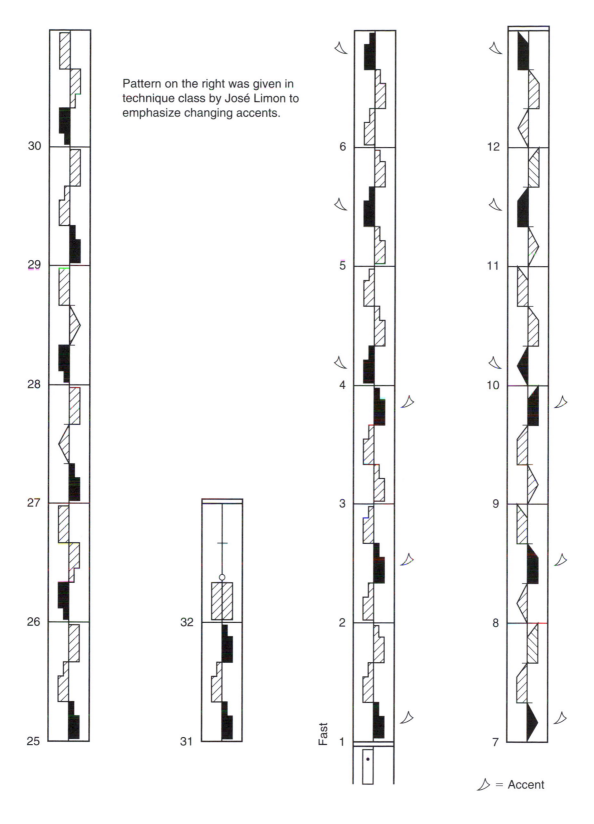

Pattern on the right was given in technique class by José Limon to emphasize changing accents.

= Accent

(continued)

FIGURE 10.7 *(continued)*

Courtesy of the Dance Notation Bureau.

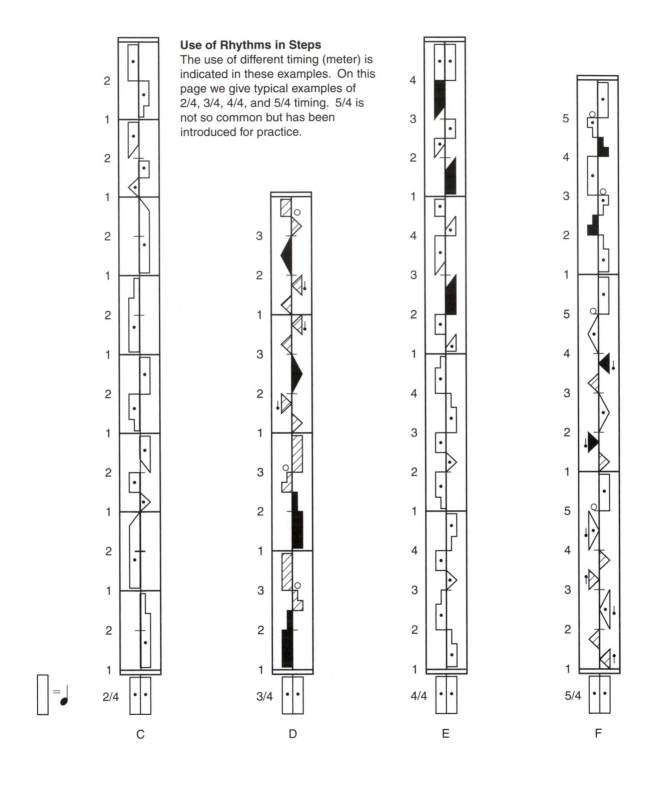

Use of Rhythms in Steps

The use of different timing (meter) is indicated in these examples. On this page we give typical examples of 2/4, 3/4, 4/4, and 5/4 timing. 5/4 is not so common but has been introduced for practice.

FIGURE 10.7   *(continued)*

Courtesy of the Dance Notation Bureau.

(continued)

318

Steps in Different Rhythms

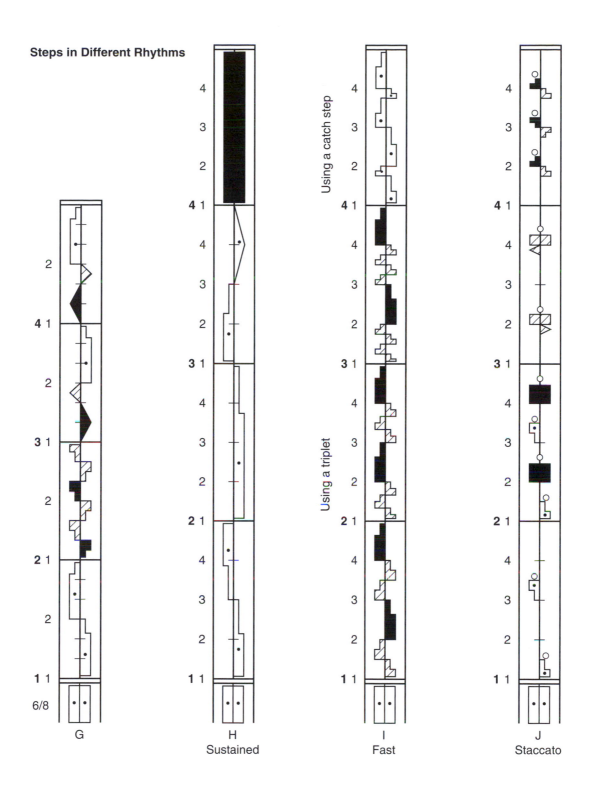

G

6/8

H
Sustained

I
Fast

Using a catch step

Using a triplet

J
Staccato

FIGURE 10.7   *(continued)*

Courtesy of the Dance Notation Bureau.

Collaborating With Music

Music uses movement to enhance a child's rhythmic acuity, coordination, aesthetic sense, and expression. Music uses choreography to enhance music performance. But neither of them replaces or duplicates the substantive dance curriculum.

Shared Structures

Musical and choreographic forms historically share comparable structures. A good example is how pre-classic music and dance evolved together. Musical forms such as musical theme and variation, AB, rondo, and call and response also serve dance. Music and dance share common elements: dynamics, texture, tempo, and duration (length). In some cultures music is inseparable from dance, such as Ghanaian drumming (Africa) or Kathak's tala (India). When the drums change rhythm or texture, they communicate the next dance pattern.

Unhealthy Dependence (on Music)

Creative accompaniment and collaboration with music teachers is fruitful when both music students and dance students compose original works on the same theme and put them together in an artful way. However, overreliance on music must be avoided.

Songs   Students can make up moves to the latest popular songs all they want outside of class and enjoy doing it immensely. Besides being creative, it increases activity levels. However, this practice is not for school-based dance and is inappropriate for a school performance. The craft of choreography you teach in educational dance is not about stringing moves together that mimic the words or story line of a song. Besides, movers are not learning anything about choreography during this process (which is evidenced by the fact they can do this without knowing anything about choreography). This kind of dance is totally at the mercy of the music for the idea, the rhythmic structure, and its length. This kind of dance is decorative at best and limp at worst. Although the song may be compelling, if there is an artistic statement, such a statement has usually been made in the music, and the movement merely enhances the pleasure of listening to it for its fans. Surely there are exceptions, but few. Popular songs are best not used in an educational dance program. The one exception may be an advanced high school class project, "Creating Music Videos," emphasizing the blend of choreography, music, and videomaking processes to result in a finished video containing a class' original choreography. Remember to adhere to all copyright laws regarding such a project.

Dance Accompaniment   Music is so often used as accompaniment for dance we hardly realize that sometimes we make music subservient to dance. Think about how you use music for accompaniment so as to keep the musical form's integrity without adapting and chopping it up to suit your own purposes. When we think of music as a sister art form, then we remember to create a partnership that serves both the music and the dance. Take care not to cut and paste music without giving thought to its compositional integrity, just as you would want someone to keep the artistic integrity of your dance choreography.

Discourage the use of self-selected musical accompaniment until students are advanced enough to make full dances. This is after they have mastered dance studies with all the simple forms (either without music or with accompaniment you chose).

Divorce dance's reliance on music; otherwise students will put steps and routines directly to the music. Be very intentional about introducing accompaniment options. Dance as art in education is about increasing self-expression using the PODs, the BSTER elements, and the craft of choreography, not dancing to the music.

Collaborating With Visual Arts

Dance is sometimes referred to as a visual art because it unfolds before the viewer in performance styles of dance. Visual art and dance are the two most alike of the four arts because they are spatial arts, they start from scratch, and they emphasize creating. Although music and theatre instruction can involve creating and composing, they rely heavily on the large body of works already created. The artistic principles of design guide creative work in visual art and dance. Both share elements: line, texture, relationship, shape, perspective, and space. Both create three-dimensional forms. Both work with mass and weight—dance does so with numbers of dancers whereas art does so with density and size of shapes. Both direct the eye of the beholder by making visual points of emphasis. Both strive for artistic excellence during the creative process so products are aesthetically solid. The use of space and relationship is similar in dance and visual arts.

Visual art works are excellent stimuli for choreography because you can unpack them—much the same as you unpack a dance work—to translate

320

ideas into movement. The lines in a visual art work may become floor pattern or air pattern in dance. The textures of a visual art work translate to dancing dynamics and textural interest. The mood in a visual art work translates, as do repetition and patterns. Two- and three-dimensional shapes in visual art become shapes and shaping in dance.

For beginners, use only one or two visual concepts. For seasoned students, extrapolate multiple choreographic criteria. Unpack visual art works so beginners discover connections to these works. Encourage advanced students to really unpack art works for criteria and concepts for dance composition.

Collaborating With Theatre

Theatre relies on the use of the body in space and time and with dynamics. It emphasizes the relationship of character to situation. Theatre class usually begins with movement warm-ups to emphasize concentration, muscular coordination, flexibility, relaxation, and deep breathing. From there students work to develop a full range of dynamics and learn to coordinate body energy with vocal energy. They work on time by pacing their interactions in relationships. They work with space and blocking for ensemble work. Older students analyze a character's personality traits and translate them into movement qualities. This enables the character to read from the stage and helps the actor portray the character consistently and intuitively.

Dance and theatre use the human body and movement to communicate. Dance can be presented artfully with theatre. But too often when dance is part of musical theatre or is used to sparkle up dull scenes, it becomes less about dance as art and more about dance as spectacle and entertainment. Therefore, dance and theatre sometimes have less in common than dance and visual art.

Creative movement underlies creative dramatics and creative dance. Creative dance reinforces theatre skills by equipping students to use variables of time, space, and degrees of dynamics. Through creative drama, students increase their expressivity on stage in dramatic roles as well as in dance. Students embody the BSTERs as movement vocabulary for both.

Creative dramatics and dance rely on creative movement as a base, but each takes its own point of departure. The departure comes when creative drama *portrays* a story from beginning, middle, to end, and creative dance *abstracts* a story into choreographic movement that may or may not follow the story. The story can be the stimulus but not always the script in dance.

Integrating the Arts Through Dance Themes

Themes are important links across subject areas, especially the arts. Talk to arts specialists about what students are to learn. Brainstorm. Find commonalities that work for at least two or three arts disciplines. Select a unifying theme that all arts specialists seem eager to tackle such as social justice, transformations, cultural studies, carnival, or pioneers. All teach it at the same time. Create and then perform or exhibit for each other for feedback and critique. Use the principles of design as review criteria for critique.

Water

Choose a theme such as water, because all the arts have significant works related to water. Create a collaborative unit to perform and exhibit. Use ideas like these to stimulate your own thinking.

DANCE

- Reconstruct Doris Humphrey's early work "Water Study" performed without musical accompaniment. Its movement makes its own accompaniment. Learn how the dance is imagistically conceived to evoke the moods of the ocean.

- Learn and perform the Israeli folk dance, "Mayim, Mayim" (translated: water, water) and sing its song as accompaniment.

- Investigate Ailey's "Wading in the Water" (from *Revelations*).

MUSIC

- Ask the music specialist to recommend "water" music that would also be good accompaniment for creative dance works around the theme of water.

- Study such works as Debussy's "La Mer" and Handel's *Water Music*.

- Learn traditional Negro spirituals such as "Deep River" and "Wade in the Water."

THEATRE

- The musical *Big River* connects the Mark Twain stories around the Mississippi River for all ages.

- The portrayal of the Jade Emperor in Bright Sheng's *The Silver River* is also a stunning work. Spoken and sung in stylized Chinese, it is a fusion of Chinese opera, traditional opera, and theatre.
- A third option is *The Miracle Worker,* the life of Helen Keller, which uses water as a metaphor for truth and knowledge as the culmination of the play.

VISUAL ART

- Study watercolor as a medium in art.
- Study works that feature the subject of water.
- Inquire into different techniques to create a wet-looking surface in painting media.
- Survey three-dimensional works that are set in water (such as fountains, water sculpture, and ice sculpture).

Organic Versus Geometric

Use concepts from disciplines such as science and math to stimulate explorations across the arts. All the arts explore what it means to be human and a part of nature. They juxtapose the natural, organic world against what is human-made, mechanical, and inorganic. Consider designing a unit called "Organic Versus Geometric" using ideas such as these to stimulate your thinking about conceptual collaborations.

Dance and visual art explore hard-edged and geometric shapes as contrasted to rounded, organic shapes with softer edges. Explore them with bodyshaping, by drawing lines in space, and by movement qualities. Change the quality of movement according to which is portrayed, natural or mechanical. Explore Laban's concepts of spoking, arcing, and carving as a part of the linear shaping of the body.

Music explores sound from nature (e.g., sounds of whales, waterfalls), from the world of humans (e.g., created forms, rhythmic structures, music compositions), and from combinations of the two (e.g., electronic, ambient, nonmetered music synthesized from Machu Pichu that uses technology to shape natural sounds).

Great drama is born out of the conflict between the human need for organic time structures and the ever-pushing society that is driven by clocks,

Dance and visual art explore geometric and organic shapes, which can inspire bodyshaping that is symmetrical (like this) or asymmetrical.

322

schedules, and human-made constructs of time. The world of technology clashes with the world of nature. The systems we construct occasionally devour us. It is the subject of great drama to just miss something or someone, to hurry and be too late, to unsuccessfully try to increase life's pace to keep up with others, to die young. For example, in the drama *Proof*, the daughter of a mathematician figures out a complex mathematical problem that is surrounded by suspicion, yet she has difficulty figuring out and sorting out her own personal life. That play is only suitable for high school students, but it juxtaposes the mathematic against the organic.

Transformation

Both **visual and performing arts** work with transformation; in fact, all art has the means to transform. The transformation can be a magic act in theatre where one thing is quickly transformed into another. Or it can be a drama based on the transformation of things over time—such as going from one stage of life to another, death and resurrection on stage, a mask change to portray a different character. Explore the art of transformation in a collaborative unit.

- Visual art uses paint to transform a canvas into a portrayal of something it is not. Visual art depicts change in large murals that show the passage of time. It also creates small sculptures within larger ones.

- *Trompe l'oeil* is art that appears to be something it is not. It fools the eye. It transforms a real place into a totally different one. It can make a smooth surface appear rough. It can give the appearance of a real window on a solid cement wall.

- Dance takes a concept from a real situation and abstracts it from real life into nonliteral movement for choreography. Dances such as *The Nutcracker* and *Petroushka* deal with transformation of toys to live characters. Act 1 of *Giselle* portrays a happy peasant girl, but Act 2 transforms her into a dancing spirit.

- In Kabuki theatre, one costume is sewn inside another, and with a lightning flash gesture the threads are pulled and a complete costume transformation happens before your eyes to change the character.

- Music suites that start with slow adagio sections may end with fast ones such as gigues. A

musical theme is transformed through numerous variations.

Simple Form

Identify basic ways to make a statement in each of the arts. One of the most basic is beginning–middle–end (B–M–E), as we learned in chapter 7.

DANCE: MAKE A SIMPLE MOVEMENT PHRASE

a. A breath phrase
b. A kinetic phrase
c. A locomotor phrase
d. An axial phrase
e. An axio-locomotor phrase

MUSIC

Compose a simple melodic phrase with a beginning, middle, and end. For older students, use it as the theme. Vary it according to tempo, texture, and tone.

THEATRE

a. Create a complete solo sketch with beginning, conflict, resolution, and end.
b. Reenact a historic improvisation around a historic figure.

VISUAL ART

Create two-dimensional shapes that have length, width, and depth of volume.

Contrasting Form: AB Form

Use an AB form to express the relationship between two extremes or opposites. Collaboratively identify the set of opposites that you wish to use (e.g., curved lines–straight lines, bound flow–free flow, smooth–sharp, in one place–through space).

- Dance: Create one movement phrase (A) followed by a contrasting movement phrase (B).
- Music: Compose a two-part study that contrasts rhythmic structures.
- Theatre: Create a speech that makes two different points. Start with one idea and either modulate or transform it into another. Work with the concept of changing situations.
- Visual art: Create an installation that uses cones, cylinders, cubes, or spheres to create two contrasting concepts. Feature either line or shape as a part of the contrast.

Dancing Across the Curriculum

Chapter 3's teaching roles and responsibilities included initiating crossovers to other subjects. Be that center point for collaboration. Import into dance and export dance so nondance teachers bring dance into their classrooms.

A national study, Reviewing Education in the Arts Project (REAP), found the arts to have a positive impact in teaching other subjects. However, the study warned against subverting the arts or pretending to teach other subjects through them. The study cautions, Do not justify arts education in the schools by how well other subjects are taught through them. Justify your existence by the dance standards you meet. Justify dance as substantive aesthetic education in dance. Unless you can authenticate that dance meets other standards, don't claim that it does (refer to table 10.2, page 299).

National standards make you accountable to teach dance and make meaningful connections to other disciplines (NSDE 7). To do this without compromising national or aesthetic standards of either discipline, use the cornerstone frameworks to emphasize dance as rigorous, substantive, artistic, and educationally necessary to broadly prepare educated citizens for this century.

Curricular balancing in dance is more than importing to dance and exporting dance. First students need competence in dance. Weight the curriculum heavily in the dance discipline (i.e., dance cornerstones) to have the dance depth to support work across disciplines. Without this emphasis, cross-curricular collaborations are weak and superficial. Balance can't be strictly calculated because each unit of study makes its own connections to take dance goals forward. The goal of a substantive curriculum is to achieve both dance and other curricular goals without trivializing either.

There is also the issue of balancing curricular-based initiatives with those that are student centered. And scheduling enough time for dance instruction—which we discuss in chapter 11—affects curricular balance. Include enough content-rich instruction in dance. All else is predicated on that.

Questions to Ponder

1. How do national standards in other academic core subjects support educational dance?

2. How can dance facilitate the goals of other subjects while advancing the art of dance? Without compromising dance standards?

3. What topic (or themes) from social studies would be useful to bring to dance for middle school students?

4. What themes from science would be useful for primary ages to dance?

5. What common processes are vital to all the visual and performing arts?

6. What concepts discussed by teachers in other subjects could be effectively taught through movement?

7. How does this information add to or reshape your Statements of Belief (as explained in the Introduction)?

Rich Resources

- American Dance Legacy Institute. Strandburg, Julie A., and Carolyn Adams (Eds). *Dancing Through the Curriculum: A Guide to Dance Videotapes Curated and Designed to Enrich the School Curriculum,* Providence, RI: JayEss Press, 1997.

- www.arts4learning.org: Arts for Learning (A4L) brings numerous resources, tools, and research to help you facilitate learning in and through the arts. It also shows effective ways to integrate the arts into other academics.

- http://artsedge.kennedy-center.org: The ARTSEDGE Web site contains an excellent collection of lesson plans in dance and in dance integrated with other subjects.

- www.acr.uc.edu: Go to Alliance for Curriculum Reform for links to standards in other disciplines.

- Gilbert, Anne Green. *Teaching the Three R's through Movement Experience* (reprinted in 2004 by NDEO). This book shows lessons you might incorporate into your units that address specific concepts and ideas across subjects.

Creating and Maintaining an Effective Arts Learning Environment

"... it is unfair to hold teachers accountable for their students' meeting the standards unless they too are ensured adequate time, materials, and other necessary conditions for teaching."

—National Dance Association, *Opportunity-to-Learn Standards in Dance Education* (1995, p. i)

This chapter enables you to set up effective learning environments for dance. Topics include how to organize your studio or classroom, how to maintain discipline in a movement-based class, and how to set expectations to promote aesthetic growth. We will look at what affects your ability to successfully teach a standards-oriented curriculum: scheduling, dance facilities, and safety issues. The chapter identifies competencies you need to plan and facilitate dance instruction. You will address practical matters that affect your ability to teach dance as art in education.

Creating a Positive Arts Environment

Teaching dance as art in education depends on how you set up a learning environment that supports artistic growth. You can only meet educational dance goals when students cooperate and invest themselves in the process. Artistic success hinges on practical factors you regulate: setting and maintaining safe boundaries, managing productive classes, and establishing trust. Here are some of the main questions you face:

- What is a positive environment?
- What are the non-negotiable, basic rules you have to establish and maintain?
- How can you maintain structure in a room without desks?
- What are effective behavior management techniques for classes in dance?

Keep the Environment Productive

What is a positive environment? It's an environment that is conducive to artistic expression. The better you establish and maintain this environment, the more your students benefit; the saner you are; the more respect you earn from peers, administrators, students, and parents; and the better results you'll get from students.

Emulate arts teachers who keep students on task, waste no instructional minutes, and have a spirit of joy about them. Seek out teachers who are encouraging and available to students. Ask these teachers what structures they use to support student discipline while holding artistic standards. Ask what helps them run efficient classrooms and how they go about making rules, enforcing rules, and determining consequences for failure to comply. Ask which rules require the most teacher reinforcement. Ask how these teachers spin corrections toward the positive rather than the punitive.

No student deserves a self-centered teacher who whines when things don't go his or her way, who is the students' buddy, or who lets them slide by without working. Students lose respect for such a teacher, merely tolerate the class, and become lazy. Give your students the gift of being appreciated for being good at something and for doing their best. This keeps the environment productive.

Go for win–wins. Validating good work produces win–wins: Students achieve and feel good about themselves. Misbehavior and punishment produce lose–lose: Students neither achieve nor feel good about themselves.

Good work—plus validation for it—builds student esteem, which reduces misbehavior in class. Attention-needing students misbehave to get attention because it works. As you showcase individual students as models of good work, their need for attention is satisfied positively. When you genuinely appreciate the unique contributions of a student, let

Students do their best work in a safe, nurturing, and positive environment.

her know. This creates a collaborative and positive environment.

Stabilize the Environment

In your classroom, consistently enforce rules and use consequences. Fiercely protect students' collective rights to grow by not tolerating any attempts by disruptive individuals to sidetrack you or reduce your effectiveness. Create a safe place with clear boundaries where each student can experience, create, and take risks to grow artistically. Learn how to facilitate

1. a firm, supportive learning environment emotionally;
2. a stimulating environment intellectually and artistically; and
3. a safe environment physically.

These elements stabilize the class environment.

Let your professionalism prevent you from becoming upset over personality clashes or allowing power struggles with students. Classroom issues are professional for you—not personal. Students generally act and react personally—especially at middle and high school levels. But you must not respond personally to a student: It never works. In the school setting you are the professional, and you must respond as such. This keeps the learning environment secure for all and puts students on notice that the teacher won't be baited into an argument or lose sight of the lesson goals and objectives. This, too, stabilizes the environment.

Enliven the Environment

Project in the classroom similar to the way you perform on stage. Be "big"—bigger than you really are. Extend beyond yourself. Be the one who can handle anything in the classroom. Grow confidence alongside teaching skills so each time you walk into school you transform your personal self into a professional self with a student-focused, can-do attitude and with artistic education foremost on your mind. This attitude enables you to use your authority to build a positive classroom environment.

An example: A colleague was one of the most dynamic and effective educational dance teachers. She was direct, positive, and assertive; fed the class energy; got her students going; and artistically stimulated them in all aspects of dance to such an extent that her students were empowered to accomplish great tasks. Year after year she turned an ordinary group of students into the most magical, gifted, and extraordinary dancers and choreographers imaginable. She was relentless in her classroom as she directed student energy toward success, because she had the artistic training and professional background to do it. However, it was hard to recognize this person outside of school. She was ordinary. With her peers she receded. She was shy, quiet, and totally nonassertive. Although her teacher persona was dynamic, her personal persona was opposite. Yet she more than transcended any lack of personal confidence as soon as she walked into a classroom.

Establish an affirming, productive environment by respecting students. They will love the magical, creative atmosphere and the expressive abilities you help them uncover within. This enlivens the environment.

Channel the energies of the hyperactive individual into dance production and artistic activity. Direct such a student to use his full body energy to focus attention on the creative process or the performance skill. Some of the most creative and artistically talented dance students have mild attention-deficit/hyperactivity disorder. Value their energy and keep them focused on the project at hand. Direct them to finish one artistic project at a time rather than get too many going at once. These students, when channeled, energize the environment.

Create a Nurturing Environment

Reduce student anxiety by assuring students that you will not compromise their integrity or make them look or feel stupid. Many students feel insecure about being in dance. Assure them you are there for their maximum educational benefit. Don't make fun of anyone. Teasing serves no good purpose.

In an increasingly impersonal world, many people lack enough personal attention. Dance class may be one of the few places where some kids are recognized, valued, and nurtured. You stand at the doorway of education to invite them in. Do it positively, with good energy, and with a focus on their artistic growth (see chapter 3).

See your students as individuals. Notice and comment on individual achievement. Communicate directly to each person. Convey your commitment to develop each one physically, artistically, and intellectually. Do so with positive reinforcement, direct eye contact, praise for good work, and energy—especially for those who need it most. Inspire excellence. Speak each child's name positively every day. Showcase individual success so it becomes contagious. Show how proud you are of students' achievements just as you insist they go further, refine their work artistically, and integrate new knowledge and skills. Consider the following questions:

- How can dance help us all feel good about ourselves while we are learning valuable movement skills and dance knowledge?
- How can you notice and validate students for doing good work?
- How can you build community within the confines of your room?
- Which boundaries are yours to hold?
- What kind of questions can you pose to the group to stimulate individual inquiry?

Answers to these questions produce a nurturing environment.

Communicate Rules and Policies

Communication is critical to creating a positive learning environment. Set parameters along with personal and programmatic expectations. Then hold students accountable to these parameters. Without rules and policies, student success is limited (not to mention your sanity and job satisfaction).

New Student Orientation

Get students and parents off on the right foot by having new student orientation for first-year students in middle and high school. Go over the course outline, your expectations, and the year's long-range plan with new students. Explain the artistic processes (c/p/r) that your program features. Explain how educational dance differs from community dance education. Invite parents to ask questions and express concerns. Display leotards, tights, ballet shoes, and everything needed for the year.

Student Handbook

For all middle and high school students, a detailed student handbook is also a must to communicate expectations and policies. It should specify how your school-based program differs from other dance education models by referencing the national standards, the six characteristics of educational dance, and the goals for the year. Distribute the handbook and review all main points with everyone—new and returning students. Send the handbook (or an abbreviated version of it) home for detailed reading. Get commitment signatures from both parents and student.

Explain the handbook's contents so everyone knows logistics, schedule, and personal expectations in class—especially

- what to wear in class,
- what to do and what not to do (no gum, no dangling earrings or bracelets),
- which days are different (e.g., ballet on Fridays),
- expectations for dressing out and participating and consequences for failing to do these,
- number of absences allowed before they affect the grade (and how many points are lost per absence beyond that number), and
- when a doctor's excuse is needed for an absence.

Explain what is expected outside class, such as

- transportation responsibilities for off-campus events,

- how many rehearsals there will be and their exact dates and times,
- consequences of missing a rehearsal (no performance),
- consequences of missing a performance (grade lowered), and
- outside concerts to attend, dates, locations, and all information.

Explain programmatic expectations and standards for dance as art, such as

- content and achievement standards,
- performance expectations,
- assessment strategies, and
- all grading policies.

Follow school district absentee and tardy policies. They determine such things as how many absences forfeit credit for the class. In addition you may decide to deduct points for missing a rehearsal after students have committed to perform—because commitment is usually factored into a final grade.

Tardy policies vary. Clarify what constitutes "late to class." What are the consequences for tardiness and what kind of excuse is needed? Set policies that deter bad habits. Use these policies to speed up slow movers. For example, one high school uses a step system: a warning for the first tardy, assignment to after-school work detail for the second, and parent shadowing with an additional written report in their permanent school record for the third. Each teacher consistently enforces the steps.

See appendix B for a "Sample Student Handbook (High School Gifted and Talented Program)" with some of the rules and policies you might want to adapt or adopt. Also see "Class Management Notes From an Inner-City High School Teacher" in appendix B. List other guidelines and expectations you would include in your student handbook.

Formulate Rules and Policies for Dance

How much time each day do you allocate for dressing out? What signals that this time has lapsed? What are the consequences if the limitation is not met? How do you assess daily to grade the quality of participation given that you have limited time between classes?

Structure a classroom to have maximum time for learning and time on task. Set boundaries to get maximum output. Set standards for quality participation by each student. Set time limits on such things as changing shoes or clothes. Then you have maximum time to nurture artistic processes in students. A blend of structure, discipline, and rules contributes to the well-being of all students and affects the quality of their arts education experience.

Classroom Management

You will have individuals whose behavior you need to manage to keep the entire group moving forward. Every class has three main requirements:

1. The effective organization of space and time to maximize student time on task
2. The safety of the students (emotional and physical)
3. High-quality instruction in and through dance

The need for a structured environment cannot be overemphasized. You need structure so you are free to be creative in your arts instruction and to keep the sense of vibrancy about what is being taught. Students need structure as the basis for maintaining safe boundaries in which they have the freedom to create, dance, and critique. If the structure breaks down and chaos reigns, there can be no creative work or artistic growth. Students have to be on task to reach learning objectives.

Classroom Rules

Post rules. They optimize functioning, set safe boundaries, and provide consistency. State classroom rules affirmatively, like the following:

- Be truthful and responsible.
- Respect your classmates and their property.
- Listen and follow directions.
- Be on time.
- Bring dance materials and clothing to every class.

Routines

Set and post daily routines to prevent your having to oversee repetitive start-up tasks each day. Establish exactly where to dress and exactly what is to be worn, including shoes, hair clips, and clothing. Adhere to this routine so students won't have to ask you what to do. It will help keep you sane, and you'll be glad to focus your attention on important matters instead during those first critical minutes. Establish where belongings are to be stored during class. Make a place for street shoes, book bags, and coats. Routines foster student responsibility, build efficiency, and set up good work habits so you have between-class time to assess the previous class. There's no reason for a daily battle of wills (e.g., "Do we have to dress out today?"). There's no reason to allow chatty or poky students to sponge up valuable dance time.

Allot a short time for students to dress out for your class. Three minutes is enough. Set a timer as soon as the period bell rings, and then be ready to start class in 3 minutes whether all students are ready or not. Deduct a point from the total points allocated for the day for any who take longer than the allotted time to change, and make this rule non-negotiable. You must not allow slow students to hold the entire class back and reduce productive time. Make a management plan to move students quickly from dressing out to the first activity.

Activity Rules

What are your activity rules for students? What's the same each day and what is different? Always make movement rules clear; post them and stick to them. State class rules affirmatively. For example:

1. "Look for open spaces before you move. No bumping or touching another person."
2. "Listen to directions and cues. Watch body signals; listen to verbal cues, drum cues, and music cues."
3. "Concentrate on moving silently. No talking or noise while moving. We use our active-listening skills in dance, which isn't possible with noise."
4. "Class starts when the timer chimes. Be ready!"
5. "Help make our space safe for everyone. It must be safe physically, emotionally, and intellectually for you and for others. Each one contributes to everyone's safety. Any action that compromises safety is not allowed."

Daily Records

How will you keep records so you can recall exactly what happened 6 weeks ago? You don't have all day for record keeping. If you require full participation and quality effort in all lessons—whether activity based or not—how will you organize your grade book to notate daily studio participation, daily dance academics, and major quizzes or assessments? After you explain daily effort standards and quality standards required for success in dance, be sure you have a parallel system to keep track of exactly those things—especially in movement-based classes. Record student progress, level of participation, and commitment to quality daily. This applies to all ages in K-12. Because one class follows another, you should have 2 to 3 minutes between classes for record keeping.

In cases where you have less than 3 minutes between classes, ask the classroom teachers (K-5) to walk students to your class and hold them outside the door for 30 seconds to a minute while you reset music and make notes. Study the sample daily record book in figure 11.1, which has a place to notate grades. You can do this for 30 students in 2 to 3 minutes each day. Then you are ready to greet the next class. For older students who have a dressing routine, time is not so tight. You can generally supervise their dressing routine while you make specific notes from the previous class.

Accountability standards have changed the way we measure educational success. For example, we used to list participation as a main aspect of students' dance grades. The main criteria were dressing out and going through the motions of class. If kids remembered their dancewear, didn't grumble about dressing out, and danced, they got a satisfactory participation grade. Some teachers weighted participation as the largest percentage! Today that is not enough. Dance's standards are raised, and so are the stakes. Aesthetic education holds students accountable to a high level of participation in creating, performing, and responding to dance. We grade according to the learning objectives students accomplish. We grade according to the growth in ability to articulate—in words and movement —the kin-aesthetic learning taking place. It is not acceptable to compromise the standards, so let's see how we set up for success.

Student Accountability   Vital to accountability is keeping daily records and organizing your grade book. Unless you hold students accountable daily (i.e., give a daily grade), they tend to work at substandard quality level. Your memory blurs details over time. Quality is hard to qualify and quantify later without clear daily records and comments. Keep records as snapshots over time of where a student is so you can see how he or she is progressing.

Set nondebatable parameters for class work when injury or illness prevents participation in the dance class. Reasonable and enforced nondebatable rules offer the greatest educational structure.

Students who know and adhere to the functional boundaries get maximum time on task within a limited school day. For example, non-negotiables related to time must be set, such as expecting students to be on time, dress out in a set amount of time before incurring penalty points, and turn in written work and finish creative assignments on time. Penalty points determine the consequences—which build incrementally (e.g., you might remove the chronic infractor from the next student performance). In this overall structure, you can be the holistic authority model and facilitate learning in an unimpeded productive environment.

 How do you think teacher authority and student accountability coexist?

Teacher's Daily Records   Daily assessment helps you identify who lags and who needs more challenge. Use symbols for shorthand to write as much as possible—in fact, an elaborate symbol system saves you much time. Inform students that you record two daily grades per person: quality of effort and participation and quality of academic and artistic achievement. Notate behavior or infractions in one place and artistic growth and achievements, breakthroughs, and academic work in another. Discipline yourself to quickly record in your grade book between every class—while one group is preparing to leave and the next is about to enter and while they are going through their preassigned dressing preparations for class. Reveal the exact percentage that this quarterly (i.e., 9-week) daily participation grade is weighted.

Assess on a 3-point scale for elementary and a 5-point scale for middle and high school students:

- Elementary: 0-1-2-3. Record each student a 0, 1, 2, or 3 as soon as class ends to quickly notate the quality of class participation, where 0 is absent, 1 is below average, 2 is average, and 3 is outstanding (i.e., earned through diligence, concentration, and full participation). Monitor participation throughout each lesson to notice who is invested in progress and process. Tie semester rewards to having accumulated a certain number of daily points as a positive reinforcement for quality outcomes.

- Middle and high school: 0-1-2-3-4-5. More is expected at this age, so record more detail. Using numbers in your grade book helps you document progress and behavior—from 0 to 5. These numbers help you monitor when a student replaces an undesirable habit with a desirable one.

Dance Class—Grade Book Sample for Daily Participation Grades (Middle School)

Daily Grade Scale

5 = 100 (A+)

4 = 92 (B+)

3 = 84 (C+)

2 = 79 (D+)

1 = 69 (F+)

0 = 0 (F-)

Point Breakdown

Dressing out on time earns up to 2 points.

Effort and progress earns up to 3 points.

Student name	9/1	9/2	9/3	9/4	9/5	9/8	9/9	9/10	9/11	9/12
Antoine Bates	5	5	5	• 4	5	5	5	• 3	4	5
Carolyn Dobbs	• 4	• 4	X 3	X 3	X 3	5	5	5	5	• 4
Emily Finch	5	5	5	5	5	5	5	4	5	5
Gwendolyn Hastings	5	5	4	• 3	• 4	• 4	X 3	X 3	X 2	4
Indira Jennings	5	5	5	5	5	5	5	5	5	5
Kevin Lomax	5	5	5	• 5	4	5	5	5	5	5
Morgan Nolan	4	3	X 2	X 2	X 1	X 0	X 0	X 2	X 2	X 1
Ophelia Phillips	5	5	• 4	• 4	5	5	5	5	5	5
Quincy Reynolds	4	5	5	4	4	4	5	5	5	5
Sarah Thomas	X 2	X 3	X 3	4	5	5	4	5	4	X 3
Uma Vance	5	5	5	5	5	5	5	5	5	5
William Xavier	• 4	• 4	• 4	• 4	• 4	• 4	• 4	5	5	• 4
Yvonne Zee	5	5	5	5	X 3	5	5	5	5	5

• = Late dressing out (minus 1 point)

X = Did not dress out (minus 2 points)

FIGURE 11.1   Daily record book.

Used with permission of A. Wrenn Cook.

List details of daily problems for any daily grade below 3 to document actions and consequences. Such records provide a thumbnail progress report so you see patterns that need to be addressed. Make a list of your own shorthand symbols to record problems in your grade book. For example, h = no homework, t = tardy arrival, c = no dance clothes, d = discourteous or disrespectful, w = weak participation, m = medical, a dot = late dressing for class (more than 3 minutes, minus 1 point), X = did not dress out (minus 2 points), e/x = brought no written excuse. See figure 11.1 from a middle school dance specialist's grade book, noting the grading scale, the point breakdown, and symbols used. Symbols are time savers and sometimes lifesavers.

From figure 11.1 you can see how recording daily quality numbers helps you do the following:

1. Assess student progress over time and assign a final grade

2. Provide grading documentation to administrators when needed

3. See patterns of behavior and chart a student's cumulative level of participation

4. Pinpoint exactly what happened on what date

5. Document when a certain action was done and support the student's grade

6. Settle disputes over how many times a student did something (e.g., was late to class)

7. Specify to parents how many times h happened and on what dates (there it is in black and white)

8. Verify that a student did not show up with a doctor's excuse

Arts Grading   Record growth in each cornerstone. Make separate headings:

C1. Daily growth in movement, dance, or studio classes (e.g., dancing, technique, skills)

C2. Creative work (e.g., creating and composing, dance making)

C3. Academic work (e.g., dance knowledge and special projects)

C4. Aesthetic feedback and critiques (e.g., dance analysis and criticism)

State that written assignments and compositional work are due on the assigned date. If you will accept them late, decide how many points are deducted each day they are late—for example, 5 points per day. State such policies in the handbook.

Weight the grading scale according to your priorities, giving more weight to what you consider important. For example, if quality of artistic participation is a priority, make it a higher percentage of the total grade. State your main categories and assign each one a percentage or weight before classes begin (adding up to 100%). When grading time comes, average each category separately before averaging weighted totals. Ranges usually are as follows:

1. Quality of daily participation (also artistic quality)—60% to 80% of quarterly grade
   - Dancing and performing
   - Creating and composing
   - Responding and critiquing

2. Written work and projects; knowing about dance—10% to 30%

3. Exam, performance, and final projects—10% to 15%

Realistic Expectations   All students do not deserve A's. You have probably been a good student all your life and think that the standard is A and anything that is not quite up to standard is B. That's not accurate! C is the accepted median level and is the grade to measure against. For example, is the student on par (C), above par (B), or way above par and excellent in every way (A)? Or is the student below par (D) or just not working (F)? If all is generally acceptable, that is a C.

Grade inflation is one aspect of giving students something for nothing. Similar to unwarranted praise, it sabotages standards of excellence in dance and undermines quality. The NSDEs set forth realistic standards in dance. To accomplish these standards is not A. To accomplish them really well is A. State realistic dance standards in your unit objectives. Then measure in a discriminating way the extent to which students consistently achieve them. Then you can encourage students to redo, refine, and relearn when necessary to reach a higher grade. Let students redo their work for a higher grade because of the remedial learning opportunity it provides—especially after peer review of written and creative work. Arts education's aim is for students to achieve—it doesn't matter if they achieve on the first try or not, so long as they get it.

Consider using numeric grades—1, 2, 3, 4, 5, with 3 being median—rather than letter grades for all assessments. Numbers are clearer after you explain that the median 3 is for acceptable work. This system lets you add grades and average them at the end of the grading period without conversion. Then, if letter grades are used at your school for send-home reports, translate numbers directly, because 1-5 corresponds directly to F-A.

The exception is kindergarten through fourth grade peer assessments of student work and self-assessments. They use a 3-point scale, with 2 as median. Three-point scales are the most basic. This policy establishes realistic expectations for younger students and sets up your use of a numerical 5-point scale later. When you are averaging peer or self-assessments as part of a grade, average them in with your assessments and convert them to a 5-point scale for recording purposes.

Accepting Authority

The learning environment requires you to claim a classroom presence and authority. As you empower others, don't give students control over you by giving them your power. You are the authority, but that does not mean you should be loud. Quiet, firm leadership is usually the strongest. Be an authority figure even as you are a facilitator of learning. A substantive, aesthetically driven, and inquiry-based dance program requires an authority figure. Don't try to be the most popular teacher.

Empowering Students Without Undermining Your Authority

Dance specialists exist to help others communicate in dance as a means of artistic expression and find their artistic voice. How can you empower students to do this without undermining your authority? This question is especially relevant in a holistic arts education environment. Can you effect student achievement in a standards-oriented curriculum? How does obedience fit into the elementary classroom alongside empowerment? Teachers and students share the responsibility 50-50 for student achievement. But students must be motivated to learn and empowered to find their artistic voice in dance. Reflect on Peterson's perspective in the next Reflect and Respond. What is the difference between a holistic learning environment and a traditional one? How does this apply to arts education? When does obedience to authority help educational dance and when does it hinder it? Is empowerment different for different ages?

Rules for behavior are traditional; rules for learning are holistic. In a holistic learning community, students are guided by inquiring and by processing their own thinking. A learn-because-I-say-to-learn authority goes against divergent thinking and the freedom to problem solve, make dances, critique,

Reflect and Respond

Do you agree with this excerpt from Ralph Peterson's "Thoughts on Teacher Authority and Student Empowerment"? Why or why not?

"Teachers exercise authority—let there be no doubt about it. Learning is at best haphazard and chaotic if teachers are unable to exercise authority in their teaching. What is important is that there are many kinds of authority. Authority is a broad continuum that comprises obedience to externally created rules as well as respect for one's own ways of thinking and acting.

"The primary function of authority in a holistic learning community is not to control students or to require obedience, but to empower students to take the initiative, think for themselves, and assume responsibility for their own learning. Students who are empowered have the personal authority needed to express themselves confidently, judge their own work and the work of others, and take action in their own best interest as well as the interest of others.

"The word 'empowerment' separates traditional teaching from holistic teaching. Simply put, holistic teachers require students to be responsible for their own learning. That is to say, ideas central to holism such as valuing intuition and feeling as ways of knowing, plus recognizing the importance of living and learning where social relationships are based on caring, as well as content, are made operational by students' taking responsibility for their learning. Teachers are responsible for caring for students the best way they know how, but the learning is up to the students. . . . learning that results in a true change in competence will happen only when a student assumes responsibility for learning. . . . Learning is personal. Others can help, but the learner has to do the work.

"Is there any reason to believe that obedience to authority strengthens students' intellect and enriches their imaginations? Is there any reason to believe it helps them develop the conviction to stand up for what they know and believe to be right? These questions are not only important educational questions, they are critical to a democratic society."

Excerpts adapted, by permission, from *Life in a crowded place: Making a learning community*, by Ralph Peterson. Published by Heineman, a division of Reed Elsevier, Inc., Portsmouth, NH, 1992.

reflect, and journal. Don't do for students what they should do for themselves. The classroom environment you build either supports inquiry and self-directed investigation in a positive learning environment or not. Therefore, think about

- how your rules establish the necessary order to function optimally,
- how your interactions with students support them but hold the line on level participation and creative and kin-aesthetic production,

- how you facilitate inquiry and hold students accountable for their learning,

- how you monitor and adjust according to student-centered needs while at the same time hold students accountable to national standards, and

- how all this contributes to an environment that is artistically alive and challenging so students produce the kind of work that validates who they are and builds real self-esteem.

To create a conducive, positive environment is more than how you operate a classroom. It affects all you do in aesthetic education.

Discuss authority models with supervisors before beginning clinical observations in the schools. The teacher is the ultimate authority who is accountable for achieving artistic objectives and standards. Structure is necessary for a classroom to produce results. The teacher must define freedoms and limitations based on how much structure each group needs to function optimally.

Praising Accomplishment in the Arts

Research shows that many American schools overemphasize positive reinforcement to increase self-esteem more than praising a job well done. You can inadvertently lower student expectations by overpraising. Such a combination of "something for nothing" tends to produce individuals addicted more to entitlement than to achievement, which sets them up for disappointment, confusion, and low esteem. False praise sets up unrealistic expectations, making students unwilling to work. In the arts, this is a big issue. Work in the arts is not easy. It requires sweat, thought, critical thinking, judgment, and work in the artistic processes.

We expect students to investigate matters of depth and substance in dance. There are real goals to achieve in each cornerstone. There is artistic integrity to support through refining and editing one's original work. There is performance after all! Students need encouragement and genuine praise to achieve the real educational dance goals that get them on par with national standards. Personal accomplishment in dance—and accompanying legitimate praise—build real self-esteem. Motivate toward true accomplishment. You would not dream of setting expectations so low that you'd rob individuals of the quality of work that brings a surge of inner pride—the substance of real self-esteem. Legitimate praise in dance produces high achievement and legitimate self-esteem.

Child psychologist John Rosemond said,

> While self-esteem among America's youth has been on the rise for the past 30 years, accomplishment and responsible decision-making have been on the decline. Why? Because the sort of self-esteem bloating many of America's kids is not based on a realistic appraisal of their strengths and weaknesses; therefore, it does not lead to accomplishment. Rather, it is based on unconditional, uncritical acceptance of whatever they do and think; therefore it leads to mediocrity. . . . Praise by itself does not produce high achievement. High expectations coupled with accurate, supportive feedback produce high achievement, which merits praise.

Adapted with permission of John Rosemond, *The State Newspaper*/SC, 2002.

High expectations coupled with accurate, supportive feedback produce high achievement, which merits praise.

Compare Rosemond's perspective to Lerman's Critical Response Process (see chapter 9). How does critical response contribute to a choreographer's legitimate confidence and self-esteem?

Managing Arts Instruction: The Precursor to Artistic Expression

Two issues need attention:

- facilitating the five phases of a kindergarten through grade 5 creative dance class as introduced in chapter 7 and
- planning ahead for students who are unable to dance in K-12.

Managing a Creative Dance Class (Kindergarten Through Grade 5)

Creative dance—which is central to the entire dance curriculum—looks like managed chaos. Facilitating skills must be refined through practice. Although you cannot control another person's movement, you can provide a safe structure for self-managed, self-governed movement. As the unquestioned authority, you can very gradually loosen the initially tight reins so students learn to manage their own actions, creating and expressing themselves in unique ways through their invented dances. But first hold the line. Before artistry can develop, one must control one's movement. Here are ways to guide beginners to learn how to work with the body in space.

> **"It was an important day when I discovered I did not teach Dance, I taught People."**
>
> —Mary Stark Whitehouse, dance therapy pioneer (Wallock 1981, p. 45)

Readiness

You must take utter and complete command of a creative dance class until beginners at the primary or elementary age demonstrate ability to self-govern in motion. Work them toward self-governance by repeating and reinforcing these management concepts as they move:

- "Move on cue with the drum to stop and start." (i.e., cued motion time)
- "Listen when moving. Make no sound."
- "Move without touching others or objects."

- "Move with strong muscles that keep you from collapsing when the drum stops." (Dancers don't flop on the floor.)
- "Move so you can stop when the drum stops."
- "Move only while the drum is sounding."
- "Freeze. Hold your shape as long as required."

Establish and enforce a quiet sitting position (QSP) for kindergarten through grade 5 students. They take a QSP as soon as shoes are removed to show they are ready to begin class . . . and any time they need to refocus on the lesson objective.

Modulate your voice. Use silence and whispers effectively. Lower your voice when classes are noisy so they must quiet down to hear what you are saying. Never try to out-shout a noisy group. It doesn't work.

Creative dance might initially seem to little ones like an invitation to misbehave. In regular classrooms they are trying their best to follow directions, sit still, line up, follow one after the other without bumping, and get the correct answer to a specific question. They are seldom asked to be expressive in movement with the full body in motion, so to circumvent bedlam in creative dance you must plan each progressive step of the lesson. Guide exploration and closely monitor movement responses. As soon as exploration breaks down—which it will during the first lessons—have students dance back to place for more instruction. Stop and start again until all can bodyshape and move in control. Until this is accomplished, you simply cannot get much further. Explore many different ways to help children gain control of their bodies. Give plenty of practice. This is more than a cognitive skill—it is psychomotor.

To judge the readiness of kindergarten through fourth grade students, observe their guided exploration. Can they manage themselves in one place? If so, can they control their body parts in a limited amount of space? Incrementally give more spatial challenges as the ability to self-govern increases:

1. If students can't move in control while sitting in one place exploring moving body parts, they won't move in control while standing.

2. If they can't move in control while standing in one place, they will not move through the room in control.

3. If they can't move through an uncrowded room, they can't move through close spaces.

Assess the absolute basics to reinforce them before you progress to other more challenging lessons:

- Can students hold absolutely still?
- Can they freeze absolutely as the drum stops?
- Do they start moving exactly when the drum starts sounding?
- Are they able to move absolutely without talking?
- Are they able to move absolutely without noise?
- Are they looking into the open, safe spaces so that they are not touching others?
- Can they start and stop on cue with strong muscles?

Ensure that students gain mastery of each skill as you go. The payoff comes when they self-manage and move with ease within the parameters of safe space. (Safe space is that which has no obstacles in it and no slippery floor.) Students won't use dance expressively and artistically until they can govern their own movement and master intentional bodyshaping.

Place Tapes

A useful technique for managing classes in open space is to put "place tapes" equidistant around the entire space—one per student with a few extras. Tape the floor in rows with sequential numbers, and assign each student a numbered seat on the floor. This is where she sits every day to start class—as though it were a desk. Numbered place tapes identify one's place in the room, so during guided spatial exploration you can ask everyone to dance back to his place tape. Separate troublemakers. (Later you might change the place tapes from numbers to words such as the names of the states, famous astronauts, poets, or textures of movement that convey qualities.) Place tapes are where students assume a QSP (quiet sitting position) at the beginning of class. When a class gets careless, noisy, or out of line, return students to this spot, refocus the exploration problem, and

start again. It is not a punitive place, just a starting place. When you dance them back to place, many students are unaware that you are using this move to regain their attention. Each student's place is just an excellent starting and stopping neutral place. It is a useful ending place for creative exploration. It's a good place to refocus. Place tapes have numerous applications in creative dance.

Self-Governance

Student safety is in your hands. Keep students safe and on task toward the lesson's objectives. Students don't come to dance class knowing how they should act: You must teach them. Give them tools with which to self-govern. You can't control the class. Individuals control themselves after they master skills of self-governance. You don't have to use authority harshly when you firmly insist on safety and on rules of behavior. Students need to control themselves before you can work on arts expression, so try to achieve this in minimum time.

Kids have to rehearse the complex task of simultaneously listening, thinking and processing, translating what they hear into action, and moving. Cue movement starts and stops. Ease young children into movement exploration in place before they move away from their place tapes. Ask them to move tiny things (nose, toes, then nose and toes) with drum cues. Stop and start drumming to give them practice listening and responding. When they are successful, go on to larger body parts and get students used to moving on cue. Monitor whether they can listen, think, and respond simultaneously.

Appeal to very small children's imaginations. Ask them to squeeze all of the air out of their shapes so they are in a tiny ball. From that position invite them to slowly slide out one body part at a time that you name and then quickly bring it back in. Repeat until they are listening and appropriately responding in movement without making any sound. Expect it to take a few tries: Practice is the key. Work with them until they get going up or down in place and in or out. Learning to move in control requires lots of practice. Talking about it does little good because it is more than a brain function. It is also a muscle coordination activity. Knowing what to do and being able to do it are not synonymous for young children.

It is logical to start with the most obvious dance element: the body. Work with the body to start (i.e., body parts, body moves, steps, body shapes, muscles, bones, and joints). Recombine explorations in different ways to help students experience and respond appropriately. Mastering the body in time comes before being expressive and creatively unique. Wait to use the dance element of space until students gain some mastery over the body. Children who are not developmentally able to handle the body are overchallenged when asked to take the body through space with others moving. Spatial choices require more complex decision making than just moving one's body. (The exceptions are levels and directions, which can be explored fairly easily.)

Build self-governance into the earliest lessons so new students are immediately successful and learn self-discipline and moving parameters. During this self-governance process, you are planting seeds for clarifying intent and harnessing body energy. You are making safe movement structures. Now you are ready to emphasize dance making and artistic goals described elsewhere in the cornerstone chapters. Spend time with Mary Joyce's *First Steps in Teaching Creative Dance to Children*, an indispensable resource that shows you how to guide exploration and dance making. For example, Joyce creates a "living sculptures" lesson that keeps kids in place to concentrate on their muscles. It is a spatially controlled lesson. A lesson on muscles calls attention to self-control through bound movement. Her lessons explore concepts of muscles tightening for strength and control early on.

When children are ready to move through space, find a limited method that only moves several students at a time while the rest freeze. Call out one student at a time to move around and among other dancers, going into the open or safe spaces. Move four or five students at the same time but only as many as can be successful. As you notice concentration or movement quality breaking down, call "freeze." This is a good opportunity to have everyone reshape in place several times to change positions. When all are refocused, begin to call, one by one, names of new students to travel around the still shapes. This gives practice on how to stop and start, look for open spaces in which to move, move without touching, and move without talking. It also helps you assess readiness for freer spatial movement.

Students over second grade never seem to tire of mirroring each other's movement! It is another way to increase concentration. Mirroring activities are good with all ages from kindergarten to adult, especially those needing to work on concentration and muscle control. Mirroring eventually can incorporate more than body parts. Try adding such

aspects as variety with levels, directions, shaping, timing, near and far, opening and closing, and symmetry and asymmetry.

Common Problems and How to Deal With Them

Problems are opportunities. Let's defuse some. Four common problems hinder artistic growth in creative dance:

1. *Students are confused or don't understand.* Help them. Dance the group back to their place tapes to re-explain using a different approach or example.

2. *Students are distracted and are not paying attention.* Admonish them. Dance them to their place tapes to refocus their attention. If they won't concentrate, admonish them to pay attention; explain that dancers must be aware of many things at once to perform. If they are still distracted, take disciplinary action (see "Misbehaving Students" section of this chapter on page 350).

3. *Students are fearful or insecure.* Help them. Build in chances for success—then acknowledge worthy attempts.

4. *Students are defiant and will not follow the rules.* Admonish them. Sit them out. Give your greatest attention to those following directions, and acknowledge successful attempts. Try not to give attention to the agitator. Follow disciplinary action steps or behavior modification described later in this chapter.

Avoiding "No Wrong Answers" It is counterproductive to say, "There is no wrong response or answer in creative dance." (What about a child who defiantly runs forward when you are guiding the group to "make round shapes with your back?") Instead, encourage creativity with instructions like, "Let's find more than one right answer in creative dance." "There are many different right answers in movement exploration. Show me your way of . . ." Avoid giving carte blanche to those who have difficulty accepting boundaries. Realize there can be wrong answers in creative dance! Be ready for them and quick to redirect them by praising desired movement responses.

Physicalizing Responses You may find that children want to verbally speak answers instead of physically moving answers during exploration. Patiently and consistently insist that students bodythink and bodyspeak. Bodyspeaking is responding through intentional movement with an expressive body without verbalizing. Remind students to quietly show their response.

Ask questions that require students to move their response—with bodies instead of words. For example, "Show me with movement instead of with words how you understand the concept of symmetry. When the drum sounds, show me a wide symmetrical shape . . . a narrow one . . . an upside down one. . . . Change it to an asymmetrical shape with the upper body, now the lower; a one-legged shape; hold it with your best balance."

Create an exploratory environment in which students respond by bodythinking (which includes brain thinking) instead of by brain thinking alone. Enable students to build confidence in communicating nonverbally with their bodies through constant practice. This is prerequisite to learning to express themselves artfully.

Using a Drum to Lead Class Exploration   Modulate sounds on a hand drum. Play it to communicate all the gradations between soft and strong, smooth and sharp, tight and loose, rhythmic and arrhythmic. Explore drum textures: sounds with your fingers, fingernails, knuckles. Scrape it, tap it, play it to nonverbally communicate, and thus let sound help you elicit responses you want. Let the drum speak for you. Let it tell others when to stop and start. Incorporate your body gestures to reinforce what you play during movement exploration. For example, shape your spine as you ask students to, twist or round your back with them, travel or freeze along with them. When you partner with a drum in class, you master an essential skill in teaching creative dance (as well as technique class).

To cue motion time, stick by this rule: "The drum rules the class. When it sounds, you move. When it stops, you stop."

This is the unwavering rule when you are using a drum. This rule is sometimes as hard for new specialists to get used to as it is for novice students. Practice working a drum on your peers. Modulate its sound so you can convey intent and reinforce what you're describing. For example, tap lightly for a delicate movement response or firmly for a strong one. Vary the sounds students hear. In any 5-minute period you may need to use soft, loud, slow, moderate, sharp, and smooth sounds; one-finger tap; fingernails swirling on the drum

head; and percussive repetitions. All help students find an array of textures for dance making. After you can drum effectively and can consistently enforce basic rules, you make major strides in managing a creative dance class. It's pretty safe to say that any time you make exceptions to the drum rule you will find yourself in big trouble. To teach the rule, I exaggerate for kindergarten through third graders:

- "When the drum stops, freeze; this is the rule. Not even an eyelash moves."
- "What if you are standing on one leg when the drum stops? (You freeze.)"
- "What if you begin to lose your balance before it starts? (Tighten your muscles for stability as you freeze.)"
- "What if you are in a one-leg balance and are not stable? (Touch a toe down until you regain balance.)"
- "What if you are in the air when the drum stops? (Freeze right there! Or, if you must come down, just land softly in the same shape!)"

Using a Safety Override   Because the drum freeze is the main rule, only one thing takes precedence over it: your verbal command "freeze!" Students are accountable to stop instantly. They must learn that it's serious business when you command "freeze!" (When used, this directive must always sound electric.) Save it for crises—to avert injury or calamity, when two people are heading on a collision course. It reflects your responsibility and authority to enforce safety. Use the freeze command only in emergencies; otherwise cue with "stop" and "go."

Plans for Students Who Are Temporarily Unable to Dance

For valid reasons, students can't participate in dance classes from time to time—dance injuries, bronchitis with a doctor's excuse, sprained ankle, and the like. On days when students cannot dance, what do you do with them?

Establish clear guidelines for not participating in a class and post them conspicuously. Specify the acceptable and unacceptable reasons in the student handbook. State how many times are too many to sit out. Print the consequences for sitting out too often so that parents and students know the first week of school. Don't negotiate consequences on a case-by-case basis. Make certain you address this the first day so students understand you can't lose class time to negotiate what is appropriate or inappropriate. Enforce requirements every time or you might as well not have the guidelines and consequences.

Students Who Are Sick or Running a Fever Cannot Produce

Sick students should go to the nurse's room to keep from spreading germs. Determining whether a child is actually injured or sick is not always easy. Trust intuition. You don't want students to dance injured or sick but neither can you pander to their whims. For example, one middle school dance specialist permits students to sit out once without a doctor's excuse, but more than once during a 5-day period requires a doctor's excuse. She reasons that if they are too sick to dance for 2 days, they are sick enough to see a doctor. Compare notes often with the school health personnel to keep tabs on students with legitimate injuries as well as those who seem to be chronic misusers of sick excuses.

Students Who Are Injured—Not Sick—Can Produce During Class Time

Expect and plan for them in each unit so they have something to do on dancing days. Make this an opportunity to teach something beneficial. Keep alternate lesson plans ready that accomplish other learning objectives. Hold students accountable for completing assigned class work by grading them as you do those participating in movement class. Don't make alternate activities punitive—or too much fun. (You certainly don't want to encourage students to sit out!) To determine appropriate assignments, consider how long the student will be out of commission. Also call on other methods of inquiry in dance to accomplish present (or future) objectives.

Depending on the age and season, some injured students can still do some of the following:

- Help out during performance preparation (such as design the programs for an upcoming performance event, write copy for upcoming programs about the works, develop study guides for upcoming performances, sew costumes)
- Review dance skills or concepts (such as use their Labanotation or motif writing skills to notate some combinations—for later use by the class or for documentation; use LabanWriter software to score a work)

- Assist with accompaniment by adding percussion during class
- Sketch gesture drawings of the dancers for display
- Research the choreographer for an upcoming unit to glean his or her pertinent contributions to dance and prepare to make a multimedia presentation to the class
- Use their own specific injury as a venue for learning anatomy, kinesiology, and injury prevention and maintenance (use a page from an anatomy coloring book to study and shade in with colored pencils; investigate that body part, the injury, its prevention and care; go online to a health Web site to make a rehab plan for such an injury to add to a student injury guide)
- Go to the library with a specific dance videotape and a list of prepared guided viewing questions to respond to and be graded on (make the lists ahead and keep them on hand)
- Do an Internet search on a relevant dance topic to achieve a learning objective
- Make posters of the NSDEs to display

A long-term injury requires a customized alternative long-range plan. The plan depends on the context, the injury, the unit objectives, and what the student will miss. Don't penalize students for being injured. It is usually not their fault they can't participate.

 In what other ways can you productively involve injured dance students?

Reflect and Respond

List all acceptable and unacceptable reasons to sit out of a dancing class. Group them under headings such as Dance Injuries (acceptable), No Dance Clothing (unacceptable), Respiratory Infections (acceptable), Late to Class (acceptable with excuse), and Menstrual Problems (unacceptable). Make a standard plan for each of the acceptable reasons only (e.g., keep clean leotards and tights in the costume closet that students can wear; they are charged a grade penalty or a fee each time they forget to bring appropriate dance clothing; or require that they keep a spare set in their lockers).

Developing Teaching Skills

What other teaching skills enable you to (1) successfully set up and maintain an environment that promotes aesthetic education, (2) effectively manage an arts classroom, and (3) actively monitor learning outcomes? Following are common errors and a list of 33 skills to practice and master.

Common Dance Teaching Errors

- Overexplaining and talking too much while students sit
- Forgetting that dance is learned by moving
- Giving information out rather than generating it from students through questions
- Forgetting to ensure that students commit to what they are doing
- Forgetting to state the lesson's objective
- Not keeping students focused on the lesson's learning outcomes
- Wasting learning time on random exercises not related to the objectives
- Wasting learning time on daily routines that can be shortened or streamlined

Success Factors for Creating and Maintaining an Effective Learning Environment for Dance

Use this list first for information and then as a checklist to self-assess your strengths and weaknesses. The effective dance specialist

1. ____ facilitates inquiry and involves students in problem solving and creative and critical thinking in dance;

2. ____ serves as a positive role model for students in the classroom;

3. ____ creates and maintains a physical environment that supports student inquiry and provides an inviting place to learn;

4. ____ maintains a room arrangement that allows all students to see, hear, and participate fully in creating, performing, and responding;

5. ____ promotes cooperation, collaboration, and mutual respect among students;

6. ____ conveys appropriately high standards for student process and performance;

7. ____ conveys confidence in own dance knowledge and ability to assist students in achieving dance objectives;

8. ____ consistently involves students in reflective thinking to contextualize learning and personalize dance;

9. ____ enables students to teach themselves and peers and give qualitative feedback as critical friends through the use of aesthetic criteria;

10. ____ conveys respect for the feelings, ideas, and contributions of students so there is emotional safety as well as physical safety;

11. ____ conveys an understanding of the social and cultural backgrounds of students and keeps the classroom inclusive by addressing different cultural forms of dance;

12. ____ maximizes positive and productive interactions with students and parents;

13. ____ gives appropriate encouragement and incentives for quality participation in class and in performance; and

14. ____ establishes and maintains professional distance between teacher and student.

Notebook/Portfolio:
Perspectives Notebook

How effectively do you maintain a learning environment? As with other Success Factor checklists in this chapter, use the criteria as performance indicators for self-reflection and mentor evaluation. After mentors have critiqued you and you have polished your skills to earn all 3s, add the signed and dated evaluation to the Teaching Skills section of your Perspectives Notebook. See the evaluation plan in appendix A for rating details.

Success Factors for Managing an Arts Classroom

Use this list first for information and then as a checklist to self-assess your strengths and weaknesses.
The effective dance specialist

1. ____ maintains clear, appropriate rules for student behavior and participation and enforces them fairly and consistently;

2. ____ creates a nurturing learning environment that supports creativity, inquiry, and aesthetic growth;

3. ____ uses preventive discipline techniques and organizes movement classes within parameters for safety and creativity;

4. ____ provides students opportunities to be responsible for their own behavior, governance, dance skill development, artistic growth, and refinement of work;

5. ____ establishes appropriate and effective routines for completing essential noninstructional tasks, such as dressing out, taking roll, bringing out barres, and turning in projects;

6. ____ manages transitions between instructional events to maintain a smooth flow of activity during lessons and minimize loss of instructional time;

7. ____ effectively manages instructional materials, resources, and technologies;

8. ____ provides positive reinforcement for acceptable and commendable performance;

9. ____ guides learning activities by being engaged and active, moving among students;

10. ____ leads guided discovery in creative dance class by moving among students, modulating voice and drum;

11. ____ teaches individuals as a part of the entire class without jeopardizing class time-on-task; and

12. ____ participates fully in the lesson and shares his or her energy with students.

Notebook/Portfolio:
Perspectives Notebook

How effectively do you manage a classroom? As with Success Factor checklists in other chapters, use the criteria as performance indicators. Use them for self-reflection and also mentor evaluation. Use the rating details in appendix A. Add them to your Perspectives Notebook.

Success Factors for Monitoring Dance Learning

Use this list first for information and then as a checklist to self-assess your strengths and weaknesses.
The effective dance specialist

1. ____ monitors learning by observing performance in the studio and reactions during class activities and lessons;

2. ____ facilitates learning with appropriate questioning techniques and aesthetic stimulation;

3. ____ keeps national standards at the forefront of student participation and learning so that student performance during all related class activities is focused on achievement (e.g., presentations, technique class, improvisation, performance tasks, group discussions, research, and collaborative tasks);

4. ____ monitors learning and development by reviewing work completed by students (e.g., homework, projects, video documenting, choreography, and dance portfolios);

5. ____ evaluates students' stages of progression, particularly their kinesthetic, cognitive, and aesthetic skills, to provide timely and informative instructional feedback to enhance their creative and artistic development;

6. ____ provides appropriate and sufficient reviews and summaries of content and skills to keep activities contextually coherent and gives students time to reflect on what they learn; and

7. ____ extends students' learning and artistic development through appropriate acceleration and enrichment activities.

Based on, but liberally adapted from, the South Carolina Department of Education Web site.

Notebook/Portfolio:
Perspectives Notebook

How effectively do you monitor dance learning? As with the Success Factor checklists in chapters 8 and 12, use these criteria as performance indicators for self-reflection and mentor evaluation. After mentors have critiqued you and you have practiced and polished your skills to earn all 3s, add the signed and dated evaluations to the Teaching Skills section of your Perspectives Notebook. See the evaluation plan in appendix A for rating details.

Developing Planning Skills

Success factors for short- and long-range planning are vital for the dance specialist. Long-range plans are for 1 to 5 years and take your goals forward. Short-range plans are your series of units that take your objectives forward. Use the 30 items on these checklists to identify planning skills.

Success Factors for Curricular Long-Range Planning

Use this list first for information and then as a checklist to measure how well you design an effective long-range curricular plan **(LRP)** for the school year.

The effective dance specialist

1. ____ aligns the LRP with district, state, and national dance content and achievement standards;

2. ____ creates contextually based units in a logical sequence to accomplish the aims of the entire LRP;

3. ____ communicates the LRP to students, parents, professional arts team, and administrators;

4. ____ writes an LRP that presents appropriate instruction so students can achieve district, state, and nation outcomes;

5. ____ has a system in place to routinely communicate with parents;

6. ____ develops an appropriate timeline to complete all dance units;

7. ____ acquires instructional materials and resources to deliver contextually based, aesthetically driven dance units;

8. ____ plans a system to evaluate long-term student progress and achievement;

9. ____ plans ways to maintain records of daily progress and achievement;

10. ____ designs a way to keep records of student overall progress and achievement;

11. ____ plans and implements rules and procedures to manage student behavior;

12. ____ plans essential noninstructional routines;

13. ____ designs ways to incorporate students' different abilities and development levels, backgrounds, needs, and interests;

14. ____ evaluates the LRP periodically and adjusts as necessary; and

15. ____ uses *Opportunity-to-Learn Standards for Dance Education* (2nd printing, 1995) in LRP to address scheduling, facility, and safety issues.

Adapted from the South Carolina Department of Education Web site.

Notebook/Portfolio:
Perspectives Notebook

How effective are your year-long plans? See appendix A for the rating details and follow the same plan as described above.

Success Factors for Short-Range Unit Planning

Success factors suggest ways to create short-range plans **(SRPs)** that successfully accomplish the goals of the LRP. SRPs may be organized in quarters (9 weeks) or units of study (1-3 weeks). Each school district defines how long SRPs should be.

The effective dance specialist

1. ____ plans instruction that builds on student's previous skills;

2. ____ writes unit objectives appropriate to student ability while setting appropriately high standards for all;

3. ____ includes different intellectual, aesthetic, kin-aesthetic, social, and cultural perspectives;

4. ____ selects and develops materials, resources, and technologies to present dance in varied formats;

5. ____ plans sequenced instruction consistent with desired outcomes;

6. ____ accommodates different rates of learning and learning styles;

7. ____ plans instruction to actively engage students in inquiry;

8. ____ plans instruction to actively engage students in varied levels of critical thinking;

9. ____ plans instruction that promotes both independent and collaborative learning;

10. ____ integrates the processes of creating, performing, and responding to dance;

11. ____ uses triad unit plans that integrate objectives, instruction, and assessment;

12. ____ states clear objectives based on age-appropriate content;

13. ____ creates authentic assessments as part of on-going learning;

14. ____ creates effective instructional strategies to take learning objectives forward; and

15. ____ includes plans to adjust the SRP to better serve student-centered learning needs.

Adapted from the South Carolina Department of Education Web site.

How effectively do you design instruction? As with checklists in this chapter, use the criteria as performance indicators for self-reflection and mentor evaluation. Follow the same plan as described earlier.

Scheduling

Class schedule affects the artistic and educational outcomes of your program. Either too few classes or classes spaced too far apart in time jeopardize your ability to meet course requirements. Scheduling should not be left to chance, because it is the channel by which you deliver a quality arts education.

Using School Delivery Standards to Maximize Learning

Opportunity-to-Learn Standards (OTLS) were part of the Goals 2000—Educate America Act enacted into law in 1994. They stimulate state efforts to

> ensure that no young American is deprived of the chance to meet the content and performance or achievement standards established in the various disciplines because of the failure of his or her school to provide an adequate learning environment. (National Dance Association Opportunity-to-Learn Standards 1995, p. i)

Find the *Opportunity-to-Learn Standards (OTLS) for Dance Education* in the second printing of the NSDEs (1995). These national school guidelines elaborate the school's administrative responsibilities to provide what is needed for student success according to national dance education standards.

The OTLS explain what constitutes sufficient delivery and offer vital explanations to incorporate into your planning. The OTLS give practical guidance for setting up a national standards-based program related to

- curriculum and scheduling,

- staffing in dance education to ensure that teachers are qualified and that there is a sufficient number for the size of the school (students served),

- facilities specifications,
- safety measures to be factored into a program, and
- equipment needs.

Go to the Curriculum and Scheduling section of the OTLS to discover the critical links between scheduling and being able to deliver a meaningful arts curriculum. Study the OTLS to learn what schools should provide.

Whereas dance specialists are accountable to the *National Standards in Dance Education,* schools are accountable to the *Opportunity-to-Learn Standards for Dance Education* (1995). You may need to take the OTLS to your first job interview to show them to the principal. Ask, "Do you want to have a standards-based dance education program?" And then supply the OTLS. Many school principals have no background in standards-based dance curriculum. Therefore, as the one who knows, be proactive to negotiate a schedule that enables students to meet minimum standards. Because both documents are in one book, the *National Standards for Dance Education* (2nd printing, 1995), you can show the principal both sets of standards that affect the learning outcomes established for your grade levels. You would certainly not want to negotiate a contract for a school program that does not (or worse, cannot) meet the delivery standards.

An optional program follows state and national standards to produce well-rounded students who are facile movers, innovative creators, and astute responders.

Determining a Minimal Program in Dance

What good is it for a school to have a highly qualified dance specialist but provide too few classes for students to be able to meet standards? Scheduling makes or breaks a dance program.

Dance as basic curriculum is integrated into the school-day curriculum rather than as an after-school activity or for special students (i.e., gifted and talented). Students get a minimum of five classes per week for at least a 9-week quarter—preferably more. (Six weeks is not long enough for students to meet standards in dancing, dance making, and dance appreciation.) Students need daily instruction in dance to develop movement skills and techniques.

Class length should be a minimum of 45 minutes (except kindergarten with 30-35 minutes). Allocate enough time for students to achieve the objectives from the cornerstones and meet minimum NSDE

standards. Frequent contact for fewer weeks is preferable to infrequent contact for an entire school year (i.e., every day for 9 weeks is better than once a week for a year). Young people require continuity to achieve arts goals and objectives.

Determining an Optimal Program in Dance

A substantive program in dance optimally lasts the entire school year. It meets from 3 to 5 days a week all year for 45 minutes at the elementary school, 1 hour at middle school, and at least 1 1/4 hours at high school. The optimal program follows state and national standards to produce well-rounded students who are facile movers, who create dance to communicate ideas, who are knowledgeable about dance in time and place, and who are able to use the dance vocabulary to analyze and critique dance works. Students meet NSDEs and cornerstone objectives;

thus, the program produces dance-literate students. Dance should be taught every year K-12.

High school graduation requirements should include at least a year of study in either dance, drama, music, or visual arts. High schools should also provide classes for any who want additional arts study for academic credit beyond the requirement. High school gifted programs in dance are gauged to a higher standard and therefore include increased time and more frequent contact than general dance courses.

Understanding the Aesthetic and Educational Impact of Scheduling

Designing a total school schedule is a multitiered process. The dance schedule must fit into the entire school arts program. Dance, as a related art, often toggles with visual art, music, and theatre. Fifteen percent of each student's total instruction time should be in arts education. Effective arts programs require adequate time in each art form.

Designing a dance curriculum is one thing, but scheduling for optimum potency is another. You have to teach students often and regularly enough for them to achieve artistic goals. Consider the following as you negotiate or design schedules with your principal.

Scheduling With Artistic Goals in Mind

Considering the goals and objectives of your long-range curriculum plan, project how long it will take to achieve them. Look at your curricular plan and the school's schedule side by side. Make the two fit together to achieve each year's goals to keep students building skills and knowledge in the allotted time.

- Class size: For safety reasons, class size is critical. Class size is an issue for educational and artistic reasons as well. Do not combine classes. Dance class should be no larger than classes in other academic subjects.

- Arts-infused schools: You need specialized skills in dance and dance education to deliver a standards-oriented program. Therefore, you need to be a certified dance specialist. Specialists in arts-focused or arts-infused schools get release time to help classroom teachers bring dance into their classrooms. Schedule collaborative planning time so you can plan ways to meet common objectives and specific student needs.

- Student–teacher ratio in dance: As dance specialist, you are the hub of the school dance arts wheel (see figure 3.1 and chapter 3) and should be

scheduled to maximize effectiveness. One specialist is not enough for large schools. Elementary schools need one teacher per 450 students. Middle and high school ratios usually depend on district curricular requirements in the arts.

Allocating Time

Time is precious in the school day. There is never enough time to accomplish all you want. Prioritize at each grade level to design a tight curriculum. Layer skills and knowledge, grade by grade, and spiral back to pick up old familiar threads on which to add the new. Make transitions tight by rehearsing students at the beginning of the class as to what is planned and what is expected. Keep them on task. To stop and start wastes time. Instead plan lessons like choreography with smooth, well-timed transitions and quick entrances and exits. Teach students that dancers keep their focus during transitions. They efficiently handle routines to get their moment in the spotlight.

- Teaching time: Dance specialists in elementary, middle, and high should teach no more than 250 minutes a day. Middle and high school teaching time adjusts downward for those who teach specialized classes during the school day, such as performance or dance company activities that tend to be large.

- Planning time: Daily planning periods of at least an hour should be allocated for dance preparation and evaluation. A sample day is six 45-minute periods plus a 3/4- to 1-hour planning period in K-5. Dance specialists need the same considerations that schools give classroom teachers.

- Showcasing: The school should support, encourage, and celebrate student efforts and accomplishments. Build time into the overall school schedule to showcase work with additional time to give lecture–demonstrations as appropriate to your school.

(The scheduling section draws from material assembled by a team of dance professionals and published in the *South Carolina Visual and Performing Arts Framework*, 1993, pp. 37-40.)

About Facilities

Dance facilities directly affect teaching. Know proper construction requirements to ensure safety and optimum performance for your students and yourself. Never build a dance studio without appropriate specifications (called "specs") available from national dance organizations. Don't rely on information from salespersons or sales Web sites. You can retrofit existing school facilities for dance. Set up specialized dance spaces to positively impact instruction, safety, and learning required by state and national standards for dance. Consult the OTLS about appropriate dance facilities. Share this information with your principal.

Studio Floors

The structure and surface of flooring must be addressed for safe dancing. Beware of hard floors. They are the single most potentially damaging aspect of a facility. Do not ever consider dancing on any surface laid directly over concrete. Chronic (long-term) and acute (immediate) injuries develop from dancing on such improper dance flooring. Make certain

1. the floor construction is resilient by being cushioned correctly,
2. the surface is finished and treated for safety, and
3. the amount of floor space per student is adequate.

This applies to renovation and new construction alike. Contact the National Dance Association (NDA) (see Rich Resources) for the informative booklet *Dance Facilities* to glean structural specifications for a studio. Contact information is in appendix C.

Floor Construction

The most critical aspect for safety in the studio is the construction of a sprung wooden floor with enough cushion and airspace between the surface and the underfloor. Although you need a large unobstructed space, the most important aspect of flooring is shock absorption to give a soft landing for the user. If

> there is little deflection or "give," as with concrete, tile, or thin mat materials, the muscles of the lower extremities must act to absorb the majority of the shock. (Seals 1986, p. 81)

Do not dance or teach dance on floors constructed of tile over concrete. Hard floors jeopardize the safety of students and the health of the dance teacher over time. Repetitive use causes debilitating injuries and chronic problems that may not be immediately obvious. Improper floors shorten a dancer's professional life and contribute to chronic shin splints, joint problems, back pain, stress fractures, and countless other musculoskeletal problems. In the short term, hard floors tire those dancing on them, contribute to achy bodies and inflamed joints, and

cause acute shin splints. Hard floors cause some students to have to sit out of class, which affects instruction time. One of the worst offenders is tile laid directly over concrete.

Optimum construction specifications for dance studios of all kinds specify that the subfloor should start with two-by-fours laid with narrow side down 18 inches apart. This is to leave a 4-inch air pocket. Next, solidly lay 12-inch pine boards (soft wood is needed) on the diagonal across the two-by-fours. It is good to lay tar paper on top of this, but it is not necessary. The third or surface layer should be hardwood of maple or oak (hard rock maple is the best).

Floor Surface

The floor surface also affects the daily well-being as well as the long-term health of a dancer. Surface injuries damage the foot, but a nonskid surface can also cause serious knee and ankle injuries that occur when one tries to turn but the foot sticks and does not turn with the rest of the body. An uneven floor can actually slice open the ball of the foot in chassés or glissades using bare feet.

A proper surface is neither too slick nor skid-resistant. "The surface of a dance floor must be firm in order to provide resistance to the force exerted by the dancers' feet as they push off during various movements, leaps, and jumps" (Seals 1986, p. 81).

One ideal surface is a seamless (i.e., tongue-in-groove) hardwood floor with a tung oil finish. If nails are used in construction, they should be equidistant to keep boards from buckling or becoming uneven—a hazard to the sole of the foot and potentially to the ankle. Nails should be set (i.e., nailed below the surface) before the floor is sanded and finished. Varnishes are not used. Gym finishes must not be used because the nonskid surface is extremely dangerous for both axial and locomotor movements.

Finally, take good care of the studio floor. No food, drink, or street shoes should be allowed on the floor. Dirt adversely affects traction and mars the finish, and it is unsanitary and uncomfortable on bare skin. (Have you ever turned on a small pebble?) Mop with clear water and no detergent.

Setting Up a Dance Space

Dance is not costly for education. It doesn't need disposable art supplies, scripts with royalty fees, or music scores—but it does need space.

Space Requirements

Dance requires academic space and studio space for teaching. Ideally, some rooms accommodate both so you have your DVD or VHS media equipment ready to integrate short dance examples during activity. Studios with an adjoining seated classroom and media equipment also work well. Your private office should be large enough to meet with parents and talk with students. It should lock and have a desk and chair, storage shelves, on 8-by-10-foot closet for costumes and props, video storage, and file cabinets.

It is helpful to have an auditorium for performances with adjustable acoustics, adequate lighting, and a large open stage with a sprung floor available for performances. Order library and resource center items to support the curriculum (i.e., books, periodicals, videos, films, computer software, and sound recordings). Ask for a budget to provide

- basic CDs and music for various dance styles and studies,
- costume materials,
- musical percussion instruments,
- educational dance video series such as *Dancing!* or the JVC Video Anthology of World Music and Dance,
- a growing video library of major dance works, and
- instructional equipment such as boards, display areas, computers, and dance software.

Dancing requires an unobstructed space; generally, 110 square feet of floor space per student is ideal. Small children do not need quite as much space for movement. Children in kindergarten through fifth grade don't need mirrors and barres. At middle and high schools, ceiling height should be a minimum of 12 feet. Spaces should be equipped with mirrors on one wall and barres on the opposite wall. Shared rooms are instructionally unacceptable (e.g., school cafeterias, one side of a large gym, one half of a multipurpose room, a school auditorium that is not private).

A dance program needs a changing area, optimally with lockers, showers, and restrooms that are available to both genders. Locked storage facilities for performance (e.g., costumes, music, props) and for teaching (e.g., charts, media equipment, anatomical models) should adjoin the classroom. Computers and CD players need to be secured as well (South Carolina Visual and Performing Arts Curriculum Framework Writing Team 1993).

Reasons Not to Use the Gym

The gym is spacious enough, but because it is a sports arena it is not conducive to artistic expression. The space is too cavernous. It is arena scale, not individual-expressive scale. It is too large a space to contain and focus movement exploration. Such a drafty, disruptive place compromises the artistic processes (c/p/r).

The gym is not suitable for other reasons. Acoustics are abysmal. Sound systems don't give quality accompaniment. There is no place to modulate sound to work with textures of movement.

Gym floors have nonskid finishes, which are dangerous to knees, ankles, and hips, particularly when dancers are barefoot. Foot traffic in street shoes makes the gym floor grimy and unsuitable for floor work in dance. Gym floors are constructed differently (i.e., harder with less airspace) than dance floors because they are built for padded athletic shoes in basketball and other sports. Dance shoes—such as jazz shoes and ballet shoes—are not padded, so the body joints absorb too much shock on a hard gym floor.

Other activities are scheduled in the gym during the day. It's noisy. Dance doesn't need to compete for the space or for students' attention with all that goes on around a gym. Even the equipment visually distracts. It is just as unsuitable for dance to share a teaching space as for another core subjects to do so. Just like trying to teach tennis in a swimming pool, it is the wrong place!

Safety Issues

Follow strict safety guidelines when designing dance facilities. Design studios large enough to safely and comfortably accommodate the largest group taught. Students need unobstructed space for physical movement that is clean and free of debris and harmful objects such as tacks or broken glass.

Adequate ventilation and proper temperature controls are important to the dancing body. You need access to the thermostat that controls the studio temperature. Dancing facilities should

- be accessible for those with physical disabilities,
- provide suitable lighting and acoustical properties,
- have adequate electrical outlets,
- have immediate access to ice and first aid equipment and supplies, and
- have immediate access to telephones (South Carolina Visual and Performing Arts Curriculum Framework Writing Team 1993).

Functionality Issues

Establish a dance-parent organization. Ask the group to fund-raise to supplement the allotted budget, which never is enough. This group can keep you from being overwhelmed with details of finding money, putting on performances, making costumes, assisting in the classroom, and carpooling to off-site events and rehearsals. Establish a real organization with officers and a chain of leadership. These parents are vital to an outstanding educational dance program. They are also vocal advocates for strong dance programs.

Survive and Thrive

You need key skills to be effective in the classroom. Successful specialists who are well prepared stay in the profession, but the attrition rate for those who are not prepared is high—most leave after 3 years. That is why the information in this chapter is so important. You need not only to survive but also to thrive.

Essential Classroom Survival Skills

Accept the fact that you are a teacher, not a personal friend to students. This is a cardinal rule of professional behavior. It is also a key survival skill. As you accept your roles and responsibilities for standards-oriented instruction, prepare yourself to maintain your professional place and practice democratic leadership.

Keeping a Professional Distance

Establish and maintain professional distance. That enables you to be supportive, warm, encouraging, challenging, creative, genuinely interested, and committed to your students. But it also empowers you to take necessary action on the part of the school and district when needed. Keeping a professional distance permits you to make corrections, steer students away from problem areas, and be intolerant of misbehavior and disrespect. It enables you to hold students accountable for their actions, lead them into new directions, and make tough decisions. A professional distance lets you divide students into work groups outside their comfort zones and exert your authority and leadership. It helps you keep dance education goals at the forefront rather than trying to please everyone—which is not possible.

Professional distance keeps the established roles of teacher and student from blurring. There are sad cases where teachers compromised educational goals because they mistook themselves for a student's personal friend instead of their professional friend.

Students aren't the ones who establish professional distance. You do it by your attitude and actions, by your leadership qualities, and by being worthy of trust. Even though you know your students well because you perform and create together, you stand apart. Your role transcends pettiness, favoritism, and power struggles. A teacher's professional distance extends to personal time away from the classroom as well as in. Never talk about students to outsiders or divulge personal information or observances about them to anyone else besides your superiors who may need to know.

Picking Favorites

Picking favorites in a dance class violates all laws of professional behavior. It is unprofessional to critique or correct only the best dancers. It is unethical to choose only the best for performance, to spend more time with those who come into school dance with strong studio backgrounds while ignoring the less skilled in dance. How would that affect the morale in a classroom? How would that affect the quality of instruction? How would that affect the accountability standards for the program and the administrator's value of it?

Developing Key Survival Skills

The key survival skills in figure 11.2 assume that there is a strong aesthetic education curriculum in operation. Which ones do you want to add to your own personal top 10? Discuss them with a classmate

1. Keep a professional distance.
2. Use rules and consequences.
3. Plan lessons well.
4. Respect each student.
5. Foster cooperative spirit.
6. Affirm students' worth.
7. Expect success.
8. Model the best; praise the best.
9. Establish classroom order.
10. Be as fair as possible, as often as possible.

FIGURE 11.2   Key survival skills.

and then craft your own list of 10 key survival skills for your Perspectives Notebook (see chapter 16).

Be prepared for any- and everything! Don't let one child impede the education of the rest of the class. Learn the difference between queries and questions. Students chatter queries that are nosey and personal, which should simply be ignored. Dislike the action, not the child. And sincere praise is the most powerful tool you have for classroom management.

Communicating With Students

Learn how to give instructions and direction to get maximum student response. This is an art in itself. Be authoritatively direct and positive. Figure 11.3 shows the nine mistakes adults make when giving children and youth instructions and how to avoid them. Be direct to be clear.

In addition, like at no other time in history, teachers must be multilingual. Because communication is basic to teaching and working with people of all ages, you need to speak and understand diverse languages. To be successful today you must be a world citizen, familiar with diversity in dance and articulate across cultures. You must communicate with students, their parents, other teachers and colleagues, and dance artists from around the world. Language **fluency** affects pedagogy. Develop a working vocabulary in local prevailing languages, especially Spanish.

Avoid	Instead try
Phrasing instructions as questions: "How about putting away the props so we can get ready to go?"	"It's almost time for class to end. You need to put away the props."
Phrasing expectations in abstract rather than concrete terms: "I want you to be good while I rewind the videotape."	"Please stretch your Achilles (while I rewind the videotape)."
Stringing several instructions together: "I want you to listen to the music and figure out its rhythmic structure, work on the dynamics of the performance, and then take the costumes to the costume room."	"The first thing to do today is to focus attention on the rhythmic structure. If you finish early let me know so I can tell you what comes next." (Give 5-year-olds one instruction at a time, 6- to 10-year-olds no more than two instructions at a time.)
Preceding instructions with "Let's" (which is passive and nonauthoritative): "Let's put on your shoes, OK?"	"It's time to put on your shoes."
Giving instructions followed by reasons or explanations (putting the reason last calls attention to it rather than to the instruction): "Its time to come sit in a circle in the middle of the room so we can discuss the performance."	"It's time to discuss the performance; please join me in the middle of the room and sit in a circle."
Making instructions into sales pitches: "Hey, this is a really cool video that you are just going to love to see and are going to find very exciting."	"It's time to see an example of bodyshaping like we've been doing today. Please look for these three things . . ."
Giving instructions in the form of wishes (which is a passive complaint): "I wish you would stop coming into class late every day."	"Be in class by the time the bell rings."
Expressing an instruction like an exasperated question: "How many times do I have to tell you not to come to class late?"	"Be in class by the time the bell rings."
Using "OK?" when giving an instruction: "Be on time, OK?"	"Be in class by the time the bell rings."

FIGURE 11.3 Mistakes to avoid when giving instructions.

Ideas adapted for dance from syndicated columnist John Rosemond, *The State Newspaper*/Columbia, SC, 2002.

Behavior Management in Dance

To authoritatively enforce rules and consequences for maximum artistic achievement, learn basic **behavior modification techniques**. Use them when students willfully disrupt to minimize time lost dealing with behavior and maximize time on artistic task.

You need to acquire two different kinds of classroom management techniques: one for the classroom and the other for the studio. In some schools you will have the classroom and the studio combined, but in others you have two separate facilities (preferably adjoined). In any case, acquire skills for students in motion as well as students at rest. It is one thing to manage one or two students, but a classroom full of individuals all with somewhat differing agendas and needs puts an enormous responsibility on you. Your classroom structure and ongoing environmental organization determine how the class as a whole operates. Structure is key in this instance. Boundaries are essential and the maintenance of them is ongoing (i.e., if you let one individual get by with something, it breaks down the system).

Behavior Management Techniques

Learn from arts specialists and physical educators who model effective management. Observe various models for exercising authority. Read management books adaptable to dance such as Jones and Lynne's *Positive Classroom Discipline* and *Elementary Classroom Management* by Weistein and Mignano.

Modeling   Physical education management strategies are similar to dance's because both environments are typically large, open, and relatively unstructured (i.e., no individual desks). Both rely on techniques to increase performance and decrease disruptive behaviors. There are good behavior management articles in the *Journal of Physical Education, Recreation & Dance (JOPERD).* Model after physical educators who keep a class focused on task and lessons moving forward while they single out individuals to coach, correct, encourage, and praise. Observe classroom teachers with effective strategies. Remember, the most effective behavior management technique at any given moment is the one that works.

Channel High-Energy Classes   Expect hard-to-manage classes from time to time. When an entire group of elementary students come to class hyper and unfocused, needing to get their wiggles out,

quickly get your drum and put them in motion. Lead a guided exploration with everyone using large, expansive traveling. After students are warmed up, take them into the air with jumps, leaps, and turns. Without saying a word about how hyper they are, channel their pent-up energy by putting them into purposeful motion. Explore their largest, strongest movement punctuated with sharp stops. Gradually work the class into a more controlled, modulated rhythm so their moving time will have prepared them to settle down and move right into the day's dance topic. Wisely channel, rather than fight, energy. (But don't let on or you'll blow its effectiveness.)

Reflecting   Hold the last few minutes of class for reflection—even while kids put on shoes in a circle (see chapter 9). This moves experiences out of the body and right brain and into the left brain. Routine reflection puts students on notice to think during dance activities and to be ready to respond at the end of class to what they did and learned. By keeping students on task during class and accountable for what they learn each day, reflecting will improve concentration and decrease opportunities to misbehave. Routine reflection also has instructional benefit: You assess what was learned, what may not have been clear, and what needs to addressed in the following lesson. Occasionally ask students to summarize the lesson to reinforce its main points. High expectations are a good deterrent to misbehavior.

Misbehaving Students

How do you handle inappropriate behavior in dance? You can't ignore it and you can't allow it. You need authority to deal with misbehavior.

Counteracting Testing Behaviors   Testing behaviors are like communicable diseases. It's bad enough when one student tests you, but when unstopped, testing becomes epidemic. If one gets by with it, all try. Misbehaving students usually have at least one of these goals:

1. To get attention and be noticed (show off)
2. To control the class (power)
3. To get even (revenge)
4. To withdraw from people and from risk (fear)

Testing behaviors take many forms: someone taking too much time to do a task, dawdling, failing to follow directions, or ignoring class rules. Some students might disrespect peers, get peers' attention inappropriately, or run into others. Some students might fabricate excuses to leave the room, refuse to participate, disrupt the lesson, or talk out of turn. Some might laugh at peer performances or be unwilling to dance. School districts have a uniform **disciplinary action plan (DAP)** to deal with such. Memorize the plan. Make it prominent in your student handbook. Use it.

Use your supervised teaching internship to get familiar with district policy and practice for

- positively reinforcing students who are behaving appropriately and
- identifying testing behaviors and learning procedures for dealing with each one.

Different from misbehavior are the chatter queries that disrupt and are meant to divert (e.g., "What time is it?" "When are we going to . . . ?" "Why haven't we . . . ?"). Ignore these questions completely. Keep your dance lesson going. Students soon see that you stay on task and aren't manipulated by their attempts to disrupt. Inappropriate queries dry up without your having to say a word! If this method doesn't work, have a private conference with the student after class to explain that you are there to teach dance.

Dealing With Serious Behavioral Problems in Dance Count on having a few children with real problems. For these, aesthetic development must wait on positive psychological–social behavior (see chapter 4). Student needs come first. Deal with these problems promptly:

- Children who need your attention constantly
- Children who need consistent structure
- Children who need to control their world

Children who act out often suffer anxiety from seeing too much violence and chaos. They may not have enough meaningful adult–child interaction to have their inner fears quelled. When physical and emotional needs are not met at home, students bring their needs to school and into your dance classroom. Just as a child without enough food comes to school hungry, so the child without enough loving attention and validation comes to school hungering for emotional security, which he tries to satisfy there.

Because you teach the whole child, address these needs through dance. Try to get the big picture of a child's whole environment. Dance's advantage is that it gives nonachievers a venue to shine. They can create, show their work, and be seen and validated. They can perform and show what they can do and who they are as individuals. Focus attention on the positive aspects of their performance and accomplishment while consistently challenging them to do their best within your consistent organizational structure.

Performance requires positive group effort and structure to succeed. Group and ensemble work give students a sense of belonging to something larger than themselves. For some this enhances identity. Intangible rewards like performing are incentives for appropriate behavior. Children feel a sense of

> **"Student teachers, as well as many beginning teachers face the problem of handling inappropriate student behavior. . . . In fact, it is one of the greatest barriers that preservice teachers must overcome. Without order in the classroom, instruction cannot take place. . . . Furthermore unless teachers establish structure [order] within the first two or three weeks of the school year, student testing behaviors (e.g., talking out of turn, reckless behavior in the gymnasium [studio], failure to follow teacher instructions) increase until the classroom's climate becomes chaotic. . . . This chaotic classroom situation results in the teacher spending more time on managing inappropriate student behavior and less time on instruction and student skill practice."**
>
> —Anne Boyce (1997, p. 28)

control when allowed to create, perform, and share personal responses about dances. Performance is not an option for any who cannot follow basic rules or be trusted, however. Use group performing to increase dependability, self-governance, and social responsibility.

Often, children whose personal worlds are chaotic try to control a dance class by acting out. When they test rules, they are usually seeking safe boundaries, consistency, and reasonable limits. Their caregivers may not enforce limits, set safe psychological boundaries, have order, or value structure. Your dance structures likely help these students function better in and outside dance class. You can use dance to improve safe psychological–social interactions. Monitor small group work and help dysfunctional children learn how to produce dances in small groups. Before they can achieve artistically, they have to function socially and collaboratively, so this is not time wasted.

Modifying Behavior To be effective as a dance specialist, learn behavior modification techniques and use them as consequences for serious misbehavior. The three basic ones are time-out, restitution, and positive practice.

Time-out sends an offender to a safe, easy-to-monitor, nonreinforcing area of the room (e.g., the corner of the studio). She stays for an appropriate amount of time until ready to exhibit prosocial behavior. Time-out is simple and easy to implement. Sitting out can deter almost any type of inappropriate behavior. Yet it fails to teach what the desirable behavior is, and it removes the student from the learning process, decreasing time on task. Those who do not like participating may misbehave just to escape dance activities they don't like (Henderson et al. 2000).

Restitution replaces an undesirable behavior with a desirable one. An offender must restore the environment he disrupted. For example, he picks up his own shoes left in the center of the room and also straightens all the shoes along the wall to provide a safe dancing space.

Positive practice has the offender repeatedly practice a desired behavior. For example, a student who runs into the room and slides across the floor goes back to the entrance and walks to her place quietly two or three times. (This can be used for an entire class.) It is better than time-out because students learn what not to do as well as what to do instead. You must closely supervise elementary students' performance of positive practice if you want to make long-lasting positive changes. When

you put forth effort to correct behavior—rather than ignore it—most learn to be responsible for their actions. The action steps in the correcting system are these:

1. Tell the student to stop the unacceptable behavior (e.g., "No pushing"). You hope the behavior corrects at this cue. If you consistently give this command before you deliver punishment, most students stop and correct behavior to avoid the consequences.

2. If the behavior is not corrected, give systematic verbal instruction or physically assist the process.

3. Return the student back to the class as soon as the correction is successfully accomplished or the task completed.

In each of these three behavior modification techniques, consistency is the key ingredient. When you always firmly, calmly go through each step of a behavior sequence, students realize they cannot manipulate you into ignoring misbehavior, so behavior usually improves (Henderson et al. 2000). A good deterrent is a fast-paced inquiry-based dance class with maximum time on task. Switching viewpoints from dancing to creating to responding not only increases aesthetic education and artistic growth but also it leaves little time for trouble.

Adapted, by permission, from H.L. Henderson, R. French, R. Fritsch and B. Lerner, 2000, "Time-out and overcorrection: A comparison of their application in physical education," *JOPERD* 71(3): 31-35.

Teaching Practices to Avoid

When your energy is used to manage a class of behavior problems, there are several things to keep in mind that you might forget when under stress.

Abandon what is neither educational nor safe. Create a productive artistic environment. Do not

- embarrass a student in front of the rest of the class;
- remove students from participating for too long a time;
- overemphasize "having fun," because it makes dance seem unimportant;
- allow a low time-on-task ratio;
- create low movement to class-time ratios; or
- disregard student safety in situations that would likely produce injury, dehydration, or overuse.

Excerpted and adapted from Neil Williams, *JOPERD*, February 1994.

Clinical Experiences

As you prepare to become a dance specialist, you will have clinical experiences in schools that will help you see what school-based dance is really like. With luck you will get to see a number of programs so you see different ages and get an opportunity to assist in various settings. This is where you find out what to expect. Learn from every situation. And remember as you go into the schools that you go in with a number of responsibilities.

Your First Visits in the Schools

Each state requires a specified number of hours of **observation** in the schools. To observe teachers in the public school is not a right; it is a privilege. Your conduct and attitude once there reflect on you and your university—and to some degree on dance educators.

Follow these general rules when you observe in schools:

- Report to the school office immediately to sign in. This is law. (Remember to sign out, too.)
- Don't chew gum—ever.
- Dress in a way that does not call attention to yourself (e.g., no really short skirts or shorts for women and no shorts or t-shirts for men).
- Do not take food into the school.
- When in the halls, in the classroom, or on the school grounds, conduct yourself as a teacher. This includes no loud conversations, talking on cell phones, talking about students, or gesturing.
- Be on time for all observation appointments. Get settled before students arrive for class so as not to disrupt their start-up routines.

Classroom Observation

Your clinical hours progress from observation to assistance in the classroom to eventual internship. First is observation. When you arrive at the dance classroom, certain behavior is expected. It is common courtesy to knock before entering, even if the door is ajar or open. Once there, remember these guidelines:

- Always speak to the teacher to say you are glad to be there. Introduce yourself by your last name (e.g., Mr. Smith). At the end thank the teacher for allowing you to observe or work with her students.
- Sit so you can observe the teacher and the students well, but from the sidelines. Pick an inconspicuous place so you are neither in the way of the progress of the class nor featured.
- Evaluate the level of artistic output from the students. Is instruction aesthetically driven, contextually coherent, and inquiry based?
- Make detailed observation notes for your journal. Describe specific ideas you could adopt. Develop a shorthand code to make notes decipherable for later use such as C = content, I = instruction, A = assessment, $HOTS$ = higher-order thinking skills, Seq = sequencing a lesson, and $Mgmt$ = classroom management.
- Maintain your professional demeanor when you observe in cohort groups from your university.
- To keep students from becoming self-conscious, do not talk with your peers during class.
- Refrain from pointing or calling attention to what goes on during class. Maintain a neutral facial expression when observing. (Be especially neutral with adolescent classes, because students at that age are self-conscious, self-critical, and hyper-aware. Their insecurities cause them to think you are laughing at them whether you are or not.)
- Save comments about the class or the lesson until students leave and you are alone with the teacher.

Internships

Your student teaching semester is called an **internship.** It is your chance to apprentice with one master teacher and have supervised experiences that allow you to develop your own teaching skills. The idea works as a scaffold (see chapter 4) where the supervising teacher asks for your assistance but does not turn the class over to you all at once. You build your skills incrementally so that you grow from the apprenticeship. Make each moment an important apprenticing opportunity. Learn how to do each aspect of the job, from daily records to costume storage to long-range planning to ordering and filing resources for teaching. This apprenticeship is one of your most important learning opportunities and gives you knowledge and experience. Be willing to do more than is required of you so that your senior capstone experience prepares you to be the professional you can be.

It's useful to organize a teaching file of all your course materials to which you could refer as you start your student-teaching internship. A sample of the items you should have in your file is given in appendix B ("Sample Teaching File Checklist"). The better you organize this file now, the more readily accessible the materials are later. In addition, keep all your dance, dance education, education, and related textbooks (e.g., anatomy, theatre, music) there. During your internship semester, you may find it beneficial to keep the file in the trunk of your car so that you have access to it when you plan at school and at home. Several portable file boxes are preferable to one large one for ease of handling.

Technology-Based Learning

Stay abreast of the latest in software and use of technology in dance. For example, the National Dance Association sponsored two Dancing with the Mouse Conferences held in Texas and South Carolina. Look for technology in the arts conferences and seminars that are announced through NDA and NDEO list-servs, in such places as the SE Center for Education

in the Arts (Chattanooga), Arizona State University, SUNY–Brockport, and other universities.

Identifying Substantive, Aesthetically Based Dance Software

Choose software that furthers aesthetic education. Weigh its educational benefit against your limited amount of in-class moving time. Is the software best used by students outside class? How will it increase skills needed to create, perform, and respond according to the standards? When software can increase the educational experience—like pulling up a Web site of a major dance company and downloading excerpts of a dance to show students—use it.

Consider technology-based assignments when students are injured and cannot dance. Investigate software such as LabanWriter and DanceForms. DanceForms (a newer version of LifeForms) by Credo Interactive is a 3-D human animation software that enables users to produce movement sequences—even complete dance works—in animated form. You can use the program to produce animations that help explain concepts in choreography, technique, and dance analysis. Students can choreograph original dances for the virtual dancers or attempt to restage existing variations.

Cornerstone-based software is available for student use in and outside of class. There are inquiry-based interactive products on the market from companies like Bedford Interactive (BI) Productions in the United Kingdom. BI's products give you substantive, aesthetically driven dance units developed around significant choreographic works. For example, BI's interactive CD-ROMs feature works such as the Ludus Dance Company's creation and performance of *Wild Child*. The choreography is based on the real-life story of a boy found and brought into civilization after having lived for years abandoned in the wild and growing up in the care of animals without words to communicate. The

Middle and high school students can use interactive software such as *Wild Child* to motivate their own creative compositions.

Wild Child Resource Pack comes with two CD-ROMs, an audio disc, and a book of extensive teaching worksheets for lessons. The practical *Resource Pack* features activities for teaching composition, performance, and dance appreciation/critique. Middle and high school students respond well to *Wild Child*'s format because the story that motivated its creation and the work's artistic creative process are used to stimulate students' own creative responses and composition. This resource's investigative format of creating, performing, and responding is inquiry based.

Bedford Interactive's other outstanding CD-ROMs with multimedia resource packs for teachers are highly recommended for grades 9 through 12. These products explore artistic dance concepts through copious video imaging and provide viewers with the ability to slow a dance down, leave trails and traces of movement, and interact in various ways:

- *Motifs for a Solo Dancer* analyzes use of themes and motifs for choreography using the dance elements to analyze a work in order to see how to construct works that hold together.
- *Graham Technique: Analysis of Ten Basic Exercises* deconstructs the basic Martha Graham techniques to see the underlying characteristics and to analyze the techniques.
- *Choreographic Outcomes: Improving Dance Composition* studies eight pieces of choreography in detail so that students create form in their dance compositions.

A number of other CD-ROM products for dance have applications for instruction and for student practice. For example, William Forsythe's *Improvisation Technologies* is a CD-ROM that provides comprehensive explanations of his concepts with accompanying video exemplars. There are also several classical ballet CD-ROMs that provide terminology and accompanying video exemplars.

Using Handheld Computers

Write notes to parents on small handheld computers. Electronic devices such as personal data assistants (PDAs) let you enter in your student database parents' names, phone numbers, and e-mail addresses so you can send e-mails home about students even while you wait in line for the car wash or a traffic jam. Ask students to use these devices to download information about a choreographer being studied. When someone cannot dance because of injury, put her to work on a handheld computer. Give quizzes

on these devices, and with special software record the grade instantaneously into your computer. Ask students to journal with PDAs and e-mail their journal entries to your computer or to your PDA to read and respond away from school. Direct transfer is quicker than burning CDs, and handheld computers can be carried with you to meetings and to lunch. They allow you to use time that would otherwise be wasted.

Personal handheld electronics are like a mobile office. In addition to using your handheld device for data storage, you can use it backstage during performances to talk to the lighting board if there is no call system in your school auditorium. These little electronic devices with instant messaging give portable ways to communicate in many performance settings. Look into grants that can equip all your students with these devices and use them to further aesthetic education.

Notebook/Portfolio:
Perspectives Notebook

List the 12 priority headings for your student handbook (high school):

- First, consider everything students need to know the first day of class. Make a list.
- Group these items according to main topics. The headings will likely emerge from this list.
- Reflect further to see what else is needed.
- Swap your list with a peer to share ideas, and then brainstorm further.
- Finalize your list and place it in your Perspectives Notebook.

Questions to Ponder

1. How can you be in charge of a class without being the center of attention?
2. How should teacher authority and student empowerment coexist?
3. What goes into your student handbook for students and parents to read and sign?
4. What are the most important safety issues for dance instruction in public schools?

5. How will you record daily grades to reflect the quality of participation in the limited time you have between classes?

6. How much time do students need to dress out? What signals will you use that this time has lapsed? What are the consequences if the limitation is not met?

7. What does the information on scheduling and facilities add to your Statements of Belief (as explained in the Introduction)?

Rich Resources

RESOURCES

- National Dance Association (NDA), part of the American Alliance for Health, Physical Education, Recreation and Dance (AAHPERD), publishes dance resources such as the *Dance Facilities* book and the NSDEs, which includes the OTLS (for school delivery).

- *Wild Child Resource Pack* from http://bedfordi.20m.com and www.dance-interactive.web.com.

- Boyce, Anne. "Inappropriate Student Behavior—A Problem for Student Teachers." *Journal of Health, Physical Education, Recreation and Dance* 68(6): 28-30, 1997.

- Jones, Fred, and Jo Lynne. *Positive Classroom Discipline*. Santa Cruz, CA: Fredric H. Jones, 1999 (www.fredjones.com).

- Wong, Harry K., and Rosemary T. Wong. *How to Be an Effective Teacher: The First Days of School*. Mountain View, CA: Harry K. Wong, 1998 (www.firstdaysofschool.com). This is a valuable manual as you transition from student to teacher.

- Weistein, Carol Simon, and Andrew J. Mignano, Jr. *Elementary Classroom Management*. Second Edition. New York: McGraw-Hill, 1996.

- Joyce, Mary. *Dance Technique for Children*. Palo Alto, CA: Mayfield, 1984. This book is a must for all K-12 dance educators. Read it from stem to stern and incorporate it into your thinking about dance as art in education. It is a dance specialist's bible, along with Joyce's other book, *First Steps in Teaching Creative Dance to Children*.

- Information about quality construction of both the substructure and surface of dance floors can be found in such flooring systems as the L'Air System, at www.aecinfo.com/1/resourcefile/00/28/78/lairx01.htm. Note that some sites offer information and others are selling products.

Investigating the Arts Savvy Curriculum, Instruction, and Assessment Triad

"[Discipline-based arts education] addresses the four sorts of things that people do with art; they make it, they appreciate its qualities, they locate its place in culture over time, and they discuss and justify their judgments about its nature, merits, and importance."

—Elliot Eisner (2002, p. 27)

This chapter investigates the interaction of the **teaching triad:** curriculum, instruction, and assessment. What is taught (curriculum), how it is taught (instruction), and how well it is taught and learned (assessment) become the interdependent, inseparable three-part process you use to teach dance in education. In this chapter you learn to write goals and objectives that merge dance's content and achievement standards.

Rather than outline a strict lesson format, this chapter shapes your perspective about blending the triad of curriculum, instruction, and assessment. We inquire into how each part of the triad intersects in practice to enable you to shape coherent units of study that richly bring the Dance Cornerstone Curriculum Framework to your students. This interdependent teaching triad enables you to advance all six characteristics of educational dance:

- Your curriculum is to be broad (comprehensive), deep (substantive), and sequential.
- Your instruction and assessment are to be aesthetically driven, contextually coherent, and inquiry based.

Curriculum Content

Chapters 6 through 9 described one aspect of the teaching triad—the Dance Cornerstone Curriculum Framework. You saw how to sequence dance content so students achieve desired outcomes at different age levels. You learned to incorporate achievement standards into learning objectives. You advanced enduring understanding in dance. The framework doesn't say how to teach but rather indicates what should be accomplished and what to include. The instructional details that you add are the unique aspects of your program for your particular students based on your expertise and your students' needs. And you add student accountability to this mix.

So how do you break down this bountiful feast into digestible chunks so students end up eating the whole curriculum a piece at a time, and it is part of them by the time they finish it? We'll start with goals and objectives.

Identify what you consider to be dance's mega-ideas and concepts that contribute to enduring under-

standing in dance. Translate these into realistic goals that also incorporate national content standards that are to carry through from year to year. These are the very goals you must translate into concrete, specific, and measurable student learning objectives that incorporate national achievement standards in dance for different ages. After describing this "dance feast" you are ready to create contextual units containing individual lessons around a theme, topic, or idea (the digestible chunks). Goals drive your long-range plan. Objectives drive each unit of study. They state the desired outcomes of what students should know and be able to do as a result of instruction. Thus, as you see in figure 12.1,

- each lesson takes its unit objectives forward;
- each unit takes long-range goals forward; and
- each goal contributes to the education of students about the enduring understandings as well as the important dance ideas, processes, and perceptions of dance.

Figure 12.1 depicts how one goal breaks out into many objectives. These are two of the objectives:

- To meet or exceed NSDE achievement standards related to this goal (represented with one star)
- To articulate one or more of dance's mega-ideas and concepts (enduring understandings) related to this goal (represented with two stars)

Children don't get bored with school when they find enough imaginative challenges there.

Mega-Ideas and Concepts

Goal

Objectives

FIGURE 12.1   Dance's mega-ideas and concepts, goals and objectives, and national standards keep you focused on what you should teach according to what students should learn. *One objective is "to meet or exceed NSDE achievement standards related to this goal." **One objective is to be able "to articulate one or more of dance's enduring understandings related to this goal."

Operationalizing Dance Content

Incorporate dance's enduring understandings into your long-range plan (LRP) and then advance them in your short-range unit plans. Build each grade level's LRP on the previous year's accomplishments. Consider the LRP as a creative staircase with a unique step for each year, as in figure 12.2. You determine the design of each step to ensure it is solid, fits with the one before it, and connects to the one after it.

Translating Goals and Objectives

Also make friends with goals and objectives, because the teaching triad depends on them to convey what is worth knowing and doing. (Please review the "Using Goals and Objectives" section of chapter 5.)

Goals describe destination points. They describe long-range pictures of where K-12 students need to go (e.g., to use the body as an instrument of expression). Keep all K-12 students striving toward that goal. Advance each cornerstone's goals every year (see chapters 6-9). Goals drive the LRP.

Objectives drive the selection of content, instruction, and assessment (i.e., the teaching triad) for teaching units. Objectives say what students should know and do when they complete a unit, the material, and the experience.

- Objectives start with, "The student will . . ."
- Objectives list outcomes demonstrating that students are reaching a larger goal.
- Objectives help teachers design content, instruction, and assessments to standard.

It is imperative to write learning objectives in measurable language so they can be demonstrated and assessed. Use definitive verbs such as *demonstrate, show, apply,* and *create*—not vague phrases like *understand how* or *be aware of.*

As you learned in chapter 5, whereas goals describe the destination, objectives drive the curriculum to get students there. Both must incorporate the national standards: Goals incorporate content standards; objectives incorporate achievement standards. Look at this example of one goal and

Educational Dance Staircase

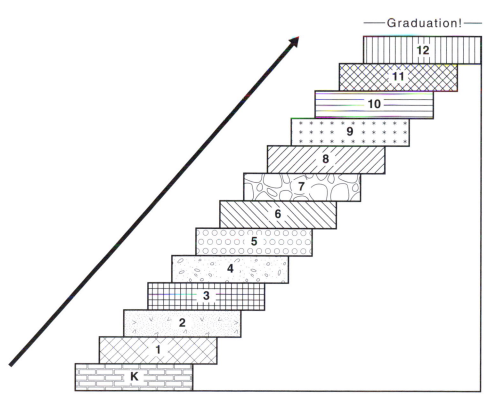

FIGURE 12.2   Advance students on a well-constructed curricular stair so that each step is built on the one before and leads students to the one following it.

its defining objectives and ask yourself, "How do the objectives show if learners accomplished the goal?":

- Goal: To use the body as an instrument of expression.
- Objectives: The student will
  1. demonstrate increased skill in conveying shapes with the body in space (bodyshaping) and in varying use of levels in a combination or sequence;
  2. demonstrate evidence of muscular coordination and balance and show proper jumping and landing skills; and
  3. demonstrate rhythmic acuity in new, complex dance patterns.

Transferring Achievement Standards Into Objectives

Achievement standards describe and measure student performance levels. Incorporate achievement standards into your learning objectives to ensure you include all of each age level's significant learning outcomes in dance. When you compile all of the year's assessments for a class, students should meet or exceed state and national dance standards for that grade level. When you find the need to add more objectives to the cornerstones, consider how they advance state and national achievement standards. Keep them of the highest quality.

Learning objectives drive a complete cornerstone curriculum and incorporate all national standards. Keep objectives as follows:

- Substantive—involving challenging, stimulating, and complex content so you engage students intellectually and kin-aesthetically.
- Sequential—so students experience progressively more complex and sophisticated aspects of the content. Build each unit in complexity grade by grade so what is learned in one grade is the basis for what follows at the next level.
- Spiraling—to revisit familiar concepts in new, more challenging ways. Build on previous concepts to add real depth to the content.
- Comprehensive—to ensure that broad content includes varied dance styles, cultural forms, dance appreciation, dance making, performance, and criticism along with creating and dancing.

Look at the goal and three objectives stated previously.

- Notice that the goal—"to use the body as an instrument of expression"—factors in NSDE Content Standard 1: *To identify and demonstrate movement elements and skills in performing dance.* Notice that objectives 1 and 2 ("Demonstrate increased skill in conveying shapes with the body in space [bodyshaping] and in varying use of levels in a combination or sequence" and "Demonstrate evidence of muscular coordination and balance, and show proper jumping and landing skills") subsume NSDE 1.g for kindergarten through grade 4: *To demonstrate kinesthetic awareness, concentration, and focus in performing movement skills.*
- Notice that objective 3 ("Demonstrate rhythmic acuity in new, complex dance patterns") subsumes NSDE 1.f for kindergarten through grade 4: *To demonstrate accuracy in moving to a musical beat and responding to changes in tempo.*
- Notice that objective 2 subsumes NSDE 1.a for grades 5 through 8: *To demonstrate the following movement skills and explain the underlying principles—alignment, balance, initiation of movement, articulation of isolated body parts, weight shift, elevation and landing, fall and recovery.*

Designing a Curriculum

Use these steps to design an incremental curriculum for each grade level. Even if your state has no dance curriculum framework and your district has no grade by grade scope and sequence, you can design and deliver a standards-oriented curriculum by combining the Dance Cornerstone Curriculum (DCC) Framework and the national dance achievement standards.

Step 1: Go to the NSDEs Incorporate the NSDEs so every grade level meets expectations.

- Make the content standards your first goals.
- Then make the achievement standards your first objectives.
- Write them into your 1-year LRP as goals and objectives.

This cues you to give students at each grade level content and experiences so they achieve standards.

Step 2: Go to the DCC Framework Use the framework to determine what is needed and break out the skills to be accomplished for every grade level.

- Add the framework goals.
- Add framework objectives appropriate for the age level.
- Cross-check to be sure you have subsumed 100 percent of the NSDE achievement standards.
- Write additional objectives as long as they take the national achievement standards forward. You might also convert sample learning outcomes from the DCC Framework to objectives when needed. (Because they are presented in four 3-year blocks, break them out into a yearly sequence according to what is age appropriate.)
- Write all of the objectives into your 1-year LRP for each grade level.

Step 3: Review Your Draft LRP to See That It Is Indeed Comprehensive, Substantive, Aesthetically Driven, and Sequential Is there anything missing? Does each student get a logical learning sequence as he goes from kindergarten through twelfth grade?

Step 4: Make an SRP With Objectives for Each Grade Level Now you are ready to design short-term units of study that enable students to accomplish all you say they should in your LRP to grow aesthetically, intellectually, emotionally, socially, and kin-aesthetically.

Determining Teacher Competencies

What dance specialists seem to worry about most is, "What will I teach?" So relax, you have the DCC Framework to call on. But the more pressing question is what you will teach that is of the most educational benefit that enables students to grow kinesthetically, artistically, intellectually, emotionally, and socially. How will you teach a 6DC Cornerstone Model effectively to ensure that students measure up? These are specific competencies you must master en route to successful teaching.

SUCCESS FACTORS FOR BUILDING AN ARTS CURRICULUM IN DANCE

Use this list first for information and then as a checklist to assess your strengths and weaknesses. Rate yourself a 1, 2, or 3 on each item.

The effective dance specialist provides dance cornerstone content that

1. ____ is aligned with district arts and dance content standards;
2. ____ is standards-oriented and meets the national dance achievement standards for the grade level;
3. ____ is consistent with and achieves long-range goals in dance;
4. ____ is appropriate for the objectives of the instructional unit of study;
5. ____ is substantive and aesthetically based as well as current and accurate;
6. ____ is presented in a logical and sequential order;
7. ____ is well-paced and appropriate for all students;
8. ____ comes from multiple sources that reflect varied social, cultural, and intellectual perspectives;
9. ____ is sequential and builds on skills and knowledge;
10. ____ is substantive and worthy of student attention and inquiry;
11. ____ is inquiry based;
12. ____ is contextually coherent;
13. ____ is aesthetically driven;
14. ____ is appropriate to the physical, intellectual, emotional, social, and artistic needs of students;
15. ____ increases kin-aesthetic growth; and
16. ____ increases dance literacy and fluency.

The effective dance specialist also

17. ____ provides sufficient demonstrations, explanations, examples, and samples of high-quality performance for students to increase their artistic perception;
18. ____ emphasizes content from the four dance cornerstones; and
19. ____ emphasizes the dance elements as key to creating, performing, knowing about, and responding to dance.

Adapted from The South Carolina Department of Education Web site.

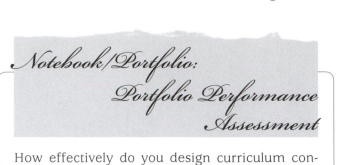

Notebook/Portfolio:
Portfolio Performance
Assessment

How effectively do you design curriculum content? As with checklists in other chapters, write an assessment rubric using all the preceding criteria to measure your growing skills. After mentors have critiqued you and you have practiced and polished your skills to earn all 3s, add the signed and dated evaluations to the Achievement and Skills section of your Professional Teaching Portfolio. See appendix A for the details.

Instruction

Harry Wong says it best:

> Learning has nothing to do with what the teacher *covers*. Learning has to do with what the student *accomplishes*. (Wong and Wong 1998, p. 210)

Have you seen students who didn't learn because the teacher lacked the skills to communicate effectively? Have you known teachers who knew the content but could not get it across? Who could not relate to students? Who did not have the skills to engage students? Begin to acutely observe how your teachers deliver dance. What strategies are effective? Clever? Ineffective? A waste of time? Why not start your own teaching journal of effective strategies you observe?

You accumulate skills by monitoring and adjusting instructional strategies to fit the learner and the learning situation. How you translate content into action determines your effectiveness in the classroom. As you carry the 6DC Cornerstone Model forward, remember one cardinal instructional rule: Waste no time; stay on task.

The way you approach instruction affects learners' cognitive, affective, and psychomotor development. Vary instructional strategies, settings for learning, and groupings. When possible, use an inquiry approach to facilitate active learning. Take a multisensory approach.

Instructional Approaches

To keep instruction student focused, move at a pace that allows students to succeed and to grasp the concepts being taught. As soon as they learn a concept, put it into practice—kinesthetically and cognitively. Learn it, do it. When they apply it, they understand and retain it. Then you can assess responses and performances and quickly intercede so all continue successfully.

Seven other things strengthen instruction.

1. Stay Actively Engaged During Any Approach

Whether students are researching with computers or being guided through a viewing session, be active and alert and facilitate learning. Move through the room surveying all activity and supervising. Individualize comments to keep students focused and to boost them when they are stuck or have reached a dead-end on a topic.

2. Promote Excellence and Stimulate at a High Level

Teach facts and skills as a foundation for higher-order inquiry (analysis, synthesis, and evaluation). As soon as students have the basics, engage them beyond the basics (see chapter 4). Build incentives for excellence. Reward achievement. Move beyond rote learning, imitation, and re-creation of someone else's work. Move into inquiring, creating, and analyzing as well as reflection, critique, and self-evaluation. Promote collaboration instead of competition.

3. Guard Time for Maximum Learning

A common pitfall in dance is allocating too much educational time to rehearsing formal presentations, concerts, and performances for audiences. Resist overemphasizing big dance productions to dazzle parents and administrators. Rehearsals absorb instructional time for little value received. Create informal venues instead to show works and works in progress to mark artistic growth and afford opportunities for feedback. Usually the school day isn't long enough to accomplish a standards-oriented program and dwell on rehearsals for big performances, too.

4. Emphasize Process and Product

Both process and product are essential to a balanced dance program. Do not emphasize products (dances) at the expense of process. Show and critique works so students get to integrate and apply concepts as they learn them (process). Put new learning into practice immediately to aid retention. Let classroom performances keep students goal-oriented for technical proficiency in upper grades and to demonstrate and make concrete the cornerstone learning objectives. Use informal showings to foster teamwork (because team playing is mostly learned through the performing arts and sports), boost self-confidence, and give you authentic assessment opportunity. Validate the artistic process of performance but not at the expense of the process. Resist letting performance drive education, because it overemphasizes C1 and weakens the educational side of C2, C3, and C4, which could cause its downfall. Use performance more as incentive to practice, polish, and perfect what students do than to make everything a production.

5. Don't Overuse Didactic Teaching Methods

Lectures eat up instructional time, putting you rather than the student at the center of the process. Dispense facts to launch a dance investigation but quickly activate students. When you must lecture, season a lecture with questions when students can provide the answers (e.g., "Why is that a good idea? When would you want to do that?"). Add impact by stacking learning styles. Use video and DVD clips as well as visual technology like PowerPoint. Find or create computer software to support lecture objectives that enliven student involvement. As you develop software for your students, share it with other dance specialists (i.e., post on a Web site such as www.dancecurriculum.com).

6. Involve Students in Multisensory Learning

Vary instruction. Have your students move, create, dance, perform, read, write about, view, and discuss works of dance and other arts. Investigate dance using all the senses. Review chapter 4's section titled "Maximized Learning." This enlivens learning as it validates the expertise and experience students bring to a lesson.

7. Identify Developmental Indicators

Apply the developmental indicators to determine where children are and move them to where they need to be. The "Developmental Indicators" in appendix B assist the strategic instructional decisions.

Direct and Indirect Approaches

Match the content to the most effective delivery. Above all, master many different strategies so you are skilled at facilitating both convergent and divergent learning. Four unidentified teachers shared practical advice at an education workshop:

- "The number of problems to solve cannot exceed the grade level of the child in elementary school." —Elementary school teacher
- "What the body experiences, the mind will never forget." —Classroom teacher
- "The number of words of instruction cannot exceed the age of the child." —Elementary school teacher
- "The arts—especially dance—are a teacher's vehicle for testing and remediating on the spot." —Dance specialist

Directed Teaching

Much information is required before one has the vocabulary and understanding to use the information creatively. In dance, we use a directed approach to the foundations for the dance ideas, concepts, and experiences that are required. From these solid foundations students are able to use the information in different ways, such as to create, to perform, or to critique. It is vital information. For example, students must comprehend certain facts and be able to apply them (Bloom's first three levels: knowledge, comprehension, application) to use them for higher-order thinking (Bloom's highest three levels). These are some directed teaching approaches in dance:

- Facts-based teaching
- Convergent learning methods
- Research-based assignments (to capitalize on individual interest in a given topic)
- Technology-based learning (such as Web searches, LabanWriter)
- Teacher-guided practice
- Guided discussions
- PowerPoint lectures
- Technique (command teaching)

Guided Discovery and Inquiry

An inquiry approach does not replace directed teaching but relies greatly on guided discovery for divergent and convergent processing. Design instruction and inquiry so students immediately apply what they learn. Use these tools:

- Guided discovery
- Query (i.e., inquiry)
- Guided reflection questions (at the end of significant sections of material)
- Creative movement exploration

- Experimentation
- Discussions
- Improvisation
- Mind mapping
- Problem solving
- Individual research
- Guided viewing (when looking at a dance work or peer works)
- Brainstorming
- Creative process
- Critiquing
- Self-assessment
- Reciprocal learning
- Peer-on-peer mentoring

Groupings

Whether you use direct or indirect approaches, vary groupings to keep learning fresh and to engage students in different ways:

- Whole group
- Small groups
- Individual creative activities
- Collaborative ventures
- Partners
- Audience
- Split groups (e.g., two groups with one active and the other observing as critical friends)
- Student mentors (for one on one)

Instructional Strategies

Because teaching dance is more than teaching technique, intentionally call on multiple strategies within units so students achieve all learning objectives. Incorporate varied strategies:

- Technique classes
- Repertory classes
- Reconstructions
- Discussions
- Presentations
- Informal showings
- Performances
- Class observation
- Critiquing sessions
- Creative dance

- Peer assessment and feedback
- Reflection and review
- Guided exploration
- Guided viewing
- Research
- Dance technology and software
- Educational dance manipulatives
- Videotaping
- Notating and scripting movement
- Web search
- Multidiscipline projects

Leading Inquiry

Lead inquiry to get at genuine understanding as opposed to superficial or surface comprehension. Do not be satisfied by signs of apparent understanding, such as students giving back the right words, definitions, or specifics. By changing the questions, you could realize students do not really grasp what you thought they did. Wisely select the kinds of questions you ask as well as the types of inquiry you engage students in.

Prioritize Concepts

McTighe and Wiggins (1999) described educating for understanding using three priority levels to help teachers emphasize the most vital concepts they seek. (See figure 12.3 for the visual representation of these three points.) Educational dance adapts this as a model to ensure we don't get lost in the details of dance. Look at everything you teach to decide which priority category it falls into (McTighe and Wiggins 1999, p. 75):

1. Dance understanding that is enduring (highest priority)
2. Dance knowledge and skills that are important to know and do (important)
3. Dance knowledge that is worth being familiar with (lowest priority)

Priority 1. Understanding That Is Enduring The ring embedded in the center of figure 12.3 refers to the mega-ideas and concepts that promote enduring understanding in dance, concepts that are to be retained about dance long after some of its details have been forgotten. These concepts form the educational priorities: dance's big ideas and main artistic processes.

Such understanding has lasting value beyond the classroom. These are the very concepts—both kinetic and cognitive skills—that are lasting and of greatest value in seeing the big picture of dance. From them come the central questions that go to the core of the dance discipline (the essential questions in dance).

- These dance concepts, skills, and understandings are at the heart of dance.

- They reside in our goals and objectives, our content standards, and our unit topics.

- Get at them by questioning, "What mega-idea does this connect to?" "Why is this important to dance?" "What does it relate to?" "What is most important about this topic or skill?" "How does it affect dance or dancing?" (Chapters 6-9 contain additional suggested mega-ideas and concepts.) Emphasize the main points in each unit by asking essential questions in the cornerstones and as part of the artistic processes (c/p/r).

Priority 2. Knowledge and Skills That Are Important to Know and Do in Dance   The middle ring specifies the knowledge and skills to accomplish—key tasks, important aspects, experiences in all of dance's cornerstones and artistic processes. They are measured by assessments and are vital to a dance cornerstone curriculum. The concepts cross units and grade levels and build depth year by year. They make up dance's basic skills of creating, performing, and responding.

- Design units around the essential questions in dance.

- Identify priorities that drive instruction in and about dance.

Priority 3. Knowledge That Is Worth Being Familiar With   The outside ring contains interesting details found in a dance unit that round out the learning process and the specific dance topic. Over time some of these details may get lost, but they help one learn the specific aspects of one dance topic worth knowing and doing. These details add interesting flavor and specificity to each unit of study but are not the most vital. Include them because they add value to learning as well as diversity to dance techniques. This is generally not information worth assessing or testing.

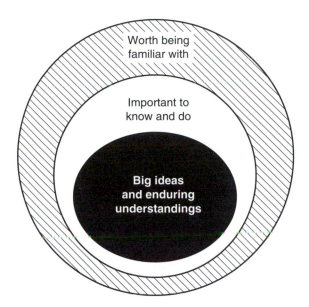

FIGURE 12.3   Prioritize instruction so that you emphasize what is most important for students to learn and to do within a unit: (1) concepts that build lasting understanding in and about dance (highest priority); (2) dance knowledge and skills that are important to know and do as part of this unit (important); and (3) dance knowledge worth being familiar with to make the unit come alive and to add interesting details (lowest priority).

From G. Wiggins et al., 2004, *Understanding by Design professional development workbook* (Alexandria, VA: ASCD), 79. © ASCD. Reprinted by permission. The Association for Supervision and Curriculum Development is a worldwide community of educators advocating sound policies and sharing best practices to achieve the success of each learner. To learn more, visit ASCD at www.ascd.org.

Question According to Priority

You must know where you are going (answers) to ask the kind of questions to get students there. Use a reverse process like the TV show *Jeopardy:* you know the answers you want students to give, so what questions do you ask to get them there? Your questions are often more open-ended (divergent) than *Jeopardy's,* however. Use questions to

- get students involved,

- stimulate their personal interest, and

- model effective inquiry so they learn to ask their own questions (that lead them deeper into the topic or into a related area of dance interest).

How do you question so students investigate what is relevant? How do you further enduring understanding? Ask yourself three questions first:

1. Which mega-ideas and concepts do my students need that are vital to their understanding of dance and can be applied in many dance situations?

2. What do they need to know about this unit or topic that is relevant and important?

3. What interesting details make this unit come alive but are not vital to know forever or to understand in detail?

Then design instruction and questions to emphasize the most important aspects (i.e., questions 1 and 2). Include kin-aesthetic, cultural, and aesthetic inquiry.

Use Bloom's Taxonomy

In chapter 9 you used an inquiry approach to mobilize the cornerstones at all six levels of thinking and processing to engage students at each level. Now let's use the verbs in figure 9.3 to write objectives for all six levels of Bloom's taxonomy:

To *know* the cornerstones viewpoints, the student will

- recall and memorize facts related to dance,
- understand ideas and information in dance,
- know the dance elements, and
- observe details.

To *comprehend* and understand aspects of the cornerstones, the student will

- tell about or summarize what he knows;
- apply dance vocabularies;
- describe or show what he knows about dance; and
- demonstrate his grasp of the dance elements.

To *apply* what she knows about the cornerstones, the student will

- apply her understanding of the dance elements to performance,
- solve a movement problem,
- compare and contrast two dance concepts,
- improvise and explore movement concepts, and
- show, tell, or illustrate her grasp of movement or dance.

To *analyze* aspects of the cornerstones, the student will

- break out information into its constituent parts so it can be understood,
- unpack a dance work,

- break down a movement sequence,
- detect structure and form in a dance,
- distinguish the key elements in a dance composition, and
- relate cause and effect.

To *create and compose,* the student will

- compose, improvise, choreograph, and create dance movement;
- design movement patterns;
- connect concepts from different cornerstones;
- relate one thing to another;
- plan, refine, and edit;
- solve a creative problem; and
- discuss how a dance was created.

To *judge* the artistic quality, the student will

- critique dances,
- evaluate by aesthetic standards and criteria,
- recognize the best,
- judge according to established criteria,
- give qualitative feedback,
- establish the worth or quality of dances or performers,
- measure according to standards, and
- pass judgment.

Use Different Kinds of Questions

In addition to identifying and asking the essential questions about the mega-ideas and concepts at all three levels of priority in figure 12.3, also use facts-based questions and those that require different levels of complex application and thinking according to the six levels of Bloom's taxonomy. Hit two targets with one arrow: Ask targeted questions and in the process model how to inquire into dance. Use five kinds of questions:

- Lead students into the core of a topic. (essential questions)
- Help them formulate questions of their own. (spin-off questions)
- Focus on the depth and look for the ramifications of a topic. (probing questions)
- Lead students to put a topic or experience in context. (reflection questions)

- Lead them to extrapolate and imagine. ("what if" and divergent questions)

Essential Questions

Essential questions are central and take us to the core of an issue or idea or unit. They seek the most significant facts and information, and they educate for understanding. For example:

- "What is this about?"
- "What is most relevant here?"
- "What is necessary about this?"
- "How does this show dance as a universal form of human expression?"

Spin-Off Questions Spin-off questions result from central questions of a unit. They sometimes relate to the big ideas and sometimes to side topics. They elaborate and extrapolate; they uncover juicy facets of a main topic. They sometimes raise other questions. For example:

- "What reasons might be behind the choreographer's choice of black and white as the only colors used in the dance?"
- "How closely is the dance tied to the music? Which was the starting point for that dance: the movement or the music?"
- "Is it important that this choreographer collaborated with a visual artist? Why?"

Probing Questions (HOTS) Use probing questions to zero in on a topic to deepen understanding. These questions go straight to the heart of the topic and hunt out viable information there. They push beyond the obvious to what is more illusive, powerful, or intuitive. Use probing questions during discussions rather than as discussion starters. For example:

- "What do you think the choreographer is trying to communicate by doing this?"
- "What does she want you to think? To feel?"
- "How strongly do you get that message?"
- "If you were the choreographer, how would you describe the piece to the set designer so he'd understand what to create for it?"
- "Where might this lead?"

Reflection Questions (HOTS) Reflection questions relate present experience to what we already know. They help us cognitively process dance experiences. They help us put things in context: to recall what we did and relate it to something else. For example:

- "Why did we do this?"
- "When have we seen something like this before?"
- "How does this relate to what we did yesterday?"
- "What is missing?"
- "What did you learn by that?"
- "What kind of artistic statement does this make?" (reflection questions that ask us to contemplate the ramifications of something)
- "What does this mean?" (questions for analytical thought)

"What If?" and Divergent Questions (HOTS) Divergent questions are open ended and seek new solutions. They depart from where you are and launch an exploration to unknown territory.

- "How might you have used the rope in a completely different way?"
- "How would this solo change if danced by three dancers?"
- "A choreographer wouldn't dare do such a thing in the middle of this choreography, would he?" (provocative questions that incite debate and serious discussion)
- "If you were asked to finish this choreography, what would you do to resolve it given all that has been communicated up to this point?"

What if?, a particular kind of divergent question, is an exercise in creative thinking. It is active inquiry. Although a form of reflection, What if?s explore the less obvious, extend possibilities, test results, and relate information to other settings. Whereas an essential question is like the spot the stone lands in the water, What if?s are ripples that extend out indefinitely. You examine the edges rather than the center of the topic and think about their ramifications. Whereas reflective questions are more summative about personal thinking, What if?s are more formative about actions and possibilities. You not only ask students "What if?"; you want them to ask "What if?" back! You can project a theory or idea into the future with, "What are the ramifications of . . . ?" or "What would happen if . . . ?" You can ask them to test their beliefs by going past the given information to what could be:

- "What if the dancer had burst in from behind instead of slowly moving toward her from the side?"

- "What might happen if *this* became *that?*"
- "What might happen if *this* came before *that?*"
- "What artistic difference would it make if they danced in front of a blank proscenium rather than using an elaborate set like this?"

Reflect and Respond

Turn Mega-Ideas and Concepts Into Essential Questions (see figure 12.1)

Part 1: Write four strong mega statements about dance that you want to impress on your students for enduring understanding. Write one from each cornerstone viewpoint (dancer, choreographer, historian–anthropologist, and critic).

Part 2: Turn each statement into one or more essential questions to use (in an appropriate learning context, not out of the blue!) to facilitate inquiry. For example, "The dancer's body is the instrument of expression through which ideas, concepts, and feelings are artfully expressed" (dancer, C1).

1. "What is the dancer able to express through the body?"
2. "What is the dancer's instrument of artistic expression?"
3. "How does the dancer in this dance work use the body to express the concept of ____?"
4. "What dance elements related to the body help the dancer artfully portray [this idea]?"

Five Misconceptions About Inquiry

Let's address the five most common questions and concerns about using inquiry in teaching.

1. *Does "inquiry based" mean there are not set or absolute answers to questions?* No. The avenue of learning includes inquiry. It does not mean inquiry only. Convergent and divergent thinking are vital to an inquiry approach. Students still acquire facts-based information by rote learning, reading and writing, memorizing anatomical terms, learning movement sequences, analyzing movement, Labanotating, and critiquing dances according to specific criteria. It is the active spirit of investigation that makes learning inquiry based. For instance, you might begin inquiry with, "There are four basic facts about this topic, which are . . . Why are they so critical to success?" Inquiry uses factual concepts for meaningful exploration and personalization.

2. *How can a teacher test what is learned in individualized open-ended inquiry?* Embed assessment in the actual learning experience. Before setting students to open-ended tasks, describe concretely what success will look like. Explain desired outcomes. Specify the timetable (from a few minutes to a few days). For example, use goal-oriented review criteria to measure open-ended research, keep students on task, and hold them accountable for timely, independent investigation. Use performance assessment to evaluate movement skills and content application. Use critique (peer, self, and teacher).

3. *Do some dance styles better lend themselves to inquiry than others?* No. Facilitate inquiry into all dance styles. Modern dance and creative dance are hallmarks of the exploratory, creative art forms, but ballet, jazz, tap, and indigenous dance styles lend themselves to this approach. Also adopt this method yourself. Investigate alongside your students to feed your own inquisitive self and light new creative fires.

4. *Can both seasoned and inexperienced dance specialists facilitate inquiry?* Yes. Seasoned specialists use experience to determine desired learner outcomes. They often work backward, going from the goals to the sequential action steps to get students there. These specialists design questions that motivate and steer students toward the outcomes. New specialists find that discovery works even when they don't yet have all the answers. To facilitate learning in dance, you need

> a broad scope of dance,
> the ability to analyze movement,
> skills to qualitatively measure student output,
> skills to shape discovery and quantify it,
> the disposition to reflect and evaluate along the way,
> dedication to learn ahead of your students, and
> the ability to reroute inquiry when necessary to get students where they need to be.

Always expect multiple discoveries and exciting side trips that spark ideas to later pursue. See how this process turns ho-hum students into involved learners.

5. *Do students have to be still during inquiry (i.e., not moving)?* Not necessarily. Inquiry does not require that they be seated. Indeed, they do search Web sites and read, so sometimes they don't move.

But some of the best inquiry happens while they are creating or applying understanding to a movement problem. For example, ask students to seek variations and alternative ways to express an idea. Investigate movement to integrate body, intellect, and emotions and to increase aesthetic judgment. Inquire kin-aesthetically.

Teacher Competencies

Good teachers are usually a product of good teaching! You likely have had many exemplary teachers in various subjects whose methods you can inherit. Use them. Then develop others on your own. Particularly master these skills needed to teach dance.

SUCCESS FACTORS FOR DELIVERING INSTRUCTION AND FACILITATING INQUIRY

To maximize aesthetic education, the effective dance specialist uses varied instruction

1. _____ that includes lessons organized in a logical sequence progressing toward desired outcomes;

2. _____ that achieves the learning or developmental objectives of the dance unit;

3. _____ that is appropriate for the level of dance content and skills to be learned;

4. _____ that is appropriate for the student's ability and development;

5. _____ that accommodates different rates of learning;

6. _____ that uses verbal, visual, kinesthetic, and tactile approaches to support and extend all learning styles;

7. _____ that is appropriate to where students are in the learning stage (initial, application, practice, review, and transfer);

8. _____ that actively engages students in instruction and learning;

9. _____ that promotes different levels of thinking and problem-solving skills, emphasizing higher-order and critical thinking;

10. _____ that promotes both independent and collaborative learning;

11. _____ that is student outcome oriented;

12. _____ that demonstrates mastery of varied questioning techniques;

13. _____ that includes connecting learning to mega-ideas in dance;

14. _____ that stimulates meaningful inquiry that increases understanding of dance; and

15. _____ that is appropriate to kin-aesthetic activity as well as classroom study.

Adapted from The South Carolina Department of Education Web site.

Notebook/Portfolio:
Perspective Notebook

How effectively do you deliver instruction and facilitate inquiry? As with other Success Factor checklists, use the criteria as performance indicators for self-reflection and mentor evaluation. Use the rating details in appendix A.

SUCCESS FACTORS FOR MAINTAINING HIGH LEARNER EXPECTATIONS

You must establish and maintain appropriately high expectations for students and also hold to high artistic standards. The effective dance specialist

1. _____ promotes students' achievement of performance artistry and productivity in the studio and classroom,

2. _____ reinforces and upholds artistic standards in the artistic processes (c/p/r),

3. _____ clearly conveys what students are expected to know and do according to artistic standards and objectives,

4. _____ explains dance's learning objectives at the beginning of each unit and lesson and assesses objectives through criteria and rubrics,

5. _____ restates and clarifies objectives during dance units,

6. _____ holds realistic expectations according to the ability and development of students,

7. _____ challenges and invites all students to achieve appropriately high artistic levels,

8. _____ ensures that students understand current objectives' relevance to past objectives,

9. _____ ensures that students grasp the importance of achieving the unit objectives,

10. _____ establishes high participation expectations,

11. _____ sets appropriate expectations for completing tasks in and out of the classroom and studio and ensures that these expectations are met, and

12. _____ stimulates student reflection to make information contextually coherent.

Adapted from The South Carolina Department of Education Web site.

Assessment

Although we live in a standards-oriented educational system, some educators protest the amount of attention assessments get and question their overall efficacy. Educators don't want standards to become the tail that wags the dog. Standards should keep us focused on major goals—but should not drive arts education. There is more to arts education than tests and measurements. Much of what is of educational and aesthetic value cannot be effectively measured—neither quantified nor qualified.

There are obvious benefits of assessment. By assessing learning we determine if sufficient achievement levels are met in dance. We ensure that all students know and can do what they need to, according to standards. Without standards of measure, how would we know what sufficient progress is? How could we be accountable?

Assessment and **evaluation** are similar measurement terms. The arts usually use the terms "assessment" for students and "evaluation" for programs and teachers (as does this text). Evaluation is for large-scale measurement over time.

Relation of Standards to Assessment

Standards state what is to be achieved. Assessments measure students to see if they achieved standards. However, assessment issues are much larger than merely assessing students in dance according to standards. Arts assessment functions to improve learning as well as measure it.

It isn't possible to reduce all of dance's educational benefits to what is stated as standards. Student assessment is a mechanism whereby we check in with students to see where they are and use the results to help them get to the next level. This process builds accountability into teaching and learning. Ideally, assessment enables students to learn more and to achieve better results—whether tied to external standards or not.

Here are three important questions about arts assessment.

1. *Is assessment necessary in the arts?* Yes, for many reasons.

> Assessment helps arts educators achieve uniform standards so when students move from school to school there is some consistency in programs.

> Assessment lets everyone know what has and has not yet been accomplished: teachers and students, parents and administrators.

> Assessments identify what has been learned and what needs remediating.

2. *Is it a waste of time to test students?* No. Most arts teachers assess learning to continue the learning process, not only to measure what was learned. Assessments are strong learning tools in the hands of those teachers who make time for students to analyze what they have learned, synthesize it in a new way, and learn to reflect and to critically think for themselves. Assessment should be educational time spent to deepen learning in all arts processes. When assessments take the form of tests, they should also use critical and creative thinking instead of regurgitating facts. When tests ask students to apply what they know (Bloom's application, analyze) and think critically (Bloom's synthesize, evaluate), they help students synthesize information.

3. *Is it necessary to assess the arts to validate them as educational?* Yes. It is necessary so that other educators, administrators, parents, and students see the specific learning outcomes mastered. Assessment validates that cognitive and kin-aesthetic learning in dance is measurable and educational. Assessment is powerful advocacy in the highly political educational system. We must assess, and we must stay alert and politically savvy. That said, we must not lose sight of our reason to be in the school:

. . . not to finish something, but to start something, . . . not to cover the curriculum, but to uncover it. What one starts is an interest that is sufficiently powerful to motivate students to pursue that interest outside school. (Eisner 2002, pp. 90-91)

Personally Referenced Standards (Criteria Based)

You set your own personally referenced standards (i.e., teacher referenced) to establish and maintain high learner expectations. Base them on your professional beliefs about what is educationally important and what is best practice in dance education. These standards—unique to your school—are where you build and maintain your program's integrity. They are critically important because your standards of excellence ensure that your students more than meet the minimum standards set by outside sources. These standards list the criteria you believe are most important to achieve and to measure.

Student assessment creates a feedback loop to measure (for you and others) how well the content and instructional strategies worked for each learner based on unit goals and objectives. You will assess all instructional increments—a lesson, a unit, a semester. Assess student progress at designated intervals to monitor quality and to ensure the smooth transition of students from one learning level to another.

Nationally Referenced Standards (Norm Based)

Outside entities, such as state and national organizations, disseminate standards that apply uniformly to all students in that sample. External standards are baseline benchmarks to measure whether all students in that sample acquire basic-level skills and knowledge (and in some cases proficiency). From these standards come norm-based assessments.

- External content standards, such as the NSDEs, identify the scope of learning required. Their benchmarks guide where we are going with our curriculum and keep us from leaving out major parts of our dance curriculum.

- External achievement standards are benchmarks to measure actual student achievement. (i.e., "The student will . . ."). Such standards do not consider mitigating circumstances. They are cut and dried. They are basic, concrete criteria to assess whether students achieve what

> "[S]tandards can make a contribution to arts education if they do the following: if they represent in a meaningful and non-rigid way the values we embrace and the general goals we seek to attain, if they provide those who plan curricula with an opportunity to discuss and debate what is considered important to teach and learn, and if they suggest criteria that can be used to make judgments about our effectiveness. Standards should be viewed as aids. . . . They should not be regarded as contracts or prescriptions that override local judgments."
>
> —Elliot Eisner (2002, p. 173)

they are supposed to. Students who measure up achieve; those who do not fail the standard. External standardized assessment instruments measure achievement standards.

Parameters for Designing Student Assessments

Validity, reliability, and objectivity are necessary for any effective assessment. Ongoing student assessment should become part of the learning process as much as a measurement of achievement. Assessments should represent the complete range of unit objectives and standards and measure the extent to which students meet them. Assessments should be compatible with the approaches used for instruction. The actual assessments should be fair to all students. Assessments should measure content and skills from all four cornerstones. They should be administered to coincide with when students have attained the greatest aptitude and achievement. Assess performance from kindergarten through twelfth grade. Clearly establish criteria for making judgments about student work and responses. Grading should be the result of using multiple assessment techniques and should include teacher, peer, and self-assessments (South Carolina Visual and Performing Arts Curriculum Framework Writing Team 1993).

Objectives Become the Assessments

Turn learning objectives (i.e., desired student outcomes starting with "The student will. . . .") into assessment criteria for units and for lessons (starting with "The student will achieve. . . ."). List all criteria that show mastery of the objective, and then devise a way to measure each criterion. The criteria you list enable you to concretely communicate to students what is to be learned, what is learned, and what needs to be relearned or refined.

Arts assessments can be dynamic. In dance we get to see students perform right in front of us for feedback and critique; we videotape them to demonstrate skill proficiency.

what others are doing as it is being done. We get students to perform right in front of us; we videotape them to demonstrate proficiency. We use performance portfolios. Although measurements are somewhat subjective, we make them less so when we create rubrics to objectify what we look for in performance.

Assessment can be formal or informal. Formal assessments assess all students at once using some kind of instrument or test; everyone gets graded. Informal assessments are more process oriented and random. Use both. For example, teacher-made tests of curriculum content are formal, whereas there are two kinds of informal assessment:

1. Authentic assessment, where the teachers observe and assess how well learners process information and concepts during the creative, compositional, and performance activities. Can students process, think, and perform while dancing? Can they demonstrate successfully? Can they apply new learning to their creative work?

2. The **participant–observer method,** where the teacher collects data from multiple sources such as journals, in-class comments and discussions, personal inquiry outside of class, peer assessments, and self-assessments of quality. Assess broadly, giving students the chance to demonstrate mastery of the many skills from the dance cornerstones and artistic processes. Find the most appropriate strategy to authentically measure the learning objectives you are teaching (i.e., to assess student performance, collect and interpret specifics about their performance). Then direct the assessment data toward improving skills and raising program standards.

These criteria hold students accountable. Therefore, the criteria you list should cut right to the heart of the task to adequately measure the skills you want to address. It takes time to practice and refine these skills.

Write objectives in measurable terms or language (e.g., "The student will demonstrate the use of beginning, middle, and end in a composition"). Then determine how you can best assess this without taking away instructional time. Assessments should aid instruction, not impede it. For example, embed assessment in the activity to remediate and increase achievement for those who have not acquired the skill. Critiquing and feedback are two in-process assessments that help students remediate during the process to increase skills.

Arts Assessment as Part of the Learning Process

Arts assessment should be exciting and entertaining, not dull and boring. We want students to see

Assess All Four Cornerstones

Assess student progress toward aesthetic literacy in each cornerstone. Just as the cornerstones are different methods of inquiry, so too do they need different methods of assessment. Use authentic ways to assess each cornerstone. Use a variety of assessment techniques to gain a comprehensive picture of (a) student progress and (b) program effectiveness relative to each cornerstone. Content, instruction, and assessments vary according to which cornerstone is at the forefront: Some are physical, some are creative, some are cognitive, and all have aesthetic and critical thinking dimensions. Why are a variety of measurements over time (vs.

one measurement) a better picture of what students know and can do?

Formative Assessment

Use **formative assessment** or in-process feedback during—and sometimes throughout—an activity, project, or unit. Formative feedback by both teachers and peers increases overall performance quality. Turn ongoing assessment into constructive feedback that students need during the creative process to guide them as they edit, refine, and polish. Ongoing assessment takes many forms, such as corrections during warm-up or at the barre or comments to refine movement exploration and class work. Ongoing assessments give students ongoing feedback to aid their growth. This is a form of authentic assessment.

Facilitate peer assessment to improve attention to detail. Aside from helping the doer, peer review benefits the reviewer. The reviewer pays closer attention to detail, analyzes structure, uses critical thinking, applies dance vocabularies, and organizes thoughts to provide helpful feedback. Peer reviewers usually transfer the new insights to their own work, thereby raising the aesthetic expectations for the reviewer as well as the one reviewed.

Students who are asked to reflect on their own work after receiving feedback, critique, or evaluation get a better perspective on their work. They understanding what is missing or what is needed. They immediately apply assessment. The act of self-evaluating through critical thinking usually results in improved products and skills.

Formative assessment helps identify low-performing students so you can intervene and give early assistance.

Summative Assessment

Summative assessment or product assessment evaluates the overall success of a project at its completion. Overall achievement of an activity, project, lesson, or unit is measured at the end. This assessment takes into account all aspects of the activity or project and evaluates each aspect in relation to the whole. Clarify review criteria at the outset of each activity to show students exactly what they need to know and do. Assess artistic criteria and involve peers and self.

Use summative assessments to take snapshots of student progress from time to time, such as at the end of each unit. Use formal as well as informal means to assess these end products, but include both what students know (knowledge) and what

they can do (skills). Summative assessments can be performance based as well as oral and written, studio as well as classroom, and individual as well as small group, but in all cases you must grade each individual because you must keep records of progress for each person (for reports to parents and for school records).

It is more realistic to use summative assessments at the main crossroads rather than at every little intersection. Use summative assessment to help you keep track of where students are, not only as part of your grading and reporting system, but also to let students know what they need to work on. Use this kind of assessment to promote continued learning at the main crossroads. When you report on student progress (e.g., progress reports, report cards, parent–teacher conferences), include the results of summative assessments. Gather the results from a number of sources: formal and informal assessments, criteria-based assessments, performance-based assessments, teacher assessments, peer assessments, and self-assessments.

By their nature, summative assessments lead you to information by which to grade students. Therefore, plan at the outset all the areas you need to include. Separate summative assessments into these categories and subcategories to ensure that you cover all aspects of learning and growth in your overall assessment plan:

1. Categories for all three artistic processes:
   a. Performing (C1)
   b. Creating (C2)
   c. Critiquing (C4)
2. Category for knowing about dance (C3, as well as aspects of knowing about C1, C2, and C3)

Note: Categories should factor in the aspects of student development (studied in chapter 4). So, when assessing C1, C2, C3, and C4, incorporate aesthetic–artistic, kinesthetic–motor, and aspects of cognitive–intellectual progress. Also make a separate place on your report card to report about behavioral aspects and development (both emotional and social).

Embedded Assessment

Assessment is best when it is authentic, or part of learning. **Embedded assessment** can be either formative or summative. A highly effective way to get reliable feedback in the learning process is to embed assessment into the learning process itself. Create ongoing checkpoints to focus on quality and to see how well students apply what they learn. Give timely feedback and focus on constructive corrections as part of the lesson. Insist that students inquire into the present quality of their arts output—whether dancing or discussing—and make a habit of reflecting about their long-term growth.

When you embed performance assessment, it teaches students to expect to get and give feedback. It habituates them to self-evaluate (e.g., "How am I doing here?" "What needs refining?" "Will this be better if I . . . ?"). Such personal inquiry increases students' investment of time and energy so they create increasingly better products through increasingly richer processes.

Embedded assessment is part of the lesson. It is both an instructional strategy and assessment strategy at the same time. For example,

- we watch students' movement explorations and give them constructive feedback,
- we observe their barre or center work and make corrections,
- we see what students are doing as they do it and remediate on the spot so they get it correct,
- we build refinement into the lesson so they edit and polish to do better or get it right, and
- we ask them to reflect on what they learned and respond.

Conduct performance assessment while students are engaged in the activity. The quality of the activity shows whether they understand the concept and can apply it. Analyze movement responses, as dance teachers have been doing for centuries, to determine the quality of the output and the grasp of the concept. Performance assessment demonstrates by doing. For example, students demonstrate their understanding of accelerating and decelerating by using these processes in their dance composition, "Getting Nowhere." Thus, the instructional strategy is both a choreographic assignment and a test.

Constructive peer feedback is as useful to the person giving it as the one receiving it. Embed peer assessment so students evaluate each other's work to increase everyone's standards of achievement. Invite students to use their growing aesthetic awareness, their developing dance vocabulary, and their critical thinking skills to assess quality. This process

is an avenue to sharpen their aesthetic perception and broaden their perspective. It also raises their expectations.

Communicate daily expectations and routinely evaluate progress. Consistently hold students accountable to high standards. Ongoing assessment helps them and you see their incremental progress. (This includes daily record keeping and empowering student learning as discussed in chapter 11.)

Assessment Techniques

Use an array of assessment techniques, both formal and informal. A cross-reference of teacher assessment, peer assessment, and self-assessment produces excellent results. Match assessment types that best qualify the activity. Look at some of the varied ways to assess.

Teacher Assessments of Students

Assess in the most effective, authentic ways possible to improve artistic output as well as to measure artistic success. Think of assessment as a way to increase learning as you measure it so that assessment makes the most of valuable instructional time. Use these methods:

- Demonstration of knowledge
- Demonstration of skills
- Observations in class
- Student interviews
- Tests and quizzes
- Proficiency testing
- Narrative summaries
- Question and answer
- Student portfolios
- Student journals
- Video of student work with feedback
- Contracts with students
- Rubrics
- Grading
- Critiquing of work
- Placement and audition
- Ongoing feedback
- Embedded assessments
- Reflection questions
- Performance assessment (embedded)

Peer Assessments

Fully use peer feedback and critique to deepen all students' learning as well as their critical thinking skills. Use all of the following techniques and find others to increase artistic output, to measure artistic success, and to engage all learners in meaningful reflection:

- Observations
- Critiques of peer work
- Evaluative feedback
- Critical response process
- Rubrics
- Review criteria (teacher made, student made)

Self-Assessment

Critical thinking as part of routine self-reflection produces learners who are more intentional with their work and who take ownership for developing quality work. Use all of the following methods. Consider the kinds of activities that will be most beneficial to assess in these ways to improve artistic output and to measure artistic success:

- Reflection
- Feedback and discussion
- Editing and refining works
- Research papers
- Self-evaluations
- Reflection journals
- Reaction journals
- Rubrics
- Review criteria

Collaborative Assessment and Portfolios

Assessment gives important one-to-one feedback along the arts learning journey. Student portfolios and journals for advanced students in high school (and in some cases earlier) give depth to dance assessment. Because both techniques are retrospective and current, they help the person learn where he is along the path. Use them to get students started again if they get bogged down. Suggest that they create videos of their work for portfolios. Collaborative assessment benefits both teacher and student.

BENEFITS FOR THE TEACHER

- You discover students' interest and qualify their understanding.
- You encourage them to develop a single project in depth.
- You help them synthesize a wide range of processes and produce more independent products.

When you have assignments that are critical for students to read, watch, or study, one of the best ways to ensure they give a thoughtful appraisal is to ask for a reaction journal, in which they first summarize the article or event and then make personal observations.

BENEFITS FOR STUDENTS

- They gain more autonomy in their work.
- As they evaluate their own dance making, they refine their critical thinking skills.
- In-depth portfolio reviews with you can lead students into additional artistic experimentation with movement and movement forms.
- They become more aware of their artistic development over time.
- You can encourage further dance study outside of school and identify those who need to apply for artistically gifted programs in the arts and in dance.

This does not reduce the need for formal and informal assessments or for tests of cognitive understanding. Students still need teacher-made tests for curriculum content using essay questions, vocabulary, written and oral reporting, choreography, and showcases of work. But use journals and portfolios—which work concurrently—to inspire advanced students to compete with themselves and increase dance skills over time.

Reflect and Respond

For what purpose might you use these teacher assessments in dance:

- Proficiency testing (open-ended testing that gauges skills in demonstrating knowledge and skills)?
- Portfolio and video assessment?
- Reaction journals?

Assessing the Artistic Processes

Assess the artistic processes: creating, performing, and responding (c/p/r). Some specialists organize their grade book headings according to these three areas of artistic output (in addition to a behavioral heading that measures one's emotional growth and relationships with others [social]).

Creating and Composing (Choreography)

Closely observe compositions to give feedback that improves the dance and the student's artistic skills. Target the exact issue, and do not address too many issues at once. If the work is a muddle, determine whether your assignment was too advanced, too long, or unclear or whether it lacked specific choreographic criteria. There are specifics of choreography to evaluate to increase compositional skills clarity. Use these specific items also to grade students:

- Rhythmic timing
- Effort qualities
- Use of spatial directions
- Level changes
- Points of emphasis
- Clarity of statement
- Length of dance (or sections)
- Order of sections
- Sequencing
- Stylistic quality
- Accuracy
- Coordination
- Musicality
- Attitude
- Spatial interest
- Rhythmic interest
- Dynamic interest
- Placement of dynamic accents
- Placement of timing accents
- Number of dancers
- Entrances and exits
- Unity of overall work
- Variety of facing and groupings
- Variety and interest within work
- Contrast of sections
- Three dimensionality (or sculptural aspect)
- Use of repetition

- Use of movement theme or of motif
- Development from beginning, through middle, to end
- Climax or high points in the work
- Use of phrasing
- Use of abstraction (rather than imitation)

Dancing and Performing (Technique)

Assess technique in middle and high school by closely observing technique class. Make timely corrections so students immediately apply the correction to increase their performing skill. This embedded, performance-based assessment and feedback are vital to developing performers but also to increasing everyone's dancing. Use it also for grading. To assess and correct **technique,** comment on specifics such as these:

- Movement flow
- Balance and stability
- Stability of turns and the ability to turn on center
- Phrasing
- Elevation
- Centeredness
- Mobility and fluidity
- Postural alignment
- Placement (both static and dynamic)
- Total body coordination
- Isolations of body parts
- Joint articulation
- Rhythmic timing
- Accents
- Textures
- Qualities
- Sequencing
- Stylistic quality
- Accuracy
- Use of space
- Emphasis
- Musicality
- Attitude about moving through space
- Relationship of body parts to each other
- Relationship of dancer to other aspects of dance
- Clarity of focus

- Clarity of movement intent
- Quality of the line
- Use of shape and shaping
- Quality of the bodyshape or of body designs
- Performance conviction and confidence

Responding and Critiquing   Assess the quality of student critique. Are students analyzing, describing, interpreting, or evaluating? Do they use the UDV to accurately describe what is happening with the body in space? Are they seeing relationships? Are they responding to the use of time and dynamic qualities (see chapter 6)? Judge an individual's response quality when you assess critical responses based on these items:

- Levels of critical thinking (Bloom's taxonomy)
- Ability to unpack a dance work using the Four-Step Critique process: describe, analyze, interpret, and evaluate
- Use of the dance elements to describe and analyze dance (BSTERs)
- Use of principles of design (e.g., unity, variety)
- Use of Lerman's Critical Response Process (when applicable)
- Ability to attentively view dances
- Ability to apply review criteria in an informed way

Using Review Criteria

Think of review criteria as a road map to successfully get all kids where they are going. Criteria help students organize their work and focus their energy on quality rather than guessing what the teacher is looking for. Review criteria make assignments clear by conveying what you expect, exactly what you will evaluate, and how you weight each aspect according to importance (three priorities). The criteria become instructive because they detail what is to be done. They become evaluative because they say exactly what achievement is to be measured. They raise awareness of what is required and in effect become an informal contract to keep students focused on the tasks at hand.

Review criteria quantify and qualify the lesson objectives (desired outcomes) and turn them into measurable actions. Thus, review criteria identify both what is expected (quantity) and to what level or standard (quality). Review criteria identify what is most important to achieve.

Review criteria are democratic; they give everyone the same chance for success and level the playing field. Review criteria show that everyone is held to the same standard of measure and is evaluated on the same basis. Review criteria inform the process up front because they describe the end results. That makes assignments clear to students and to parents. Review criteria yield a specific evaluation that explains each person's particular strengths and weaknesses.

Here are two examples of assignments with review criteria: a research paper (figure 12.4) and a composition (figure 12.5) that contain both compositional (structural) and aesthetic criteria.

Transposing Review Criteria Into Rubrics

Translate learning objectives into review criteria. Translate review criteria into **rubrics** in order to inform and assess. Rubrics turn objectives and criteria into measurements (criteria-based assessments). Rubrics list some of the "digestible chunks" we spoke about. Rubrics can take the form of either a list of criteria to judge or **matrixes** (structures or forms) that lay out all the levels of achievement for each criteria of an assignment. In both cases, rubrics show what is expected. Putting criteria in black and white makes them concrete. The evaluators use rubrics to look for strengths and weaknesses so the one assessed knows which part of the assignment needs more work.

Rubrics serve two purposes:

- To express what criteria are to be used at the beginning of an activity
- To rate accomplishment of that criteria (formative and summative assessment) during or after the activity

Design different rubrics for different graded assignments and activities—a project, a paper, a creative activity or choreography, a performance portfolio. Pinpoint all the criteria for each objective in an assignment. This way the rubric operationalizes objectives. It restates the details of each objective (i.e., desired outcomes) of the assignment. That is, one objective may have two or more criteria.

In order to make peer review integral to learning, show students what to look for in the form of concrete specifics in a rubric. Having a rubric tells students what to analyze and gives them quality markers. As students learn to read, use the vocabulary they know.

Cultural Heritage in Dance (Grade 10)

Goal (big idea): To know dance as universal expression across time and culture.

Directions to students: After completing research from three sources on this dance, submit a three-page, typed, single-spaced paper that presents your findings. Address all of the following criteria. The number of points earned depends on

- accuracy and importance of the information,
- completeness of coverage, and
- clarity of expression.

Review Criteria for Paper

____ The paper has a beginning, middle, and end. The beginning explains the purpose of the paper and the end summarizes the main points of the middle, or body, of the paper. (1-10 points)

____ The paper is error free in spelling and grammar. (1-10 points)

____ The resources are strong and the author makes strong points that are organized so points flow from one to the next in a logical sequence; the paper is easy to read and understand. (1-15 points)

The body of the paper explains

____ all the significant aspects of this dance form. (1-15 points)

____ about those who perform it, identifying what the dance means or expresses to them. (1-10 points)

____ the type or style of dance, the reasons it is performed, its contribution to society, or its function within a larger cultural context. (1-10 points)

____ how this form relates to the broad spectrum of dance (may compare) and how it contributes to aesthetic and cultural understanding. (1-10 points)

____ why we investigate dances of different cultures and times and what of value they teach outsiders. (1-10 points)

____ how one studies culture and history through dance. (1-10 points)

Composing hint: Transitions improve flow between sections just as in choreography.

Maximum points that can be earned = 100. Total points earned = ____

FIGURE 12.4 Teacher-referenced review criteria are not only helpful for dance composition and critique but they are also useful for other kinds of compositional assignments both in and out of class. The one above lists criteria that serve as compositional and review criteria for a written paper at the high school level.

Adapted with permission from Ellen Hollis Harrison, 1997.

By third grade, make dance rubrics standard operating procedure for critiquing.

HOW RUBRICS HELP STUDENTS

- Used regularly, rubrics accustom students to critically evaluate. Evaluative thinkers usually produce better products.
- Rubrics objectify dance as a language of expression and make students less subjective and able to make more accurate judgments.
- Rubrics show students what to look for and identify what incremental levels of achievement look like.
- Rubrics are effective diagnostic tools to zero in on details and help assessors evaluate the aesthetic impact of a creative assignment.
- The written criteria establish a common language with which to discuss what is observed.

Review Criteria for Third Grade Composition: "Contrasts"

Composer/performer name: _____   Date: _____

Assessor is (circle one):   Peer   Self   Teacher

The solo composition

_____ 1. is sequenced with a beginning, middle, and end.

_____ 2. incorporates traveling and level changes in the sequence.

_____ 3. incorporates at least one sharp change of dynamics to emphasize the contrast (aesthetic criteria).

_____ 4. maintains a clear intent of contrast throughout (aesthetic criteria).

_____ 5. is within the time parameters (1/2 to 1 minute).

_____ 6. emphasizes a contrast in energy and dynamics for artistic effect (aesthetic criteria).

Rating scale for each item:

5 = excellent   4 = above average   3 = good/average   2 = rework   1 = start over

Total score: _____ divided by 6 = rating of _____

FIGURE 12.5   Use teacher-made, personally referenced criteria to identify the scope of an assigned composition (whole) and delineate its particular tasks (parts) so as to clearly communicate expectations to learners. Use the same criteria to assess the results.
April Barber, 1997.

- When rubrics are used at different points in the learning process (e.g., for works in progress [formative assessment] and again for finished work [summative assessment]), students chart progress by comparing rubrics from different phases of a project.

HOW RUBRICS HELP TEACHERS

- You can use individual rubrics to assess what each person learns.
- You can evaluate all the rubrics from one class to see how effective the instruction was and what you may need to emphasize in the future.

Rubrics measure creative projects (e.g., choreography, research) and help keep students on track during creative inquiry. As you determine the objectives and plan a composition assignment, create a rubric from the same criteria. Give it to choreographers to chart their own progress. Give it to critical friends to measure achievement levels. Through consistent use, criteria-referenced rubrics instill aesthetic principles and raise expectations of artistic quality. The same person who is at one time composer and another time critical friend benefits from using the same rule of measure for both.

Creating Rubrics

There are two useful forms of rubrics: matrix rubrics like in figure 12.6 and regular scoring rubrics like in figure 12.7. Learn to use both. Base them on the learning objectives (e.g., specific artistic concepts, dance elements, or design principles to be learned).

When you design a rubric, be specific. Analyze each step students are to encounter; list the steps as criteria on the rubric. Your analysis breakout does two things:

- It instructs creators about what to include.
- It instructs critical friends about what to look for.

Use the same rubric for evaluative self-reflection, peer, and teacher evaluation.

How to Create Scoring Rubrics   Summative assessment rubrics apply to the finished product. They are usually the same as for the work in progress. Summative assessments from teachers and peers become the basis of a final grade at the end of a unit.

Formative assessments increase the quality of final products by measuring progress along the way

Rating scale		1	2	3	4	5	Score
C O N T E N T	Includes beginning, middle, and end (B–M–E)	No clear B or E	Either B, M, or E unclear	B or E unclear	B–M–E defined	B–M–E clearly defined and balanced	
	Incorporates traveling and level changes	No level changes or travel used	Only level changes or travel, not both	Travel and level changes included	Travel and level changes incorporated	Travel and level used to enhance artistic quality of composition	
	Incorporates at least one sharp change of dynamics to emphasize contrast	No dynamic contrast	Dynamic contrast weak	One sharp contrast observed	Contrast emphasized with two to three sharp changes in dynamics	Dynamic contrasts incorporated in the work and dynamic changes effectively emphasized	
C R I T E R I A	Maintains a clear intent	No intent observed	Intent unclear	Intent sometimes clear	Intent clear	Clear intent maintained throughout to communicate directly to the audience	
	Keeps within time parameters (20-40 seconds)	No attention paid to length	Too short to be effective	Too long to be effective	Between 1 and 1 1/2 minutes	Between 1 and 1 1/2 minutes; use of time to increase artistic impact maximized	
	Contrasts energy and dynamics for maximum artistic effect	No attention to artistry in the movement design or performance	Little attention to artistry in the movement design or performance	Some attention to artistry in either movement design or performance	Some attention to artistry in both design and performance	Consistent attention to contrasts in design that maximize artistic impact of performance	
Maximum achievement points = 30							

Rating scale: 15 = does not meet standards

20 = making progress toward standards

25 = meets standards

26-30 = exceeds standards

FIGURE 12.6   Matrix rubric for third grade composition.

and using the results to upgrade the final product. For example, sixth grade students are to create a dance study to contrast negative and positive space while using nonmetered and unpredictable timing surprises. The rubric lists all criteria:

a. Artistic use of negative space

b. Artistic use of positive space

c. Overall contrast between negative and positive space

d. Use of nonmetered timing

e. Use of timing surprises for interest and contrast

f. Overall artistic effectiveness

Look at figure 12.7, which shows a teacher's formative assessment of one student's work-in-progress. Notice how well he achieved space contrast, yet his timing is too predictable and therefore uninteresting. The assessment tells Jose his strengths and weaknesses so he knows exactly what to refine. Jose gets peer assessments from two critical friends. Jose then revises his work, gets additional feedback, and ends up with 5s on each line. Notice that figure 12.7 is not a matrix rubric, as is figure 12.6.

Sample assessment for ___Jose___

__X__ Formative or summative _____

Peer _____   Self _____   Teacher _X_

Scoring scale (low to high): 1 2 3 4 5

1. _5_ Artistic use of negative space
2. _5_ Artistic use of positive space
3. _5_ Overall contrast between negative and positive space
4. _3_ Use of nonmetered timing
5. _1_ Incorporating timing surprises for interest and contrast
6. _3_ Overall artistic effectiveness

Comments:

Strengths: Contrasts negative and positive space.

What needs improving: Timing is too predictable.

FIGURE 12.7   Sample scoring rubric (Jose).

How to Turn Choreographic Criteria Into a Rubric   Some specialists prefer to use two forms for one kindergarten through grade 5 composition assignment: one for choreographic criteria and the other for review criteria. For example, consider the following two forms in figures 12.8 and 12.9.

Directions to Students

1. With a partner, choose a poem or short written text to inspire a movement sequence. Select text with vivid action words. Analyze how it suggests different BSTER dance elements.

2. Analyze line by line. Do not incorporate the entire text.

3. With a partner, target specific words that will drive or inspire your movement sequence.

4. Together, circle all dance elements you will include in your dance. Keep them in the order they are in the poem.

Choreographic Review Criteria (Duet)

Your duet composition must accomplish the following:

- Include a clear beginning, middle, and end
- Last at least 30 seconds but no longer than 2 minutes
- Involve two level changes
- Emphasize two force elements (e.g., sharp, smooth, light, strong)
- Include a noticeable change of focus (e.g., from a body part to a point in space)
- Include a time when you and your partner move at different tempos from each other
- Communicate its intent with artistic integrity

FIGURE 12.8   Grade 5 dance elements composition: choreographic criteria (part 1).

Used with permission of Ellen Hollis Harrison, 1997.

Composition Title: _____

Evaluator (circle one):

Teacher   Peer student

Directions: Score a 1, 2, or 3 in each category

1 = needs improvement

2 = good

3 = excellent

_____ Text was analyzed and dance elements were circled. (teacher only)

_____ 1. Text clearly inspired the movement.

_____ 2. Movement was inventive and original.

_____ 3. There was an identifiable beginning, middle, and end.

_____ 4. Composition was within its time parameters.

_____ 5. At least two level changes provided points of interest.

_____ 6. Two force elements were effectively contrasted.

_____ 7. There was an appropriate change in focus.

_____ 8. Performers moved at two different tempos, at the same time.

_____ 9. Composition maintained its sense of sequence and unity (artistic quality).

_____ 10. Students worked well together and stayed on task during the creative process.

_____ 11. Student performers stayed focused and performed as a team with kinetic integrity (artistic quality).

_____ 12. Reviewer comments:

FIGURE 12.9   Grade 5 scoring rubric for dance elements (part 2).

Adapted with permission of Ellen Hollis Harrison, 1997.

 How do these criteria help fifth graders review each others' work to give feedback? How do the criteria instruct the reviewer about his or her own composition?

How to Create Matrix Rubrics   Five-point matrix rubrics work best for more complex compositions. They help the critical friend (i.e., assessor) give an accurate assessment of quality and help the one assessed see exactly what needs to be done to improve and where. Use the matrix rubric to qualify (from 1 to 5) and quantify (number of items to be addressed) so students see how to observe.

How do you translate what you want students to do into a matrix rubric? List each criterion. Then describe five different levels of achievement, with 1 being low and 5 being high. Make the levels incremental like the ones in figure 12.6. It is helpful to first describe the median criterion for what is acceptable (3) and then write what is less acceptable (1 and 2) and more than acceptable (4 and 5).

Figures 12.10a, 12.10b, and 10.3 (the haiku matrix rubric in chapter 10) show other matrix rubrics. Both examples in figure 12.10 measure outcomes according to the unit's objectives (as stated in performance standards). Figure 12.10a is for high school and 12.10b is for elementary school. Both state all desired learning objectives as review criteria. When each person gets evaluation results, she not only receives an achievement level but also knows exactly which actions earned it. See appendix B for "Sample Rubric for Technique Areas" that you can use for middle and high school.

Reflect and Respond

1. Transfer the assessment in figure 12.7 into a matrix rubric that describes five different levels of achievement for each criterion. Do the same with figure 12.9.

2. Design a rubric for a sixth grade choreography assignment: "Horizontal and Vertical, Symmetrical and Asymmetrical."

   > What objectives would you address?

   > What would you want student choreographers to include?

   > What structural criteria would you want students to include (length, elements, concepts)?

   > What aesthetic criteria would you include (artistic effectiveness in design and in its performance)?

Unit theme = Movement in Nature

Detail of Summative Assessment in Choreography

Teacher = Ellen Hollis Harrison, Dance Specialist, Ridgeview High School, Columbia, SC

	Criteria	0	1	2	3	Weight	Score
Choreographic criteria	Content	The movement is not based on nature.	The movement suggests nature one time.	The movement suggests nature.	The movement is clearly based on nature throughout.	9	
	Level changes	There are no level changes in the movement.	There is one level change in the movement.	There are three or fewer level changes in the movement.	There are clear multiple level changes in the movement.	4	
	Movement dynamics	There is no variety of movement dynamics.	There is one change of movement dynamics.	There are three or fewer changes of movement dynamics.	There are clear multiple changes of movement dynamics.	5	
	Beginning, middle, and end	There is no clear beginning, middle, or end.	The movement contains one of the concepts.	The movement contains two of the concepts.	The movement has a clear beginning, middle, and end.	5	
	Title	There is no title.	The title does not fit the movement sequence.	The title fits the movement sequence.	The title fits the movement sequence with a creative flair.	3	
Performance criteria	Time/duration	Inefficient use of time.	Needs more/less time to complete the idea.	The idea was fully developed in the duration of the movement.		4	
	Performance	There is no commitment to the movement.	There is some commitment to the movement.	There is full commitment to the movement.		4	

Total Score:

The teacher reserves the right to add or subtract 1/2 point to/from the criteria value.

a

[continued]

FIGURE 12.10 Matrix rubrics: *(a)* This matrix rubric accompanies a unit for high school beginners. *(b)* This matrix rubric accompanies a lesson on pathways for sixth graders.

Figure 12.10a reprinted with permission of Ellen Hollis Harrison, 1997. Figure 12.10b reprinted with permission of Deborah Martin.

Teacher's Scoring Sheet for Pathways Exercise

Student's name _____ Student's group number _____ Date _____

Teacher: Deborah Ann Martin, movement specialist, Triad: Winston Salem, Greensboro, High Point, NC

	4	3	2	1	Score
Creating					
Each letter of the name is represented.	All letters are represented.	Most letters are represented.	Some letters are represented.	Minimal letters are represented.	
Uses curved and straight pathways.	Moves many body parts as well as the whole body in various pathways.	Moves some body parts as well as whole body in various pathways.	Moves only the whole body in various pathways.	Moves in minimal pathways—body parts and/or whole body.	
Locomotes using general space	Uses a variety (>2) of loco-motor steps throughout general space.	Uses only two kinds of loco-motor steps throughout general space.	Uses only one kind of loco-motor step throughout general space.	Uses only one kind of loco-motor step with minimal use of general space.	
Levels in space	Uses all levels of space in a variety of ways.	Uses all levels of space.	Uses only two levels of space.	Exists at same level of space throughout dance.	
Vocal/natural accompaniment	Vocal and rhythmic accompaniment are fully integrated into the dance.	Vocal and rhythmic accompaniment relate to the dance.	Vocal and rhythmic accompaniment simply exist.	Disconnected or little use of vocal or rhythmic accompaniment.	
Beginning, middle, and end	Exceptionally clear beginning, middle, and end.	Clear beginning, middle, and end.	Unclear delineation between beginning, middle, and end.	Shows little evidence of beginning, middle, and end.	
				Score for creating:	
Performing					
Commitment to movement	Performs with full commitment and intensity.	Performs expressively with commitment.	Performs with some projection.	Performs with no projection.	
Alignment, balance, and control	Consistently demonstrates principles of alignment, balance, and control.	Demonstrates principles of alignment, balance, and control with commitment.	Occasionally demonstrates principles of alignment, balance, and control.	Demonstrates minimum physical commitment and control.	

b

[continued]

FIGURE 12.10 *(continued)*

384

	4	3	2	1	Score
Performing					
Spatial awareness	Always aware of self and others and responds to changing spatial relationships.	Aware of self and others and responds to changing spatial relationships.	Aware of self and others and occasionally responds to changing spatial relationships.	Demonstrates little or no awareness of spatial relationships.	
				Score for performing:	
Responding					
Use of dance vocabulary	Expands and elaborates using dance vocabulary.	Identifies and describes using dance vocabulary.	Identifies some of the elements using dance vocabulary.	Describes dance using general vocabulary.	
Connections to cultural traditions	Draws parallels, discussing more than one connection to cultural traditions.	Makes a connection to cultural traditions.	Attempts to make a connection to cultural traditions.	Describes dance with no relationship to cultural traditions.	
				Score for responding:	
Group dynamics					
Degree of participation	Actively participates by sharing ideas/movements, listening and responding, leading initiatives, and expanding on ideas of others.	Participates by sharing ideas/movements, listening and responding, following initiatives of others, and accepting ideas of others.	Participates in a passive manner by accepting ideas/movements of others and listening and responding in a limited manner.	Shares few ideas and shows little response to ideas of others.	
				Score for group dynamics:	
				Total score:	

Scale:

37-48 = Level 4/Proficient

25-36 = Level 3/Adequate

13-24 = Level 2/Beginner

4-12 = Level 1/Novice

0 = Not scorable

This scoring sheet/rubric makes use of an analytic format, which allows options in scoring. Each component can be scored separately to provide diagnostic information for teachers/students. For a holistic score, add component scores together, and then determine a range of scores for each performance level.

FIGURE 12.10 (continued)

Teacher Competencies and Accountability

You must be able to select, adapt, and develop a variety of measurements to assess student learning according to teacher-referenced and nationally referenced standards.

SUCCESS FACTORS FOR ASSESSING STUDENT LEARNING

Use this list to guide assessment planning. The effective dance specialist plans and consistently assesses by

1. ____ planning and scheduling appropriate assessments of students' progress and achievement during instructional units (formative),
2. ____ using performance assessment rubrics as detailed and appropriate to dance,
3. ____ using both formal and informal assessments,
4. ____ designing assessments appropriate to the ability and developmental levels of dance students,
5. ____ using appropriate assessments to measure the objectives of instructional units according to the aesthetic goals,
6. ____ using assessments appropriate for the content and skills covered and consistent with the instruction used,
7. ____ designing appropriate criteria to evaluate artistic achievement and factor in the results to instruction and planning,
8. ____ analyzing assessment results to make judgments about students' aesthetic progress and achievement,
9. ____ analyzing assessment results to determine the need for instructional feedback,
10. ____ analyzing assessment results to evaluate the extent to which instruction met all students' needs,
11. ____ incorporating assessment results into subsequent unit or lesson planning,
12. ____ maintaining daily accurate records of student artistic progress and achievement, and
13. ____ maintaining accurate long-term records of student progress and achievement.

Notebook/Portfolio:
Perspective Notebook

How effective are you at assessment? As with other Success Factor checklists, use the criteria as performance indicators for self-reflection and mentor evaluation. Use the rating details in appendix A.

Standardized Dance Assessment

You need to prepare your students to be assessed by NAEP according to nationally referenced standards (norm-based assessments).

A comprehensive national dance assessment presents logistical challenges. Students need a quiet space to watch and respond to videos and a spacious, well-lighted room free of obstructions for the movement exercises. Students will take performance assessments and open-ended paper-and-pencil tests. Fourth grade assessments need 60 minutes, and grades 8 and 12 need 90 minutes. Because it is high-stakes testing and student scores go into the national database, give students every advantage to succeed. Keep group size between 4 and 12 for movement activities, and arrange students with enough space to fully perform the exercises. Rearrange them so everyone gets observed for a fair assessment.

Figure 12.11, a sample of the NAEP standardized assessment for grade 8, shows how national standards are translated into assessments (three responding, one performing, and one creating). Decode the assessment:

- NSDE standards (i.e., A, B, C) identify what is to be learned and measured.
- Numbered items indicate the criteria to be assessed.
- Numbers in parentheses, such as (5a), refer to the content standard followed by its corresponding eighth grade achievement standard (e.g., content standard 5, achievement standard a). Assessors rate each student's achievement level as basic, proficient, or advanced (National Assessment Governing Board 1994).

I. Creating

A. Invent solutions to movement challenges, generating, and selecting from alternatives.

1. Create own warm-up and explain how that warm-up prepares the body and mind for expressive work purposes (6c).

B. Follow improvisational and compositional structures.

1. Given verbal direction, demonstrate in movement the principles of contrast and transition (2a).
2. Given verbal direction, demonstrate movements that exemplify choreographic processes such as reordering (2b).
3. Given verbal direction, demonstrate movements in the following forms of AB, ABA, canon, call and response, and narrative (2c).

C. Collaborate to achieve solutions.

1. Demonstrate the following partner skills in a visually interesting way: creating and complementary shapes, taking and supporting weight (2e).
2. Demonstrate the ability to work collaboratively in a group of three to four during the choreographic process (2d).

II. Performing

A. Accurately recall and reproduce movement.

1. Memorize and reproduce dance sequences that are at least 32 counts in length (1g).
2. Given the prompt of a rhythmic pattern beat on a drum, reproduce that pattern in movement (1c).
3. Given the prompt of a spatial pattern drawn on paper, reproduce that pattern by traveling through space (1c).
4. Given verbal prompts, demonstrate two previously learned dances, each at least 32 counts in length, representing two different styles and vocabulary of basic dance steps, body positions, and spatial patterns in their demonstration (1b, 5b, 5a).

B. Demonstrate physical technique.

1. Given verbal prompts, demonstrate through movement the following qualities: sustained, percussive, and vibratory (1e).
2. While following the demonstrated movements of a facilitator, demonstrate the skills of alignment, balance, articulation of isolated body parts, weight shift, elevation and landing, and fall and recovery (1a).

C. Communicate through movement (expression).

1. Create a dance of at least 32 counts that successfully communicates a topic of personal significance (3d).

III. Responding

A. Identify compositional elements and notice details.

1. After viewing a dance, describe the movements and movement elements using appropriate dance vocabulary (e.g., level, direction) (1h).

B. Identify contexts (stylistic, cultural, social, historical) of dance.

1. Describe the role of dance in two different cultures or time periods (5d).

C. Make informed critical observations about the dance's and dancer's technical and artistic components.

1. After observing a dance, discuss personal opinions about both the choreography and the performers (4b).
2. Identify and use criteria for evaluating dance (such as skill of performers, originality, visual or emotional impact, variety, and contrast) (4d).
3. Compare and contrast two dance compositions in terms of space (such as shape and pathways), time (such as rhythm and tempo), and force and energy (such as movement qualities) (4c).

FIGURE 12.11   Excerpts from NAEP dance assessment for grade 8.

Excerpted from *NAEP Arts Education Assessment Framework,* Pre-publication Edition (NAGB 1994, pp. 75-76).

Program Evaluation

Assessment falls into two major categories: student assessment and program evaluation.

Program evaluation happens concurrently with student assessment. Indeed, student achievement depends on program vitality; therefore, program evaluation is the rest of the arts assessment. Arts assessors want to see evidence of strategic planning that sets the stage for what is happening in the classroom. They look for long-range plans (LRPs) and short-range unit plans (SRPs). Assessors also look for demonstrated on-target content, age-appropriate instruction, and ongoing student assessment as part of the learning process.

Districts require specialists to articulate measurable objectives that incorporate content and achievement standards. You must tie teaching directly to each objective and measure the outcomes to validate that learning happened as expected. For example, measure the extent to which each student masters exactly what you state as an objective—not only for the student's grade but also to measure the efficacy of your school-based program.

Ongoing dance program evaluation helps determine whether students get it to further determine whether your LRP needs to be revised, adjusted, refined, or tossed. For example, to evaluate program effectiveness, the National Dance Association looks to see if the program

- begins where the child is—with what each child knows and can do;
- provides the content, the environment, and the structure that allow for development to occur;
- assesses each child's progress on a regular basis; and
- explores further and responds appropriately when children are not continuing to develop skills and understanding in dance (National Dance Association 1990).

Internal Program Evaluation

Use the following program criteria to evaluate effectiveness of school programs you observe and those in which you teach. Use a 3-point rating scale to measure each item on the checklist: 1 = needs improvement, 2 = meets standards, 3 = exceeds standards. What other criteria describe quality programs?

1. ____ Content is comprehensive and represents all cornerstones.

2. ____ Learners acquire both knowledge and skills according to standards.

3. ____ Learning is meaningfully linked to previous learning and experience.

4. ____ Lesson outline is clear to teacher and made clear to students.

5. ____ Goals and objectives are clearly stated by the teacher and understood by the students.

6. ____ Instructional strategies move students continually toward the desired outcome of the lesson.

7. ____ Dance instruction extends student knowledge and skills of using the body, space, time, energy and dynamics, and relationships.

8. ____ All teaching materials support the stated objectives.

9. ____ Vocabulary is age appropriate (cognitively, aesthetically).

10. ____ Activities are age appropriate (kinesthetically, socially).

11. ____ Teaching strategies are age appropriate (emotionally, socially).

12. ____ Learning is both active and interactive.

13. ____ Higher-order thinking and action are observed.

14. ____ Students are on task; instructional time is not wasted.

15. ____ Cognitive development happens simultaneously with psychomotor and kin-aesthetic development (i.e., body and mind are fully engaged during the learning process).

16. ____ Dance material taught is substantive and challenging (neither trivialized nor trite).

17. ____ Activities are meaningful and lead the student to either learn about dance and movement or develop skill in dance and movement according to learning objectives.

18. ____ Classroom order and discipline are maintained.

19. ____ Time is used wisely and productively.

20. ____ Students are invested learners.

21. ____ Class atmosphere is nurturing and the environment conducive to learning.

22. ____ Safety measures are consistently taken.

23. ____ Dance elements are actively applied as a language for dance.

24. ____ Any who sit out because of injury or illness have worthwhile work to do that furthers the goals of the unit.

25. ____ Noninstructional daily routines operate efficiently to maximize instruction time.

26. ____ There is evidence of prior strategic planning that places this lesson in a broad learning context.

27. ____ A long-range plan is in effect that guides the year's study.

28. ____ Learning in dance extends the students' knowledge and skills in dance, movement, and the arts.

29. ____ Learning is also happening through dance that extends knowledge and skills in dance and the other subject areas.

30. ____ Students articulate what they are learning that relates to their understanding of dance and its relationship to other subjects.

Students need to see high-quality viewing samples that continually inspire them to refine their own performing skills.

31. ____ There is evidence that students understand dance more than superficially.

32. ____ Dance's enduring understandings are carried forward in the program and given priority.

See appendix B for sample formative and summative self-evaluation rubrics to periodically measure your effectiveness once you establish a school program ("Sample Self-Evaluation Forms").

External Program Evaluation

Districts conduct external program evaluations in all disciplines. Their purpose is

to gather, analyze, and disseminate information that can be used to make decisions about educational programs. Evaluation should always be directed toward *action* that hopefully will result in the improvement of services to students through the continuation, modification, or elimination of conditions which effect learning. It should be emphasized that the conditions which effect learning are not necessarily restricted to the instructional process. (Renzulli 1975, p. 2)

Figure 12.12 shows the cycle of decision making around programmatic action and program evaluation. Different stakeholders are involved. The specialist finds out information that modifies the teaching–learning setting. The principal finds out

FIGURE 12.12   Notice the dynamics between program evaluation, decision making, and action for program improvement.
Renzulli (1975, p. 4).

information about student performance and the conscientiousness of the dance specialist. The district administration finds out the quality of various programs at the school. At all levels decisions are made based on the action–evaluation cycle.

Program evaluation's main purpose is to get information for decision makers to see that programs include everything students need to succeed. Program evaluation measures such things as the scope (i.e., breadth and depth) and sequence of the curriculum, the quality of instruction, the effectiveness of instructional strategies, and overall program organization and management. Program evaluation also examines the external support structure such as how the facilities, schedule, resources, and class size aid learning in dance. Therefore, it is imperative that the *Opportunity-to-Learn Standards for Arts Education* are the basis for that part of the evaluation (see chapter 11). Renzulli's advice is this:

> . . . decision making is a fundamental goal of evaluation and therefore it is important to identify decision makers and the actions over which they have control at the beginning of any evaluation endeavor. (1975, p. 5)

Thus, figure 12.12 also shows the dynamics between the evaluation, decision making, and action for program improvement (Renzulli 1975).

Some evaluations are part of self-studies within the school. But count on occasional outside evaluators who assess academic units (e.g., the fine arts department). Whereas internal evaluators come from the ranks of teachers, students, and building administrators, external evaluators are usually district or state administrators, paid consultants, or members of accrediting bodies and professional associations.

Preparing for Evaluations

Expect to show what you know and can do, because district and state evaluations often determine such things as merit pay. Expect formal in-depth evaluations of all newly certified teachers, much the same as your evaluations during student-teaching internship. Also expect your daily and semester record-keeping to be evaluated. Maintain up-to-date records as you go—rather than wait until time for the evaluation. Set up a file system from day 1. Your local district likely specifies which of these records you need—if not, keep all of them:

- Teacher written reports
- Student test scores
- Student grade point averages
- Program statistics
- Student scholarships awarded
- Class observation reports by administrators
- Copies of unannounced teacher evaluations
- Surveys
- General observations
- Documentation of student performances (video, photo, programs)

- Assessments from student performances
- Writing samples
- Audition notices
- Student handbooks and contracts; parent handbooks

This is harsh, but it must be said: *If a school-based program cannot achieve at least the national standards for its students, it should not exist.* Programs with itinerate teachers—some of whom see students one to five times a year—are inadequate because minimum standards cannot be met. Why waste taxpayers' money?

Integrating the Triad

Students are at the center of the learning triad because they are the beneficiaries of standards-oriented curriculum, instruction, and assessment. Instruction aims to achieve all six characteristics of educational dance (6DCs). Content, instruction, and assessment are the working triad that organize and deliver instruction, as shown in figure 12.13. All unit plans cross-reference and correlate the three. One affects the other.

TEACHING TRIAD

- Curriculum content and objectives are delivered through instruction.
- Instruction optimizes delivery of content in the dance cornerstones.
- Assessment of student outcomes monitors the effectiveness of content and instruction.

Design and deliver curriculum content to achieve developmental learning objectives and standards through effective instructional strategies. Assess both content and instruction to monitor

- student progress,
- value and suitability of the content,

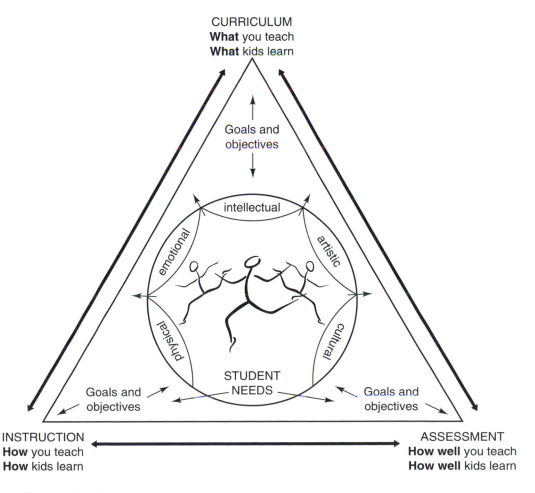

FIGURE 12.13   The teaching triad.

- effectiveness of instruction, and
- whether part or all of the plan should be modified.

External standards plus internal objectives drive the triad as you plan

- what student should know and be able to do (objectives),
- how you will teach the objectives (instruction), and
- how you will measure student mastery (assessment).

Backward Dance Design Process

Jay McTighe and Grant Wiggins, in their well-known design books *Understanding by Design (UBD) Professional Development Workbook* (2004) and the *UBD Handbook* (1999), advocate designing units and lessons in three stages. This UBD model certainly works for dance. It keeps students at the center of learning by acknowledging that the first stage is to identify the desired results. That is, ask, "What will the student know or do as a result of this experience, lesson, or unit?" McTighe and Wiggins say that instead of first deciding the topic to teach and second how to teach and assess it, you should reverse the whole process in light of a backward design process. That is, first ask what mega-ideas and concepts students are to learn and then move backward to finally end up with what to teach based on what is first most important to learn. This is outcomes-based instruction.

The UBD model's process is in three stages (McTighe and Wiggins 2004, p. 12):

1. Identify desired results.
2. Determine acceptable evidence.
3. Plan learning experiences and instruction.

Stage 1 incorporates goals and objectives and standards as part of the process. What big ideas are worth pursuing? Identify learning objectives that bring about the understanding.

Stage 2 involves determining the acceptable evidence, which means, "What will show that the student grasps the idea, topic, skill, understanding?" That is, you determine what kind of assessment best shows what students learned. Here you design the most authentic outcome-based assessments on all the results you want the students to show based on the original objectives. Include all the kinds of assessments (from the earlier section, such as quizzes, questions, self-assessments). Use all of the evidence that is available to monitor and record a student's progress.

Stage 3, the last stage, backs you up to actually planning the learning experiences and instruction. (This is probably where you thought you would start.) Here is where you sequence learning experiences based on Stages 1 and 2. You embed the assessment as part of the instruction and learning. It is where you identify all the necessary knowledge and skills to foster enduring understanding in all cornerstones. Stages 1 and 2 guide your decisions about what to teach and how (instructional strategies that include embedded assessments). This is the stage where you identify the essential questions that take students to the heart of the topic and engage them in inquiry (McTighe and Wiggins 1999).

> **"Standardized assessment of dance provides a unique challenge. First, the art form itself is temporal; it leaves few lasting traces and no permanent objects to assess. Second, evidence of learning in dance can be particularly difficult to separate from innate ability because all children are constantly developing and practicing their instrument—the body. Because the child's body is both an instrument of creating in dance, and an everyday functional body, a dance assessment must be careful to distinguish between growth and learning that is the result of dance training and that which comes from another source."**
>
> —National Assessment Governing Board (1994, p. 42)

392

Dance's strategic triad design incorporates what UBD calls the backward design process.

- Stage 1: Objectives (identify desired outcomes). What do students need to know and do that take the goals and objectives of the DCC Frameworks and the NSDEs forward?

- Stage 2: Determine authentic assessments (determine acceptable evidence). Where and how do you look for proof that the objectives have been met through embedded, formative, and summative?

- Stage 3: Instructional strategies (plan specific learning experiences). How do you design dance instruction and experiences so that you can meet curriculum objectives and authentically assess the evidence (McTighe and Wiggins 1999)?

The stages of the backward design process in dance became the ongoing teaching triad. This backward approach departs from the old way of thinking about assessments being last because they were given at the end when the unit was completed.

Operationalizing the Triad

Figure 12.14 identifies what each part of the triad does. The triad requires all three parts to be in balance. The success of any one depends on the success of the other two.

In a nutshell, curriculum content and objectives are delivered by instructional strategies based on identifying the acceptable evidence that objectives are being met and designing authentic assessments. After that you select the best instructional strategies to optimally deliver dance content. Assess student outcomes to determine students' level of achievement and to monitor the effectiveness of the content and instruction.

- Assessment results show whether to modify the plan and, if so, which part.

- Assessment shows which individuals need corrective work.

Triad Unit Planning

It is time to apply what you learned about instruction and assessment in dance to learning objectives and cornerstone content. Design (actually *choreograph*) units so the triad functions as a magnificent

trio. Coordinate each part of the triad to partner the other.

Sketching a Triad Unit

Read the format in figure 12.15, then sketch a rough draft of a triad unit plan in three sequential steps:

a. State the content objectives from the framework. Objectives are outcomes students are to accomplish in the unit.

b. Translate objectives into acceptable evidence that shows students master the content and skills in dance. Assessments measure what students accomplish and to what extent they accomplish each objective.

c. Design the best instructional plan for the unit. This step describes how you plan to go about instructing to accomplish each objective and embed assessment.

To see how the parts of the triad come together in a real unit plan, look at figure 12.16. It is a real-life sample of a 6- to 9-week long-range plan for artistically gifted dance middle school students. Notice that the plan assesses several unit objectives at once, a goal you should strive for when you plan.

There are at least three ways to make a triad unit plan. Use the one that suits you best. Each way starts with objectives. (They drive the triad.) When you finish, ensure that each item in the triad supports the other and there are no gaps. All three ways get at the same results:

1. Down one column at a time (vertically). Systematically fill out all objectives. Next list acceptable evidence and assessments for each objective. Next design instruction for each objective.

2. Across one line at a time (left to right, horizontally). Complete line 1 across all three columns and relate all three. Then go to number 2, and so on through number 10.

3. A holistic approach (criss-cross). Draft a list of objectives before writing them on the plan. Then group them according to the assessments and instructional strategies so you accomplish several objectives with one strategy. This is efficient and beneficial.

Step 1

For your first practice, make your own one-page chart in the same format as the one in figure 12.15.

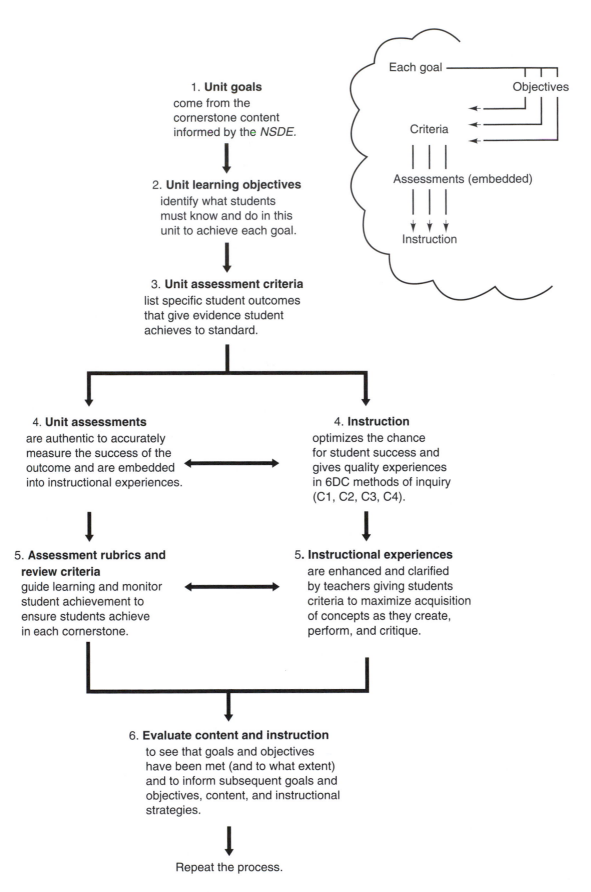

1. **Unit goals**
come from the
cornerstone content
informed by the *NSDE.*

2. **Unit learning objectives**
identify what students
must know and do in this
unit to achieve each goal.

3. **Unit assessment criteria**
list specific student outcomes
that give evidence student
achieves to standard.

Each goal ——————— Objectives

Criteria

Assessments (embedded)

Instruction

4. **Unit assessments**
are authentic to accurately
measure the success of the
outcome and are embedded
into instructional experiences.

4. **Instruction**
optimizes the chance
for student success and
gives quality experiences
in 6DC methods of inquiry
(C1, C2, C3, C4).

5. **Assessment rubrics and
review criteria**
guide learning and monitor
student achievement to
ensure students achieve
in each cornerstone.

5. **Instructional experiences**
are enhanced and clarified
by teachers giving students
criteria to maximize acquisition
of concepts as they create,
perform, and critique.

6. **Evaluate content and instruction**
to see that goals and objectives
have been met (and to what extent)
and to inform subsequent goals and
objectives, content, and instructional
strategies.

Repeat the process.

FIGURE 12.14   Curriculum content and objectives are delivered by instructional strategies that you choose based on identifying acceptable evidence that objectives are being met.

The Triad: Objectives, Assessment, and Instruction Using the Backward Plan

1. Identify desired results. (Objectives)

2. Determine acceptable evidence. (Assessments)

3. Plan learning experiences and instructional strategies. (Instruction)

Objectives	Assessments	Instruction

Derive the content and skills from several sources:
 	
Content from the DCC Framework
  1. Knowledge
  2. Movement skills
Standards
  1. National
  2. State
Desired outcomes
  1. What students will know as a result of this experience (knowledge).
  2. What students will be able to do as a result of this experience (skills).
	Say how you will measure students' achievement of each objective:
	
	Evaluate content
	  1. Is it age appropriate?
	  2. Is content learned?
	  3. To what extent do students learn and apply the content?
	Evaluate instruction
	  1. Was teaching effective?
	  2. What could be improved?
	Evaluate students
	  1. Level of individual progress
	  2. Whole class' progress
		Identify how you will teach (i.e., what methods, processes, and materials you will use) to accomplish each objective:
		
		Instructional strategies
		  1. Use C1, C2, C3, and C4 methods of inquiry.
		  2. Identify delivery strategies that accomplish the objectives and show evidence of learning.

FIGURE 12.15   See how objectives, assessments, and instruction interact to support each other. Then, put the triad unit plan to work for you as you sketch a rough draft of a unit that begins by identifying the desired outcomes (objectives).

Draw 10 lines spaced 2 inches apart across the page horizontally so it looks like a grid. Now prepare to integrate the triad. Open the NSDEs to pages 23 through 26 to identify specific objectives. For practice, let's develop an eighth grade triad unit plan on the theme "designing space." Choose 10 achievement standards for grade 8 from NSDEs 1 through 5 that you will advance by this study. List them all on the chart as objectives.

Step 2

Now that you have objectives, you're ready to fill out the details of the designing space unit plan. Take ideas from figure 12.16.

What is the acceptable evidence you want to see that demonstrates the objectives were achieved? What will students know and be able to do as a result of the instructional unit? What are the outcomes and how will you know to what extent each student achieved them? In effect, what assessments will you embed to measure success? Another term for this is *outcomes-based assessment*. How would you assess

students on each of your 10 achievement standards? (Record in the "Assessment" column.) Can you make one assessment optimally work for two objectives? Is each assessment the best way to measure the outcome of the standard-turned-objective? Does the assessment serve the objectives you stated?

List both formative and summative assessments for your unit plan (i.e., the ongoing performance assessment that is in process and the culminating assessment). If you see that one assessment can measure several objectives at once, group those objectives together to prepare you to move to the next step.

Step 3

Now that you have determined what kind of assessments measure how successfully students meet your desired outcomes, what kind of instructional strategies would lead students to meet your outcomes? Now it's time to fill in the last column. Create an instructional strategy for each item (or cluster of items) so that every objective has a corresponding

Objectives	Assessments	Instruction
The student will achieve the following: 1. Demonstrate increased skill level in using the body in space, in time, and with dynamic fluency 2. Demonstrate increasing levels of coordination, balance, stamina, elevation, and technique appropriate to age and development 3. Demonstrate kinesthetic awareness of the body in motion and in stillness 4. Demonstrate mastery of dance technique and expanded movement vocabulary and appropriate multisensory integration 5. Demonstrate knowledge and use of anatomically and kinesthetically sound movement principles for safety, efficiency, and longevity as a dancer 6. Become aware that dance takes many forms, is a valid form of expression for males and females, and can present and communicate ideas in many different ways 7. Demonstrate comprehension of a variety of dance styles and proficiency in executing more than one style 8. Identify careers related to dance in contemporary society 9. Recognize the difference between creative process and final product 10. Recognize necessity for commitment to a project by dancers and creators 11. Apply aesthetic principles and choreographic criteria to judge the quality of dance both as observer and as the creator–participant 12. Judge anatomical and performance factors basic to the technical performance skill of the performer 13. Use accurate dance terminology when discussing the technical skill of the performer as well as the aesthetic principles and their application to dance works 14. Increase use of correct dance terminology and a variety of synonyms and reference points (historical and cultural) in the discussion of the aesthetics of dance (Objectives from *South Carolina Visual and Performing Arts Framework,* 1993, Grades 6-8) Although not the main focus, these tested basic skills are addressed within this unit's objectives: **Reading:** Vocabulary and comprehension **Mathematics:** Concepts and problem solving **Language:** Prewriting, composing, editing	Objectives 1-7: Demonstrate evidence of having refined and mastered ballet and modern techniques as appropriate to age and development, as well as apply safe practices for injury prevention while warming up and dancing (teacher observation) Objective 8: Identify and define production roles (questioning and worksheets) Objective 9: Apply established choreographic criteria while choreographing sequences for performance in the final dance production (teacher and peer evaluation) Objective 10: Participate in a group warm-up or assume responsibility for preparing his or her group to perform Objectives 11-14: Write self- and peer critiques of the production	Objectives 1-7: Participate in ballet and modern warm-ups as well as rehearse sequences to be performed in the final dance production Objective 8: Identify and discuss various production jobs associated with dance performance (e.g., choreographer, director, costume designer, lighting designer, composer, stage manager) Objective 9: Participate in the creative process by composing movement sequences to be performed in the final product (dance production) Objective 10: Assume personal responsibility for being mentally and physically prepared for dance rehearsals, maintaining the attitude that dance production is a team effort, and believing that each participant is crucial to the success of the production Objectives 11-14: View the videotapes of the final dance production

FIGURE 12.16   See how this extended triad unit plan for middle school AG/T incorporates standards into objectives. Also notice how it clusters objectives 1 through 7 and 11 through 14 so several objectives are addressed and assessed together.

Used with permission of A. Wrenn Cook.

strategy and all outcome-based assessments are incorporated. Design a way to deliver each of the 10 achievement standards you have as objectives. Find one strategy to cover several objectives. Use at least three different instructional strategies. When your plan is complete, read through the whole triad plan. Do the items relate to each other effectively? Do they make a cohesive unit plan? What else must you consider to make the unit work better? Will it be a good unit to break into several individual lessons? Estimate how many.

If this were a real unit of study, you would now design individual lessons that use these strategies in a logical order so students achieve all objectives and standards.

PEER ASSESSMENT

- Swap plans with a classmate and peer assess each other's plan. Use a rating scale where 1 = needs improvement, 2 = meets standards, 3 = exceeds standards. When the plan rates a 3, place it in your Perspectives Notebook.
- Create a sample authentic assessment for a triad unit.

Creating a Sample Authentic Assessment for a Triad Unit

As you write your unit plans, be creative in assessing students. Cover more than one objective in your formal assessments. Find the most organic way to embed assessments into the learning activity so they deepen learning as part of the instruction. Make assessments authentic by finding the most natural and nonintrusive way to determine student mastery. See how the anatomy dance in figure 12.17 turns the summative assessment for a unit on anatomy into a choreographic problem that is peer critiqued for content and artistry. This is an example of using an assessment to increase learning and artistry as well as creative and critical thinking.

Anatomy Dance (Authentic Assessment)

Test on Bones, Joints, and Joint Movements (Articulations)

Sixth Grade Gifted Dance Composition

Directions: Create a dance that accomplishes these tasks in order.

1. Touch some phalanges to a femur.

2. Circle the pelvis right and then jump from side to side on the metatarsals.

3. Cross a radius over an ulna while flexing any hinge joint.

4. Twist the cervical vertebrae to the right, then left, while moving the metacarpals in the air.

5. Touch the lumbar vertebrae to the floor and extend the right femur–tibia joint.

6. Cross one set of tarsals over the other and then move the right shoulder joint.

7. Move another ball-and-socket joint while touching several carpals to the sternum.

8. End your dance with a sequential flexion in as many joints as possible.

FIGURE 12.17   This small group in-class choreography assignment is actually the test (summative assessment) in an anatomy unit for AG/T sixth graders. Groups perform their works as others watch closely to pinpoint any criteria discrepancies and then suggest how to choreographically fix them. As a result, everyone has applied what they know about anatomy and is ready to refine the rough draft of the work into a polished performance.

Used with permission of A. Wrenn Cook, 1997.

Reflect and Respond: Triad Unit Exercise

Now that you know how objectives, outcomes-based assessment, and instruction correlate, return to the NAEP assessment in figure 12.11. Deconstruct its information and turn its achievement standards into a triad unit plan (as demonstrated in figure 12.16).

- Can you design a unit to accomplish the objectives?
- What will be acceptable evidence of learning? How will you assess the extent of student success?
- What instructional strategies best accomplish this?

When you can do this, you will be arts savvy and ready to invite a NAEP assessment team!

Arts Savvy Curriculum, Instruction, and Assessment

To be arts savvy, you must move back and forth between various arts-focused objectives from C1, C2, C3, and C4. You must use the triad unit backward plan. You must produce students who can create, perform, and respond to dance. You must produce students who achieve national assessments.

Teacher Competencies

How arts savvy are you? Use the following self-assessment as a checklist. What can you successfully do now that will aid your delivery of the triad unit plan? Assess yourself periodically at different stages of your preparation to become a dance specialist as well. Check all that apply.

ASSESSING MY CONTENT

1. ____ I incorporate ongoing performance assessments in the unit's lessons to increase content learning.
2. ____ I continually evaluate curriculum content for effectiveness and adjust as needed.
3. ____ My dance curriculum is significant and substantive with strong goals and objectives.
4. ____ I make useful links to other academic subjects.
5. ____ My curriculum increases students' aesthetic education.

6. ____ Lessons incorporate inquiry and reflective thinking about dance content.
7. ____ Students view a variety of significant dance choreographies as examples.
8. ____ Content becomes increasingly more challenging.
9. ____ Content spirals and builds on previously developed skills.
10. ____ Topics and activities are sequenced in a logical progression.
11. ____ Content is current and accurate.
12. ____ Content includes diverse perspectives and features diverse cultures.
13. ____ Content is appropriate to student development and interest.
14. ____ Content prepares students to achieve national dance standards.
15. ____ I effectively translate content goals into learning objectives.

ASSESSING MY INSTRUCTIONAL STRATEGIES

1. ____ I regularly assess my instructional strategies to adjust and improve.
2. ____ I use open-ended activities and encourage creative and artistic response.
3. ____ I elicit higher-order thinking grounded in solid facts.
4. ____ I overlay critical thinking experiences while students are in motion and dancing.
5. ____ I give numerous opportunities to apply and inquire into content and skills.
6. ____ I create targeted learning activities and keep them student centered.
7. ____ I give students a mental, aesthetic, and physical workout.
8. ____ My directions are clear to avoid frustration and confusion.
9. ____ I encourage students to create and explore.
10. ____ I select activities that promote positive self-image as movers and creative problem solvers.
11. ____ I select activities that build skills in different dance styles.
12. ____ I select activities that build dance skills in and appreciation for different cultures.

13. ____ I use experiences that increase success and boost student confidence.

14. ____ I personalize activity by encouraging all to express ideas and feelings about what they are learning and accomplishing.

15. ____ I select activities that are incremental and move students to the next level of development; I use familiar material as a launch pad.

16. ____ I make composition criteria clear and challenging.

17. ____ I give composition experiences that increase ability to organize movement and present it in a structured way.

18. ____ I emphasize artistic as well as structural compositional criteria and hold students accountable to them.

19. ____ I emphasize the design principles and increasing artistic quality.

20. ____ I give clear compositional assignments using choreographic criteria.

21. ____ I use rubrics to assist the critique of peer and personal creative works.

22. ____ I emphasize accomplishment and achievement according to internal and external artistic standards.

Use these criteria to keep you on track once in the school. Use the rating scale 1 = seldom, 2 = usually, and 3 = always.

Questions to Ponder

1. How can you include objectives from all cornerstones in each unit to plan for a complete dance education?

2. Must you lose instructional time to assess students? How can assessments be instructive? When can you effectively use peer assessment as an instructional strategy?

3. Using NSDE 4 achievement standards for grade 4, how would you make a triad unit plan?

4. Of what value are student portfolios in high school? What are some materials you would have students acquire for their dance portfolio?

Notebook/Portfolio:
Perspectives Notebook

IDENTIFY FIVE MEGA-IDEAS AND CONCEPTS IN DANCE

Part 1

You are in the process of writing your Statements of Belief about dance education; now it's time to write your Statements of Belief about dance. What five concepts about dance are worth retaining for a lifetime? Or, what are the mega-ideas and understanding in dance that are vital for every person to know? Create a list. This list is important:

1. The list identifies what you believe is most vital to learn about dance. (The list items often convert to excellent teaching goals to lead your curriculum.)

2. The list helps you articulate what is most important about dance in education.

Part 2

On another sheet, turn these 10 statements into essential questions that would get at the core of each statement, the lasting understanding, and would lead students to examine each belief statement. (For example, if a belief statement is "that dance is a medium of expression to transmit personal and cultural ideas found throughout the world," following are some essential questions it fosters: a. How is dance a universal phenomenon? b. Where do you find dance? c. What does dance transmit and why is it important to individuals? To passing on traditions and cultures?

5. What would your technique assessment rubric look like for modern dance technique in high school modern dance class? How does it compare to the sample rubric in appendix B?

6. What is the connection between curriculum, instruction, and assessment in the teaching of dance and the arts?

7. Can you transform a set of choreographic criteria into review criteria to create a rubric? What would it include? How does it help one's

composition to know the review criteria before starting to create the dance?

8. What review criteria might you design to guide students in researching and writing papers about dance at middle and high school levels? At upper elementary?

9. What is best left to teachers to assess? To districts? To states? To national or federal bodies? How long should state assessments take? How much will it cost to conduct a state or national assessment?

Rich Resources

- McTighe, Jay, and Grant Wiggins. *Understanding by Design Handbook* (1999) and *Understanding by Design Professional Development Workbook* (2004). Alexandria, VA: Association for Supervision and Curriculum Development, 1999. Help with identifying desired results, determining acceptable evidence, and planning learning experiences and instruction. Recommended resource to prioritize and organize content, instruction, and assessment.

- Wong, Harry K., and Rosemary T. Wong. *How to Be an Effective Teacher: The First Days of School*. Mountain View, CA: Harry K. Wong, 1998. Gives you practical guidance on planning and managing classes. Valuable as you transition from student to teacher.

Integrating the Cornerstones to Create Units of Study in Dance

"If our
civilization is to
continue to be both
dynamic and nurturing,
its success will ultimately
depend on how well we
develop the capacities of our
children, not only to earn a
living in a vastly complex world,
but to live a life rich in meaning."

—Consortium of National Arts Education
Associations (1994, p. 5)

This chapter shows how to integrate the corner-stones' methods of inquiry. Students are to be dance literate in all the cornerstones—to be a dancer, choreographer, historian, and critic. In this chapter we distinguish between dance literacy and dance fluency and see how to bring about both. We also look at an Eight-Step Plan as an effective way to deliver units as well as individual lessons. You learn the eight steps and how to vary them to increase aesthetic education and build organic connections between the artistic processes. The goal is to merge the cornerstones into coherent, aesthetically driven units of study.

Relating the Cornerstones

Individual cornerstones contain the specialized dance skills needed for a complete education in dance (i.e., the ability to dance, create, know about dance, and critique). One cornerstone is no more important than another. But we also need to integrate the cornerstones to reinforce their aesthetic relation-ship to each other. You are to ensure that students gain a perspective on dance as a complete art form and as a universal form of human expression. To aesthetically synthesize the four cornerstones—like they are in the world of dance—emphasizes their artistic connections and links their artistic processes. Educators tend to separate the cornerstones for teaching purposes—which is valid. Yet we also have to know when to bring the parts back together to relate them to the whole. This is necessary so students don't get a fragmented perspective of dance. The cornerstones' union and interaction determine dance's artistic and educational value.

Dance Literacy

Literacy is the ability to function in each dance cornerstone as dancer, critic, historian–anthropologist, and choreographer. Thus, **dance literacy** combines knowing about dance and the ability to create, perform, and respond to dance as an art form as promoted in the NSDEs and NAEP assessments.

Dance literacy needs to catch up to other kinds of literacy in America. Sports literacy is way ahead. But your efforts to bring young people world-class content and instruction can make a difference. Make dance literacy an educational priority so at the same time students

- grow articulate bodies, able to express physically and rhythmically with ease;
- make dances;
- read dance and dances, pay close attention, analyze and critique, using the universal dance vocabulary; and
- be as familiar with major dance works as they are with classics in other subjects.

Dance literacy involves learning techniques from around the world (e.g., classical, popular, and folk styles). Because dance expression is so multifaceted, it is unthinkable that any one style be taught at the exclusion of others in such a varied world dance tapestry. Likewise, impart a sense of dance in its time and place so students

- compare dance styles,
- analyze similarities and differences,
- note the salient features of a dance style,
- verbalize about dance, and
- critique its effective use of body, space, time, energy and dynamics, and relationships (BSTERs).

As part of dance literacy, grow articulate bodies that are able to express themselves physically and rhythmically with ease.

 How can you make great choreographic works as recognizable as artworks by Picasso, symphonic scores by Ravel, or plays by Shakespeare?

However, also think beyond literacy. Aesthetic education is also about the interrelationship of all facets of an art form. Create a curriculum that integrates rather than isolates different aspects of dance. Who wants to study dance history one quarter, technique one quarter, choreography one quarter, and critiquing one quarter? That compartmentalizes learning.

Dance Fluency (Advanced Dance Literacy)

Dance fluency kicks dance literacy up a notch. It is an advanced form of dance literacy, a matter of degrees, like "dance literacy squared." Fluency is the ability to correlate and use the cornerstones to

Dance Literacy

- Functions well in each cornerstone

- Is articulate and expressive in each cornerstone

- Is successful in each artistic process (c/p/r)

- Understands and uses each cornerstone

Dance Fluency

- Functions optimally across cornerstones

- Is articulate and expressive across the cornerstones

- Integrates the artistic processes (c/p/r)

- Uses a global perspective of dance to shift between viewpoints

FIGURE 13.1   Descriptors for dance literacy and fluency.

benefit each other. It is the ability to aesthetically integrate and synthesize the parts into the whole. See figure 13.1 for descriptors of dance literacy and fluency.

Compare dance fluency to learning a foreign language. To know vocabulary and speak words and some short phrases in a foreign language (literacy) is different from speaking in complete sentences and conversing in the language (literacy with fluency). It is also a matter of degrees. To communicate fluently in that language you have to perceive, understand, translate, and actually formulate a response that is coherent and articulate. Likewise, in dance, a fluent choreographer designs and refines a dance composition and then critiques and polishes it so as to perform it well. He compares it to a model work for similarities and to raise personal aesthetic standards. Thus, all four cornerstones interact to produce a fluent dancer–choreographer with the aesthetic perspective of a historian–critic, and vice versa (a historian–critic with the aesthetic perspective of a dancer–choreographer).

Fluency emphasizes creating and communicating meaning (NSDE 3) in all the artistic processes (c/p/r). It is precisely

- because you're a choreographer that you're a better critic,

- because you're a dancer that you're a better choreographer,

- because you're a critic that you're a better dancer,

- because you're a dance historian that you're a better critic, and

- because you know masterworks that you're a better choreographer.

All who study dance K-12 should be fluent by graduation. They should understand how one dance cornerstone affects the other. Fluency depends on

- viewing enough high-quality dance to be familiar with a number of works and able to critique them,

- unpacking great works to see how major choreographers create dance works and what they communicate,

- relating our own choreographic process and products to those of professional choreographers,

- developing the ability to dance as well as talk dance,

- knowing dance from different cultures and the aesthetic standards that surround them, and

- developing the ability to compose dances that express clear intent and self-critique them.

Therefore, fluency is the ultimate form of dance literacy. It means that by twelfth grade a student not only can dance and create but can speak with personal conviction about what it is to dance and perform, create and compose, analyze and critique, and know his own dance heritage and that of others around the world—a reasonable goal for any core subject.

Linking Perspectives Across the Cornerstones

When you look at the cornerstones as methods of inquiry, it may appear that C1 is strictly dancing and performing and the rest of the curriculum is not movement based. However, C2 is movement based, and C3 has a strong movement component when you approach it from learning to dance dances of different cultures, learning segments of great works, learning repertory, and trying out different dance styles. Now that we have looked at each cornerstone individually we will put them together for instruction in a way that dynamically captures dancing from every angle.

Consider how you can affect and maximize fluency by integrating the artistic processes from the cornerstones. For example, find ways to investigate history (C3) by analyzing (C4) historic choreography (C2) and to investigate technique (C1) by analyzing and critiquing (C4) performances (C3). Incorporate critical thinking across the cornerstones even in written work such as journals, papers, and tests.

Dance Critics and Dance Historians (C3, C4) Teach students to inquire as historian and critic at the same time. Clarify the similarities and differences in their roles. Critics and historians reflect on the same dance works, just in different ways.

- Historians look at works not only from the past but from today as part of the unbroken chain of human expression in movement. Historians go to the past to see how dance served its own place and time.

- Critics usually focus on current works in a company's repertory. Critics emphasize current trends in light of what went before and sometimes use comparative analyses to predict future trends. Critics help us get a perspective on artistic expression during different times in history.

Performers, Choreographers, and Critics (C1, C2, C4) Teach students to self-evaluate to refine their work. Performers who are critics of their performance skills must learn to self-correct. Choreographers who are critics of their work should refine their compositions and become better, more astute choreographers. The better critics they become, the better choreographers they become—and vice versa.

Performers, Choreographers, Historians, and Critics (C1, C2, C3, C4) After the choreographer designs and refines a dance, she critiques and polishes it to perform it well. She compares it to the master work for ideas. This is how the cornerstones support each other in the best sense of the word.

Maximizing the Six Characteristics of Educational Dance

How will you use the Dance Cornerstone Curriculum (DCC) Framework to maximize all the 6DCs? (Refer to figure 5.4 for a linear depiction.) Walk through the DCC Framework by focusing only on one age group, such as kindergarten through second grade. Can you do the following?

- Integrate all four cornerstones for that age group to broaden their experience (comprehensive).

- Integrate the concepts down that age's column to deepen the experience (substantive).

- Arrange the framework concepts into logical learning sequences from less to more complex (sequential) to serve the child as he progresses from kindergarten to grade 2. (Also spiral back

After a choreographer designs a dance, she critiques and polishes it to perform it well. The interplay of all cornerstones contributes to her dance fluency.

Consider the many ways one can and should be literate in dance. Literacy requires not only performing literacy but also other kinds of knowledge and skills related to the artistic processes (c/p/r).

Why do you need all dance cornerstones to produce dance-literate students? Dance-fluent students?

C1: How Do Dancing and Performing Relate to Dance Literacy and NSDE 1 and 3?

- NSDE 1: "Identify and demonstrate movement elements and skills in performing dance."
- NSDE 3: "Understand dance as a way to create and communicate meaning."
- To be able to dance is itself a form of movement literacy.
- By performing, students increase their facility with dance, their expressive range, and their body–kinesthetic understanding.
- We use the dance elements as a kinetic language to express ourselves. We continue to increase our capacity to express ideas the more we embody them and perform them.
- To dance is to be kinetically literate.

What Can I Do?

- Invite students to communicate by dancing.
- Increase their ability to express ideas to an audience through bodyspeaking.
- What else can I do?

C2: How Do Creating and Composing Relate to Dance Literacy and NSDE 2 and 3?

- NSDE 2: "Understand choreographic principles, processes, and structures."
- NSDE 3: "Understand dance as a way to create and communicate meaning."
- *Choreo* (dance) *graphing* (writing) is literally "writing dance."
- Composing dances to communicate meaning develops expressive literacy.
- Learning how to use the principles of design and composition increases the ability to structure movement into coherent statements of nonverbal expression.
- Improvising is creative literacy.

What Can I Do?

- Invite students to express who whey are, what they think, and how they experience the world by creating dances.
- Ask students to respond to stimuli through movement exploration and improvisation.
- What else can I do?

C3: How Do Dance History, Culture, and Context Relate to Dance Literacy and NSDE 3 and 5?

- NSDE 3: "Understand dance as a way to create and communicate meaning."
- NSDE 5: "Understand dance in various cultures and historical periods."
- Encountering the creative work of others, responding to live performances, learning dances from other cultures, and discovering notable works of dance from the present and the past create a broad perspective for dance. This increases cultural literacy.
- Systematic exposure to dance enables learners to understand external references to dance—a vital part of their total education.

What Can I Do?

- Invite students to recognize dance works and the people responsible for their growing dance heritage by using
  a. photographs of famous choreographers;
  b. posters of famous dancers (Gregory Hines), choreographers (Maurice Bejart), dance works (*Aureole*), and cultural dances (Kabuki); and
  c. references to choreographic works that exemplify your concept.
- Build units around dance works to increase recognition of works and styles so students develop visual literacy for dance.
- What else can I do?

C4: How Do Analysis and Criticism Relate to Dance Literacy and NSDE 3 and 4?

- NSDE 3: "Understand dance as a way to create and communicate meaning."
- NSDE 4: "Apply and demonstrate critical and creative thinking in dance."
- Observing dance works and talking about what does and does not work will develop aesthetic literacy.
- You can analyze dance works and use the dance elements to communicate the experience (verbally or in writing).
- You can use the aesthetic principles as criteria to measure a work's effectiveness and to teach discrimination in critiquing.
- The ability to articulate about dance requires critical thinking and is a form of critical literacy.

What Can I Do?

- Invite students to analyze and critique dance works
  a. by professionals,
  b. by peers, and
  c. by themselves.
- What else can I do?

to revisit familiar skills and then layer and overlap them to reinforce their relationship.)

- Overlay concepts from C2, C3, and C4 during technique class, such as adding a creative component to extend performing skills and viewing a demonstration to critique for technique pointers. Also remember how important it is to learn a dance style's roots and place (contextually coherent) while learning how to perform it.
- Expect students' artistic best in everything (aesthetically driven).
- Ask the kinds of questions that draw students in and keep dance relevant to them (inquiry based).

Teaching by Integrating the Cornerstones

Whether you build units around a dance style, a theme, or a piece of choreography and its choreographer, include a viewing sample of professionals performing to demonstrate quality performing and composition. Use the sample to raise artistic standards and expectations for dance and to introduce prominent figures in the field of dance as models. Students need models—much like sports figures—to set the standards of excellence. Consider the alternative: If learners see no good examples, they will have no idea of expected standards of quality. They will lack interest out of ignorance. In the same way, how limiting it would be to only see and critique student works. Without exemplars, we're handicapped in achieving the overall aesthetic standards we desire.

Exemplary or great works illustrate how all facets of dance interact. Select a work worth critiquing, worth emulating, worth learning about, able to stimulate creativity, and able to model the technique of its style. Ask students to speak from multiple perspectives about a work (e.g., as dancer–choreographer and historian–critic) so they adopt all viewpoints in the same work.

Unravel a Dance Work to Plan Integrated Instruction

Every dance work is just waiting for you to find all the ideas lurking there. Think of it as unraveling the threads of a great tapestry to see what it's made of. Pull out the threads of ideas from dance works to help you plan units. Look for different colored threads from each cornerstone. Then weave all these threads back together into a new tapestry for teaching. Let your unit objectives lead you sometimes, and let inspiration from the work itself lead you at other times. As you start to integrate the threads into a unit, be sure they help you take some objectives forward, as in the following examples:

- Threads from C1. Use the featured techniques in the work to teach students how to increase technical skill. Raise performance proficiency expectations. Use the performance to point out concepts that increase knowledge of the dancing body (e.g., anatomical support for technique, kinesiology, kin-aesthetics, somatics, safety in motion, or injury prevention). Show students how to dance by modeling after professional dancers. Thus create a broader context for student performing skill development—more than just a studio class. Use the work to demonstrate concepts such as lifts and partnering for older students.

- Threads from C2. Analyze the choreographic ideas and compositional structures within the great work. Use them as ideas for creating dance. Analyze the personal style of one of the dancers and have students identify the personal uniqueness and movement strengths each person brings to dance performance. Determine which dance elements are most prominent and which could be used for choreographic inspiration.

- Threads from C3. Inquire into the social, cultural, and historical milieu of the work in its time and place. Find its implications for its time and also for ours. See if the dance is a mirror that reflects parts of our humanity. Use it to increase awareness of ourselves and of dance traditions, major dance works, and notable choreographers. Look at what it contributes to the field of dance and aesthetics. Critique its artistic strengths and memorable moments.

- Threads from C4. Think critically about the work and reflect on its artistic value and its personal significance. Interpret its meaning and compare it with other works. Compare the choreographer's process with your own. Evaluate your own work, rework if necessary, and perform it for critique. Integrate creative process and product by critiquing works of self and others. Thus, value dance and others.

Benefits of Incorporating a Great Work

Let's explore how interrelated study benefits students. Let's assume that a great work of dance is incorporated into each unit as an example of either theme, style, history, performing, dancing technique, artistic expression, or some other aspect of dance. The work may be a small part or a major emphasis of the unit, but it makes dance instruction visual and aesthetic. You will need regular access to a large-screen video or DVD player to see viewing examples. Integrate slices of a work into a dance study to increase contextual coherence, to build dance literacy, to raise aesthetic awareness, and to inspire performance excellence. What a way to show the dynamics of how pliés soften landings, how the lift looks, how multiple turns are accomplished through spotting, how to skim across the floor and soar through the air!

The Framework's Relatedness

Because instruction on dancing and performing (C1) is only part of the picture, how can you build context? How can you enrich one cornerstone with facets of the others? When you look at the complete Dance Cornerstone Curriculum (DCC) Framework, you see that it combines all four component parts (C1, C2, C3, and C4). The complete DCC Framework appears to be **linear** (i.e., a masculine model of sequence), when in fact it is also spiral (i.e., feminine model of relatedness). That is, the concepts are designed to be returned to, integrated, and woven together during instruction according to the age group you are teaching (e.g., K-2, 3-5, 6-8, and 9-12). You must tie complementary concepts together from C1, C2, C3, and C4 as demonstrated in figure 13.2. (You also must return to beginning concepts for older beginners to dance.)

Take a moment to practice integrating facets of the DCC Framework. First, return to figure 13.2, this time to focus only on grades 3 through 5. See how the shaded boxes from the C1, C2, C3, and C4 components relate to each other and can be part of the multiple outcomes of a lesson. What kinds of learning activities would accomplish them all?

Next, consult the DCC Framework in chapters 6 through 9. Compare the same age group (second column for grades 3-5) to find other concepts and skills that complement each other across cornerstones. Find organic connections that support each other within one cornerstone and also across all four.

Points of Entry

Because all unit objectives are to be accomplished through the unit's individual lessons, plan ahead. You may start from any cornerstone with equal success (see chapter 5). Let your unit goals and objectives inspire the entry point for each unit.

Example 1: Polyrhythms

If one objective for middle school is "to increase varied timing and rhythmic response" and another objective is "to understand dance as a universal form of expression across time and place," why not create a polyrhythms unit? Start by exploring West African dance and drumming techniques from Nigeria or Ghana; then critique one of Chuck Davis' dances related to a Ghanaian culture, such as the welcoming dance "Funga Alafiya." Take those experiences to stimulate a creative compositional project to create polyrhythmic dances as well as polyrhythmic accompaniment scores. Perform for each other while one group dances and another group drums. Layer several different patterns to get a resultant rhythm. Critique the dances and the drumming to get pointers for improving the dances; then fine-tune them. Learn and perform "Funga Alafiya." Present it to a social studies class studying Ghana or Nigeria and bring cultural information along with your dance.

Example 2: Tall Tales of the Wild West

If your objective is "to link dance and social studies around a theme," consider a theme such as "Tall Tales of the Wild West." Your point of entry could be a major work such as Eugene Loring's *Billy the Kid*. View and unpack it first. Take technique ideas from its performance to work on in the studio. Use the theme to inspire students to create their own dances from other stories or historic tales of early America. Many of these tales lend themselves to group dances for upper elementary and middle school. You could include other cultural aspects of the U.S. westward expansion through dance. You could use it as a springboard to look from a different perspective, like how Native Americans viewed the expansion into their territories. This lesson opens up concepts for a choreography project about America's

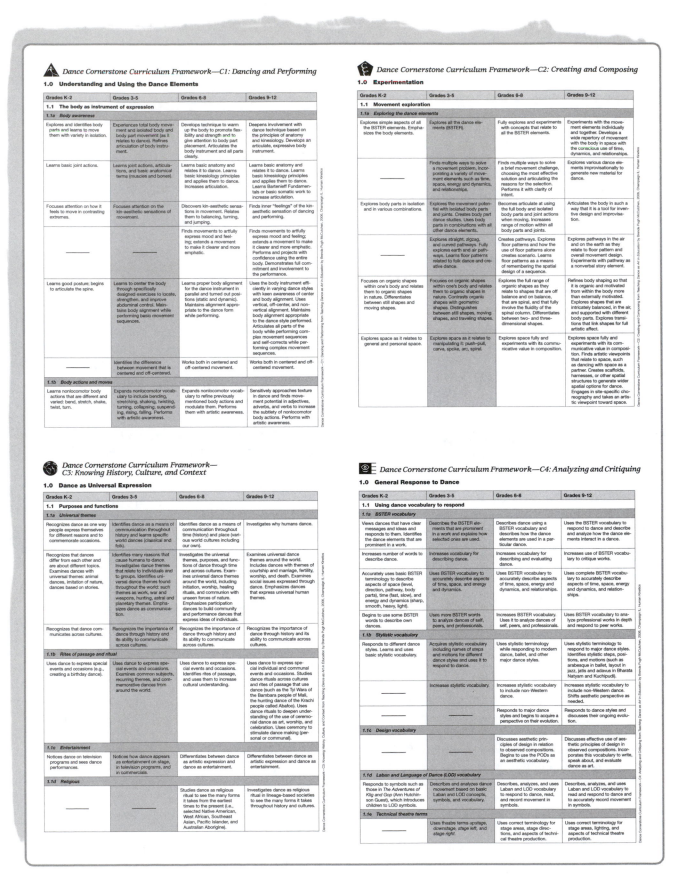

FIGURE 13.2 Cross-referencing and interconnecting dance concepts from different cornerstones build context for dance. Design units that hold ideas together so lessons are not random events.

pioneering spirit in all new bold ways (e.g., space exploration, underwater discoveries). In your guided viewing and critique of *Billy the Kid* you could compare the work with one from the same genre such as Agnes De Mille's *Rodeo*. That naturally leads to a study of major theatrical dance performance of the mid-1950s era (20th century) and could spawn a new unit.

There are numerous approaches to a unit. Any cornerstone can be a starting place—there is no best place to start. Be wise. Vary your approach for different units. Each cornerstone contributes different artistic processes to integrate into units. Over time, cohesive units build context that broadly educates dance students. (Find additional examples in chapter 14.)

Using the Eight-Step Plan to Maximize Artistic Results

You can use the delivery system described in this chapter with experienced students as well as novices. This system incorporates the content and methods of inquiry from all four dance cornerstones. It serves aesthetic education and dance literacy, and it creates

---

Reflect and Respond

Using the criteria in figure 13.1 on literacy, determine how many of the following three snapshots describe someone who is either dance literate or "dance literate squared" (fluent). Can you defend your selections?

Snapshot 1: Sean

Sean is able to identify shots from famous dance works in the Sunday arts section of the newspaper. When he sees a TV ad featuring a famous repertory work, he often knows who choreographed it. He went on a game show and chose "dance" as a category and had the right answer! He takes his wife, who is not a dancer, to live dance concerts because he wants to attend. At the last one he was familiar enough with the repertory listed in the program that he explained to his wife what they were about to see before the program. He knew the genre and the style of dance. He was familiar with the choreographer and some of the circumstances around one of the works. Sean is at home in a dance performance and gets excited about live performances. He can talk about dance well enough that his wife is beginning to understand how to talk about space and shape. They critique the dances. Sean knows how it feels to dance and to create dances, so he always identifies with the performers and appreciates their physicality and artistry.

Snapshot 2: Erica

Erica loves dance. She knows the dance cornerstones and is still involved in dance as a young adult from four perspectives. She is articulate in each artistic process. When she speaks about dance she uses a dance vocabulary and finds that the dance elements help her grasp dancing skills and also describe about dance. When she performs you can tell she expresses her idea by bodythinking. When she composes she uses the principles of design to keep her works balanced and artful. After she studied a number of great works in different dance styles and genres, she realized she particularly likes dances of other cultures. She attends dance performances every chance she gets and takes her friends with her. They enjoy discussing their perceptions about the artistic quality of dances.

Snapshot 3: Eduardo

Eduardo recognized a poster of Alvin Ailey's *Revelations* as he walked into a building downtown. He also recalled Donald McKayle's *Rainbow 'Round My Shoulder* when reading a social commentary on the criminal justice system. Eduardo's interest in the arts of other cultures leads him to see dance from as many parts of the world as are available to him. When watching a documentary film about the coil technique used by Australian Aborigines that sends them springing into the air, he recalled learning to jump for height by using deep pliés when he studied dance in school. He knows what springing into the air feels like. He recalls creating dance expressions and appreciates what the choreographic process entails. He is familiar with the dance elements and can talk about dance in those terms but is not so comfortable with the principles of design. He usually feels more comfortable talking about the quality of the dancer's dancing than he does about the choreographic design of a work.

---

context by integrating the main aspects of dance. This system helps students achieve artistic results while also meeting or exceeding national standards in dance. It is not the only effective approach, but it is one that emphasizes artistic results.

Be sure each student assumes four dance viewpoints within each dance unit of study—moving between them multiple times during one unit and even one lesson. As we look at the sample integrated units of study in chapter 14 and the next section of this chapter, notice how the student fluently moves back and forth between being

- dancer–performer,
- choreographer,
- dance historian–anthropologist, and
- dance critic.

Literacy in dance combines the understanding of dance as an art form with skills acquired through the artistic processes.

To fail to assume all viewpoints renders the student's education incomplete and contextually void.

Neither the complexities of dance nor the expansiveness of the K-12 curriculum reduces itself to only one lesson format. There are many ways to deliver lessons. Use a variety of methods to keep instruction fresh and concepts organically connected according to the emphasis of each unit and according to students' age and stage of development. Technique classes for middle and high school levels are wonderful places to integrate tidbits from works, such as a short viewing slice. It is excellent when dance lessons follow an integrated format. In the case of fully integrated lessons, you should know about one that positively impacts artistic fluency: the Eight-Step Plan.

The Eight-Step Plan (8SP) and its miniature version, the Five-Step Plan (5SP), are two instructional formats that integrate creating, performing, and responding (c/p/r). Whereas the Eight-Step Plan is a model for individual lessons within a unit of study, it is equally effective stretched over several class periods. It is also elastic enough to stretch across an entire unit. (The 5SP, however, is designed specifically to integrate content and methods within the time frame of a lesson.) In whatever time frame you apply the 8SP, it is necessary to stress the artistic and aesthetic quality of each step.

The Eight-Step Plan is an active learning model. It shifts the learner's perspective from one viewpoint to another during the lesson (i.e., critic, dancer, historian, choreographer). Thus it uses all cornerstones. It is predicated on dancing and being in motion as much of the learning time as possible. Study the 8SP carefully to get the full impact of how the segments interact. Let's first look at the full 8SP.

Before and After the Eight-Step Plan

Plan the lesson's opening and closing. Start all lessons with an introduction to announce the main topic of the lesson and synopsize what students are expected to accomplish. Let the introduction set the tone for expected artistic output. Select a hook that draws the class into the lesson's main topic (such as having large cutout Labanotation directional symbols that signify different directions to introduce the lesson's main topic: direction). Likewise, design a conclusion so students recall and relate what was learned in that lesson to what is already known. This is the time to re-emphasize the artistic objectives of the lesson, and it can include assessments. Start every lesson with an introduction and end it with a conclusion—they are constant. Between them resides the flexible and adaptable Eight-Step Plan.

Introduction: Always give students at the opening of class the main information that focuses their participation in the lesson. Include at least three pieces of information about the lesson:

- Main topic
- Objectives
- Standards

Conclusion: Always give students class closure activities that deepen learning. These activities move the day's experiences into long-term memory. They help students see relationships and make sense of what they learned. They put what was learned (part) into a context (whole). Closure activities are usually reflection activities as described in chapter 9. They may also include informal assessments. However, the three main reflection activities are the 3 Rs: *review, reflect, relate*. Ask questions such as these:

- Review—"What did you learn about [select the main topics] today?" (WDYL)
- Reflect—"Why is *that* important to know how to do?" (Reflections may also be a way to open as well as close a lesson. They are useful during class as well.)
- Relate—"How does what you did in class today relate to. . . ?"

Eight-Step Lesson Format

The Eight-Step Plan incorporates all four cornerstones and artistic processes into an integrated lesson format. It uses creative and critical thinking in six of the eight steps. An 8SP is a "during class" delivery model of instruction. These are the eight steps:

= INTRODUCE IT =

1. Explore It   (C1, C2)
2. View It   (C3, C4)
3. Compose It   (C2, C1)
4. Show It   (C1)

5. Analyze It   (C4)
6. Refine It   (C1, C2, C4)
7. Perform It   (C1)
8. Critique It   (C4)

= REFLECT ON IT =
(OR OTHER SUITABLE CLOSURE)

Figure 13.3 shows how the eight steps are generally ordered to positively impact artistic growth and to promote NSDEs 1 through 7. (Other orders are also listed later.) The figure also demonstrates how the steps enroll students in the different artistic processes and what is at play as you use the 8SP. Note: "Perform It" loosely translates to "dancing." It refers not only to performance of dances but also to technique classes and any time one is dancing a dance.

Try to alternate action and nonaction segments of a lesson to modulate the energy of the class. The 8SP switches between fine- and gross-motor movement segments, so once students warm up for activity, they should not sit too long. Use the brief inactive segments to rest the student for the vigorous work in Steps 1, 3, 4, and 7.

The eight steps are a concrete way to see that you're integrating experiences. As we look at varying the order, note that the duration of the steps varies widely. One step may last 20 minutes and the next only 3 minutes.

Varying an Eight-Step Lesson

Organization is good, but not rigidity. There is no point to rigidly controlling the creative process of lesson planning. This is not a canned prescription. That would diminish the very aesthetic process you are working to create.

The Eight-Step Plan is in fact a mix-and-match process. It identifies the ingredients but not the exact recipe. A recipe would take the same ingredients and get the same results every time. That would be "cookie cutter!" This process is more fluid and creative than that. It relies on your knowledge of dance and instruction. Use your imagination to design each triad unit based on your learning objectives in different ways, with different entry points for different units. Also design daily lessons that vary the entry points.

= Introduce It =

When	What	How	Processes	Viewpoint	Thinking	Artistic process	BEGINNING STUDENTS	MORE EXPERIENCED STUDENTS
1	**Explore It**	Create	Explore and embody concept	Dancer (C1, C2)	Creative thinking	Creating		
2	**View It**	Respond	Observe and analyze	Historian and critic (C3, C4)	Critical thinking	Responding and knowing about		
3	**Compose It**	Create	Compose	Choreographer (C2)	Creative thinking	Creating		
4	**Show It**	Perform	Perform Observe	Dancer and then critic (C1, C4)	Critical thinking, bodythinking	Performing		
5	**Analyze It**	Respond	Receive feedback Give feedback	Choreographer and then critic (C2, C4)	Critical thinking	Responding		
6	**Refine It**	Create	Edit and refine	Choreographer, critic, and dancer (C2, C3, C4)	Critical and creative thinking	Creating		
7	**Perform It**	Perform	Perform Observe	Dancer and then critic (C1, C4)	Critical thinking, bodythinking	Performing		
8	**Critique It**	Respond	Critique and evaluate	Critic (C4)	Critical thinking	Responding		

= Reflect on It =

FIGURE 13.3   The Eight-Step Plan incorporates all cornerstones and artistic processes into an integrated lesson format. It alternates between convergent and divergent processes.

Although the order of the eight steps changes, all are present. They contain all necessary ingredients for a complete lesson (and unit) without prescribing which order the steps come in. The 8SP is flexible enough to adapt to different needs. Although it is primarily the format for a lesson, cut it back for beginners or expand it into more than one lesson. Think of it as a very effective lesson (and unit) structure to move students toward dance fluency.

Because not all lessons have a creative activity that needs to be refined and performed, the 5SP is quite often useful.

Using the First Five Steps for Beginners

There are numerous applications for the 5SP. Let's look at a few. First, to introduce students to integrated lessons, use no more than the first five steps. As soon as a 5SP is comfortable, work your way up to the full 8SP as needed with groups above second grade. Both increase the lesson's aesthetic impact and sharpen critical thinking skills.

Introduce beginners to the 8SP through an abbreviated 5SP. Return to figure 13.3 to notice that the first five steps are listed for beginners. This works for all ages of beginners.

Also use the 5SP for advanced students who need to spend more time in depth on a step. The fewer the steps, the more time you have to work on one single aspect of the lesson. The 5SP, however, is crucial for creative dance in kindergarten through grade 5.

Structuring a Creative Dance Class (K-5)

Refer to the detailed Five-Step Plan for creative dance in chapter 7. 5SP is the basic format for creative dance. However, you may incorporate an 8SP on occasion by adding opportunities to view again, to give peer feedback, and to rework and perform creations again for grades 3 through 5.

Increase the complexity of subject matter and number of steps as you advance grade levels. Include the kin-aesthetic, aesthetic, thinking and processing, emotional, and social aspects of the educational experience (see chapter 4) during instruction. Use the 5SP to move students through the stages of progression in each of these. Emphasize the dance elements to increase dance literacy and solidify student understanding of the fundamentals of movement.

- *Introduce the main topic:* Identify the topic, objectives, and standards. Teach vocabulary for the lesson—for example, an element such as Levels: (Space). Set up the lesson's outcomes and expectations.

- *Step 1—Explore It:* Use guided exploration: Explore the main topic, for example, Levels: (Space), and use other elements as helpers to support exploring the main topic.

- *Step 2—View It:* Introduce an example: Select a slice of dance that exemplifies artistic use of levels. Identify it and introduce it to the students. Guide their viewing with at least one, but usually no more than three, guided viewing questions prior to viewing. Use the same questions as follow-up at the end of the slice (e.g., "Where do you see examples of level changes that are unexpected?" "Where does level change add interest to the dance?").

- *Step 3—Compose It:* Conduct the dance-making phase: Select and order movement into repeatable patterns (e.g., select from one's exploration the captivating movements that may be structured into a dance sentence with a beginning, middle, and end) or into structured improvisations.

- *Step 4—Show It:* Have students show the dance: They perform the work for facilitated peer critique and comment. Use this time to teach students how to see dance and how to read it. Use the earliest steps of the Lerman process when students are ready.

- *Step 5—Evaluate It:* Conduct the critiquing phase: Students receive aesthetic feedback from peers and teachers (e.g., pointing out effective use of levels in space and what was most memorable).

- *Reflection activity as closure:* Use the 3 Rs (reflect, review, and relate) to respond to the impact of the lesson and its value. It is a time for informal assessments, occasional in-class journaling, and other deepening activities.

Vary the 5SP when you need to increase student artistic output. Why not substitute feedback and refinement to increase artistry one day when you don't use a viewing sample? Substitute and rearrange any of the eight steps to use as a 5SP. For example, after Introduce It (introduce the main element and the learning objectives), you could use these steps:

1. Guided exploration step (Explore It)
2. Dance-making step (Compose It)
3. Editing and refining step (Refine It)
4. Performance step (Perform It)
5. Critique step (Critique It)

Applying the Five-Step Plan With Older Beginners (Grades 6-12)

Because all schools don't yet have uninterrupted K-12 dance programs, you can't predict the age of your beginners. You may be asked to begin at kindergarten and stop at grade 5 or you may start at grade 6 and go through high school. Your beginners may be taller than you are. So whatever age they are, start them with a 5SP and gradually add steps and content complexity until you work them into a full 8SP.

Use the Five-Step Plan   The amount of time you have dictates how you use the 5SP. Daily class schedule determines how many steps you can productively use for one lesson. For short schedules—such as 40-minute classes—you may need to stretch the five steps across two lessons. Take advantage of each step to maximize learning and achieve objectives.

Use Inquiry   Emphasize inquiry at each step. Occasionally start a lesson with an introductory question. Let questions help you personalize instruction as well as pique interest and focus attention on a topic. Use reflection questions at any point during the 5SP to increase personal investment and critical thinking. Include the essential reflection question, "What did you learn today?" or WDYL.

Use Aesthetic Context   Emphasize aesthetics in all five steps (and the 8SP also for that matter) so students grow artistically. Raise standards by keeping high-quality models in front of your students. Select dance works with care so the content is useful and the works motivate students to improve their dancing skills and literacy. As we have said, to base a unit on a master work enables you to go in many different directions within one aesthetic context. Some units use 5SPs and culminate with an 8SP so as to edit and refine the creative product at the end of the unit. Some units have only one point at which the 8SP is aesthetically viable.

Make Lessons Sequential   Once a skill is introduced, reuse it in different ways to extend it. Also use the skill as a support to another main topic. For example, after bodyshaping is introduced and understood, use it as a criterion in dances on other featured elements. That is a way to build skill on skill. Arrange lessons according to their level of complexity, and start from known skills and move to new skills.

Using the Five-Step Plan for Complex Subjects

The 5SP serves more complex subjects that need in-depth work in one artistic process (c/p/r). For instance, when students begin to make longer and more complex compositions, the students need the better part of a class period to complete and refine their compositions. Then use only a short amount of time to get feedback on the work to refine it. Show It and Refine It (two steps) can be handled informally one on one with partners or within the choreographic grouping. That portion may only last 5 minutes of the class period. In that case, use Compose It for most of the class period with time at the end to add Analyze It, Refine It, Perform It,

and Critique It—or any of the steps that serve the purpose. In some cases, you may delay the performance while students continue to refine the product the next day. Don't be constricted by the format; make it work for you. Mix and match the steps to achieve what you set out to accomplish.

Unfamiliar subjects that need longer explanations or a longer opportunity to see a viewing sample use the 5SP. For example, a sample unit you will build in chapter 14 on Bharata Natyam uses five-step lessons because the style and subject are less familiar. That is not to say that all unfamiliar topics need a 5SP instead of an 8SP.

A straight technique class, as was noted, is not an integrated lesson, so neither the 5SP nor 8SP is used. However, the mindset of an integrated lesson can and should be brought into technique class so you take every opportunity to cross-reference dancing and performing to the other artistic processes.

Using Different Points of Entry for the Eight-Step Plan

Use different artistic processes as points of entry for different units and lessons: creating, responding, and performing, as shown in figure 13.4. Rearrange the 8SP according to the unit by varying it as needed. It is not rigid. Note repeat signs (i.e., the arrows) at places where you may find it beneficial to repeat steps to get more refinement of creative work according to developmental stage.

When you start with "performing" by learning a sequence that is not your own choreography—for instance, phrases from a repertory or a master dance work—teach them straight out (after warm-up). The idea is to have some creative activity that either enhances or adds to the length of the original sequences. The "performing" start has many ways to incorporate creating and responding. Let your objectives and your imagination lead you.

Using Different Points of Emphasis

Unit objectives determine the points of emphasis. Some units do more with creating than others. Some do more with performing. Others delve into a dance work for technique and choreographic stimulus and to build context. In any case, the point of emphasis needs an aesthetic connection. Emphases should also vary so students advance each artistic process.

The culmination of a unit (its high point) can also dictate where you start in order to end up at the right place. For example, you may wish to save viewing

When You Start With Creating

= Introduce It =

Explore It

View It

Analyze It

Compose It

Show It

Refine It

Perform It

Critique It

= Reflect on It =

When You Start With Responding

= Introduce It =

View It		View It
Analyze It		Explore It
Explore It		Compose It
Compose It	or	Show It
Show It		Analyze It
Refine It		Refine It
Perform It		Perform It
Critique It		Critique It

= Reflect on It =

When You Start With Performing

= Introduce It =

Show It

Analyze It

Refine It

Perform It

Critique It

View It

Explore It

Compose It

= Reflect on It =

FIGURE 13.4 Vary the way you use the 8SP so you have different creating–responding–performing points of entry and different class formats.

the entire dance work that is the focal point of the unit until you have finished several lessons that feature various aspects of the choreography. Each lesson may view a different slice of the dance work, unpack it, and use it for stimulus for creating dances in that lesson so that by the end of the unit students are very familiar with parts of the work. The culminating lesson may be the big performance. In this case you work backward to the grand finale.

Stretching the Eight-Step Plan to a Unit

Because the 8SP integrates the artistic processes, it can easily stretch to help you shape a whole unit. Whether it is a unit plan or an individual lesson plan, rearrange the steps to emphasize a point or better relate it. The objectives drive how you use the 8SP.

Just like individual lessons, unit points of emphasis and unit points of entry vary. The point of entry into one unit may be performing and in the next responding. To keep instruction organic and fresh, change the order, the emphases, and entry points. When a topic needs it, use the 8SP as a unit format so separate lessons focus on just one process (step).

The next chapter develops sample units of five sequential lessons. They demonstrate how the 8SP stretches the cornerstones (content) and methods of inquiry (instruction) into a unit. (The sample lessons demonstrate both the 8SP and 5SP.)

To stretch the steps of an 8SP into a unit plan, review and incorporate these aspects:

- Content and methods of inquiry from all four cornerstones (chapters 6-9)
- Embedded performance assessments (chapter 12)
- Objectives and achievement standards (chapter 12)
- Triad unit plan (content, instruction, and assessment) (chapter 12)
- Inquiry (chapter 5)
- Critical and creative thinking (HOTS) (chapter 4)
- Aesthetic context (chapter 1)
- Dance literacy and fluency (chapter 13)

The 8SP emphasizes the artistic processes in the context of a lesson. It is rooted in the dance cornerstones, which link dance in the present to dance in the past (through history) and the future (through creating). There is value, too, in linking dance to nondance concepts when they enhance dance, enlarge one's general education, place the art of dance in a broad context, or achieve a combination of these.

Using the Eight-Step Plan to Increase Student Attention

To build on the concepts in chapter 4 about increasing cognitive function, let's apply brain development research (cognitive) to the specific instructional strategies we use in our classroom to increase a child's ability to learn. Dr. Bruce Perry explains in his article, "How the Brain Learns Best," three neural responses in children that affect their ability to learn:

1. attention
2. the need for context
3. the brain's novelty-seeking property

He also describes how to bring about all three. Teachers who cause children to activate different kinds of neural responses in the brain during one lesson, rather than continue to do the same kind of activity, get better results. Using different neural responses not only helps them pay attention but also increases overall brain function. Such brain research seems to support

- having multiple learning objectives within a single lesson,
- integrating different types of activity around a topic during a lesson,
- engaging students in inquiry, and
- using integrated, contextual lessons, such as the 8SP and 5SP.

Attention

Have you wondered why students lose concentration? Our brains tire easily with one kind of task and become less efficient. If we start, stop, and reset, we learn better.

> Attention is mediated by specific parts of the brain. Yet, neural systems fatigue quickly, actually within minutes. With three to five minutes of sustained activity neurons become "less responsive"; they need a rest (not unlike your muscles when you lift weights). They can recover in minutes, too, but when they are stimulated in a sustained way, they just are not as efficient. (Perry 2005b)

Need for Context

Rather than continue one kind of learning, shift gears but retain context. Thus, as we shift to different sets of neural responders to give them all a workout, we must do so around a topic that holds the different aspects together. "Facts are empty without being linked to context and concepts" (Perry 2005b). When a child listens to you give a fact, "she uses one neural system (call it A). When she is told about a concept related to that fact . . . a functionally interconnected neural set (B) is used. When she listens to a vignette . . . yet other related neural systems are active (C and D)" (Perry 2005b). This points to the need to change the kind of activity and mode of learning within a context, such as the 8SP does around a theme or great work.

Novelty-Seeking Property

Continually shifting gears within one lesson keeps students alert and on task. This minimizes the likelihood of misbehavior and promotes learning quality and artistic development. One more reason to integrate learning and shift gears within one lesson is supported by the brain's novelty-seeking property.

It is because one is a better critic that she is a better choreographer and dancer—and vice versa.

When a child is in a familiar and safe situation, as in most of our classrooms, his or her brain will seek novelty. So, if this child hears only factual information, she will fatigue within minutes. Only four to eight minutes of pure factual lecture can be tolerated before the brain seeks other stimuli, either internal (e.g., daydreaming) or external (Who is that walking down the hall?). If the teacher is not providing that novelty, the brain will go elsewhere. Continuous presentation of facts or concepts in isolation or in a nonstop series of anecdotes will all have the same fatiguing effect and the child will not learn as much, nor will she come to anticipate and enjoy learning. (Perry 2005b)

From "How the Brain Learns Best" by Bruce Perry, from Scholastic.com. Copyright © 2005 by Scholastic Inc. Adapted by permission of Scholastic Inc.

Zigzag Learning

This brain function research seems to support integrated lessons that call on the different artistic processes because integrated lessons incorporate all three items that Dr. Perry describes: They shift brain gears within lessons, build context around a theme or topic, and offer novelty through changing activities. This research seems to support what the arts do so well—nonlinear learning that is interconnected and organic.

> The most effective presentation must move back and forth through these interrelated neural systems, weaving them together. These areas are interconnected under usual circumstances, like a complete "workout" in the gym where we rotate from one station to another. Similarly, in teaching, it is most effective to work one neural area and then move on to another. (Perry 2005b)

Perry calls this "bob and weave" teaching. I call it "zigzag learning" with the 8SP.

From "How the Brain Learns Best" by Bruce Perry, from Scholastic.com. Copyright © 2005 by Scholastic Inc. Adapted by permission of Scholastic Inc.

Questions to Ponder

1. Which is better for aesthetic education: isolating or integrating cornerstones? Why?

2. How do creating, performing, and responding artistically relate to each other?

3. What does it mean to build contextual coherence? What are ways to integrate a unit of study?

4. Where are the natural connections between the cornerstones? The artistic processes?

5. How does this information add to or reshape your Statements of Belief (as explained in the Introduction)?

6. How does the 8SP carry national standards forward? How does the 8SP carry dance fluency forward?

7. How does the 5SP prepare beginners to move into an 8SP?

8. How does the 8SP keep students changing roles within the course of one class (dancer, choreographer, critic, dance historian–anthropologist)? How does the 8SP integrate exemplary works into daily or weekly study? How does the 8SP carry your internal objectives forward?

Rich Resources

- *Wild Child Resource Pack* integrates creating, performing, and responding around a Ludus Dance Company choreography, *Wild Child*. It is one of the most substantive and contextual on the market. Available in CD-ROM. See chapter 11 for more information or go online to http://bedfordi.20m.com.

Creating a Unit of Study Using an Arts Education Perspective

**"Skills
. . . are not
ends in themselves.
They are the means
for understanding human
purpose and creating new
visions of it."**

—Brent Wilson (1997, p. 12)

This chapter helps you create your own units of study with an aesthetic emphasis. It also presents one detailed model unit designed around a triad unit plan. This unit of study demonstrates how all the cornerstones interact to increase dance fluency. You examine the unit objectives that are accomplished. The Eight-Step and Five-Step Plans are used to break the unit into objectives-driven, standards-oriented lessons. You learn how to design units for contextual coherence.

Creating an Integrated Unit of Study

Units are groups of related lessons that address common objectives. They focus learning experiences on an important focal point (or topic) in dance. Most topics come from the dance cornerstones, such as a dance style, a theme, choreographic work, or a combination (e.g., a choreographic work in a particular dance style). It is up to you to cluster related lessons around the topic to ensure coherence to the unit.

Conceptualize the unit first. Let goals and learning objectives (which incorporate achievement

As you plan, remember that it is the child who is the beneficiary of your careful planning and instructional delivery.

standards) drive the design of your unit. Think of the whole (unit) before you consider its parts (lessons). To conceptualize a unit is a global, not a linear, process. You want to end up with a cohesive unit.

Next, you'll construct the unit. You will need to adequately construct units so students incorporate all the artistic processes (c/p/r) and integrate all methods of inquiry within it. This is where you put the triad unit plan to work for you. As you plan backward,

1. identify desired results (objectives—in all artistic processes),

2. determine acceptable evidence (assessments—in all artistic processes), and

3. plan learning experiences (instruction—in all artistic processes).

Also keep in mind that your unit is rooted in your annual long-range plan (LRP). See figure 14.1. Translate your LRP goals and the national content standards into unit objectives. Then translate all unit objectives (whole) into various lessons (parts) in the unit. Lessons deliver well-designed experiences so students accomplish all of the unit's objectives and achievement standards. When you finish, all objectives will have assessments and instructional strategies designed to accomplish them. (At the end of the year, all units will combine to have achieved the goals and objectives of your LRP, which advance enduring understanding in dance.)

Write unit objectives in measurable language. (And write them in language students can understand.) Then determine the acceptable evidence or criteria that describe success. Use verbs from Bloom's taxonomy to write measurable objectives: "The student will + verb + criteria" (see chapter 9). Formally assess students as part of each unit, not in every lesson. Informally assess students all the time.

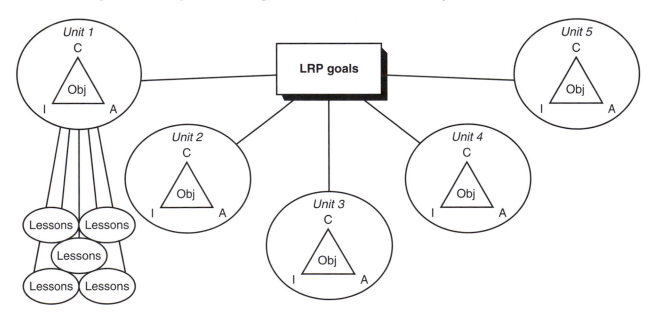

FIGURE 14.1 Goals drive long-range plans (LRP), objectives drive units, and unit objectives are divided to drive individual lessons. Mobilize the triad of curriculum (C), assessments (A), and instruction (I) through your lessons.

Relating Units to Lessons

Educational goals are best met by organizing curriculum into units rather than teaching a series of isolated and unrelated lessons. This builds context into study. Contextually coherent units and lessons relate aspects of the dance cornerstones to each other and to the world beyond. In both cases, it is crucial for you to state the parallels and make the connections clear so students don't miss them. Don't assume students automatically see the connection. By calling attention to connections, you teach students to look for connections, which steadily improves their ability to see relationships and link experiences for themselves. Over time their being able to establish the relationships between units builds perspective in dance. An occasional isolated lesson is still appropriate for special opportunities (e.g., a master class, an introductory class on motif writing or somatics that will be applied in later units). Even these isolated classes will eventually contribute to the larger context during the semester or year as you apply the learned information.

We are less about giving students isolated and unrelated enrichment experiences than we are about giving them skills in and perspectives on dance. That's why you must set out to accomplish all unit objectives through the unit's lessons. List all unit objectives as you write your plans and work backward so you design instruction and assessments to accomplish them. Base units around concept clusters or related ideas that move multiple objectives forward. Base lessons around instruction that accomplishes multiple objectives with one task.

Lesson Sequence Within a Unit

Sequence lessons to build new skills on old. Build skill on skill. Use existing skills to strengthen and develop students as well as to provide the foundation on which to build new skills. Skills are not developed in isolation one at a time. They are used and refined in subsequent lessons so there is steady growth. Structure lessons so all unit objectives and skills are realized through the combined lessons. Sequence lessons so they cumulatively build all the skills named in the unit objectives.

There is no magic number of lessons in a unit: Some units are as short as 3 lessons and others as long as 12 depending on the scope of the unit and the amount of school time allocated to dance instruction. Most are typically between 5 and 7 lessons (i.e., class periods). Because each lesson takes part of the unit objectives forward, it also contributes

to achieving the goals of the LRP. Figure 14.2 shows how the national standards affect this process.

Enjoy translating unit plans into action through your lessons. Break the whole (units) down into parts (lessons) that enliven the topic and translate the objectives into substantive experiences. Let unit objectives lead the way because they specify what students are to know and do as a result of the unit, and thus you are accountable to achieve these objectives.

Use the Five-Step and Eight-Step Plans (see chapter 13) for as many lessons as you can, and for others, incorporate aspects of the eight steps. Design units by the triad (see chapter 12). Embed assessment and use rubrics as much to inform and deepen learning as to evaluate during the critical thinking steps (i.e., Analyze It, Critique It). The 8SP puts all the cornerstone methods of inquiry into one lesson when productive. In any case, integrate them into the unit. Employ particular steps of the 8SP that serve the lesson's points of emphasis. Figure 14.3 depicts how individual lessons from several consecutive units might vary content, and thus instruction, to emphasize particular cornerstones or artistic processes to achieve desired objectives. A standards-oriented curriculum thus plays out day by day, varies lesson by lesson, takes different points of entry, and features different points of emphasis—all to carry out the long-range vision (LRP goals). Note: Formal critique is not a part of every lesson but part of every unit.

Unit Sequence

Sequence units to relate one to another and order them in a way that systematically builds skills and experiences for coherence. This makes study relevant rather than random. It is less important how many skills you teach than what students learn and use. Set out to order units in such a way as to reinforce concepts from earlier units. See the framework in chapters 6 through 9 to see how concepts develop.

One exception is at the kindergarten through second grade level, where emphasis is on building a foundation in the dance elements (BSTERs) through creative dance. At this foundation stage, students are learning the basic elements and vocabulary (kinetic and conceptual) of dance. Lessons are grouped in the context of learning these building blocks of dance, which takes longer than a normal unit. For example, an expanded unit, "Learning and Exploring the Dance Elements," could span a large part of the curriculum at the outset. Because such a unit lays the foundation in the kindergarten

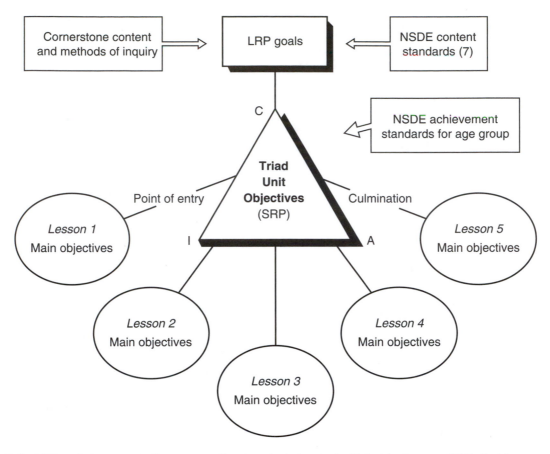

FIGURE 14.2 LRP goals incorporate the seven national content standards. Unit objectives are SRPs that incorporate external achievement standards; therefore, assessments in the triad unit plan measure what students know and do according to the internal objectives and external standards.

through second grade curriculum, it should be seen as a pivotal developmental process for the remaining school years.

Keep your educational priorities in mind: The highest priority is to emphasize dance's mega-ideas and concepts that increase enduring understanding. The second priority is to teach the most important skills and concepts from each unit. The last is to include interesting facts and details that flesh out the topic and enliven the unit. Refer to figure 12.3 to recall the three curriculum layers according to priority. As you begin to plan units, use these priorities to help you weight or emphasize areas of importance so as not to get lost in the fascinating details of the unit and overemphasize them. Follow the arrows in figure 14.4 to see how the details and supporting information (outer ring) support the main ideas of each unit (middle ring). They, in turn, support lasting learning in dance (inner ring). Have your unit plans reflect the priorities. By the end of a unit you will have accomplished all three and measured accomplishment accordingly.

Merging the Cornerstones in a Unit

How does integrated study benefit students? It increases dance literacy every time a choreographic work (including current artistic choreography) is introduced and incorporated as an illustration of

- theme (such as transformation),
- a certain dance style (such as modern dance),
- a historical period or place (such as early 20th-century United States),
- technique, or
- a work of dance art to critique and appreciate.

The work itself may be a minor part of a unit or the unit's point of emphasis. Either way those unfamiliar with dance get to see skilled dancers perform choreography. The work models how to dance and perform and shows dance as art communicating meaning. It gives something of aesthetic value to critique (e.g., choreography, performance quality).

422

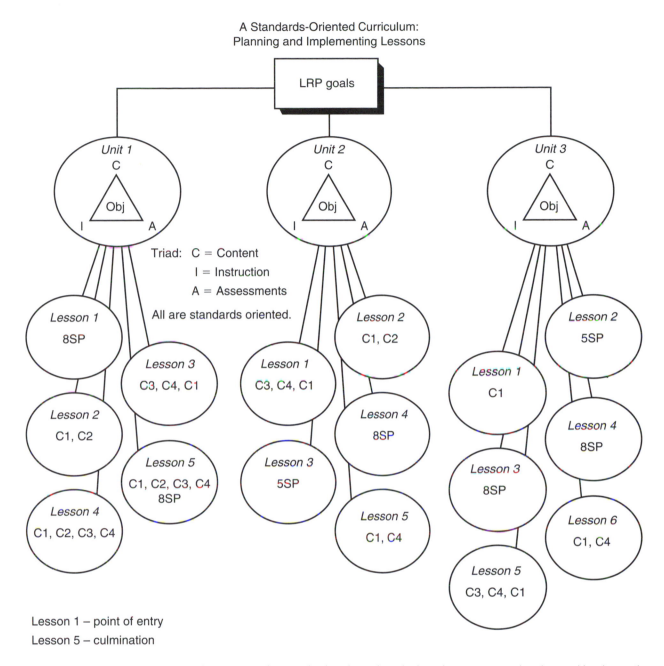

A Standards-Oriented Curriculum:
Planning and Implementing Lessons

LRP goals

Unit 1
C
Obj
I A

Unit 2
C
Obj
I A

Unit 3
C
Obj
I A

Triad: C = Content
I = Instruction
A = Assessments
All are standards oriented.

Lesson 1
8SP

Lesson 3
C3, C4, C1

Lesson 2
C1, C2

Lesson 5
C1, C2, C3, C4
8SP

Lesson 4
C1, C2, C3, C4

Lesson 2
C1, C2

Lesson 1
C3, C4, C1

Lesson 4
8SP

Lesson 3
5SP

Lesson 5
C1, C4

Lesson 2
5SP

Lesson 1
C1

Lesson 4
8SP

Lesson 3
8SP

Lesson 6
C1, C4

Lesson 5
C3, C4, C1

Lesson 1 – point of entry
Lesson 5 – culmination

FIGURE 14.3   This diagram shows the context of a standards-oriented curriculum that supports planning and implementing lessons.

Thereby, the work relates responding to creating and performing. It models choreographic structure and shows how movements are put together for motional, visual, and aural coherence. It shows a complete composition that is artfully designed.

The resulting familiarity with works permits students to gain a point of view about dance. Familiarity equips them to relate works to each other and to even compare different works by one choreographer. This broad knowledge shows the scope and depth of the lexicon of dance. Over time students grasp outside references made to dance much as they would in music, theatre, or art. This translates into enduring awareness and understanding.

Around a Theme: Theme-Based Units

As you learned in chapter 13, there are numerous thematic approaches to a unit. Any cornerstone will do—there is no best place to start; just pick the best one for that particular unit. Try not to overuse any one entry point. Integrate such that units, tallied one

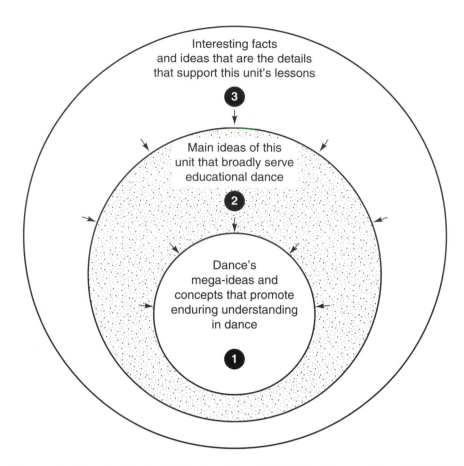

FIGURE 14.4   Develop a unit with educational priorities in mind so all details in (3) serve (2) and (1). (1) Highest: mega-ideas in dance (goals and content standards); (2) Important: big ideas of this topic (learning objectives and achievement standards); (3) Good: supporting information (various stylistic, historic facts, people involved).

on the other, result in a broadly educated dancing student. See "Points of Entry" in chapter 13 (page 407) for two examples of theme-based units: Polyrhythms and Tall Tales of the Wild West.

For example, if your objective is to use the dance elements to create and communicate meaning, your entry point might be creating and composing around the topic of water. First explore various ways to move while either in or beside a body of water (imaginary water): splashing, pouring, wading, rippling, swirling, floating. Explore each concept first as an improvisational problem and then shape it into a simply structured choreography.

After the compositional project is under way, show how one (or more) choreographers took that theme or topic to inspire a dance. To culminate the unit, view Ailey's "Wading in the Water" (from *Revelations*) to see how the images of water are expressed (i.e., inquire into the same concepts as the exploration). Notice also the stylized walks representing wading in the water and the water's characteristic waves through the undulations. Compare the work to Doris Humphrey's *Water Study* and other

works of artistic interest. Teach the Middle Eastern folk dance, "Mayim, Mayim" ("water, water"), learn about the dance's cultural origins, and examine the motions that express the waves (forward and back), circling around the oasis, and swishing water with

MAYIM, MAYIM
V-SHAV-TEM MAYIM BI-SA-SON
MI-MA-YI-WEY HA-Y'SHU-AH
:\:
MA-YIM, MA-YIM, MA-YIM, MA-YIM
V-MA-YIM BI-SA-SON
:\:
HEY! HEY! HEY! HEY!
MAYIM, MAYIM, MAYIM, MAYIM,
MAYIM, MAYIM BI-SA-SON
:\:

FIGURE 14.5   Teach the words to "Mayim, Mayim" so students can sing with the music, then self-accompany.

424

your toe. Sing the Mayim song to self-accompany the dance. See figure 14.5. Explore Gene Kelly's soft-shoe dance in *Singing in the Rain* and perhaps use it as a bridge to a later unit on tap dance.

Around a Dance Style: Style-Based Units

Integrated units created around a dance style use the style to build context. Select a number of examples of performance works to demonstrate the style so older students know what it looks like and what its artistic range is. Unless there are viewing samples, a stylistic study is shallow. To critique professional quality gives a context for learning and trying on the style. Integrate C1, C2, C3, and C4.

Example 1: Jazz Dance

This example includes valuable insights about jazz dance from Pat Cohen (NYU) and Karen Hubbard (UNC-Charlotte).

If one objective for high school is to learn different styles of a 20th-century American dance form, you can investigate jazz dance (and music) as a rhythmic form with many styles. If your point of emphasis in this unit is C4—analyzing and critiquing—investigate jazz from a movement point of view so you "try jazz on" in the studio (C1):

- Fully explore the West African roots of jazz.
- Focus on the Africanist elements basic to jazz: lowered center of gravity, isolated body parts working in polyrhythms (syncopation), polyrhythms, spinal alignment forward or vertical, pushing the rhythm, articulated spine and limbs, the "swing" quality (release energy into and retrieve it from the earth), use of the circle, interaction and exchange of energy between dancers and musicians, improvisation (putting one's individual touch on a movement, embellishing it), expressing the uniqueness of how the individual embraces values of the culture, the "aesthetic of the cool" (laid back with a sense of urgency), the "get-down" quality with the pelvis engaged, vocalization.
- Explore traditional jazz from the 1920s to 1940s and its vernacular steps (e.g., Suzie Q) and styles (e.g., lindy hop).
- Distinguish between different jazz dance styles (e.g., Fosse) and jazz techniques developed by people like Matt Mattox, Gus Giordano, Luigi, and Lynn Simonson. Learn them.

The unit's entry point might be the Harlem Renaissance. Lead a guided viewing exercise using the section in *Dancing—New Worlds, New Forms* (Program 5) (see Rich Resources), showing 1930s footage at New York's Savoy Ballroom interspersed with commentary by the dancers who were actively involved with the jazz style. Put a video monitor in the studio so you can "view and do." Learn the basic step from the couple dance, the lindy hop. Talk about its improvisational nature, its competitive exuberance, and its connection to the jitterbug. Improvise movements to some of the same swing music you hear on the video in the Savoy Ballroom and invent new moves in the style of the lindy hop. (Do not try the acrobatic moves.)

Explore the Big Apple, the group dance performed in a circular formation that originated among black people in the 1930s in Columbia, South Carolina, at a nightclub called the Big Apple Club (formerly a Jewish synagogue). Explore this dance's use of vernacular vocabulary and how a caller would call out steps like "Shorty George," "Suzie Q," and "truckin'" so the dancers would know which way to go—whether clockwise, counterclockwise, or into the center.

Next look into the different cultural influences on jazz dance, particularly its Africanist elements. There is much to choose from. Discuss the Irish influence on traditional jazz and how black slaves and Irish indentured servants had interactions that resulted in an indigenous U.S. dance form. While essential ingredients of jazz are identifiably West African, aspects of European dance are also evidenced. Sine jazz came from vernacular street dance, see how it was influenced once it came into the studio. See how jazz continues to evolve, who is involved, how it incorporates street moves (hip-hop, break dancing, popping), how it incorporates elements of modern dance, and how it is both codified into recognizable steps yet still retains its improvisatory nature. Identify syncopation in jazz music as a shared characteristic with the dance. Investigate both "hot" and "cool" jazz styles; have students dance both. Teach students to embody the syncopated rhythms and body isolations of jazz (ribs, hips, shoulders, hands) and its emphasis on individual expression. Show how stylistic variations come from the individual dancer. Encourage personal interpreting and embellishment.

Take the study to Broadway, just a short way from Harlem. View samples from several theatrical jazz masters whose styles you want to learn and compare. For example, see excerpts from Bob Fosse's choreography, such as *Damn Yankees, Pippin,* or *Pajama Game.* Trace influences of Jack Cole (early American choreographer who popularized jazz and influenced other 20th-century jazz choreographers besides Fosse), who made an impact on musical theatre of Broadway (stage) and Hollywood (film). View an excerpt from a period sample of early jazz such as Cole's *Kismet* (1955 story of the Arabian Nights) to see how jazz from that period compares with today's. Inquire. "What is jazz? What is necessary?" Find the underlying principles of jazz technique that are basic and constant over time despite stylistic variations. Explore worldwide dance crazes that originated among blacks: Cake Walk (pre-jazz), Charleston, lindy hop, Big Apple.

Identify aspects of jazz style visible in vernacular dance (social dance), musical theatre dance, and concert jazz. Compare three musical theatre and vernacular dances from three decades or periods and take them into the studio. Identify the Africanist elements in all three. For example:

1. Vernacular: lindy hop (Savoy Ballroom of the 1930s and 1940s)
2. Musical theatre: Fosse's Broadway (1950s through 1980s)
3. Vernacular: hip-hop (1990s to 2000)

Take the unit's creative work from these three elements (C3). For example, teach three phrases of 8 counts in one style and then have students compose an additional culminating 8-count phrase to that combination—in the same style—that varies and repeats the movement motifs used in the first three phrases (i.e., PODs variation and repetition). Repeat this process for all three time periods.

To culminate your comparison of jazz styles unit with an embedded performance assessment, teach the class a 24-count sequence that changes levels and facings. Teach it as a straight, unison movement sequence devoid of any stylistic characteristics. After everyone learns the sequence, divide a class into six groups for a creative project.

- Assign each group a number from 1 to 6 to determine the order they will show their work.
- Prepare ahead three cards with the three styles studied in the unit (i.e., one of each).
- Give each student a test sheet numbered 1 to 6 with two columns to answer.

PART 1: GROUP PROCESS FOR BOTH PROFICIENT AND ADVANCED CLASSES (NSDE)

1. Each group draws a card, which is facedown, reads it together, and puts it back, keeping secret which style they drew.

2. Within their group, students collaborate to overlay the original sequence according to the style they drew. They rehearse without music and prepare to show the class.

3. They perform in numerical order. Peers analyze to determine which style and write it on the test sheet's first column. Then they assess the group's performance quality using a 5-point rating scale in the second column. (Students mark their own group with a star in the first column and self-assess their group's performance in the second.)

4. Students swap papers to peer grade. Take this as both a discussion starter and an assessment rolled into one (e.g., "Whose style did Group 1 present?" "Describe the characteristic that led you to that assumption").

5. There may be a controversy over which period a group portrayed, so as you review each group determine if the clarity of the performance (quality number beside the group's name) interfered with the audience recognition or if the audience was not focusing. Some groups may need to perform again to better embody the style (i.e., correction) until it is obvious to the audience. Use peer feedback to help them. Keep the process organic, for what is more important than the test grade is that performers learn to be clear and the audience gives assistance. Everyone grows in the process, so the test is both an instructional aid as well as an assessment. (This is an example of the assessment increasing learning.) To close, add music of the period to each performance and fully perform the sequences for each other.

By the end everyone should have a larger vocabulary for dance (conceptual and kinetic), articulate jazz's basic elements, demonstrate period stylistic characteristics, perform stylistic variations convincingly, and better critique dance.

PART 2: CONTINUATION FOR ADVANCED CLASSES

1. Combine all groups who performed the same style into one group (e.g., all who danced the Fosse style). There are probably three groups.

2. Students take their stylistic versions, which are different creations inspired by the same style. While remaining true to the style, students pool all versions and work out a new

performance in which they take creative license, using these criteria: They make the dance longer and more complex and interesting. They add entrances and exits. They no longer dance in unison. Some students are still while others move (timing) but keep the style intact. The dance must change (a) pathways, (b) directions and facings, and (c) timing of the original. (Give students written choreographic and review criteria.)

3. Culminate with a showing for peer critique using the criteria. Apply critiques by teachers, peers, and students as part of the unit's summative assessment.

Ask students to reflect on what they will remember about this unit. Leave them with an enduring understanding that jazz is an ever-evolving, multidimensional theatrical form based on techniques born in Africa and the Caribbean; leave them with a lasting sense of how it feels to perform, create, embellish, and respond to jazz dance.

Reflect and Respond

Look again at the jazz unit. Identify the different cornerstones to see how they are integrated in the unit. Mark which are C1, C2, C3, C4, or a combination of more than one. How are the cornerstones integrated in that unit?

Example 2: Rhythmic Step Styles If one of your objectives for high school is "to perform a variety of performance styles with an emphasis on rhythmic step patterns," consider comparing three styles, such as tap, flamenco, and kathak. (This could lead to the kathak study suggested in Example 3.) All three emphasize rhythmic footwork and are improvisational within a highly structured movement vocabulary. The point of entry can be the studio exploration of rhythmic patterns. It can start with a teacher-led improvisational warm-up in which you call out rhythmic patterns, such as "slap, clap, stretch, clap, slap, clap, clap (hold)" and additional other rhythmic patterns that change level to get blood flowing and rhythms going. (Slap different body parts for a different sound and specify which ones.) Weave together several objectives in one unit from C1, C2, C3, and C4. Add another objective, "to use the choreographic form, call and response." Then investigate how all three styles use rhythmic call and response. View samples of all three styles

that illustrate call and response. Thus students learn three styles in the studio at their level of readiness (C1), create original calls and response in one or more of the styles (C2), and critique guided viewing samples of all three (C3, C4). Embed peer performance assessments into the instructional strategy for each cornerstone (C4).

Because call and response is integral to all three styles, especially flamenco and kathak, numerous samples demonstrate it. However, there is one mesmerizing clip, in a current video compilation of old musicals (That's Entertainment [Part One]: Classic Musicals), of an a cappella tap dance call and response between the greats Eleanor Powell and Fred Astaire from the film Broadway Melody (1940) that is nothing short of stunning. Not only is it illustrative, but it is worth seeing and critiquing as a genuine aesthetic experience. (See Rich Resources.) Incorporate reflective inquiry with questions such as, "What does this study teach us about the interplay between dance and accompaniment?" "About steady beat and syncopation?" "What does it show us about the necessity of training the body as an artistic instrument of expression?" By the end of the unit, students have broadened their perspective of rhythmic styles across cultures; they have danced, created, and critiqued three different styles; and they have sharpened their ability to respond to intricate rhythms using the body. A unit on rhythmic call and response is a natural springboard into units on other rhythmic styles, such as West African dance and drumming or Irish step dancing, both of which incorporate call and response.

Injured dancers who cannot dance participate in this unit in three ways:

1. They create the rhythmic calls to which the dancers respond.

2. They research the more unfamiliar kathak dance to learn the talas and bols (see Example 3) for calls and responses in this unit.

3. They become the kathak expert to assist you in teaching Example 3.

Example 3: Kathak If one of your objectives for middle or high school is "to demonstrate knowledge and skills in a non-Western performance style," consider introducing kathak, a classical dance of north India with Middle Eastern and Persian influences. It has characteristic fast rhythmic footwork and quick turns and spins. Its origins are with ancient, traveling storytellers called kathaks, so the element of storytelling is present. Another feature is the call and

427

Investigate the roots of jazz dance and its use of Africanist elements.

hand and then transfer them to the feet. Then ask students to respond to the talas as they are called out. (For example, the drummer says, "ta tai tai tai tat, Aa tai tai tat . . ." and then the dancer responds to the pattern.) Next work on turning. Kathak is accentuated by its pirouettes (turns). Teach students to "spot" while turning to maintain balance. Have them add turns to the rhythmic patterns. After students have danced talas and turns, view a kathak dancer performing with drum accompaniment. Use guided viewing questions before viewing, such as the following queries. View both styles—the *tandava* (masculine, vigorous style) and the *lasya* (feminine) style and explain them both. Unpack this predominantly solo dance form. Start with "What do you see?" (aesthetic scanning).

Investigate further the relationship between dancer and musician on stage. Become familiar with the rhythmic exchange. Have students learn particular talas and bols directly from the video and transfer them from sound to body movement as demonstrated. Ask students to isolate different parts of the foot (ball, heel, flat) to articulate the foot for quick rhythmic patterns. Students can learn to execute some of kathak's intricate footwork patterns and several two-dimensional turns around the central axis. Ask students to put these patterns into a repeatable rhythmic pattern at a tempo they can handle. Have students practice several sequences from kathak to show.

Query students:

1. "What do you notice about the two-dimensional verticality (up and down aspect) of kathak?"

2. "Which does this sample seem to be: the tandava (masculine, vigorous style) or the lasya (feminine) style?"

3. "There are two components of kathak—one portrays a story through gestures and the other is pure, abstract movement. The *nritta* is pure dance without storytelling. A*bhinaya* is the kind that is full of expression and storytelling. Which is this one?"

For advanced level classes, dip into the storytelling aspect of the kathak's expressive artistry: abhinaya. Sample abhinaya—the dancer's ability to interpret words set to music or pantomime. Teach how kathak dancers learn traditional stories and characterizations and then express them in a particular stylistic

response between the onstage percussionist and the dancer. Investigate it from the viewpoint of both performers: the drummer and the dancer. Rhythmic dance cadences are central to kathak performance. As soon as one gives the rhythmic cadence the other responds in a game-like fashion—the percussionist plays the talas (rhythmic patterns) and also recites rhythmic bols (rhythmic syllables) as he plays. The dancer attentively listens to it, then tries to produce the same set of bols/talas using her ankle bells. The two exchange rhythmic patterns back and forth (call and response). The result is complex rhythms and dazzling footwork. The dancer's ankle bells add yet another layer of rhythmic accompaniment to accentuate the footwork.

Because kathak emphasizes footwork, the unit's point of entry is for students to listen to kathak's rhythmic syllables and learn to speak them. Make a chart of the basic talas to read and learn. Ask students to first tap out the talas with different parts of the palm of the technique. Learn one of the stories. Contrast kathak with ballet's character dancing. Point out that both men and women perform all the roles—dancing both male and female characters of the stories—so they can pantomime both parts. Investigate how the north Indian kathak's abhinaya has evolved from the early storytellers, has absorbed aspects of the Indo-Persian culture from the north and west, and yet is a product of the north Indian Hindustani cultures of the region (which is different from the south Indian cultures we study in Bharata Natyam). Find different schools of kathak (schools are called *gharana*) that show other cultural influences. View several samples of abhinaya. Incorporate kathak's three other characteristics:

1. Hand gestures are more decorative than expressive, less intricate and precise as the use of *mudras* in other forms of classical Indian dance such as Bharata Natyam, Kuchipudi, and Kathakali (C1).

2. Kathak depicts life based on a continuous flow of movements and therefore seldom stops or is static—like life itself (C1).

3. Highly skilled kathak performers improvise distinctive rhythmic patterns on the spot during a portion of a performance. This is in addition to well-defined and -rehearsed repertory with the drummer (C2).

Use these three ideas to further investigate how kathak is performed: Divide into groups and give each group a different rhythmic structure on which to improvise that features criteria from the dance works observed. Create a short study based on these stylistic attributes. Ask each group to use a percussion instrument to accompany each dance as they show their creation to the class. Compare how the created work is like kathak and how it differs. Use the interest generated in creating, performing, and responding to students' own work to go back and look at other kathak performances. Compare students' dances with other more familiar highly rhythmic dance styles:

a. Rhythmic step patterns in tap dance, stepping, and Irish step dancing

b. Jazz dance's use of improvisation and its close relationship to its accompaniment

c. Bharata Natyam, one of the other classical dance forms of India, which also uses abhinaya but uses a different, more exact set of *hasta*

mudras to pantomime the story and convey its sentiment (This produces a worthy comparison only if students already know Bharata Natyam.)

By the end of the unit, leave students with an enduring understanding of kathak as a rhythmic art form from northern India, after they have seen and analyzed some of the technique, worked with aspects of abhinaya, improvised on the rhythmic cadences of kathak, danced its characteristic movements, and compared it with more familiar dances as a point of context.

Around a Choreographic Work

Organically basing a unit around a masterwork is more rooted in the art of dance than arbitrarily making a list of objectives to try to pull together an aesthetic context. Units around a masterwork automatically have contextual coherence. There is a main aesthetic focal point, because an art work is there to critique as a model. Student inquiry is substantive around a work and its choreographic process. Pick a dynamic choreographic work that students will enjoy and learn from that can serve multiple instructional purposes and achieve numerous internal objectives and external standards.

Deconstructing a Choreographic Work for a Unit

Making a choreographic work central to the unit builds in a strong aesthetic component and increases dance literacy. That is, you first analyze the work and pull out its threads as the basis of your unit. There are so many possibilities within one dance that after you analyze the work, you must determine which aspects to use according to your LRP's goals.

This is an extended example of how to plan a unit with some pointers about the process to start. It builds on the basic process described in chapter 9's "Developing Critical Inquiry Skills" (page 281).

- Analyze a work and take thorough notes on "Thumbnail Sketch of a Dance Work" in appendix B.

- Look at the work several times to uncover what is there: once for the elements of space, again for the elements of time, again for movement themes and structure, again for dance techniques and body articulation, and again for rhythmic aspects and accompaniment.

- File all notes so you can use them later for different teaching purposes.

Analyzing and recording helps you accumulate substantive teaching materials. Plan to return to the information in subsequent units to demonstrate a new point, reinforce an old concept, demonstrate a related point, or compare and contrast. Many students love to revisit works they know.

1. Pick a work that will engage the age level (i.e., a brand-new or a known masterwork). Never choose a work you do not like!

2. Analyze its use of the BSTER elements.

3. Continue to unpack it. Peel off its layers, writing down everything you see in the work. Sit down with the remote control, stop, start again, rewind, replay sections, and list all possibilities. (Save all notes for future reference.)

4. Divide the work into digestible viewing slices. If the work is not structured into short sections, determine where a "learning chunk" starts and stops or where a natural break occurs. It's tricky because the segment has to coincide with both dance phrasing and music phrasing so it holds together. Write the time markers from the DVD or VCR display, title each slice of dance, and make notes about what each section demonstrates. Then you have the slices ready to use for different purposes (e.g., one that features phrases of fast movement each followed by dynamic stillness, another that shows how partners create lines in space, another that shows arm gestures and their development as part of a theme). Number the slices and time them with a stopwatch (e.g., Slice 3: from entrance with props to exit—45 seconds). Because you will use these segments in your units, make good notes to identify each section by length, and describe its movement concepts.

5. Look at the whole dance's artistic impact. Spend focused time getting to know the work as if you were part of it. Enjoy it. Discern what the work has to teach children about the art of dance and find concrete examples to show in class. Write down impressions. Analyze its impact based on how it demonstrates effective principles of design (PODs). Add them to your notes.

6. Create queries. Take your impressions and the comments you wrote and turn them into multiple questions. For example, if your note says, "This slice demonstrates sudden stops and starts, contrasts quick movement and dynamic stillness," rewrite it backward as inquiries so students have the engaging experience of discovering these things on their own:

   > "Q: What two things are contrasted in this section? Where do you see that?"

   > "Q: Are the movements quick or slow? How quick? Where is a dynamic stillness? Where else?"

   > "Q: Are the dancers who are not moving, just stopping their movement as a way into stillness, or are they using dynamic stillness? Describe the difference in how the dancers do that—how is it different from the way you would stop an everyday movement?"

   > "Q: What kind of energy does it take to hold a dynamic stillness?"

   If your note says, "I see a long cloth used as a prop that adds texture to the dance," rewrite it as inquiries:

   > "Q: What kind of textures does the long cloth add? What movements are possible because of the long cloth? Where did you see that?"

   > "Q: What do you think the cloth symbolizes?"

   > "Q: Where else do you see the cloth used in the dance? What does it add there?"

   > "Q: Would this dance work as well without the cloth? What else could be used instead that would be as effective?"

   Ask questions that lead to dance concepts you plan to incorporate into the lessons.

7. Judge what the work has to teach from the viewpoint of the four cornerstones:
   > As a dancer (C1)
   > As a choreographer (C2)
   > As a dance historian–anthropologist (C3)
   > As a dance critic (C4)

8. Turn this information into a triad unit plan (objectives, assessments, instruction). Break

out the unit objectives into lessons. Determine the point of entry into the unit (see figure 14.6).

Deconstructing a work is described as an individual process, but some find it especially satisfying to get together with other dance specialists and unpack a work together. They brainstorm and generate multiple ideas. Consider forming a cohort group that keeps a lookout for videos and DVDs that would be useful in the classroom. Meet every month to share videos and DVDs and unpack one (or more) as a group.

Why Are Choreographic Works Necessary to Units?

To take an arts education perspective is to familiarize students with the masterpieces of the discipline as well as to involve them in the process of art making.

- How could the music teacher forget to use works of music by great composers?
- How could the theatre teacher overlook plays and playwrights? How could she model great performance techniques or creative aspects of the art form without masterpieces?
- Wouldn't the art teacher show exemplary art works by notable artists?
- Wouldn't literary arts study be flat without the work of poets, novelists, and short-story writers?
- How else would learners know what the art form was about?

How many choreographic works have your students seen? Ask them! (Depending on your proximity to a large city, you may get varied answers.) Probably students have not seen many works, maybe none.

Works demonstrate the craft of choreography at its best. They give us something worthy of critique. They shed light on the expressive potential of dance and model performance standards. They show all four cornerstones integrated into a work of art. How can you create in a void without having seen the art of dance?

Newly created works as well as enduring works of choreography by well-known choreographers—which are referred to as masterworks and great works—give artistic substance worth exploring in the classroom. By unraveling the different aspects of these exemplars, students increase dance literacy.

- Each work introduces fresh aesthetic material to critique.
- Each one offers new ideas to compose with.
- Each one introduces interesting movement ideas and inventive ways to use space, time, and dynamics.
- Each offers a unique look into historical, social, stylistic, and cultural issues in dance.

One work offers more than enough materials and ideas for a rich unit of study while being a center point or a context for one's dancing, creating, and responding.

Develop units around a style. Works demonstrate the best of a dance style (e.g., classical ballet, social dance, Balinese legong, modern dance, jazz dance, Irish step dancing). You may opt to show an excerpt of a performance as part of an 8SP to demonstrate the part of the style you are working with. However, in-depth style units in high school benefit from students' seeing and unpacking a whole work.

Develop units around a theme. Sometimes it is hard to locate a work based on a theme such as social injustice. That is when your thumbnail sketches are useful—even if you've not fully analyzed the work. Each sketch has a line for noting themes, and thus you would probably find the dance *Rainbow 'Round My Shoulder* (Donald McKayle) for social injustice. (Copy and use figure 8.3 to keep track of learning possibilities in each work. A thumbnail sketch form is also in appendix B.)

Viewing a theme-based dance work models one way the theme has been expressed before. One caveat to modeling works in the context of themes is this: You may not get to show the complete choreographic work because of time constraints, particularly if the masterwork is lengthy. Use your judgment as to how much of the work is educational and aesthetically needed to attain objectives given the instructional time available and to honor the artistic integrity of the complete work.

Making the Process Your Own

Lessons allow your creative self to take over. Use your creativity to apply what you know to choreographing lessons that accomplish what kids need.

Lessons are where it all comes together. Lessons are the only part of this process a child sees and experiences. All that goes before is for your understanding, and it underpins the quality program. What goes after is students' aesthetic and kin-aesthetic growth (see figure 14.6).

Lessons in dance are largely kin-aesthetic (i.e., movement based). Lessons aren't just about what students know in dance. Lessons are about what students know and are able to do in dance. Even lessons about dance history try out doing dances of the past. To view a dance work gives students a chance to try out phrases from it and create movement responses to it. Motion is the medium for learning dance. Active learning is the process. Inquiry is the method. Dance literacy and fluency are the outcomes.

"Do I need all that teaching information and educational theory to teach?" you ask. Absolutely. The purpose of educational dance is to educate children broadly through dance and to design a complete 6DC program with the four cornerstones. Also remember that you operate in a school-based program that will already have one eyebrow cocked at you. "Could dance really be educational?" administrators and educators might ask. "How can you possibly contribute to a child's meaningful education if all you do is dance?" The eyebrows will come down one by one as educators come to appreciate the vital, complex body–mind skills learned via dance. However, this will only happen if you—our excellent dance specialist—bring all these skills into the school environment.

Identify Works to Use

Now is the time to identify masterworks suited to instruction. From your own study of repertory, dance history, and criticism, make a broad list of choreographic works to call on for teaching. Keep concert programs with notes you make in them. Become familiar with the documentaries from the Smithsonian and the JVC Video Anthology of World Music and Dance to round out your offerings of authentic works around the globe (see Rich Resources in chapter 8).

Select a known choreographic work by using three criteria: its artistic merit, its ability to model your objectives, and its suitability for children. When selecting works, consider these questions:

- Do the works have artistic merit and enough ideas to work with?
- How do they use the dance elements?
- Which works are so strong they can become the central aesthetic context for a unit?
- Which ones could play a supporting role?
- Is there a mix of choreographic periods from the present to the past? From different cultures?
- Which ones are good examples of the art form?

I. Preclass: Planning

Long-range planning (annual plan)

Short-range planning (unit and lesson)

- Standards
- Goals and objectives
- Curriculum content
- Assessment strategies rubrics
- Integrating the cornerstones
- Instructional strategies

II. During class: Implementation

- Introduce main topic
- Describe learning outcomes through objectives
- Address standards through objectives
- Use Eight-Step Plan for instruction
- Incorporate reflection activity
- Integrate student assessment

III. After class: Teacher reflection and assessment

Student progress

- Grading
- Progress reports
- Student assessment
- Follow-up

Teacher performance

Program evaluation

- Suitability of content
- Effectiveness of instructional strategies

FIGURE 14.6 As you look at the whole planning and implementation process, you get an overview of how everything fits together for the educational benefit of children.

Plan Instructional Use

Determine the emphasis of the unit. Select a great work and find the threads of the work. Great works are finely woven art fabrics. Treat them as great art works. Use them to model the best of dance. Examine each cornerstone's most beautiful threads. Which thread will you pull first as your point of entry? Unravel a work to find the very threads that will draw your students into it to interact with the work. How will you turn this into a dance unit full of performing, creating, and responding? Which thread is the end? How could the ending be the unit's high point?

Show Slices for Maximum Benefit   Use digestible viewing slices of the masterwork as a prelude to showing the full work to focus on individual movements and aspects of the dance. Use them to inform the lesson's main objectives. Select only high-quality slices. Use them to show students how to look at dance and build descriptive vocabulary. Use slices to focus on specific aspects of a dance, as if studying a detail of a large painting in art class or microscopic view of a subject in science class. Like cake, too big a slice is not digestible, and too small a slice is unsatisfying.

Guide Viewing   Draw attention to particular aspects of the work by asking guided viewing questions before viewing any part of the work—either a slice or the full work. Afterward lead into discussion with the same questions. Ask students to describe and analyze (aesthetic scanning in chapter 9) and eventually to interpret and evaluate what they see. Call attention to the dance elements and how they are used (see chapter 6) by your guided viewing questions.

Show the Full Work   Show the entire work at least once. It is not enough to see just slices or excerpts, although slices prepare students to view the artistic whole. The work's artistic impact and compositional integrity come through in the whole work.

Critique the Whole Work   Choose the best time to critique the full work for maximum effect: at opening, during the unit, or as culmination of the unit. Place the work where students bring the greatest experience and understanding to it. Vary placement in different units so as not to be predictable.

Shape a Unit Around Ideas in the Work   How many lessons do you see in this work? How will you use the work for educational and artistic growth? How will you relate aspects of the dance to the broad context? How will you sequence the lessons in a logical fashion to build to a high point? Will the critique of the full work be the culmination? Will you start students with a creative activity as the point of entry to give them a personal experience before introducing the work?

A unit's point of entry sets the tone of the entire unit. Figure 14.7 suggests points of entry—different

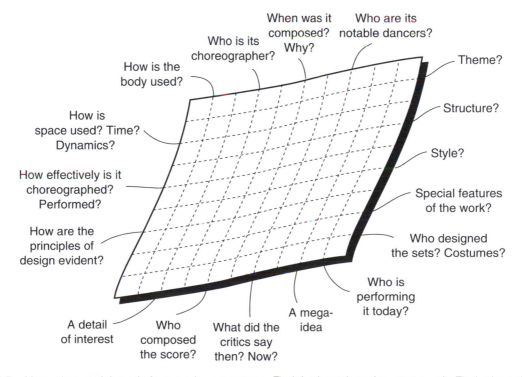

FIGURE 14.7   Unravel several threads from each cornerstone. Find the best thread to start a unit. Find others that support artistic quality in dancing, creating, and critiquing.

threads from each cornerstone that can be pulled and rewoven into a new dance fabric by your students. By the end of the study students are to understand a particular work from having danced it, read about it, viewed it, critiqued it, and created their own dances stimulated by the work.

Check Out the Background of the Work An upbeat and unlikely dance work such as David Parsons' *Sleep Study* can intrigue students by showing them that everyday movements are the stuff many dances are made of. What sparked Parsons' imagination to create this dance? What has he said about it? Investigate what companies perform it in their repertory now. As you learn about the work, can you think of ways to integrate its background into a lesson without lecturing or giving a handout on it?

Teacher as Learner As teacher, you are one of the community of learners. Your active involvement as a learner–teacher is critical to the successful facilitation of learning for and with others. Yours is never a passive role. For example, you do not "show" or "have students watch" a video, you actively "view" a slice together in order to facilitate inquiry and integrate the experience into the fabric of the lesson. (You will notice the lesson plans in the next section also are expressed from this perspective of the teaching–learning partnership.)

Sample Unit: Examining a Work by David Parsons

The choreographic focus of this sample unit is David Parsons' *Sleep Study* and the video showing its creation: *Behind the Scenes with David Parsons.* The video chronicles Parsons' choreographic process and concludes with the performed work.

The unit's lessons in creating, performing, and responding (c/p/r) evolve out of this work. The standards-oriented unit is inquiry based, comprehensive, substantive, and aesthetically driven. We will plan the unit together. It furthers many of the kindergarten through eighth grade NSDE achievement standards. You find substance and variety to explore in the context of the work. Look for these things:

- How the cornerstones' viewpoints overlap to support and enhance each other
- How students benefit from being dancer, choreographer, historian, and critic in the same unit
- How the six characteristics blend around this delightful piece of choreography

Adapt the dance work's ideas to fit your students. The sample unit is to guide rather than prescribe. It synthesizes what you've learned so far. As you preview the video, find additional ways to spark creative, artistic work as you incorporate creating, performing, and responding.

Planning the Unit

Use live performance as often as possible. The Parsons Company tours and performs across the United States, so try to teach this unit in conjunction with a performance near you. We rely on video study because live works are often unavailable outside large cities.

1. Preview *Behind the Scenes with David Parsons.*

2. Brainstorm all the teachable ideas it brings up. Write them down as seed ideas (use "Thumbnail Sketch of a Dance Work").

3. Consider the NSDE achievement standards for kindergarten through eighth grade. Which ones does the video address?

4. Consider the cornerstone frameworks. Which aspects of the artistic processes does the video address?

5. Write your answers to 3 and 4 as unit objectives (i.e., The student will . . .).

6. Create a triad unit plan by merging your seed ideas and concepts from the video into a cohesive unit with objectives, assessments, and instruction.

7. Sketch an overview of the lessons—that is, what each lesson would likely include. Reshape the overview until it is coherent. Identify key words (such as structure, codify, choreographer). Incorporate them into different lessons. Determine how many lessons are needed for the unit.

8. Choose the entry point (i.e., Lesson 1's starting point).

9. Design each lesson fully into a lesson plan, incorporating the 8SP when useful.

10. Decide if the fight scenes footage for actors and the cartoon of Aldo are useful to your age level and objectives. If they are useful, notate ways to use them (e.g., gesture, choreographing a scene, ensemble work, performance skills). If they are not useful, omit those viewing slices.

Analyzing the Work From Four Perspectives

Analyze the work from the viewpoint of a dancer, choreographer, dance historian–anthropologist, and critic. Here is a partial instructional content analysis of *Sleep Study*.

Dancer Identify the movement motifs from this work. Teach similar phrases of movement that you create that use the motifs in a style similar to the dance work. Use the new phrases to demonstrate how to manipulate a simple movement phrase: using repetition, using retrograde, speeding it up, slowing it down, changing its level, changing facing and directions, changing number of dancers doing the movement, mirroring, dancing in unison, dancing in a canon, and emphasizing transitions between sections (a POD).

Choreographer Use images with sleep postures and gestures. With that stimulus, create and com-

pose. Select other postures and gestures as creative stimuli for dance making. Let the work lead you into analyzing how the PODs (notably repetition, variety, and unity) are used to increase a piece's artistry and coherence.

Dance Historian–Anthropologist Find out about Parsons' work and its impact on the current dance landscape. Learn about his earlier life as a Paul Taylor dancer and investigate whether Taylor's style has any influence on Parsons' choreographic style. Find out other influences on Parsons that can be seen in his dance style. When was the dance made and first performed? What does it contribute to our understanding of the communicative nature of dance?

Dance Critic What are the work's artistic strengths and weaknesses? What does the work contribute to the world of dance as a whole? What does it contribute to our understanding of the creative process? What did critics say when it premiered? How about now? How is it accepted? Is it a great work of dance or a lesser work of dance? Why? What constitutes a great work?

Use an Arts Savvy Triad Unit Plan (Objectives, Instruction, and Assessment)

Now you are ready to write a triad unit plan: with objectives, assessments, and instruction. Remember to design backward. Make it aesthetically driven. Start with your objectives that reflect the achievement standards. Determine what acceptable evidence shows that students have met these objectives (in order to embed assessments). Then find the instructional strategy that optimizes the delivery of this content from all four dance cornerstones. Now integrate content, instruction, and assessment. Refer to chapter 13 for the details of a triad unit plan.

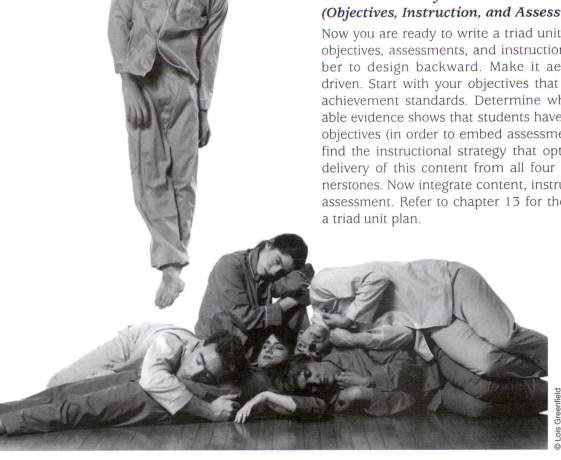

The David Parsons Dance Company performs *Sleep Study.*

Unit Objectives   See the triad unit plan in figure 14.8. Most of the objectives are taken from the NSDE achievement standards (K-8). Add additional objectives from the DCC Frameworks that this unit will also cultivate. Then put together a working unit plan that ensures students accomplish all objectives.

Assessment   Embed informal performance assessment during lessons (formative) to exchange feedback with critical friends. Notice in the five lessons how the formative and summative assessments are part of the instructional plan, which serves artistic learning at the same time it measures knowledge and skills.

Instruction   Lesson examples are geared for grades 4 through 8 but may be simplifed or enhanced for all ages. Some lessons follow the 8SP, but for the sake of making a point of emphasis, not all lessons do. The total unit, however, shows an integrated cornerstone unit. It aims to increase dance literacy and fluency.

Key Words and Concepts   *Behind the Scenes with David Parsons* introduces key words and concepts: structure, codify, phrase, retrograde, choreographer, spacing, repetition, duet, trio, variation, upstage, patterns, groupings, on a diagonal, unison, juxtapose. Add others: staccato, gesture, posture, rehearsal.

Learning objectives	Assessments	Instruction
Reorder these so the instructional plan addresses several at once. 1. Accurately describe the dance elements used when creating, performing, and responding (NSDE 1h). 2. Effectively demonstrate the difference between pantomiming and abstracting a gesture (NSDE 3a). 3. Present own dances to peers and discuss their meanings with competence and confidence (NSDE 3c). 4. Take an active role in a class discussion about interpretations of and reactions to a dance (NSDE 3b). 5. Observe and discuss how dance is different from other forms of human movement such as everyday gestures (NSDE 3a). 6. Improvise, create, and perform dances based on their own ideas and concepts from other sources (NSDE 2b). 7. Adapt one choreographer's methods of shaping a dance according to the PODs of unity, repetition, and variety. 8. Respond to a dance work and make value judgments about it. 9. Demonstrate the ability to work effectively alone and with a partner (NSDE 2e). (National Dance Association 1995)	*Go to the five lessons in this chapter. Locate all the embedded assessments you can find and list them here. Match them with the objectives and instruction.* (Mark performance assessments with an asterisk.) (Add others that will increase artistic learning and critical thinking.)	*Go to the five lessons in this chapter. Read the instructional plans. Transpose them into this format to show the way the lessons carry out the instructional plan to accomplish all objectives.*

FIGURE 14.8   Read all nine learning objectives in the first column, then use the lessons in this unit to supply information for columns 2 and 3. See how to design a triad plan for this unit.

Behind the Scenes with David Parsons is easy to slice into viewing chunks: introduction, the creative process, a study of staged fight scenes for the theatre with kids learning the techniques and a cartoon on patterns, and footage of *Sleep Study* in performance. The video's format makes dance accessible to nondancers. Different slices address different lesson objectives.

TIMED BREAKOUT OF THE VIDEO SLICES

Slice 1. Introduction (2 minutes): Everyday movements—gestures and postures. View from the introduction by Penn and Teller through the everyday movements (gestures and postures) mixed with footage of dancers doing similar body moves.

Slice 2. Creative process (5 1/2 minutes): Finding movement—turning everyday postures into dance. Parsons' choreographic process of finding the raw material of the dance from sleep postures. Codifying and stylizing everyday movements. Also shows an excerpt of how Gene Kelly turned splashing in rain puddles into a dance and how Ailey drew from wading in water for "Wading in the Water."

Slice 3. Creative process (6 minutes): Choreographic techniques to develop raw material. Penn and Teller introduction: a related topic of teaching stylized gestures and postures to stage fight scenes on stage using kids. Parsons' choreographic process using the dance elements to vary movement: change time, space, numbers of dancers (unison, canon, and juxtaposing one against the group). Shows how to shape raw material and achieve unity through repetition and variety through variations on the moves. Shows the company rehearsing the work as it is coming together. Intersperses choreography of fight scenes with Parsons' choreography. (The fight scenes show how to add variety to gestures to make them effective on stage, which is useful and an interesting interlude.)

Slice 4. Interlude (2 1/2 minutes): Creating patterns through repetition and variety. Cartoon about patterns with Aldo the dancing dog.

Slice 5. Performance of *Sleep Study* (2 1/2 minutes): Costumed performance of the finished dance before an audience. (The video ends with a silly 2 1/2-minute dance by Penn, Teller, and the theatre kids, which is not shown.)

Breaking the Unit Into Lessons

Assimilate all you've gathered so far by drafting a plan that helps you break the unit into lessons. Shape and reshape at this stage until it seems solid enough to write into lesson plans. This overview of the unit shows a sketch of its five lessons, which are later presented in detail. Four of them use an 8SP and one uses a 5SP. Lessons are written from the viewpoint of the teacher as learner to reinforce your role as an active participant in facilitating learning and being part of the learning community. Lessons describe what you and your students do together.

The overview will seem sketchy to you at first, so read it lightly now and return to it after you have read its details that follow. This is the whole feast of the unit; its digestible chunks come directly afterward.

 # Unit Overview of Sample Lessons on *Sleep Study*

Lesson 1—Using Everyday Movements: Gestures (8SP)

Creating, Performing, and Responding Activities
- Define gestures and postures, show and use examples.
- As a class, brainstorm gestures that communicate.
- Show how to abstract gestures by extending them in time, space, and with different body parts (BSTERs).
- Select several gestures as examples.
- Work in partners to structure a sequence.
- Introduce how everyday movement becomes raw material for dance.
- View Slice 1 of video *Behind the Scenes with David Parsons*.

Lesson 2—Abstracting Everyday Movements: Postures (8SP)

Creating, Performing, and Responding Activities
- View Slice 2 of the video *Behind the Scenes with David Parsons*.
- Relate work development to learner's own creative process.
- Explore a concept through movement.

- Identify everyday gestures and postures to codify for dance.
- Explore abstracting real postures by exaggeration, shaping, and codifying movements so they are intentionally abstract rather than imitative.
- Codify abstract postures into dance.
- Compose rough drafts and perform for feedback (critical friends).
- Review phrases that emphasize gestures (Lesson 1).
- Create phrases that emphasize postures.
- Create an AB form with A being gesture study and B combining gestures and postures.
- Use creative and critical thinking.

Lesson 3—Developing Choreographic Techniques: Patterns (8SP)

Creating, Performing, and Responding Activities

- Teach step patterns suited to students' age (e.g., grapevine, two-step, triplet, bourée, Africanist step patterns) and show how to dance these patterns by varying their tempo, space, and place.
- View Slice 3 of the video *Behind the Scenes with David Parsons* (developing choreography in time and space emphasizing pattern, repetition, and variety).
- Critique the artistic processes used in creating and shaping movements into patterns.
- Guide viewing of the artistic processes used in creating a dance work, noting performance skills addressed in the process.
- Return to Lesson 1 and 2's raw material of gesture and posture.
- View Slice 4 of video on pattern.
- Link to patterns in math, visual art, and music.
- Compare with stylized gestures for fight scenes (optional).
- Conceive a new dance creation that draws on what was learned (gestures and postures) from viewing and from explorations of gestures and postures.
- Apply choreographic principles observed to dance making.

Lesson 4—Unpacking Sleep Study: Comparing Our Creative Process to Parsons'

Creating and Responding (5SP)

- View Slice 5 of the video: the performance of *Sleep Study*.
- Note the beginning as well as the development of the middle and end.
- Unpack the performance of *Sleep Study* (Four-Step Critique).
- Introduce Parsons, his background, and style of dance; inquire into his significance to dance.
- Link the work to visual arts: *The Scream* abstracts gesture and posture to communicate; theatre uses fight scenes.
- Learn about *Sleep Study* and discuss its creative origins.
- Begin working on a new composition inspired by *Sleep Study*.
- Assess what was learned.
- Reflect on the choreographic process based on sleep patterns.
- Move fast and slow as a warm-up to the movement project.
- Explain how AB form is also a pattern.

Lesson 5—Creative Expression: AB Form (8SP, Culmination)

Creating, Performing, and Responding Activities
- Relate the finished choreography (product) to the process.
- Relate the finished choreography of *Sleep Study* to their own compositional process.
- Introduce the link to science (REM and non-REM sleep).
- Apply choreographic principles: pattern and repetition, variety, unity.
- Refine and edit to perform.
- Critique the final performance.
- Link to other works using everyday gestures and postures (optional).
- Assess what was learned.

Unit conceived by Heather Riley Shealy, Dance Specialist, Saluda District 1 Schools, South Carolina, and developed collaboratively.

Now we are ready to describe this sample unit in detail through five model lessons.

Lesson 1 (8SP)—Using Everyday Movements: Gestures

The point of entry is gestures and how they communicate.

Main Objectives

Use gestures as the point of emphasis. Students do the following:

- Identify gestures and abstract everyday gestures into dance movement.
- Create, perform, and respond to dance.
- Effectively demonstrate the difference between pantomiming and abstracting a gesture (NSDE 3a).
- Observe and discuss how dance is different from other forms of human movement such as everyday gestures (NSDE 3a).
- Improvise, create, and perform dances based on ideas and concepts from other sources (NSDE 2b).

Teacher's Preclass Prep

View and cue the opening section of the video starting with Penn and Teller introducing everyday movements (gestures and postures). (Slice 1 sets up the unit's point of emphasis: turning everyday movement into dance movement by abstracting and stylizing it. It is delightful footage for a point of entry. Use it to start discussion about how everyday gestures help us communicate.)

In Class: Introduce the Lesson "Today we will explore everyday movement and how humans use gestures to communicate. What are gestures? How do they differ from postures? (Gestures are predominantly made with the limbs and extremities such as the hands, arms, face, legs, feet, head, hips, and shoulders. Postures are body shapes using part of the torso and involve the spine.) We will do a round robin one at a time with everyone showing a gesture that you communicate with. Our objective is to investigate how gestures communicate and to use them as a basis for dance making. We will abstract them and stylize them to create a dance. Our objective is also to elaborate on and extend small movements into general space."

Step 1—View It Guide viewing with this question: "Look at this short video clip and answer this: What everyday movements can we use for dance? What are gestures and what do they communicate?" (View

the clip. Then ask students to respond to the same questions.)

Make a circle and ask everyone to add a gesture. Do it as a call and group response. This brainstorm is a movement elaboration exercise. No repeats are allowed—each student has to add a new gesture or pass. As long as students are producing new gestures, go around again. The purpose is to generate a wealth of ideas for dance making and to stimulate creative thinking.

Step 2—Explore It Select several gestures to explore as a group. Explore several simple gestures and extend them in space. You should move with students to teach by example how to manipulate each gesture in multiple ways to increase its movement possibilities. For example, lead students to increase the size and spatial range of a gesture to expand into their reach space; travel with the gesture and take it from one place to another; transpose it to different body parts; start it near the floor and travel it up and back down in space, turn with it; alter the rhythmic timing to speed up the gesture and slow it down; and alter its dynamics.

Step 3—Create It Assign individual dance-making activities with a distinct beginning, middle, and end. Select, then give everyone the same three gestures to work with. The beginning phrase introduces all three. The dance evolves from variations of the gestures and nothing else. The ending must incorporate all three gestures.

List the criteria for the dance in a rubric. Choreographic criteria state what is to be included. Aesthetic criteria state the level of artistic quality expected. Following are examples:

CHOREOGRAPHIC CRITERIA

- The dance has a clear beginning, middle, and end.
- Beginning phrase uses all three gestures.
- Ending still pose incorporates all three gestures.
- Movements clearly come from the gestures without extraneous movement.

AESTHETIC CRITERIA

- Gestures are abstracted and extended in space in such a way as to transform them into inventive and interesting movement material.
- An aesthetic relationship between the gestures is established.

Can you take the preceding criteria, put them into a matrix rubric, and rate them from 1 to 5? Describe all five levels of achievement.

Step 4—Show It In groups of five, sit in small circles about the room. Show dances for feedback from critical friends in the group.

Step 5—Analyze It Ask students to give and get feedback from peers in the group. Use both the choreographic and the aesthetic criteria to shape the feedback session within the groups. Students communicate what worked and what is not yet clear.

Step 6—Refine It Students refine, edit, and rework the dance to perform for the entire class. (You may have each group select work to represent the full group—the one they think is most representative. If you choose this, give the group time to focus more energy on refining the chosen work so there is time for group input.)

Step 7—Perform It Students perform for the class with attention to performance quality and full investment in presenting their work.

Step 8—Critique It Now everyone gets the chance to analyze and critique the works presented. Talk about their similarities and differences. Turn the choreographic and aesthetic criteria into review criteria.

Reflection Reflection deepens learning. Culminate with queries such as

- "What did you learn today about gestures and how they communicate?"
- "What did you learn about extending a small movement into a large, full-body motion in space?"
- "What did you learn about the arts process of creating by abstracting everyday movements?"

Lesson 2 (8SP)—Abstracting Everyday Movements: Postures

This lesson focuses attention on the core of the body, rather than on the limbs, and how posture communicates.

Main Objectives

Use postures as the point of emphasis. Students do the following:

- Abstract postures to use as raw material (motifs) for a dance study.
- Present dances to peers and discuss their meanings with competence and confidence (NSDE 3c).
- Improvise, create, and perform dances based on ideas and concepts from other sources (NSDE 2b).
- Demonstrate the ability to work effectively alone and with a partner (NSDE 2e).

Teacher's Preclass Prep

View and cue Slice 2 of the video showing Parsons finding the sleep postures he will use as raw material (i.e., motifs or themes) for his dance.

In Class: Introduce the Lesson "In Lesson 1 we explored how everyday gestures communicate and how we can abstract them to use as dance material. This process is similar to art class where everyday items are used in different ways as an art medium, transformed into something else. Today we explore postures and how they are used in dance to communicate mood and convey a situation. We will learn to exaggerate them to make a dance statement that communicates. Let's try some postures that lean, curl, twist, stretch, or bend." (Older, experienced movers may relate to partners to improvise with these five kinds of postures.)

Step 1—View It Guide the viewing of Slice 2 of the video. (This section shows Parsons' process of taking an idea of sleep postures and codifying them into a repeatable, sequenced pattern.) Ask three **guided viewing questions (GVQs)** before viewing. Facilitate discussion afterward with them.

- "How do you describe the postures Parsons selects for his dance?"
- "How does he transform them from the everyday posture into dance raw material?"
- "How does this apply to what we did yesterday?"

Step 2—Explore It Guide exploration around different postures (such as those seen in yesterday's film clip or around the body moves element. Guide the exploration so the concepts are fully explored. Vary levels (include upside down), directions (include moving upward and downward), and other BSTERs. Assign students (possibly in groups of three) to improvise around postures. After they have improvised and explored, ask them to select three postures as raw material for a new dance (motifs). Select one as the dance's emphasis with the other two in support. (For any who need help, assign three postures: leaning, curling, and twisting.)

Step 3—Compose It Start to work on a short posture dance using the three motifs. The intent is to take pedestrian postures and stylize and abstract them to get raw material for a dance. This dance is not to tell a story. The postures can be inspired by any number of everyday events: how people look in the subway; how baseball players or pitchers stand; how runners look before, during, and after a race; how teachers stand and look at students when they misbehave. (This process goes into Lesson 3. Today's objective is to find the raw material for the dance. If there is time to design some phrases, that is good.) Find what is most relevant to your students (i.e., what they are studying in another subject, what their previous work has been). Have students vary the motifs with level and timing changes.

Choreographic criteria: Have the student start on stage in a still shape that is best to launch the first movement phrase. The middle of the dance evolves out of the three designated postures (e.g., lean, curl, twist). The student creates variations on these postural shapes and sees where they lead. Does a story develop out of the movement? That is all right, but that is not the intent. Make clear that the intent is to explore postural shapes in relation to each other. The student ends in a still shape or posture that brings the last part of the dance to a fitting close.

Reflect and Respond

Can You Create a Rubric to Use as Review Criteria?

Include such choreographic criteria as these:

- Beginning still shape emphasizes one of the three designated postures.
- End shape is still and emphasizes one of the designated postures.
- Inventive postures are created throughout.
- Intent is clear and emphasis is on the three designated postures.
- Space is used well to support the idea.
- Time is varied and not too predictable.
- Dynamics are varied.
- Movement invention is fresh and creative throughout.
- Level changes add interest.

Step 4—Show It Facilitate peer work by grouping two trios to work together and show the main postures they will use as raw material. If they have started codifying some phrases, have them show these phrases as works in progress to their critical friends.

Step 5—Analyze It Critical friends give and receive feedback about selected postures (raw material) and how they were put together in movement phrases. Use choreographic criteria as review criteria for quality feedback.

Step 6—Refine It Ask trios to refine and rework, incorporating the feedback they received.

Step 7—Perform It Students perform for the entire class as before (Lesson 1). Add performance criteria for more experienced age groups.

Step 8—Critique It Facilitate peer critique and feedback about suitability of the postures for a dance study and the manipulation of them in the dance. Talk about the importance of selecting postures that can be manipulated in time and space.

Reflection Ask students, "What did you learn? How was today's process similar to or different from that of Parsons' when he designed *Sleep Study*? How was your dance similar to or different from his finished product? How are postures different from gestures?"

Lesson 3—Developing Choreographic Techniques: Patterns

This lesson develops the raw material into a dance by repeating to create patterns.

Main Objectives

Use patterns in dance as the point of emphasis. Students do the following:

- Adapt one choreographer's methods of shaping a dance according to unity, repetition, and variety (PODs).
- Improvise, create, and perform dances based on their own ideas and concepts from other sources (NSDE 2b).
- Demonstrate the ability to work effectively alone and with a partner (NSDE 2e).
- Take the motifs (raw material) and develop them into a pattern by repeating each motif.

Teacher's Preclass Prep

View and cue Slices 3 and 4 of the video. Show only these two slices in this lesson to see how Parsons took the codified postures and began to shape and craft the work according to choreographic principles.

In Class: Introduce the Lesson "Today we are going to work with pattern in dance. Who can describe what a pattern is in dance? We are going to watch David Parsons continue to work his raw material into patterns that repeat yet change and develop to please the eye. Then we will take yesterday's postural motifs (raw material) and develop them into a pattern."

Step 1—View It Show David Parsons again, pointing out what he does with his raw material and how he shapes it into a dance.

Have students watch with these three questions (GVQs) in mind:

1. "What is pattern in choreography?"
2. "How does repetition create pattern?"
3. "What role does variation play when you create dance patterns? Why is it needed?" (To keep a pattern interesting and from being boring and predictable.)

Step 2—Analyze It Analyze and discuss the process of shaping the work into patterns, especially the emphasis on repetition, groupings, and unison versus nonunison (i.e., juxtaposed). Notice how the use of variety and repetition creates unity. Call attention to unison and juxtaposition as a design element in the piece. Set up the exploration and composition through the discussion of the work.

Step 3—Explore It Teach the full group step patterns in which movements repeat (e.g., grapevine, two-step, triplet, bourée, stamping rhythms). Show how to vary these step patterns in time and space. Then guide students to explore each step with variations that keep the pattern but change the element (e.g., different pathways, tempos, and directions; in pairs or with a partner).

In motion, review gestures and postures from Lessons 1 and 2. Repeat and vary each one with different BSTERs. Show how to explore and extend the gestures by stylizing and abstracting them. Do the same with postures. Move with students to keep them focused on how to stylize a movement or posture. Help students experiment with what they

can do with the three posture motifs they selected yesterday (raw material) to create a pattern.

Step 4—Compose It Direct students to use repetition to create pattern in dance; create repeatable patterns with their three postures; use repetition and variation to create a pleasing pattern with contrasts of level, timing, and accents; be inventive; and incorporate what they observed Parsons do. Make a chart for students, listing the choreographic and aesthetic criteria using level, time, and accent change and PODs. For example:

CHOREOGRAPHIC CRITERIA

The dance:

- Presents a clear beginning, middle, and end.
- Creates a pattern whose beginning and end are linked (so the pattern may be danced again and again).
- Fully uses the three postures.
- Contrasts levels.
- Contrasts timing and accents.

This shape (with its strong horizontal, vertical, and diagonal lines) could be the thematic basis for a design study in middle and high school.

AESTHETIC CRITERIA

- Contrasts of timing and accent add interest to the pattern (POD).
- The pattern's three postures offer variety (POD).
- The pattern is interesting to watch as it repeats (POD).
- The pattern holds together (POD unity).

Have older students incorporate abstract gestures. Perhaps they can refine the previous study or rework it into a solo or a small group dance.

Step 5—Show It Facilitate as students show works in progress for in-process feedback from critical friends.

Step 6—Refine It Facilitate as students revise so the work achieves all objectives and standards.

Step 7—Perform It Ask students to perform for the full group. List performance criteria for quality indicators.

Step 8—Critique It Discuss how the work has changed and which changes added value. Ask students to critique strengths and weaknesses as opportunities to improve.

Reflection Ask students, "What did you learn by watching Parsons choreograph? What pointers did you pick up during the discussion of Parsons' choreographic process? What were you able to incorporate into your dance that made it better artistically?"

Lesson 4—Unpacking *Sleep Study:* Comparing Our Creative Process to Parsons'

This lesson features the finished choreographic work and incorporates a visual art work.

Main Objectives

Use critiquing the work as the point of emphasis. Students do the following:

- Accurately describe the dance elements used when creating, performing, and responding to dance (NSDE 1h).
- Take an active role in a class discussion about interpretations of and reactions to a dance (NSDE 3b) (DCC Framework).
- Respond to a dance work and make value judgments about it.

- Unpack a dance work (i.e., describe, analyze, interpret, and evaluate).

Note: Lesson 5 continues to develop the concepts in Lesson 4 by building onto the dance work from Lesson 4.

Teacher's Preclass Prep

View and cue Slice 5 of the video showing the costumed performance of the work before an audience. This is a 5SP to allow time for activities. Bring in a reproduction of the visual art work, *The Scream.* Also locate pictures of other Parsons works on his Web site.

In Class: Introduce the Lesson "Today's lesson is in three parts. First we will see the performance of *Sleep Study.* We will unpack the dance (i.e., describe, analyze, interpret, and evaluate the performance of the work from Slice 5 of the video). Then we'll find out who Parsons is."

Step 1—View It Have the class watch *Sleep Study* performed on stage. Give guided viewing questions (GVQs) before and after. Ask what is seen for the first time—what is new about the work. What worked better in production than in rehearsal? What does the finished work communicate?

Step 2—Critique It Ask students to describe, analyze, interpret, and evaluate the work.

Step 3—Analyze It Ask students to inquire into different aspects of what they see.

- Creative process:
  - > "How did his choreographic process get him to the final work?"
  - > "How did he refine it as he went?"
  - > "How does it compare with your creative process of finding raw material to shape into patterns?"
  - > "What did you learn about shaping raw material into patterns and structured sequences of dance?"
- Working with movement:
  - > "How does his dance work communicate? Does it tell a story?"
  - > "What does he mean by stylizing movement? Codifying shapes (postures and gestures)?"
  - > "How does he abstract the movements he uses so they are not actual sleep postures but communicate that they are?"

> "How close to the original postures does he stay when he codified the shapes and motifs for his raw material?"

- Principles of design:

  > "What does that teach you about designing a dance?"

  > "How does timing change add variety?"

  > "How does unison (all at the same time) movement differ in interest from juxtaposed movement (different moves going on at the same time or one against the group)?"

  > "When you design dances in groups, should you try to keep a lot of unison? Why or why not?" (Note: Use this to make a point about the value of PODs variety and contrast.)

- Overall:

  > "What have you learned about being a choreographer?"

  > "How successful was this dance?"

  > "What did it communicate to you? How did it make you feel?"

  > "Are you surprised to find movement potential in sleeping?"

(Note: Get many different answers to each question and let answers lead you into other queries.)

Let's look at a notable work of visual art, *The Scream*. (Ask the same kinds of inquiry questions as before.) Add these: "What does it remind you of? Does it look like a nightmare? Have you ever had a figure like that in a dream? How has the artist abstracted this scream? What is not realistic? Does it still convey a scream although it doesn't look exactly like one? Did he capture the essence of the scream?" (Questions should investigate gestures and postures.) "Look at its facial and hand gestures; its body posture. How do they convey the mood of the scream? Describe the mood."

Step 4—Explore It   Have students synthesize what they learned so far from this unit into another creative dance. Ask students to draw on these aspects of their learning:

1. Watching the making and performance of *Sleep Study*

2. Being aware of gestures and postures as raw material for dance

3. Understanding of how repetition creates pattern and how variety keeps a dance pattern from being too repetitive, predictable or boring (Recall the fight scene where the man changed levels to add variety.)

4. Studying *The Scream* and how it abstracts and stylizes both gestures and a posture to convey the concept of a scream in art

Step 5—Compose It (Section A of the AB Form)
Building on all the aspects of the previous lessons, students compose a new dance study. Explain that they are to take gestures and postures you have experienced in a dream as the raw material (or a daydream, if a dream is not recalled). Describe the process:

1. Sketch the postures or gestures you recall from one or more dreams (or from imagination).

2. Select three contrasting postures you will use as the raw material for your dance.

3. Try the gestures on the body. Stylize them. Practice repeating the gestures in different ways. Take this raw material and apply choreographic principles: pattern and repetition, variety, unity.

4. Develop the gesture into a repeatable 8-count phrase of movement that incorporates all three choreographic principles. Structure and codify its movements.

5. Teach the dance to a partner.

In Class: Closure and Reflection   "We will continue this dance study tomorrow. Rehearse at home if you have time. What did you learn from seeing *Sleep Study* performed today?"

Lesson 5—Creative Expression: AB Form

Reinforce this particular unit's earlier objectives by adding several from Lessons 1 through 4 as needed to tie concepts together in your culminating lesson.

Main Objectives

Integrate the artistic processes through choreographing, performing, and critiquing as the point of emphasis to culminate the unit. Students do the following:

- Improvise, create, and perform dances based on their own ideas and concepts from other sources (NSDE 2b).
- Demonstrate the ability to work effectively alone and with a partner (NSDE 2e).
- Demonstrate critical and creative thinking.
- Perform an AB form (contrasting sharp and quick with smooth and slow).
- Create a work that is linked to science—REM and non-REM sleep patterns.

Teacher's Preclass Prep

Develop a rubric from the review criteria to use in class. In small groups, ask critical friends to use the rubric (peer critique) for in-process feedback and again at the end after original work is performed. Ask peers to add comments to the final performance evaluation. Also do a teacher evaluation.

In Class: Introduce the Lesson "Yesterday we started on a dream study. We each learned our movement phrase and one from our partner. Do you remember it? Today we are going to add a new criterion to that same dance phrase and make it into a dance—the new criterion has to do with nighttime dreaming. Who will explain REM sleep (link to science)? REM stands for rapid eye movement, which occurs when we dream at night. Non-REM sleep is deep sleeping when we are not dreaming. Create an AB form (contrasting quick and sharp with slow and smooth). Create your own work. Link with science and REM and non-REM sleep patterns."

Step 1—Explore It "Today we explore and extend the extremes of tempo: rapid and slow. Find movement material to remember for the study you will do later today."

Step 2—Compose It Teach AB form. (In this case A is for slow; B is for quick.) Explain that AB form is useful to contrast two ideas. Use it as the structure for this dance duet inspired by non-REM (A) and REM (B) sleep patterns.

Instruct students to review the two phrases they developed yesterday with their partners; use this phrase as the basis of their dance study; use the phrase in both the A and B sections and vary it in each; use repetition to establish a pattern (the A section will be slower and steadier than the contrasting B section, which will add some quick timing to it); create the A phrase with a fitting beginning, middle, and end; and then do the same for the B phrase.

(Another option is to have one partner emphasize slow and smooth and the other partner emphasize quick accents in his or her phrase. These will be duets.) The intent of this dance is to express in AB form the contrast in the two forms of sleep. The raw material is the postures and gestures from a recent dream you can recall.

Step 3—Show It Ask students to perform duets in a small group (possibly six) for critical feedback. After they critique all of them, the group selects one dance to represent them and performs it for the class.

Step 4—Analyze It Give out rubrics containing review criteria by which to critique the dance (formative, in process). Remind students to be specific with comments about its strengths and weaknesses and opportunities. Facilitate informal feedback with the class to spawn additional ideas.

Step 5—Refine It "Go back and incorporate aspects of what you learned about choreography according to what will make the dance better (e.g., if needed, add additional gestures or postures, extend it into more space, abstract the movement more so it has more interest to the viewer and communicates). Clarify the intent. Use the raw material from gestures and postures of one of your dreams. Get assistance from your group when you need to."

Step 6—Perform It Students perform in small groups.

Step 7—Critique It Students use the rubric as summative assessment. They give and receive assessments from peers and from you.

Step 8—Culmination "To culminate the unit, reflect on your process and your final product. Self-evaluate in light of the final critiques and evaluations as well as the comments on the rubric. (If your students keep reflection journals, add this entry.) Ask, "What did you learn in this unit (about choreographing a dance, finding movements for dance, gestures, postures, BSTERs, PODs, and others)?"

In Class: Reflection Ask, "What did you learn? What does the rubric tell you about your performance quality? About your choreographic design? About the way you used the principles of design (PODs) in your own work and in this unit of study? Self-reflect: How did you use the PODs to critique others' work?"

Reflect and Respond

Add one more lesson to this unit that addresses a different objective and extends the unit. Return to the section called "Analyzing the Work From Four Perspectives" (page 435). Incorporate an idea listed there. What does the new lesson add to the unit? Is it in an 8SP or a 5SP?

Building Your Own Unit of Study Around a Choreographic Work

From your own dance studies in dance history and criticism, which dynamic dance work comes to mind as a focal point to a unit? How about Alvin Ailey's *Revelations* to excite students about dance in a way almost nothing else can?

First you'll realize that the full *Revelations* is too long to be the main focal point because it is a suite of dances, each so different from the other—at least at this stage of development. So let's focus on one dance from that suite—"Wading in the Water"—to get ideas about putting together a unit of your own. Such a work creates a focal point for learning and generates literally hundreds of teaching ideas. Because the unit can adapt from grades 3 to 12, we will incorporate a wide age range of NSDE achievement standards.

Of course, see a live performance when available. The Ailey company tours and performs extensively across the United States, so you could teach this unit in conjunction with a performance near you. Ailey concerts end with *Revelations* as the finale because it is Ailey's enduring signature work. Videos of the work are also commercially available from numerous sources.

Working With a Sample Unit Sketch: "Wading in the Water" From Ailey's *Revelations*

Even if you know "Wading in the Water," now you must know its details. View it several times and take notes. Use the "Thumbnail Sketch of a Dance Work" in appendix B. Determine how the cornerstones merge to support and enhance each other, notably how the dancers (C1) realize the choreography (C2). After you are thoroughly familiar with

the work, consider what about it would best inspire students to dance, choreograph, and critique. What would best enable them to experience this dance as part of their own dance heritage? Then set out to construct a unit of five aesthetically driven, inquiry-based lessons.

For planning purposes, we will make this unit for grade 5. If you teach in middle or high school, extend the unit into a longer unit that includes modern dance technique classes (lessons) that are enhanced by seeing performance slices of the work. It contains many technique ideas such as the articulated torso, stylized dance walks, and contraction and release.

Preunit Planning

The steps of preunit planning are the same as the Parsons' unit. Review them. Then add these:

1. Sketch an overview of the lessons and shape it until coherent. Find the vocabulary words related to dance and other subjects that are vital to include (e.g., *entrance, exit, props, undulating, baptism, spirituals, river, symbols, procession*).

2. Slice the work into digestible viewing chunks. Time these portions. Use slices, microscopic views of the work, either as preparation for viewing the entire work or afterward to focus on its details. Consider the order to present slices. Slices do not have to be shown in order because you will show the full work at some point.

3. Plan to show the entire work at least once to relate its parts (slices) to the whole. Do not overlook the dance work as a complete artistic entity.

4. After you have slices that hold together by phrasing or music section, count how many you have. Which will you use in this unit and which will you save for another unit to support other dance topics? You don't have to use all the slices in one unit.

5. Take your notes from each slice and transform them into questions. Borrow some from chapter 5 to get started. Then compose more guided viewing questions (GVQs) for each slice. Ask students to describe what they see in each slice and in the full work as you did in the aesthetic scanning section of chapter 9.

6. Decide which lesson is best to view "Wading in the Water" all the way through. Determine

where it best sheds light on the creative process: at the beginning, midpoint, or end of the unit? If this is an early unit before students gain experience viewing and reading dances, consider viewing the complete work as culmination to a unit. (But if students are experienced in unpacking works and have seen a number of dances, you may have better results showing the work near the beginning.)

7. Return to the example of theme-based lessons given earlier in the chapter for additional ideas to include.

Analyzing the Work From Four Perspectives

Do your own content analysis of the work. Analyze the work from four perspectives: from the viewpoint of a dancer, choreographer, dance historian–anthropologist, and critic. It may look something like this.

Dancer   Teach phrases of movement that you create based on the style of the technique. Identify the movement motifs from this work. Also view the processional to the river, which precedes the actual dance. Perform a processional using similar movement qualities. Use the processional to teach dance walks (technique), entrances and exits (choreography), and transitions between sections (a POD). Look at the recessional after the dance to see how its movements are similar to the processional.

Choreographer   Use imagery of water and water movements (e.g., river flow, ocean wave, ripples, pouring, splashing, bubbling). Take that stimulus for exploring movement qualities. Create movement phrases incorporating each of the words. Give students a structure in which they can compose a short dance from specified water images translated into movement qualities. Experiment with using fabric as a prop to add qualities and symbolize images (such as "Wading in the Water" does). Select a fabric and improvise with it to see what kinds of images it evokes. If there are enough images to collect and weave into a dance, do so. Will you create a short one as an example for students? Will it be evocative of an image or purely abstract and emphasize only movement and qualities of movement? Explore different entrances and exits. Design them as bookends to a short dance so they create a similar beginning and ending to a dance.

Dance Historian–Anthropologist   Find out about Alvin Ailey's life and work. Learn about the rural South and the traditions of church meetings and baptisms. Find out how and why Ailey was so deeply influenced by gospel music. Since the dance was first performed in 1960, what political climate surrounded it? (The civil rights movement was in full force, and legislation was pending that would desegregate schools in the 1960s. Although the work does not deal with integration, the dance work's acceptance resounded across the world. Could the performance of this work have contributed in any way to racial–political gains?)

Dance Critic   Look at the work as a critic. What are its artistic strengths and weaknesses? What was said by critics when it premiered? At other times in history? Today? How was it accepted across the world? Now? (It has been performed all over the world to enormous support and acclaim.) Look at "Wading in the Water" to see how it is choreographically designed and how effectively it holds together. What are its movement motifs, and do they recur throughout the piece? Of what significance are the props? How do they add to the movement? How does the fabric create images of water in this dance? What other images does the fabric call up? How effectively do the blue gauze strips enhance the visual impact of the piece? How many images of water do you see in the dancers' bodies (undulating and rippling, splashing, pouring)? What do the umbrellas and tall white flags symbolize in the baptism ceremony? Are they effectively used to portray the story and to enhance the dance movement? How effective are the costumes?

Studying the Background of the Work

Investigate the work's origins, significance, and place in dance history. Find out what companies are actively performing it in their repertory. As you encounter the work, think how to integrate the following information into the curriculum without lecturing or giving a handout.

"As early as I can remember I was enthralled by the music played and the songs sung in the small black churches in every small Texas town my mother and I lived in. . . . I remember hearing 'Wade in the Water' being sung during baptism" (Ailey 1997, p. 97). Ailey describes how *Revelations* came about. In the full work, "the costumes and set would be colored brown, an earth color, for coming out of the earth, for going into the earth." The second part was white and pale blue for the baptismal and the purification rite of using the water to wash away sins (Ailey 1997, pp. 97-98). This is the section that includes "Wading in the Water." The music of the spirituals, with the profound feelings of faith, hope, joy, and sometimes sadness, compelled Ailey to create his masterpiece *Revelations*. In it he originally compiled a number of Negro spirituals but later shortened the work to its present-day order when he was invited to perform it in 1961 at Jacob's Pillow. The Jacob's Pillow sequence was "I Been 'Buked," "Didn't My Lord Deliver Daniel," "Fix Me Jesus," the processional, and "Wading in the Water"—thus it was the finale of *Revelations* in that program.

> In "Wade in the Water," long blue-and-white gauze ripples; white streamers jiggle as if blown by a breeze; dancers glide forward and back, leading with the pelvis; Judith Jamison's arms and waist undulate and flow, doing more to recall the image of a river than even the gauze can. You don't have to be black or baptized to understand what is happening, to feel the joy of purification and the sense of surrender to the river of the spirit. (Cook and Mazo 1978, p. 12)

> Then, blue and white gauzes, a white pole decked with streamers, and a huge white umbrella turn the stage into a riverbank on a hot afternoon. . . . Arms reaching out and heads tossed back speak of religious ecstasy. When the baptized girl is carried off, protected from the sun and from evil by the white umbrella, cleansing has been accomplished. (Cook and Mazo 1978, p. 111)

Ailey's earliest memories were of small Texas towns and processions of people all in white going down to the lake for baptism. He spoke in his autobiography about his memory of the choir singing "Wade in the Water" as the minister was baptizing everybody. "After baptism we went into church where the minister's wife was singing a soulful version of 'I've Been 'Buked, I've Been Scorned'" (Ailey 1997, p. 18).

Using an Arts Savvy Triad Unit Plan

Now you are ready to write a triad unit plan: with objectives, assessments, and instruction. Return to the sample unit on *Sleep Study* earlier in this chapter. Review the section called "Use an Arts Savvy Triad Unit Plan" (page 435). Plan unit objectives, assessments, and then instruction with the help of "Wading in the Water." Pull out the key words and concepts and then time each video slice and describe it (like the *Sleep Study* unit). When you finish these, you possess the proper tools with which to design the lessons.

- Unit objectives
- Assessment

- Instruction
- Key words and concepts
- Timed breakout of video slices
  a. Slice 1
  b. Slice 2
  c. Slice 3
  d. Slice 4
  e. Slice 5

Breaking the Unit Into Lessons

Following are suggested integrated lessons around "Wading in the Water." Either work alone or with a partner to flesh out each lesson based on the title and suggestions given. Rely on ideas from the DCC Framework and the NSDE for Grade 5.

Unit Overview of "Wading in the Water"

Lesson 1—Exploring Water Concepts

Emphasis on creating (NSDEs 3 and 4) (5SP).

The entry point is creative: brainstorming and creating a sequence. Give the unit an exploratory and improvisatory beginning. Also teach textural phrases that you design based on some of the words. Explore different movement qualities. Lead movement exploration on textures and qualities to increase use of the energy and dynamics elements from the BSTER. Also incorporate these items in a 5SP (Explore It, Compose It, Show It, Analyze It, and Refine It):

- Bring in a tub of water and have the class brainstorm words that evoke water images (include rippling, splashing, wading, and pouring) to start the unit.
- Instruct students to take the concepts into the body as movement.
- Have students explore, compose, and perform.
- Have students elicit feedback (from critical friends).
- End with a student composition using the words in a structured sequence (approximately 32 counts, but without music).

Lesson 2—View Water Images

Emphasis on performing (NSDEs 1, 4) (5SP).

Pull together images and movements evoked by water—the water itself and also the way one moves in and with water. Incorporate ideas from Lesson 1 to design choreographic criteria. Show a slice that invites students to look for specific water images: rippling, splashing, wading, and pouring. Add guided viewing questions (GVQs). Then create textural dances based on these water images. Teach abstraction so water images inspire movements rather than imitate exactly. Convey the qualities of water and fluidity. Also incorporate these items in a 5SP (Explore It, View It, Analyze It, Compose It, Refine It):

- View one slice of the dance to find water images from the creative work in Lesson 1.
- Explore working with fabric to enhance water images before and after viewing. Use this to become comfortable using fabrics as a prop. Ask students to change the quality of the fabric so it is used in at least three different qualitative ways (such as smooth, rippling, and splashing).

The idea for this lesson came from a workshop presentation by Pamela Sofras, UNC–Charlotte.

Lesson 3—Linking the Dance

Emphasis on performing and linking (NSDEs 1, 3, 4, and 7).

Look at two viewing slices: the entrance and exit. Focus on entrances and exits that are similar—like bookends. (Consider using fabric as a prop for the rest of the lessons, and, if so, use the entrance to present the fabric that will be used in the dance and the exit to take it away.) Create entrances and exits for the dance from Lesson 2. Depending on the age of the student, work for artistry in the entrance and exit as a processional. Teach "Mayim, Mayim" as the closing for that lesson because it is aerobic and needs to be preceded by other forms of movement. Keep movement the medium for learning as much as possible and profitable. Emphasize dance links—the entrance and exit are links, and "Mayim" is a link to another culture. Make other links appropriate to grade 5 or develop another concept that you find in the dance to link, such as how "Mayim's" wave to the center and back

out is a link to the wave made by the fabric when two dancers run downstage and back upstage. Also incorporate these items:

- View two slices of "Wading in the Water": the entrance to the dance (the procession to the water) and its exit (ending).
- Explore entrances and exits and set bookend patterns.

Make at least one link:

- Link to social studies (rural South)
- Link to other arts (Negro spiritual music)
- Link to language: making word dances based on water images (rippling, undulating, splashing, pouring, diving, washing)
- Link to other works using water as a theme (e.g., Doris Humphrey's *Water Study*)
- Involve higher-order thinking (critical thinking)
- Learn Israeli folk dance, "Mayim, Mayim," and sing with the accompaniment

Lesson 4—Critiquing the Work

Emphasis on responding and knowing (NSDEs 3, 4, and 5).

View and unpack the whole work, "Wading in the Water," including processional and recessional. Relate it to students' own creative process. Also teach several phrases inspired by one section of the dance to enhance dancing skills. Tie in the work's links to other disciplines when they surface. Determine how much dancing and performing can go into Lesson 4 and still accomplish other items. Be in motion as much as possible. Draw from Lessons 1 through 3 any ideas that still need developing. Incorporate these items:

- Unpack the work (Four-Step Critique).
- Know about Alvin Ailey's significance to dance.
- Know about *Revelations* and its creative origins.
- Learn several phrases (with or without fabric).
- Apply concepts from one part of the dance.
- Review "Mayim, Mayim" as closure.

Lesson 5—Create an Organically Structured Dance With Entrance and Exit

Synthesis of creating, performing, and responding (NSDEs 2, 3, and 4) (8SP culmination).

Bring all the concepts you've developed to a logical conclusion in Lesson 5. Use as many steps of the 8SP as possible in Lesson 5. Have students do the following:

- Use props (or fabrics).
- Create a short dance work inspired by "Wading in the Water."
- Perform the new dance for feedback.
- Refine and edit to perform.
- Critique the final performance of the new work.
- Relate the new work to "Wading in the Water" and compare its similar points.

What of importance will students know from this unit that they would have missed without it? How will you tie this unit to previous learning? How does it further dance technique? Composition? Dance history? Dance criticism? What enduring understanding in dance does it leave?

Where have you embedded assessments? Do you have enough feedback to grade students on this unit? If not, add such things as choreographic and review criteria. Which objectives still need measuring? Add assessments for all objectives and use one assessment to measure more than one objective.

Reflect and Respond

- When was the first time you saw Alvin Ailey's *Revelations?* Was it live or on video? What was your reaction? What is still memorable about it?
- Which section is your favorite? What attracts you to it? Why does it stand out? How were you introduced to it? Do you wish you were one of the dancers or its choreographer? If you were to write about it as a dance critic, what would you say?

Building Your Own Unit of Study Around a Style

Create your own unit of study around one of the classical dance styles from south India, Bharata Natyam. Ideally, you have learned Bharata Natyam's foundation techniques, so you are familiar with its concepts and its movement vocabulary. You need some demonstration skills and conceptual vocabulary to teach a unit on Bharata Natyam for any age student. As you read the next section, consider how some of its information will factor into the unit you will teach on Bharata Natyam.

This unit includes valuable insights by Anuradha Murali, Mrudani School of Performing Arts, Orangeburg, South Carolina.

Background of the Style

Bharata Natyam is one of the world's most ancient and important classical dances with a highly codified movement and technique vocabulary. Its roots go back 2,000 years to the *Natya Shastra* and the *Abhinaya Dharpana,* which describe the dance's codified postures and gestures in detail. Gestures and postures not only comprise two of the most striking features of the technique but the same postures and gestures also appear in temple *bas relief* (carvings) all over India and in parts of southeast Asia. The most notable are those on the temple at Chidamabaram where the entire 108 *karanas* (postures) denoted in the *Natya Shastra* are carved. Inquiry into Bharata Natyam can be far-reaching because the dance form has a long and eventful history.

Bharata Natyam's stylized movement vocabulary, and therefore its technique, is in stark contrast to Western classical dance (ballet). Bharata Natyam's codification compares in some ways to the codification of classical ballet in 17th-century Europe and Russia. However, Bharata Natyam existed long before classical ballet, and the spirits that animate the two are vastly different. Whereas ballet grew up around the royal courts of Europe and developed courtly mannerisms and stylizations of social interaction, Bharata Natyam grew out of a sacred tradition of devotional dance performed in Hindu temples of south India by **devadasis,** young female temple dancers.

Bharata derives from three syllables (i.e., *bha + ra + ta*) that are vital to the dance: mood (*bhava*), melody and sentiment (*raga* and *rasa*), plus rhythm (*tala*). *Natya(m)* means dance. *Abhinaya* and *nritta* are its essential components. Abhinaya is the expressive part of the dance, conveying its sentiment or mood. The Bharata Natyam performers learn to express the fullest range of human emotions in the abhinaya sections. The *mudras,* or codified hand gestures in the dance, communicate stories in a form of sign language as part of abhinaya. Twenty-four head movements and numerous

Photo courtesy of V.P. and Shanta Dhananjayan, Bharatha Kalanjali, 22 Jeevaratnamnagar, Chennai, India.

Bharata Natyam, classical dance of India, was codified in the second century a.d.

facial expressions (e.g., movements of the eyebrow, cheek, eye, chin, mouth) help convey the mood. These movements take meaning when they are done in relationship to the corresponding postures of the limbs and the particular mudras. Conversely, the nritta, or pure abstract dance without abhinaya (expressions), includes decorative hand, feet, body, and eye movements to enhance the steps. In nritta rhythmic footwork, poses and abstract movements and gestures do not tell a story but are for virtuosity and beauty of performance. See the photo on this page depicting the dance.

To become proficient requires years of exacting study with a guru (teacher). However, in K-12 education one can learn enough aspects of the dance style to appreciate it. The aim in K-12 education is to teach Bharata Natyam without compromising either its classical traditions (serious study with a guru) or its artistry. For that reason it is necessary to see an authentic performance as part of a unit.

Two of the most noted Bharata Natyam teachers and performers were Rukmini Devi Arundale and Balasaraswathi, who both lived into the late 20th century and taught around the world. Their ability to translate the aesthetic aspects of the stylized technique to students brought new life into the art form. Just as there are stylistic variations in properly executing a step according to the ballet method one studies (such as the Russian school versus the French school), so Bharata Natyam has different stylistic schools. For example, Rukmini Devi Arundale established the Kalakshetra style of Bharata Natyam in Chennai, India, which has a highly structured way of teaching the art form. The Kalakshetra style is different from that of Balasaraswathi.

Both male and female dancers acquire the skills to express the gamut of human emotions and situations. Males and females perform Bharata Natyam and learn to use its full expressive range: the *tandava,* or the vigorous, masculine dynamic, and the *lasya,* or feminine, romantic, and delicate dynamic. Although Bharata Natyam is associated more with female performers because of its roots with the devadasis, both men and women portray masculine and feminine characteristics and characters, as is the case in much of Asia. Thus a solo dancer can tell a story and switch back and forth between different emotions as well as between characters—male and female—by varying the dynamics.

When you attend a complete Bharata Natyam recital, keep in mind it consists of a series of variations—all different, yet in some ways similar to the various aspects of a ballet program (such as the adagio, allegro, pas de deux, variations, grand pas de deux). However, all full Bharata Natyam programs follow this exact performance order:

1. *Alarippu*—The introduction, a nritta (pure dance), is performed only to the rhythmic accompaniment of the *mridangam* (drum). The dancer executes a number of concentrated rhythmic patterns. It takes a whole-body approach—eyes, arms, legs, body, head.

2. *Jatiswaram*—A nritta in which the dancer rhythmically executes *jatis* (steps), paralleling the rhythmic syllables of the drum.

3. *Sabdam*—Abhinaya (dance story) is used to portray the story with elaborate facial expressions and hand gestures, which mime a story that is told through the music. Rhythmic passages along with the poetic syllables are introduced in this section.

4. *Varnam*—The most intricate, complex section. It gives the fullest leeway to the dancer to improvise on a given theme and color its meaning. Varnam means coloring. It uses both nritta and abhinaya.

5. *Padams (mime)*—An interpretive dance of a lyrical passage set to music. It is a focused opportunity for abhinaya (mime) through the language of the limbs, hands, and face.

6. *Tillana*—The rhythmic and expressive pinnacle of the dancer's repertory, which brings the performance to a conclusion. The musical tillana is a musical composition sung in a particular mode (raga) set to a rhythmic cycle (tala).

Preplanning the Unit

Assuming you have studied Bharata Natyam and know its basic terminology and techniques, create an integrated unit for grades 3 through 5 to incorporate at least these aspects of Bharata Naytam:

- Its basic vocabulary and techniques
- Aramandi, the basic position, (turned-out first position demi-plié)
- Mudras (hand gestures) and their *viniyoga* (use of hand movement)
- Abhinaya (storytelling through expressive dance)
- Guided viewing of video samples of Bharata Natyam techniques, including mudras and viniyogas, and a lecture–demonstration of a varnam
- Viewing and critique of a well-performed varnam

Find Suitable Stories to Dance

The Panchatantra Tales are 2,000-year-old fables from India that are similar to Aesop's fables. *The Panchantantra Tales* feature animals and creatures as the main characters of the stories. Fables are appropriate for all ages. Turn one of these tales, such

as "The Monkey and the Crocodile," into a structure that uses Bharata Natyam's mudras to convey the story. Use it so students create a short expressive dance as part of the unit. "The Monkey and the Crocodile" tells of trust and friendship, greed and jealousy, betrayal and quick thinking. It is short and has a good enough ending. Young learners can perform a tale such as this in *aramandi* position, using 10 or so mudras and 3 rhythmic step patterns to tell its story. You can enhance it for older learners by incorporating more details of the story, adding more body positions (*mandala beda*), mudras, and rhythmic step patterns.

Find the Right Video Resource

Rely on these two excellent video resources to plan the unit:

1. Video #1 (DVD format)—"Bharatanatyam: Precepts and Practice" (sic) gives a thorough video demonstration of mudras, viniyogas, and *slokas* (chants). It is a must-have resource. It comes with a CD-ROM that explains details of the mudras and their viniyogas to help you plan a unit.

2. Video #2—"Bharatanatyam Varnam: The Sum and Substance" contains two video CDs. Volume 1 presents the theory and movements of the varnam in a lecture–demonstration format, while Volume 2 presents the full performance of a beautifully danced varnam. (See Rich Resources.)

Prepare Ahead

Use these two videos for your own review and practice of the particular mudras and viniyogas needed to portray "The Monkey and the Crocodile": river (sindouthu), monkey (mukula), tree (asamyuta thripataka), king (same as tree), mountain (karkata above head), river bank (ardhapataka), fruit (padmakosha), smile (chandrakola), crocodile (samuta thripataka), friend (keelakau), wife (katakhamukha and shikara), heart (arala), and "to give" (samyuta mukula). Learn them well enough to teach them without the video. Prepare charts with these terms to use as visual aids.

As you preview these videos, begin to select video slices that will benefit in-class instruction (e.g., video #1's demonstration of asamyuta mudra [single hand] with sloka, and the samyuta mudras [double hand] with sloka). Also find the slice that demonstrates the viniyogas for pataka and thripataka and shows all the varied usages for these two mudras. Locate the slices that give the most digestible educational chunks to achieve your purposes and meet your learning objectives. Number those slices, time them, and make cue notes on how to return to them.

Use video #2, volume 1, to find the rhythmic syllables with their corresponding steps to teach in Lesson 3. Emphasize only the three-beat rhythms. Practice them so you can add them to the story:

- To combine monkey with moving to the right in three beats (tha-ki-ta)
- To show the river (ganga) movement to the front in three beats (di-di-thai in prenkhana)
- To show the mountain in three beats (tha-ki-ta)

Increase Dance Vocabulary

Increase your students' dance elements vocabulary. Also teach Bharata Natyam terms. Make posters of the Bharata Natyam terms you will use along with their meaning. Make charts of the key terms from the *Panchatantra* tale (for Lesson 2). Teach the names of the particular mudras used in the story, if not all mudras. Present most key words and concepts in the early lessons so that students get enough practice using them by the unit's end. Include not only the term *mudra* but also denote single-hand mudras (asamyuta mudras) and mudras using both hands (samyuta mudras). Include other basic terms, like *viniyoga, abhinaya, nritta, aramandi, sloka,* and *varnam.*

Triad Unit Plan: Objectives, Assessment, and Instruction

As soon as you are comfortable with the material in your videos and have selected a *Panchatantra* tale, prepare a triad unit plan:

- Write objectives using the DCC Framework and NSDE.
- Design formative assessments for the lessons and a summative assessment for the unit.
- Plan instruction that uses the 5SP.

Unit Objectives

Write your desired learning outcomes as objectives. Inform students of all of them at the unit's outset to direct their efforts. Keep cornerstone objectives realistic according to student age and stage. For example:

1. To demonstrate proficiency in creating, performing, and responding (C1, C2, C4)

2. To demonstrate skills in a non-Western classical dance form (C1, C3)
3. To diversify technical skills in dance and challenge the dancer (C1)
4. To place dance in a broad context by comparing it with a familiar form (C3)
5. To increase dance vocabulary related to gestures, postures, and steps (C1)
6. To express an idea or concept through dance movement (C1)
7. To create and compose dance phrases using a new movement vocabulary (C2)
8. To describe a performance by a skilled Bharata Natyam dancer (C4)

 What additional objectives do you need?

Later, after you flesh out the unit's lessons, come back and add other learning objectives or standards that you did not initially include but became obvious by virtue of the unit's planned activities. Often you accomplish more than you set out to do, so routinely go back and add them.

Assessments

Identify the acceptable evidence and design your assessment criteria. Embed assessments in the artistic processes (c/p/r). Make formative and summative assessments part of the instruction so they increase learning as they measure knowledge and skills. Create an assessment rubric for the final performance of the folk tale.

 What assessments will be most effective?

Instruction

Group unit objectives so that one instructional strategy addresses several objectives (see chapter 12). Use the 6DC Model (see chapter 1). Present the lessons in a logical sequence and interlace aspects of the other arts that Bharata Natyam incorporates: music, theatre, and visual aspects. Since Bharata Natyam is danced to Carnatic music, find music in that style. Facilitate inquiry in the form of GVQs for viewing video slices, as lead-ins to learning Bharata Natyam techniques, and to stimulate interest in the art form. Re-examine the inquiry samples given for C1, C2, C3, and C4 as bullet points in chapter 5's "Each Cornerstone—A Method of Inquiry" (pages 106-107) to get ideas for queries.

 What questions get you started?

Breaking the Unit Into Lessons

The unit's point of emphasis is to use Bharata Natyam's gestures and rhythmic footwork to tell a story. Accept the challenge to introduce Bharata Natyam to beginners without compromising it as an art form. Plan five lessons suitable for grades 3 through 5. (It is preferable to omit a style than to unknowingly misrepresent it, trivialize it, or divorce it from its artistic context.)

Include aramandi position, which is the most essential position to Bharata Natyam (first position, demi-plié). Beginners can practice the rhythmic steps and mudras from this position. Teach hasta mudras (hand gestures) along with the sloka (rhythmic chant) that goes with them so that students chant the names of the mudras as they perform them in a warm-up (young students only learn some, not all, mudras). Teach viniyoga, or the way mudras move to tell a story. Teach basic rhythmic footwork and patterns.

To support the artistry of this unit, ask students to analyze and critique footage of a skilled Bharata Natyam dancer performing a varnam. To ensure students learn to follow the hand movement with their eyes, teach the basic sloka and devise movement to accompany it (to be used in Lesson 3): "Where the hand moves, the glance (eye) follows. Where the glance goes, the mind follows. Where the mind goes, the mood follows. Where the mood goes, atmosphere is created." At some point in the unit ask students to:

1. Practice basic mudras (from video #1) and recite their names as you do them.
2. Focus eyes on the movement of the hands to instill the habit of the glance following the movement of the hands.

What else will you include in this unit? What is your point of entry? Will lessons be arranged similar to the lesson breakout below? Will you culminate the unit

- with a critique?
- by emphasizing how universal gestures and stylized postures are to dance?
- with a performance assessment of the student performance of the mudras and viniyogas?
- with an actual performance of several learned phrases of movement featuring mudras and rhythmic step patterns?
- with all of these?

Unit Overview of Bharata Natyam

Five lessons are outlined here to show what is important to include and how the content develops. Use the lesson suggestions as a guide. From this unit sketch, you are to provide the rich details with the help of the resources listed (two videos). This unit forms around "The Monkey and the Crocodile," but other tales may later be substituted. Mudras are its point of entry.

Embed an assessment in the lessons, such as reciting a sloka while performing the series of mudras learned. Note who has trouble, remediate on the spot, and reassess them. The following lesson descriptions enroll the teacher as learner and use participatory verbs to show you are also actively involved in the teaching–learning process as you facilitate learning.

THUMBPRINT OF THE UNIT

1. Gestures
2. Positions
3. Rhythms
4. Unpacking a varnam as stimulus for creating
5. Creating and performing

LESSONS

- Lesson 1
  - > Introduce mudras. Teach those mudras that apply to the tale (wait to introduce the tale).
  - > Teach the four essential positions of the body (mandala beda) in Bharata Natyam: aramandi, sthanakam, aalidam, and prenkana.
  - > Practice mudras while in basic aramandi position.
  - > Introduce "The Monkey and the Crocodile" tale. Ask students to imagine how they would tell such a tale through the gesture language of the mudras before you unveil the story.
  - > Connect the story to its corresponding mudras. Practice them.
- Lesson 2
  - > Review the body positions and mudras. Combine these four mudras with their body positions: king in prenkhana, river in prenkhana, tree in sthanakam, and monkey in aramandi. Practice.

> Teach several rhythmic step patterns that all use three-beat syllables.

> View a slice from video #2 that demonstrates the three-beat syllables; ask students to identify them as they occur.

> With hands on hips, in aramandi position, let them practice selected three-beat rhythmic steps until they are in the body's muscle memory.

> Introduce abhinaya (expression). Teach the sloka of the eyes following the hands (explained in "Preplanning the Unit").

> Then view a slice of video #2 that demonstrates the eyes following the movement of the hands. Use GVQs so students look for the abhinaya of the face and hands during viewing. Discuss it afterwards.

> Review all movements from earlier in the lesson. Add the eyes following the hand movements this time.

- Lesson 3

> View a slice from video #2 that demonstrates the rhythmic steps (explained in "Preplanning the Unit") of the monkey (tha-ki-ta), the river (di-di-thai in prenkhana), and the mountain (tha-ki-ta).

> Teach these three patterns. Let students practice them.

> Combine mudras and body positions learned so far with the steps.

> Practice them next with the eyes following the hands.

> Get and give feedback to peers, then refine the skills of performing the body positions, mudras, rhythmic steps, and focus.

> Introduce the varnam as a section of dance where the performer colors the telling of the story. View a substantial section of the video #2 lecture–demonstration explaining the varnam. Analyze it together. Help students extract from it the artistic points that make Bharata Natyam so compelling and that they can incorporate into their created dance story in Lesson 4.

- Lesson 4

> With this new vocabulary of stylized movement, return to "The Monkey and the Crocodile" tale. Call on this new Bharata Natyam movement vocabulary to create a dance story structured around the tale using mudras, rhythms, focus, and positions. Emphasize abhinaya.

> View and unpack a slice of the actual performance of a varnam in video #2. Look at detail and nuance. Apply these experiences to the process of creating the dance story.

> Divide "The Monkey and the Crocodile" tale into three parts: the friendship, the betrayal, the resolution. Work on only one part at a time until it is complete. Get and give feedback from peers. Practice it.

> Incorporate aspects of the previous lessons into creating, performing, and responding to this story dance.

- Lesson 5

> Incorporate all the unit's skills into this culminating lesson to achieve your learning objectives. Also incorporate a summative unit assessment.

> Complete the creative process.

> Polish and refine the presentations. Show them for critique.

> Compare the original presentations with a section of the varnam performance.

> Facilitate student reflection on the unit as closure.

Teacher Reflection

What did you learn while planning this unit? How will you tie concepts in this unit to previous student learning? How will you make this unit a bridge to future learning? How will this unit contribute to your and to your students' enduring understanding of dance? Of Bharata Natyam? Since this unit introduces Bharata Natyam, what kind of follow-up unit on this style would be best to teach next school year to the same students who experienced this unit?

How can you learn more about Bharata Natyam and practice your skills? Consider bringing in an accomplished artist-in-residence who performs and teaches Bharata Natyam to present a week-long residency or a unit for middle or high school. Use that opportunity to apprentice with the artist-in-residence.

Now that you have fleshed out this unit in detail, place the unit plan in your Perspectives Notebook to show your ability to facilitate culturally diverse units.

Questions to Ponder

1. What does a dance work contribute to a unit of study? Why are dance works included in most units?

2. How do lessons relate to a unit? How do units relate to a LRP? How does the 8SP contribute to integrated instruction?

3. How can you maximize movement time for dancing when you are also incorporating creating and responding to dance?

4. If your own K-12 dance education had included dance works as part of your study, how would your education now be different? How can you help change that omission from K-12?

5. How do units of study address the six characteristics of educational dance?

6. How does the sample unit address the cornerstones? Is it a complete 6DC unit?

Rich Resources

RESOURCES

- Video: *Behind the Scenes with David Parsons* (28 minutes) from www.firstrunfeatures.com.

- Video: *Dancing* (1993, Martha Swope Associates). Program 1 (*Dancing: The Power of Dance*) introduces Bharata Natyam to beginners, and Program 5 (*Dancing: New Worlds, New Forms*) introduces the 1930s era of swing dancing.

- Video and study guide: *Ragamala: A Painting and Poetry in Motion* (1996). Available from Ragamala Music and Dance Theatre. www.ragamala.net has excerpts from Bharata Natyam and explains mudras, gesture language of the face and hands (abhinaya), a brief history of the dance form, and other related aspects of the art form. The performers blend music, painting, and dance in this resource.

- Video: *Dances of India: Learning Bharata Natyam* (Instructional Dance Video) features Padma Chiborlu and is produced by the Culture Center of India LLC. Available from amazon.com.

- Video: *That's Entertainment (Part One): Classic Musicals*. (ISBN 0-79074514-3) Available from amazon.com.

- Brenda Dixon Gottschild, *Digging the African-ist Presence in American Performance,* makes a compelling case for understanding the African influences and aesthetic presence in American modern dance, ballet, and jazz dance (Westport, CT: Greenwood Publishers, 1996).

- Marshall and Jean Stearns, *Jazz Dance—The Story of American Vernacular Dance,* gives a solid basis for teaching jazz through its encyclopedic perspective of vernacular dance—the authentic jazz dance (Da Capo Press, 1994).

- *The Panchatantra,* a collection of tales gathered over 2,000 years ago in India's Vale of Kashmir, is similar to *Aesop's Fables.* Animal characters tell stories with a moral. Adapt them as structures for telling stories in dance through Bharata Natyam gestures, postures, and rhythms. Find the tales in books and for download at www.panchatantra.org.

- *Mirror of Gestures* is an English text version of the Abhinaya Darpana, which demonstrates mudras and explains how to use them.

WEB SITES

- www.parsonsdance.org

- www.swathigroup.com

- http://greetingindia.tripod.com/dance.html for information on kathak, Bharata Natyam, and other Indian dance styles.

- www.kathak.org for information on kathak and the Chitresh Das Dance Company and Chhandam School of Kathak Dance. Mr. Das also teaches in several universities in the United States.

- www.alvinailey.org, Alvin Ailey American Dance Theater (AAADT), for a wealth of jazz-influenced concert choreography by Talley Beatly, Donald McKayle, Alvin Ailey, and others.

- Order the two Bharata Natyam videos from www.kalakendra.com. Kaladendra has high-quality Bharata Natyam DVDs and CDs with skilled demonstrations and performances. Video #1 is "Bharatanatyam—Precepts and Practice." Video #2 is "Bharatanatyam Varnam: The Sum and Substance." It is a double volume video CD: Volume 1 gives a video lecture and demonstration to help understand the varnam, Bharata Natyam's techniques, and the artistry required. Volume 2 presents a full performance of the varnam in recital. Useful for grades three through college.

Reflecting on Teaching

"We
must challenge
our students to
believe, that as they
invent themselves, they
invent the future. They must
go beyond revisiting past
traditions and find a new quality
of poetry in the marks that they
make, whether it be in the art
they create, or in fashioning a
professional role as an artist
or art educator. They must
be challenged to make new
thunder for future moons,
the ones we have not yet
seen."

—Richard Loveless
(1992, p. 137)

This chapter asks you to reflect on how and why you teach. What are the deeper responsibilities and obligations that come with your profession? The ethical dimension affects all you do as a teacher. It affects your impact on the work environment and its impact on you. Ethics should guide the entire school in caring for and nurturing students to maximize their potential and well-being. Ethics affect how you deal with situations that arise at school. Ethics determine the extent of your professional commitment.

The ethical dimension permeates all that happens in an institution, determining how all people there feel about the place they call school. It affects how you work with others, how you teach, how you feel about your students, and how you treat them. It guides you and the entire organization in caring for and nurturing students.

This chapter speaks about the impact of professional ethics on the collective realm of teaching as well as individual ethical concerns that you face as a teacher. This chapter has three purposes:

1. To encourage you to take an intentional, nurturing attitude about interacting with your students

2. To help you bring out the best in a *school* and, when necessary, improve its environment for the sake of all involved—the community, the parents, the school partners, the administration and staff, and the students

3. To support your reflective practice

Ethical Dimension of Teaching

We have learned much about one branch of philosophy: aesthetics. Now we turn to another branch: ethics. Ethics, or moral philosophy, are the values that drive our practice. Sometimes such values are stated in formal codes of ethics, but mostly they find expression through the lives of educators, like yourself.

As you look into the face of a student, what do you see? What is your professional and moral responsibility to him?

Martin Luther King, Jr., said,

The function of education . . . is to teach one to think intensively and to think critically. But education which stops with efficiency may prove the greatest menace to society. The most dangerous criminal may be the man gifted with reason but no morals. We must remember that intelligence is not enough. Intelligence plus character—that is the goal of true education. The complete education gives one not only power of concentration but worthy objectives upon which to concentrate. . . . We must work passionately and indefatigably to bridge the gulf between our scientific progress and our moral progress. One of the great problems of mankind is that we suffer from a poverty of the spirit which stands in glaring contrast to our scientific and technological abundance. The richer we have become materially the poorer we have become morally and spiritually. (Willimon and Naylor 1995, p. 55)

Considering Codes of Ethics

Most professional organizations have a belief statement one must promise to uphold. Why not so for teaching? There is not yet a common code of ethics promulgated by the educational dance field. Neither is there a way for the field to hold specialists accountable to particular behaviors. We rely on higher education teacher preparation programs to instill in preprofessionals the qualities they deem desirable. However, greater than a formal code is each dance specialist's personal integrity grounded in a solid philosophy of teaching.

As you reflected and responded through this text to matters of teaching importance, you acquired a new vocabulary, a new set of ideas about what educational dance requires of you, and new concepts about what you must enable students to do. Now you must ask, "What is my moral responsibility to those I teach? How does my own code of ethics affect my philosophy of teaching?" What is your broader role in education? Examine what you believe about students and learning in light of what is right, humane, moral, and of lasting benefit. How do you teach dance at the same time you also educate the whole child? In addition, how are you both teacher–facilitator and reflective practitioner?

The questions posed in the next pages are to encourage you to draw together what you know with what you believe. These questions do not have concrete answers. They are some of the questions you must grapple with as you become a reflective practitioner guided by your moral compass and sense of ethical responsibility to those whose lives you touch. Teaching is not a profession to impart knowledge. It is a profession to facilitate inquiry. Furthermore, it is a profession to facilitate learning in a humane, conscientious way so that you contribute hugely to the quality and success of a child's life.

Applying Ethics

Willimon and Naylor believe "There is no way to have education without concern for the character of the educators" (1995, p. 56). Teaching is a moral responsibility, meaning an obligation of trust and a commitment to quality. We owe it to students by virtue of our professional credentials to take the job seriously. Gary Fenstermacher of the National Network for Education Renewal (NNER) recommends that we understand our professional commitments in education much as the legal and medical professions do. Our ethics should affect how we are licensed as certified dance specialists. He asks how it is possible to separate the occupational requirements of teaching from the moral and ethical.

> Imagine law with its grand principles of jurisprudence, . . . but without its canons of legal practice. Imagine medicine with its extraordinary knowledge base but without its Hippocratic oath. It seems nearly impossible to imagine the field of medicine without a profound moral commitment to relief from pain and suffering and the preservation of life. . . . Of what value would the knowledge and skill of the physician be without any moral commitment to relieve suffering and preserve life? (Fenstermacher 1990, p. 132)

What code of ethics will you live by? Let your integrity and ethical values guide you to put your sound philosophy into practice in the school, in the classroom, and when you deal with others. Give serious thought to what educational philosophy guides your program. State it in your student handbook and post it in your classroom. Does your program project the fundamental principles you believe should guide your institution? If not, what are you willing to do about it? Because educational philosophy is also the heart and soul of any institution, does your school have a clear philosophy statement that guides its educational policy and goals as well as its political structure? Does this philosophy permeate all activities related to school life? Does this strong sense of who you are as an institution guide planning and implementation of programs and services? How will this affect your ability to create an effective aesthetically driven dance education program?

You will have many opportunities to apply ethics in schools. One way is to be fair and impartial to those around you. Another is to call forth the best from your students by setting standards for behavior as well as artistic growth. Another is to positively interact with students—which also has a positive impact on your school. Another is to facilitate in the classroom positive peer interaction built on trust and mutual support. Foster honesty during peer feedback while supporting the child's efforts. Use critique to build not tear down the child. Eisner adds, "The social conditions, the prevailing norms, the comments and attitudes of peers, the organizational structure of schools, the hidden messages that are conveyed to students in evaluation and testing practices—these also teach" (2002, p. 157).

Creating Inviting Schools

Can't you feel the vibes of a school as soon as you walk through the door? How many schools have you visited? How many schools have you entered where you felt an energy, a sense of pride, a sense of active participation evidenced by the artwork on the walls? Did you notice the cleanliness of the corridors, the faces of the students you met, the faces of the adults who were a part of the school? Did the efficiency and kindness of the office staff and the personal touches in the building take away the sterility of the building? These are the inviting schools.

Have you walked into schools where students were unruly, noisy, belligerent, defiant, and smug and where the atmosphere was more like a juvenile justice ward than an educational setting? Did staff seemed demoralized or glazed over? Have you entered schools where pleasantries are not exchanged, where the building and people seem indifferent or, worse, hostile? Too many of these uninviting schools exist. And it is time to reclaim them and turn them back into places for nurture, caring, and growth. Not only do you owe it to your students; you must demand no less for yourself as a professional. This is a way to apply your professional ethics.

Inviting schools are not all new, not all in the best neighborhoods, not all urban, not all rural, not all anything. Some are not even technologically up to speed. Financial circumstances have almost nothing to do with the fact that they are inviting. The same is true of uninviting schools.

Inviting schools seem glad you are there and sweep you into the momentum being generated, into the process of a nurturing pedagogy. They without exception reflect the attitude, philosophy, and energy of the principal, staff, and teachers. Figure 15.1 paints a broad picture of the attributes of such schools.

Inviting schools are not the product of what is displayed on the walls or the cleanliness of the building. Their atmosphere derives from something more important and intangible that happens in the personal interactions between the people and what is being fostered in the classroom. Inviting schools are not just basic skills school. They are alive with creative process and the arts. The arts are not about competition but collaboration, creative problem solving, team work, excellence, and reflection. They promote group process. They applaud success. "The arts are among the resources through which individuals recreate themselves. The *work* of art is a process that culminates in a new art form. That art form is the recreation of the individual. Recreation is a form of *re*-creation. The arts are among the most powerful means of promoting re-creation" (Eisner 2002, pp. 240-241).

Relational Teaching

As educators, we sometimes think that if we get the curriculum in place, master the instructional strategies, and embed the assessments just right we will be successful. We don't go to the next level of considering how we interact with students while we do this, what we are fostering in our classrooms, how we model relationship-building for students' psychological–social development.

We may think that if we organize the classroom efficiently, achieve national standards, and learn to plan backward, that is enough. We don't go to the next level of asking how a nurturing pedagogy teaches children to value collaborative relationships more than competitive ones, how to learn and interact with those around them through models of shared power and responsibility.

We may think that we if master the technology, get a faster computer with more memory, and have all the right DVD clips to demonstrate everything we need to show in dance, that is enough. We don't go to the next level of consciously creating a learning community using collaborative peer critique to achieve greater artistic ends as well as to increase civility, communication, and trust.

We may think if we learn about NAEP assessments, teach the right combinations, use the 8SP, we are successful. We don't go to the next level of tasking individuals to use what they learn to help everyone, not just themselves.

Inviting schools	Uninviting schools
Produce energy	Consume energy
Have a clear sense of philosophical purpose	Lack a coherent educational philosophy
Encourage growth	Inhibit growth
Invite and attract positive people	Exude negativity
Emphasize creating and creation	Emphasize status quo, even destruction
Move forward with purpose	Go nowhere, are aimless

FIGURE 15.1   Inviting and uninviting schools.

We may think if we ask the essential questions and investigate other cultures, that is enough. We don't go to the next level of using dance inquiry to help learners better relate to the world and to others, to develop greater tolerance and increase mutual respect.

We may think if we keep daily records and set up our grade book efficiently, that is enough. We don't go to the next level to ensure we don't do that for our own glorification to be superior to others but to make the learning environment more efficient so there is time to give positive encouragement and constructive criticism to students.

We may think that if we get all 3s on the Success Factors, create effective rubrics, and master the Four-Step Critique, that to get all the mechanics right is enough. We don't go to the next level to realize that no matter how important mechanics are, one of our main goals is to facilitate relationships between children and the adults who are responsible for them and thereby increase the joy of learning, interacting, and spending time together.

Using Models for Constructive Interaction

Several educational leaders have been turning the pendulum away from what was the "me" generation focus on individual rights toward what may be called a "we" generation focus on constructive interaction with others. This paradigm shift is a trend toward emphasizing what can be accomplished

- through teamwork and collaboration,
- through reflection and problem solving, and
- through building working relationships with others.

Investigate further the impact of two of these dynamic educational leaders. One is Dr. John Goodlad, founder of the NNER: National Network of Educational Renewal (University of Washington–Seattle). The network's impact has been widely felt across the United States, having produced collaborations between colleges of arts and sciences and colleges of education within universities in partnership with selected K-12 schools, called professional development schools (PDS). Goodlad bases his premise on the simultaneous renewal of K-12 and higher education (grades 13 through 16). When teachers and administrators in the PDS collaborate with preservice teacher programs at the university, they effect simultaneous professional development of professors, student teachers, and teacher–mentors in the schools. NNER advances substantive learning, effects character development, practices a nurturing pedagogy, and expects educators to exercise their moral responsibilities to the teaching profession. NNER and its sister program, the Institute for Educational Inquiry, continue to produce some of the more substantive thinking about educational reform and what it means to be an educator today. Their Arts in Teaching and Teacher Education Institute (1998-2002) emphasized substance in the arts, the role of active learning through inquiry, and the value of education to transform lives through the arts (all of which we have discussed in this text).

Another leading contributor to relational teaching and learning is Dr. James P. Comer, professor of psychiatry at the Yale University School of Medicine and founder of the Comer School Development Program (SDP). His reform efforts for urban schools accentuate child and adolescent development through building relationships. He advocates building learning communities in the schools that emphasize working for a common good rather than competing. This translates to our showing students how to work together (much as you do in the peer critique and composing segments of your units) to get better results than each working alone. Show students how to be patient with each other (rehearsing a work), respect differences (unique creative responses to the same stimulus), take turns (showing work and then critiquing a peer's work), and collaborate to strengthen the learning process (group work) and its creative products (critiquing performances).

Dr. Comer bridges psychology and education at Yale School of Medicine's Child Study Program. He says many improved educational practices

> have been less successful than they might have been because they have focused primarily on curriculum, instruction, assessment, and modes of service delivery. Insufficient attention has been paid to child and adolescent development. When these matters are addressed at all, the focus is often on the student—on a problem behavior—and not on how to create a school culture that promotes good growth along the critical developmental pathways. (Comer 2005, p. 758)

Comer describes six developmental pathways: physical, cognitive, psychological, language, social, and ethical.

Student-centered learning should not be construed to promote self-centeredness. It is about developing all four aspects of a child through educational dance—all of which are important. To negate any aspect is to fail the child; to overemphasize one over another is unbalanced (i.e., it is not just about dancing and performing in the kinesthetic–motor aspect). Because one of the four aspects is psychological–social, constructive interaction is vital to success in the other three.

Reflect and Respond

Extend your thinking about dance's four main developmental areas: kinesthetic–motor, aesthetic–artistic, cognitive–intellectual, and psychological–social (see chapter 4) by seeing how the Comer SDP model adds to and further develops them. See Rich Resources for the Web site.

Reflecting on Relational Teaching

Reflect on how your actions aid child and adolescent development. How do they promote healthy, growing relationships and human interactions in an environment of trust? These are all the more needed because we live in a world we often can't trust, a world that isolates us from each other as we increasingly live "behind the wheel" and "in front of the screen." As we grow more distant from each other—ironically attributable in part to overreliance on advanced artificial communication systems (e.g., cell phones, computers, television)—children need to be brought back into relating and interacting with those in their environment. They need you to bridge this chasm to show them how "dance is a way to be fully human and alive" (Charles Fowler) and be put back into meaningful relationship with others.

Even well-meaning parents of the 1990s tended to push children to get ahead (translated: "get ahead of others," be competitive), to take up for yourself (translated: "be prepared to stand up to other people" and not be taken advantage of, be confrontational). You may be a product of that thinking. If so, it's vital that you reflect on what kind of learning environment that attitude produces. Weigh it against a nurturing environment where positive interaction is expected, responsibilities are shared, and collaboration helps individuals achieve personal excellence in a way that is supportive and tolerant.

The arts, through arts education, have a humanizing effect on students when used to increase communication skills, artistic expression, elevation of beauty, cooperation and collaboration, and performance standards of excellence. How can you engage learners not only with the artistic processes but also with each other so that their artistic successes don't set them apart as special and further isolate them? One of your most important roles is to bring people together to respond to each other first with civility and then with trust. Realize that your critique sessions contribute to collaboration as much as to development of artistic work. Both are necessary for well-rounded student growth (artistic, emotional, social, intellectual) and for the long-lasting good of all in your care.

Reflect on how you exert power in the classroom. Can you facilitate learning in a way that your authority is unquestioned without being too heavy handed, which can cause power struggles and behavior problems?

Create learning communities where you, as well as your students, find renewal and inspiration. Reflect on how you can facilitate learning in a way that increases civility (and ultimately civilization). How can you help students build relationships in your classroom that focus on positive interaction yet honest feedback? How can you structure the learning community so young choreographers experience the microcosm of the classroom as a place to work with others instead of against them for the betterment of all? How can you create a learning community where collaboration is valued as a way to problem solve to better achieve quality end results? How can you model the importance of working for positive responses from adults instead of negative ones?

For example, you can teach students how to work for positive responses in a choreography lesson through criteria. When you list criteria for choreography, you are also setting boundaries so students have the freedom to exercise their personal options to express themselves within appropriate limits. Criteria are democratic in that everyone has the same boundaries within which to work. As you ask students to give each other critical feedback based on the criteria, you are in effect demonstrating how a collaborative team works to benefit all. It's not about competition and "me first." This models boundary setting and appropriate response, working in a democracy at the same time you are focused on artistic quality and standards of excellence in dance.

We need relational teaching to move children away from self-centeredness, which is a presocial behavior (see chapter 4). Some describe self-centeredness as the root of all social evils, such as bullying (and bullying's extreme form, terrorism), road rage, violence, and aggressiveness. Children need to move away from these presocial behaviors and toward working for the common good, away from indifference toward engagement. They need

- to be shown how to do it right instead of be yelled at for doing it wrong,
- to be given power to correct their own mistakes and not be made to look stupid or powerless, and
- to achieve standards of excellence and beauty through collaboration and positive interactions.

Nurturing Pedagogy

Neil Postman, an affiliate of NNER, says a poor education is not necessarily caused by a lack of information. He says poor education results because the tether between human purpose and information has been too often severed. He laments how information bombards us from every direction, appears so indiscriminantly, and seems aimed at no one in particular. He decries that information comes at such high speeds, in so many ways, that it is often indecipherable. Such information given without context is devoid of meaning or purpose. "So what?" the child asks. "More information?"

So as we plan instruction, we must know its purpose. Ask yourself these questions:

- Of what value is this information to the receiver?
- What makes the information relevant? (What good are facts that are irrelevant?)
- How does the information relate to dance? To the arts? To aesthetics?
- How does it contribute to the broad learning goals of students?
- What is most important to know about this?
- How does it relate to what students already know?

Find photos of a dance work to stimulate creative inquiry. Ask, "What do you think led up to this one, and what happened after it?" After creating phrases, compare them to the viewing slice to draw students into the dance work.

This further reminds us to ask, What enduring understanding drives the instruction, and what is most important for students to retain? To make sense of what they hear, see, or read, learners must judge its personal value to them and be able to apply it. Help them create a context in which to place new ideas and information so they are educationally relevant.

 So what if someone can execute a triple pirouette? Is that enough?

Dance seems to be a natural medium to nurture individuals. It's a place where everyone can be encouraged to do their best as they acquire skills in moving, thinking, creating, and critiquing. Give nurturing corrections to help students develop proficient skills in dance technique. To berate them for errors tears them down, but to show them how to succeed builds confidence. Give consistent intuitive

463

guidance and feedback during improvisation and exploration to increase self-reliance and comfort in stretching oneself to new levels of creativity. Mentor students in choreography to help them refine creative, aesthetic, and compositional skills. Give constructive criticism to help them edit, refine, and perform. Build an increasingly adept performer and self-assured creator who is competitive with himself and who assists others during their creative process. Give children training wheels until they have steady balance.

A nurturing pedagogy goes beyond teaching dance. You are obligated to teach the whole child, which includes the psychological–social (see chapter 4). That involves helping shape character and developing values as part of the nurturing process. It's a matter of ethical practice.

Promoting Values Education

During the 1990s, education took a hands-off approach to teaching values. Values education seemed too controversial in light of society's cultural plurality, belonging to the realm of "learn at home." Meanwhile, gang membership grew, weapons came to school, and violence became prevalent in a system that theoretically existed to educate for success, to promote productivity, and to encourage positive interaction. It became obvious that too many youth were not getting values education at home. Instead they were learning values from TV, commercials, or from hard and fast video games (many violent). Many of these students' role models neither valued education nor followed societal rules. Students weren't learning values that would make them good citizens. Their behavior at school, which was intolerable, pointed to the breakdown of a values-neutral educational system.

That time of values-neutral education took a toll on teacher preparation programs in higher education as well as on K-12 education. Emphasis was on the mechanics of doing more than showing students how to seek positive interaction by building healthy relationships. Today, educators must take responsibility to instill early the behaviors that help students acquire personal interaction skills they need to thrive. Today's curricula must embed values education for all grades such as the importance of being on time, of following through on commitments, and of being reliable and trustworthy. These become character traits when consistently forged in the school and at home. These also happen to be the main traits employers seek.

Children must learn the consequences of their actions and know the difference between behaviors that are positive and those that are negative, what is of lasting value and what is for short-term gain, and what is selfish and what is generous. It is not a large leap to go from quality of personal interaction in dance as an expressive art to quality of personal interaction with peers and students in general.

What values will you instill in young people to help them be responsible and responsive to those around them? Dance can instill positive attributes of sharing, nurturing, collaboration, and responsibility and still stress accountability to artistic quality.

- How can you increase aesthetic quality in dance as well as promote an aesthetic quality of life?

- How can you help build moral character (i.e., knowing right from wrong, making good choices, accepting responsibility, working hard, contributing to a team effort)?

- How do you foster these values in dance? What might be the results of your efforts? Do you incorporate values such as challenging subject matter with appropriately high achievement standards in a caring, nurturing environment that expects learners to take responsibility for their actions? Do you encourage satisfaction in their accomplishments? Do you discourage bullying and other inappropriate ways to show power?

- What kind of citizens will you create for tomorrow? Will you instill the love of freedom and choice and show them how to take personal responsibility for their choices in a democratic society? Will you prepare them to be visionary leaders to help shape their culture and world or merely mirror their surrounding culture and environment?

Reflect and Respond

Because "the character of the knower intrudes powerfully upon the nature of what is known" (Willimon and Naylor 1995, p. 56), how does our own character affect what we teach? How important is it for us to develop character in our young charges? Of what value are all of the knowledge and skills of dance and aesthetics without a moral commitment to enable students to reach their potential?

School Renewal

We've mentioned the school renewal efforts of Drs. Goodlad and Comer. Now we need to consider the school renewal efforts you will be involved in at the local level and your conduct. Your personal ethics are either supported or undermined by the ethical code of your larger workplace. Formal codes of ethics work well in schools where all adhere to the codes, but it is vital that you have your own personal ethical standards in dance that aren't compromised by outside influences. Reflect on how what you believe about teaching dance should affect your conduct toward others and toward your work. Base your standards of conduct on what you believe (teaching philosophy). In some workplaces you may need to initiate discussions about ethical concerns with peers and administrators. You must hold firm to your own high ethical standards in order to make your workplace a better, more equitable place for those whose lives you touch.

As a dance specialist you may teach hundreds of students a week, so your interaction with them is different from that of the classroom teacher, who sees them daily. Try to establish an internal communication system so students are consistently dealt with and are tracked by various teaching teams. It also helps if teaching teams share similar pedagogical philosophies. Set up communication channels to report deficits as well as strengths in students to the teaching team. Interact frequently with teachers to ensure students' continuing growth.

Facilitating School Renewal

All steps to school renewal are built on the foundation of positive interactions: between children and adults as well as between peers. The arts are vital to school renewal. Vibrant inviting schools don't exist without dynamic arts leaders.

Although every school is not an exciting, invigorating, nurturing, inviting, special place, every school can become so through the desire and energy of those who occupy it. No individual should be demoralized—either student, teacher, administrator, or staff. Exercise confident leadership so school renewal is positive and meets the needs of its constituents. With values clarification, thoughtful discussion, inclusive planning, and dedication of all concerned, a school that lacks spirit can turn around. It can become renewed by finding its purpose.

Mission Statement

Should your school not yet have a mission statement that states its educational philosophy, initiate constructive dialogue with colleagues and administrators about the school, its mission, and its philosophy. Find commonalities and agreements. Bring up the role of the arts. Guide the writing of a purposeful mission statement that addresses all school operations. Ensure that it promotes a democratic organizational flow that determines how all people and programs are systematically handled. And ensure that the mission statement presents a philosophy of how constructive interaction is to happen. Look at the sample mission statement featured on this page. How does its central purpose focus on curriculum? On students? Does it say enough about constructive interaction?

Steps to Renewal

Planning Phase. Renewal comes about by first deciding a change is needed. You must get all stakeholders to the table to get every voice involved in determining the educational philosophy that will guide the school. Address such issues as these:

- What are the roles of faculty and students in the educational process?
- What are the responsibilities of faculty and students to ensure that learning is high quality?
- What is valued here?
- What is the role of the arts?
- What is the school's social responsibility?

> **"[The central purpose] is to develop the life of the mind to the fullest sense: to foster clear and critical thinking, to disseminate valuable information, to facilitate research and to enrich the imagination, broaden sympathy and deepen insight. Middlebury seeks to help each student develop the capacity to contribute to society and find personal fulfillment."**
>
> —Mission statement of Middlebury College (in Willimon and Naylor 1995, pp. 63-64)

465

- What is our collective ethical responsibility?
- What are our academic responsibilities?
- What are the main educational benefits to students, faculty, and the community?

Implementation Phase of School Renewal. To articulate educational philosophy is the first step in moving the school from the planning phase to the implementation phase.

Involve all stakeholders in a process to compose a five-sentence schoolwide mission statement. Involving everyone keeps renewal organic with simultaneous buy-in for change as well as ownership of the decisions.

Implementation starts with the administration and teachers working together in an incremental way to effect change. In other words, ask what will success look like and how will it be measured. Then staff and students set up responsibilities according to agreed-on expectations that cover these areas:

- The social (how people are expected to be treated and to interact)
- The political (who is in charge of what)
- The moral (what is valued and honored)
- The organizational (what structure best supports our mission, our goals)
- The academic (what is taught and to what standard of measurement)
- The aesthetic (where and how the arts are integrated into the curriculum)

Reflect on each of the following school renewal goals. How vital is educational dance to realizing each one of them? Is there a place in the curriculum that better serves these educational purposes? If you are serious about a comprehensive, substantive, sequential program in educational dance that is aesthetically driven, contextually coherent, and inquiry based, how can you not be absolutely vital to the success of your school?

School Renewal Goals

- To prepare students to think critically
- To prepare students to live and work in a democratic society
- To prepare students for higher education or workplace
- To enable students to develop excellent communication skills

- To raise the level of each student's self-confidence
- To increase literacy among students
- To teach students how to interact with others
- To teach students how to work in concert with others
- To teach students how to be ethical and fair
- To enable students to be actively engaged in learning
- To increase students' ability to solve problems and think divergently

Education is about change. When positive change is needed, offer to help. Can't you provide some of the energy to rally school forces in planning for constructive renewal? Don't accept a school that is less than it can be. Help the administration transform it. (Return to chapter 10 to the description of three kinds of schools: arts centered, arts infused, and arts integrated. Which model will your school use?)

Promoting Policy Changes

The teaching profession is sometimes at odds with state policy makers as to how to place value on the educational outcomes of schools—especially arts education. It's a vicious circle. On the one hand, lawmakers are reluctant to allocate money when so few students seem to graduate with the required skills and values to be productive in the workplace and contribute as good citizens. On the other hand, teachers struggle under lawmakers' solutions to this problem in the form of creating more accountability, more tests, more standards, and more standardization. Child-centered learning seems far removed from policy makers' offices. Teachers want more autonomy to use their professional knowledge to benefit students. They argue that good teaching requires complex and sophisticated skills built on a knowledge base that continues to grow and change at a rapid rate.

The debate between lawmakers and teachers centers more around testing (of teachers and of students), measuring success, and optimizing performance than on what constitutes effective, nurturing teaching practices or educationally rich learning environments. Little is heard during this debate about fundamental purposes of teaching: enlightening the young, developing human virtue, providing quality arts education, challenging students, preparing children for productive, responsible lives in a democracy, emphasizing equality and fairness. Little is heard about the ethical obligations of teaching and the profound importance of teachers to the moral development of students. But why? Any human action undertaken in regard to and for the benefit of other human beings has principled implications. What is fair, right, just, and virtuous should always be considered. When a teacher asks a student to share something with another student, moral considerations are present. A teacher's conduct in every way is an ethical matter. If for no other reason than that, teaching is a moral activity. As a child observes the ethics displayed by the teacher, so the child grows—it is hoped that she demonstrates honesty, fair play, consideration of others, tolerance, and sharing. The teacher's ethics and honor are character models for students (Fenstermacher 1990).

The teacher–policy maker debate needs to center around teachers developing ethical practice and exhibiting behaviors that are professional in every way. Policy makers must promote certification standards that promote a nurturing pedagogy in today's schools and must support teacher acquisition of professional knowledge and demonstrated competent practice. Teaching should be more focused on sharing knowledge and skills with the young than on acquiring status, rank, or numbers of graduate hours, which policies usually emphasize. As you promote aesthetic growth in children, help create a new generation of lawmakers and policy makers who value a nurturing pedagogy, high standards, aesthetic education, and values education.

James P. Comer (SDP) noted that curriculum reform and more testing for students and teachers may work fine, but there is no magic in them. He said,

> The magic is in a culture that supports child and adolescent development, and that can only happen through relationships. . . . Think of your own experience and the people you interacted with and their advice to you about what it takes to make it in the world. Think of the people who cared about you and who taught you how to elicit positive responses from people who can make your life better or worse. These are the people who point you toward success. (Comer in Raspberry 2005, sec. 1, p. 3)

Developing Fitness for Teaching

Just to pass education courses doesn't mean one has the right to be certified to teach. Certification is not an entitlement. Certification is a registry of

Teach how a dance's beginning and end relate to each other and to the middle of the dance—they are not to be arbitrary poses.

fit educators. Universities should screen out teacher candidates devoid of a sense of purpose. Higher education should prepare fully committed professional arts educators and role models who light the creative fires for students, nurture their communication skills, and challenge them to make refined qualitative judgments. Because the arts in education inspire the young, how can we do less?

Affecting One's Own Classroom

You have a degree of autonomy in your own classroom and studio. If you believe that teaching is a moral undertaking, interactions in your classroom will promote cooperative, interactive, creative, challenged, and channeled students who are into productive learning. Consider the moral implication of your actions before coldly demanding that students adhere to your rules. Although this method may get order in the class or result in high test scores, a strict autocratic approach misses the mark of a nurturing pedagogy—one that is student centered and inquiry based.

 What are some effective ways to get order, hard work, and excellence? Can you at the same time encourage students, nurture values of cooperation, and foster respect for qualities such as creative invention and perseverance? How can performing arts nurture students' abilities?

Reflective Practitioner

Being a reflective practitioner gives you perspective and enables you to see the big picture and translate what you believe to what you do. Reflection is a thoughtful approach to teaching that helps you examine your professional abilities and better understand what you do. Reflection gives you a context for making positive changes in what you do. There are many kinds of reflection, but consider three kinds: professional, programmatic, and personal reflection.

Professional Reflection

In addition to reflecting on the moral implications of teaching, consider other important areas, such as your own satisfaction with teaching, the quality of your professional development, and your own particular insights and intuition. Determine such things as whether your own artistic growth is personally satisfying enough and whether your skills enable you to facilitate inquiry and present an aesthetically driven curriculum.

Ask yourself questions about nurturing, being a positive role model, and creating a collaborative learning community. Think through the enduring understandings you want to advance through your units. Begin reflective habits now. Start looking for relationships of one thing to another:

- How is composing a good test like teaching a good technique class?
- How is a good curriculum like a well-choreographed work?
- How is teaching a good class like designing a well-crafted piece of choreography?

In addition, reflect on the impact the national dance standards have on your teaching practice:

- How does what students should know and be able to do in dance affect what teachers should know and be able to do in dance education?
- How does what students should know and do in K-12 affect what you must master in college?
- How do national standards inform your understanding of curriculum, instruction, and assessment?

Because you may be the only dance specialist in a school, find another in a nearby school to talk over your concerns, share successes and teaching tips, and serve as reflective sounding boards to each other. It will enrich both of you professionally to have another whom you can trust to listen and give sound advice. Discuss the moral implications of teaching and your ability to be a positive role model for others so that you empower each other to grow.

Programmatic Reflection

A teacher as reflective practitioner evaluates the effectiveness of the curriculum content, the instructional strategies, and the assessment measures he uses. He self-assesses, assesses students, and also evaluates the overall dance program. The cornerstone model gives varied opportunities for students to self-evaluate and peer evaluate in formal as well as informal ways. It is helpful to the older student and the teacher to occasionally reflect together on the strengths and weaknesses of the program with the idea of making it better.

Reflection is required to evaluate each student thoughtfully. By taking a reflective attitude about student progress, you will pick up cues from students throughout a lesson that will tell you much of what you need to know about how and what they are learning.

Student answers to your questions give you feedback to evaluate how effectively you taught the lesson and how actively they engaged in the learning process. Sometimes the actual learning process is different from the lesson plan. Although you design structured lessons, the actual learning process may take a different tangent, miss its mark, or not progress beyond a superficial level so student

> **"There is nothing to call out reflection until a new bothersome or doubtful situation arises."**
>
> —John Dewey (1910)

outcomes are not what you envisioned. Thus, your reflective thinking about student feedback enables you to self-evaluate the process as well as to student evaluate.

Teacher Self-Reflection

In chapter 9 we saw how reflection is a useful form of assessment, particularly self-assessment. Therefore your own reflection is your way of editing and refining your work! Develop a habit of reflecting immediately after teaching a class as well as at the end of units of study. Improve your efficiency and your delivery skills.

On Daily Skills

Facilitating creative dance for children is perhaps your newest teaching skill. Mary Joyce suggested evaluating yourself immediately after teaching a creative dance class:

- Did you and your students fully explore the element?
- Did the children try movements they would not have tried without your question?
- Did you challenge them to extend their ability?
- Did students select and use movements of their own choice at some point during the lesson? (Joyce 1994)

Other self-reflections help you identify whether your instructional plan is sufficient:

- How effective was your instructional plan?
- How age appropriate was the content you selected?
- Was this topic a logical progression for students or were they ill prepared for this lesson?
- How might you have made the point they missed clearer?
- Was the topic over their heads?
- Did this lesson increase understanding of the BSTERs? Artistic use of the BSTERs?
- Was each section of the lesson equally strong (introduction, guided exploration, dance making, editing and refining, and critiquing)?
- What of artistic value did students learn?
- Were critical thinking activities productive?
- Was reflective thinking rich?

It is also helpful to prepare a reflection sheet like the one in figure 15.2 to place in your Perspectives Notebook. Use the sheet to prompt your thinking and reflect on your growing skills. Rate yourself periodically to determine what areas you need to work on. There are also two sample reflective self-assessments in appendix B that you can use once you are in a school. The first ("Sample Formative Teacher Self-Evaluation") is an ongoing, formative assessment to use at regular intervals. The second ("Sample Summative Program Evaluation Form on Cultural Diversity") is a year-end summary of how inclusive the programming has been. Use such documents to strengthen your teaching performance and your practice.

On Teaching Goals

You have been formulating personal Statements of Belief since the start of this book. As you learn new ideas and stretch your thinking about educational dance, what have you added to your statements? Why?

Challenge students to stretch their bodies and their minds through dance.

Teacher Self-Reflection: Teaching Creative Dance

Consider these self-reflection questions and rate yourself on a scale of 1 to 3.

1 = not as successful as you would like   2 = successful   3 = very successful

____ Did you present the element with a visual aid?

____ Did you use all four learning styles effectively (visual, auditory, kinesthetic, tactile)?

____ Did you use tactile reinforcement often while teaching?

____ Did you maximize each moment for learning?

____ Did you use your voice to encourage students to explore and create?

____ Did you use your body language and eye contact to increase their level of involvement in the lesson?

____ Did you increase dance vocabulary and enhance reading skills?

____ Were there any safety issues you needed to address?

____ Did you notice each child and speak his or her name during class?

____ Did you call on students who did not raise their hands?

____ Did your critical thinking questions deepen the experience for students or did the comments remain on the surface?

____ What questions elicited the richest responses?

____ Did you give students enough guidance for reflecting and journaling?

____ Did you remember to ask, "What did you learn today?"

____ Did you relate this lesson to previous learning?

____ Did you relate this information to another subject (science, social studies, math, or language arts)?

____ Did you build aesthetic awareness with your students?

____ Did you remember that you're a teacher first and a dance teacher second?

____ Did you ensure that students felt good about the experience and themselves?

____ Did you keep the students moving as often as possible during the lesson so that they were learning in motion rather than learning while sitting and listening?

____ Did you refocus students often enough that they were able to maintain interest and involvement throughout the class?

____ Did you achieve your goals and objectives?

____ Did your assessments adequately measure the goals and objectives?

____ Was the content age appropriate or should it be revised up or down?

____ Were the instructional strategies effective or do they need to be revised?

____ Were rubrics clear and review criteria on target?

____ **Total points for 26 questions**

Assessment standard:

66-78 points = outstanding   51-65 points = very good   Below 50 = try harder

FIGURE 15.2   Dance teacher self-reflection instrument.

Notebook/Portfolio: Professional Teaching Portfolio

Why is it necessary for preservice dance specialists to build a 6DC cornerstone curriculum strong in dance content, with effective instructional strategies and assessments? What must your Statements of Belief say about a strong dance curriculum? What must your Statements of Belief also say about a nurturing pedagogy with constructive interaction? As you reflect on these concepts, add your own reflections to your Statements of Belief. Place them in your Professional Teaching Portfolio.

- Curriculum content: Learners need depth and breadth in their curriculum. The content must be broad enough to include varied dance styles, include all the arts processes, and enable students to communicate in and about dance. Content must be strong in techniques and skills, creative work, historical and cultural heritage, and aesthetics. You have to master the art form as well as teaching skills.

- Instruction: You should practice inquiry strategies, creative problem solving, and effective arts classroom management. You must enforce safety issues and keep learners on task during class.

- Assessment: Ongoing assessment determines how curriculum content and instructional strategies should be changed, adapted, repeated, modified, and revised for optimum learner success. Embedded assessments increase learning as they provide performance data to evaluate. Ongoing performance assessment makes immediate remediation possible and constantly provides data to evaluate on behalf of individual students, whole classes, and the dance program itself.

- Nurturing pedagogy: To teach from a student-centered perspective develops the whole child in different aspects. How students receive information from adults affects how successful students will be with it. Why is it necessary to create a vibrant, inquiry-based learning community where students collaborate and inquire together about the matters that are most important in dance?

Take a look at your Statements of Belief. What are the most important goals you should accomplish in the long view of your teaching career? Translate what you believe into a forward thinking action plan. Identify your teaching goals by writing them. Start each goals statement with the words, "One of my goals is to . . . " Place the list of goals in your Perspectives Notebook. Periodically reflect on how much of your time you spend accomplishing these goals. Use them to identify anything you believe needs to change to redirect your energies to accomplish your goals.

Importance of Articulating About Dance

A reflective practitioner in the arts also learns to be a vocal advocate for arts education. There are many reasons you must be vocal and articulate. You must be able to speak persuasively about the profession for it to be understood and valued by others. The opportunity to advocate for arts education and dance education arises over and over. You must say what students learned and why it is important. You must tell the principal, the other teachers, the parents, the students, and the community at large, which includes the funders and curriculum personnel at the school, district, state, and national levels. When you write grants to enhance your program, you must be able to write what is important about what you are doing and how it changes lives.

Not only must you be articulate about dance to the world outside your classroom, but you must constantly, consistently, and consciously enable your students to articulate what they are learning. At the same time you develop your students' movement vocabulary for moving and dancing, develop student reflection. Reflecting at the end of class (such as using the essential reflection question: "What did you learn today?" or WDYL?) firms up their perspective on what they do. As they reflect they build vocabulary to verbalize their developing appreciation for dance experiences: their own and the dance works of others.

Teach reflective articulation, just as you teach body part and joint articulation in technique classes. If not, your students will be inarticulate regarding the dance experience. In technique class you get students to articulate their joints to make clear, precise movements that are technically correct in order to develop the ability to express movement well. A dancer's joint articulation is tantamount to developing an articulate body and good technique.

Body part articulation is an expected part of learning to dance. Now add the next step.

Your own reflective articulation encourages you to be the best you can be. It keeps you rooted in the present by processing the past. It keeps you rooted in the present by having a perspective on where you are going in the future.

Questions to Ponder

1. How well does your teacher preparation program help you articulate and deliver a coherent philosophy about educational dance?

2. How do you describe the K-12 schools you attended? How inviting or uninviting were they? What must have been the educational philosophy of the administration and teachers at that school? How important a role should teachers take in effecting and maintaining a collective school environment that is inviting? Make a list of things that might entail.

3. When interviewing for a teaching position with a principal, what might you ask about the mission of the school and its educational philosophy?

4. What kind of classroom atmosphere do you wish to establish and maintain? How important is it to help instill values and civility into your students' lives?

5. Why is composing a good test like teaching a good technique class? Why is teaching a good unit like designing a well-crafted piece of choreography?

6. How often do you formally reflect on your own dancing experiences in technique class? Do your professors ask you to reflect on what you value in their courses? How often do you relate new skills to those you already know? Should you keep a journal about your growth process in technique or choreography class? How often do you get to engage in reflection conversations with your professors? Your peers?

7. How does what students should know and be able to do in dance affect what teachers should know and be able to do in dance education? How does it affect what you must master in college? How does it connect to your studies of curriculum, instruction, assessment?

Rich Resources

- National Network for Education Renewal (NNER), University of Washington, Seattle, WA. Go to the NNER Web site, http://depts.washington.edu/cedren/NNER/index.htm to learn about K-16 school renewal initiatives and to access Goodlad resources such as these:

  > Goodlad, John I. *Education and Democracy: Advancing the Agenda*. Seattle, WA: Institute for Educational Inquiry, 2000. (Visit http://depts.washington.edu/cedren to download a free PDF version of this document.)

  > Goodlad, John I. *Educational Renewal: Better Teachers, Better Schools*. San Francisco: Jossey-Bass, 1994.

  > Goodlad, John I, Roger Soder, Kenneth A. Sirotnik, Editors. *The Moral Dimensions of Teaching*. San Francisco: Jossey-Bass, 1990.

- Comer School Development Program (SDP), a model for transforming urban schools, is part of Yale University School of Medicine's Child Study Center. Comer, professor of psychiatry at the School of Medicine, developed SDP, a school- and systemwide intervention formulated to bridge psychiatry and education. These materials are accessible from the Web site (http://info.med.yale.edu/comer/):

  > Comer, James P. *Leave No Child Behind: Preparing Today's Youth for Tomorrow's World*.

  > Comer, James P. *The Field Guide to Comer Schools in Action*.

  > Comer, James P. "Child and Adolescent Development: The Critical Missing Focus in School Reform," *Phi Delta Kappan* 2005; 86(10): 757-763.

- Order "The Child's Bill of Rights in Dance" from NDEO at www.ndeo.org.

- Order Stevenson, Lauren, and Richard Deasy's *Third Space: When Learning Matters* (2005) from www.aep-arts.org. It describes how the arts transformed 10 schools serving economically disadvantaged students through engaging them as a community of learners and creators.

Developing an Arts-Oriented Teaching Portfolio

"The one essential ingredient is the inspiring teacher—one who has fully experienced the power of the art and can transmit that experience."

—Patricia Knowles and Rona Sande

In this chapter you compile two professional resources to use: a notebook to use in teaching and a Professional Teaching Portfolio for teacher certification. Take time now to polish your items-in-progress from earlier chapters and assemble them to show what you know and can do. Turn your Statements of Belief into a final document titled "My Philosophy of Teaching Dance as Art in Education." As you reflect on what you have learned, select the most important and informative ideas and experiences to include in the document.

You decide as a reflective practitioner what you believe is most critical to educational dance. You began this process in the first pages of this text. Now you are ready to create and use your career materials. Let's prepare two documents:

1. Perspectives Notebook—an informal teaching and advocacy document for dance specialists

2. Professional Teaching Portfolio—a formal document for those completing teacher certification requirements or teaching internships (i.e., student teaching)

Both documents show what you know. The portfolio shows what you can do. Use both for job interviews,

473

professional presentations, graduate school application, and advocacy. Approach these culminating projects as a way to assess where you are now, but also consider them works in progress that you will add to throughout your career.

Preparing a Perspectives Notebook

Your Perspectives Notebook contains materials that help you grow as a professional. Use the notebook to organize all the items prepared throughout the text into a readable file of materials. Continue to develop the notebook as you gain more experience and put what you know into practice. Include the material that has broad application first. Then save your personal reflections in the last section, which is your teaching reflection journal, full of ideas and insights to return to. Use the last section to keep track of teaching tips and lesson ideas, which might otherwise be forgotten.

Let a few well-chosen photos (like this one) represent what learning in your classroom looks and feels like.

Notebook Contents

Get organized! Gather the materials you created throughout this book. Get a 2-inch, white, three-ring notebook with five sectional dividers for each heading:

1. Perspectives on Teaching
2. Knowledge of Dance Education
3. Teaching Skills
4. Resource Documents
5. Reflection Journal

Place your materials according to each heading, and then create a table of contents for page 1 after everything is organized and complete.

1. Perspectives on Teaching

Statements of Belief (From the Introduction)   Return to your original Statements of Belief and to your insights that you added along the way. Use them now to shape your formal philosophical statement about teaching and learning in and through dance. (The original statements will surely point up how much you have grown in thinking during this learning process.) To write this crystallizes what you believe and further enables you to communicate it to others. Include both:

- Your "Philosophy of Teaching Dance as Art in Education"
- Your definition, "Dance education is . . ."

Sign and date these statements.

Materials to Collect   Collect the materials you prepared in the following chapters under Notebook/Portfolio headings:

- "How National Dance Standards Affect My Teaching"—Perspectives Notebook from chapter 2
- "My Roles and Responsibilities as a Dance Specialist"—Perspectives Notebook from chapter 3
- "What I Believe About Student-Centered Learning"—Perspectives Notebook from chapter 4

2. *Knowledge of Dance Education*

CORNERSTONES OF DANCE EDUCATION

- "Reflecting on Cornerstone 1: Dancing and Performing"—Act 1: writing from chapter 6
- "Reflecting on Cornerstone 2: Creating and Composing"—Act 1: writing from chapter 7
- "Reflecting on Cornerstone 3: Knowing History, Culture, and Context"—Act 1: writing from chapter 8
- "Reflecting on Cornerstone 4: Analyzing and Critiquing"—Act 1: writing from chapter 9

INTEGRATING CONTENT

- "Integrating Dance Across the Curriculum" (Perspectives Notebook from chapter 10)
- "Dance's Role in Advancing All the Arts" (Perspectives Notebook from chapter 10)

3. *Teaching Skills*

- How effectively do you integrate cultural diversity? (from chapter 8)
- How effectively do you maintain a learning environment? (from chapter 11)
- How effectively do you manage a classroom? (from chapter 11)
- How effectively do you design instruction? (from chapter 11)
- How effectively do you monitor dance learning? (from chapter 11)
- How effective are your year-long plans? (from chapter 11)
- How effectively do you design curriculum content? (from chapter 12)
- How effectively do you deliver instruction and facilitate inquiry? (form chapter 12)
- How effective are you at assessment? (from chapter 12)
- Triad unit exercise (Reflect and Respond from chapter 12)
- Integrated unit plans (Reflect and Respond from chapter 14)
  - > Bharata Natyam
  - > Ailey's "Wading in the Water"

4. *Resource Documents*

National Standards and Assessments Assemble the external materials that you have been asked to acquire in earlier chapters, such as the *National*

Standards for Dance Education (NSDEs), *Opportunity-to-Learn Standards for Dance Education* (School Delivery Standards—which are reprinted in the NSDEs), *INTASC Teacher Licensure Standards in the Arts,* and the *NAEP Arts Education Assessment Framework*.

State Standards and Assessments Gather state documents that pertain to educational dance in your own state including frameworks and achievement standards. Include compendiums such as an arts education framework if it includes dance. Contact your state office of education to order them.

5. *Reflection Journal*

- Teaching practices
  - > Key survival skills (see chapter 11)
  - > Most important headings from student handbook (see chapter 11)
- Self-assessments
- Peer assessments

Now Put Your Notebook to Work

Show what you know. Find opportunities to use your notebook to

- make professional presentations at PTO meetings, conferences, and education courses;
- aid advocacy efforts;
- raise awareness of dance education issues;
- share documents and ideas with administrators; and
- identify talking points for poster and PowerPoint presentations.

Regularly add to section 5: Reflection Journal as you encounter opportunities to self-assess and get informal peer feedback on your work. Keep building this section with useful ideas to further your teaching practice.

Preparing Your Professional Teaching Portfolio

A Professional Teaching Portfolio is required for K-12 certification in dance. This formal, impressive, polished compilation documents your readiness to teach and confirms your credentials. It also informs its readers about educational dance—especially during job interviews. Include the items listed and other special artifacts that attest to your proficiency for teaching dance. Do not put everything in your portfolio, especially items that better fit the notebook, which is less formal.

Make your portfolio a purposeful collection of your credentials. Gather that which you believe reflects your best work, development, and thought. Let the portfolio speak for you. Be sure it demonstrates what you can do but also shows how you evaluate your own skills as a reflective practitioner. Let it authentically document how you apply your knowledge and skills in real-world school settings. The most common requirements for portfolios are listed next. You may alter the suggested content outline to accommodate your needs and those of your accrediting agency. Each artifact should be of the highest quality. The portfolio is about polish, professionalism, and promotion (of dance education and your teaching abilities).

Portfolios generally need this kind of information and documentation:

1. Philosophy of teaching (Statements of Belief, teaching reflections)

2. Knowledge of your subject (written papers, reports, subject reflections)

3. Achievement and skills as a teacher (signed evaluations, awards)

4. Sample lesson plans (your own lesson and unit plans)

5. Resource documents (standards, frameworks, state assessments)

6. Resume and educational background (resume, transcript)

Portfolio Contents

Get a 1-1/2-inch, black, three-ring binder and at least 16 tabbed dividers. The basis of your portfolio will be the 10 INTASC core principles recommended for teacher licensure in the arts (refer to chapter 3). Most of your portfolio's contents will be organized around these 10 core principles. Label 10 dividers—one per principle. Label one divider each for Resume, Philosophy Statement, Artistic Skills, Outside Documentation, and Electronic Portfolio.

The order of items in your portfolio is not nearly as important as the quality of the documents. If your state is one of more than 33 that adopted the INTASC

standards as their model for teacher licensure, these standards will be your primary benchmarks. NCATE also adheres to the INTASC standards as the benchmarks for initial teacher licensure (certification). Even if your state doesn't require you to meet these standards, measuring your proficiency by national standards demonstrates that you are on par with others in your field. When you seek jobs in other states, this becomes very worthwhile.

Your exact portfolio specifications are determined by your university and are based on state requirements. Your professor will tell you if items in your portfolio are to be arranged differently. Wait to prepare your table of contents after you assemble all your artifacts!

Because you want to present your portfolio artistically, weigh matters of artistic design and unifying themes as you begin. Make it visually coherent. Keep it aesthetically appealing so as to draw readers in.

Document yourself performing as part of your portfolio in order to show what you can do artistically.

476

Include several photos of your students with you teaching them. You might even design dividers with photos appropriate to each section. Let your artistry and personality shine through your portfolio so an interviewer becomes intrigued about—and sold on—what you offer.

PORTFOLIO OUTLINE

Table of contents

1. Resume
2. Philosophy statement
3. INTASC principles (principles 1-10 listed separately)
   > INTASC Principle 1
   > INTASC Principle 2
   > INTASC Principle 3
   > INTASC Principle 4
   > INTASC Principle 5
   > INTASC Principle 6
   > INTASC Principle 7
   > INTASC Principle 8
   > INTASC Principle 9
   > INTASC Principle 10
4. Artifacts supporting artistic skills (media based and print based)
5. Outside documentation of teaching skills
6. Electronic portfolio

Tab 1—Resume

Make resumes easy to read and to the point. A reader—presumably a principal—won't need to know every detail of your experiences. One can always request more information. Do include these:

- Full name and contact information (address, phone number, e-mail address)
- Dance education career objective
- Formal education
- Artistic experience (include dance and all the arts)
- Performance skills (include performing, choreography, culturally diverse skills in dance)
- Teaching experience
- Special recognition or awards (especially in performing arts)
- Personal skills (such as computer skills, playing a musical instrument, managing

backstage during performance, publicity for performance)

Tab 2—Philosophy Statement

"My Philosophy of Teaching Dance as Art in Education"—which is in your Teaching Perspectives Notebook—makes another grand entrance here. Both notebook and portfolio need to prominently display your philosophy. Figures 16.1 and 16.2 show sample philosophy statements.

Tab 3—Artifacts (Contents) Based on the INTASC Core Principles

Not just dance and the arts but all subject areas use the same 10 INTASC core principles as the national standards for initial teacher licensure. Your portfolio should show your expertise and demonstrate your mastery of all 10 principles.

Order a copy of national arts standards for teacher licensure: *Model Standards for Licensing Classroom Teachers and Specialists in the Arts: A Resource for State Dialogue*, June 2002 (see Rich Resources). Read the details of each principle. But pay close attention to Principle 1, which delineates what you as a dance specialist should know and do in dance as well as in the other arts (www.ccsso.org/intasc).

For each of the 10 principles, either prepare or collect several documentary artifacts and at least one reflection statement (one to two pages).

Artifact is the term for what you select to best represent the quality and diversity of your expertise. Artifacts are to be well chosen, not a conglomeration of everything you have ever done. No one wants to wade through garbage to get to the good stuff. So make it easy on the reader. Cull duplicative items so the artifact you select best represents all of that type of material. Usually, less is more.

Assemble several artifacts for each principle. Choose samples that display your understanding and competence in each principle, such as lesson plans, student work samples, and assessment criteria. Content quality is more important than quantity. Your portfolio is not a scrapbook of all your products but a selective documentary of your professional abilities.

Reflection statements for each principle include three parts:

1. The rationale for choosing each artifact
2. A reflection of how you have grown in experience and perspective in that principle
3. How you plan to refine these skills to continue to grow

What I Believe About Teaching Dance as Art in Education

I believe that dance is a primal art, arising out of the core of our humanity as a means to communicate. I see it as a deeply personal, intrinsic part of the self. Too many in our culture—cut off from their dancing roots—have undeveloped their capacity to express through movement what is vital to life. This is why educational dance is so essential to the full development of each person in K–12.

Educational dance must not be solely activity based but should also integrate intellect, body, feeling, and spirit to heighten self-awareness. Every person is entitled to experience process and product to harness dance as a powerful means of artistic expression. Dance should help us achieve balance between our inner and outer worlds.

I believe that educational dance deserves to be a core subject because it refines motor skills and presents challenging subject matter for higher-order thinking, creating, and performing. It enhances perceptual skills, reveals new relationships, and empowers learners to discover solutions to complex problems of time and space.

I believe that teachers must approach teaching as an art. They should come to teaching with a strong background in the dance discipline. I believe that standards should be used as benchmarks so good teachers use them as springboards to motivate students to exceed them.

I believe that creative dance and educational inquiry are basic to dance learning. Dance from other cultures must be integrated into dance teacher preparation as a way to view the world of dance and teach it. I value the kind of cross-disciplinary ties that stimulate intellectual growth and open up rich creative opportunities for dance. I see reflection as necessary to learning and value specialists who incorporate it into practice to grow wisdom alongside skills, who know not only what to teach but why.

—Brenda Pugh McCutchen, MFA Dance

FIGURE 16.1   This sample philosophy statement incorporates my basic beliefs about teaching dance in school-based settings.

My Philosophy of Education

Education is much more complex than mastering traditional math and language skills for reproduction in defined testing situations; it is about teaching our children to be successful in all realms of their lives. It is about giving them the tools to be independent thinkers and seekers of knowledge to prepare them for an uncharted future.

How do we present and make sense of this educational complexity? Primarily, we must broaden the curriculum to emphasize independent investigation of knowledge by the students while focusing on the interrelationship of all areas of study. The "real world" does not exist in small compartments of knowledge. In the real world, history, art, mathematics, psychology, and personal relationships all blend together to create what is known as the culture of our society. Outside of the classroom, students live in this culture , and it is essential that they learn how to effectively use investigative tools to explore not only the nature of our culture but also our culture's relationship to other cultures. Therefore, it is our job as educators to prepare students to be successful in the future outside world, not just in the immediate academic classroom. . . .

Through the study of many different realms of life and the complex connection between these realms, children begin to see and understand the vastness of the world in which they live. Through these studies our future adults gain tools of inquiry, confidence in their ability as individuals, and the freedom of imagination to apply their knowledge to the needs of their lives. If we can provide this for our students, we will have given them not only the tools with which to view the world but the tools with which to view and redesign the world as they desire it to be.

—Nicole Manuel Almeida, BA, Dance Education

FIGURE 16.2   This statement comes directly from Nicole's Professional Teaching Portfolio. It was written at the completion of her teaching internship en route to teacher certification.

See an example of a reflection statement on INTASC Principle 4 from a student-teaching intern's portfolio (Nicole Manuel Almeida) in appendix B.

INTASC Principle 1 *The teacher understands the central concepts, tools of inquiry, and structures of the discipline(s) he/she teaches and can create learning experiences that make these aspects of subject matter meaningful for students. (Subject Matter Knowledge)*

Principle 1 should contain a minimum of five lesson plans: the first four feature your teaching abilities in each of the four dance cornerstones and the last shows how you integrate the cornerstones to create a context for studying dance. This does not imply that the first four lesson plans should include only one cornerstone, but one should be prominent. Document your understanding of the how, why, when, where, who, and what of educational dance (see chapters 5-10 for details).

Possible artifacts: Lesson plans, student projects, assessment criteria, tests

INTASC Principle 2 *The teacher understands how children learn and develop, and can provide learning opportunities that support their intellectual, social, and personal development. (Child Development)*

Choose documents that show your understanding of appropriate material for various age and developmental levels. Include well-designed instruction in which students explore, test, and refine different creative solutions to artistic problems. Also show how you get students to reflect on, critically analyze, and explain their artistic choices and preferences.

For example, include two lesson plans focusing on the use of space in choreography—one for third grade and one for tenth grade, to demonstrate your ability to present the same concept at two different developmental levels (see chapters 4 and 7).

Possible artifacts: Lesson plans, student projects, assessment criteria, video of model lessons

INTASC Principle 3 *The teacher understands how students differ in their approaches to learning and creates instructional opportunities that are adapted to diverse learners. (Diversity of Learners)*

Include at least two documents showing lesson material presented, practiced, or assessed in several ways to address students with different learning styles or special needs: for example, a lesson plan in which students read information on the parts of a proscenium stage, draw the stage with all its parts, discuss its dimensions, and create a movement study out of a sequence of stage directions.

To celebrate cultural diversity, document how you focus on a range of cultural and racial perspectives. Lesson plans on specific cultures and their authentic dances would serve well.

Dance is for everyone including those with physical, emotional, or cognitive disabilities. Show how you adapt content, instruction, and assessment to

Dance is a visual–kinetic art. This dancer demonstrates the ability to bodyshape, bodythink, and bodyspeak as she performs.

meet individual needs. Show how you challenge the gifted and talented without disrupting the flow of the class or isolating individual students. Then show how you use these students' skills in groups to enrich education. Include documents that reveal your understanding of special needs and your ability to bring lessons to life for those with special physical, cognitive, psychological, or perceptual needs without sacrificing high standards (see chapter 4).

Possible artifacts: Lesson plans, student projects, assessment criteria

INTASC Principle 4   *The teacher understands and uses a variety of instructional strategies to encourage students' development of critical thinking, problem solving, and performance skills. (Instructional Strategies)*

Feature at least three different instructional strategies. They may be in separate lesson plans or multiple strategies in one lesson. Select the most effective and creative of your teaching experience. Show how you vary teaching roles during instruction: instructor, facilitator, director, coach, and performer.

Possible artifacts: Lesson plans, student projects, assessment criteria, video documentary of teaching

INTASC Principle 5   *The teacher uses an understanding of individual and group motivation and behavior to create a learning environment that encourages positive social interaction, active engagement in learning, and self-motivation. (Learning Environment)*

Students must feel safe and supported by the teacher and their classmates. List classroom rules and expectations, lesson plans that involve student inquiry and active learning, examples of peer support, and effective group and individual activities. Show examples of how inquiry motivates learners to initiate independent research or special projects. Include collaborative projects that resulted in choreography or performance and those that resulted in independent reflective and critical thinking.

Show your innovative classroom management techniques and ways you keep students on task. Show evidence of how you build scaffolding into teaching practice. See appendix B for a completed sample of INTASC Principle 5 by a student-teaching intern showing the artifact (document) she selected for her portfolio as well as her three-part reflections on this aspect of teaching (Nicole Manuel Almeida).

Possible artifacts: Lesson plans, student projects, assessment criteria, effective management techniques

INTASC Principle 6   *The teacher uses knowledge of effective verbal, nonverbal, and media communication techniques to foster active inquiry, collaboration, and supportive interaction in the classroom. (Communication)*

Include documents that demonstrate your ability to integrate media and technology into instruction (e.g., TV, video, PowerPoint and other computer programs). Evidence your effective verbal corrections and directions throughout a class. Demonstrate your skills at using a drum to nonverbally communicate during a creative dance class. Show examples of guided viewing questions that lead students to unpack dance works. Show lessons that demonstrate how you use video clips of great dance works to help learners understand the context of dance and make informed aesthetic critique (see chapter 9). Document your effective use of body language to communicate support and enhance students' feelings of safety.

Possible artifacts: Lesson plans, student projects, questioning strategies, technology examples for classroom and software you use

INTASC Principle 7   *The teacher plans instruction based upon knowledge of subject matter, students, the community, and curriculum goals. (Planning/Integrated Instruction)*

Demonstrate that you can make subject matter relevant to the lives of your students, community, and the cultural environment in which they live. Include examples of activities that draw on students' previous cultural, social, or physical experiences. Illustrate long- and short-range planning designed collaboratively to cross disciplines while simultaneously meeting dance goals and objectives. Show planning that reflects knowledge of national, state, and local standards. Include your 1-year long-range plan (see chapters 3, 6-10, and 12).

Possible artifacts: Long-range plan, lesson and unit plans, student projects, goals and objectives with assessment criteria

INTASC Principle 8   *The teacher understands and uses formal and informal assessment strategies to evaluate and ensure the continuous intellectual, social, and physical development of the learner. (Assessment)*

Demonstrate a variety of methods for evaluating student progress that align with instructional goals. Show how you gain information about students as learners and provide feedback to them to aid their growth. List the criteria used in both informal and formal assessments. Include an informal assessment of a choreography assignment, a written test, or a project assignment with a teacher-directed (and a student-directed for older students) rubric.

Possible artifacts: Lesson plans, assessment criteria, rubrics, student reflection, tests, video clips, peer and teacher feedback, sample of student work

INTASC Principle 9 *The teacher is a reflective practitioner who continually evaluates the effects of his/her choices and actions on others (students, parents, and other professionals in the learning community) and who actively seeks out opportunities to grow professionally. (Self-Reflection/Professional Development)*

Demonstrate that you are a conscientious practitioner who seeks to grow professionally (see chapter 15). Document participation in professional workshops and organizations. Demonstrate that you are open to a variety of approaches to teaching and learning in dance. Show how you work with students and colleagues to reflect on student work, seek professional development, and share resources. Include two iterations of one lesson plan: the original plan and a revised version after you have reflected on how the lesson achieved its goals in actual practice. Say how you would modify it for future use to be more effective. See appendix B for a completed sample of INTASC Principle 9 by a student-teaching intern showing the artifacts (documents) she selected for her portfolio as well as her three-part reflections on this aspect of teaching (Nicole Manuel Almeida).

Possible artifacts: Lesson plans, student projects, assessment criteria, catalogs from conferences, proof of membership in professional organizations, assessment from or for other colleagues

INTASC Principle 10 *The teacher fosters relationships with school colleagues, parents, and agencies in the larger community to support students' learning and well-being. (Community Involvement)*

To maintain a flourishing dance program is next to impossible without support from parents, colleagues, and others in the community. Seek help from parent volunteers for special projects and performances. Demonstrate your ability to communicate with and seek their assistance.

Demonstrate your cross-curricular lessons. Document collaborations. Show how you incorporated

guests with specialized dance skills into your curriculum. Document field trips to live performances. Display the study guides and show how they were used. Include evidence of involving parents in student learning experiences.

Possible artifacts: Lesson plans; student projects; letters to parents, colleagues, or agencies in the community; fund-raising plans and business contacts; collaborative lesson planning; identification of artists-in-residence; sample PTO presentations

Italicized standards reprinted, by permission, from Council of Chief State School Officers, 2002, *Model standards for licensing classroom teachers and specialists in the arts: A resource for dialogue* (Washington, DC: Council of Chief State School Officers).

Tab 4—Artifacts Supporting Your Artistic Skills

As a dance specialist you are a vibrant artist, and the person interviewing you for a job will want to know that. Include a DVD of you performing and another that shows your choreographic works. Include programs from performances in which you danced and a picture of you performing for documentation, for visual appeal, and to underscore your artistry. Include a dated copy of your latest audition and placement form in technique.

Tab 5—Outside Documentation of Teaching Skills

Include formal assessments from outside evaluators (e.g., college supervisors, principals, curriculum specialists) that testify to your teaching competence. Select a few of the most representative. See the information that follows and the OTA-D evaluation instrument in appendix B (also see "Considerations for Hiring a Qualified Dance Specialist" in appendix B).

Include the best of some of these: your latest audition and placement forms, signed skills checklist, written evaluations, signed supervisor observation sheets with comments, and documents that verify that you achieved specific certification standards.

Tab 6—Electronic Portfolio

In addition to a hard copy of your portfolio, compile a PowerPoint presentation (or similar electronic format) on a CD featuring highlights of your portfolio. Add artifacts, reflections, and pictures from the hard copy. Make your electronic portfolio artistic and visually appealing to your audience. Make a sleeve or pocket for it in the portfolio itself.

Assessing Portfolio Contents

Similar to the way you assessed your developing skills throughout your study, self-assess your portfolio. First check for omissions (add anything missing).

Assessment Rubric for Portfolio

Criteria	5	4	3	2	1
A. Quality of artifacts and reflections	Highly effective use of artifacts that demonstrates an advanced understanding of concepts and content. Compelling awareness and careful observation. Artifacts/reflections are consistently convincing and interesting.	Appropriate use of artifacts that demonstrates a clear understanding of concepts and content. Shows awareness and observation but with less substance than a 5-point essay. Support is very strong but may lack a high degree of creativity and richness.	Use of artifacts demonstrates a sufficient understanding of concepts and content. Shows only adequate awareness and observation. Essay is strong but not necessarily original: support reinforces the focus but lacks creativity.	Artifacts fall short in demonstrating an understanding of concepts and content. Ideas are predictable and support is missing detail.	Inadequate presentation and completeness. It is unacceptable and must be redone. Artifacts fail to demonstrate an understanding of concepts and content. Absence of basic comprehension, relevant ideas, and creativity.
B. Completeness of material	Exemplary document in every way. All components are thoroughly represented. • Description of unit • Lesson plans • Reflections • Videotape • Analysis of student learning	All components are thoroughly represented. • Description of unit • Lesson plans • Reflections • Videotape • Analysis of student learning	All components are represented. • Description of unit • Lesson plans • Reflections • Videotape • Analysis of student learning	Components missing.	Components missing.
C. Mechanics	Uses exemplary writing skills with no errors. Exemplary use of capitalization, punctuation, spelling, and grammar. • No spelling errors • No capitalization or punctuation errors • No errors in application of grammar	Uses standard English and good writing skills with no mechanical errors. Commendable use of capitalization, punctuation, spelling, and grammar. Three errors or fewer in capitalization, punctuation, spelling, and grammar (collectively).	Appropriate standard English usage and writing skills. Commendable use of capitalization, punctuation, spelling, and grammar. Five errors or fewer in capitalization, punctuation, spelling, and grammar (collectively).	Does not use standard English and writing skills. There are more than five errors in capitalization, punctuation, spelling, and grammar (collectively).	Inappropriate English usage. Inadequate use of capitalization, punctuation, spelling, and grammar. There are more than 10 errors in capitalization, punctuation, spelling, and grammar (collectively).
D. Artistic presentation	Presented with exemplary degree of professionalism	Presented with high degree of creativity, artistry, and style	Appropriate professional style	Meets minimum standards	Poor presentation

FIGURE 16.3   After editing your portfolio down to its essential elements, use this rubric to evaluate the quality and completeness of your material. Then evaluate its organization and presentation. Use results to refine your final portfolio.

Next check for items that are either extraneous or of poor quality (remove them). If the poor-quality item can be replaced with one of high quality, do so.

Rubric to Assess Your Portfolio

Now that you have edited your portfolio down to its actual contents, assess its quality based on the following criteria. Use the rubric in figure 16.3 to assess the following:

A. Quality of artifacts and reflections

B. Completeness of material

C. Mechanics

D. Artistic presentation

Use a 5-point scale:

5 = exceeds expectations, exemplary in all aspects;

4 = meets expectations;

3 = acceptable;

2 = weak or incomplete;

1 = inadequate and incomplete.

Overall Teaching Assessment in Dance (OTA-D)

Specific standards of excellence for teaching dance are sometimes unavailable. For dance to be on par with other academics, standards of excellence need to be identified, assessed, and validated. "Self-reflection on one's own teaching, though important, is seldom sufficient . . . What we need is critical yet supportive feedback from those who know how to see the teaching of the arts in practice" (Eisner 2002, pp. 56-57). Look at the Overall Teaching Assessment in Dance (OTA-D) Checklist (appendix B). It shows—and measures—specifically what you need to be able to do to be an effective teacher. Use it to self-assess.

If your state lacks detailed teaching competencies in dance, recommend that evaluators use the OTA-D to validate your collective teaching skills for your portfolio. It is comparable to evaluations for other core subject areas. Get a qualified outside evaluator (such as your dance education professor, **supervising teacher**, or supervising principal) to evaluate you during your internship in a K-12 teaching setting. You must have an official document from outside sources verifying that you have been

Let your portfolio speak for you.

officially observed in a classroom and are competent to manage these areas: planning, curriculum development, instruction, assessment, managing a learning environment, monitoring learning, maintaining high standards, and professional and aesthetic development. Include this evaluation (or other specified state assessment document) in section 5 of your portfolio, Outside Documentation.

Now Put Your Portfolio to Work

Use your Professional Teaching Portfolio

- as documentation for K-12 teacher certification in dance,
- as reference during job interviews and as documentation to share with principals,
- for graduate school applications,
- for professional presentations and conferences, and
- to determine talking points for meetings.

Let your portfolio speak for you and for educational dance in dynamic ways. Proudly present it to others.

Closing Statement

Your portfolio speaks to who you are, what you know, and how you educate the young. Craft it to show the best of who you are and what you do.

There will no doubt be other worthy artifacts or documents to include that have not been mentioned here. Consider other items such as travel to other countries, studies from other cultures, lists of resources, research you have done, audition materials, creative writing (e.g., poetry, prose), memberships in national organizations like NDEO, or interviews with notable dance educators. You may choose to include a video or DVD of yourself teaching various age levels as a demonstration of your teaching ability. Take stock of all you offer dance education. Go forth and make it happen.

Inspired teachers not only teach, they inspire others. Continue to seek your own inspiration. *Inspire. Inquire. Acquire.*

> Talent is a blessing. And so is the pedagogic talent in dance. Our task, however, lies in serving: to serve the dance, to serve the work, to serve man, and to serve life.
>
> Keep the artistic fire from being extinguished, dear friend—hold high the torch! (Mary Wigman 1966, p. 111)

Rich Resources

INTASC document: *Model Standards for Licensing Classroom Teachers and Specialists in the Arts: A Resource for State Dialogue.* Available on the Web for printing at www.ccsso.org/intasc.html. Bound copies may be obtained from the Council of Chief State School Officers, One Massachusetts Ave. NW, Suite 700, Washington, DC 20001-1431; phone 202-336-7016; fax 202-408-1938.

Appendix A

Reference Lists of Concepts

Appendix A gives you easy access to the most-often-used lists in the text that are integral to understanding the content as well as to teaching dance as art in education.

1. Bloom's Taxonomy of Thinking
2. Dance Elements: BSTER
3. Developmental Aspects of Educational Dance
4. Four-Step Critique (Primarily for Professional Works)
5. Lerman's Critical Response Process
6. Main Technique Areas
7. National Standards for Dance Education (1994) Content Standards
8. Opportunity-to-Learn Standards
9. 6DC Model
10. Ten Principles of Design
11. Three-Act Reflection
12. Turning Success Factors Into Performance Indicators

Bloom's Taxonomy of Thinking

These appear in chapter 4 (figure 4.4) and chapter 9 (figure 9.2). The levels of thinking are for all ages. Teachers target different levels by the questions they pose to students and the active learning experiences they set up. The aim is for teachers to facilitate learning that calls on the three highest and most complex of the thinking skills. Bloom's taxonomy list goes from lower- to higher-order thinking:

1. Knowledge
2. Comprehension
3. Application
4. Analysis
5. Synthesis
6. Evaluation

Dance Elements: BSTER

These appear in chapter 6 (figure 6.2). All five element categories are present in each dance. The dance elements are the universal vocabulary of dance: different aspects of how the body moves in space, in time, with energy (dynamics), as well as in relation to something. The dance elements are both a conceptual vocabulary and a kinetic vocabulary. BSTER is an acronym for the elements associated with

- body,
- space,
- time,
- energy, and
- relationships.

Developmental Aspects of Educational Dance

These appear in chapter 4. Educational dance should advance students' growth in four areas of development: the kinesthetic–motor, the aesthetic–artistic, the cognitive–intellectual, and the psychological–social. Consciously move students from one stage and level to the next.

STAGES OF KINESTHETIC–MOTOR DEVELOPMENT FROM PREFUNCTIONAL TO ADVANCED PERFORMANCE

- Stage 1: prefunctional
- Stage 2: functional
- Stage 3: preperformance
- Stage 4: proficient performance
- Stage 5: advanced performance

STAGES OF AESTHETIC–ARTISTIC DEVELOPMENT FROM NAIVE TO SOPHISTICATED

- Stage 1: preoperational
- Stage 2: operational
- Stage 3: connectional
- Stage 4: insightful
- Stage 5: advanced

LEVELS OF COGNITIVE–INTELLECTUAL DEVELOPMENT FROM BASIC TO HIGHER ORDER

- Level 1: knowledge
- Level 2: comprehension
- Level 3: application
- Level 4: analysis
- Level 5: synthesis
- Level 6: evaluation

STAGES OF PSYCHOLOGICAL–SOCIAL DEVELOPMENT FROM PRESOCIAL TO PROSOCIAL

- Stage 1: self-centered
- Stage 2: allowing
- Stage 3: other oriented
- Stage 4: empathetic
- Stage 5: prosocial

Four-Step Critique (Primarily for Professional Works)

This appears in chapter 9. Use this critique format to unpack a dance work and analyze its parts and its whole effectiveness. Use it to generate discussion and lead students into higher-order thinking and critical analysis. It is a different process from the facilitated Lerman Critical Response used to give personal feedback to a choreographer.

- Step 1: describe (aesthetic scanning)
- Step 2: analyze
- Step 3: interpret
- Step 4: evaluate

Lerman's Critical Response Process

This appears in chapter 9. Use Lerman's Critical Response Process steps to give direct feedback to the choreographer. Facilitate the discussion as a third-party mediator.

- Step 1: statements of meaning
- Step 2: choreographer as questioner
- Step 3: neutral questions from responders
- Step 4: permissioned opinions

Main Technique Areas

These appear in chapter 6. As soon as you begin to teach technique (around fifth grade), incorporate these areas in developmentally appropriate ways. They are the main technique areas to build in a dancer:

- A strong sense of center
- Muscular strength: core muscle strength (central torso)
- Muscular strength: limbs
- Use and articulation of the feet
- Body alignment (lower body, torso, shoulder girdle, arms, neck, and head)
- Hip rotation (turned out and parallel)
- Placement of arms and legs in relation to the torso

- Placement of weight between feet
- Flexibility and stretch
- Balance
- Joint articulation and movement flow
- Turning (axial and locomotor, and on different axes)
- Elevation (lift, lengthening torso)
- Elevation (jumps, leaps, air work)
- Landing (safely articulating through each joint)
- Breath support
- Coordination of movements
- Use of multiple body supports
- Shaping (torso and limbs)
- Accurate rhythm, beat, and timing
- Steps (basic to complex)
- Focus
- Muscular endurance
- Cardiovascular endurance for performance
- Range of movement qualities
- Full range of dynamics

National Standards for Dance Education (1994) Content Standards

These appear in chapter 2. Seven NSDE content standards apply to all students in K-12. Under each one are various age-appropriate achievement standards (not shown here) that students are expected to achieve by grades 4, 8, and 12.

- **Content Standard 1:** Identifying and demonstrating movement elements and skills in performing dance
- **Content Standard 2:** Understanding choreographic principles, processes, and structures
- **Content Standard 3:** Understanding dance as a way to create and communicate meaning
- **Content Standard 4:** Applying and demonstrating critical and creative thinking skills in dance
- **Content Standard 5:** Demonstrating and understanding dance in various cultures and historical periods
- **Content Standard 6:** Making connections between dance and healthful living

- **Content Standard 7:** Making connections between dance and other disciplines

This material is reprinted from the *National Standards for Dance Education and the Opportunity-to-Learn Standards in Dance Education* with permission of the National Dance Association (NDA). The original source may be purchased from: National Dance Association, 1900 Association Drive, Reston, VA 20191-1599.

The Dance Standards were completed as part of the Arts Standards, a project developed by the Consortium of National Arts Education Associations (American Alliance for Theatre & Education, Music Educators National Conference, National Arts Education Association & National Dance Association). This project was under the guidance of the National Committee for Standards in the Arts, & prepared under a grant from the U.S. Dept. of Education, the National Endowment for the Arts and the National Endowment for the Humanities.

NDA is an association of the American Alliance for Health, Physical Education, Recreation & Dance (AAHPERD).

Opportunity-to-Learn Standards

School districts can find guidance for what they need to provide to enable their students to achieve national standards in dance. Certain conditions are necessary for success, such as qualified teachers. Locate the *Opportunity-to-Learn Standards for Dance Education* (reprinted in the NSDE), which specify what school districts should provide in the way of staffing, facilities, schedules, curriculum, material, resources, and equipment.

> Standards for schools are as important as standards for students. In its 1992 report, *Raising Standards for American Education,* the National Council on Education Standards and Testing called for national standards and a system of assessment, and it specified "School Delivery Standards" as a necessary component of national standards.
>
> School Delivery Standards are labeled "Opportunity to Learn Standards" in the "Goals 2000: Educate America Act" enacted into law in 1994, but their purpose remains the same: to ensure that no young American is deprived of the chance to meet the content and performance, or achievement standards established in the various disciplines because of the failure of his or her school to provide an adequate learning environment. The Opportunity to Learn Standards in the arts are intended to specify the physical and educational conditions necessary in the schools to enable every student, with sufficient effort, to meet the national voluntary content and achievement standards in arts education.

From the Introduction to Opportunity-to-Learn Standards for Dance Education, 1995, p. i.

6DC Model

SIX DEFINING CHARACTERISTICS OF EDUCATIONAL DANCE

1. It is comprehensive (broad in scope).
2. It is substantive (challenging and significant).

3. It is sequential (ordered and incremental).

4. It is aesthetically driven (seeking fine quality).

5. It is contextually coherent (relevant and related).

6. It is inquiry based (participatory and investigative).

Ten Principles of Design

The PODs appear in chapters 7 and 9. There are 10 aspects that govern composition in all the arts: unity, variety, repetition, contrast, sequence, climax, proportion, harmony, balance, transition.

The most basic principles are easy for primary students to grasp and are appropriate for all grade levels: unity, variety, repetition, contrast. The more complex principles are useful once students get into composition and choreography (grades 6 through 12 and beyond): sequence, climax, proportion, harmony, balance, transition.

Three-Act Reflection

This appears in chapters 6, 7, 8, and 9. In each cornerstone chapter, you are asked to reflect and then write a paper for your Perspectives Notebook. The specific criteria for Act I is listed in each chapter, but the process for each of the papers is the same. This describes the process.

Act II is a peer assessment and Act III incorporates the assessment feedback to refine your paper to be included in the Perspectives Notebook with all reflections together.

Act I: Write

Prepare a three- to four-page typed paper for your Perspectives Notebook that expresses what each cornerstone contributes to educational dance. Address the specific composition criteria listed in the Notebook or Portfolio feature of the chapter. Use it first for Act I as composition criteria and for Act II as review criteria. Criteria are specified in each cornerstone chapter (chapters 6-9).

Act II: Assess (25 minutes)

The most successful papers merge the criteria to build context rather than address criteria as individual points.

FORMAL IN-CLASS PEER ASSESSMENT

Step 1: On the date your class submits these papers to your professor, engage in a formal, in-class peer evaluation. Attach a rating sheet (the review criteria in Act I) to your paper, and do a cooperative peer review. Swap papers so three peers evaluate your paper and make comments. You will do the same for others. Rate 1, 2, or 3 on each criterion based on correctness of information, thoroughness of coverage, and clarity of expression. (Successful coverage of all three rates a 3.)

Step 2: After evaluating peer papers and getting yours evaluated, return papers to the owners to check ratings and comments before giving them to your professor to grade.

Step 3: Your professor grades your paper and adds comments.

Act III: Refine

After your professor returns your paper—with all comment sheets attached—synthesize all comments and refine your paper (out of class) to attain 3s on all items. Incorporate concepts and information from peers' papers that make your paper better. Place your reworked paper into the Perspectives Notebook.

Turning Success Factors Into Performance Indicators

Lists of Success Factors for teaching are found in chapters 8, 11, and 12. Ask mentors and supervisors to assess your applied teaching skills according to the same criteria. Directions to transform Success Factors into performance criteria follow:

1. Use a rating scale: 1 = needs improvement, 2 = OK, 3 = very successful

2. Ask mentors to critique your teaching of one or more lessons to children and assess your ability to effectively deliver diverse content at that grade level.

3. Ask them to rate each item, then give you feedback for any item rated 1. Continue mentor evaluations until you consistently get 3s on every criteria.

4. After mentors have critiqued you and you have practiced and polished your skills to earn all 3s, add the signed and dated evaluations to the Teaching Skills section of your Perspectives Notebook.

Appendix B

Forms, Checklists, Sample Items, and Articles

Appendix B contains the forms, long checklists, sample items, and articles referred to in the text. The first item presented is the Thumbnail Sketch of a Dance Work. This is followed by the checklists, inventories, or rubrics:

- Developmental Indicators
- Learning Modalities Inventory
- OTA-D Checklist

Various sample items that were referred to throughout the text are presented next:

- Sample Artifacts From a Professional Teaching Portfolio
  - > INTASC Principle 4
  - > INTASC Principle 5
  - > INTASC Principle 9
- Sample Rubric for Technique Areas
- Sample Self-Evaluation Forms
  - > Sample Formative Teacher Self-Evaluation (Qualitative)
  - > Sample Summative Program Evaluation (Qualitative and Quantitative)

- Sample Course Requirements for BA in Dance Education
- Sample Mega-Ideas and Concepts
- Sample Student Handbook (High School Gifted and Talented Program)
- Sample Teaching File Checklist

Finally, two articles are reproduced here:

- Class Management Notes From an Inner-City High School Teacher
- Considerations for Hiring a Qualified Dance Specialist

Thumbnail Sketch of a Dance Work

Deconstruct each great work you encounter with this thumbnail sketch. Keep copies of the form so you can readily list which aspects of technique, performance, and choreographic style the work demonstrates. Compile the thumbnail sketches into a notebook or file for quick reference when planning units and lessons. (See chapter 8 for details.)

Thumbnail Sketch of an Exemplary Dance Work for Teaching

Title of dance: _____

Choreographer: _____

Length of work: _____

Number of dancers: _____

Part of a longer work? _____

Performers:_____

Title of videotape:_____

File location:_____

Dance style: _____

Appropriate for young children? Yes / No

USEFUL WHEN TEACHING (CIRCLE ALL THAT APPLY)

Body articulation

Isolated body parts

Performance quality

Shaping (still and moving)

Spatial design

Use of props

Thematic material

Dramatic story line

Movement motif

Levels

Symmetry

Asymmetry

Use of dance chorus and soloist

Accent

Polyrhythms

Steady beat

Nonmetered accompaniment

Using percussion for accompaniment

Music concrete (found sound)

Unison versus nonunison movement

Partnering

Lifts

Elevations (jumping, leaping)

Contact work (as in contact improv)

Everyday gestures and movement

Use of focus for clarity

Translation of subject matter into dance

Abstraction

Example of costume-enhancing movement

Masks or masklike makeup

Non-Western or ethnic classical dance

Non-Western or ethnic folk dance

Other:

USEFUL FOR TEACHING COMPOSITIONAL FORM AND STRUCTURE

ABA

Theme and variation

Canon

Rondo

Other:_____

QUERIES AND QUESTIONS TO HELP ME FACILITATE AESTHETIC SCANNING AND CRITIQUING

1.

2.

3.

4.

5.

Overall aesthetic impact of the work:

Developmental Indicators

Use the list on the next page to prepare yourself to change the level of student participation. Let it help you take students from where they are to where they need to be. (See chapter 12 for details.)

Learning Modalities Inventory

Assess your own strengths in this questionnaire. Identify your preferred ways of learning. Be particularly aware of the one you least prefer so that you can make a special effort to use it in the classroom. (See details in chapter 4.)

Place a checkmark by all the statements that strongly describe what you prefer.

AUDITORY

_____ I need to hear myself say it in order to remember it.

_____ I often need to talk through a problem aloud in order to solve it.

_____ I memorize best by repeating the information aloud or to myself.

_____ I remember best when the information fits into a rhythmic or musical pattern.

_____ I would rather listen to a recording of a book than sit and read it.

Examples of Developmental Indicators (NDA)

From	Toward
1. Watching from the sidelines	Active participation in the whole class
2. Generalized response of the whole body	Use of body parts in isolation when desired (moving only one body part at a time)
3. Inability to stop movement in response to signal	Ability to stop movement (freeze) in response to signal
4. Stopping movement by extreme tension or falling down	Stopping movement with a freeze that allows continued movement when desired
5. Use of constant or inappropriate vocal sounds while moving	Use of appropriate vocal sounds at appropriate times
6. Frequent imitation of adults or other children	Demonstration of original responses
7. No observation of other children in dance	Observation and response to dances of other children
8. No verbal response to dance	Use of words to describe own response and dance movement qualities
9. Inability to select and use personal space; frequent bumping into objects or other children	Ability to select and use personal space while respecting personal space of others
10. Working alone at all times	Working successfully with one or more partners at times
11. Inability to balance on one body part	Ability to balance on one foot or other body part for increasing length of time
12. Creating a dance with one kind of movement, no variations (e.g., a dance that contains only forward tiptoe steps)	Creating a dance with a sequence of two or more kinds of movements or variations of the same movements
13. Use of movement in forward direction only	Use of movement in all directions, when appropriate
14. No differentiation between slow and fast movement in dance	Demonstration of differentiation between slow and fast and degrees in between; use of acceleration and deceleration when appropriate
15. No differentiation between curved and angular shapes	Demonstration of differentiation between curved and angular shapes
16. No differentiation between strength and lightness	Demonstration of differentiation between strength and lightness
17. Maintaining concentration and awareness for a brief period in dance	Maintaining concentration and awareness for increasing periods in dance

Published by the National Dance Association, an association of AAHPERD.

VISUAL

_____ I need to see an illustration of what I'm being taught before I understand it.

_____ I am drawn to flashy, colorful, visually stimulating objects.

_____ I almost always prefer books that include pictures or illustrations with the text.

_____ I look as if I'm daydreaming when I'm trying to get a mental picture of what's being said.

_____ I usually remember better when I can actually see the person who's talking.

KINESTHETIC

_____ I have difficulty sitting still for more than a few minutes at a time.

_____ I usually learn best by physically participating in a task.

_____ I almost always have some part of my body in motion.

_____ I prefer to read books or hear stories that are full of action.

From *The Way They Learn,* published by Focus on the Family, Colorado Springs, CO 80995. Copyright © 1994, Cynthia Ulrich Tobias. All rights reserved. International copyright secured. Used by permission.

OTA-D Checklist

OTA-D and Success Factors (found in chapters 8, 11, and 12) have the same roots but are not alike. The Success Factors are formative and describe your developing skills in detailed focus areas. The OTA-D is a summative evaluation instrument to measure all your skills. The two work together so you have the skills you need (formative) by the time you are ready for a summative evaluation of your classroom competencies (OTA-D). (See details in chapter 16.)

Should your state lack quantifiable teaching competencies specifically in dance, use the OTA-D as an evaluation instrument to document your collective teaching skills for your Professional Teaching Portfolio. Ask qualified outside evaluators, such as your dance education professor or school principal or supervisor, to evaluate your classroom performance during your student-teaching internship. Use a three-point scale: 1 = needs improvement; 2 = meets expectations; 3 = surpasses expectations.

© 2004 South Carolina Department of Education.

Overall Teaching Assessment in Dance (OTA-D) Checklist

___ Outside evaluator:

___ Self-evaluation:

Date:

Setting:

Suggested rating scale:

1—Needs work or does not yet meet expectations

2—Acceptable or meets expectations

3—Accomplished or exceeds expectations

A. Creates Long-Range Plans (LRPs)

1. ___ Aligns LRP with district content standards in the arts.

2. ___ Sequences instructional plan to accomplish LRP.

3. ___ Communicates LRP to students, parents, professional arts team, and administrators.

4. ___ Writes LRP using arts education content appropriate to the instructional plan for the district, state, and nation, which addresses the desired student outcomes.

5. ___ Plans procedures for routinely communicating with parents.

6. ___ Develops appropriate time line for completing instructional units in dance.

7. ___ Obtains special instructional materials and resources needed to deliver an aesthetically driven unit.

8. ___ Develops effective processes to evaluate student progress and achievement.

9. ___ Designs a process for recording students' daily progress and achievement.

10. ___ Designs a process to record students' overall progress and achievement.

11. ___ Plans rules and procedures that manage students' behavior in dance class and in performance settings.

12. ___ Plans procedures for essential noninstructional routines.

13. ___ Determines ability and development levels, backgrounds, needs, and interests of students.

14. ___ Evaluates LRP periodically and adjusts as necessary.

15. ___ Uses Opportunity-to-Learn Standards in LRP to address scheduling, facility, and safety issues.

B. Creates Short-Range Plans (SRPs)

1. ___ Plans instruction built on student development and learning from previous units.

2. ___ Plans unit objectives appropriate for ability levels of students and also sets appropriately high expectations for all.

3. ___ Includes a variety of intellectual, social, artistic, and cultural perspectives.

4. ___ Selects or develops materials, resources, and technologies to present aesthetically based content in a variety of formats.

5. ___ Plans logically sequenced instruction to affect appropriate learning outcomes.

6. ___ Considers ways to accommodate different rates of learning.

7. ___ Plans instruction that actively engages students in instruction and learning.

8. ___ Plans instruction that actively engages students in varied levels of higher-order thinking.

9. ___ Plans instruction that promotes both independent and collaborative thinking.

10. ___ Includes plans to adjust the SRP to better serve students' learning needs.

C. Constructs Curriculum Content

The successful dance teacher provides content that

1. ___ is aligned with district content standards.

2. ___ meets the national dance achievement standards for the grade level.

3. ___ meets long-range goals.

4. ___ is appropriate for the goals and objectives of the instructional unit of study.

5. ___ is current and accurate.

6. ___ is presented in a logical sequence.

7. ___ is presented at an appropriate pace for all students to grasp.

8. ___ comes from multiple sources that reflect varied social, cultural, and intellectual perspectives.

9. ___ gives sufficient explanations, examples, and demonstrations for students to grasp.

10. ___ emphasizes the key elements of the subject matter.

11. ___ is sequential and builds on known skills and knowledge base.

12. ___ is rich in substance and worthy of the student's attention and time.

13. ___ is appropriate to the needs of the students in the class.

D. Delivers Instruction

The successful dance teacher uses varied instructional strategies

1. ___ in a logical sequence.

2. ___ appropriate for the learning or developmental objectives of the unit.

3. ___ appropriate for the dance content and skills being learned.

4. ___ appropriate for the ability and development of students.

5. ___ that accommodate different rates of learning.

6. ___ that use verbal, visual, kinesthetic, and tactile approaches to accommodate different learning styles.

7. ___ appropriate to where students are in the learning stage (initial, application, practice, review, and transfer).

8. ___ that actively engage students in instruction, inquiry, and learning.

9. ___ that promote critical thinking and problem-solving skills.

10. ___ that promote both independent and collaborative learning.

11. ___ that show capability of facilitating inquiry.

12. ___ that show mastery of different kinds of questioning strategies.

E. Plans Effective Assessments

1. ___ Plans and schedules a variety of appropriate assessments of students' progress and achievement as needed during instructional units.

2. ___ Creates performance assessment rubrics that are specific and appropriate.

3. ___ Selects, adapts, or develops assessments appropriate to the ability and developmental levels of students.

4. ___ Selects, adapts, or develops assessments appropriate for the objectives of instructional units.

5. ___ Selects, adapts, or develops assessments appropriate for the content or skills covered during instructional units and consistent with the instruction used during units.

6. ___ Designs appropriate criteria for evaluating students' progress and achievement, factoring in assessment results to lesson and unit planning.

7. ___ Analyzes assessment results to make judgments about students' progress and achievement.

8. ___ Analyzes assessment results to determine the need for instructional feedback.

9. ___ Analyzes assessment results to evaluate the extent to which instruction met all students' needs.

10. ___ Incorporates assessment results into subsequent unit and lesson planning.

11. ___ Maintains accurate daily records of students' progress and achievement.

12. ___ Maintains accurate long-term records of students' progress and achievement.

F. Sets and Maintains High Learner Expectations (Accountability)

The successful dance teacher establishes a learning environment in which

1. ___ strategies promote students' responsibility for their performance, artistry, active participation, and productivity in studio and classroom.

2. ___ students receive clear explanations of what they are expected to learn and be able to do (according to artistic standards and objectives within a class).

3. ___ objectives for student learning and development are stated at the beginning of each instructional unit or lesson and are assessed through criteria and rubrics.

4. ___ expectations for overall performance and participation are established and reinforced throughout the semester.

5. ___ expectations are appropriate for the ability and developmental levels of students.

6. ___ expectations challenge all students to achieve at appropriately high levels.

7. ___ students understand the relevance of the objectives to previous and future learning objectives.

8. ___ students understand the importance of achieving the unit objectives.

9. ___ learning objectives are clarified during instructional units as needed.

10. ___ appropriate expectations for participating in instructional activities are established and maintained.

11. ___ appropriate expectations for completing instructional assignments and tasks in and out of the classroom and studio are established and maintained.

12. ___ facts and experiences are integrated into a larger context so that students acquire an understanding of dance.

13. ___ students are accountable in all aspects of dance: creating, performing, responding to, and knowing about dance.

14. ___ students reflect on dance and its relevance to the world and to themselves.

G. Monitors and Enhances Learning

1. ___ Observes students' general performance and reactions during class activities and lessons.

2. ___ Uses appropriate questioning techniques.

3. ___ Observes specific students' performance during activities (e.g., speeches, technique class, improvisation, performance tasks, group discussions, and collaborative tasks).

4. ___ Reviews work completed by students and responds (e.g., assignments, projects, and portfolios).

5. ___ Uses information from monitoring kin-aesthetic and cognitive skills to provide timely and informative instructional feedback to enhance development.

6. ___ Provides appropriate and sufficient reviews and summaries of content and skills.

7. ___ Extends students' development by appropriate acceleration and enrichment activities.

H. Creates an Environment That Promotes Learning

1. ___ Uses appropriate and accurate oral and written communication.

2. ___ Serves as a positive role model for students in the classroom and studio.

3. ___ Creates and maintains a physical environment that engages students and provides an inviting place to learn.

4. ___ Maintains a room arrangement that allows all students to see, hear, and participate in instruction.

5. ___ Promotes cooperation, teamwork, and respect among students.

6. ___ Conveys appropriately high expectations for students' participation and performance.

7. ___ Conveys confidence in knowledge of the content and skills being taught.

8. ___ Conveys confidence in ability to teach and to assist students in accomplishing learning and development objectives.

9. ___ Promotes in students a sense of responsibility for teaching themselves and their peers.

10. ___ Conveys respect for the feelings, ideas, and contributions of students.

11. ___ Conveys an understanding of and sensitivity to the social and cultural backgrounds of students.

12. ___ Maximizes positive and productive interactions with students.

13. ___ Provides appropriate rewards and incentives for learning and skill development.

14. ___ Establishes and maintains an appropriate professional distance between teacher and student.

15. ___ Gives ample opportunity for peer collaboration in feedback, sharing compositional assignments, group work, and critical response.

I. Manages a Classroom

1. ___ Establishes clear, appropriate rules for students' behavior.

2. ___ Maintains and enforces rules for students' behavior in a fair and consistent manner.

3. ___ Uses appropriate preventive discipline techniques.

4. ___ Provides students with an opportunity to develop a sense of responsibility for their own behavior.

5. ___ Establishes appropriate and effective routines for completing essential noninstructional tasks, such as dressing out, taking roll, and attending arts events.

6. ___ Manages transitions between instructional events to maintain a smooth flow of activity during lessons and minimize loss of instructional time.

7. ___ Effectively manages instructional materials, resources, and technologies.

8. ___ Provides positive reinforcement for acceptable behavior and performance.

9. ___ Monitors small-group guided learning activities by being engaged and active, moving among students during all forms of instruction.

10. ___ Facilitates movement exploration during creative dance activities by moving among students, using sound cues, and modulating voice.

11. ___ Teaches individuals as a part of the entire class without jeopardizing time on task for the class.

12. ___ Participates fully in the lesson and shares his or her energy with students.

J. Facilitates Aesthetic Education Through Dance

1. ___ Teaches students how to consider the artistic quality of what they do, see, or make.

2. ___ Lists aesthetic criteria along with other criteria to be measured for assessing.

3. ___ Facilitates inquiry to focus on artistic quality.

4. ___ Elicits qualitative responses from students.

5. ___ Develops the artistic quality of individuals' performance skills.

6. ___ Develops the artistic quality of individuals' dance-making and creating skills.

7. ___ Emphasizes the artistic quality of what is viewed and analyzed.

8. ___ Develops students' artistic eye about watching and evaluating dances of others.

9. ___ Teaches students how to switch aesthetic perspectives to judge quality in cultures with a different aesthetic.

10. ___ Holds high artistic standards for own creating, performing, and responding to dance.

11. ___ Analyzes choreographic works from an artistic point of view and gets students to do likewise.

Sample Artifacts From a Professional Teaching Portfolio

See these examples for ideas on how to prepare your reflection statements and artifacts for your portfolio.

INTASC Principle 4: Sample Reflection Statement

This example is only the "Why I Chose This Document" as artifact in the portfolio rather than all the items. It shows the student teacher's thoughts about applying INTASC Principle 4.

Why I Chose This Document

The success of any classroom is dependent on establishing and maintaining high expectations for student behavior and performance. All students want to feel strong, smart, and capable. One way of promoting this feeling is for the teacher to view them as such. Students will automatically rise or fall to whatever expectations they are presented with. By setting high expectations the teacher sends the message that he or she views the students as intelligent and expects a high quality of work from them. Many teachers underestimate what their students are capable of and these low expectations are reflected in the behavior and academic progress of the students.

The document included in this section of my portfolio was chosen because it represents my expectations for both daily and long-term work within the dance classroom. The daily grade for each student is based on students' taking responsibility for their own behavior, effort, and technical progress. Procedures and expectations are established for attitude and effort, timeliness, dressing out, and technical improvement, all of which students know their grade is dependent on.

How I Have Grown

Going into this semester I had expectations concerning behavior and academic progress that were not completely appropriate for different age levels. For instance, I expected the middle school students to be well behaved, but I greatly underestimated the level of academic achievement that they were capable of. Interestingly enough, I expected the exact opposite from the elementary school students. I expected their behavior to be slightly out of control, but I expected them to have a greater understanding of the material than they did. Although it is important to set high expectations for students, it is also important that these expectations be realistic and age appropriate. Through my own work and watching my cooperating teachers work with students over the past three months, I have begun to develop more appropriate expectations for the students. I have been working recently on increasing my expectations for behavior and decreasing the amount of independent work that I expect from children of elementary school age. I have also been working on increasing my expectations of the quality of student work at the middle school age. I feel that I am now successfully navigating the thin line between expectations that are high, but not too high, for specific developmental ages.

Future Plans for Improvement

One of the difficulties that I faced in establishing high expectations was an uncertainty in age-appropriate standards for cross-disciplinary connections. For example, I assigned a homework project for the eighth graders in which they were to write a story and then create a piece of choreography about a character in their story. Because I am very familiar with the discipline of dance, I had little trouble creating a rubric for the choreography section. What I did have trouble with was creating a rubric for the writing section. I attribute this trouble to my lack of knowledge concerning eighth grade writing skills. In the future I plan to seek out the assistance of other teachers to aid me in creating age-appropriate rubrics for cross-curricular material. I would like to view samples of student writing projects as well as speak with the math teacher regarding the level of math that the different grades are working on. Enlisting the aid of other teachers will enable me to set appropriately high expectations when integrating other curricular studies into my own lesson plans.

Setting appropriately high expectations for students can be difficult for a teacher that is certified in K-12. Vast differences exist in ability between so many different age levels, and for a new teacher this can be quite intimidating at times. It is important to remember that this hurdle can easily be overcome with nothing more than time and more teaching experience. After all, I feel as if I have come a very long way already and I have only been student teaching for three months.

Adapted with permission of Nicole Manuel Almeida.

INTASC Principle 5: Full Sample

Creative Movement, Beginning Choreography Review, Intro to Bound and Free-Flowing Energy (6th Grade)

Teacher: Nicole Manuel
September 25, 2002

Goals To review the elements and introduce students to the concept of bound and free-flowing movement.

Lesson Objectives
1. Students will demonstrate their understanding of the previous elements they have studied by performing a dance that includes all of these elements.
2. Students will be able to move their bodies showing a significant difference between bound and free-flowing movement.

Purpose of the Lesson   To provide students with the skills needed to create dances using a wide range of expressional movements.

Preassessment   Students have been working for a full week on the elements of body, space, and time. They have not yet been introduced to the energy element under which bound and free-flowing movements are categorized.

Advance Organizer
- Warm up using previously learned elements.
- Review dances created on the previous day.
- Perform dances.
- Discuss energy.
- Explore free-flowing movement.
- Explore bound movement with body socks.
- Explore bound movement without body socks.
- Wrap up by having students explain how their bodies felt different doing each type of movement.

Personalization   "Every single day, no matter what you are doing, you are using energy. When you wake up in the morning, when you run to the bus stop, and when you wander down the hallway at school you are using energy. You probably don't pay much attention to your energy on a regular basis, but throughout a day you use many different kinds of energy. Two of these are bound and free-flowing energy."

Connection to Prior Knowledge   "For over a week now we have been exploring the various elements of dance movement. We have previously discussed the elements of body, space, and time. Today we are going to discuss the element of energy. Why is it important to know about all of the elements instead of just knowing a few of them?" (Student answers.) "Right, because all of the elements are connected. It is impossible to dance without using all of them, so it is important to know the many ways that all of the elements can be used. Knowing this allows you to create extremely interesting choreography."

Opening Activity   The teacher will lead students through a warm-up in which they will review the movement elements explored in previous classes. The students will move around the room when the music plays and freeze when the music stops. The warm-up will include bent, twisted, and stretched shapes and movements; slow and fast movements; straight, curved, and zigzag pathways; and low, medium, and high levels.

Student Practice Guided by the Teacher
- The teacher will lead students through a warm-up to review previously learned elements.
- The teacher will lead students through an exploration of free-flowing movement.
- The teacher will lead students through an exploration of bound movement using body socks.
- The teacher will lead students through an exploration of bound movement without the body socks.

Student Independent Practice
- Students will finish creating their dances that include all of the previously studied elements. They will then perform these dances for the rest of the class.
- There will not be any independent practice of bound and free-flowing movement until the following lesson.

Summary   The teacher will question students about how their bodies felt different when performing bound and free-flowing movement.

Materials
- As many lycra body socks as possible (one for every student is ideal)
- CD: *Planet Drum,* by Mickey Hart
- CD: *Sacred Earth Drums,* by David and Steve Gordon

Advanced Ballet: Arm Shaping in Second Position (8th Grade)

Teacher: Nicole Manuel
November 12, 2002

Goals   Students will know the appropriate alignment of the arms in second position and will be able to support this alignment by initiating and supporting the shape from the muscles of the upper back.

Objectives
1. Students will engage the muscles of the upper back to support their arm work in second position.
2. Students will keep their elbows lifted while dancing.
3. Students will keep their wrists elongated.
4. Students will keep their shoulders down.

Purpose of the Lesson   To provide students with the skills necessary to begin their journey toward correct performance presentation.

Personalization "In most of the dances that we have watched this semester, many of you have commented on how strong the dancers are. One of the ways that you can begin to achieve upper body strength is through the correct use of your arms when dancing in class every day."

Connection to Previous Knowledge "The use of the arms in second position is a very old tradition in ballet dancing. You have studied how ballet developed out of the court dances that were presented to the royal families. The second position of the arms was a way that dancers opened up their bodies and presented themselves to the kings. It was the dancers' way of saying, 'Here I am to dance for your pleasure.'"

Preassessment Most of the students have had at least two years of ballet technique, but they still have a lot of difficulty using the arms correctly. Many of them forget about their arms entirely, and those who do remember cannot keep them in correct alignment when they begin moving.

Advance Organizer

- Discuss the correct position of the arms while students practice looking in the mirror.
- Students view a clip of *Sleeping Beauty.*
- Students will be given cotton cords to wear across their shoulders and down their arms during barre work. This should help them keep their elbows lifted so that the cord does not fall off.

BARRE WORK

- Pliés
- Tendus
- Dégagés
- Stretches
- Grand battements

CENTER WORK

- Tendus
- Adagio
- Summary

Opening Activity The teacher will instruct students on the correct positioning of the arms, and the students will use the mirrors to make sure that they are holding their arms correctly. The teacher will then give each student a cord to wear draped across the shoulders and down the arms. To prevent the cord from falling to the floor, the students must keep their elbows lifted throughout all of the exercises during the class.

Student Practice Guided by the Teacher

- The teacher will instruct the students in the correct positioning of the arms, and the students will practice facing a mirror.
- The teacher will teach plié, tendu, dégagé, stretching, and grand battement combinations to the students emphasizing the use of the arms at the barre.
- The teacher will teach a tendu and an adagio combination emphasizing the use of the arms in the center of the room.

Student Independent Practice The students will perform each of the combinations taught to them by the teacher.

Materials

- CD player
- CD: *25th Anniversary: Celebrating,* by David Howard
- 20 5-foot-long cotton cords

Introduction to Technical Theater (7th Grade)

Teacher: Nicole Manuel
September 10, 2002

Goals To introduce students to the fundamentals of the technical side of theater productions.

Objectives

1. Provide students with information pertaining to the setup of a proscenium stage.
2. Provide students with information about the various jobs and responsibilities of the many people needed to put a production together.

Purpose of the Lesson To provide students with the information they will need in order to be a successful member of a theatrical production.

Advance Organizer

- Discuss the three different types of stages and show pictures of them.
- Teacher will lead students through the process of drawing and labeling a proscenium stage.
- Teacher will lead students through labeling stage positions.
- Discuss the different jobs necessary for productions.
- Create a mock stage using strips of cloth.
- Students will choreograph a short dance using new technical information.

Personalizing "There will be several dance performances this year that, in one way or another, all of you are going to be a part of. To make any show successful it is important that you know as much as possible about the technical aspects of putting together a show. Even though you are all taking a dance class, when it comes time to put on a performance, dancers do much more than just dance. You have to know about lighting, scenery, and costumes, and you need to be able to speak to the technical directors using the proper terms for the setup of the stage. Today we'll begin learning about some of these technical aspects."

Opening Activity The teacher will begin class by explaining why it is important that dancers know the technical aspects of production. The students will be shown pictures of the three different types of stages and will be asked to identify the one that they will be using for their dance performances.

Student Practice Guided by the Teacher

1. The teacher will lead students through the process of drawing and labeling the different parts of a proscenium stage.
2. The teacher will lead students through the process of creating a mock stage in the classroom using strips of cloth to represent the different areas of the stage.
3. The teacher will then instruct students to move to different parts of the stage in order to test their understanding of where each part is located.

Student Independent Practice Students will create their own 32-count dance in which they must know their stage directions. Each student will be assigned a number, 1, 2, or 3. Students assigned number 1 must do the following:

- Enter from the third wing, upstage left.
- Use the apron.
- Exit downstage right (first wing).
- Use high-, medium-, and low-level movements.

Students assigned number 2 must do the following:

- Enter downstage right (first wing).
- Use upstage center.
- Exit into stage left (second wing).
- Use high-, medium-, and low-level movements.

Students assigned number 3 must do the following:

- Enter upstage right (third wing).
- Use right center stage and left center stage.
- Exit downstage left (first wing).
- Use high-, medium-, and low-level movements.

Students will perform their choreography in groups of three. One student has each number.

Emphasis of Key Points and Summary Students will be given handouts that will list all of the terms covered in class and will have diagrams of a proscenium stage.

Materials
- Crayons
- White paper
- Handout with diagrams of the stage
- Handout with a list of technical terms
- 6 short pieces of cloth, 4 long pieces of cloth, 1 long piece of string
- Cards with instructions for creating choreography for the three different groups

Resources

Cunningham, Glen. 1993. *Stage lighting revealed: A design and execution handbook.* Cincinnati: Betterway Books.

Hartnoll, Phyllis and Peter Found. 1992. *The concise Oxford companion to the theatre.* New York: Oxford University Press.

Schlaich, Joan, and Betty Dupont. 1998. *Dance: The art of production.* Hightstown: Princeton Books.

Walters, Graham. 1997. *Stage lighting step by step.* Cincinnati: Betterway Books.

Reflection

Why I Chose These Documents Dance can be hard work, and using a variety of creative instructional strategies can help to keep the students engaged and interested in learning. The three lesson plans included under this dimension of my portfolio contain examples of activities that I used with middle school students to help clarify and reinforce the material that they were studying.

The first lesson plan was used with sixth grade students and it focused on the use of free-flowing and bound energy in movement. Energy can be very difficult to understand kinesthetically, and so I had the students dance inside of lycra body socks in order to experience feeling bound.

The second lesson plan I used with sixth through eighth grades during a ballet unit focusing on upper body presentation. During this specific lesson the students worked on the proper placement of the arms in second position. The students were required to dance with ropes draped across their backs and down their arms. To keep the ropes from falling, the students had to keep their elbows lifted the whole time. Although the students moaned and groaned about their arm muscles getting tired, by the end of the class their arms looked much better.

The third lesson plan that I included was an introduction to technical theater taught to seventh grade students. During this lesson they learned the various parts of the stage and the appropriate directional terms. At the end of the class the students had to build a large stage out of pieces of cloth. I randomly chose students to place the different pieces in the appropriate spots. For instance, I would tell one person to place the scrim on the stage and she would have to know where to put it. After the stage was put together I gave the students verbal cues and they had to move about the stage according to the specific directional cue given to them.

How I Have Grown All of the lesson plans that I included in this dimension of the portfolio contain activities that are hands-on oriented. Coming into this semester I would say that creating hands-on activities was one of my strong points. As the semester has progressed I have developed a variety of visual instructional strategies as well. I created PowerPoint presentations to present material for both middle and elementary school students as well as created posters and bulletin boards that reinforced material that the students were studying. I also created PowerPoint presentations that existed on only one slide. This one slide was an overview of the focus for the day. On it I included bulleted points concerning the specific details that I wanted students to focus on during that day's technique class. I also included at least one picture for added visual appeal and as an example of correct ballet technique. This slide stayed up throughout the class to visually remind students what they should be focusing on.

Future Plans for Improvement I greatly enjoy using my creative powers to come up with new and interesting instructional strategies and plan to continue developing new ideas in the future. One learning style that I feel I greatly neglect in my strategies is the logical–mathematical style. Because I don't gravitate toward that learning style myself, I tend to neglect it when teaching students, and that is something that I need to work on. In forthcoming lessons I plan to work the mathematical learning style into my lesson plans on a more regular basis.

Not only does incorporating a variety of learning styles into my instructional strategies help my students, but it will provide a good opportunity for me to learn as well. Working with a learning style that I am uncomfortable with will actually make me smarter in the long run because I will have to develop skills I am not used to using. The same is true for the students: The more learning styles they are forced to use, the more they will develop a large range of skills that will be useful in all realms of their lives.

Adapted with permission of Nicole Manuel Almeida.

INTASC Principle 9: Full Sample

Rules and Procedures

Middle School

NONINSTRUCTIONAL ROUTINES

In a dance classroom there are many noninstructional routines that must be established in order to take full advantage of the maximum amount of instructional time available. The following list outlines the noninstructional procedures expected of students.

- Students are expected to enter the classroom quietly and remove their shoes before walking across the studio floor.
- Students are expected to change into their dance clothes and securely fasten their hair out of the face within three minutes.
- Students are expected to quietly begin warming themselves up as soon as they finish changing clothes.
- If a student needs to leave the classroom to use the restroom, he or she is expected to write a pass for the teacher to sign.
- Students are expected to raise their hands for permission to ask questions or share information.
- If students need to sharpen pencils, they are expected to do so quietly without asking.
- When dancing, students are expected to move without entering the personal space of other students.

- In order to gain students' attention if noise levels become too high, the teacher will clap a pattern and the students will repeat this pattern and remain silent. This is especially useful when working in the theater.

CONSEQUENCES FOR MISBEHAVIOR

All students who misbehave are subject to a series of consequences directly relating to the number of the times the unacceptable behavior has occurred.

- First offense: verbal warning
- Second offense: lunch detention or call home
- Third offense: guidance referral—student is sent to the guidance counselor
- Fourth offense: discipline referral—student is sent to the administrator in charge of discipline. This can result in an in-school suspension or out-of-school suspension. Any student receiving a discipline referral will also be cut from all performing opportunities.

Elementary School

NONINSTRUCTIONAL ROUTINES

The following is a list of noninstructional routines expected of students at the elementary school level.

- Students will enter and exit the classroom quietly.
- Students will sit in assigned spots on the floor when they enter.
- Hands will be raised if a student wishes to speak.
- Students will know and use a "ready to listen" and a "ready to move" shape when instructed. When the teacher says, "Ready to listen," students will sit on the floor with their legs crossed. When the teacher says, "Ready to move," students will stand up tall with their arms by their sides.
- When called on, students will take off their shoes and line them up neatly against the wall.
- Students move when the drum "speaks."
- Students freeze when the drum stops "speaking."

Students are expected to use appropriate social behavior:

- Be respectful to the teacher.
- Be respectful to other students.
- Do not interrupt others.
- Use good personal space.

CONSEQUENCES FOR MISBEHAVIOR

- Warning
- Time-out
- Time-out for the remainder of the class time
- Note sent home
- Visit to the principal

Reflection

Why I Chose This Document Establishing routines and expectations for behavior during the very first day of classes is the best way to manage student behavior. When students know what is expected of them, classes tend to run much more smoothly and there is minimal loss of instructional time. As documentation of this Performance Dimension I have included a list of noninstructional routines and consequences for misbehavior for both middle and elementary school students. I have found that these routines are extremely effective in promoting positive student behavior without the constant direction of the teacher.

How I Have Grown During my first day of student teaching I walked into a room full of very noisy students. I immediately felt overwhelmed because I could hardly hear myself speak to my cooperating teacher. Suddenly my cooperating teacher turned toward the class and clapped out a pattern with her hands. Immediately, the students repeated the clapping pattern and silence reigned over the classroom. I was struck completely dumb. It seemed to me that an act of magic had just transpired before my very eyes. There was no yelling, no frustration, no struggling to be heard over students' noise. A simple clapping pattern, and calm was instantaneously returned to the room. I am so thankful for exposure to classroom management tricks like this. Although I have worked with children in many different settings, I had never really thought outside of my ingrained box for behavior management. This semester I have begun to view behavior management much differently than I had previously done. I now see classroom management as a creative problem to solve rather than a struggle of wills. This has made all the difference in my level of frustration with student chatter and disruption.

I have also learned that it is okay, and even necessary, for me to be stern with students. Being nice all of the time and letting students get away with nonadherence to the rules do neither party any good. Failing to be stern when the situation calls for it undermines my authority as a teacher, and it sends students the message that they are not accountable for their behavior. This has been a bit of a struggle for me because my instinct is to want to be nice so that the students will like me. I have realized recently that students will like and respect me even more as a teacher if I stand my ground and set clear boundaries for behavior. Even if they don't immediately look kindly toward me, in the long run I will be providing them with the structure they need to lead successful lives as adults, and that is what is truly important.

Future Plans for Improvement   I have found that students behave the best when you include them in the process of establishing classroom rules. By having students help create rules, they receive the message that you see them as well behaved and responsible individuals. In doing this, if students break a rule, they are not only breaking the teacher's rules, but they are breaking the rules of their peers and friends. This does not hold the same popularity potential that breaking a teacher's rules can sometimes hold for children. In my future classrooms I plan to use this rule-making technique with my students, as well as continue to explore for other creative alternatives to the traditional shouting technique.

Adapted with permission of Nicole Manuel Almeida.

Sample Rubric for Technique Areas

Name: _____   **Date:** _____

TASK (CRITERIA)	1	2	3	4	5
	Beginning (lacks motor coordination)	Basic (becoming more adept)	Secure (beginning to develop isolated performance skills)	Mastery (increased coordination and fine motor skills for performing)	Professionally advanced (sophisticated, high-level performance)
Alignment: torso					
Alignment: legs					
Alignment: total body					
Placement of limbs					
Balance					
Turnout					
Elevation					
Landing					
Articulation of movement flow					

	Beginning (lacks motor coordination)	Basic (becoming more adept)	Secure (beginning to develop isolated performance skills)	Mastery (increased coordination and fine motor skills for performing)	Professionally advanced (sophisticated, high-level performance)
Turning					
Core body strength					
Joint flexibility					
Cardiovascular endurance					
Muscular strength					
Muscular endurance					
Application of LOD concepts					
Application of dance elements					
Ability to make corrections					
Rhythmic accuracy					
Sense of timing					
Sense of space					
Sense of shape and shaping					
Sense of dynamics					
Sense of relationship					
Ability to use isolated body parts					
Articulation of the full body (joints)					
Use and articulation of the feet					
Endurance (cardiovascular and muscular)					

Sample Self-Evaluation Forms

Part of being a reflective practitioner is regularly evaluating your own effectiveness. Use these to assess your overall strengths and weaknesses to find ways to increase your effectiveness.

- Sample Formative Teacher Self-Evaluation (Qualitative)
- Sample Summative Program Evaluation (Qualitative and Quantitative)

Sample Formative Teacher Self-Evaluation (Qualitative)

At the end of each grading period, reflect on your effectiveness (formative). Use a rating scale of 0 = never, 1 = rarely, 2 = sometimes, 3 = always.

A. INSTRUCTIONAL STRATEGIES

1. Activities are open ended and encourage the creative process.
2. Activities call for higher-order thinking and reflection, not simply a recollection of factual information.
3. Ample opportunity is given students to move and learn to process cognitively while physically engaged.
4. Students are given many opportunities to inquire about the material under consideration.
5. Activities are meaningful and student centered, fully engaging students mentally and physically.
6. Instructions are clear to avoid frustration and confusion.
7. Activities are positive and build a positive self-image as a mover and as a creative problem solver.
8. Activities promote developing positive attitudes toward different dance styles.
9. Activities promote developing positive attitudes toward different cultures.
10. Activities help boost students' confidence.
11. Activities are personalized and students are encouraged to express ideas and feelings in their unique ways.
12. Activities take students to the next level, and familiar material becomes the springboard for going further.

13. Activities challenge students to be creative, to organize, and to present in a structured way.

(Total: 39-30 = excellent, 29-20 = fair, 19-15 = weak, below 15 = unacceptable.)

B. CONTENT

1. Units and lessons include ongoing assessment of students.
2. Curriculum is evaluated regularly for effectiveness and adjusted as needed.
3. Instructional strategies related to content are evaluated regularly for effectiveness and adjusted as needed.
4. Curriculum is substantive in dance.
5. Curriculum has appropriate ongoing interdisciplinary links to other academic subjects.
6. Students are engaged in inquiry and reflective thinking about the content of dance.
7. Students have access to a variety of dance works on video to develop dance literacy and familiarity with diverse dance forms.
8. Content spirals (material from dance vocabulary is used multiple times in varied contexts to build on skills previously developed).
9. Themes and activities are sequenced in a meaningful and logical order.
10. Content includes diverse perspectives from diverse cultures.
11. Content is current and accurate.
12. Content is sequential and becomes increasingly more challenging by building on concepts and skills previously learned.
13. Content is appropriate to the developmental level and interest of the students.

(Total: 39-30 = excellent, 29-20 = fair, 19-15 = weak, below 15 = unacceptable.)

C. STUDENT ASSESSMENT

1. Assessments authentically measure student outcomes.
2. Assessments enhance learning.
3. Overall assessments are continuous and ongoing (formative).
4. Assessments are weighted according to educational priorities.
5. Assessments accurately measure desired outcomes.

6. Assessments are integrated into instruction.

7. Assessments are both formal and informal.

8. Data from assessments positively affect teaching practice in content and instruction.

9. Assessment data are recorded and communicated accurately and systematically.

10. Assessment is conducted to monitor student achievement of learning objectives.

11. Both student assessment and program evaluation monitor learning and enable teachers to adjust to achieve better results.

12. Assessments are timed to coincide with when students have optimal mastery of content and skills.

13. Assessments incorporate concepts and skills from NSDEs.

(Total: 39-30 = excellent, 29-20 = fair, 19-15 = weak, below 15 = unacceptable.)

Sample Summative Program Evaluation (Qualitative and Quantitative)

PART I: QUALITATIVE QUESTIONNAIRE

1. What are your key accomplishments to date in _____? (Example: What are your key accomplishments to date in bringing cultural diversity into your curriculum?)

2. How effective has the program been in terms of the following areas?

   a. Curriculum content

   b. Instructional strategies

   c. Student assessment measures

3. What indicators are you looking at to know whether the approach is working? How complete are they?

4. List the SWOTs to date:

   a. **S**trengths

   b. **W**eaknesses

   c. **O**pportunities

   d. **T**hreats

5. What external factors led you to choose this approach? (For example, district or state mandates, national goals, parental support, availability of resources, budget.)

6. What internal factors led you to choose this approach? (For example, personal philosophy, students' needs, school environment.)

7. Has program evaluation changed your approach? How so?

8. Has program evaluation changed your teaching objectives? How so?

9. What are your key objectives for the future?

PART II: QUANTITATIVE QUESTIONNAIRE

1. How many opportunities did students get to experience culturally diverse

   a. programs? _____

   b. lessons? _____

   c. guest artists? _____

2. How many students overall experienced this? _____

3. How many community members and staff experienced this? _____

4. How much money was spent to facilitate culturally diverse education in dance? _____

5. Cite the places publicity occurred or happened: _____

6. How many evaluation forms were distributed? _____

7. How many evaluation forms were returned? _____

8. How many evaluation forms were compiled into data? _____

9. How effective were our assessment strategies? _____

Sample Course Requirements for BA in Dance Education

Because educational dance requires skills in dance, in education, and a specialty in dance education, one's bachelor of arts in dance education must adequately address all three. There should also be a systematic building of skills rather than a random order to one's coursework. (See chapter 3 for details.)

• Part I shows an example of how your studies may progress.

- Part II shows a sample four-year undergraduate degree program with initial teacher certification in dance.

Part I: Example of a Broad-Based Undergraduate Teacher Preparation Curriculum

Undergraduate academic schedules are fluid in time and variable in content. However, your course work each academic year should not be random courses. They should build knowledge and skills in an ongoing and consistent manner. Your college education should provide adequate preparation. Perhaps it is similar to this:

YEAR 1

- General education
- Dance academics and techniques
- Dance company apprentice

YEAR 2

- General education
- Dance academics and techniques
- Professional education (foundations courses)
- Performing
- Clinical observations in K-12 dance by a dance specialist*

YEAR 3

- Dance academics and technique
- Performing
- Professional education (upper-level courses)
- Dance education
- In-depth clinical experiences ranging from primary ages to high school*

YEAR 4 (SAME AS YEAR 3)

- Performing (but not during the semester you student teach)
- Modern and ballet pedagogy**
- Student-teaching internship**

*Because certification is K-12, the skills required of a dance specialist are broad. Whether or not you plan to teach one specific age level, your college certifies that you are ready to teach at all levels, from primary through high school. Therefore, it is necessary to develop skills for all of them. Usually the most unfamiliar skills are leading movement

exploration for young children and teaching them to choreograph, perform, and critique dance. There should be enough practice in primary and elementary school clinical experiences not only to develop skills in teaching this age but also to enable you to see where and how the curriculum begins in K-5 so you fully understand how to build onto it at older ages.

**In a four-year curriculum, there is hardly enough time to practice teaching skills at all levels K-12. Be creative in finding other ways to sharpen pedagogy skills for all grade levels. Be pragmatic. If you get an opportunity to teach ballet and modern dance to nonmajors while you are in college (perhaps as a practicum associated with a dance pedagogy course), take it. These skills are similar to teaching high school–age students. Then use clinical hours to refine the more challenging skills for the primary, elementary, and middle schools. Use supervised clinical experiences to acquire all the skills you need at all age levels.

Part II: Sample Course Requirements for a BA in Dance Education With Teacher Certification

CORE IN DANCE (DANCE SPECIALIZATION): 57 SEMESTER HOURS

- Introduction to dance as art and phenomenon (3)
- The dancer's body (emphasis on care and prevention) (3)
- Body conditioning with gyrokinesis (1)
- Somatics and experiential anatomy and kinesiology (4)
- Choreography (6)
- Ballet history and criticism: Preclassic to present (3)
- Modern dance history and criticism (3)
- Non-Western dance history and cultures (3)
- Dance analysis and critique (Laban-based) (3)
- Ballet technique every semester (7)
- Modern technique and improvisation every semester (7)
- A specified world dance sequence every semester (technique class, which incorporates

history and its practice—e.g., Bharata Natyam, West African dance and drumming, Balinese legong and baris) (7)

- Dance company and production every semester (technical theater internship: sounds, costume and makeup, lights, backstage, stage craft, house management, box office) (7)

GENERAL EDUCATION: 56 SEMESTER HOURS

- Lab science: anatomy and kinesiology (4)
- Other lab science (4)
- Fine arts (3)
- Anthropology: cultures, rituals, art (6)
- Other social science (3)
- Humanities: music for dancers (3)
- Speech (3)
- Writing: English I and II (6)
- Literature (3)
- Foreign languages (6)
- History: world civilizations and cultures (3)
- History: American (3)
- Math and analytical: computer science or philosophy I and II (6)
- Wellness, fitness, and nutrition (3)

PROFESSIONAL EDUCATION: 36 SEMESTER HOURS

- Dance education I: foundations of dance education K-12 (3)
- Practicum for dance education I (K-12) (1)
- Dance education II: creative dance for K-5 (3)
- Practicum for dance education II (elementary) (1)
- Dance education III: pedagogy for grades 6-12 (3)
- Synthesis of dance education constructs: pre-internship seminar (1)
- Internship in student teaching (12)
- Schools in communities (3)
- Learning and diversity in learning (3)
- Exceptional learners or physical education for inclusion (3)
- Interdisciplinary relationships in the arts (3)

Total hours: 149 semester hours

Sample Mega-Ideas and Concepts

Using the dance cornerstone points of view, the dance faculty from Old Donation Center Gifted and Talented Program (grades 3 to 8) started a list of the mega-ideas they plan to drive home all six years with students. They plan to reinforce each one in multiple ways.

AS A DANCER

- The body is an instrument of expression.
- Dance performance requires an articulate body.
- One's self is the substance out of which this art is made.
- Mastery of space, time, and dynamics is vital to dance.
- Dance can be read and written using notation.

AS A CHOREOGRAPHER

- Movement is the medium of expression.
- Dance making is a creative process.
- Dance involves form and structure (design).
- Dance conveys ideas, feelings, and moods.

AS A HISTORIAN AND CULTURAL ANTHROPOLOGIST

- Dance has intrinsic value and significance to society.
- Dance is both an art and a human phenomenon.
- Dance is a universal mode of human expression.
- Dance is enduring and ephemeral.

AS A CRITIC

- Dance is analyzed for structure and design.
- Dance is analyzed for content and meaning.
- Dance uses critical thinking to evaluate and interpret movement.
- Dance uses multiple vocabularies.

A Working Draft from Old Donation Center (Virginia), composed in a workshop with the author and ODC dance faculty: Karen Buchheim, Laura Pettibone Wright, Gwen Jones, and Pamela Washburn.

Sample Student Handbook (High School Gifted and Talented Program)

Student handbooks give parents and students an overview of expectations and permit all parties to sign contracts at the beginning of the year. This sample is from a high school for artistically gifted and talented students. (See chapter 9 for details.)

The dance curriculum correlates with the curriculum standards set forth by YYY School District.

Participation in Class

Students are expected to participate fully in every aspect of the dance program. Daily grades are assigned and are based on four factors—dressing out, effort, attitude, and progress. The only legitimate excuse for not participating in class is illness or injury. If a student cannot participate in class, a doctor's note is required. If the student does not have the appropriate clothing, he or she is still required to participate in class. However, points will be deducted from the daily grade for that student.

Dressing Out

Class will begin three minutes after the tardy bell rings. Girls will enter the classroom and immediately begin to dress. Boys will change in the restroom closest to the dance room and wait outside the door. When students are dressed, they will spread out on the dance floor and begin a personal warm-up. Class will end three minutes before the bell in order to give the students time to change back into their school clothes.

Female dancers are required to wear a leotard and ankle-length tights. Ballet slippers are required for ballet technique, jazz shoes or jazz sneakers for jazz technique, and bare feet for modern technique. Hair must be pulled away from the face and off of the shoulders. Oversized jewelry and chewing gum will not be permitted.

Male dancers are required to wear a fitted T-shirt and gym shorts or tights. Footwear requirements are the same as those for female dancers.

Note: Dance skirts are permitted for ballet technique; however, no plastic shorts or leg warmers.

Effort, Attitude, and Progress

Dancers will be evaluated daily on the basis of task commitment and progress. Task commitment is an essential component in the study of dance.

Many people have the ability and creativity to pursue excellence in dance; however, only those who are determined and dedicated will successfully achieve their goals. Having a positive attitude is an important component in a dance program. Dance often involves working on group projects; therefore, cooperation and respect for others are essential. Establishing this kind of classroom environment will ensure that everyone has fun in the process of learning.

Completion of Assignments

Students are required to complete all in-class homework assignments. In the case of excused absences, homework assignments will be due on the student's first day back in school. The student is responsible for getting missed assignments from the teacher. Late assignments will be subject to a grade penalty of five points per day. Assignments that have not been turned in by the end of the marking period will receive the grade of zero.

Tests and Projects

Written tests will be given periodically based on notes and handouts from class. In-class review sessions will precede all major tests. In some cases, a project, research paper, or performance may substitute for an exam. Students will be given at least two weeks' notice for major projects.

Journals

Students will be responsible for maintaining a personal dance journal throughout the semester. In the journals, students will be allowed to record and reflect on their experiences in dance class that week. Each journal entry will be one page in length and kept in a spiral or composition notebook. Loose papers will not be accepted. Journals will be turned in each Friday and returned to the students on the following Monday.

Performance Requirements

Students are required to participate fully in all performances and attend all scheduled rehearsals. Performances are an extension of the dance curriculum. Therefore, they are not considered an extracurricular activity, even though they may take place outside of the school day. Failure to attend rehearsals and performances may result in students' dismissal from the performance or the dance program. A missed rehearsal or performance will have a definite effect on a student's grade. Advance requests from parents will be taken into consideration and schedule conflicts will be handled according to individual circumstances. Students who miss a rehearsal or performance without prior approval must supply a doctor's excuse. The absence of even one dancer at a rehearsal may compromise the quality of the performance. For this reason, the attendance policy will be strictly enforced. Please note the rehearsal and performance dates below and make arrangements to attend in advance.

All students are assigned performance roles in productions with the following exceptions: Discipline problems in dance class that caused the student to lose the privilege of performing in production (discourtesy, unsafe practice, disrespect for others). Or the student's daily grade in dance (participation) falls below the B level. **These students are assigned understudy roles and a backstage jobs for productions.**

PERFORMANCE DATES

_____

_____

_____

REHEARSAL DATES AND TIMES (AFTER SCHOOL)

_____

_____

_____

_____

_____

Pleas sign and return this statement to verify your willingness to accept the course requirements for this school year.

_____

I have read and fully understand the course requirements as set forth in the 2005 Student Handbook of the dance department of YYY High School.

Student's signature

_____

Date _____

Parent or guardian's signature

_____

Date _____

Sample Teaching File Checklist

Organize your textbooks and the course materials from your dance studies into a portable teaching file. File materials so that you can access them, especially for your semester of student teaching internship. (Consider keeping it in the trunk of your car to have it both at home and at school.) Here are sample items to keep in your file. (See chapters 3, 11, and 12 for details.)

CORE MATERIALS

1. Notes and papers for all dance education courses
   - [ ] Dance education I and II
   - [ ] Diversity courses
   - [ ] Dance analysis and critique
   - [ ] Experiential anatomy and kinesiology
   - [ ] Dance pedagogy
2. CDs and audiotapes from diversity classes
   - [ ] Spanish and Latin dance
   - [ ] Building community through dance
   - [ ] Scottish dance
   - [ ] Balinese dance
   - [ ] West African or Caribbean dance
   - [ ] Kuchipudi or Bharata Natyam
   - [ ] World folk dance
   - [ ] Native American dance
3. [ ] National Standards for Dance Education (with OTLS)
4. [ ] State dance education framework K-12
5. [ ] State visual and performing arts framework
6. [ ] Photos or videos from in-school experiences
7. [ ] List of videos useful for instruction

AUXILIARY MATERIALS

1. [ ] Resources for teaching materials (catalogs, list of Web sites)
2. [ ] Materials from dance history classes
3. [ ] Materials from dance composition classes
4. [ ] Materials on dance injury and prevention

5. [ ] Materials on dance criticism

6. [ ] Materials on higher-order thinking

7. [ ] Materials on anatomy and kinesiology

8. [ ] Articles related to dance education (from NDA, *JOPERD*, NDEO, *JODE*)

9. [ ] Several percussion instruments

10. [ ] Audiotapes for accompaniment

11. [ ] Materials from introduction to dance class

12. [ ] Non-Western ritual in dance and religion materials

Class Management Notes From an Inner-City High School Teacher

Absence policies vary. In our school, if a child cuts class, s/he receives zeroes. However, if absences are excused, the teacher must provide the student with make-up work or the student must schedule a time with the teacher within a week from the absence to practice what was missed. Students are not failed because of too many absences.

Excused tardies are acceptable. Three unexcused tardies equals one unexcused absence. A student schedule for each semester is included in my Student Handbook. The schedule includes lesson/unit topic for each class meeting, test dates, notebook due dates, performance dates, dates of assemblies and holidays, and in-class student/teacher conference dates.

I am not able to discuss the Handbook and requirements with parents—only with students. So I sent home an abbreviated version of the Handbook with the pertinent information that concerned the parents that also told them their child received a more in-depth Student Handbook. Students signed a statement saying they received the Handbook packet, and the parents signed a copy of their abbreviated version stating they read and agreed to the information. Later in the year when I had to call parents for specifics, I was able to refer to the abbreviated versions and the note that I sent home. I found the more I referred to the document the more support I had for my position.

Do not try to go over it all in one class period. Students tune it out. Instead it works to read one particular procedure, rule, etc. and then have them practice it. It is also helpful to refer to the schedule in the packet every class meeting to alert them to what is to happen during the next class.

I found it beneficial to display a poster of "Performance Expectations," to which I referred quite often. When students would say they did not know about one of the expectations, I was able to stand my ground by saying "you received it in your Handbook, we have discussed it many times in class, and it has been on the wall since the beginning of the year." Students/parents cannot dispute this.

Dance educators should make rules and consequences about the pick-up time for after-school events (for students who don't drive). Make a rule if the child is not picked up *on time* for a specified number of times that there is a specific consequence, such as s/he will be dropped from the performance roster.

Reprinted with permission of Kellie Romanstine.

Considerations for Hiring a Qualified Dance Specialist

This article is for principals hiring their first dance specialist and for those who are unfamiliar with the K-12 dance standards. (Readers: Place it in your Perspectives Notebook for job interviews or offer to mail the principal a copy before your interview.) (See chapter 16 for details.)

Comprehensive dance education requires a K-12 dance curriculum taught by a certified dance specialist with broad training in dance and dance education. High-quality student preparation depends on high-quality teacher preparation.

Many school administrators ask whom they should hire to design and deliver the most substantive dance curricula. Do they hire someone from the local dance studio? Do they hire someone with a respected background in ballet? Do they hire the English teacher who has also been a dancer? This article assists by correlating the standards of the K-12 dance curriculum with the qualifications of the one who teaches it.

A comprehensive dance education program requires a dance specialist with particular dance education skills and extensive dance training. Cross-check the candidate's credentials with his or her ability in a demonstration class. Look for evidence of comprehension and application in the following areas:

- Thorough grounding in anatomy and kinesiology

- Attention to anatomical placement and alignment for both static and dynamic (kinetic) work

- Technical knowledge and skills in diverse dance styles, including some non-Western styles

- Proficiency in modern dance and ballet

- Broad understanding of all dance styles and their relationship to one another

- Thorough grounding in dance criticism and an ability to facilitate analysis and critique

- Skills in composition and choreography

- Thorough grounding in dance history as well as comprehension of the cultural underpinnings of many dance styles

- Articulate movement vocabulary, both verbal and kinetic

- Knowledge of human development in order to build from simple to complex, to sequence K-12, to discern instructional level and appropriate time to use partners and to avoid use of partners, and to build systematic and consecutive grade level instruction

- Grounding in both the theory and methods of teaching various dance styles

- Use of some social and recreational dance forms to complement artistic dance forms

- Ability to collaboratively facilitate learning in and through dance in an educational setting with guest artists, classroom teachers, visual and performing arts teachers, physical education specialists, community-based dance schools, and artistically talented and gifted dance programs

- Understanding of common dance injuries and prevention and the ability to use these skills when needed

- Performance and production skills (lighting, costume, makeup, sets)

- Basic understanding of musical forms and accompaniment

Standards provide valuable information in K-12 curriculum, instruction, and assessment. However, selecting dance faculty who will teach the content is new territory for most school administrators.

There are too few model curricula for grades 13 to 16 to follow. Look for transcript evidence of the following:

1. Modern and ballet technique (4 years each)
2. Diverse world dance techniques (4 years)
3. Dance history and anthropology
4. Dance criticism
5. Choreography
6. Anatomy, kinesiology, and somatics
7. Courses in dance education
8. Dance analysis
9. Clinical experiences in dance education (K-12)
10. Evidence of student teaching in dance education, not solely education

Also look for evidence of performance, choreography, and teaching skills.

Find teachers who have integrated dance education backgrounds rather than simply isolated course work in dance and in education. Isolated course work produces dancers with incomplete skills for schools. Directed teaching in dance education is critical to understanding and applying dance to K-12. Studio training is not sufficient. A studio model is incompatible with educational dance settings. Well-intentioned dance programs have been derailed when they have hired beautiful performers to be K-12 educators. Qualified, certified dance specialists with grounding in the art form of dance and the art of teaching educational dance produce the best results in school-based programs.

Administrators should be sensitive to the dance specialists' need to continue their own performing skills. Taking dance classes outside of school demands extra time and energy from the specialist, but it also enriches teaching and feeds the overall school program.

In summary, when determining the parameters of a quality educational dance program, look for a fully certified dance specialist with broad educational credentials and experience in supervised teaching. This person must also be well versed in the artistic discipline of dance itself. Consider posting the job on the National Dance Education Organization Web site at www.ndeo.org or National Dance Association Web site at www.aahperd.org/nda.

From the *South Carolina Journal for Health, Recreation, Physical Education and Dance*, 1994.

Appendix C

🦅 Professional Organizations and National Initiatives

Appendix C lists some of the professional organizations that are useful for dance specialists. Along with key players in arts education, it also includes initiatives and legislation pertaining directly to dance.

1. American Dance Legacy Institute
2. Consortium of National Arts Organizations
3. Council of Chief State School Officers
4. Dance Heritage Coalition
5. Goals 2000—Educate America Act
6. Kennedy Center Alliance for Arts Education Network
7. National Assessment of Educational Progress
8. National Assessment Governing Board
9. National Association of Schools of Dance
10. National Center for Education Statistics
11. National Council for Accreditation of Teacher Education
12. National Endowment for the Arts
13. National Organizations for Dance Education
    - National Dance Association
    - National Dance Education Organization
14. National Initiative to Preserve American Dance
15. SCANS Report for America 2000
16. U.S. Department of Education

American Dance Legacy Institute

ADLI is located at Brown University, P.O. Box 1897, Providence, RI 02912. The ADLI provides the opportunity to practice and participate in contemporary and historic master works of dance. Its motto is "That which is saved is that which is valued. That which is valued is that which is known and shared." ADLI commissions an ongoing series of short studies or études extracted from dance masterpieces for serious dance students, teachers, and professional dancers. Web site is www.adli.us/index.html.

Consortium of National Arts Organizations

DAMT includes the national organizations in dance, art, music, and theatre. They guided the writing of the National Standards for Arts Education. DAMT is composed of the American Alliance for Theatre & Education (AATE), MENC: The National Association for Music Education, National Art Education Association (NAEA), and National Dance Association (NDA).

517

Council of Chief State School Officers

CCSSO is a consortium of 33 states that are interested in reforming their teacher licensing systems using performance-based standards and assessments. Among other documents, they assembled a national arts education committee to write *Interstate New Teacher Assessment and Support Consortium (INTASC)*, which provides model standards for licensing classroom teachers and arts specialists in the United States. Web site is www.ccsso.org/intasc.

Dance Heritage Coalition

DHC is an organization to strengthen the national network of dance documentation and preservation. Founded in 1993, it promotes documentation, gives grants, and is a clearinghouse for the array of dance resources on the Internet at www.danceheritage.org. This site provides information, tools, training resources, and services for dance research and documentation, along with searchable, full-text finding aids to more than 50 collections of primary resources at DHC member libraries online. DHC member institutions include American Dance Festival; Dance Collection at New York Public Library for the Performing Arts; the Harvard Theatre Collection, Houghton Library, Harvard University; Jacob's Pillow Dance Festival; Library of Congress Music Division; Ohio State University; and San Francisco Performing Arts Library and Museum. You may link to library catalogs and national databases that include dance materials and download outlines and documents focused on dance documentation and preservation.

Goals 2000—Educate America Act

(See chapter 2 for details.) As the enabling legislation for dance as arts education, this act names the core subjects of the arts, including dance, for all K-12 children in the United States.

BY THE YEAR 2000

- Goal 1: All children in America will start school ready to learn.
- Goal 2: The high school graduation rate will increase to at least 90 percent.

- Goal 3: All students will leave grades 4, 8, and 12 having demonstrated competency over challenging subject matter including English, mathematics, science, foreign languages, civics and government, economics, arts, history, and geography.
- Goal 4: The nation's teaching force will have access to programs for the continued improvement of their professional skills.
- Goal 5: U.S. students will be first in the world in mathematics and science achievement.
- Goal 6: Every adult in America will be literate and will possess the knowledge and skills necessary to compete in a global economy and exercise the rights and responsibilities of citizenship.
- Goal 7: Every school in America will be free of drugs, violence, and the unauthorized presence of firearms and alcohol and will offer a disciplined environment conducive to learning.
- Goal 8: Every school will promote partnerships that will increase parental involvement and participation in promoting the social, emotional, and academic growth of children.

Kennedy Center Alliance for Arts Education Network

KCAAEN is a programmatic affiliate of the education department of the JFK Center for the Performing Arts, Washington, DC. It partners with state affiliates to promote the arts and support policies, practices, and partnerships that ensure the arts are woven into the fabric of American education. It builds community partnerships for effective school arts programs, serves as an information exchange, and actively participates in the development of arts education policy in partnership with other national arts and arts in education organizations. Web site is http://kennedy-center.org/education/kcaaen.

National Assessment of Educational Progress

NAEP is an important resource for understanding what students know and can do in all core subjects. NAEP assessments have explored students' abilities in subject areas including reading, science, U.S. history, and mathematics. Based on assessment results,

NAEP reports levels of student achievement and the instructional, institutional, and demographic variables associated with those levels of achievement. In 1997, NAEP conducted a national assessment in the arts at grade 8. The assessment included the areas of music, theatre, and visual arts. (Though an assessment was developed for dance, it was not implemented because a statistically suitable sample could not be located. The 2008 and 2016 assessments are not planning to include dance unless a significant number of comprehensive programs come forth to advocate for it. Do so at www.ndeo.org.)

Dance professionals need to advocate for having qualified dance specialists administer the assessment rather than non-dance specialists. Even if a smaller number is assessed, it is better that it be done correctly than administered and scored by a non-dance person.

The National Center for Education Statistics (NCES) publication "Arts Education in Public Elementary and Secondary Schools" contains further information about statistics on comprehensive dance education programs now in existence. Find the document at http://nces.ed.gov/pubsearch/pubsinfo.asp?pubid = 2002131.

The NAEP 1997 Report Card: Eighth-Grade Findings from the National Assessment of Educational Progress is available electronically at http://nces.ed.gov/naep. It is also on a CD-ROM from Educational Testing Service. NAEP's Arts Education Assessment Framework (1994) may be accessed from NAGB's Web site: www.nagb.org.

National Assessment Governing Board

NAGB is the governing board that sets up the NAEP assessments, which are scheduled for 2008 and 2016 (but possibly without dance or theatre). On the Web site www.nagb.org, NAGB posts specifics about the National Assessment of Educational Progress (NAEP) as well as the proposed Voluntary National Tests in Reading and Math.

National Association of Schools of Dance

NASD is the most widely recognized accrediting body for institutions of higher education with degree programs in dance and dance education and for professional schools of dance. It promotes high standards for degree-granting institutions. It reviews all aspects of a dance program including undergraduate- and graduate-level work, accounting for every aspect of dance and how the parts fit together as a whole in a college or university setting. Approximately 50 institutions are accredited by NASD. Most are college and university programs but others are professional schools, such as the Alvin Ailey American Dance Theatre School, the Martha Graham School, the Pittsburgh Ballet, and the Laban Institute of Movement Studies. NASD recognizes the most outstanding programs for higher work in dance and dance education.

NASD also gathers statistical information from member institutions and compiles it into useful information. These data are used for advocacy, provide professional development opportunities for dance department heads, and help articulate to academe and to others the scope, range, and overall success of the faculty and programs they accredit.

NASD works in conjunction with the other national accreditation organizations in the arts: NASM (music), NASAD (art and design), and NAST (theatre). Although affiliated, they maintain their own separate discipline-specific accreditations and review processes. All are available at the same Web site, www.arts-accredit.org.

Although not a regulatory agency, NASD serves as a qualitative review agent for NCATE, the teacher accreditation body for teacher certification in higher education. NASD aims to "sustain and advance the strongest possible dance education for our young people in schools, community dance programs, and private studios. Teacher education and research are primary responsibility of faculty and NASD institutions, but these efforts must be supported by policy development and implementation that maintain and build conditions for study at the elementary and secondary level. NASD's efforts in these areas are most often behind the scenes, but the association is always working to build a critical base of dance participation and understanding in young people" (NASD 1999, p. 2).

National Center for Education Statistics

The NCES is the primary federal entity for collecting and analyzing data related to education in the United States and other nations. Web site is http://nces.ed.gov.

National Council for Accreditation of Teacher Education

National Council for Accreditation of Teacher Education (NCATE) is the most widely recognized agency that measures the effectiveness of education departments or schools and the departments such as dance that offer teacher certification.

The state in which you reside adopts accreditation standards to ensure institutions of higher education provide adequate teacher preparation in all subject areas. Most state departments of education use NCATE as the standard for quality. NCATE adheres to INTASC standards for new teachers.

NCATE is another system of quality assurance for higher education regarding the teaching profession. NCATE accreditation helps ensure colleges of education develop a coherent program of study according to current and emerging knowledge in fields (such as dance education). NCATE accredited programs must demonstrate that the knowledge bases are understood by, as well as articulated by, faculty and students alike. Their standards address four categories:

1. The design of professional education at the institution
2. The development of preservice teacher education
3. The professional education of faculty
4. Specific standards related to the individual disciplines

NCATE recognizes NASD accreditation as reciprocal. That is, an institution accredited by NASD categorically meets NCATE standards in dance. Professional accreditation standards such as NASD and NCATE ensure that institutions of higher education, such as the one you attend, provide worthy training for you as a professional. (For more information about NASD, their roles, programs, procedures, and standards, contact the National Association of Schools of Dance, 11250 Roger Bacon Drive, Suite 21, Reston, VA 22090.)

For more information about NCATE accreditation policies and procedure, contact the National Council for Accreditation of Teacher Education, 2010 Massachusetts Ave. NW, Suite 500, Washington, DC 20036-1023; Web site: www.ncate.org; e-mail: ncate@ncate.org.

National Endowment for the Arts

The NEA is the federal agency that Congress created to support the visual, literary, design, and performing arts to benefit all Americans. The mission of the endowment is twofold:

1. To foster the excellence, diversity, and vitality of the arts in the United States
2. To broaden public access to the arts

NEA makes direct grants and resources available to arts education and dance.

a. Professional dance
   - Dance on tour
   - Dance presenting
   - Choreography
b. Dance education
   - Access to the arts
   - Cultural heritage and preservation of the arts
   - Community arts partnership initiatives
   - Youth at risk

NEA also redistributes funds allotted to them by the U.S. Congress directly to each state.

Each state's arts commission gets a share of funds for these categories: cultural heritage and preservation, education and access, creation and presentation, and planning and stabilization.

Access current news on NEA's Web site, www.NEA.gov, or contact National Endowment for the Arts, Nancy Hanks Center 1100 Pennsylvania Ave. NW, Washington, DC 20506-0001, telephone 202-682-5400. Valuable arts advocacy and educational materials are available through the NEA as well as their partner agency, the National Assembly of State Arts Agencies (NASAA) at 1010 Vermont Ave. NW, Suite 920 Washington, DC 20005, telephone 202-347-6352.

National Organizations for Dance Education

Both professional organizations for dance education guide the national reform agenda in dance education. Dynamic leaders from both the National Dance

Education Organization (NDEO) and the National Dance Association (NDA) create national certification models for dance specialists and establish standards of excellence for dance education. Both are membership-based organizations governed by professional volunteer boards of directors and operated by executive directors. Thanks to their strong leadership and political savvy, the art of dance taught by certified dance specialists as a core subject in arts education is growing.

Both organizations convene annual conferences devoted to professional development in numerous aspects of dance. Both have state affiliates. Both give discounts on dance books to members. Join one or both, since your active participation adds momentum to the profession.

a. National Dance Association (NDA) is part of the American Alliance for Health, Physical Education, Recreation and Dance (AAPHERD). It publishes dance resources such as the NSDE, and the OTLS (for school delivery). Web site is www.aahperd.org/nda.

b. National Dance Education Organization (NDEO) is an autonomous organization that facilitates dance as arts education across the nation. NDEO publishes for its membership the *Journal of Dance Education,* the only professional journal devoted to dance education. Web site is www.ndeo.org.

NDEO's monumental undertaking to get a database for Research in Dance Education (RDE) moves the field along by giving educators access to data that have heretofore been inaccessible, such as unpublished master's theses and doctoral dissertations. The RDE database is housed at the Center of Research in Dance Education (CRDE) at Temple University in Philadelphia and is accessed by members through a link on the NDEO Web site (www.ndeo.org).

National Initiative to Preserve American Dance

NIPAD supports documentation efforts to solidify the cultural contributions made by dance artists and scholars in the United States with a sizeable grant program to assist. The NIPAD is a program of Dance/USA, funded by the Pew Charitable Trusts. It is administered by the Kennedy Center for the Performing Arts, Washington, DC. Web site is www.danceusa.org/programs_publications/nipad.htm.

SCANS Report for America 2000

SCANS Report for America 2000 was prepared for the U.S. Department of Labor in 1991 and presented to the U.S. Congress by the secretary of labor and the Secretary's Commission for Achieving Necessary Skills (SCANS). The report identifies what is expected of the literate person of the future. It forces us to examine how broadly the arts educate the young and profoundly affect society. The arts are necessary for humanistic education. SCANS gives education three mandates (Secretary's Commission on Achieving Necessary Skills, U.S. Department of Labor 1991):

1. All American high school students must develop a new set of competencies and foundation skills if they are to enjoy productive, full, and satisfying lives.

2. The qualities of high performance that today characterize our most competitive companies must become the standard for the majority of our companies, large and small, local and global.

3. The nation's schools must be transformed into high-performance organizations in their own right.

SCANS identified competencies and a three-part foundation of skills and personal qualities needed for a quality job performance in "A Three-Part Foundation Needed by Students." For example:

BASIC SKILLS

a. Reading: locates, understands, and interprets written information in prose and in documents such as manuals, graphs, and schedules.

b. Writing: communicates thoughts, ideas, information, and messages in writing and creates documents such as letters, directions, manuals, reports, graphs, and flow charts.

c. Arithmetic and mathematics: performs basic computations and approaches practical problems by choosing appropriate mathematical techniques.

d. Listening: receives, attends to, interprets, and responds to verbal messages and other cues.

e. Speaking: organizes ideas and communicates orally.

THINKING SKILLS

a. Creative thinking: generates new ideas.

b. Decision making: specifies goals and constraints, generates alternatives, considers risks, and evaluates and chooses best alternative.

c. Problem solving: recognizes problems and devises and implements plan of action.

d. Seeing things in the mind's eye: organizes and processes symbols, pictures, graphs, objects, and other information.

e. Knowing how to learn: uses efficient learning techniques to acquire and apply new knowledge and skills.

f. Reasoning: discovers a rule or principle underlying the relationship between two or more objects and applies it when solving a problem.

PERSONAL QUALITIES

a. Responsibility: exerts a high level of effort and perseveres toward goal attainment.

b. Self-esteem: believes in own self-worth and maintains a positive view of self.

c. Sociability: demonstrates understanding, friendliness, adaptability, empathy, and politeness in group settings.

d. Self-management: assesses self accurately, sets personal goals, monitors progress, and exhibits self-control.

e. Integrity and honesty: chooses ethical courses of action.

Education Commission of the States (ECS) promotes the Partnership for 21st Century Skills, which stands on the shoulders of the SCANS report. Twenty-first century skills are driven by information technology and globalization and uphold the necessary role of the arts in education to prepare youth for the creative economy of the 21st century. The creative economy includes industries such as the arts, design, architecture, computer graphics, software, hardware, marketing, and information.

U.S. Department of Education

The USDOE is the federal agency that sets and oversees educational policy in the nation. The United States secretary of education is appointed by the president of the United States and serves on his cabinet as an adviser. The USDOE does not have legal authority to mandate programs or policy, but it, like the NEA, works to influence the president and Congress in favor of educational initiatives.

- Goals 2000—Educate America Act was a joint effort of the USDOE, the Assembly of State Governors, and the president's office working with the Congress. The fact that goal 3 of the Goals 2000 legislation lists the arts as core subjects is directly attributable to former USDOE Secretary Richard Riley, a consistent advocate for arts education in the public schools.

- Arts Education Partnership (AEP): The USDOE in collaboration with the NEA created a national coalition of arts education partners, which includes representative stakeholders from a broad spectrum of constituencies in education, the arts, and government. The AEP conducts forums across the United States. Go to www.aep-arts.org and ask to be put on their listserv, or go to www.ed.gov.

Glossary

abstract—That which is nonimitative and nonliteral; to extend reality by distorting gesture, posture, or movements.

achievement standards—Specific levels of student competence for all seven NSDE content standards differentiated by grade clusters: K-4, 5-8, and 9-12.

aesthetically driven—The artistically centered education that advances diverse ways to create, practice, and appreciate quality and beauty.

aesthetic education—The artistic processes and principles taught in school-based programs to affect artistic learning in and about dance in all its facets.

aesthetic pluralism—An approach to the study of art that attempts to broaden individual perspective and build appreciation for culturally diverse forms of artistic expression.

aesthetics—The branch of philosophy that deals with the nature of beauty and our response to it. That which is beautiful, well-designed, and artistic.

affective domain—The realm of feeling, emotions.

Africanist—A term to signify African and African-American influences, resources, presence, trends, and phenomena both past and present; it denotes the considerable impact of African and African-American culture on the arts and society.

all the arts—The multiple art forms (fine arts, folk arts, design arts, literary arts, musical arts, theatrical arts, media arts, visual arts, and performing arts). In this text, the arts signifies dance, music, theatre, and visual arts.

analysis—Separation of a whole into its component parts. In dance, analysis is to examine complex movement forms, their elements, and the relationships between and among them.

antecedent phrase—Musical term for an introductory phrase, which is followed by one or more phrases called consequent phrases. The latter is connected to the first phrase usually as a result of or an answer to the first phrase.

applied aesthetics—Aesthetics that are put to practical use. Making artistic choices and having artistic quality guide one's decisions about dance and dancing.

aptitude—Ability.

artistic processes—Creating, performing, and responding to dance, which are denoted by (c/p/r) in the text.

arts education perspective—A viewpoint that furthers aesthetic education through the artistic processes of creating, performing, and responding to art works. It is rooted in expressive languages that communicate meaning. It emphasizes the art form itself.

arts-centered school—There is in-depth exposure in the arts for all students, and the arts are the focal point for the school. It stresses competencies in all the arts (dance, music, theatre, visual arts) and aligns them with the general education core of the school.

arts infusion—The arts improve the general curriculum in addition to being taught as separate disciplines (dance, music, theatre, and visual arts).

arts integration—The arts are incorporated into the general education curriculum and are used to enhance the understanding of themes and topics of concern to the whole school. There is also substantive learning in the arts (dance, music, theatre, and visual arts).

Asianist—Signifying Asian influences, resources, presence, trends, and phenomena both past and present.

assessment—Term for measuring student outcomes according to learning objectives. Collection of performance data through a variety of means. This text uses assessment for students and evaluation for programs.

authentic assessment—Measurement in which teachers observe and assess how well learners process information and concepts during the creative, compositional, and performance activities.

BA—Bachelor of Arts degree, the liberal arts undergraduate degree in dance; the BA in Dance Education has a balanced dance curriculum of technique, choreography, dance academics, dance education, and an education component that includes clinical and student teaching internships. It normally comes with initial teacher certification or licensure in dance.

balance—The appearance of stability or the equalization of elements in a dance work; one of the 10 principles of design.

ballistic stretch—A bouncing stretch.

Bartenieff Fundamentals—An established series of flexion and extension preparatory exercises that begin on the floor and move to standing; developed by Laban protégé, Irmgard Bartenieff. The exercises articulate connections between upper and lower body as they focus on efficient internal initiations of movement beyond the often-used muscle–joint motivation.

behavior modification techniques—Strategies to alter behavior for long-term change.

BFA—Bachelor of Fine Arts degree, the professional undergraduate arts degree in dance; for example a Bachelor of Fine Arts degree in Dance emphasizes performance and choreographic skills.

B–M–E—Beginning–middle–end; the simplest compositional form.

bodymind—The source of bodythinking. The engaged body and mind toward the same desired outcome through movement. (See *bodythinking*.)

Body-Mind Centering (BMC)—A somatics approach developed by Bonnie Bainbridge Cohen; it shows how to use different body systems to support maximum performance quality and to fully tap into the body's natural sources for biomechanically efficient and artful movement. Body-Mind Centering can reprogram the body when needed by working with the human developmental patterns: *homologous, homolateral,* and *cross-lateral* (see each one for further clarification).

bodymindspirit—Integrating all aspects of the self through dance.

bodyspeaking—Expressing nonverbally with intention and clarity; communicating through movement in dance.

bodythinking—Using the entire nervous system to integrate one's total expressive instrument to communicate an idea or concept through motion.

BSTER—The dance elements: body, space, time, energy, and relationship.

choreography—One of the parent disciplines of dance as art; the processes and skills involved in the creation of dance works. Also a completed dance composition.

cinquain—A simple literary form with five lines on one topic in the shape of a diamond. Line 1 has one syllable; line 2 has two syllables; line 3 has three syllables; line 4 has two syllables; line 5 has one syllable.

classroom—Large teaching space for dance (studio, multipurpose room, large classroom).

climax—High point(s) in a dance work; one of the 10 principles of design.

codified—Set.

codified dances—Set dances and set movement sequences, such as folk dances and choreography that is completed.

cognitive—Mental function; use of intelligence.

collective aesthetics—Prevailing collectively accepted principles of structure and form that apply to the arts. It comes from the arts and design community about what is of artistic quality based on the principles of design as well as principles from various world cultures.

community of learners—A group that is involved in learning together. It includes the teacher as learner as well as students (a classroom is a community of learners).

comprehensive—Broad in scope.

conceptual dance vocabulary—Cognitive and intellectual understanding of the dance elements that enables one to think about as well as to verbalize or write about dance.

concrete—Bringing information directly through the five senses.

consequent phrase—Musical term for a phrase that is related to an introductory phrase that precedes it, called an antecedent phrase (see *antecedent phrase*). A consequent phrase means it is a following phrase and is usually the result of or an answer to the first phrase.

Consortium of National Arts Education Associations (DAMT for Dance, Art, Music, and Theatre)—Consortium consisting of American Alliance for Theatre &

Education (AATE), MENC: The National Association for Music Education, National Art Education Association (NAEA), and National Dance Association (NDA).

content standards—Seven overarching student learning goals identified by the NSDE for all grade levels.

contextual coherence—Understood in relationship to another experience or fact. Relevance and relatedness.

contrast—Achievement of emphasis and interest in a dance work through differences in dynamics, spatial elements, timing, textures, and other dance elements. One of the 10 principles of design.

convergent thinking—Thinking that focuses on specifics, concrete facts, and details.

cornerstones—Core body of knowledge and skills that all students should know in the dance discipline.

(c/p/r)—Shorthand for the three artistic processes of creating, performing, and responding to dance.

critical thinking—Way of thinking that is generally analytical and evaluative (higher-order thinking).

criticism—Description, analysis, interpretation, and evaluation of dance works. Criticism applies rules and principles that govern decisions instead of merely emotional reactions to dance works.

critiquing—Judging artistic quality of what is seen or done (critical thinking).

cross-lateral—Developmental pattern from Body-Mind Centering that connects upper to lower across the body in a giant X from upper right to lower left diagonally and from upper left to lower right. The third and most complex pattern of development, which enables us to turn. Human developmental patterns start in infancy and continue throughout life.

culture—An ever-changing system of shared beliefs, values, traditions, customs, learned behaviors, and artifacts that are transmitted from one generation to another.

cultural pluralism—Existence of multiple sets of cultural values within the world or society.

Dance Cornerstone Curriculum Framework (DCC Framework)—McCutchen's scope and sequence for the 6DC model of educational dance. It consists of goals and objectives (scope) and a detailed progression of content and experiences for K-2, 3-5, 6-8, and 9-12.

dance cornerstones—Four main aspects of dance: dancing and performing; creating and composing; knowing about history, culture, and context; analyzing and critiquing. Four distinct methods of inquiry are taken from the parent disciplines of dance: dance performance, choreography, dance history and anthropology, and dance criticism.

dance criticism—Process to describe, analyze, interpret, and evaluate specific dance works. It uses aesthetic principles—mainly the principles of design—to evaluate the artistic quality of a specific work. Its purpose is to offer insight into a choreographic work by illuminating its creative process and its choreographic components. One of the parent disciplines of dance as art.

dance education—General term to describe all situations where one person teaches dance to another. *Dance education* is too generic to convey the complex nature of educational dance as it functions in K-12. The term includes every model of teaching dance, private and public, group or individual, in all settings.

dance elements—The basic movement concepts of dance that emerge out of the five key categories: body, space, time, energy (dynamics), and relationships. Also referred to as BSTERs.

dance fluency—Knowing and demonstrating skills in all four dance cornerstones with the ability to cross-reference and integrate them (e.g., making one's own dance, critiquing it, performing it, and relating it to the broader world of dance). Fluency is an advanced form of dance literacy. Fluency is the ability to correlate and use the cornerstones to benefit each other; the ability to aesthetically integrate and synthesize the parts into the whole.

dance history—Field of study that identifies and classifies dance works in cultural and chronological context. Dance history is one of the parent disciplines of dance as art.

dance inquiry—Problem-solving, questioning, and investigative approach to dance by students. It combines higher-order and critical thinking around significant content.

dance literacy—Combination of knowing about dance and the ability to create, perform, and respond to dance as an art form; knowing, doing, and demonstrating skills in all four dance cornerstones.

dance specialist—One who is both dancer and dance educator, certified by the state education accrediting body to teach dance as art in K-12 education in the United States.

design principles—Ten principles that govern artistic processes of composing and critiquing the arts; dance's 10 principles of compositional design (see *principles of design [PODs]*).

devadasis—Temple dancers of south India's ancient Hindu temples who performed for the Hindu deities a dance that is the forerunner of the Bharata Natyam.

disciplinary action plan (DAP)—Uniform procedural steps in K-12 schools that enforce a specified code of student behavior, including consequences of misbehavior.

divergent thinking—Expansive thinking that seeks many possible answers.

dynamics—The way energy and force are directed and modulated to add texture to movement. One of the five BSTER categories.

educational dance (ED)—Encompasses all aspects of dance used to educate and inspire the young in K-12. It assumes that dance is taught as an art form by using knowledge and skills in all the various dance processes—dancing, creating, performing, responding, and critical thinking about dance to affect the education of the child. This term should not be confused with the European terminology that refers to "educational dance" as creative dance for children.

elaboration—Embellishment; making more detailed or sophisticated; developing dramatic strengths and meaning. One characteristic of creativity.

embedded assessment—Measurement that is part of a lesson. It serves as both an instructional strategy and an assessment measure.

enduring understandings—Mega-ideas and concepts that undergird a K-12 program, which students should never forget. To surpass knowing to understanding based on knowing. Understanding based on knowing is fluid so it can transfer to new contexts and transform into new theories.

ethnicity—Expressions and manifestations of attitudes, values, and behaviors that are based on a specific tradition, ancestry, history, and cultural heritage.

ethnocentric education—Assertions that people of diverse ethnic origins must be seen as subjects of history and of human experience. It takes the perspectives of the culture being studied to affirm both the struggles and achievements of different ethnic groups.

evaluate—To measure, classify, or judge.

evaluation—Measurement term for making value judgments and interpreting data from both student assessments and program evaluation. This text uses *assessment* for students and *evaluation* for programs.

experimentation—Process of exploring a particular idea or concept, then focusing on that concept to extend it in multiple ways.

exploring—Seeking all options (movement exploration).

expression—Act of communicating thoughts or feelings through movements, images, or actions.

fluency—Ability to generate a large number of possible solutions to a given problem.

form—Structure of a dance work.

formal analysis—Analysis of a work of dance art based primarily on the dance elements and the choreographic principles of design.

formative assessment—In-process feedback.

four arts disciplines—Dance, music, theatre, and visual arts.

gamelan—Form of musical accompaniment found in Indonesia (Bali, Java) composed of bronze xylophones, gongs, cymbals, and drums, which uses a 5-tone melody.

geometric—Including rectilinear or curvilinear motifs. Man-made shapes.

gestures—Movements predominantly made with the limbs and extremities such as the hands, arms, face, legs, feet, head, hips, and shoulders.

gifted—Conceptually, compositionally, and choreographically outstanding; the exceptional ability to conceptualize. Some individuals are both gifted and talented.

graining—Nikolais/Louis term that means texturing the body so that every grain or cell in the body attends to a certain direction or particular focal point. It is part of somatic awareness.

guided viewing questions (GVQs)—Queries to give students before they view a dance work to focus attention. The same questions are used to start discussion immediately following viewing.

harmony—Arrangement of shape and movements that is pleasing to the eye and holds together well; oneness. Quality of having all the parts of a dance work appear to belong together. One of the 10 principles of design.

higher-order and critical thinking—More refined and complex thinking skills of analysis, synthesis, and evaluation.

homolateral—Same-sided. Pattern of movement using only the right or the left side of the body. One of the developmental patterns of human movement from Body-Mind Centering. The second pattern of human development that starts in infancy and follows the rest of one's life.

homologous—Pattern of movement using only the upper half of the body or the lower half. One of the developmental patterns of human movement from Body-Mind Centering relating to moving one-half of the body—either the upper or lower half. The first pattern of human development that starts in infancy and enables locomotion later in life (mobility).

improvisation—The act of spontaneously creating movement while alone or in a group.

improvising—Spontaneously creating while alone or in a group.

inquiry approach—Method used by a dance specialist to facilitate student learning by posing questions to direct thought and action. The method a specialist uses to increase active learning, higher-order and critical thinking, and artistic production.

inquiry-based dance—Dance that is about investigating, participating, and problem solving. Inquiry produces an active learning environment in which students uncover diverse topics essential to their growth. Both a teaching style and a student learning process that stimulate learning. Aesthetic inquiry leads learners to make discriminating artistic choices about what they create and how they interact with the works of others.

intelligence—Cognitive function.

intentional motion—The artistic quality of moving to communicate. Movement that intends to be dance and not pedestrian. The simultaneous sensation of moving and refining the movement to express an idea.

internship—Student-teaching semester with a mentor teacher.

interpret—To explain or clarify. The ability to decode or uncover meaning in dance works.

JODE—*Journal of Dance Education,* published by NDEO.

JOPERD—*Journal of Physical Education, Recreation and Dance,* published by the American Alliance of Health, Physical Education, Recreation and Dance, the parent organization for NDA.

journaling—Reflective writing activity to record what was experienced or read and how it impacted the learner.

juxtaposition—One thing in contrast to another.

kin-aesthetic—Emphasizes the artistic quality of moving, the simultaneous sensation of moving (kinesthetic) and the refinement of the movement (aesthetic). Merges three words: *kinetic + kinesthetic + aesthetic.* Dancing with attention to the qualitative aesthetic choices one makes. Kin-aesthetic education in Cornerstone 1 helps dancers and performers integrate the aesthetics of intentional motion into their dancing.

kinesiology—Science of human movement.

kinesthetic—The way one perceives or feels one's own movement in one's body.

kinetic—Moving; movement or motion; physical action.

kinetic dance vocabulary—Movement vocabulary; dancing language; expressing oneself in motion. Having a kinetic dance vocabulary enables one to translate a concept into dance movement. It incorporates the conceptual dance vocabulary.

Labanotation—Symbol system for notating dance that can be read and written.

Language of Dance (LOD)—An experiential approach to movement understanding, education and creativity, leading to chorography, that integrates motif notation to promote dance literacy. Leads to Labanotation.

line—Path of a point moving in space. The outline or contour of an object: lines made with body shapes or by drawing motional lines in space. In ballet, line results from placement and extensions.

linear—Masculine model of sequence.

LOD—See *Language of Dance.*

LRP—Long-range plan (3-5 years); in schools often the full year curriculum plan.

matrixes—Structures that lay out all the levels of achievement for each criteria of an assignment.

methods of inquiry—Ways to investigate and personalize learning. In the arts, to investigate from different artistic viewpoints using the cornerstones as a dancer, a choreographer, a dance historian–anthropologist, and/or a dance critic.

mobility—Articulating the body, increasing its range of movement in the joints, and moving through space.

modalities—Ways of perceiving and processing information: kinesthetic, tactile, visual, auditory.

motif—Theme; one or more identifiable movements that recur in a dance that visually stand out and help hold the work together.

motif writing—Shorthand symbols that emanate from Labanotation but are less specific (e.g., one symbol indicates pathways but leaves the method of travel and the duration of travel up to the mover).

multicultural education—Learning about many cultures; concerned with increasing educational equity for a wide range of cultural groups.

multiethnic education—Modifying the total educational environment to reflect the ethnic diversity within American schools (i.e., that environment includes school policy, institutional norms, attitudes, and expectations of faculty and staff, counseling programs, courses of study).

multiple intelligences (MIs)—Different ways of knowing theorized by Harvard psychologist Howard Gardner to explain the main ways humans learn. His original seven intelligences are linguistic, logical-mathematical, musical, spatial, bodily-kinesthetic, interpersonal (between people), and intrapersonal (self-knowledge).

"Nation's Report Card"—The logo on documents pertaining to the national assessments planned and administered by NAEP (The National Assessment of Educational Progress). Another term for NAEP assessments.

NDA—National Dance Association.

NDEO—National Dance Education Organization.

objective—Based in fact.

observation—Act, habit, or power of seeing and noting. Also the institutional plan for preservice teachers to formally watch and take note of good practice in the field prior to and during student teaching internship.

Opportunity-to-Learn Standards (OTLS)—Published inside the *National Standards for Dance Education* (1996). Also called school delivery standards.

organic—Freeform, curvilinear, or natural shapes as opposed to geometric shapes or other man-made forms.

originality—Quality of being unique, fresh, or new. The ability to think, do, or create in a way that has not been done before. One characteristic of creativity.

participant–observer method—Method of assessment in which the teacher collects data from multiple sources such as journals, in-class comments and discussions, personal inquiry outside of class, peer assessments, and self-assessments of quality.

pattern—Forms, lines, or symbols that move in a pre-arranged sequence. A recurring motif or movement sequence.

personal aesthetics—Individual response from our unique inner aesthetic perception, enhanced by educational experiences in the arts.

PODs—See *principles of design (POD)*.

postures—Body shapes using part of the torso and involving the spine.

principles of design (PODs)—Ten aesthetic principles that apply to composition in all fine arts, literary arts, and design arts: unity, variety, repetition, contrast, sequence, climax, proportion, harmony, balance, transition.

process-oriented composition—Composition that involves selecting movements created through exploring, experimenting, or improvising with movement.

proportion—Relationship between sections of a dance regarding length and emphasis. The relative size of one part in relation to the whole. One of the 10 principles of design.

refinement—Precise improvement through simplification or elaboration.

reflection—Recalling, reviewing, and relating. The act of deliberating and contemplating; a conclusion reached after much thought.

reflective practitioner—The teacher who continually evaluates the effects of personal choices and actions on others (students, parents, and other professionals in the learning community). One who is self-motivated to seek opportunities to grow professionally.

reflective thinking—Thinking that relates new learning to what has gone before to put the experience into a broader context.

relationships—Connection between or among two or more objects or concepts. A condition of belonging to the same family or category. One of the categories of dance elements.

repetition—Recurring again and again. One of the 10 principles of design.

rhythm—Kinetic and auditory marks of timing movement. Recurring beat patterns, the result of the way movements are grouped together. Rhythm is one of the dance elements for time.

rubrics—Tools that turn objectives and criteria into measurements. Rubrics can either be criteria to judge or matrixes (structures) that lay out all the levels of achievement for each criteria of an assignment. They show what is expected and give a format by which to measure results.

safe space—Space that has no obstacles in it and no slippery floor.

scaffolding—A learning tactic by which the teacher facilitates in increments so that students eventually learn the modeled skills or behaviors on their own.

school-based program—Dance education program in a public or private K-12 school district that serves students in primary, elementary, middle, or high school during the school day as part of the basic school curriculum. After-school programs are not referred to as school-based programs.

scope and sequence—Sequential plan (e.g., a curriculum framework) that shows the content to be included (the scope) and how to develop it for each consecutive year (the sequence).

sequence—Order of sections of a dance. One of the 10 principles of design.

sequencing—Sophisticated form of ranking. Continuity of progression.

sequential—Ordered and incremental.

shape—Three-dimensional design made with the body in space. One of the dance elements.

6DC Cornerstone Model of Inquiry Based Educational Dance—McCutchen program model that describes a complete educational dance program as standards oriented, student centered, and rooted in the dance cornerstones. It must be comprehensive, substantive, sequential, aesthetically driven, contextually coherent, and inquiry based.

six defining characteristics (6DC) of educational dance—Comprehensive, substantive, sequential, aesthetically driven, contextually coherent, and inquiry based.

somatic—Of the body. An internal awareness of the body.

somatics—The bodymind process that activates an internal awareness of the body.

spiral—Feminine model of relatedness. A method that links new learning to old.

SRP—Short-range plan, usually a unit plan.

stability—Alignment; center; balance on different support bases; bilateral and cross-lateral support to maintain body equilibrium.

stages of progression—Levels of expertise from immature to mature.

stasis—State of non-movement in space (static).

static stretch—Non-ballistic stretch; lengthening a muscle without bouncing or visibly moving.

subjective—Based on personal references, not on specific criteria.

substantive—Challenging and significant.

summative assessment—Assessment that evaluates overall success of a process or product at its completion. Overall achievement of an activity, project, lesson, or unit is measured at the end. Summative assessment may take into account all aspects of the activity or project and evaluate each aspect in relation to the whole.

supervising teacher—Teacher to whom you are assigned for your student-teaching internship during the last semester.

symmetry—Design in which both sides are identical or nearly the same.

synthesis—Combination of separate elements to form a coherent whole; a joining together of previously separated elements.

talented—Outstanding performers in dance. Some students are both gifted and talented (see *gifted*).

taxonomy—Classification; principles pertaining to such a classification (cf., BSTER dance elements taxonomy, Bloom's taxonomy of levels of thinking).

teaching triad—Curriculum, instruction, and assessment. What is taught (curriculum), how it is taught (instruction), and how well it is taught and learned (assessment) become the interdependent, inseparable three-part process that you use in teaching dance in education.

technique—Way of using the body that is highly refined and includes placement, alignment, joint articulation, rhythmicality, and expressivity.

texture—Internally motivated characteristics of a movement's energy and dynamics that affect its quality, such as its roughness or smoothness or whether the dynamics are sharp, hard, or soft. Texture is a dance element.

three dimensional—Possessing the qualities of height, width, and depth.

time on task—Using every available moment for learning. Concept of keeping students focused on learning objectives and fully engaged without wasting any instructional time. The amount of time students are engaged in learning.

transformation—Change in structure, appearance, or character. A change from one form into another.

transition—Bridge between two aspects of a dance (phrases, sections). One of the 10 principles of design.

UDV—See *Universal Dance Vocabulary*.

unit of study—Group of lessons around a topic or theme for conceptual coherence.

unity—Oneness or wholeness of a work of art. One of the 10 principles of design.

Universal Dance Vocabulary (UDV)—Use of the dance elements to describe and conceptualize movement concepts. This BSTER vocabulary incorporates Laban terminology and applies to all styles of dance.

universality—Worldwide or global; found all over the world; transcending place.

variety—Diversifying elements within a dance work to add visual interest. One of the 10 principles of design.

visual and performing arts—Four fine arts disciplines—dance, music, theatre, and visual arts—that are considered core subjects in K-12 education in the United States.

WDYL—The most essential reflection question, "What did you learn?"

References

Ailey, Alvin with A. Peter Bailey. 1997. *Revelations: The Autobiography of Alvin Ailey.* Secaucus, NJ: Carol Publishing Group.

Alliance of SC Arts Education Organizations in Visual Art, Dance, Music and Theatre. 1991. *Where We Stand on Arts Education.* Columbia, SC: SC Alliance for Arts Education.

American Dance Legacy Institute. 2005. www.adli.us.

Arnheim, Rudolf. 1971. *Art and Visual Perception: A Psychology of the Creative Eye.* Berkeley, CA: University of California Press.

Arts Education Partnership Working Group. 1993. *The Power of the Arts to Transform Education: An Agenda for Action.* Washington, DC: The John F. Kennedy Center for the Performing Arts and The J. Paul Getty Trust.

Barringer, Janice and Sarah Schlesinger. 1998. *The Pointe Book: Shoes, Training, and Technique.* Revised edition. Hightstown, NJ: Princeton.

Bartenieff, Irmgard and Dori Lewis. 1980. *Body Movement: Coping with the Environment.* New York: Gordon and Breach.

Bennis, Warren. 1982. Leader Effectiveness. Lecture at Wilson Learning Client Conference, Minneapolis.

Block, Betty A. 2001. Literacy Through Movement: An Organizational Approach. *Journal of Physical Education, Recreation and Dance* 72(1): 39-48.

Bloom, Benjamin S., ed. 1956. *Taxonomy of Educational Objectives: The Classification of Educational Goals. Handbook 1: Cognitive Domain.* New York: David McKay.

Boyce, Anne. 1997. Inappropriate Student Behavior—A Problem for Student Teachers. *Journal of Physical Education, Recreation and Dance* 68(6): 28-30.

Boydston, Jo Ann, ed. 1985. *The Works of John Dewey, 1939-1941.* Vol. 14 in *The Later Works of John Dewey, 1925-1953.* Carbondale, IL and Edwardsville, IL: Southern Illinois University Press.

Brandt, Ron. 1987-1988. On Discipline-Based Art Education: A Conversation with Elliot Eisner. *Educational Leadership* 45(4): 6-22.

Bucek, Loren. 1992. Constructing a Dance Curriculum. *Journal of Physical Education, Recreation and Dance* 63(9): 39-42, 48.

Cohen, Bonnie Bainbridge. 1988. The Dancer's Warm-Up through Body-Mind Centering. *Contact Quarterly Dance Journal* 13(3): 28-29, 32-33.

Comer, James P. 2005. Child and Adolescent Development: The Critical Missing Focus in School Reform. *Phi Delta Kappan* 86(10): 757-763.

Consortium of National Arts Education Associations. 1994. *National Standards for Arts Education: What Every Young American Should Know and Be Able to Do in the Arts.* Reston, VA: Music Educators National Conference.

Cook, Susan and Joseph H. Mazo. 1978. *The Alvin Ailey American Dance Theater.* New York: William and Morrow.

Council on Basic Education, A Standards Primer. n.d. Wall chart. Washington, DC: Council on Basic Education.

Critical Dance. 2001. Turnout—A ballet basic. Critical Dance Web site: www.criticaldance.com.

Davis, Jessica. 1996. Art for Art's Sake. *Education Week* 16(7): 32-33.

Dobbs, Stephen Mark. 1989. Discipline-Based Art Education: Some Questions and Answers. *National Association of Secondary School Principal Bulletin* 73(517): 7-13.

Dobbs, Stephen Mark. 1998. *Learning in and through Art: A Guide to Discipline-Based Art Education.* Los Angeles: Getty Education Institute for the Arts.

Donahue, Keith, ed. 1997. *Imagine! Introducing Your Child to the Arts.* Washington, DC: National Endowment for the Arts.

Drews, Elizabeth Monroe. 1975. The Gifted Student: A Researcher's View. In *The Gifted and Talented: Developing Elementary and Secondary School Programs,* ed. Bruce O. Boston, 32-39. Reston, VA: Council for Exceptional Children.

Educational Psychology Interactive: Cognitive Development/Applications. 2003, April 9. http://chiron.valdosta.edu/whuitt/interact.html. Adapted from Woolfolk and McCune-Nicolich. 1984. *Educational Psychology for Teachers.* 2nd edition. Englewood Cliffs, NJ: Prentice-Hall.

Education Commission of the States. n.d. The Arts, Education, and the Creative Economy. Denver: Education Commission of the States. www.esc.org.

Eisenberg, Nancy, Janusz Reykowski, and Ervin Staub, eds. 1989. *Social and Moral Values: Individual and Societal Perspectives.* Hillsdale, NJ: Lawrence Erlbaum.

Eisner, Elliot W., ed. 1985. *Learning and Teaching the Ways of Knowing.* Eighty-fourth Yearbook of the National Society for the Study of Education. Chicago: National Society for the Study of Education.

Eisner, Elliot W. 1988. *The Role of Discipline-Based Art Education in America.* Los Angeles: Getty Center for Education in the Arts.

Eisner, Elliot W. 1990. Implications of Artistic Intelligences for Education. In *Artistic Intelligences: Implications for Education,* ed. William J. Moody, 31-42. New York: Teacher's College Press.

Eisner, Elliot W. 1992. The Misunderstood Role of the Arts in Human Development. *Phi Delta Kappan* 73(8): 591-595.

Eisner, Elliot W. 2002. *The Arts and the Creation of Mind.* New Haven, CT: Yale University Press.

Feldman, Edmund B. 1967. *Art as Image and Idea.* Englewood Cliffs, NJ: Prentice-Hall.

Fenstermacher, Gary D. 1990. Some Moral Considerations on Teaching as a Profession. In *The Moral Dimensions of Teaching,* eds. John I. Goodlad, Roger Soder, and Kenneth A. Sirotnik, 130-151. San Francisco: Jossey-Bass.

Fisher, Christine and Andrew Svedlow. 2005, September 14. Arts in Basic Curriculum Project. Rock Hill e-mail communication. www.winthrop.edu/abc/

Flummerfelt, Joseph. 2002. Arts in Education. Lecture at Spoleto Festival Education Panel. Charleston, South Carolina.

Fowler, Charles, ed. 1990. *Educating America's Youth in the Arts and Their Cultural Heritage: The 1989 National Summit Conference on the Arts and Education Alliance for Arts Education.* Washington, DC: John F. Kennedy Center for the Performing Arts.

Franklin, Eric. 1996. *Dance Imagery for Technique and Performance.* Champaign, IL: Human Kinetics.

Gabbard, Carl. 1998. Windows of Opportunity for Early Brain and Motor Development. *Journal of Physical Education, Recreation and Dance* 69(8): 54-56.

Gardner, Howard. 1990. Multiple Intelligences: Implications for Art and Creativity. In *Artistic Intelligences: Implications for Education,* ed. William J. Moody, 11-27. New York: Teacher's College Press.

Gardner, Howard. 1999. *Intelligence Reframed: Multiple Intelligences for the 21st Century.* New York: Perseus.

Garfias, Robert. 1989. What Do We Mean by "Cultural Diversity"? *Inside Performance* 1(2): 25-28.

Gdula, Kimberly. 2001. Alonzo King: The Royal Treatment. *Dance Teacher* (October): 56-59.

Graham, George, Shirley Ann Holt/Hale, and Melissa Parker. 2004. *Children Moving: A Reflective Approach to Teaching Physical Education.* 6th edition. New York: McGraw-Hill.

Guest, Ann Hutchinson. 1983. *Your Move: A New Approach to the Study of Movement and Dance.* New York: Gordon and Breach.

Hackney, Peggy, Sarah Manno, and Muriel Topaz. 1977. *Study Guide for Elementary Labonotation.* 2nd edition. New York: Dance Notation Bureau Press.

Hammond, Sandra Noll. 1984. *Ballet Basics.* 2nd edition. Palo Alto, CA: Mayfield.

Harris, Jane A., Anne M. Pittman, Marlys S. Waller, and Cathy L. Dark. 2004. *Dance a While: Handbook for Folk, Square, Contra, and Social Dance.* 8th edition. Boston: Allyn & Bacon.

Hayes, Elizabeth R. 1993. *Dance Composition and Production.* 2nd edition. Pennington, NJ: Princeton.

Henderson, Hester, Ron French, Ron Fritsch, and Barbara Lerner. 2000. Time-Out and Over-Correction: A Comparison of Their Application in Physical Education. *Journal of Physical Education, Recreation and Dance* 71(3): 31-35.

Huckabee, Mike. 2005. Report to Arts Education Partnership Forum. Lecture at College of Charleston. Charleston, SC.

Interstate New Teacher Assessment and Support Consortium (INTASC) and Arts Education Committee. 2002. *Model Standards for Licensing Classroom Teachers and Specialists in the Arts: A Resource for State Dialogue.* Washington, DC: Council of Chief State School Officers. Available at www.ccsso.org.

Jensen, Eric. 2001. *Arts with the Brain in Mind.* Alexandria, VA: Association for Supervision and Curriculum Development.

Jones, Fred. 2000. *Tools for Teaching.* Santa Cruz, CA: Fredric H. Jones. www.fredjones.com.

Joyce, Mary. 1984. *Dance Technique for Children.* Palo Alto, CA: Mayfield.

Joyce, Mary. 1994. *First Steps in Teaching Creative Dance to Children.* 3rd edition. Mountain View, CA: Mayfield.

Kanter, Rosabeth Moss. 1989. *When Giants Learn to Dance: The Definitive Guide to Corporate America's Changing Strategies for Success.* New York: Touchstone.

Kealiinohomoku, Joann. 1983. An Anthropologist Looks at Ballet as a Form of Ethnic Dance. In *What Is Dance? Readings in Theory and Criticism,* eds. Roger Copeland and Marshall Cohen, 533-549. Oxford, UK: Oxford University Press.

Kras, John, Brad Strand, Julie Abendroth-Smith, and Peter Mathesius. 1999. Teaching Study Skills Through Classroom Activities. *Journal of Physical Education, Recreation and Dance* 70(1): 40-44.

Kraus, Richard, Sarah Chapman Hilsendager, and Brenda Dixon. 1991. *History of the Dance in Art and Education.* 3rd edition. Saddle River, NJ: Prentice Hall.

Lee, Meredith. 1998. Goethe Question Identified. *Goethe News and Noda* XI no. 1 (Spring). www.goethesociety.org/pages/quotescom.html.

Lerman, Liz. 1993. Toward a Process for Critical Response. *Alternate Roots: Regional Organization of Theatres South* (Summer): 4.

Lerman, Liz, and John Borstel. 2003. *The Critical Response Process—A method for getting useful feedback on anything you make, from dance to dessert.* Takoma Park, MD: Liz Lerman Dance Exchange.

Louis, Murray. 1980. On Teachers. In *Inside Dance: Essays by Murray Louis,* 83-88. New York: St. Martin's Press.

Loveless, Richard. 1992. Open the Window to the 21st Century by Chancing a Romance With Contemporary Media Forms: A Challenge for the Arts in Higher Education. In *The Future: Challenge of Change,* ed. Norman C. Yakel, 115-137. Reston, VA: National Arts Education Association.

Lunt, Joanne M. and Brenda Pugh McCutchen. 1995. SC Framework for Dance Education K-12. Columbia, SC: SC State Department of Education.

Mader, Sylvia S. 1998. *Biology.* New York: McGraw-Hill.

McCutchen, Brenda Pugh. 1994. Considerations for Hiring a Qualified Dance Specialist. *South Carolina Journal for Health, Physical Education, Recreation and Dance* 26(2): 6.

McTighe, Jay and Grant Wiggins. 1999. *Understanding by Design Handbook.* Alexandria, VA: Association for Supervision and Curriculum Development.

McTighe, Jay and Grant Wiggins. 2004. *Understanding by Design Professional Development Workbook.* 2nd edition. Alexandria, VA: Association for Supervision and Curriculum Development.

Nadel, Myron Howard and Marc Raymond Strauss. 2003. *The Dance Experience: Insights Into History, Culture and Creativity.* 2nd edition. Hightstown, NJ: Princeton.

National Assessment Governing Board. 1994. *NAEP Arts Education Assessment Framework: Pre-publication Issue.* Washington, DC: Council of Chief State School Officers.

National Association of Schools of Dance. 1999. *Report to Faculty,* Spring 1999, Volume 1. Reston, VA: National Association of Schools of Dance.

National Council of State Arts Education Consultants. 1992. *A Summary of State Arts Education Frameworks.* Washington, DC: Getty Center for Education in the Arts and Council of Chief State School Officers.

National Dance Association. 1990. *Guide to Creative Dance for the Young Child.* Reston, VA: National Dance Association.

National Dance Association.1995. *NDA Interim: Spotlight on Dance.* Reston, VA: National Dance Association.

National Dance Association. 1994. *National Standards for Dance Education: What Every Young American Should Know and Be Able to Do in Dance.* (2nd printing [1996] included Opportunity-to-Learn Standards in Dance Education 1995). Reston, VA: Music Educators National Conference for the National Dance Association.

National Endowment for the Arts. 1994. *Goals 2000: Opportunities for the Arts.* Washington, DC: U.S. Department of Education.

Ormrod, Jeanne Ellis. 2000. *Educational Psychology: Developing Learners.* 3rd edition. Saddle River, NJ: Prentice-Hall.

Parsons, Michael J., ed. 1987. *How We Understand Art.* Cambridge, UK: Cambridge University Press.

Patchen, Jeffrey. 1996. On the Arts. Lecture at Arts Education Symposium at Getty Education Institute, Los Angeles.

Perry, Bruce Duncan. 2005a. Curiosity: The Fuel of Development. Scholastic, Inc. www.scholastic.com.

Perry, Bruce Duncan. 2005b. How the Brain Learns Best. Scholastic, Inc. www.scholastic.com.

Perry, Bruce Duncan. 2005c. The Developmental Hot Zone. Scholastic, Inc. www.scholastic.com.

Peterson, Ralph. 1992. *Life in a Crowded Place: Making a Learning Community.* Portsmouth, NH: Heinemann.

Raspberry, William. 2005, July 18. Sensible Methods to Help Children Learn. *State.* Columbia, South Carolina.

Renzulli, Joseph S. 1975. *A Guidebook for Evaluating Programs for the Gifted and Talented.* Ventura, CA: Office of the Ventura County Superintendent of Schools.

Rosemond, John. 2001, December 7. Praise Without Accomplishment Worth Nothing. *State.* Columbia, South Carolina.

Rosemond, John. 2002, May 3. My Top Ten List: Call it Stupid Parenting Tricks. *State.* Columbia, SC.

Sammarco, G. James. 1987. The Hip in Dancers. *Medical Problems of Performing Artists* 2(1): 5-6.

Schrader, Constance. 2004. *A Sense of Dance: Exploring Your Movement Potential.* 2nd edition. Champaign, IL: Human Kinetics.

Scott, Jan. 2003, May 15. Reflections on Teaching Third through Fifth Graders. Personal communication by e-mail.

Seals, Jay G. 1986. Dance Floors. *Medical Problems of Performing Artists* 1(3): 81-84.

Secretary's Commission on Achieving Necessary Skills (SCANS), U.S. Department of Labor. 1991. *What Work Requires of Schools: A SCANS Report for America 2000.* Washington, DC: U.S. Government Printing Office.

Smith, James A. 1970. *Creative Teaching of the Social Studies in the Elementary School.* Boston: Allyn and Bacon.

Smith-Autard, Jacqueline M. 2002. *The Art of Dance in Education.* 2nd edition. London: A & C Black.

Solomon, Ruth. 1980. It's Getting Harder to Teach, Isn't it? *Journal of Physical Education and Recreation* 51(3): 62-71.

Sorell, Walter, ed. 1975. *The Mary Wigman Book: Her Writings Edited and Translated.* Middletown, CT: Wesleyan University Press.

Sorell, Walter, ed. 1992. *The Dance Has Many Faces.* 3rd revised edition. Chicago: A Cappella Books of Chicago Review Press.

South Carolina State Department of Education. n.d. Adept Performance Dimensions. www.scteachers.org/adept/perfdim.cfm#TOP [accessed July 7, 2004].

South Carolina Visual and Performing Arts Curriculum Framework Writing Team. 1993. *South Carolina Visual and Performing Arts Framework.* Columbia, SC: South Carolina State Board of Education.

Stewart, Virginia and Merle Armitage. 1970. *The Modern Dance.* Brooklyn, NY: Dance Horizons.

Tobias, Cynthia Ulrich. 1994. *The Way They Learn.* Wheaton, IL: Tyndale House.

U.S. Department of Education Office of Educational Research and Improvement. 1998a. *The NAEP 1997 Arts Report Card,* NCES 1999-486. Washington, DC: National Center for Education Statistics.

U.S. Department of Education Office of Educational Research and Improvement. 1998b. *Focus on NAEP* 3(1): 1-6. Washington, DC: National Center for Education Statistics.

Wallock, Susan Frieder. 1981. Reflections on Mary Whitehouse. *American Journal of Dance Therapy* 4(2): 45-56.

Wiggins, Robert A. 2001. Interdisciplinary Curriculum: Music Educator Concerns. *Music Educators Journal* 87(5): 40-44.

Wigman, Mary. 1966. *The Language of Dance.* [Translated from the German by Walter Sorell.] Middletown, CT: Wesleyan University Press.

Williams, Neil F. 1994. The Physical Education Hall of Shame, Part II. *Journal of Physical Education, Recreation and Dance* 65(2): 17-20.

Willimon, William H. and Thomas H. Naylor. 1995. *The Abandoned Generation, Rethinking Higher Education.* Grand Rapids, MI: Eerdmans.

Wilson, Brent. 1992. Postmodernism and the Challenge of Content: Teaching Teachers of Art for the Twenty-First Century. In *The Future: Challenge of Change,* ed. Norman C. Yakel, 99-113. Reston, VA: National Arts Education Association.

Wilson, Brent. 1997. *The Quiet Evolution: Changing the Face of Arts Education.* Los Angeles: Getty Education Institute for the Arts.

Wong, Harry K. and Rosemary T. Wong. 1998. *How to Be an Effective Teacher: The First Days of School.* Mountain View, CA: Harry K. Wong.

Woodbury, Joan and Shirley Ririe. 1989. *Teaching Beginning Dance Improvisation: Education Handbook.* Salt Lake City: Ririe-Woodbury.

Index

Note: An italicized *f* or *t* following a page number indicates a figure or table on that page, respectively.

About the Author

Brenda Pugh McCutchen, MFA, is a dance education consultant for Dance Curriculum Designs (Columbia, South Carolina) and teaches at the University of South Carolina department of theatre and dance. She was associate professor of dance at Columbia College, where in 1994 she created and directed South Carolina's first undergraduate teacher certification program in dance education. This program was accredited by the National Association of Schools of Dance (NASD) and National Council for Accreditation of Teacher Education (NCATE).

During her 35-year career in arts and education, McCutchen's roles have included professor of dance education, classroom teacher, and K-12 dance specialist. McCutchen's perspective of dance as art in education is also shaped through her experience as a performer, choreographer, artistic director, arts administrator, and dance artist in residence for students in kindergarten through high school. As a leading dance curriculum consultant, McCutchen now helps clients design standards-oriented curricula for college and K-12 dance programs. She leads teacher workshops and institutes across the country.

McCutchen tirelessly works to see that dance plays a significant role in K-12 education and that dance specialists are prepared to realize the potential of dance in that setting. From 1989 to 1994, McCutchen was arts education program director for the South Carolina Arts Commission. She also coauthored the *South Carolina Framework for Dance Education K-12,* adopted by the state board of education in 1990 as a basis for South Carolina's curriculum development in dance education. She was a committee member for the Council of Chief State School Officers (CCSSO) *INTASC Teaching Standards in the Arts.* She is currently on the board of directors for the National Dance Education Organization (NDEO). She serves NDEO as vice president for programs and services as well as director of publications and resources. She helped draft *Professional Teaching Standards for Dance* as well as *Model Program Guidelines* for dance education in the United States.

McCutchen holds an MFA in dance from the University of North Carolina at Greensboro (UNC-G) and has received awards for her contributions to the fields of dance and dance education from the South Carolina Dance Association, the National Dance Week Commission (SC Chapter), and UNC-G's School of Health and Human Performance.

*You'll find
other outstanding
dance resources at*

www.HumanKinetics.com

In the U.S. call

1-800-747-4457

Australia.. 08 8277 1555
Canada 1-800-465-7301
Europe...+44 (0) 113 255 5665
New Zealand...................................... 0064 9 448 1207

HUMAN KINETICS
The Information Leader in Physical Activity
P.O. Box 5076 • Champaign, IL 61825-5076 USA